CONSUMER BEHAVIOR

CONSUMER

CONSUMER BEHAVIOR

CONSUMER

BEHAVIOR

DOROTHY COHEN
HOFSTRA UNIVERSITY

NEW YORK   RANDOM HOUSE BUSINESS DIVISION   TORONTO

First Edition
987654321
Copyright © 1981 by Random House, Inc.

Library of Congress Cataloging in Publication Data
Cohen, Dorothy.
    Consumer behavior.

    Includes index.
    1.   Consumers. 2.   Consumers—Attitudes.
3. Consumer protection. I. Title.
HC79.C6C63   658.8'34   80-20003
ISBN 0-394-31160-4

Cover and text design: Karin Gerdes-Kincheloe

Manufactured in the United States of America. Composed by American–Stratford Graphic Services, Inc., Brattleboro, Vt.
Printed and bound by R. R. Donnelley & Sons Co., Crawfordsville, Ind.

PERMISSIONS ACKNOWLEDGMENTS

Figure 1.2, p. 12—From CONSUMER BEHAVIOR, Third Edition, by James F. Engel, Roger D. Blackwell, and David T. Kollat. Copyright © 1978 by The Dryden Press, A division of Holt, Rinehart and Winston. Reprinted by permission of Holt, Rinehart and Winston.

Exhibit 2.1, p. 25—Courtesy The Chase Manhattan Bank. Exhibit 2.3, p. 29—Reprinted with permission of copyright owner, © 1978 Clairol Inc. All rights reserved. Table 2.1, p. 31—*Advertising Age*, August 11, 1975, p. 49. Reprinted with permission from the August 11, 1975 issue of Advertising Age. Copyright 1975 by Crain Communications, Inc. Table 2.2, p. 36—Reprinted from *Journal of Marketing*, published by the American Marketing Association. "A Cross-national Comparison of Consumer Habits and Innovator Characteristics," by Robert T. Green and Eric Langeard, 39, July 1975, p. 38. Table 2.3, p. 40—Reprinted with permission of Macmillan Publishing Co., Inc., from THE NATURE OF HUMAN VALUES, by Milton Rokeach. Copyright © 1971 by The Free Press, a Division of Macmillan Publishing Co., Inc.

Table 3.1, p. 49—From A. C. Nielsen Co., in Thayer C. Taylor, "Blacks: Two Distinct Markets in One," *Sales and Marketing Management*, December 12, 1977, p. 35. Reprinted by permission from Sales & Marketing Management Magazine. Copyright 1977.

Table 4.2, p. 61—From Donald Treiman, "Standard International Occupational Prestige Scale," from *Occupational Prestige In Comparative Perspective* (New York: Academic Press, 1977). Table 4.3, pp. 64–65—Reprinted from "U.S. News & World Report," February 14, 1977, p. 39. Copyright 1977 U.S. News & World Report, Inc. Figure 4.2, p. 72—Reprinted from *Journal of Marketing*, published by American Marketing Association. "Socioeconomic Product Risk and Patronage Preferences of Retail Shoppers," by V. Kanti Prasad, 39, July 1975, p. 44.

Table 5.1, p. 86—Reprinted from *Journal of Marketing Research*, published by the American Marketing Association. "A Comparative Analysis of Roles Portrayed by Women in Print Advertisements: 1958, 1970, 1972" by Ahmend Belkaoui and Janice M. Belkaoui, 13, May 1976, p. 171. Table 5.2, p. 87—Reprinted from *Journal of Marketing Research*, published by the American Marketing Association. "'Women's Libber's' versus Independent Women: A Study of Preferences for Women's Roles in Advertisements" by Jacob M. Duker and Lewis R. Tucker, Jr., 14, November 1977, p. 474.

Exhibit 6.1, p. 102—C. F. Hathaway Division of Warnaco Inc. Table 6.3, p. 109—From Mark Munn, "The Effect on Parental Buying Habits of Children Exposed to Children's Television Programs," in *Journal of Broadcasting*, 2, Summer 1968, pp. 253–58. JOURNAL OF BROADCASTING. Figure 6.2, p. 112—Reprinted from *Journal of Marketing*, published by the American Marketing Association. "Observation of Parent–Child Interaction in Supermarket Decision-Making" by Charles K. Atkin, 42, October 1978, p. 43. Table 6.5, p. 114—Reprinted from *Journal of Marketing Research*, published by the American Marketing Association. "Life Cycle Concept in Marketing Research" by William D. Wells and George Gubar, 3, November 1966, p. 362.

Exhibit 7.1, p. 144—CLIENT: Edward S. Gordon Company, Inc. Renting/Managing Agent; AGENCY: Rose & Brosse Advertising, Inc., New York. Figure 7.3, p. 151—Seatrains Lines, Inc. Figure 7.8, p. 158—Reprinted from *Journal of Marketing*, published by the American Marketing Association. "The Use of Non-Metric Multidimensional Scaling in Marketing Analysis," Lester A. Neidell, 33, October 1969, p. 41. Exhibit 7.2, p. 159—Used with permission of Church P. Dwight Co., Inc.

Table 8.3, p. 174—Reprinted from *Journal of Marketing Research*, published by the American Marketing Association. "The Value of Unit Price Information" by J. Edward Russo, 14, May 1977, p. 194. Figure 8.3, p. 176—Reprinted from *Journal of Marketing Research*, published by the American Marketing Association. "Analyzing Proximity Judgments in an Experimental Design" by Mary Lou Roberts and James R. Taylor, 12, February 1975, p. 69. Exhibit 8.2, p. 184— © Brown & Williamson Tobacco Corporation. Reprinted by permission; all rights reserved. Exhibit 8.3, p. 185—Printed with permission of The Dow Chemical Company. Table 8.5, p. 188, and Figure 8.5, p. 189—Reprinted from *Journal of Marketing*, published by the American Marketing Association. "Importance-Performance Analysis" by John A. Martilla and John C. James, 41, January 1977, p. 78.

Table 9.2, pp. 207–208—Adapted from Henry A. Murray, "Types of Human Needs," in David C. McClelland *Studies in Motivation* (N.Y.: Appleton-Century-Crofts, 1955), pp. 63–66. Copyright 1955 by Irvington Publishers, Inc. Reprinted with permission. Table 9.3, p. 222—Reprinted from *Journal of Marketing*, published by the American Marketing Association. "A Replication of the 'Shopping List' Study" by Frederick E. Webster, Jr., and Frederick von Pechmann, 34, April 1970, p. 62.

Exhibit 10.1, p. 237—BOODLES is a registered Trademark of Joseph E. Seagram & Sons Inc. Figure 10.1, p. 244—From Larry Percy, "A Look at Personality Profiles and the Personality-Attitude-Behavior Link in Predicting Consumer Behavior," in *Advances in Consumer Research*. Reprinted with permission of the Association for Consumer Research. Table 10.2, p. 250—Reprinted from *Journal of Marketing Research*, published by the American Marketing Association. "Psychographics: A Critical Review" by William D. Wells, 12, May 1975, p. 197. Table 10.3, p. 251—Reprinted from *Journal of Marketing Research*, published by the American Marketing Association. "Psychographics: A Critical Review" by William D. Wells, 12, May 1975, p. 198. Table 10.4, p. 252—Reprinted from *Journal of Marketing*, published by the American Marketing Association. "The Concept and Application of Life Style Segmentation" by Joseph T. Plummer, 38, January 1974, p. 34. Table 10.6, p. 257—Reprinted from *1971 Combined Proceedings of AMA Spring and Fall Conferences*, published by the American Marketing Association. "Life Style and Advertising: Case Studies" by Joseph T. Plummer, 1972, p. 294.

Footnote 23, p. 273—Martin Fishbein, "An Investigation of the Relationships Between Beliefs about an Object and the Attitude Toward That Object," *Human Relations*, 16, 1963, pp. 233–240. Plenum Publishing Corporation. Table 11.1, p. 274, and Table 11.2, p. 275—James Engel, Wayne Talarzyk, and Carl Larson, *Cases in Promotional Strategy* (Homewood, Ill.: Richard D. Irwin, 1971), p. 91. © 1971 by Richard D. Irwin, Inc.

Figure 12.1, p. 290—Reprinted from *Journal of Marketing*, published by the American Marketing Association. "Fitting the Semantic Differential to the Marketing Problem" by William A. Mindak, 25, April 1961, p. 31.

Table 13.1, p. 303—Reprinted from *Journal of Marketing*, published by the American Marketing Association. "Discovering New Product Opportunities with Problem Inventory Analysis" by Edward M. Tauber, 39, January 1975, p. 70. Table 13.2, p. 311—From INNOVATIVE BEHAVIOR AND COMMUNICATION by Thomas S. Robertson. Copyright © 1971 by Holt, Rinehart and Winston, Inc. Reprinted by permission of Holt, Rinehart and Winston.

Figure 14.1, p. 327—Reprinted from "The Communication/Persuasion Matrix," in *Evaluating Advertising: A Bibliography of the Communication Process*, by William J. McGuire, © Copyright 1978, by the Advertising Research Foundation. Figure 14.2, p. 333—From Harry W. McMahan, "Rating the Stars in TV Commercials: Bugs Bunny vs. Catherine Deneuve," *Advertising Age*, August 22, 1977, p. 37. Reprinted with permission from the August 22, 1977 issue of Advertising Age. Copyright 1977 by Crain Communications, Inc. Figure 14.3, p. 338—Reprinted from *Journal of Marketing Research*, published by the American Marketing Association. "Interpersonal Communication in Marketing: An Overview" by James Hulbert and Noel Capon, 9, February 1972, p. 28. Table 14.1, p. 338—Reprinted from *Journal of Marketing Research*, published by the American Marketing Association. "Interpersonal Communication in Marketing: An Overview" by James Hulbert and Noel Capon, 9, February 1972, p. 29. Table 14.2, p. 339—Reprinted from *Journal of Marketing Research*, published by the American Marketing Association. "Nonverbal Communication in Marketing: Toward a Communicational Analysis" by Thomas V. Bonoma and Leonard C. Felder, 14, May 1977, p. 176.

Exhibit 15.1a, Exhibit 15.1b, p. 344—Courtesy of The Gillette Company. Exhibit 15.1c, p. 344—Used with permission of Church P. Dwight Co., Inc. Figure 15.1, p. 346—From *The Psychology of Learning*, by James Deese and Stewart H. Hulse. Copyright © 1967. Used with permission of McGraw-Hill Book Company. Table 15.2, p. 353—Reprinted from Alan D. Fletcher and Sherilyn K. Zeigler, "Creative Strategy and Magazine Ad Readership," *Journal of Advertising Research*, 18, February 1978, p. 30. © Copyright 1978, by the Advertising Research Foundation. Exhibit 15.3, p. 357—Courtesy-Johnson Wax. Table 15.3, p. 362; Figure 15.2, p. 363; Table 15.4, p. 364; and Table 15.5, p. 364—From *The Media Book 78*, The Media Book, Inc., 1978.

Table 16.1, p. 373—Steven H. Chaffee/Jack M. McLeod, "Consumer Decisions and Information Use," in CONSUMER BEHAVIOR, THEORETICAL SOURCES, © 1973, pp. 391. Reprinted by permission of Prentice-Hall, Inc. Englewood Cliffs, New Jersey. Figure 16.1, p. 377—Reprinted from *Journal of Marketing*, published by the American Marketing Association. "Consumer Behavior and Product Performance: An Alternative Conceptualization" by Chem L. Narayana and Rom J. Markin, 39, October 1975, p. 2. Table 16.2, p. 378—Reprinted from *Journal of Marketing*, published by the American Marketing Association. "Consumer Behavior and Product Performance: An Alternative Conceptualization" by Chem L. Narayana and Rom J. Markin, 39, October 1975, p. 4. Table 16.3, p. 392—From Robert A. Hansen and Terry Deutscher, "An Empirical Investigation of At-

tribute Importance in Retail Store Selection," *Journal of Retailing*. New York University. Table 16.4, p. 393—Reprinted from *Journal of Marketing Research*, published by the American Marketing Association. "Method for Developing Tailor-made Semantic Differentials for Specific Marketing Content Areas" by John A. Dickson and Gerald Albaum, 14, February 1977, p. 89.

Exhibit 17.2, p. 407—Reproduced with permission of the copyright owner, Bristol Meyers Company, © 1979/1980. Exhibit 17.3, p. 408—Permission granted by Sony Consumer Products Company. Footnote 23, p. 413—Reprinted from *1974 Combined Proceedings of AMA Conferences*, published by the American Marketing Association. "Perspectives on Consumer Satisfaction" by John A. Czepiel, et al., p. 121. Figure 17.1, p. 415—Reprinted from *Journal of Marketing Research*, published by the American Marketing Association. "Consumer Dissatisfaction: The Effect of Disconfirmed Expectancy on Perceived Product Performance" by Rolph E. Anderson, 10, February 1973, p. 39. Table 17.2, p. 418—From Marc A. Grainer, Kathleen A. McEvoy, and Donald W. King, "Consumer Problems and Complaints: A National View," in *Advances in Consumer Research*. Reprinted with permission of the Association for Consumer Research. Figure 17.3, p. 423—Reprinted from *Journal of Marketing*, published by the American Marketing Association. "The Relationship Between Price and Repair Service for Consumer Durables" by Lee Adler and James D. Hlavacek, 40, April 1976, p. 82.

Figure 18.1, p. 429, and Figure 18.2, p. 432—Reprinted with permission of Macmillan Publishing Co., Inc., from COMMUNICATION OF INNOVATION, by Everett M. Rogers and Floyd Shoemaker. Copyright © 1973 by The Free Press, a Division of Macmillan Publishing Co., Inc. Table 18.1, p. 442—From Valerie Valle and Melanie Wallendorf, "Consumers' Attributions of the Cause of Their Product Satisfaction and Dissatisfaction," in *Consumer Satisfaction, Dissatisfaction, and Complaining Behavior*. Copyright, 1977, by the Foundation for the School of Business at Indiana University.

Table 19.1, pp. 452–453—Reprinted from *Journal of Marketing*, published by the American Marketing Association. "Assessing the Effects of Information Disclosure Requirements" by George S. Day, 40, April 1976, p. 43. Table 19.2, p. 454—Reprinted from *Journal of Marketing*, published by the American Marketing Association. "Assessing the Effects of Information Disclosure Requirements" by George S. Day, 40, April 1976, p. 46. Figure 19.1, p. 466—*Fortune,*

April 9, 1979, pp. 54–55. John Haines for FORTUNE Magazine, 1979. Footnote 44, p. 469—From SATISFACTION GUARANTEED by Booton Herndon. Copyright © 1972 by McGraw-Hill. Used with the permission of McGraw-Hill Book Company.

Table 20.1, p. 486—Reprinted from *Journal of Marketing*, published by the American Marketing Association. "Consumer Problems and Consumerism: Analysis of Calls to a Consumer Hot Line" by Steven L. Diamond, Scott Ward, and Ronald Faber, 40, January 1976, p. 59. Table 20.2, p. 487—Reprinted from *Journal of Marketing*, published by the American Marketing Association. "Consumer Problems and Consumerism: Analysis of Calls to a Consumer Hot Line" by Steven L. Diamond, Scott Ward, and Ronald Faber, 40, January 1976, p. 60.

To Morris, Richard, and Susan,
and in memory of my mother, Rose Waldman

PREFACE

This book is designed to provide an introduction to the field of consumer behavior. It presents insights into consumer behavior developed from other disciplines and offers practical applications of these concepts to marketing situations. All areas relevant to the field of consumer behavior are discussed, with particular emphasis on those likely to generate increasing interest in the 1980s: communication theory and societal concerns.

I wish to thank a number of people who reviewed this manuscript and provided constructive suggestions: Peter M. Sanchez, Temple University; Terence A. Shrimp, University of South Carolina; Sak Onkvisit, Illinois State University; Alvin C. Burns, Louisiana State University; Thomas S. Robertson, University of Pennsylvania; M. Venkatesan, University of Iowa; William G. Zikmund, Oklahoma State University; Robert B. Woodruff, University of Tennessee; Dan Robertson, Georgia State University; Lawrence A. Johnson, Howard University; Linda L. Golden, University of Texas at Austin; Thomas L. Parkinson, Pennsylvania State University; Joel B. Cohen, University of Florida; and Philip G. Kuehl, University of Maryland. I would also like to thank the editorial team of Paul Shensa, Paul Donnelly, Stephen Deitmer, and David Lidz for their assistance. Suzanne Loeb in the Production Department was of invaluable help, as was Phyllis Knauf in typing the manuscript.

I am dedicating the book to my husband, Morris; to our children, Richard and Susan, who have given me continuing love and support during the preparation of the manuscript; and, in loving memory, to my mother, Rose Waldman.

CONTENTS

CHAPTER THREE SUBCULTURES 45

CHAPTER FOUR SOCIAL CLASS 57

CHAPTER FIVE SOCIAL GROUP 75

CHAPTER SIX FAMILY 93

PART THREE: INDIVIDUAL INFLUENCES 131

PART ONE
INTRODUCTION

**CONSUMER BEHAVIOR:
AN OVERVIEW**

CHAPTER 1

CONSUMER BEHAVIOR: An Overview

The study of consumer behavior has received its greatest impetus from the field of marketing. Yet not very long ago marketing was considered a purely economic process—as "the second of two great economic processes: production and distribution."[1] In more recent years, the significance of consumers in this process was expressed in a "new marketing concept" based on consumer orientation and the necessity of providing consumer satisfaction. E. Jerome McCarthy, for example, defined marketing as "the performance of business activities that direct the flow of goods and services from producer to consumer to user, in order to best satisfy consumers and accomplish the firm's objectives."[2] In addition, marketing theorists have come increasingly to recognize the relevance of societal concerns to the marketing process.

Acceptance of consumer orientation and social concerns as appropriate marketing considerations requires an investigation into human behavior, and more specifically into consumer behavior. Although consumer behavior is a relatively new discipline, the behavioral sciences have a long history. The traditional behavioral sciences are psychology, anthropology, sociology, economics, political science, and linguistics. Subdisciplines that deal with communication, personality development, motivational structure, thinking processes, and culture are of particular interest to the marketer. Since marketing problems may require knowledge of the way human beings behave in response to various aspects of their environment (advertising, price changes, sales promotion, range of products available, and the like), some people have held that marketing is really one of the behavioral sciences.[3] While this view is not universally accepted, consumer behavior is increasingly recognized as an appropriate field of study for those concerned with marketing.

CONSUMER BEHAVIOR DEFINED

There is no widely accepted definition of consumer behavior that provides precise limits to the area of study encompassed by the term. Generally, "consumer behavior" refers to activities of consumers in the marketplace, and as a field of study it includes an examination of the "what," "why," and "how" of such behavior.

James Engel, David Kollat, and Roger Blackwell, early writers in this field, define consumer behavior as "those acts of individuals directly involved in obtaining and using economic goods and services including the decision processes that precede and determine these acts."[4] Since the term "individuals" is too limiting for a comprehensive discussion of consumer behavior, for the purposes of this text the definition is revised to read: Consumer behavior consists of those acts of decision-making units (families as well as individuals) directly involved in obtaining and using economic goods and services, including the decision processes that precede and determine these acts.

CONSUMER BEHAVIOR AS AN EMERGING DISCIPLINE

A variety of societal, technological, and marketing factors have contributed to the development of consumer behavior as a significant discipline. These factors include changes in the nature of the consumer, technological and statistical advances, public policy and environmental concerns, the introduction of new products, the expansion of international marketing, and market segmentation.

The Changing Nature of the Consumer

While consumers and their behavior are not constant over time, change appears to have accelerated in recent years. The long-time concept of a four-person family consisting of two children, a working husband, and a wife-homemaker who does not participate in the labor force does not represent the typical American family of the 1980s. Furthermore, recent years have seen a growing acceptance of alternative life-styles that represent new types of purchasing and consumption behavior. A recent study on the use of cosmetics, for example, indicated variations between alternative-life-style women and those who follow traditional life-styles.

The heaviest use of cosmetics was found among single women living with men. The study concluded that the majority of new-life-style women view cosmetics as a symbol of their identity and think that fragrance can change the way people respond to them.[5] The changing nature of the consumer is discussed in greater detail in Part Two of this book.

The Impact of Computer Technology and Statistical Techniques

The development and improvement of information-gathering and analysis techniques have increased the potential for extensive consumer research. The growth of computer technology has offered insights relevant to cognitive learning and the manner in which consumers process information. It also permits electronic simulation of consumer behavior, and offers a means of analyzing extensive data gathered in the field.

Behavioral scientists have developed a variety of research techniques, many of which have been applied to or modified for consumer-behavior research. Discussions of such research techniques appear throughout the text, in the areas that have most relevance to their potential application.

Public Policy and Environmental Concerns

Increased concern with consumer rights in the 1970s generated the need to understand and evaluate consumer behavior in the marketplace (this subject is discussed in detail in Part Five). For example, it became important to know whether providing consumers with additional product information, such as the hazards of smoking or the nutritional content of food, would actually increase their protection, and whether advertisements were confusing and deceiving consumers. Consumer research by the Federal Trade Commission, for example, determined that a large proportion of people believed, erroneously, that Listerine could prevent colds. Accordingly, the agency required that Listerine ads correct this impression.

Concern with special segments of the population has led to efforts to determine, for example, whether very young children can distinguish between commercials and program content and comprehend the selling purpose of television ads, and whether "disadvantaged" consumers are abused by credit practices whose consequences they don't understand.

Environmental problems have led public policy makers to search for means of informing consumers of the consequences of using products that are potential pollutants, and the need to conserve such scarce resources as oil. The FTC, for example, engaged in consumer research to develop energy labels to be attached to appliances. The labels were designed so as to attract and hold the attention of consumers long enough so that information on comparative energy costs of appliances could be understood.

The Introduction of New Products

Technological improvements and the availability of many resources curtailed during World War II led to the introduction of new products at an increasing rate in the postwar years. The failure rate of these new products, however, was also relatively high. To reduce risk and increase the potential for acceptance, marketers began to secure information about consumers before new products were introduced. Techniques were also developed for continued monitoring of consumer acceptance of such products and for determination of the appropriate time to introduce revisions.

While the rising costs of the development of new products and the reduced availability of resources may portend a decrease in the rate at which new products are introduced, the need for consumer research efforts will continue. Rather than introduce new products, marketers may focus on maintaining and increasing the market shares of their current offerings. Consumer research may offer suggestions for effective product modifications, pricing policies, distribution channels, and promotional policies.

The Internationalization of Marketing Activities

Technological improvements, expansion of transportation and communication capabilities, and increasing competition in national markets have provided impetus for the expansion of international marketing. Such activities require an understanding of the social and cultural variations among foreign customers. One study indicated, for example, that attributes of toothpaste considered important by French people differ from those stressed by U.S. consumers.[6] Such attributes as "kills germs in mouth" and "removes particles from between teeth" were of greater importance to the French than to the Americans; the U.S. sample placed greater emphasis on "freshens mouth" and "brightens teeth."

Market Segmentation

Early marketers tended to cater to particular groups of consumers, usually those located in relatively compact geographical areas.[7] As transportation and communication facilities improved, it became possible to define markets more broadly and even to go beyond national boundaries. This and other factors encouraged the development of mass marketing. By standardizing products and selling them to a broad range of consumer types, an industrial organization could increase its efficiency.

The last twenty years have seen a partial reversal of these trends. For many products the mass market has become larger than necessary to achieve economies of scale. Moreover, it appears that the mass market is not so homogeneous as it was once thought to be. Many consumers are interested in diversity and are willing and able to pay for products tailored to their needs.

The emergence of these factors led to the concept known as "market segmentation," which, according to an early definition, is "based upon developments on the demand side of the market and represents a rational and more precise adjustment of product and marketing effort to consumer or user requirements."[8] While market segmentation has become an acceptable strategy, in recent years traditional analysis of segments on the basis of geographical location, age, and income level has appeared to provide insufficient direction for marketing efforts. In order to find segments whose characteristics provided marketers with greater power to predict consumer behavior, a variety of new bases for market segmentation were developed.

Today's markets can be segmented in an infinite number of ways. For segmentation to be a viable marketing strategy, however, the segments must fulfill several criteria:[9]

1. The segmentation variable should divide a market into homogeneous segments that tend to respond differently to a firm's marketing activities. For example, research disclosed three distinct segments in the watch market: (a) people who want to pay the least possible price for any watch that works reasonably well; (b) people who value a watch for its long life, good workmanship, and good styling; (c) people who look not only for useful product features but also for qualities meaningful to them in some emotional way (the upward striver who must have a Phillippe-Pathek, the young person who delights in a Mickey Mouse watch).[10]

2. The variable should be measurable. The more information that exists on watch-user categories, for example, the easier it is to obtain.

3. The variable should be accessible to the firm's promotional activities. For example, it may be easy to reach the low-price segment in the watch industry, but if there is a segment of right-handed watch wearers, it may be difficult to isolate the media that reach that group.

4. The variable should lead to increased profits from segmentation. While there may be a group of consumers who wear watches on their ankles, this segment may be too small to have much profit potential.

Many of the subsequent chapters will isolate variables useful in segmenting markets. When such variables are classified, they are usually designated as demographic, socioeconomic, psychographic, or product-specific segments.

DEMOGRAPHIC SEGMENTS

Many marketing strategies continue to take demographic market segments into account. These segments include the traditional groupings by age, sex, marital status, number and age of children, occupation, income, geographic location, and so on. Such segments are easy to measure and are generally accessible by various media. For example, a magazine, *W*, informed potential advertisers, "Who are the

W readers? One in eight is a millionaire. And our median household worth is way above average: $196,500, to be precise. They insist upon the best of everything, and why not? They can afford it."

While much of the relevant information concerning demographic segments is available through census-gathering sources, it is necessary to evaluate these statistics continually and to note changes in both their numbers and their impact. For example, despite a long-term decline in the birth rate, Yardley of London recently introduced a baby soap. While some people consider this action a response to a market segment that has been ignored, others note that recent statistics indicate a rise in both the birth and fertility rates in the United States.

Demographers note an age segment that is growing in size and significance—the "young elderly," who are retiring earlier, have sizable incomes, and wish to enjoy the "good life."

SOCIOECONOMIC SEGMENTS

Social class, religion, and race are often thought to delineate important socioeconomic segments. Income and occupation may also be combined with social class to clarify the significance of this variable as a market segment. In some cases, such additions cause a blurring of social-class distinctions. It should be noted, for example, that in well over half of the nation's families, two or more members bring home paychecks. The various kinds of socioeconomic influences and their impact on behavior are examined in Chapters 4 and 5.

PSYCHOGRAPHIC CHARACTERISTICS

Traditional demographic and socioeconomic methods of market segmentation do not always provide viable segments. In the late 1960s, Emmanuel H. Demby, chairman of the board of MPI Marketing Research, Inc., coined the word "psychographic," which he defined as "the measurement of consumers' propensity to purchase under a variety of conditions, needs and stimuli."[11] Psychographics describes consumers on a psychological rather than a demographic basis. It incorporates such concepts as life-styles, or the patterns of behavior that people establish in spending their time and money. Psychographics and life-style analyses are discussed in Chapter 10.

PRODUCT-SPECIFIC SEGMENTS

It is sometimes useful to focus on factors specific to the product in order to isolate viable market segments. Of prime importance in many segmentation strategies is the determination of product-use categories. Interestingly, it appears that a relatively small proportion of the total population is responsible for most of the use of some products. Moreover, when the market is segmented by usage rate (that is, heavy users, light users, and nonusers), varying strategies can be employed for each segment. When the Nestlé Company introduced Taster's Choice freeze-dried coffee, it found that the coffee market could be segmented into various types of coffee drinkers.[12] Heavy coffee users tended to be well-educated, affluent club women. Nescafé users were generally price-conscious blue-collar workers who were heavy television watchers. Defining the market Nestlé's wanted to reach and knowing how best to speak to it contributed to the successful launching of a new, relatively expensive instant coffee.

Benefit segments relate to the benefits various groups of consumers seek from a product. For example, when the perfume market was analyzed, segments were found to be differentiated by the various purposes women had in mind when they bought perfume. One segment of the market thought of perfume as something to be added to what nature had supplied. Another segment believed that the purpose of fragrance products was to help a woman to feel cleaner, fresher, and better groomed—to correct or negate what nature had supplied. In the latter instance, the fragrance product was used to cancel out natural body odors; in the former, to add a new scent. One woman told an interviewer, "I like a woodsy scent like Fabergé. It seems more intense and lingers longer, and doesn't fade away like the sweeter scents." Another woman said, "I literally loathe Fabergé. It makes me think of a streetcar full of women coming home from work who haven't bathed."[13]

Changes in economic and marketing conditions may lead to a reversal of the trend toward market segmentation. Some observers note that with the decline in resources and the rise in inflation, it may be necessary to curtail segmentation strategies that require a proliferation of products to satisfy many small markets, thus increasing production and marketing costs.

Furthermore, as costs and prices rise, consumers seem to be willing to select a product or service that is not precisely tailored to their desires in return for a lower price. This observation suggests the need in some cases for a new strategy that clusters market segments instead of segregating them.[14] Such efforts are emerging, for example, in the sale of generic products and in the development of "box stores" that offer only fast-moving grocery items from stacked boxes as price-saving alternatives. While such countersegmentation strategies may increase in the future, they do not signal the end of market segmentation. Moreover, consumer-behavior analysis is an important tool for countersegmentation strategists in their efforts to identify those areas where consumers are willing to forgo the benefits of products that are developed specifically for their needs in exchange for lower prices.

CONSUMER BEHAVIOR MODELS

Over the past decade a number of comprehensive models of consumer behavior have been developed. Such models have several uses. They provide a frame of reference for research and a means of integrating research findings into a meaningful whole. In addition, a model may serve a useful purpose in the construction of a theory, as new ideas may emerge in the course of its preparation. A model, however, cannot be considered to be an accurate representation of a theory. It is difficult to prove that a model is accurate; in fact, data for such proof may not exist. Models tend to oversimplify reality. Reality is constantly changing; models change slowly, if at all. Despite their limitations, several models have been offered to represent consumer-behavior theory, and some have had widespread acceptance.

The Howard-Sheth Model

A widely accepted model of consumer behavior developed by John A. Howard and Jagdish N. Sheth represents the first systematic effort to develop a comprehensive theory of consumer behavior.[15] Figure 1.1 is a simplified representation of this model. It includes four major constructs: inputs, perceptual constructs, learning constructs, and outputs.

Inputs are stimuli from the marketing and social environment. They may emerge from the physical product (quality, price, distinctiveness, availability, service) or from symbolic representations (linguistic and pictorial) of these dimen-

FIGURE 1.1   THE HOWARD-SHETH MODEL OF BUYER BEHAVIOR

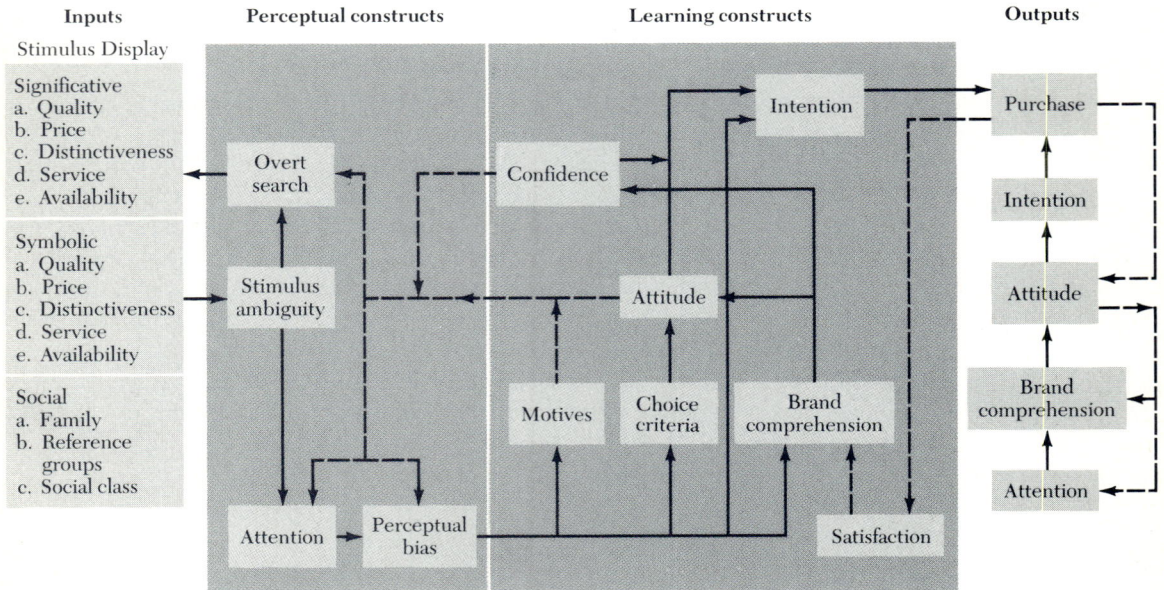

Solid lines indicate flow of information; dashed lines, feedback effects.

Source: John A. Howard and Jagdish N. Sheth, *The Theory of Buyer Behavior* (New York: John Wiley, 1969), p. 30.

sions. A third input variable includes such social stimuli as family, reference groups, and social class.

The outputs are the responses that the buyer is likely to manifest as a result of the interaction of the inputs and the internal states (included in the large central box). While from the seller's point of view the most important response may be purchase of the product, other behavior manifestations can occur, such as attention, attitude, or comprehension.

Between the inputs and the outputs are the various internal-state variables, which are not well defined but are designated as perceptual and learning constructs. They are considered to be hypothetical constructs because they are not observable but must exist for output to occur. The perceptual constructs include search for information, stimulus ambiguity, attention, and perceptual bias. The learning constructs are confidence, motives, intention, attitude, choice criteria, brand comprehension, and satisfaction.

Although empirical research has not confirmed all of the propositions included in the Howard-Sheth model, the general direction of some relationships has been supported.[16] Tests have indicated, however, that the model may need revision. It is more applicable to individual buyer behavior than to decision making within the family. It appears better able to explain choices between two brands of a product than decisions between alternative actions (for example, taking a trip to Hawaii versus buying a new automobile). Nevertheless, the Howard-Sheth model has made a significant contribution to the understanding of consumer behavior. It unifies many unrelated findings and provides the groundwork for future research.

The Engel-Kollat-Blackwell Model

Another widely quoted model of consumer behavior was developed by Engel, Kollat, and Blackwell.[17] Introduced in 1968, it has undergone a number of revisions. The latest model is presented in Figure 1.2. The E-K-B model, a decision-process model, portrays an ongoing series of processes whereby products are sought and evaluated in terms of the consumer's goals, and future purchases are influenced by previous experience.

The E-K-B model consists of five constructs grouped about the central decision-process stages: problem recognition, information search, alternative evaluation, choice, and outcomes.

PROBLEM RECOGNITION

Problem recognition—or arousal, as it is sometimes termed—can occur through information input in the form of external stimuli from various sources (for example, from mass media, personal contacts, and marketer-dominated sources). It may be activated solely by motive, without any external stimulation.

FIGURE 1.2   THE ENGEL-KOLLAT-BLACKWELL MODEL OF CONSUMER BEHAVIOR

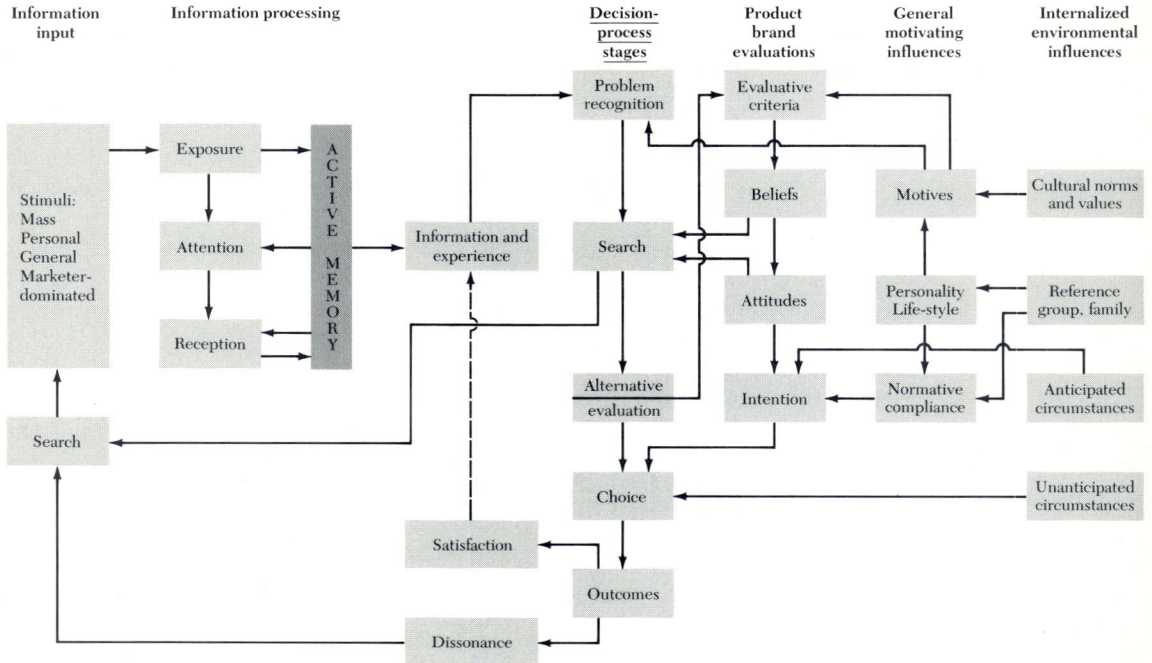

Source: James F. Engel, Roger D. Blackwell, and David T. Kollat, *Consumer Behavior*, 3d ed. (Hinsdale, Ill.: Dryden Press, 1978), p. 32.

INFORMATION SEARCH

Information is sought when the problem is recognized and the consumer must assess the available alternatives for action. Search may be internal; that is, the consumer may examine information already stored in the central processing unit. It may also be external; that is, the consumer may seek information from friends and neighbors or from published sources. As this information is passed through *active memory*, the individual "makes sense" of it, or engages in what is now commonly referred to as *information processing*.

ALTERNATIVE EVALUATION

Once information has been received, the consumer then must *evaluate the alternatives* and arrive at a purchasing decision. This process involves interactions of several types of variables including *evaluative criteria* (specifications and standards used by consumers to evaluate product and price). *Beliefs, attitudes,* and *intention* (the latter intervenes between attitudes and behavior) are included as variables that influence alternative evaluation.

In addition, alternative evaluation is affected by *motivating influences* and *environmental influences.* The former incorporate *motives, personality,* and *lifestyle,* while the latter include *culture, reference groups,* and *family.*

CHOICE AND OUTCOMES

Choice and *outcomes* are the two final stages of the decision process. Choice involves the selection not only of the product but also of the best retail outlet. Choice has two possible outcomes: *satisfaction* and *postdecision dissonance.* The latter is a state of doubt aroused by the realization that in choosing one alternative, one has rejected another that also has desirable attributes.

The Engel-Kollat-Blackwell model is less detailed than the Howard-Sheth model, and its validity has never been tested. A major contribution of the E-K-B model lies in its unification of concepts and propositions. Its emphasis on active information seeking and the evaluation process has led to some criticism. The search and evaluation phases tend to be highly rational;[18] some critics believe this characteristic may misdirect research by overemphasizing the deterministic ("every event has a cause") models of behavior.[19] Nevertheless, it has provided a useful construct for examination of various facets of consumer behavior.

The Nicosia Model

The model developed by Francesco M. Nicosia includes the firm in its representation of the consumer decision process.[20] The major emphasis, however, is on the consumer. In Figure 1.3, it is assumed that the firm is introducing a new product or brand and that the consumer has no prior attitude toward either the firm or its product. The consumer decision process in this model is divided into four fields. In Field 1 the firm sends out messages concerning its product. In Field 2 the consumer attributes interact with message content and the consumer forms an attitude, which may invoke search and evaluation procedures. In Field 3 the consumer is motivated to act and then does act—that is, purchases the product. Field 4 includes feedback of purchase information to the firm and to the consumer that will lead to modification of the consumer's predispositions toward future purchase, and perhaps to modification of the firm's future communication strategy.

The Nicosia model has been criticized for consisting mainly of "long listings of variables that might possibly enter into such a [consumer-behavior] model with little, if any, explicit treatment of how they are interrelated."[21] Its strength, however, lies in its recognition that many steps lie between attitude formation and behavior, as well as in its inclusion of the firm.

FIGURE 1.3   THE NICOSIA MODEL OF THE CONSUMER DECISION PROCESS

Field 1: From the source of a message to the consumer's attitude

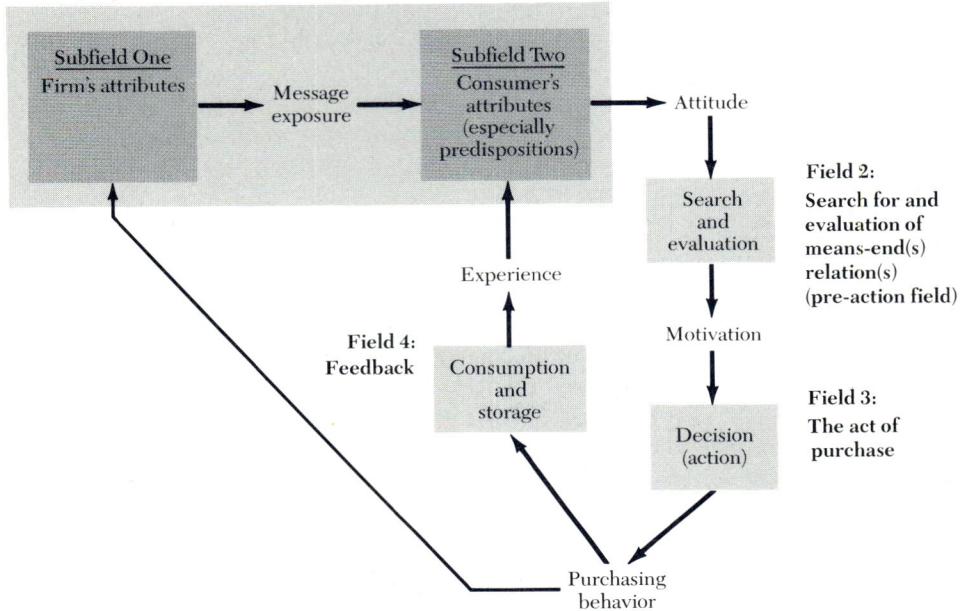

Source: Francesco M. Nicosia, *Consumer Decision Processes, Marketing and Advertising Implications* (Englewood Cliffs, N.J.: Prentice-Hall, 1966), p. 156.

THE NATURE OF THIS BOOK

Since most models of consumer behavior are subject to revision, this book is not based on a specific model, but it does discuss the numerous variables, processes, and constructs enunciated in these representations and indicates their relevance to marketing decision making.

As a framework for the discussion, the major aspects of consumer behavior are listed in Figure 1.4. Each of these aspects will be explained, its relationship to the behavior of consumers examined, and some implications for marketing strategists noted.

The major influences relevant to consumer behavior emerge from the external environment, designated as social and cultural influences, and the internal states, which are referred to as individual influences. Both sets of influences affect the consumer decision process, and feedback from the decision process interacts with the individual influences. Since knowledge from this field is being applied to public policy and consumer issues, insights on consumer behavior are examined from this perspective as well.

FIGURE 1.4   ASPECTS OF CONSUMER BEHAVIOR

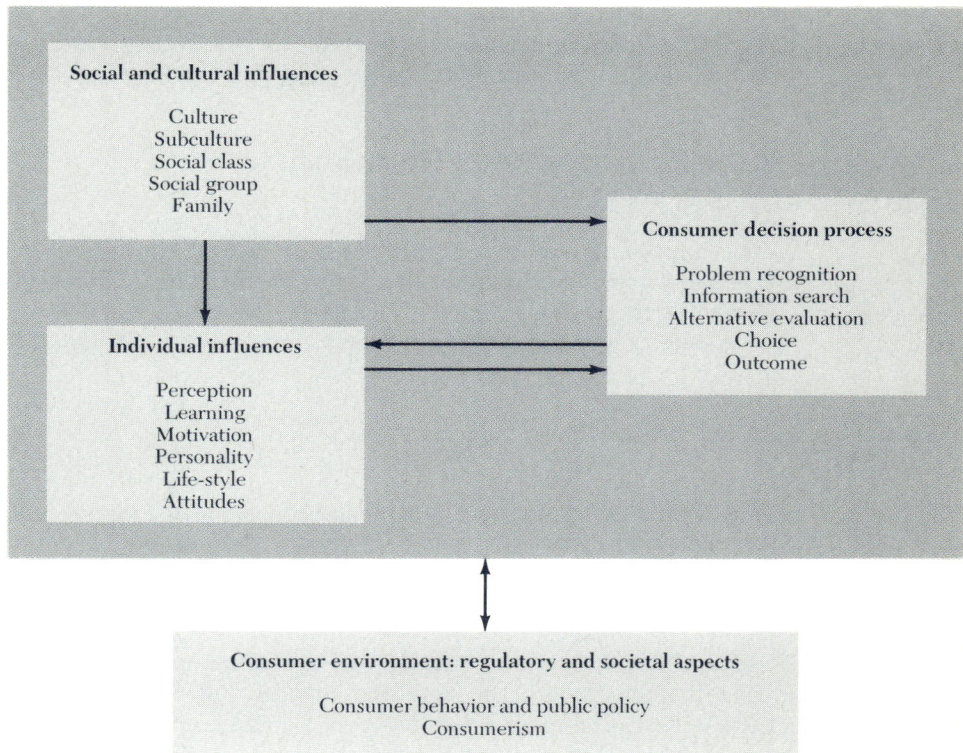

Social and cultural influences

Culture
Subculture
Social class
Social group
Family

Consumer decision process

Problem recognition
Information search
Alternative evaluation
Choice
Outcome

Individual influences

Perception
Learning
Motivation
Personality
Life-style
Attitudes

Consumer environment: regulatory and societal aspects

Consumer behavior and public policy
Consumerism

Social and Cultural Influences

The impact of such external considerations as social and cultural influences is examined in Part Two. These influences include culture, subculture, social class, social groups, and the family.

Individual Influences

Much of the material in Part Three, on individual influences, is examined from a psychological and sociopsychological perspective. This section discusses perception learning, motivation, personality, and their relationship to consumer behavior. Findings concerning attitude and attitude change as they affect consumers' decisions and actions are also presented.

The Consumer Decision Process

Part Four examines the consumer's decision process and the impact of some of the previously discussed social, cultural, and individual influences on the ongoing series of processes whereby products are sought, evaluated, and purchased. It uses the five stages in the consumer decision process represented in the most recent Engel-Kollat-Blackwell model. Specifically, these stages are designated as problem recognition, information search, alternative evaluation, choice, and outcome.

The Consumer Environment: Regulatory and Societal Aspects

The impact of public policy considerations and consumerism in generating increased interest in consumer behavior was noted earlier. Some of these interrelationships are discussed in Part Five, and applications of consumer-behavior theory to public policy and consumerist considerations are presented.

SUMMARY

This introductory chapter indicates the major thrust of this text, which is the examination of consumer behavior from the perspective of marketing activities. It has discussed some of the factors that led to the emergence of consumer behavior as a major field of study. These factors include the changing nature of the consumer, the impact of computer technology, the growing emphasis on public policy and environmental concerns, the introduction of new products, the internationalization of marketing activities, and the development of market segmentation as a widely used marketing strategy. The Howard-Sheth, Engel-Kollat-Blackwell, and Nicosia models of consumer behavior were presented and the general nature of this book was described.

DISCUSSION QUESTIONS

1. Describe a recent purchase situation incorporating some of the consumer-behavior concepts discussed in this chapter.

2. How important is the study of consumer behavior from a marketing viewpoint? From a personal viewpoint?

3. How can an understanding of consumer behavior aid public policy makers?

4. Discuss the major criteria necessary for successful market segmentation. What kinds of segments would you develop for the detergent market? The toothpaste market?

5. What are some of the major changes in the nature of consumers and their lifestyles that are important in consumer-behavior analysis?

6. What are the major contributions of contemporary models of consumer behavior? Their limitations?

7. Consumer behavior is based on knowledge acquired in other disciplines. Which of these disciplines do you think contributes most to the field of consumer behavior?

8. In your opinion, to what extent will countersegmentation strategies be increased in the 1980s? Why?

NOTES

1. Clare W. Barker and Melvin Anshen, *Modern Marketing* (New York: McGraw-Hill, 1939), p. 3.

2. E. Jerome McCarthy, *Basic Marketing: A Managerial Approach,* 3d ed. (Homewood, Ill.: Richard D. Irwin, 1969), p. 33.

3. Michael H. Halbert, *The Meaning and Sources of Marketing Theory,* Marketing Science Institute series (New York: McGraw-Hill, 1965), p. 106.

4. James F. Engel, Roger D. Blackwell, and David T. Kollat, *Consumer Behavior,* 3d ed. (Hinsdale, Ill.: Dryden Press, 1978), p. 1.

5. "Looks Are Key in Life to the 'New' Women: Study," *Advertising Age,* September 11, 1978, p. 36.

6. Robert T. Green, William H. Cunningham, and Isabella C. M. Cunningham, "The Effectiveness of Standardized Global Advertising," *Journal of Advertising* 4 (Summer 1975), pp. 25–30.

7. Ronald E. Frank, William F. Massy, and Yoram Wind, *Market Segmentation* (Englewood Cliffs, N.J.: Prentice-Hall, 1972), p. 4.

8. Wendell R. Smith, "Product Differentiation and Market Segmentation as Alternative Marketing Strategies," *Journal of Marketing* 21 (July 1956), pp. 3–8.

9. Frank, Massy, and Wind, *Market Segmentation,* pp. 27–28.

10. Daniel Yankelovich, "New Criteria for Market Segmentation," *Harvard Business Review* (March–April 1964), p. 84.

11. Peter W. Bernstein, "Psychographics Is Still an Issue on Madison Avenue," *Fortune,* January 16, 1978, pp. 78–84.

12. Patricia Brooks, "Psychographics: Is It the Elusive 'Perfect Marketing Tool'?" *TWA Ambassador,* April 1978, pp. 25–27.

13. Yankelovich, "New Criteria for Market Segmentation," p. 87.

14. Alan J. Resnik, Peter B. B. Turney, and J. Barry Mason, "Marketers Turn to 'Counter-Segmentation,'" *Harvard Business Review* 57 (September–October 1979), pp. 100–106.

15. John A. Howard and Jagdish N. Sheth, *The Theory of Buyer Behavior* (New York: John Wiley, 1969).

16. John W. Farley and Winston Ring, "An Empirical Test of the Howard-Sheth Model of Buyer Behavior," *Journal of Marketing Research* 7 (November 1970), pp. 427–438.

17. Engel, Blackwell, and Kollat, *Consumer Behavior.*

18. Jagdish N. Sheth, *Models of Buyer Behavior: Conceptual, Quantitative, and Empirical* (New York: Harper & Row, 1974), p. 44.

19. Frank M. Bass, "The Theory of Stochastic Preference and Brand Switching," *Journal of Marketing Research* 11 (February 1974), p. 1.

20. Francesco M. Nicosia, *Consumer Decision Processes: Marketing and Advertising Implications* (Englewood Cliffs, N.J.: Prentice-Hall, 1966).

21. Sheth, *Models of Buyer Behavior,* p. 286.

PART TWO
SOCIAL AND CULTURAL INFLUENCES

CULTURE
SUBCULTURE
SOCIAL CLASS
SOCIAL GROUP
FAMILY

Part Two discusses the external or environmental influences on consumer behavior. These influences include those of the culture and subculture, as well as those that emanate from social class, social groups, and the family.

CHAPTER 2

CULTURE

Culture is considered one of the major environmental elements impinging on consumer behavior. While culture is generally accepted by marketing theorists as one of the underlying determinants of consumer behavior, this seems to be an intuitive assumption for which there is currently little empirical evidence. The impact of culture on people has long been studied by sociologists; both their findings and their techniques have been adopted in attempts to determine the impact of culture on consumer behavior.

This chapter addresses itself to the following questions:

How is culture defined and what are its characteristics?
What are the major components of culture?
What are the characteristics of American culture?
Why is cross-cultural analysis important to marketers?
What kinds of research techniques are used in the study of culture?

WHAT IS CULTURE?

In a classic definition, culture is described as "that complex whole which includes knowledge, belief, art, morals, law, custom and any other capabilities and habits acquired by man as a member of society."[1] There is less than universal agreement on this concept; in fact, one book discusses 164 definitions of culture.[2] These definitions usually involve various beliefs or patterns of behavior for coping with recurring experience, shared by aggregates of people and passed on from generation to generation. Culture is not instinctive; it is learned early in life from parents and friends and through the educational environment. These learned behavior patterns are said to permeate an individual's everyday interpersonal experiences and therefore are believed to affect his behavior as a consumer.[3]

Although we are all products of our culture and our cultural antecedents are believed to affect our everyday actions and decisions, there is ample evidence to indicate that many individuals do not share the perspectives of their culture, and furthermore, these cultural perspectives themselves are changing. Many Jewish people do not observe dietary laws, Italian wives do not always wear black, and the Roman Catholic church has ceased to require anyone to eat fish on Friday.

Though culture generally cannot be seen, manifestations of it can be observed in, for example, words, actions, and things. Both traditional and changing cultural values appear to influence consumer consumption patterns, activities, and life-styles. Although the precise impact of culture on consumer behavior is difficult to determine, some of its influences can be examined. As used in an analysis of consumer behavior, the term "culture" refers to the total way of life of any society, not simply to those kinds of activities or values that the society regards as higher or more desirable. Thus it includes patterns of child care as well as works of art.

THE COMPONENTS OF CULTURE

The culture of a society can be defined in terms of its cultural beliefs, cultural values, and cultural norms.[4]

Cultural Beliefs

The belief system of a society includes all of the cognitions—ideas, knowledge, lore, superstitions, myths, and legends—shared by most of its members.[5] Such widely shared beliefs may range from reasonable acceptance of the idea that good health requires the consumption of sufficient quantities of food to the more questionable acceptance of a consumption pattern of three meals a day.

Beliefs that result in preferences may come from various sources. They may emerge from religious preference, such as the rejection of pork by Jews and of beef by Hindus. Others may evolve from geographic locations, such as the preference for brown eggs by Bostonians and white eggs by New Yorkers, although both have the same taste and nutritional value.

Cultural beliefs influence many facets of consumer behavior, including what is purchased and when, where, and how it is purchased. A food company introduced a new toaster product which was essentially a shell of bread dough filled with such things as cheese and ground meat. It was defined as a "convenient new lunch product." Consumers bought the product once but not a second time. When a telephone survey of rejectors failed to provide sufficient information, the company conducted in-depth psychological testing. They found that the advertising had led consumers to expect a toaster product that could be served as lunch; when they tried it, however, they believed it was inadequate as a lunch and more suitable as a snack for children.[6] This mismatch suggested that either the advertising had to be changed to reflect consumers' beliefs that the product was acceptable as a snack or the product had to be reformulated to conform to consumers' ideas of a "healthy" lunch.

Some beliefs may be based on valid medical experience or traditional curative approaches. A company introduced a product containing an analgesic and deacidizer that could be taken without water—a feature that was widely promoted. A postmortem examination of the product's failure revealed that many consumers believed in the customary medical advice for treatment of illness: "Drink plenty of fluids!"

Cultural Values

A value is an especially important belief shared by the members of a society concerning what is desirable or what ought to be. Though there is agreement that the term "cultural value" implies a widely held belief, the literature has not yet addressed the problem of how widely held a belief must be before it may be considered a value.[7]

When the relationship between values and consumer behavior is examined, it is necessary to incorporate the effects of values on consumption activities. Currently, however, there is little empirical evidence of a direct relationship.[8] It appears that cultural values relate to activities through norms.

Cultural Norms

Cultural norms are the rules or standards accepted by members of a society which specify the details of appropriate and inappropriate behavior. Such norms influence the behavior of the consumer in the marketplace in determining not only the product and brand choices that are made, but also the kinds of information sought, the place and manner of purchase, and the way the product is used.

Norms derive from family and friends, from the workplace, schools, and religious institutions, and reflect the values of a social system. They are guides to behavior, but they do not necessarily predict the way in which people will behave. They are, however, subject to enforcement through sanctions and rewards. Rewards may be economic or may involve social acceptance and psychological benefits. Sanctions may range from mild social disapproval to strong legal penalties. Norms can be *folkways* or *mores* and *legal codes* or *laws*.

FOLKWAYS

Folkways are norms that are not considered vital to the welfare of the group, and the means of enforcing conformity to them is not clearly defined. American folkways specify that a man should wear a business suit to a business conference. Should he wear a sweater, he may suffer mild disapproval, but no clear punishment may be applied.

Folkways are handed down by tradition, yet may change to meet new conditions. Custom tends to regulate the individual's actions in bathing, washing, cutting hair, and so on. In the recent past, folkways dictated that a man's face should be clean-shaven and his hair short, and products were designed for those bare faces and clipped heads. More recently accepted folkways incorporate longer hair, beards, and moustaches, and the products that slicked down the short hair and removed short facial hairs are replaced, to some extent, by those that enhance the longer, fly-away hair and the well-shaped beard or moustache.

The trends toward increased leisure activities and more relaxed living led to the widespread adoption of a dress code that incorporated jeans and sneakers. A 1978 survey of almost 3,000 junior and senior high school students across the country revealed that 91.9 percent of them had bought sneakers and 93.1 percent had bought jeans in the previous year.[9] The largest percentage category of both boys and girls had purchased ten or more pairs of jeans, while the largest percentage category reported purchasing two pair of sneakers.

Some marketers, however, see a possibility of the reversal of the trend toward jeans and pants and are developing strategies to cope with the change. An apparel manufacturer believes that women have been in pants so long that they have forgotten how to wear dresses. Under this assumption, the company has produced a five-minute film to be shown to sales personnel in clothing stores. The film, *How to Dress in a Dress*, provides clerks with guidance in advising female shoppers. According to the president of the company, it is "bridging the gap from manufacturer to point-of-sale."[10]

Folkways may be used by marketers as a cultural theme in their campaigns. The term "rites of passage" is used to refer to rites performed by primitive and other societies to mark or observe significant changes in social status or life situations. They may be related to religion, as in the case of the Jewish *bar mitzvah*, which marks a boy's passage from childhood to manhood. The graduation ceremony, the wedding, the retirement dinner—all are rites of passage, which mark an individual's separation from a previous status group and incorporation in a new status group. Rites of incorporation in the new status group are of particular interest to marketers, since it is at this point that the individual accepts a variety of artifacts symbolic of the new status.

In most cases, the new status encourages gift giving and the purchase of items that are relevant to the new phase. An advertising campaign for a bank revolved

EXHIBIT 2.1

"...Guess who's the new Marketing V.P.?"

Peggy Ross. It's time.

The Chase Advantage

CHASE

Job promotion seen as a rite of passage

around people who were promoted to executive positions, noting that "it's time" for such people to develop a financial plan with the banking institution. (See Exhibit 2.1.) Extensive advertising campaigns are conducted by retailers each August to reach those who will soon be "off to college."

MORES

Mores are norms that specify behavior of vital importance to the society and embody its basic moral values. The mores are actively enforced by the members of the society, through either legal action or social sanction. For example, American society places a high value on education for children and discourages their consumption of alcoholic beverages. The laws serve to secure the former, while both legal activity and social sanctions are brought to bear on the latter. Anheuser-

Busch introduced a "not-so-soft" drink called Chelsea, which combined the elements of a soft drink with a minimum of alcoholic content. The company was forced to change its advertising campaign when there was a public outcry over the possibility that children were being encouraged to become accustomed to alcoholic beverages.

LEGAL CODES

Norms may also be embodied in the *law* of a society. Most cultures have a legal code that details behavior that is in violation of the law, establishes the means for deciding whether a violation has been committed, specifies the penalties for each type of violation, and designates the agents to enforce the law. It should be noted, however, that the law does not merely reflect the mores; to some extent it helps to make them. Consumer-protection concepts are embodied in the laws of the United States and in agencies that enforce those laws. The laws and the agencies help to teach the community what the mores should be.

It is also true, however, that the law changes as the mores change. Currently the acceptance of gambling as a consumer pastime has led to the easing of lottery laws and the elimination of some restrictions against casino gambling in some regions in the United States. These changes may encourage marketing activities directed toward products and services related to leisure-time gambling.

One successful behavioral approach to the changing mores and laws related to gambling may be seen in New York State's use of a strong motivational appeal in its lottery. By instituting a method of instant gratification, whereby the buyer of a lottery ticket can determine immediately if he or she is a winner, New York increased its sale of lottery tickets significantly.

CULTURE IN AMERICA

While various societies have a number of cultural characteristics in common, cultural perspectives can vary significantly from country to country. American culture is spread by acculturation and assimilation. *Acculturation* is the process of learning a culture different from the one in which a person was originally raised. Most immigrants to the United States have had to face acculturation. *Assimilation* is the process of being accepted as a genuine member of a new social group. One is acculturated by a culture, assimilated into a society.[11]

People can be acculturated without being assimilated, and they can be assimilated without being acculturated. Although the Amish are accepted in U.S. society, they maintain their own standards of dress, entertainment, transportation, education, and so on. During World War II, the Japanese in the western United States were fairly well accultured but were nevertheless placed in special camps.

Society in America can be characterized as exhibiting *cultural assimilation* and *structural pluralism*.[12] Cultural assimilation relates to the basic values and beliefs on which a kind of middle-majority culture rests. Structural pluralism suggests that there are various ethnic or minority groups, or subcultures, that embrace values and beliefs that differ from those of the middle majority.

Furthermore, there is abundant evidence that opposite and opposing conditions coexist in American society without competing. For example:

1. Frozen dinners and ingredients for elaborate from-scratch meals, including exotic herbs and condiments.
2. Two- and three-car families, plus ecologically benign bicycles for husband and wife.
3. Booming spectator sports and booming participation sports.
4. Sleek Pucci gowns and full-skirted peasant dresses.
5. Computerized scientific management and entrepreneurial venture teams.
6. Mass-merchandising discount stores side by side with full-markup specialty boutiques.
7. Simultaneous booms in contemporary and antique furniture.
8. Mass production by thousands of workers in factories and personalized production by individual artisans in craft shops.[13]

American Cultural Values

Certain values are said to permeate American culture. They are not static, however, and change itself is considered characteristic of our culture. Some of these value changes will be noted in Chapters 6, on the family, and 10, on life-styles.

SOCIAL INTERACTION

David Riesman, in his book *The Lonely Crowd*, offered a thesis concerning social character and the way it is molded by each culture. The Riesman thesis is that human beings can be grouped into major types of social behavior (or "ways of behavior") and that each culture manifests predominantly one or more types, according to its particular phase of development.[14]

Inner-Directed Behavior. The "source of direction for the individual is 'inner' in the sense that it is implanted early in life by the elders and directed toward generalized but nonetheless inescapably destined goals."[15] In an inner-directed culture, a person gains a feeling of control over his own life. He is not so independent as he seems, however. He is obeying and conforming to an internal plan based on the values and principles he has accepted.

Such a person prefers individual sports and hobbies and task-oriented occupations, rather than jobs concerned with human frailty. He does not consume for the sake of consumption but for status and prestige and as a pathway to success. A

EXHIBIT 2.2

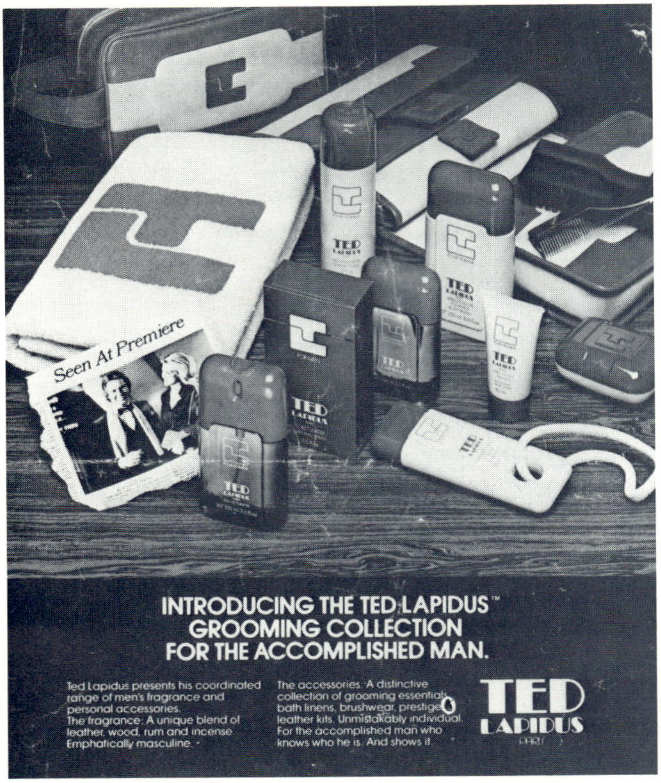

INTRODUCING THE TED LAPIDUS™
GROOMING COLLECTION
FOR THE ACCOMPLISHED MAN.

Advertisement directed toward the inner-directed consumer

campaign that suggests that the individual has worked hard, achieved success in his occupation, and therefore deserves to purchase an expensive product for himself may be effective for the inner-directed individual. (See Exhibit 2.2.)

Other-Directed Behavior. Contemporaries are the source of direction for the other-directed individual—either those known to him or those with whom he is indirectly acquainted, through friends and the mass media.[16] For this person, the peer group has greater influence than the home in implanting social values. For the other-directed individual, the product may be promoted as the kind used by members of his preferred status group.

MATERIALISM

Americans have appeared to assign a high priority to material well-being and comfort. Achievement and success are primarily measured in terms of material goods. Americans tend to buy large numbers of prestige articles that have high visibility: expensive clothing, cars, houses, and so on.

Related to the high value assigned to material possessions is the apparently growing trend toward hedonism, or devotion to pleasure. In the late 1970s a number of new products were introduced that reflect these values. Yves St. Laurent offered a perfume called Opium at $100 an ounce. According to St. Laurent, he called it Opium because, "after all, what is a perfume but an emotion, a catalyst to enchant and mystify and please?" Church shoes introduced a pair of black leather loafers with an 18-karat-gold buckle designed by Cartier, priced at $1,000. A $1,000 bill also bought a hand-painted silk shirt, with scenes featuring large birds native to Brazil. According to the designer, "The V-neck design is really unisex and can be worn either inside or outside a skirt or a pair of trousers."[17] And such advertising campaigns as Miss Clairol's indicate the acceptability of the pursuit of pleasure. (See Exhibit 2.3.)

EXHIBIT 2.3

An appeal to the pleasure principle

CLEANLINESS

Americans tend to use more toothpaste, mouthwash, deodorants, sprays, soap, and so on per capita than any other people in the world. Many advertising campaigns reflect this passion for cleanliness, and when a new product is being promoted, the attribute that is stressed is likely to be its "cleansing power." Products clean faster, better, brighter, with less energy, leave less grit, more sparkle, have scrubbable bubbles, blue brighteners, and so on. Even the less conforming youth may express a concern with cleanliness through the daily shampoo.

YOUTHFULNESS

One of the prime characteristics of American culture is the emphasis on youthfulness. The youth are given opportunities to become active politically and creatively. All segments of society, however, wish to appear youthful, particularly older people who are in daily contact with the young in a work situation. This stress on youth leads to an emphasis on cosmetics and toiletries—like hair dyes and facial creams, and such aids as the foundation garment that "makes you feel like ten years ago." Even the automobile is marketed as projecting youthfulness; it is said that at one time General Motors was considering changing one of its models to Youngmobile.

Along with the emphasis on youth is a concern for good health and longevity. Marketers are aware that many people are now diet-conscious and increasingly interested in low-cholesterol, low-calorie foods. Weight Watchers, which evolved from one individual's concern with excessive weight, has become a conglomerate providing weight-reducing services as well as specialized food preparations. More recently, Nathan Pritikin, a nutritionist, authored two best-sellers, *The Pritikin Program of Diet and Exercise* and *Live Longer Now*. A live-in Pritikin rehabilitation program was offered in many cities, Interstate Brands developed a natural-fiber bread bearing the Pritikin name, and Hunt-Wesson considered the introduction of Pritikin food products.[18]

Jogging as a health-related activity has reached almost epidemic proportions. Marketers incorporate this interest in advertising campaigns and product-development programs. Witness the jogging suit and the jogger's bra. In 1979, an electronic instrument, aptly dubbed Footprint, was developed to help in the diagnosis of joggers' ailments by generating a "map" of the distribution of the body's weight on the feet.[19]

THE WORK ETHIC

Our culture stresses work as a predominant value. This attitude is derived largely from the Puritan or Protestant ethic, which equated idleness with evil. ("The devil finds work for idle hands.") While some people see a decline in the work ethic, there are indications of its expansion, at least in some areas. More married women are working than ever before, many teen-agers and college students provide for some of their needs through part-time work, and the government has acknowledged the value attached to work by extending the age of compulsory retirement.

In addition to increasing available funds for the purchase of products and services, work activities also create more specific needs, such as "suitable" clothing, transportation facilities, and a variety of work-related items. The worker who does not carry a lunchbox carries an attaché case.

THE LEISURE LIFE

While the work ethic persists, at least to some extent, there is increasing interest among Americans in the leisure life. Requests for longer vacations and shorter work weeks indicate the interest in leisure pursuits, as well as the desire to rest. In fact, the leisure industry—that is, the companies that cater to the delivery of leisure products and services—has increased significantly in recent years.

A Gallup survey over time indicated changes in people's leisure-time habits over the years.[20] In response to the question "What is your favorite way of spending an evening?" people gave the responses shown in Table 2.1. After a sharp dip in the mid-1960s, movies/theater, playing cards/games, staying home with family, and visiting friends made strong comebacks in the 1970s.

Television viewing continued to be the number-one leisure activity of the late 1970s, but the number of hours a day spent watching television declined slightly. In keeping with the emphasis on health, there was a significant increase in participation in sports and exercise. A new racquet-ball industry emerged, and the sales of sports equipment and clothing increased significantly. AMF, makers of such equipment, reacted to this growth with a highly visible and successful advertising campaign based on the slogan "We make your weekends."

The rising tide of roller skating was considered to be one of the fastest-growing markets in 1979.[21] The manufacturing and distribution of roller skates in-

TABLE 2.1 FAVORITE WAYS OF SPENDING AN EVENING, 1938–74 (IN PERCENT)*

Favored evening activities	1938	1960	1966	1974
Reading	21%	10%	15%	14%
Movies/theater	17	6	5	9
Watching television	—	28	46	46
Dancing	12	3	2	4
Radio	9	†	2	5
Playing cards/games	9	6	5	8
Staying home with family	7	17	5	10
Visiting friends	4	10	5	8

* Some people interviewed for this information chose more than one "favorite way" to spend an evening; others chose not to select at all.
† Less than 1 percent.

Source: *Advertising Age*, August 11, 1975, p. 49.

creased markedly, and roller-skating rinks proliferated. Advertisers of numerous products, including Sprite, Dr Pepper, and the American Dairy Association, used roller skating as a campaign theme.

CROSS-CULTURAL ANALYSIS

In international marketing, many aspects of the manager's work are strongly affected by culture. Knowledge of cultural characteristics is of great value in understanding areas of consumer behavior in other countries, and such knowledge becomes increasingly important with the growing emphasis on international marketing. Furthermore, with the emergence of what Ernest Dichter, considered the "father" of motivational research, calls "the world customer," an understanding of culture should provide an important competitive tool to those who market internationally.

Cultural Universals

Cultures of various societies may differ markedly; all, however, have a number of characteristics in common—the so-called cultural universals. One list of universals presents seventy-three items arranged in alphabetical order, ranging from age grading, athletic sports, body adornment, calendar, cleanliness training, community organization, cooking, and cooperative labor through religious ritual, residence rules, sexual restrictions, soul concepts, status differentiation, surgery, tool making, trade, visiting, weaning, and weather control.[22]

These so-called universals are quite general in character. Although they exist in all cultures, they may vary widely in form, as do, for example, traditions concerning marriage, housing, and hygiene. Moreover, each culture has its own taboos, to which the marketing manager should be particularly sensitive. Blue, for example, which is the mourning color in Iran, and green, which is the national color of Egypt and Syria, would not be favorably received in products or packages.[23] Similarly, white is the color of mourning in Japan and brown and gray are disapproved colors in Nicaragua. Other cultural taboos will be discussed later in the chapter.

Culture and Multinational Marketing

International marketing considerations are becoming more and more important as firms expand their activities to various countries. Moreover, with such expansion, variations in consumer behavior in these nations are increasingly observable. Of particular relevance to international marketers is the issue of standardization versus nonstandardization in multinational marketing activities.

Many companies have found significant benefits in standardizing their multinational approach to marketing. These benefits include increased effectiveness, reduced costs, and improved planning and control.[24] Nevertheless, the majority of companies still operate on the premise that each national market is unique and must therefore be provided with its own distinctive marketing program.

The major cultural factors that relate to consumer behavior and tend to limit standardization are attitudes toward foreign goods, consumption patterns, attitudes toward bargaining, consumer shopping patterns, attitudes toward selling and language, literacy, and the use of symbolism.[25]

THE NONSTANDARDIZED APPROACH

Some authorities believe nonstandardization is best. They recommend the "tribal" approach: the addressing of marketer efforts to the distinct tastes and prejudices of the "German tribe," the "French tribe," the "Italian tribe," and so on. Knoor adopts this approach, and packages its soups so that the design is in keeping with national habits in various countries.

The tribal approach is also suggested for international advertising. According to one multinational authority, advertising to the middle class in Brazil reaches families that have servants—a much different situation from that of the U.S. middle class. In Brazil, the product is sold to a housewife who must then sell it to her maid or cook, who cannot read.[26]

The standardized approach operates on what may be an erroneous assumption that European women want the same products as U.S. women. For example, Lux liquid detergent became successful in the United States after an ad campaign stressed its gentleness to one's hands. When the same campaign was translated into German, it failed because German housewives were far more interested in how clean it could get their dishes than in how "kind" it was to their hands. Once Lux was made "tougher" to fit the German housewife's image, the product's German sales record improved.[27]

STANDARDIZATION IN MULTINATIONAL MARKETING

Nonetheless, companies would like to establish standard approaches to marketing in many countries both to achieve cost reductions and to deal consistently with consumers. Such consistency in product style, packaging, brand names, and even customer service may heighten the appropriate image the company wishes to project to its customers.

Standardization is possible when communications flow across boundaries, so that one medium may be received by several countries. Such a situation exists in France and Luxembourg and in Belgium, Switzerland, Germany, and Holland. Moreover, when professionals hold international conferences and publish journals and exchange ideas on an international basis, these activities allow companies that sell professional products to standardize their offerings.

STANDARDIZING ADVERTISING

Sometimes an advertising message may be capable of multinational acceptance. Nestlé's New Nescafé with its basic theme, "fresh-ground aroma," and similar creative treatments were used in Europe and in Australia, and subsequently Nestlé's became a leading brand of instant coffee in every European country.[28]

There appears to be increasing evidence of a movement toward a "universal language of advertising."[29] A content analysis of a sample of international advertising indicated some interesting trends.

In foreign liquor, cosmetics, travel, and cigarette advertising, products basing their appeal on status or prestige increasingly use the English words rather than their foreign-language equivalents. The extent to which this trend will continue may be questionable, particularly in view of the nationalism prevalent in some countries. Mexico, for example, requires that most brand names be translated into Spanish for promotional purposes.

American appeals and tactics—such as "slice of life," testimonials, and comparative advertising—often first appear in American television advertising and subsequently in foreign print advertisements. This is particularly true of Procter & Gamble products.

Several companies use the same advertising appeals for their products at home and abroad; often the ads are virtually identical except for the language in which they are delivered. Examples are advertisements for Polaroid, Volkswagen, Lufthansa, Marlboro, Rolex, and Parker in the United States, France, West Germany, and Brazil. United States print advertisements have even been successfully transferred to the Middle East. In this case, however, the advertisements were strongly visual. The campaign that is most frequently mentioned as internationally successful is the one based on Esso's tiger. Other frequently named campaigns are those of Coca-Cola and Volkswagen.

Potential Hazards.   Some observers declare that it is extremely difficult to design an advertising campaign that has universal appeal and note the potential for culture shock. Practices that are acceptable in some countries are taboo in others. Words that are acceptable in one area may translate into unacceptable and even obscene phrases in another. Some faux pas or failures in transferring advertising strategies to foreign countries are listed below:[30]

> "Body by Fisher" was translated as "Corpse by Fisher."
>
> Pepsi's "Come alive" came out as "Come out of the grave."
>
> Maxwell House, billed as the "great American coffee," spent a potful to find out that Germans have little respect for American coffee.
>
> Procter & Gamble found that Crest's fluoride appeal meant little or nothing to the English public.
>
> The Ajax white tornado was less successful as a symbol of power than the Esso "tiger in your tank."
>
> Coke's "Things go better with Coke" and a number of variations proved

transferable, but "It's the real thing" has been difficult to use in many markets.

Ultra Brite's flying kisses and the sexy girl who throws them aroused an adverse reaction in Belgium. This approach and "Give your mouth sex appeal" were dropped; "Nice to have sex appeal" was substituted, but recognition in Belgium was low for this type of product.

The beauty of gleaming white teeth is not perceived by the people of Southeast Asian betel-chewing regions, who are accustomed to black teeth.[31]

Two elephants symbolize bad luck in Africa, so Carlsberg was forced to add a third elephant to its label for one of its major export products.

"Let Hertz put you in the driver's seat" was translated as "Let Hertz make you a chauffeur" in a number of European languages.

The Simmons Company entered the Japanese market in 1964, carefully selected and trained eight salesmen, and sent them out to get orders. Five weeks later a major weakness was discovered: not one of the salesmen had ever slept in a bed, so none could testify personally to the benefits of Simmons mattresses.

In the Cook Islands, a raised cooking stove failed to gain acceptance because the women there had always stooped over low stoves. They found it terribly uncomfortable to have to stand upright when cooking.

Application of Cross-Cultural Studies to Marketing

Cross-national comparisons are often conducted to determine whether any similarities exist among other countries as well as differences. If they do, the marketing expertise developed in one country can be adapted to the marketing of similar products in other countries.

FRENCH AND AMERICAN PURCHASING AND CONSUMPTION BEHAVIOR

Several studies have been conducted on the differences between French and American women in store patronage, as well as variations in the manner in which American and French consumers are most likely to hear about a new grocery product or retail service.

Store Patronage. The main difference between French and American housewives in grocery shopping occurs in the type of store in which they shop.[32] American women tend to shop more often in large supermarkets than in neighborhood supermarkets and corner stores, as French housewives do. These preferences may actually be necessities, as large supermarkets are more common than small stores in the United States, whereas the reverse is true in France.

Patterns of behavior in the buying of women's clothing also varied in the two countries, although the differences were less marked. The major differences occurred in the type of store patronized and appear to reflect the greater prevalence of small specialty shops in France. American women tend to shop more frequently in department and discount stores than in the boutiques typically frequented by French women. Once adjustment was made for differences in income and stage in the life cycle, no significant differences emerged between working and nonworking wives' clothing purchases.

The researcher concluded that despite the findings of differences in purchasing behavior in these countries, the marketing manager should not conclude that it is not feasible to change those patterns. Such patterns may merely reflect the impact of retail environmental factors, rather than underlying attitudes and preferences.

Information Sources. Another cross-national study was conducted to compare the characteristics of consumers in France and the United States in the dissemination of information on grocery products and the use of retail services.[33] It was found that the U.S. customers tended to discuss grocery products significantly more than the French customers. Conversely, the French sample indicated significantly more discussion of retail services than the U.S. sample.

Differences in media habits were found in the two countries. Table 2.2 presents the media in which American and French consumers are most likely to hear about new grocery products and retail services. The U.S. respondents relied considerably more on friends and relatives and on television and print advertising than did the French respondents. Conversely, the French respondents indicated a greater propensity to notice new products for the first time in the store, and new retail services while passing by, than their U.S. counterparts. Moreover, U.S. women were likely to subscribe to a greater number of magazines and to watch

TABLE 2.2   MEDIA IN WHICH FRENCH AND AMERICAN RESPONDENTS WERE MOST LIKELY TO HEAR ABOUT NEW GROCERY PRODUCTS AND RETAIL SERVICES

Media	Grocery products		Retail services	
	U.S.A.	France	U.S.A.	France
Friends or relatives	22%	12%	32%	22%
Television advertising	40	32	22	11
Billboards	0	4	0	15
Notice while passing by (or in the store)	16	43	13	36
Magazine or newspaper advertising	22	8	32	9
Radio advertising	1	1	1	6
Cinema[a]	—	0.5	—	0

[a] Appeared only on the French questionnaire.

Source: Robert T. Green and Eric Langeard, "A Cross-national Comparison of Consumer Habits and Innovator Characteristics," *Journal of Marketing* 39 (July 1975) p. 38.

television more often than French women. These findings suggest that a promotional campaign in France should emphasize packaging considerations and displays and other forms of in-store promotion.

MARKETING TO DEVELOPING COUNTRIES

On the basis of social and economic as well as cultural differences, marketing to developing countries requires specialized techniques. In developing countries, manufacturers have to rely on an extensive range of cooperatives, agents, area distributors, retailers, and traveling peddlers.[34] It is common for items to be handled six or more times before they reach the consumer. Furthermore, these middlemen tend to have values, ideas, and beliefs similar to those of the people they serve. They have a passive attitude toward marketing, acting as an outlet for a product rather than as its advocate. To meet this problem and that of widespread illiteracy, marketers in these countries try to make good use of less conventional methods of distribution. One such method is a van equipped with loudspeakers, tape recorders for music and advertising messages, and a demonstrator/salesman.

Promotion methods may also be tailored to the needs of these developing markets, particularly in relationship to the poverty of the consumer. Wide use is made of sales-promotion techniques. For example, milk has been sold with a free sample of detergent. A spray gun is sold for almost nothing with the purchase of insecticide. Packaging is also designed for the specific needs of developing nations, as, for example, in the preparation of packages that are effective in hot, humid climates. The illiteracy of some of the population is also taken into consideration in the development of crystal-clear brand names, designs, and illustrations.

Since mass media may not reach all of a country's people, personal channels of communication are considered most important in spreading a manufacturer's message in these markets. Demonstrators are widely used. Companies also train their agents to visit villages, voluntary groups, and clubs to give authority to word-of-mouth messages that are transmitted in rural districts.

Pricing mechanisms, too, must be tailored to the country. Although the one-price system occurs in highly developed or government-controlled economies, bargaining is common elsewhere.[35] In fact, in some societies bargaining is a way of life and a source of satisfaction.

The kinds of outlets considered appropriate for shopping vary among countries.[36] In the United States, women generally shop once or twice a week; in some underdeveloped countries, marketplaces are crowded every day. Self-service was not considered feasible in India because of the high rate of pilferage. Attempts to establish supermarkets in Spain failed, partly because of the excess of labor in that nation and partly because of the customs of the people. Upper-income women in Spain welcomed their daily shopping as an opportunity to meet friends and considered supermarkets cold and unfriendly.

In Brazil, however, supermarkets were highly successful among individuals in the upper social classes, and a study of consumption behavior there indicated that a substantial potential existed for supermarkets aimed primarily at lower-class people.[37] Since the lower classes tend to shop at street fairs, the researchers suggested that supermarkets would do well to add personalized services, such as bakeries and dairy counters. The creation of food discount stores and the use of weekly specials and other types of promotion may also attract the lower classes to supermarkets.

Many of the difficulties encountered by those who have sought to improve conditions in underdeveloped countries are due to the traditionalist bias of their cultures. Frequently it is those at the lowest level of the social scale who are most resistant to change. An international agency, INCAP (Nutrition Institute of Central America and Panama), developed an extremely inexpensive meal called *incaparena*, a cereal blend that resembled the widely used cornmeal and could be adapted to any of the corn-based food of the area. The company that produced Quaker Oats agreed to produce and promote incaparena in Colombia, but its success was limited. Though many people did try it and ultimately became customers, those at the lowest economic and educational levels refused even to accept a free sample.[38]

Special care must be taken to note the economic, social, and cultural character of the so-called Third World countries in the development of marketing programs. The Nestlé Company was the target of criticism for its marketing practices in such countries as Malaysia and the Philippines. It used "milk nurses" to visit new mothers, provide them with gifts and advice, and leave samples of a powdered baby formula. According to INFACT (the Infant Formula Action Coalition, an organization developed to counteract this program), promoting the use of this formula was excessively costly for the mothers in these areas and potentially harmful to the babies because of the scarcity of pure water and the lack of knowledge of sterilizing procedures. Nestlé defended its activities as providing aid to mothers. Nevertheless, the company is responding to criticism by eliminating its promotional campaign for infant formula in the Third World countries. The product, however, is still available. A conference on infant nutrition is to be held by the World Health Organization in order to study the problem in depth and provide guidelines for Nestlé, as well as other firms that market products to Third World countries.[39]

The needs of underdeveloped countries are attracting increasing attention. Of particular relevance to the formulation of policies for developing countries is an understanding of the values that are shared by the local population. According to Denis Goulet, rather than impose values on developing countries, exporting nations ought to use the values of that country to shape technology policy.[40] Value research may also provide useful input to future strategies designed to meet the needs of underdeveloped countries.

CULTURAL RESEARCH

The major method used to study culture is fieldwork: anthropologists live closely with and carefully observe the people they are studying. Research techniques used in examining the relevance of culture to consumer behavior, however, have been derived mostly from sociologists and psychologists. In addition to traditional consumer surveys, these techniques include content analysis and value surveys.

Content Analysis

Content analysis is an objective technique for the study of culture which examines the content of communications. It focuses on the message, not the communicator, on the theory that the message reflects the values of the society. Valid content analysis must be objective, systematic, and quantitative.

Content analysis relevant to consumer behavior has been used to study such questions as: "What are the changing values in society as reflected in the analysis of fiction in mass periodicals?" "What is the frequency of appearance of blacks and other minorities in the mass media, and in what roles do they appear?"[41]

An early content-analysis study was used to determine the frequency with which blacks appeared in mass-circulation magazine advertising, and to determine the depiction of the black's role in advertising.[42] Twelve magazines were selected for the study, including *Esquire, Fortune, Good Housekeeping, Life,* and *Newsweek.* The contents of these magazines were studied for each of three years—1946, 1956, and 1965. The results of the study revealed that the frequency of appearance of blacks had not increased over the twenty-year period. The researcher also concluded that although the occupational status of blacks had risen significantly in that time period, they were seldom found in conventional middle-class settings.[43]

A more recent study of the content of television commercials between 1971 and 1976 examined the trends in role portrayals of male and female characters. The researchers concluded that the changing roles of women have become at least partially incorporated into the value system of American society.[44]

Value Surveys

While a clear understanding of the relationship of values to consumption behavior is yet to be achieved, some research has been conducted in an effort to find correlations between them.

To understand how values are correlated with consumer behavior, it is necessary to have an instrument that both defines and measures values. One such instrument was developed by Milton Rokeach, who defines a value as "a centrally held, enduring belief which guides actions and judgments across specific situations and beyond immediate goals to more ultimate end-states of existence."[45] Rokeach implies that means, or "instrumental" values, are to be differentiated from ends, or "terminal" values.

The terminal values listed in Table 2.3 measure the ends that are considered personally and socially worth striving for (e.g., leading an exciting life, family security, pleasure). The instrumental values relate to the modes of conduct that are

TABLE 2.3   CORRELATION OF TERMINAL AND INSTRUMENTAL VALUES

Terminal value	r^*	Instrumental value	r
A comfortable life (a prosperous life)	.70	Ambitious (hard-working, aspiring)	.70
An exciting life (a stimulating, active life)	.73	Broad-minded (open-minded)	.57
A sense of accomplishment (lasting contribution)	.51	Capable (competent, effective)	.51
A world at peace (free of war and conflict)	.67	Cheerful (lighthearted, joyful)	.65
A world of beauty (beauty of nature and the arts)	.66	Clean (neat, tidy)	.66
Equality (brotherhood, equal opportunity for all)	.71	Courageous (standing up for your beliefs)	.52
Family security (taking care of loved ones)	.64	Forgiving (willing to pardon others)	.62
Freedom (independence, free choice)	.61	Helpful (working for the welfare of others)	.66
Happiness (contentedness)	.62	Honest (sincere, truthful)	.62
Inner harmony (freedom from inner conflict)	.65	Imaginative (daring, creative)	.69
Mature love (sexual and spiritual intimacy)	.68	Independent (self-reliant, self-sufficient)	.60
National security (protection from attack)	.67	Intellectual (intelligent, reflective)	.67
Pleasure (an enjoyable, leisurely life)	.57	Logical (consistent, rational)	.57
Salvation (saved, eternal life)	.88	Loving (affectionate, tender)	.65
Self-respect (self-esteem)	.58	Obedient (dutiful, respectful)	.53
Social recognition (respect, admiration)	.65	Polite (courteous, well-mannered)	.53
True friendship (close companionship)	.59	Responsible (dependable, reliable)	.45
Wisdom (a mature understanding of life)	.60	Self-controlled (restrained, self-disciplined)	.52

* Numbers are test-retest correlation coefficients.

Source: Milton Rokeach, *The Nature of Human Values* (New York: Free Press, 1973), p. 28.

considered the preferable means of achieving those ends (e.g., ambition, independence, self-control). The Rokeach value distinctions have been used to differentiate various groups. For example, various combinations of terminal and instrumental values have been found to differentiate men from women and "hawks" from "doves."

Although Rokeach's value instrument has been criticized, some researchers have investigated differential product preferences by use of these concepts of terminal and instrumental values. A study of automobile attributes found indications of variations between college students and their parents in instrumental and terminal values in regard to automobiles. The researchers concluded that such surveys may be useful in market segmentation.[46] Other studies based on Rokeach's view of values indicate the importance of personal values, which may vary by geographic region, age, education, income, and other demographic characteristics.[47] It has also been suggested that value surveys have relevance for research on life-styles, discussed later in this text.[48]

Some authorities see the study of consumer values as a challenging area of research in the years ahead. For such research to be effective, however, a number of problems have to be solved. We need a better definition of consumer values; a comprehensive list of values on which behavioral scientists and marketers can agree; an acceptable model of values; a standard method of measuring values; and perhaps of most importance, a demonstration of the relationship of values to consumer behavior.[49]

SUMMARY

The influence of culture on consumer behavior can be expressed in various ways. Although culture cannot be seen, its manifestations can be observed.

The culture of a society is defined in terms of its beliefs, values, and norms. Belief systems and the values they generate can influence the social character of the individual. Norms, or folkways, also reflect the society's culture. Folkways can be adapted by marketers in the designing of marketing themes; one such concept that may be used is "rites of passage." Mores and laws are actively enforced by members of the society. They suggest the desirable standards of behavior and provide a mechanism for imposition of these standards. The marketer needs to know what aspects of culture are acceptable, restricted, or in the process of change.

American culture exhibits cultural assimilation and structural pluralism. This means that although some basic values and beliefs are accepted by the majority of citizens, various subcultures have somewhat distinctive values and beliefs. Certain characteristics permeate American culture; for example, an interest in cleanliness, materialism, and an emphasis on youth and leisure. Some new patterns are emerging in American culture, and these patterns, as well as older characteristics, are incorporated in the firm's marketing strategies.

Although the culture of one society may differ from that of another, there are a number of so-called cultural universals related to family life, work activities, and so on. Despite these cultural universals, activities or concepts that are culturally accepted in some countries are taboo in others.

With the growing emphasis on international marketing, knowledge of the cultural characteristics of various countries is becoming increasingly significant. Companies have engaged in both standardized and nonstandardized approaches in their international markets. Standardization of marketing strategies reduces costs and improves planning and control. Such standardization may be limited, however, by differences in national language, literacy, shopping patterns, and attitudes toward foreign goods and bargaining. Several cross-cultural analyses have been conducted to determine the extent to which standardization should be applied to marketing and advertising campaigns. Particular attention has been paid to developing countries in attempts to determine the most effective means of marketing in these areas.

Cultural research emerges from studies of anthropologists, sociologists, and psychologists. Culture may be studied through content analysis, a research technique that examines messages in communications on the theory that such messages reflect the values of the society. Value surveys have been used in an effort to correlate values with consumer behavior. Before such techniques can be considered effective, however, a number of problems in the development of an efficient value-measurement instrument must be resolved.

DISCUSSION QUESTIONS

1. It has been estimated that there are 164 definitions of culture. Why do you think this is so?

2. What is the difference between cultural beliefs and cultural values?

3. How are norms interrelated with consumer behavior?

4. What do you see as some of the basic cultural values of Americans? How are these values changing?

5. Describe three marketing strategies that reflect basic American values.

6. Do you see yourself as more "other-directed" or "inner-directed"? How will this tendency influence your choice of products and services?

7. Why is it important for a multinational marketer to understand cultural variations among countries?

8. Under what circumstances would a standardized marketing program be successful for multinational marketers? A nonstandardized approach?

9. What are the special cultural problems involved in marketing to underdeveloped countries?

10. Some writers referred to the 1970s as the "me generation." How was this view reflected in marketing strategies? To what extent do you think this emphasis will persist in the 1980s?

NOTES

1. E. B. Taylor, *Primitive Culture*, 3d ed. (London: John Murray, 1891).

2. A. L. Kroeber and Clyde Kluckhohn, *Culture: A Critical Review of Concepts and Definitions* (New York: Random House, 1963).

3. Walter A. Henry, "Cultural Values Do Correlate with Consumer Behavior," *Journal of Marketing Research* 18 (May 1976), p. 121.

4. Ralph Linton, "The Concept of Culture," in *Perspectives in Consumer Behavior,* ed. Harold Kassarjian and Thomas S. Robertson, rev. ed. (Glenview, Ill.: Scott, Foresman, 1973), p. 412.

5. David Krech, Richard S. Crutchfield, and Egerton L. Ballachey, *Individual in Society* (New York: McGraw-Hill, 1962), pp. 349–353.

6. David M. Stander, "Testing New Product Ideas in an 'Archie Bunker' World," *Marketing News,* November 15, 1973, p. 12.

7. Francesco M. Nicosia and Robert N. Mayer, "Toward a Sociology of Consumption," *Journal of Consumer Research* 3 (September 1976), pp. 65–75.

8. Ibid., p. 71.

9. *Apparel Survey* (Middletown, Conn.: Xerox Education Publications, 1978).

10. "Marketing Observer," *Business Week,* June 19, 1978, p. 92.

11. Bernard Berelson and Gary A. Steiner, *Human Behavior: An Inventory of Scientific Findings* (New York: Harcourt Brace Jovanovich, 1967).

12. R. J. Markin, Jr., *Consumer Behavior: A Cognitive Orientation* (New York: Macmillan, 1974), p. 469.

13. Theodore Levitt, *Marketing for Business Growth* (New York: McGraw-Hill, 1974), p. 229.

14. David Riesman, Nathan Glazer, and Reuel Denney, *The Lonely Crowd,* abr. ed. (New Haven: Yale University Press, 1961).

15. Ibid., p. 15.

16. Ibid., p. 21.

17. Betty Ommerman, "Looks," *Newsday,* September 12, 1978, p. 9A.

18. Jennifer Pendleton, "Pritikin Sells Health and Bread," *Advertising Age,* June 4, 1979, p. 108.

19. " 'Mapping' Feet That Feel Ill," *Business Week,* June 18, 1979, p. 60.

20. *Advertising Age,* August 11, 1975, p. 49.

21. Sam Harper, "Streets Now Crowded with Roller Skaters, Marketers," *Advertising Age,* May 28, 1979, p. 64.

22. George P. Murdock, "The Common Denominator of Cultures," in *The Science of Man in the World Crisis,* ed. Ralph Linden (New York: Columbia University Press, 1945), pp. 123–142.

23. Charles Winick, "Anthropology's Contribution to Marketing," *Journal of Marketing* 25 (July 1961), pp. 53–60.

24. Robert D. Buzzell, "Can You Standardize Multinational Marketing?" in *Managerial Marketing: Policies, Strategies, and Decisions,* ed. E. J. Kelley and William Lazer (Homewood, Ill.: Richard D. Irwin, 1973), pp. 332–350.

25. Ibid., p. 343.

26. A. D. (Art) Lowenthal, "The Member Speaks: Too Soon or Too Late, Good Ideas, Products Can Fail Here, Overseas," *Marketing News,* March 10, 1978, p. 3.

27. Ibid.

28. Buzzell, "Can You Standardize Multinational Marketing?" p. 339.

29. William A. Mindak, "How Close Are We to Universal Advertising Standards?" in *Making Advertising Relevant: Proceedings of the 1975 American Academy of Advertising,* ed. L. W. Lanfranco (American Academy of Advertising, 1975), p. 32.

30. The first seven examples are from S. Watson Dunn, "Effect of National Identity on Multinational Promotions in Europe," *Journal of Marketing* 40 (October 1976), pp. 50–57.

31. This and the next four examples are from F. J. Douglas McConnell, "The Economics of Behavior Factors on the Multi-National Corporation," in *Relevance in Marketing: Problems, Research, Action,* ed. Fred C. Allvine (Chicago: American Marketing Association, 1971), pp. 262–266.

32. Susan P. Douglas, "Cross-national Comparisons and Consumer Stereotypes: A Case Study of Working and Non-Working Wives in the U.S. and France," *Journal of Consumer Research* 3 (June 1976), pp. 12–20.

33. Robert T. Green and Eric Langeard, "A Cross-national Comparison of Consumer Habits and Innovator Characteristics," *Journal of Marketing* 39 (July 1975), pp. 34–41.

34. A. Graeme Cranch, "Modern Marketing Techniques Applied to Developing Countries," in *Combined Proceedings: Marketing Education and the Real World and Dynamic Marketing in a Changing World,* ed. B. W. Becker and H. Becker (Chicago: American Marketing Association, 1972), pp. 183–186.

35. Thomas S. Robertson, *Consumer Behavior* (Glenview, Ill.: Scott, Foresman, 1970), p. 110.

36. Ibid., pp. 110–111.

37. Isabella C. M. Cunningham, William H. Cunningham, and Russell M. Moore, *Social Class and Consumption Behavior in São Paulo, Brazil* (Austin: Bureau of Business Research, University of Texas, 1976).

38. Chester R. Wasson and David H. McConaughy, *Buying Behavior and Marketing Decisions* (New York: Irvington Books, 1968), p. 73.

39. Don Morris, "Is Infant Formula 'Killing Babies'? Boycott of Nestlé Hurts but It Doesn't Cut Sales," *Marketing News,* March 23, 1979, p. 2.

40. Denis Goulet, "Can Values Shape Third-World Technology Policy?" *Journal of International Affairs* 33 (Spring/Summer 1979), pp. 89–109.

41. Harold H. Kassarjian, "Content Analysis in Consumer Research," *Journal of Consumer Research* 4 (June 1977), pp. 8–18.

42. Harold H. Kassarjian, "The Negro and American Advertising, 1946–1965," *Journal of Marketing Research* 6 (February 1969), pp. 29–39.

43. Subsequent content-analysis studies of blacks in mass media are discussed in the next chapter.

44. Kenneth C. Schneider and Sharon Black Schneider, "Trends in Sex Roles in Television Commercials," *Journal of Marketing* 43 (Summer 1979), pp. 79–84.

45. Milton Rokeach, *Beliefs, Attitudes, and Values: A Theory of Organization and Change* (San Francisco: Jossey-Bass, 1968), p. 161.

46. D. E. Vinson and J. M. Munson, "Personal Values: An Approach to Market Segmentation," in *Marketing: 1776 to 1976 and Beyond,* ed. K. L. Bernhardt (Chicago: American Marketing Association, 1976), pp. 313–317.

47. Donald E. Vinson, Jerome E. Scott, and Lawrence M. Lamont, "The Role of Personal Values in Marketing and Consumer Behavior," *Journal of Marketing* 41 (April 1977), pp. 44–50.

48. James M. Carman, "Values and Consumption Patterns: A Closed Loop," in *Advances in Consumer Research,* vol. 5, ed. by H. Keith Hunt (Ann Arbor: Association for Consumer Research, 1978), pp. 403–407.

49. C. Joseph Clawson and Donald E. Vinson, "Human Values: An Historical and Interdisciplinary Analysis," in *Advances in Consumer Research,* vol. 5, ed. H. Keith Hunt (Ann Arbor: Association for Consumer Research, 1978), pp. 396–402.

CHAPTER 3

SUBCULTURES

Johnson Products Company was founded in 1954 to manufacture one product: Ultra Wave Hair Culture, a chemical hair straightener for men. In subsequent years, the company continued to introduce products specifically designed for the black market. In January 1971 Johnson Products became the first predominantly black-owned company to be listed on a major stock exchange. In the same year the company became the only black advertiser to sponsor a nationally syndicated weekly television show, "Soul Train." While in recent years the company has entered the total market, most of its products, such as hair dressings, conditioners, shampoos, and cosmetics, are designed to meet the needs of black consumers.[1]

Obviously cultural manifestations are not always consistent throughout a society. Even within a society that shares many cultural traits or elements, some characteristics distinguish one group from another. When distinguishing characteristics are shared by a group that may be identified by ethnicity, geographic origin, or some other means, that group is called a subculture.

A subculture is enduring and self-perpetuating. The members of the group may have considerable consensus with respect to value meanings and role of social institutions. In fact, they may have similar life-styles, frequently described in terms of their activities, interests, and opinions. The difference between a life-style and a subculture is the latter's capacity to endure.[2]

The influence of the norms and values of a subgroup on the life-styles of individual members may range from insignificant to dominating. It should be noted that the behavior of subcultures may not always be distinguishable from that of the national culture, but to the extent that it is, the marketer may find it useful to isolate such behavior.

Subcultures tend to exist in all countries. Canada, for instance, has the French-Canadians, who may require a marketing strategy that differs from that used to reach English-speaking Canadians.[3] Furthermore, subcultures may cross national lines. Even when nations differ in language and other aspects of culture, they may share a religious or economic subculture. The Shiite Muslims share a subculture in all nations in which they are found, and the very poor are said to share a "culture of poverty" that crosses national boundaries.

This chapter examines subcultures from the following perspectives:

How are subcultures defined?
What kinds of subcultures exist?
What is the significance of subcultural groups as market target segments?

CHARACTERISTICS OF SUBCULTURES

While there is general agreement that subcultures are specialized segments of a society, there is less consensus as to the kinds of groups that should be designated as subcultures. Typically subcultures are defined in terms of ethnic background, religion, and geographic area. In consumer analysis, age groups are included as specialized social segments whose behavior patterns influence individual consumers.[4]

One definition designates a subculture as

> a subdivision of a national culture, composed of a combination of factorable social situations such as class status, ethnic background, regional and rural or urban residence, and religious affiliation, but forming in their combination a functioning unity which has an integrating impact on the particular individual.[5]

The United States has several major subcultures that have at least some distinctive values, norms, and behavior, which in turn identify them as important market segments. These segments include such ethnic markets as blacks, Puerto Ricans, and Indians, such religious groups as Catholics, Jews, evangelical Protestants, Christian Scientists, and Seventh-Day Adventists, and such geographic groups as Californians, New Yorkers, and the Pennsylvania Dutch. The values and norms of geographic groups, however, may reflect the influences of religion, nationality, and even climatic conditions. As we have noted, from a marketing viewpoint age groups are also identified as subcultures, for the extent to which such age segments exhibit similar values, needs, and behavioral patterns may be useful in the development of marketing strategies.

Many factors enter the selection of a particular subcultural group as a target market. As we saw at the beginning of this chapter, the black subculture is significant in both size and market potential. Factors other than size, however, may be determinants in marketing strategies aimed at subcultural groups. The number of Jews in the United States who insist on kosher products (consistent with Orthodox religious requirements) is relatively small. Nevertheless, they appear to be considered a significant ethnic market segment. In 1978, *Kosher Home* magazine was introduced to consumers who were considered heavy users of traditional and kosher products. Heavy advertising from china and silverware manufacturers was anticipated, since 75 percent of readers were expected to have or need four sets of dishes and several sets of silverware, consistent with the Jewish dietary laws. In 1979, the magazine—changed to *Kosher Home's Jewish Living*—was selling well as a bimonthly.

Marketers may also try to extend the preferences of a particular subcultural segment to the total population, as, for example, in the campaign "You don't have to be Jewish to like Levy's rye bread." Such strategies may not always be successful. A novelty-item manufacturing company considered introducing Mother Klein's Kosher Style canned dog food into supermarkets. The appeal in this case was not limited to those who kept kosher homes, but rather was intended to appeal to those who perceived the word "kosher" to indicate high quality. Test print ads borrowed from Levy's famous theme: "You don't have to be Jewish to love Mother Klein's Kosher Style dog food." Radio ads featured actor Herschel Bernardi discussing the difficulties involved in determining whether or not a dog is Jewish. The problem arose, he said, when many dogs anglicized their names upon immigration; he cited the Goldberg retriever as an example.[6] Focus-group interviews, however, indicated that the product was perceived as a joke, and that while people might buy it once as a collector's item, there would be few repeat sales.[7] The firm abandoned the idea.

The rest of this chapter examines two subcultural groups that have been the subjects of consumer-behavior research and appear to have significant impact on marketing activities: blacks and the elderly.

THE BLACK SUBCULTURE

Several reasons are offered for studying the black market. Most significant is the fact that the marketing behavior of blacks is closely tied to the broad social problems of this population. Further, the black market is a large segment of the American market and has specific needs and desires that the practical marketing man should know about.

The total black population of the United States was 25 million in 1977.[8] The

1970s, like the 1960s, was characterized by a downward trend in the proportion of black husband/wife families, accompanied by a growth in the proportion of black families headed by a woman (with no spouse present). The high rate of marital dissolution, the retention of children by unmarried mothers, and increased economic independence of women are reflected in changes in the characteristics of black female heads of families. These women are more likely to be single or divorced, to be younger, and to have more children to support than white women.

Reflecting the increase in female-headed families, the percentage of black children living with both parents dropped sharply in the 1970s. For both blacks and whites, the proportion of children living with both parents appears to be associated with income level. Among black families with incomes under $4,000, less than one-fifth of the children lived with both parents. At the $15,000 income level, nearly all black children were living with both a mother and a father.

The black population cannot be characterized as a homogeneous subculture. Various segments of the black population have their own family composition, income range, and life-styles, which require distinctive marketing strategies.

Of particular interest to marketers is the growing segment of black suburbanites. Between 1970 and 1977, the black population in the suburbs increased 33 percent (versus a 10.3 percent gain by whites). Most of the new black suburbanites are in the middle to upper income categories. New suburban black households are predominantly young and small.[9]

While only slightly more than one-fourth of metropolitan black families live in the suburbs, their buying power is considerably more than their share suggests. Black family income rose twice as fast in the suburbs as it did in the central cities in the 1970s, making the segment of particular importance to marketers concerned with ability to buy.

Numerous studies were conducted in the 1960s relevant to black consumers. Some were concerned with providing an understanding of this subculture so that it might be better evaluated by the marketing decision maker.[10] Others examined blacks as members of a disadvantaged minority group in order to improve the quality of marketing services rendered to this group.[11]

Fewer studies have been conducted in recent years, but the concerns remain the same. Blacks represent more than 1 of every 5 central-city residents, and these core cities will remain important from a societal aspect, as well as for those selling to blacks. There is a growing class of upwardly mobile black families that also require understanding and evaluation.

Black Consumption Patterns

An early study designed to determine the extent to which black consumption patterns differ from those of whites indicated that the differences may be related not only to income. Some consumption patterns emerged in regard to food products, liquor, and personal hygiene products:[12]

Blacks consumed more butter than did whites at every income level. Nondietary soft-drink consumption varied drastically across income classes between the two groups. Black use was double that of whites at the lowest income level, but then tended to decline with increasing wealth.

At every income level but the highest, blacks purchased more liquor than whites. For both whites and blacks, liquor consumption rose steadily with income.

Blacks purchased more deodorants, toothpaste, and mouthwash than whites in almost every income group, but less shampoo.

A major finding was that for many household products, consumption-pattern differences between blacks and whites were small. Purchases of such products as margarine and frozen and canned vegetables were identical for the two groups. The similarities of overall consumption patterns increased as income rose.

More recent data indicate that blacks tend to use some products more and others less than the national average. (See Table 3.1.) It should be noted, however, that these data were secured by comparison of sales of items in stores in black neighborhoods with sales in all stores. It is therefore possible that such variations may reflect income variations rather than black purchasing patterns.

Brand Loyalty

There are indications that blacks are loyal to certain brands. Some brands with heavy black support include Oscar Mayer meat products, Quaker hot cereals,

TABLE 3.1   DISTINCTIVE CONSUMPTION PATTERNS AMONG BLACKS

Products with heavy usage among blacks		Products with light usage among blacks	
Product	Use index[a]	Product	Use index[a]
Rice and rice dinners	215	Dishwashing detergent	57
Evaporated milk	187	Salad dressing and mayonnaise	80
All-purpose flour	153	Prepared soups	82
Salad and cooking oils	140	Regular coffee	86
Toilet soaps	126	Prepared puddings	87
Strained baby foods	117	Canned tuna	87
Tomato paste	116	Dry cereals	87
Tea bags	115	Cake mixes	89
Catsup	111	Table syrups	92
Paper towels	108	Frozen prepared dinners	94
Instant tea	105	Foil and plastic wraps	95

[a] Based on sales of a commodity class in stores in black neighborhoods compared with the average for that commodity in all stores in the A. C. Nielsen sample. Thus stores in black neighborhoods sell 115 percent more rice and rice dinners and 43 percent less dishwasher detergents than does the average store in the Nielsen sample.

Source: A. C. Nielsen Co., in Thayer C. Taylor, "Blacks: Two Distinct Markets in One," *Sales and Marketing Management*, December 12, 1977, p. 35.

Kellogg's cold cereals, Pillsbury flour, Campbell's soups, and Lipton tea. Moreover, blacks are more loyal to national products than to private labels.[13] Nevertheless, an all-embracing conclusion that blacks are brand-loyal is premature. Certain segments within the black community tend to be more brand-loyal than others. A study in which blacks were segmented into the categories of "strivers" and "nonstrivers" indicated that strivers are more brand-loyal.[14] Strivers were more fashion and status conscious, and apparently relied on brand names for reassurance, whereas nonstrivers did not seek such reassurance. Moreover, the impact of inflationary pressures on the brand loyalty of whites, as well as blacks, is yet to be determined.

Promotion to Blacks

Promotional studies relevant to blacks involve social as well as communication considerations, and include evaluations of media use, effective advertising appeals, and the use of black models.

MEDIA

Radio appears to have the most widespread use among blacks. In fact, black consumers listen to radio more than whites, particularly in the evenings and on weekends.[15] Magazine readership appeals to the more affluent blacks, and it appears that blacks are particularly responsive to advertisements in black magazines.

An analysis of television viewing by blacks, however, revealed that a black actor in a starring or regular role in a prime-time network program does not necessarily guarantee the largest black audience.[16] Data show that commercials on "Mork and Mindy" would reach a larger black audience than those on "The Jeffersons" in some markets.

ADVERTISING APPEALS

Specialized appeals work well among the heavy product users in the black community. Such appeals, however, require more than merely the use of black models. They should be presented in realistic situations and the copy and "jargon" should be designed with care and sensitivity.[17] For example, care should be taken in depicting families in car ads aimed at blacks, since "cars are an individual ego-oriented product. Unlike the white idea of a 'family car,' cars are a 'man's car' that the family just happens to use."[18]

There are indications that humorous appeals may be less effective among blacks than among whites. A recent study to determine the effectiveness of humor in advertisements as a function of audience characteristics revealed variations between black and white responses. Blacks tended to find a radio commercial for

Blue Nun wine and a television commercial for Alka-Seltzer less funny than whites did.[19] The researchers concluded that cultural background had an impact on the persuadability of humorous commercials, and that if humor is to be used as a persuasive agent, it should be employed with the cultural or subcultural background of the audience target groups in mind.

BLACK MODELS

The use of black models in advertising has been viewed from two perspectives: marketing effectiveness and societal concern. It appears that blacks react more favorably to advertisements with all black models or with integrated models than to advertisements with all white models.[20] For a marketer who sells to both blacks and whites, however, a question frequently arises as to whether or not a black model should appear in advertising. Some people have seen this as a "damned if you do and damned if you don't" situation; that is, prejudiced whites may be antagonized by the appearance of blacks, and blacks may be equally antagonized if black models are not used.

In order to examine the extent of white backlash, research measuring the reaction of white consumers to black models in promotional materials has been conducted since the 1960s.[21] The findings, however, have not been entirely consistent. In general, the experimental literature suggests that there are very few negative reactions among white consumers to black models in promotional material.

One study indicated that negative reactions may occur when "personal" products are portrayed in ads.[22] Major negative reactions to black models, however, were found in only one study, whose authors concluded that there are high and low prejudice segments in the marketplace, and marketers could precipitate a white backlash by running ads with black models in the more prejudiced markets.[23] A more recent study resulted in disagreement with these results: the researchers concluded that marketers should not fear white backlash or any negative consequences from the use of black models in promotional material.[24]

Such fears tend to persist, however, and many advertisers do not use black models. Yet from a societal perspective, the situation seems to be improving.

Content analysis—a research mechanism for examination of cultural values, as we saw in Chapter 2—has been used to evaluate the portrayal of blacks in advertising. An early study of print media disclosed that the frequency of use of blacks in advertising had not increased between 1946 and 1965. For television, however, a content-analysis study conducted in Michigan revealed that between 1967 and 1969 there was a systematic increase in the use of blacks in TV commercials.[25] Replication of this study in two geographical areas, the South and the West, indicated that the use of blacks in TV commercials had increased by 1974.[26] In 1967, 4 percent of prime-time television commercials contained blacks; this figure rose to 13 percent in 1974. Whether this increase was a result of economic factors or humanitarian concerns is difficult to determine.

OLDER PERSONS

There were 24 million people over 65 in the United States in 1978. This figure was projected to grow to 24.5 million by 1980, or about 11 percent of the total population.[27] In fact, this group is one of the fastest growing segments of the population (see Figure 3.1) and its growth is expected to continue.

Most older people are not poor and neglected; the percentage of older Americans living below the poverty line dropped from 25 percent in 1969 to 16 percent in 1974. It is true, however, that this group tends to live at an income that will not significantly increase.

With an increase in the older segment and a decline in the birth rate, companies whose products do not appeal to more mature tastes and needs may find themselves plagued with a shrinking market share. In acknowledgment of this situation, Johnson & Johnson started a campaign to persuade adults to use its baby shampoo and baby oil. Gerber Products, which used to boast that "babies are our business, our only business," has dropped the last half of the slogan and begun to sell life insurance to older folks under the catchline "Gerber now babies the over-50's." Campbell Soup, which successfully appealed to the mothers of then-toddling baby boomers with its alphabet soup in the 1950s, now offers its Manhandlers. Even Levi Strauss is marketing a three-piece suit, and its new Levis for Men line is cut more full "to accommodate the guy who has stopped playing football and started watching it."[28]

Older families live in smaller households and may want scaled-down appliances that are highly automated. General Electric is offering minicomputerized household gadgets and Campbell is providing a Soup-for-One line. Television manufacturers see a boom in the sale of console models, traditionally the choice of

FIGURE 3.1   POPULATION GROWTH 1970–1980, BY AGE GROUPS

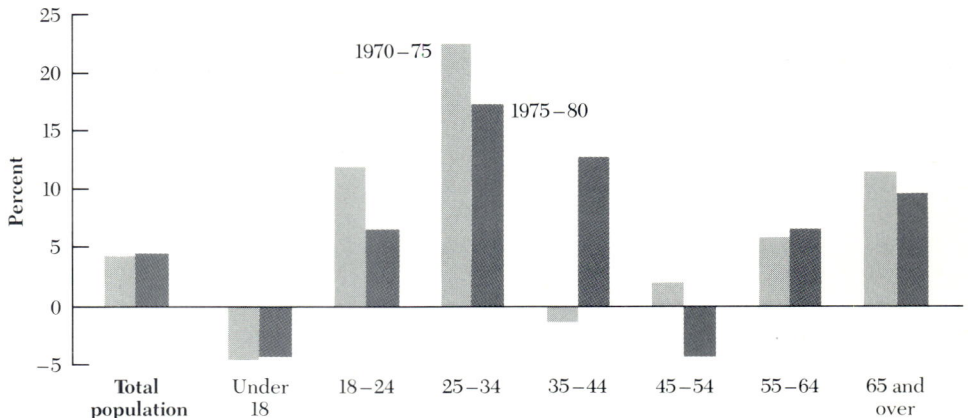

Source: Fabian Linden, "The Second Half of the Seventies," *Consumer Markets: The Conference Board Record* 12 (December 1975), p. 5.

older buyers, and are promoting their remote-control TV sets to "appeal to older people who don't want to get up."

Shopping Habits

Shopping activities of older people may be distinctive. One study indicated that older citizens are less likely to use discount stores and are significant supporters of the traditional downtown department stores.[29] The elderly appear willing to travel to the downtown shopping district and to pay higher prices for department store merchandise than those generally charged in suburban malls. They are less likely than other groups, however, to have store credit cards.

In a study to determine the extent to which the elderly used in-store information, their reported levels of familiarity with nutritional labeling, open-code dating, and unit pricing were found to be substantially lower than those of a representative national sample.[30] The usefulness and frequency of use among those who were familiar with these information sources, however, were similar for members of the elderly sample and for a national sample of all shoppers. It is suggested that since the elderly appear less informed in these areas, special attention should be directed toward them so that they can make full use of the advantages provided by such informational inputs.

Media

The elderly read selectively and prefer to get their news from newspapers and broadcasting media. They are heavy watchers of early-morning television and are highly television-news-oriented. A recent survey of TV viewing habits revealed that a large group of elderly women watch TV to offset loneliness.[31] In apparent acknowledgment of elderly viewing habits, marketers have increased the use of adults over 40 in television commercials. In earlier years, the clever young bride's perception of products was superior to that of her mother or mother-in-law; in current commercials, she frequently learns from her elders.

Some people see this tendency to use older people as a result of the habit of imitating winning commercials. One of the notable hits of the 1970s was the Maxwell House Coffee commercial that featured Margaret Hamilton, an actress best known for her role as the Wicked Witch of the West in the movie *The Wizard of Oz*. Other examples are "Mrs. Olsen" for Folger's coffee and Nancy Walker for Bounty paper towels.

As some researchers indicate, however, the older market may resist categorization and market strategies directed specifically toward them. They may, in fact, tend to be heterogeneous and segmented. H. J. Heinz's effort to package dietetic food and market it to old people under the name Senior Food flopped badly. It seemed to label these people as old. Some see the older market as split into two groups: the "young old," from 60 to 75, and the "old old," who are over 75. Further, as we saw in Chapter 1, the emergence of the "young elderly," a growing segment of people who are retiring early, have funds, and wish to enjoy the "good life," suggests the development of a third segment. One magazine introduced in the late seventies is called *50 Plus*. Its advertisers include cosmetic companies, airlines, travel and tourism organizations, and investment firms. Further research may disclose variations in life-style among these groups and suggest varying strategies to reach these segments.

SUMMARY

A number of subcultures, or specialized segments of a culture, exist in American society. The black population comprises a significant subculture that reveals distinctions in psychographic characteristics and consumption habits which may be useful in the design of an effective marketing strategy for this group. Another specialized group that is increasing in size consists of older people. Companies have engaged in campaigns designed to provide goods and services specifically geared to the older market, and advertising campaigns feature elderly people.

DISCUSSION QUESTIONS

1. What is a subculture? Under what circumstances is it important for marketers to investigate subcultural influences?

2. Do you consider yourself to be a member of a subculture? If so, to what extent does your membership in this group influence your behavior in the marketplace?

3. List several reasons why a product accepted by one subcultural group may fail in another.

4. Do you believe the black subculture is becoming more/less like the white group in terms of consumer behavior?

5. What special marketing efforts should be used to reach the black market?

6. How would you segment the elderly from a marketing viewpoint?

7. What variations in behavior of the elderly segments should be incorporated in the marketing strategy?

8. An evidently successful advertising campaign directed at a particular subgroup is considered offensive by a few members of that subgroup. To what extent should the marketer recognize these complaints? Why?

NOTES

1. John Clark, *Business Today: Successes and Failures* (New York: Random House, 1979), pp. 26–27.

2. James M. Carman, "Values and Consumption Patterns: A Closed Loop," in *Advances in Consumer Research*, vol. 5, ed. H. Keith Hunt (Ann Arbor: Association for Consumer Research, 1978), pp. 403–407.

3. M. Richard Gelfand, "French Canada as a Minority Market," in *1974 Combined Proceedings*, ed. Ronald C. Curhan (Chicago: American Marketing Association, 1975), pp. 680–682.

4. Maneck S. Wadia, "The Concept of Culture in the Analysis of Consumers," in *Changing Marketing Systems: Consumer, Corporate, and Government Interfaces, 1967 Winter Conference Proceedings*, ed. Reed Moyer (Chicago: American Marketing Association, 1967), pp. 186–190.

5. M. Gordon, "The Concept of the Subculture and Its Applications," *Social Forces* 26 (October 1947), pp. 40–42.

6. "Oy Vey, a Kosher Food for the Discerning Dog," *Advertising Age*, February 26, 1979, p. 24.

7. "Dog Food Barks Up Wrong Tree," *Advertising Age*, September 17, 1979, p. 32.

8. *1978 Statistical Abstracts* (Washington, D.C.: U.S. Government Printing Office, 1978), p. 28.

9. Census Bureau, U.S. Department of Commerce, *Social and Economic Characteristics of the Metropolitan and Nonmetropolitan Population*, Series P-23, no. 75 (1979).

10. See, for example, Henry Allen Bullock, "Consumer Motivation in Black and White," *Harvard Business Review* 39 (May/June 1961), pp. 89–104, and 39 (July/August 1961), pp. 110–124; Marcus Alexus, "Some Negro-White Differences in Consumption," *American Journal of Economics and Sociology* 21 (January 1962); James E. Stafford, Keith K. Cox, and James B. Higginbotham, "Some Consumption Pattern Differences between Urban Whites and Negroes," *Social Science Quarterly* 49 (December 1968), pp. 619–630; John V. Petrof, "Customer Strategy for Negro Retailers," *Journal of Retailing* 43 (Fall 1967), pp. 30–38; and Charles E. Van Tassel, "The Negro as a Consumer: What We Know and What We Need to Know," in *Marketing for Tomorrow—Today: Proceedings of the American Marketing Association National Conference*, ed. M. S. Moyer and R. E. Vosburgh (Chicago: American Marketing Association, 1967), pp. 166–168.

11. See, for example, Frederick D. Sturdivant and Walter T. Wilhelm, "Poverty, Minorities, and Consumer Exploitation," *Social Science Quarterly* 49 (December 1968), pp. 643–650; David Caplovitz, *The Poor Pay More* (New York: Free Press, 1963); Frederick D. Sturdivant, "The Limits of Black Capitalism," *Harvard Business Review* 47 (January/February 1969), pp. 122–128.

12. Stafford, Cox, and Higginbotham, "Some Consumption Pattern Differences."

13. Carl M. Larson, "Racial Brand Usage and Media Exposure Differentials," in *A New Measure of Responsibility for Marketing: Proceedings of the American Marketing Association Conference*, ed. Keith Cox and Ben M. Enid (Chicago: American Marketing Association, 1968), pp. 208–215.

14. Raymond A. Bauer, Scott M. Cunningham, and Lawrence H. Wortzel, "The Marketing Dilemma of Negroes," *Journal of Marketing* 29 (July 1965), pp. 1–6.

15. Gerald J. Glasser and Gale D. Metzger, "Radio Usage by Blacks," *Journal of Advertising Research* 15 (October 1975), pp. 39–45.

16. James P. Forkan, "Arbitron Study Charts Ethnic TV Viewing Habits," *Advertising Age*, October 22, 1979, p. 20.

17. "A Study of Advertising Responsiveness among Upscale Blacks and Upscale Whites," prepared for *Black Enterprise* Magazine by Earl G. Graves Marketing and Research, Inc., 1973.

18. "Use Different Ad Tact for Blacks, Meet Urged," *Advertising Age*, February 14, 1977.

19. Abraham Shama and Maureen Coughlin, "An Experimental Study of the Effectiveness of Humor in Advertising," paper presented at the American Marketing Association Annual Educator's Conference, Minneapolis, 1979.

20. Arnold M. Barban and Edward W. Cundiff, "Negro and White Responses to Advertising Stimuli," *Journal of Marketing Research* 1 (November 1964), pp. 53–56.

21. See, for example, Arnold M. Barban, "The Dilemma of Integrated Advertising," *Journal of Business of the University of Chicago* 42 (October 1969), pp. 477–496; Lester Guest, "How Negro Models Affect Company Image," *Journal of Advertising Research* 10 (April 1970), pp. 29–33; Ronald F. Bush, Robert F. Gwinner, and Paul J. Solomon, "White Consumer Sales Response to Black Models," *Journal of Marketing* 38 (April 1974), pp. 25–29; Paul J. Solomon, Ronald F. Bush, and Joseph F. Hair, "White and Black Consumer Sales Response to Black Models," *Journal of Marketing Research* 13 (November 1976), pp. 43–44.

22. William V. Muse, "Product-Related Response to the Use of Black Models in Advertising," *Journal of Marketing Research* 9 (May 1971), pp. 107–109.

23. James W. Cagley and Richard N. Cardozo, "White Responses to Integrated Advertising," *Journal of Advertising Research* 10 (April 1970), pp. 35–39.

24. Ronald F. Bush, Joseph F. Hair, Jr., and Paul J. Solomon, "Consumers' Level of Prejudice and Response to Black Models in Advertisements," *Journal of Marketing Research* 16 (August 1979), pp. 341–345.

25. Joseph R. Dominick and Bradley S. Greenberg, "Three Seasons of Blacks on Television," *Journal of Advertising Research* 10 (April 1970), pp. 21–27.

26. Ronald F. Bush, Paul J. Solomon, and Joseph F. Hair, Jr., "There Are More Blacks in TV Commercials," *Journal of Advertising Research* 17 (February 1977), pp. 21–30.

27. Fabian Linden, "The Second Half of the Seventies," *Consumer Markets: The Conference Board Record* 12 (December 1975).

28. "Marketers Look to Oldsters," *Advertising Age*, April 11, 1977, p. 2.

29. Kenneth L. Bernhardt, "Profiling the Senior Citizen Market," in *Advances in Consumer Research*, vol. 3, ed. Beverlee B. Anderson (Association for Consumer Research, 1976), pp. 449–452.

30. William O. Bearden and J. Barry Mason, "The Use of In-Store Information Sources and Dimensions of Product Satisfaction/Dissatisfaction," *Journal of Retailing* 55 (Spring 1979), pp. 79–91.

31. "Television Audience Comes in Many Stripes," *Advertising Age*, October 15, 1979, p. 520.

CHAPTER 4

SOCIAL CLASS

Environmental influences that affect consumer behavior emerge not only from the culture but also from the social structure. Culture, as we have seen, is reflected in the beliefs, values, and norms of individuals; the behavioral patterns produced by these factors tend to vary with the social structure with which they are associated. Social institutions serve to generate values and norms for consumers.

Social structure is represented in the development and persistence of patterns of social organization. The broad social patterns most germane to a discussion of consumer behavior are social class and social group; the latter is discussed in Chapter 5. Here we shall examine such issues as:

How does social stratification result in social classes?
What are the most important indicators of social class?
How can social class be measured and categorized?
How do social-class variations influence consumer-behavior patterns?

SOCIAL STRATIFICATION

Every society has a conception of the ideal type or types of person—the successful entrepreneur, the scholar, the aristocrat, and so on. The members of a society tend to rank people socially in such a way as to produce a hierarchy of respect and prestige. This process is known as "social stratification."[1]

People are stratified on the basis of numerous characteristics—authority, power, ownership of property, income, consumption patterns, occupation, education, kinship connections, and race, among others—which vary in importance from time to time and from place to place. Kinship connection, for example, is less significant for social stratification in the United States than in China and Great Britain.

Despite our expressed belief in America that "all men are created equal," there is clear evidence of social stratification in our society. Individuals are designated as members of "high society" or as "ghetto dwellers," as "professionals" or "workers," as "affluent" or "disadvantaged." These designations represent levels of social class.

Social classes are relatively permanent, substantial, homogeneous groups that have similar values, interests, life-styles, and behavior patterns. Studies conducted by various researchers indicate the importance of social class in explaining differences in consumer behavior. Others, however, declare that the relationships investigated are so complex that any generalization with regard to the overall effects of social factors on consumer behavior is premature.[2]

It may be that major changes in social class have reduced the reliability of conventional measures as predictors and that the concept of social class as conventionally used in the consumer-behavior literature is no longer helpful.[3] Thus the measurement of social class continues to be an area of interest to sociologists and consumer behaviorists as well as marketers.

SOCIAL-CLASS INDICATORS

Sociologists have used a number of indicators as determinants of social-class position. Some of these indicators are measurable, some are more abstract, and some are considered more important than others. The most frequently used indicators in the process of social stratification in the United States are examined below. It should be noted that these variables are not actual measures of social class; they are proxy variables used to make an estimation of social class.

Occupation

To some sociologists, the major determinant of social class is occupation. The U.S. Bureau of the Census stratifies occupations in such a way that professional, technical, and managerial positions are ranked highest and structural work lowest. Some occupations, however, have prestige rankings that are not related to the Census Bureau distinctions.

A classic study concerning the prestige rating of occupations showed that the rankings changed little between 1947 and 1963. (See Table 4.1.) Although simi-

TABLE 4.1 PRESTIGE RATINGS OF OCCUPATIONS IN THE UNITED STATES, 1947 AND 1963

Occupation	1947 rank	1963 rank
U.S. Supreme Court Justice	1	1
Physician	2.5	2
Nuclear physicist	18	3.5
Scientist	8	3.5
Government scientist	10.5	5.5
State governor	2.5	5.5
Cabinet member in the federal government	4.5	8
College professor	8	8
U.S. representative in Congress	8	8
Chemist	18	11
Lawyer	18	11
Diplomat in the U.S. foreign service	4.5	11
Dentist	18	14
Architect	18	14
County judge	13	14
Psychologist	22	17.5
Minister	13	17.5
Member of the board of directors of a large corporation	18	17.5
Mayor of a large city	6	17.5
Priest	6	21.5
Head of a department in a state government	13	21.5
Civil engineer	23	21.5
Airline pilot	24.5	21.5
Banker	10.5	24.5
Biologist	29	24.5
Sociologist	26.5	26
Instructor in public schools	34	27.5
Captain in the regular army	31.5	27.5
Accountant for a large business	29	29.5
Public school teacher	36	29.5
Owner of a factory that employs about 100 people	26.5	31.5
Building contractor	26.5	31.5
Artist who paints pictures that are exhibited in galleries	24.5	34.5
Musician in a symphony orchestra	29	34.5
Author of novels	29	34.5
Economist	34	34.5
Official of an international labor union	40.5	37
Railroad engineer	40.5	39
Electrician	45	39
County agricultural agent	37.5	39
Owner-operator of a printing shop	42.5	41.5
Trained machinist	45	41.5
Farm owner and operator	39	44
Undertaker	47	44
Welfare worker for a city government	45	44
Newspaper columnist	42.5	46
Policeman	55	47

TABLE 4.1 (Cont.)

Occupation	1947 rank	1963 rank
Reporter on a daily newspaper	48	48
Radio announcer	40.5	49.5
Bookkeeper	51.5	49.5
Tenant farmer—one who owns livestock and machinery and manages the farm	51.5	51.5
Insurance agent	51.5	51.5
Carpenter	58	53
Manager of a small store in a city	49	54.5
Local official of a labor union	62	54.5
Mail carrier	57	57
Railroad conductor	55	57
Traveling salesman for a wholesale concern	51.5	57
Plumber	59.5	59
Automobile repairman	59.5	60
Playground director	55	62.5
Barber	66	62.5
Machine operator in a factory	64.5	62.5
Owner-operator of a lunch stand	62	62.5
Corporal in the regular army	64.5	65.5
Garage mechanic	62	65.5
Truck driver	71	67
Fisherman who owns his own boat	68	68
Clerk in a store	68	70
Milk route man	71	70
Streetcar motorman	68	70
Lumberjack	73	72.5
Restaurant cook	71	72.5
Singer in a nightclub	74.5	74
Filling-station attendant	74.5	75
Dock worker	81.5	77.5
Railroad section hand	79.5	77.5
Night watchman	81.5	77.5
Coal miner	77.5	77.5
Restaurant waiter	79.5	80.5
Taxi driver	77.5	80.5
Farm hand	76	83
Janitor	85.5	83
Bartender	85.5	83
Clothes presser in a laundry	83	85
Soda fountain clerk	84	86
Sharecropper—one who owns no livestock or equipment and does not manage farm	87	87
Garbage collector	88	88
Street sweeper	89	89
Shoe shiner	90	90

Source: Robert W. Hodge, Paul M. Siegel, and Peter H. Rossi, "Occupational Prestige in the United States, 1925–1963," in *Class, Status, and Power,* ed. Reinhard Bendix and Seymour Martin Lipset, 2d ed. (New York: Free Press, 1966), pp. 322–334.

larly comprehensive ratings do not appear in recent literature, there are indications that rankings changed in the 1970s. While Supreme Court justice ranked
highest in 1947 and 1963 and shoe shiner lowest, a more recent study using different categories arrived at different job ratings, with university professors scoring
highest and those on welfare scoring lowest. (See Table 4.2.)

Social-class distinctions relevant to occupation may be blurring. Since 1960,
white-collar employment rose over 45 percent but blue-collar employment rose
by less than 25 percent.[4] Moreover, there has been a sharp rise in the number of
families that have two or more members in the labor force, and the combined
ranking of these members is difficult to determine. In addition, the increased salary levels of blue-collar workers relative to white-collar employees make such
distinctions less precise than they once were.

While occupational status may be less important as a determinant of social
class than it was earlier, the relative position of an individual within an occupational field can be a measure of prestige. When a restaurant owner advertises for

**TABLE 4.2   FIFTY SCORES FROM TREIMAN'S STANDARD INTERNATIONAL
OCCUPATIONAL PRESTIGE SCALE (SCALE: 0 TO 100)**

Occupation	Rank	Occupation	Rank
University professor	78	Soldier	39
Physician	78	Post office clerk	39
Lawyer	71	Receptionist	38
Dentist	70	Telephone operator	38
Head of large firm	70	Machine operator	38
Accountant	68	Car salesperson	36
Executive	67	Model	36
High school teacher	64	Beautician	35
Veterinarian	61	Firefighter	35
Clergy	60	Plumber	34
Lives off property	57	Undertaker	34
Journalist	55	Sales clerk	34
Nurse	54	Truck driver	33
Secretary	53	Cashier	31
Flight attendant	50	Assembly-line worker	30
Real estate agent	49	On Social Security	30
Bank teller	48	Barber	30
Farmer	47	Factory worker	29
Construction worker	46	Taxi driver	28
Keypunch operator	45	Doorman	27
Office clerk	43	Gas station attendant	25
TV repairer	42	Janitor	21
Proofreader	41	Laborer	19
Police officer	40	Migrant worker	18
Cabinetmaker	40	On welfare	16

Source: Donald Treiman, "Occupational Prestige," *Human Behavior Magazine,* November
1977.

an "experienced dishwasher," he clearly recognizes gradations in status among dishwashers.

Income

Income may have been a clear indicator of social class in the past, but rising incomes in recent years serve to blur these distinctions. In the mid-1940s, 4 of every 5 families had incomes under $10,000 (measured in today's dollars). Today, 3 of every 5 have earnings of more than $10,000. In the 1970s, total real disposable income—after adjustment for inflation and taxes—rose by an estimated 50 percent, and the flow of effective spending power to the upper income bracket more than doubled. It is projected that by 1985 only 22 percent of American families will have incomes under $10,000 (in 1975 dollars) and 30 percent will have over $25,-000 in income. (See Figure 4.1.)[5] As a result, class distinctions based on income may decline in significance. It is anticipated, for example, that the market for luxury goods and services and for top-of-the-line merchandise generally will continue to expand more than twice as rapidly as total consumer demand.

Furthermore, rising incomes in the 1960s made for a rapid growth in the demand for many of the goods and services generally associated with the wealthy, ranging from winter vacations to imported wines. Despite the inflation of the 1970s and 1980s, the demand for luxury items is expected to increase. Universal Foods, the largest importer and national distributor of gourmet and fancy foods, reported a 27 percent revenue gain in 1979.[6]

FIGURE 4.1   PERCENTAGE DISTRIBUTION OF FAMILIES AND INCOME, 1955–1985, BY INCOME CLASS (BASED ON 1975 DOLLARS)

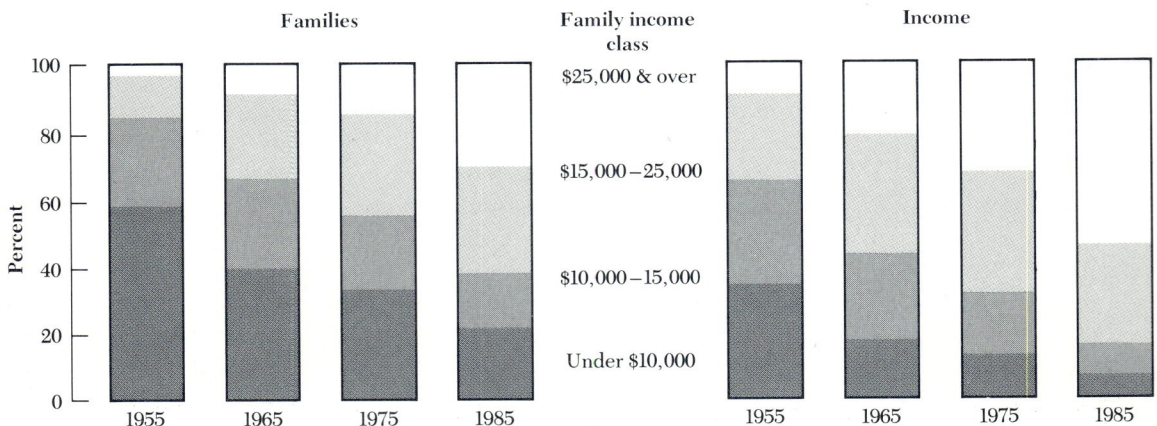

Source: Fabian Linden, "The Classes: Upward," prepared by The Conference Board, New York (April 1977), p. 2.

Possessions

An individual's possessions may reflect his income; they may also, however, represent his life-style, which may in turn be a reflection of membership in a social class. The most significant possession in terms of social-class distinction is one's home. Place of residence and type of housing are prime indicators of social class. Furniture, clothing, and many other things may be selected for their acceptability to the group.

Possessions serve as substitute indicators of income or wealth and are only indirect criteria of social class. In the future they may not serve to indicate significant class differences.

An interesting phenomenon of the 1970s was the widespread appeal of clothing and other accessories on which the designer's name was highly visible. The names or initials of Pierre Cardin, Louis Vuiton, Gucci, and Halston were emblazoned on dresses, shirts, handbags, luggage, and other merchandise, whose prices, while high, apparently were within the reach of many consumers. When designer labels no longer provided clear distinctions among social classes, one exclusive New York department store revived the customer's monogram. In 1979 Saks Fifth Avenue offered monogrammed alarm clocks and robes; silver-plated monogrammed tennis-racket labels, pocket knives, and razor and sewing kits; clothing with personalized names and letters; and many other monogrammed products that were apparently intended to serve as alternative status symbols.

Status

Status is a relative concept. The individual in a social vacuum has no status. Generally, status tends to develop in a group. Within the group, status may be *ascribed* or *achieved*. *Ascribed* status does not have to be earned; it is often acquired by inheritance or through other fortunate circumstances. *Achieved* status is the result of the individual's own efforts. Thus achieved social prestige is based on society's evaluation of an individual's accomplishments.

The way in which the individual interacts with the group—that is, the way in which the members of his group treat him and are treated by him—determines his status. The people with whom he associates—the types of people he dines with and enjoys leisure pursuits with, the country club or bowling team he belongs to—tend to place him within a specific social class.

The consumer's consumption patterns frequently are designed to indicate his social status to others. Products purchased as symbolic representations of an individual's status may lose their persuasive power, as we saw in the case of designer labels, and substitute symbols must then be found. Further, status symbols tend to vary from one geographical location to another. Table 4.3 presents one perspective on the various status symbols that were "in" and "out" in five U.S. cities in 1977.

TABLE 4.3   STATUS SYMBOLS IN AND OUT OF FAVOR IN FIVE U.S. CITIES, 1977

In	Out
New York	
Ownership of horses	Pedigreed dogs
Season opera tickets	Color television
Private-club membership	European trip
Persian rugs	Wall-to-wall carpeting
Ivy League degree	Winter sun tan
Corner office (executives)	Seashore cottage
Penthouse (the rich)	Suburban split-level
Rolls-Royce (the rich)	Swimming pool
Bathroom telephone	Famous-designer labels
Customized van (the young)	Gas-guzzling car
Atlanta	
Indoor plants	Unisex clothes
BMW car	Patched-elbow tweeds
European trip	Trail biking
Discos (the young)	Motor boat
C.B. radio (working class)	Swimming pool
Backgammon	Formal furniture
Cheap original paintings	Mink coat
Adidas sneakers	Men's pony-tail hairdos
Small farm	Suburban split-level
Transcendental meditation	Chagall posters
Houston	
Custom pickup truck	Personalized, low-number auto tags
Pool and tennis court	Men's polyester leisure suits
Personal wine cellar	Night clubs
High-rise condominium	Cheap original paintings
Sable coat	Fake fur
Trimmed beard	Prefaded Levis
Halston and Gucci apparel	Landscaped yard
Season opera tickets	Bridge
Pair of hounds	Men's pony-tail hairdos
Women's jump suits	Unisex clothes
Chicago	
Indoor plants	U.S. Indian jewelry
Owned or rented sculpture	Astrology
Cabin cruiser (the rich)	C.B. radio
Renovated brownstone	Art posters
Mixed china and crystal	Initialed accessories
Membership in private disco	Necklaces for men
Whirlpool bath	Home sauna
Harbor condominium (the rich)	Transcendental meditation, yoga

TABLE 4.3   (Cont.)

In	Out
Personal backgammon table	Frosted hair
Limousine with bar, color TV (the rich)	Owning a Playboy Club key
San Francisco	
Indoor plants	Pedigreed cats and dogs
Recreation vehicle	Swimming pool
Discos	Night clubs
Jogging	St. Bernard dogs
Personal wine cellar	Long hair (men and women)
Own winery (the rich)	Double-knit suits
Faded jeans, imported (the young)	Mink coat
Season opera tickets	Initialed accessories
Transcendental meditation and est	Costly French red wines
Pottery making	Chauffeur (the rich)

Source: *U.S. News & World Report*, February 14, 1977, p. 39. Copyright 1977 U.S. News & World Report, Inc.

MEASURING SOCIAL CLASS

Social scientists define social class along various dimensions, and these variations, in turn, are reflected in the ways in which social-class systems are measured. It is important to recognize some of the difficulties involved in stratifying consumers on the basis of social class and in developing techniques to measure these strata. First, various indicators are used to identify social class, and the researcher must decide which factors to choose. Next, should people be stratified on the basis of a single variable or composite index? Finally, one must select a method of gathering data on these variables. Generally, three methods have been used to measure social class: the subjective method, the reputational method, and the objective method.[7]

The Subjective Method

In the subjective method, individuals are asked to rank themselves in the status hierarchy. People seem to have a tendency to place themselves somewhere in the middle of these rankings. Most people are reluctant to place themselves in the "lower class," and relatively few are inclined to indicate they are of the "upper class."

The Reputational Method

In the reputational method, members of a community are asked to place each other in the status system of the community. A criticism of this method is that it is applicable to small communities only, where everyone knows everyone else.

The Objective Method

The objective method focuses on the characteristics that are considered to be most significant as determinants of social behavior or class distinctions. The objective characteristics most frequently used are occupation, income, and education. Generally speaking, the higher the income and the educational level, the higher the social class. The Bureau of the Census stratifies occupations by such groupings as professionals, managers, proprietors; clerical and sales workers; skilled, semi-skilled, and unskilled workers. In each grouping the first term is considered to be indicative of higher social ranking than the next. As we saw earlier, however, in one study college professors were ranked highest in prestige, although their salary levels are lower than those of many who were in fact ranked lower in occupational prestige.

Warner's Social-Class Categories

A number of researchers have developed specific procedures for identifying and measuring social class: Lloyd Warner's Index of Status Characteristics, Richard Coleman's Index of Urban Status, and A. B. Hollingshead's Social Class Index. Warner's index[8] combines four variables with the following weights:

Occupation	X 4
Source of income	X 3
House type	X 3
Dwelling area	X 2

Although Warner's techniques have been criticized, the social classes that emerged from his studies are frequently used in social research.

Warner's research indicates six classes or groups whose members are more or less equal to one another in prestige and community status:[9]

1. The upper-upper class is composed of locally prominent families, usually with at least second- or third-generation wealth. This class comprises probably one-half of 1 percent of the population. Members of this class tend to live graciously, to uphold the family reputation, and to display a sense of community responsibility.

2. The lower-upper or *nouveau riche* class is composed of the more recent, not-yet-quite-accepted wealthy families. It consists of the executive elite and well-to-do doctors and lawyers. Members comprise 1.5 percent of the population, and their goals are similar to those of the upper-upper group, including gracious living.

3. The upper-middle class includes owners of medium-sized businesses, organization men at the managerial level, and junior executives, who may arrive at this occupational status level by their thirties. Ten percent of the population make up this class. Husbands in this group are motivated toward career success; wives are concerned with social participation.

The major difference between the upper-middle and lower-upper classes lies in the degree of success attained.

4. The lower-middle class comprises approximately 30 to 35 percent of the population. Its members are generally nonmanagerial office workers, small business owners, and highly paid blue-collar families who are concerned with being accepted. They are considered respectable and striving. They are respectable in that they live in well-maintained homes on the "right" side of town, and they strive by doing a good job at their work and by saving for their children's college education.

5. The upper-lower class is sometimes referred to as the "ordinary working class" and comprises 40 percent of the population. Upper-lowers are more interested in enjoying life from day to day than in saving for the future. They do try to live comfortably.

6. The lower-lower class of unskilled workers and the sporadically employed comprises 15 percent of the population but less than 7 percent of the purchasing power. These people are apathetic and tend to try to get their kicks wherever they can.

There are numerous subcategories within these social classes, made up of people who do not necessarily follow the established patterns. It is not to be supposed that the millions of individuals who make up each social class are necessarily similar or identical in their consumption patterns.

Problems with Measurement of Social Class

A number of facets of social-class determination and its measurement must be improved before social-class distinctions can be of great significance to marketers. The deficiencies in this area include the following:[10]

1. Neglect of the processes by which social strata develop, that is, how or why certain positions become associated with certain levels of prestige.

2. Assumption of the stability of social class and disregard for the effects of social mobility.

3. Measurement of status by examination of consumers' positions in the social system without regard for their performance in those positions.

4. Measurement of the social class of an entire family by examination of the characteristics of the adult male wage earner, without regard for the characteristics of other family members.

Efforts to determine why certain occupations become associated with certain prestige rankings, to evaluate the effects of social mobility, and to develop more accurate measurement criteria that include an evaluation of other family members may make social class a more useful concept of marketers in the future.

SOCIAL CLASS AND CONSUMER BEHAVIOR

Social class represents a possible basis for segmenting consumers into homogeneous groups and relating such segments to consumer behavior. According to this view, social classes represent various interests, values, and life-styles, which are manifested in their choice behavior. Thus segmenting consumers along social-class lines and varying the product, pricing, promotion, and channel strategies used accordingly may be a successful marketing strategy.

Research into social-class aspects of consumer behavior, however, has not offered extensive support for this viewpoint. Findings have been limited, and methodology questions such as those discussed above arise from the lack of universal acceptance of social-class indicators and measurement techniques.[11] Furthermore, the blurring of class distinctions noted earlier may be intensified by social mobility and economic factors.

The Effects of Social Mobility

The United States has undergone significant changes in its social stratification system. Increased educational opportunity, more equal distribution of political and other forms of social influence, the creation of new opportunities by science and technology—all provide continuing opportunities for social mobility.[12]

The use of social class to determine patterns of consumer behavior may require a further analysis of the effect of social mobility on purchasing and consumption patterns. For example, consumers may perceive some automobile makes as those one moves "upward from" and others as representing a level of achievement.

A consumer who is upwardly mobile with respect to income, education, or some other indicator of status is likely to engage in consumption patterns characteristic of the group he is striving to enter.

Economic Effects

The rising tide of inflation and the increasing scarcity of resources tend to limit social-class distinctions in purchasing behavior. Earlier studies, for example, indicated that reactions to offers of coupons and special inducements vary among the classes.[13] Upper-lower-class women were most receptive when the activity did not seem too difficult. Lower-middle-class women often felt the same attraction, but they also felt the need to be sensible about such offers and to question their utility. Upper-middle-class women felt the most remote and tended to look down their noses at the quality of premiums and the size of possible savings.

Recent reports indicate that the acceptance of purchase inducements may be correlated more closely with recession and inflation than with social class. An executive of the Quaker Oats Company, which markets such basic foods as hot cereals, baking mixes, and syrup, declared that Quaker's promotional plans called for variations during periods of economic distortion. He noted that the "consumer becomes much more cost-conscious during these periods. She shops with lists more than she does in good times. She has many more coupons in her hands and is looking for more specials."[14] He declared that Quaker's alternative marketing plans for recessionary periods included increased use of coupons and other incentives. Nevertheless, some research relevant to social class and consumer behavior offers insights that may be useful to the marketing manager.

Social Class versus Income

Some consumers dine at expensive restaurants and take long Pacific cruises. Others eat at McDonald's and camp out in a state park close to home. While it is possible that such variations in consumption habits are based on social-class differences, it is also conceivable that they are expressions of income. (Such variations in consumption patterns may be a reflection of personal life-style, discussed in Chapter 10.)

Some researchers suggest that income is a better predictor of consumer behavior than social class. In a study of consumer packaged goods, it was disclosed that with few exceptions, social class was basically inferior to income as a correlate of buying behavior.[15] Another study of furniture and appliances, children's, women's, and men's wear, and travel supported these findings. Income was superior to social class in segmenting the market for nearly all items. The only exceptions were black-and-white television sets, commercial air travel, and possession of a U.S. passport, which were slightly better correlated with social class.[16]

In other cases, social class was relevant only to the extent that it was correlated with income. In southwestern cities, for example, where almost all homes and apartments are air conditioned, the presence of air conditioning equipment itself has no class significance, but the expensiveness of the equipment is directly correlated with family income.

Other products may be classless as well. In children's play clothes, durability may be the most important factor. The democratic (or classless) approach may provide the strongest motivation for some products, such as beer—that is, "Let's all be good fellows together" may be the right tone for the appeal.

Nevertheless, social class may be a better predictor of consumers' choices than income in some areas. Families of similar income but different social classes may exhibit different spending patterns. Given a specific income level, for example, an upper-middle-class family headed by a professional may spend the family resources on a home in the most prestigious area, expensive furniture, and cultural amusements. A lower-middle-class family in the same income bracket may have a better house in a less prestigious neighborhood and more but nondesigner furniture. The working-class family with the same income may have a bigger, later-model car, more expensive appliances in its kitchen, and a bigger TV set in its living room. The family will probably attend baseball games, go hunting and bowling, and perhaps own a boat.

Relative Income

Relative income adds a new dimension to the study of differences and similarities in consumer behavior. One study examined the concept of relative occupational-class income—that is, the relationship of a family's total income to the median income of other families in the same occupational class.[17] A family whose income was above the median for its occupational class was placed in the "overprivileged" group. A family whose income was below the median for its occupational class was considered "underprivileged." Families in the middle income range for their occupational class were categorized as "average."

The study indicated that relative occupational-class income may be very revealing of buyer behavior. For example, the buying behavior of relatively well-off blue-collar workers is more like that of affluent white-collar and professional workers than that of less well-off blue-collar workers. The "average" income class, regardless of occupation, owned many more foreign, economy, intermediate-sized, and compact cars than would be expected, while the "overprivileged" group, regardless of occupation, owned more medium-sized and large cars and fewer foreign economy cars than would be expected. While this research was limited to automobile-buying behavior, it suggests that relative incomes within segments may be more useful to the marketer than either income or occupation alone.

Selection of Retail Outlets

Socioeconomic status has been demonstrated to have an important effect on people's selection of retail outlets. Social factors are fundamental in that they affect the degree of consumer spatial mobility in at least two ways. First, consumers on the upper rungs of the socioeconomic ladder are more likely than those near the bottom to own an automobile, which greatly increases their ability to shop at a distance from home. Second, such people are more readily able to bear the costs involved in shopping around, and for this reason as well they tend to travel greater distances to buy.[18]

Studies have indicated that certain stores may be designated as appropriate or inappropriate places to patronize, depending on one's place in society's general structure. Shoppers prefer to patronize places where the people with whom they come in contact are neither markedly above nor markedly below them in the socioeconomic hierarchy.[19]

Lower-status people tend to prefer local, face-to-face places to shop, for it is here that they feel they will get a friendly reception and easy credit if they need it. In fact, the shopper does not take a chance on feeling out of place by going to a store where she might not fit.[20] Display, excitement, and a pleasant store atmosphere were specified as reasons for enjoying shopping by a greater proportion of the women in the upper-middle, lower-upper, and upper-upper classes. The higher a woman's social status, the greater the preference for shopping in regular department stores.[21]

PATRONAGE PREFERENCE AND PRODUCT RISK

It is clear that patronage of retail establishments is not always related to a consumer's social class. Most establishments have customers of more than one social class. Discount stores, for example, are frequently patronized by people of high occupational and income groups as well as by those in the lower social strata. It does appear, however, that higher social groups do not patronize discount stores to the same extent as those on the lower social levels, or for the same types of products. There is evidence that the kinds of products purchased in discount stores by different social classes are related to the perception of social risk.

A study was conducted to examine the influences of socioeconomic product risk on patronage preferences of retail shoppers. Two hypotheses based on previous research were tested. The first was: "For the purchase of products of high social risk, consumers in different social classes differ significantly in their patronage attitudes toward discount stores. The pattern is hypothesized to hold regardless of the level of economic risk generally associated with the products." The second hypothesis was: "For the purchase of products of low social risk, consumers in different social classes do not differ significantly in their patronage attitudes toward discount stores. This pattern is hypothesized to hold regardless of the level of economic risk generally associated with the products." Both hypotheses were supported by the research.[22]

For products with low social risk—that is, such products as sleepwear, toys, vacuum cleaners, and typewriters—there were no statistically significant differences in patronage attitudes toward discount stores among consumers of different social classes, whether the economic risk attached to their purchase was high or low. (See Figure 4.2.) For products with high social risk—costume jewelry, handbags, stereos, china, and the like—consumers in the high social class exhibited generally less favorable attitudes toward their purchase in discount stores.

Many traditional retailers acknowledge this patronage mix by offering discount outlets for appliances and tires in warehouse annexes. Discounters, on the other hand, have tried to indicate their appropriateness for products of high social risk. Mass merchandiser Korvettes greatly increased its advertising expenditures in the late 1970s. Its campaign theme, "The other Korvettes," was designed to present its discount stores as acceptable places to purchase "fashion" clothing. The campaign, however, was unsuccessful, and more recently Korvettes began to reinforce its mass-merchandising image. The theme "shop the other Korvettes" was dropped, but the symbol—a clothes hanger—was retained.

FIGURE 4.2   PRODUCT-RISK CATEGORIZATION

Economic risk	
Low	**High**
Sleepwear	Vacuum cleaners
Ironing tables	Electric blenders
Undergarments	Automobile tires
Toys	Power tools
Cookware	Men's electric shavers
Hosiery	Typewriters

Social risk	
Low	**High**
Men's dress shirts	Draperies
Costume jewelry	China
Women's blouses and sweaters	Ladies coats
Handbags	Stereo hi-fi
Wall decorations	Men's sports coats
Men's dress slacks	Ladies' dresses

Source: V. Kanti Prasad, "Socioeconomic Product Risk and Patronage Preferences of Retail Shoppers," *Journal of Marketing* 39 (July 1975), p. 44.

Fertility and Social Class

Fertility behavior indirectly affects the consumption of goods and services.[23] The decision to have children and their number and timing involve trade-offs in the purchase and consumption of goods and services that compete for the consumer's dollar. Fertility also has *direct* implications for the purchase and consumption of products and services used in the prevention of pregnancy and in child rearing.

It has been hypothesized that fertility is a function of social class.[24] It is thought that social pressure to maintain one's status within a particular socioeconomic class or the desire to rise to a higher one causes trade-offs to be made away from large families and toward the purchase of things symbolic of that status (for example, durable goods, travel, education).

This thesis has generated interest and numerous comments among consumer behaviorists.[25] While much more research is required to strengthen this theoretical construct, it is notable because its interdisciplinary approach indicates the potential contributions from other fields to an understanding of consumer behavior.

SUMMARY

Social-class distinctions explain some of the differences in behavioral patterns exhibited by consumers. To understand these distinctions, it is necessary to examine the determinants of social class, to provide for a measuring technique, and to develop an appropriate classification system. There are indications that in some activities, income may be a better predictor of consumer behavior than social class.

A number of problems exist in the application of social class to marketing. Among them are the tendencies to neglect the process whereby social strata develop, to assume that an individual's social class remains constant, and to measure the social class of an entire family by examining the characteristics of the adult male.

DISCUSSION QUESTIONS

1. What is meant by social stratification?

2. To which social class do you belong? What is your basis for this judgment?

3. Which do you consider to be the most important indicator of social class? Why?

4. Describe a situation in which status is ascribed; achieved.

5. Describe the characteristics of a retail store that is apparently designed to appeal to a particular social class.

6. How would you improve techniques of measuring social class?

7. Under what circumstances would income be a better predictor of consumer behavior than social class? When might it be less efficient?

8. Select several ads that are apparently designed to appeal to different social classes and discuss the bases for these appeals.

9. In your opinion, which, if any, of the many status symbols are now considered "in" in your circle of friends?

NOTES

1. Bernard Berelson and Gary A. Steiner, *Human Behavior: An Inventory of Scientific Findings* (New York: Harcourt Brace Jovanovich, 1967), p. 453.

2. Gordon R. Foxall, "Social Factors in Consumer Choice: Replication and Extension," *Journal of Consumer Research* 2 (June 1975), pp. 60–64.

3. Arun K. Jain, "A Method for Investigating and Representing an Implicit Theory of Social Class," *Journal of Consumer Research* 2 (June 1975), pp. 53–59.

4. Fabian Linden, "The Arithmetic of Affluence: Consumer Markets," prepared by The Conference Board, New York (September 1975).

5. Fabian Linden, "The Classes: Upward," prepared by The Conference Board, New York (April 1977).

6. "Marketing Briefs," *Marketing News,* June 1, 1979, p. 2.

7. David Krech, Richard S. Crutchfield, and Egerton L. Ballachy, *The Individual in Society* (New York: McGraw-Hill, 1962), pp. 313–316.

8. W. Lloyd Warner, Marcia Meeker, and Kenneth Eels, *Social Class in America: A Manual of Procedure for the Measurement of Social Status* (Chicago: Science Research Associates, 1949).

9. See Richard P. Coleman, "The Significance of Social Stratification in Selling," in *Marketing: A Maturing Discipline*, ed. Martin Bell, Proceedings of the American Marketing Association Winter Conference, 1960, pp. 171–184.

10. Gerald Zaltman and Melanie Wallendorf, *Consumer Behavior: Basic Findings and Management Implications* (New York: John Wiley, 1979), pp. 86–87.

11. Akun K. Jain, "A Method for Investigating and Representing an Implicit Theory of Social Class," *Journal of Consumer Research* 2 (June 1975), pp. 53–59.

12. Bernard Barber, *Social Stratification* (New York: Harcourt, Brace, 1957).

13. Pierre Martineau, "Social Classes and Spending Behavior," *Journal of Marketing* 23 (October 1958), pp. 121–130.

14. John Coulson, "Marketing Issues," *Journal of Marketing* 43 (January 1979), p. 91.

15. James H. Myers, Robert R. Stanton, and Arne F. Haug, "Correlates of Buying Behavior: Social Class vs. Income," *Journal of Marketing* 35 (October 1971), pp. 8–15.

16. James H. Myers and John F. Mount, "More on Social Class vs. Income as Correlates of Buying Behavior," *Journal of Marketing* 37 (April 1973), pp. 71–73.

17. William H. Peters, "Relative Occupational Class Income: A Significant Variable in the Marketing of Automobiles," *Journal of Marketing* 34 (April 1970), pp. 74–77.

18. Raymond Hubbard, "A Review of Selected Factors Conditioning Consumer Travel Behavior," *Journal of Consumer Research* 5 (June 1978), p. 9.

19. Ibid., p. 10.

20. Martineau, "Social Classes and Spending Behavior," pp. 121–130.

21. Stuart A. Rich and Subhash C. Jain, "Social Class and Life Cycle as Predictors of Shopping Behavior," *Journal of Marketing Research* 5 (February 1968), pp. 41–49.

22. V. Kanti Prasad, "Socioeconomic Product Risk and Patronage Preferences of Retail Shoppers," *Journal of Marketing* 39 (July 1975), p. 43.

23. Richard P. Bagozzi and M. Frances Van Loo, "Fertility as Consumption: Theories from the Behavioral Sciences," *Journal of Consumer Research* 4 (March 1978), p. 199.

24. Ibid., p. 216.

25. Clyde V. Kiser et al., "Comments on 'Fertility' as Consumption: Theories from the Behavioral Sciences," *Journal of Consumer Research* 5 (March 1979), pp. 284–302.

CHAPTER 5

SOCIAL GROUP

When social influences on consumer behavior are examined, the social group is found to have greater impact than social class. The group influences the behavior of individuals in many ways, not least by the patterns of interaction among its members. According to Kurt Lewin:

> The essence of a group is not the similarity or dissimilarity of its members but their interdependence. A group can be characterized as a "dynamic whole"; this means that a change in the state or any sub-part changes the state of any other sub-part.[1]

A group may consist of two or more people, but the fact that two or more people are in close proximity to each other does not make them a group. A group has two distinguishing features: (1) individuals in a group are interdependent in one or more ways, and (2) the individual perceives the existence of a group. Interdependence requires some kind of interaction; it may be verbal, physical, or emotional. The second requirement indicates that the individual must perceive that there is a group and that he is a member of it.

The term "group" refers to two or more individuals who share a set of norms, values, or beliefs and whose behavior is interdependent. The study of *group dynamics* concerns the members' interdependence and the changes that occur over time in the flow of information and in the influence of the group on the personalities of individual members.[2]

An examination of groups and their interaction has relevance for consumer behavior. A common form of group influence is seen in television commercials that show people advising their friends about which brands are best. A pregnant woman is told by another pregnant woman with a toddler, "I always use Pampers." An apparently knowledgeable mother tells other mothers in varying situations, "My Bobby uses Aim to fight cavities." An older woman tells younger couples that Maxwell House (or Folger's) is the best coffee. In real life, a more subtle form of influence occurs when a woman decides to try a new fashion after noticing that the "right" people are wearing it.

Difficulties are encountered in studying the manner in which group membership molds the consumer's value structure and causes him to respond in the purchase decision. The individual may be a member of many groups and may aspire to membership in many others; and the behavior patterns of these various groups are not necessarily consistent. Since uniformity of attitude and action prevails to a much greater extent in well-knit groups than among unorganized masses of consumers, however,[3] such a study is necessary in order to pinpoint significant behavior characteristics.

This chapter examines such issues as:

What are the major types of social groups?
How do social groups influence consumer behavior?
What are reference groups?
How do reference groups influence purchase decisions?
What are the effects of conformity, roles, and the socialization process on consumer behavior?

TYPES OF SOCIAL GROUPS

In evaluating social-group influence, we must distinguish between primary and secondary groups. *Primary* groups are characterized by face-to-face relationships among members: family groups, friendship groups, work groups. *Secondary* groups are the many other groups to which the individual belongs that do not interact on the same basis. The major difference between these groups is the face-to-face contact in the primary group, which permits an evaluation of the way cues are received, the immediate feedback that occurs, and the resultant interaction. Unilateral action and delayed feedback distinguish a secondary-group relationship.

Primary groups are more likely to be significant determinants of consumer behavior. The most important spheres of this intimate face-to-face interaction are the family, the play groups of children, and the neighborhood or community groups of adults. The primary groups supply many of an individual's economic, social, and psychological needs.

Secondary groups are larger and more impersonal, and membership in them is valued in accordance with the usefulness the association is perceived to provide. Secondary groups include formal organizations, professional associations, fraternities and sororities, and the church. They use mainly impersonal channels of communication to maintain interaction and generally are geographically dispersed.

REFERENCE GROUPS

Reference groups emerge from either primary or secondary groups. They are of particular importance to the individual since he identifies with the standards and beliefs of his reference groups, and then uses these norms as standards against which he defines and evaluates himself. Any group by which an individual evaluates himself, whether he actually belongs to it or not, is termed a reference group.

Membership groups, automatic groups, anticipatory groups, and negative or dissociative reference groups serve as means by which the individual evaluates his own status and behavior.

Membership groups are groups to which the individual actually belongs. They may involve face-to-face association with other members, as do the family, business organizations, and social and religious organizations. Personal association may not occur, however, in some membership groups, such as a political party to which one may belong but whose meetings one does not attend.

Automatic groups are groups to which an individual belongs automatically, by virtue of age, sex, education, marital status, and so on. This reference-group relationship involves the individual's perception of what society expects people of his age, sex, and so on to do in given circumstances.

Anticipatory groups are groups in which one hopes to be accepted. Many people are upwardly mobile. A person who aspires to membership in a group to which he does not belong may refer to it in making his decisions as a step toward securing membership in that group.

Negative or dissociative reference groups are those to which one does not wish to belong. People may avoid certain actions because they do not wish to be associated with certain groups. An antismoking advertising campaign incorporated a dissociative reference group. Such statements as "Smoking is glamorous" were accompanied by illustrations featuring disreputable-looking derelicts with cigarettes dangling unattractively from their mouths.

The Functions of Reference Groups

Reference groups, as we noted earlier, are a particularly important set of social groups, since the individual identifies with the standards and beliefs of his reference groups. The specific functions that reference groups perform in influencing individual attitudes, values, and behavior, however, have been the source of considerable disagreement. Some theorists see reference groups as influencing behavior because the individual is motivated to be accepted and treated like a member. Others believe they influence an individual's aspiration levels and thus may produce satisfaction or frustration. If the individual achieves the income of his reference group, for example, he may be satisfied; if he does not, frustration may occur. Similarly, reference groups are seen as altering and developing attitudes as the person refers to them in evaluating himself and others. Two primary functions of reference groups seem to incorporate the viewpoints of most theorists: the normative function and the comparison function.

THE NORMATIVE FUNCTION

The normative function of reference groups is that of setting and enforcing standards for the individual, usually called "group norms." Accordingly, reference groups, like other social groups, produce conformity among individuals. By creating taboos and applying sanctions (such as exclusion from the group), the reference group produces conformity to its approved patterns of behavior.

THE COMPARISON FUNCTION

Reference groups provide a means of social comparison. Social comparison is considered to be a motivating force in consumer behavior. This concept suggests that the individual tends to compare herself with other individuals in regard to various attributes in order to judge the consequences of her behavior when other evidence is not available. The type of person one is likely to compare oneself with is at about the same level as oneself in the area of comparison. This person or group is sometimes called a "co-oriented peer"—that is, an individual or group whose outlook and values are similar to one's own.

Examination of the influence of the informal group on the consumer decision process has indicated that this social comparison theory has merit. A study revealed that there is a positive relationship between one's co-orientation with informal group members and the need to obtain information from them, the group's credibility as a source of information, and the group's influence on purchasing decisions.[4]

Advertisers have made effective use of reference groups in marketing a wide range of products. Group influences are evident in the marketing strategies of the Miller Brewing Company, which succeeded in increasing its market share from seventh in 1972 to second in 1977. Its Miller High Life, long promoted as the "champagne of beers," was attracting the sort of people who drank only one or two beers on any given occasion. In order to reach the "real" beer drinker who would consume five or six beers a day, Miller changed its slogan to "If you've got the time, we've got the beer." Its advertisements presented such groups as a team of demolition experts relaxing after blowing up a building and long-haul drivers relaxing at the end of their run. Its newer product, Miller Lite, features former athletes who declare, "Lite Beer from Miller. Everything you always wanted in a beer—and less." A recent Miller acquisition, Lowenbräu, is positioned as a special beer for "good friends and those special moments."

In recent years the term "reference group" has begun to give way to "reference other."[5] This shift is not surprising, because it has become apparent that an individual is influenced by a variety of reference others, including individuals, groups, and larger social categories, as well as abstract and imaginary entities. "Reference individuals" have been widely used in promotional activities featuring celebrities. These practices are discussed in Chapter 14.

Reference-Group Influence and Purchase Decisions

A number of problems occur in the devising of strategies that use reference groups to influence the purchase decision. An individual may have many reference groups. One may be simultaneously a mother, a student, a liberal, and a saleswoman. The goals of these reference groups may be in conflict: our busy mother may require more time for her studies but also be concerned with preparing nutritious meals for her children. It may be difficult to determine which of her reference groups is most influential. Furthermore, it may be difficult to use this information operationally—for example, to decide which medium is most likely to reach the relevant reference group most efficiently.

It is possible, however, that reference groups provide values, attitudes, and other predispositions relating to the purchase of the product or service that is being sold. The influence of the group may therefore be important in the development of an effective marketing campaign.

Relatively little research has been conducted to determine the extent and kinds of reference-group influence that emerge in purchase decisions. An early study indicated that there are variations that relate to the product; more recent research revealed that consumer groups vary in their susceptibility to reference-group influence.

PRODUCT VARIATIONS

The results of a widely quoted early study disclosed that the conspicuousness of a product is the attribute that has the greatest general bearing on the product's susceptibility to reference-group influence.[6] The product must be conspicuous in two ways. First, it must be seen and identified by others. Second, it must stand out and be noticed. Visibility is not enough, for even if it is seen, if virtually everyone owns it, it is not conspicuous in the second sense.

The extent to which specific products or brands are susceptible to reference-group influence, according to this study, is suggested in Figure 5.1. Reference-group influence may operate with respect to brand but not to product (brand +, product −), as in the upper left cell; or with respect to both (brand +, product +),

FIGURE 5.1 REFERENCE-GROUP INFLUENCE ON PRODUCTS AND BRANDS

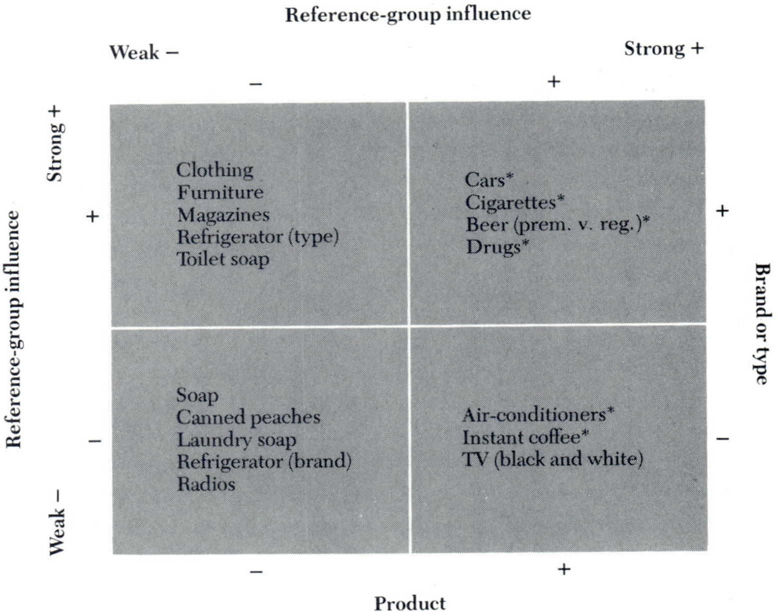

Reference-group influence

Weak —   Strong +

* The classification of all products marked with an asterisk is based on actual experimental evidence. Other products in this table are classified speculatively on the basis of generalizations derived from the sum of research in this area and confirmed by the judgment of seminar participants.

Source: Francis S. Bourne, "Group Influence in Marketing and Public Relations," in *Some Applications of Behavioral Research*, ed. Rensis Likert and Samuel P. Hayes, Jr. (Paris: UNESCO, 1957).

as in the upper right cell; or with respect to product but not to brand (brand —, product +), as in the lower right cell; or it may not operate in any significant way (brand —, product —), as in the lower left cell. These influences may change.

Brand +, Product + Items. For cars, both the product and the brand are socially conspicuous. For cigarettes, reference-group images have been built up by advertising; for drugs, decisions are made by doctors as to what should be described. Reference-group influence may be important in determining whether or not beer should be purchased and whether regular or premium beer should be selected, but it did not appear to be strong in regard to the choice of a particular brand of beer.

Brand —, Product + Items. Whether or not a person serves instant coffee seems to depend on one's view of one's own reference groups. The choice of a coffee brand is not conspicuous, however, and therefore may not depend on reference-group influence. In the case of air conditioners, "visibility from the outside" determined the location of clusters of these products, but the brand itself had little prestige attached to it. Black-and-white television sets also appeared to follow this pattern, but with the saturation point in television approaching, reference groups may no longer exert an influence.

Brand +, Product − Items. This group includes products that a very large proportion of the population uses, such as clothing. The type of clothing purchased may be influenced by reference groups, as, for example, jeans, leisure suits, and outdoor clothing. Furniture, magazines, refrigerators, and toilet soap are used in almost all homes. The visibility of these items, however, and the variety of types available make them susceptible to reference-group influences.

Brand −, Product − Items. Salt and laundry soap are socially inconspicuous. It is possible, however, that heavy advertising may provide images of the kind of people who use certain brands of these products. Radios and refrigerators are socially visible, but they have reached near-saturation levels.

Changes have probably occurred in consumer perceptions of the susceptibility of these specific products to reference-group influence since the study was conducted, in the 1950s. Current research into attitude change supports some of the suggested strategies that have emerged from these studies, however, once it is determined that the product's susceptibility to reference-group influence is strong or weak. If there is no apparent strong reference-group influence, advertising should emphasize the product's attributes and advantages over competing products. If reference-group influence is operative, the advertising should stress the kinds of people why buy the product, reinforcing and broadening the existing stereotypes of the users. Care should be taken, however, not to reinforce a stereotype of consumers that is too limited and exclusive for a mass-produced item or one that is unacceptable.

CONSUMER-GROUP VARIATIONS

Susceptibility to reference-group influence varies among consumer groups. A study revealed significant differences between housewives and students in terms of three types of influence that reference groups had on brand selection of twenty products.[7] The three types of reference-group influence considered were informational, value expressive, and utilitarian. An *informational* influence emerges in an active search for information or through observation of the behavior of significant others; that is, whether other people, particularly those who are personally important to the consumer, appear to endorse the product. A *utilitarian* influence exists if the individual perceives that others mediate significant rewards or punishments and if he is motivated to achieve the reward or to avoid the punishment. A *value-expressive* influence is one that bolsters the individual's ego or operates because the individual has a liking for the reference group.

According to the researchers, variations in motivation or need may result in variations in response to reference-group influence. Younger people, such as students, are usually less familiar with many products than housewives, have less product information, and therefore face greater purchase risk. Students also have more frequent social contacts than housewives, and thus more easily obtain information from friends. Furthermore, group structures in which they interact, such as sororities, fraternities, and dormitories, impose rules and norms, while the visibility of students' behavior in these groups makes them more responsive to group influence.

SOCIAL-GROUP INFLUENCE AND CONSUMER BEHAVIOR

Social scientists have developed numerous constructs with which to examine and explain the influence of social groups and their interaction with the individual. Some of these constructs have particular application to consumer-behavior theory and are discussed below. They include Herbert C. Kelman's three processes of social influence, the effect of conformity, the impact of roles, and the process of socialization.

Kelman's Processes of Social Influence

The ways in which the group interacts with the individual have been characterized as the processes of social influence. Kelman describes three processes as significant: compliance, identification, and internalization.[8] *Compliance* is said to occur when the individual conforms to the expectations of a group that has the power to reward her if she conforms to its norms and values and to punish her if she does not. *Identification* occurs when a person wants to define herself by her relationship to some other person or group and consequently ascribes to herself characteristics or attitudes of the person or group. *Internalization* occurs when the individual accepts influence because it is perceived as "inherently conducive to the maximization of her values," that is, the "content" of this influence is perceived as being instrumental in the attainment of her goals.

A study examined these three processes in relation to their influence on the evaluation of a brand of instant coffee. According to the researchers, after observing others evaluating a product favorably, people perceive the product more favorably themselves than they would have done in the absence of this observation. The authors concluded, however, that although people frequently buy products that others in their groups buy, this behavior may not establish a role relationship with others (identification) or incur a reward or punishment mediated by others (compliance).[9] Product evaluations by others provide information about the product, and the purchase may be made simply to acquire what the individual perceives as a good product. Thus it may be that consumers "internalize" the group's information to use in evaluating alternatives in the marketplace. Further discussion of the use of such information for alternative evaluation will be presented in Chapter 16.

Conformity

Social influence is frequently referred to as conformity and is looked upon as the relatively simple act of going along with or agreeing with a visible majority.[10] Numerous factors lead people to conform. These factors include the processes of compliance, identification, and internalization, discussed earlier. In addition, informational pressures may lead people to conform. If, for example, the individual feels he does not know enough about current fashion, he may look to his work group or his peer group to supply such information. Groups may pressure individuals to conform in order to avoid punishment, to win group acceptance, and to avoid the embarrassment of being "different." Deviant behavior may lead to mistreatment by the group; such mistreatment may take psychic, social, or legal forms. Some people are valued for their deviance, and the nature of the deviance may result in the group members being better informed about products and services. No group, however, tolerates such behavior in most of its members.[11]

Most of the studies of conformity as a group influence have not been concerned with buying situations. Laboratory studies of social influence in areas other than buying situations have demonstrated that individuals are highly susceptible to group pressure. Some findings with specific relevance to consumer behavior are discussed below.

THE IMPACT OF GROUP JUDGMENT

More individuals tend to conform to a group norm when objective standards are absent than when they are present. However, "reactance" may occur, that is, a motivational state that impels the individual to establish his freedom. According to reactance theory, any attempt by the group which threatens the freedom of the individual tends to lead him to avoid compliance.

A laboratory study was designed to test this concept in the consumer decision-making situation.[12] The two hypotheses to be tested were: (1) in a consumer decision-making situation where no objective standards are present, individuals who are exposed to a group norm will tend to conform to that norm; and (2) in a consumer decision-making situation where no objective standards are present, individuals who are exposed to a group norm and are induced to comply will show less tendency to conform to the group judgment. The established situation required the subjects to evaluate and choose the best suit among three identical men's suits. The results of the study supported the two hypotheses.

According to the researcher, the marketing implications of this study indicated that consumers accept information provided by their groups on the quality of a product, of a style, and so on, which is hard to evaluate objectively. Thus peer groups, friends, and acquaintances may be a major source of influence and information in the attention-directing stage of the buying process for major items.

Any attempt by the group to restrict independent choice, however, may be resisted under certain conditions. In the marketplace, consumers may purchase a product or adopt a new style, but reserve the right to choose other brands or variations. This finding was supported by William Whyte in his study of the adoption of air conditioners, which indicated that while an "individual may sell his neighbor on the *idea* of [an air] conditioner, he does not necessarily sell him on a particular brand or a particular store; where you see a row of adjacent [air] conditioners, only a few of them will be of the same make, and only a few from the same store."[13]

GROUP INFLUENCE ON BRAND CHOICE

Knowledge of the extent to which the social group influences brand preference would be particularly useful to marketers. One study attempted to disclose the extent of the members' conformity to the brand preferences of small, informal social groups.[14] The study, which was conducted under controlled but "real life" conditions, examined the preferences of a number of housewives for bread. The results indicated that informal groups definitely influenced their members toward conformity with respect to brands of bread preferred. Although it had been hypothesized that the cohesiveness of the group (the strength of the bonds that unite its members) would be a determinant of the degree of brand loyalty exhibited by its members, this hypothesis was not supported. When cohesiveness was combined with leadership, however, these factors did serve to influence brand loyalty.

The findings of this study were limited to bread. Other research has indicated that products vary in their susceptibility to social-group influence in brand-choice decisions. For example, the power of group cohesiveness is greater in predicting brand choice of products high in social involvement (for example, cigarettes, beer) than of products low in social involvement (for example, deodorants).[15]

ACCEPTANCE OF NEW PRODUCTS

In "The Web of Word of Mouth," Whyte postulated that the informal group decides when a new product will become accepted by its members.[16] Those who do not conform and acquire the product before group norms permit are considered outsiders. Those who fail to buy the good after the group has accepted it may be seen to be rejecting the group's judgment, and may therefore provoke irritation, resentment, and even mild ostracism. Other research has indicated that small, informal neighborhood group variables were strongly correlated with adoption of new products. These variables were found to have differential effects, however, depending on the product category—food, clothing, or appliances.[17] Thus in considering the relevance of various group phenomena on the adoption of new products, the marketer cannot generalize from the effects of group purchasing behavior in other contexts, but must consider those influences that may be relevant to his product. A detailed discussion of the product-adoption process is presented in Chapter 18.

Roles

A *role* may be defined as a set of behavior patterns that apply to categories of persons.[18] Role includes the attitudes, values, norms, and behavior that are expected of individuals in their interaction with other people. A discussion of group dynamics and social influence requires an examination of roles.

An individual occupies many roles, even in the course of a day. Like status, roles may be ascribed or achieved. Ascribed roles are those that a person is born with or has thrust upon her, such as age, sex, and kinship roles. Achieved roles include those that concern one's occupation, marital status, public service, and avocational interests. Many roles are partly ascribed and partly achieved.

To some extent, the social structure tends to judge which role behavior is appropriate, and thus to establish role expectations. For example, the role expectations of husband and wife vary considerably by social class. A lower-class housewife tends to emphasize household chores and domestic duties, whereas the upper-middle-class housewife tends to emphasize being a good companion to her husband.

The executive of an organization may feel his role requires him to dress in a certain fashion, to read "class" periodicals, to dine in prestigious places. The blue-collar worker may feel that it is appropriate for him to focus on hunting and boating, and to drink beer with the boys. Some of these "roles," however, represent stereotypical patterns of behavior, and recent research has indicated that such stereotypes no longer exist in pure forms. Moreover, the individual may occupy many roles simultaneously, some of which are in conflict.

CHANGES IN WOMEN'S ROLES

The changing nature of women's roles in today's society has generated considerable interest. The impact of these changes is enhanced by the fact that nearly one-half (46 percent) of the female population aged 16 and over are in the work force, and it is anticipated that this percentage will increase.

Market researchers pay particular attention to determining whether the marketplace behavior of working women can be distinguished from that of homemakers. The effects of such role changes on the behavior patterns of the family as a social group are examined in Chapter 6. Acknowledgment of the changing nature of women's roles has societal as well as marketing management implications. To address these issues, a number of research studies have examined the manner in which women are portrayed in advertising.

Women's Roles as Portrayed in Advertising. Efforts have been made to determine the degree of social change with regard to women's roles as they are reflected in advertising messages. A 1970 study of the roles portrayed by women in magazine ads concluded that "feminists are at least partly justified in saying that advertisements do not present a full view of the variety of roles women actually play in American society."[19] Another study examined print advertisements of 1970 and 1972 and concluded that standards of expected female behavior prevalent in 1958 continued to be the stereotypes of the 1970s. The authors concluded that print advertisements failed to keep up with the times in portraying women in the wide variety of roles they were actually playing.[20]

Table 5.1 provides a comparison of women's nonwork occupations as shown in print advertisements. Emphasis shifted from family roles in 1958 to more decorative roles in 1972.

More recently, however, a study of women's roles as portrayed in television commercials indicates some progress. The authors, who examined trends of male and female characters in television commercials between 1971 and 1976, concluded that marketers and society have begun to accept the changing role of women.[21] According to their analysis, there was a narrowing of differences from 1971 to 1976 between role portrayals in TV commercials and actual roles in the population. Nonetheless, women still were seen in more narrowly defined roles than men. For example, women still were portrayed as significantly younger than men, less frequently employed, more frequently occupied within the home, and so on.

An interesting finding of one study is that women with positive attitudes toward the women's liberation movement have shown a pattern of preference for female roles portrayed in advertising similar to that of women with negative attitudes toward women's liberation.[22] It appears that women with positive attitudes toward the movement do not uniformly reject traditional female roles.

An effort was made to determine whether a woman's attitude toward women's liberation affects her perception of advertisements containing women.[23] While

TABLE 5.1   NONWORKING ACTIVITIES OF WOMEN PORTRAYED IN ADVERTISEMENTS IN 1958, 1970, AND 1972 (PERCENT OF WOMEN)

Roles of nonworkers	1958			1970			1972		
	Alone or with females	With males	Total	Alone or with females	With males	Total	Alone or with females	With males	Total
Family	18.0%	32.0%	24.2%	21%	25%	23%	0%	13%	8%
Recreational	7.5	54.7	28.3	9	64	46	5	15	36
Decorative	74.5	13.3	47.5	70	11	31	95	32	56
	100.0%	100.0%	100.0%	100%	100%	100%	100%	100%	100%

Source: Ahmend Belkaoui and Janice M. Belkaoui, "A Comparative Analysis of Roles Portrayed by Women in Print Advertisements: 1958, 1970, 1972," *Journal of Marketing Research* 13 (May 1976), p. 171.

the results were not considered definitive, they did indicate that there was a weak relationship between women's liberation and perception of advertisements. An interesting finding, however, was that feminist groups have a more positive attitude toward advertising than the antifeminist group.

Another study attempted to determine whether the feminist's sources of information and shopping behavior differed from those of the nonliberated woman.[24] Although feminists did not tend to consider TV and magazine advertising to be as important sources of marketer-dominated information as nonliberated women, generally there was little distinction between the two groups as to sources of information used. In shopping behavior, there also appeared to be little difference. The liberated women, however, tended to make more shopping trips per week and considered the speed with which they could get their shopping done of greater importance than the nonliberated women did.

A study of young college women supported these findings.[25] It indicated that in reactions to roles of women as portrayed in advertising, there was little difference between those women classified as feminist and those classified as traditionalist. (See Table 5.2.)

Whether or not marketers should be concerned with expressing the changing nature of women's roles has both marketing and societal implications. The fact that working women continue to be portrayed as primarily engaged in secretarial or clerical occupations and nonemployed women in decorative roles may not seriously undermine the efficiency of an advertising campaign. And since some feminists appear to be willing to accept advertisements that portray them in their traditional homemaker, fashion, or sex-object roles, their acceptance may be seen by some marketers as approval of the continuation of these practices.

Vocal groups, however, continually decry such activities, particularly when

TABLE 5.2   RESPONSES TO ADVERTISEMENTS FOR FEMINISTS VERSUS TRADITIONALISTS

Advertisement images	Profeminists (N = 36)		Traditionalists (N = 31)		Neutrals (N = 37)		Chi square
	Like	Dislike	Like	Dislike	Like	Dislike	
1. Mother	8	28	4	27	6	31	1.059[a]
2. Sex object	22	14	24	7	30	7	4.121
3. Glamour girl	27	9	27	4	30	7	1.574
4. Housewife	33	3	26	5	30	7	1.762
5. Working mother	21	15	16	15	22	15	.481
6. Modern woman	20	16	15	16	17	20	.719
7. Professional	27	9	22	9	30	7	.973

[a] A cell size less than five precludes valid application of the chi-square test.

Source: Jacob M. Duker and Lewis R. Tucker, Jr., " 'Women's Libbers' versus Independent Women: A Study of Preferences for Women's Roles in Advertisements," *Journal of Marketing Research* 14 (November 1977), p. 474.

the portrayal is demeaning to women. Moreover, the changing nature of women's roles in today's society does influence their role in family decision making. This role will be discussed in greater detail in Chapter 6.

There are some indications that marketers are responding to these changes. To reduce role conflict and to break away from traditional stereotypes of women, some advertisers are using *dual roles, role switching,* and *role blending*. Dual-role ads portray women in situations that indicate their working status in conjunction with traditional roles, such as mother/chemist, wife/vice-president of marketing, and lover/professional. (See Exhibit 5.1.) Role-switching ads portray the purchase

EXHIBIT 5.1

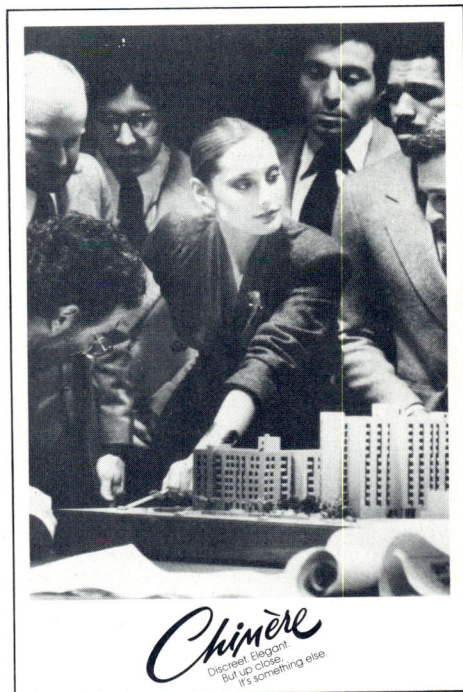

In-store promotion pieces expressing the dual personality of the "Chimère woman"
Source: Pat Sloan, "Chimère Aimed at Professional Women," *Advertising Age,* April 23, 1979, p. 40.

or use of a product by persons of the sex opposite to the traditional stereotype, such as a man washing the floor, a woman traveling to a chain of service stations to help solve their problems, or a female pilot. Role-blending ads show scenes that are usually portrayed as sexually stereotypical and present men and women in a combined activity, such as shopping together or bathing children together.[26]

Socialization

A discussion of social influences and consumer behavior must take note of the process of socialization. Socialization, defined in terms of the influence of social groups, is described as "the process by which a new member learns the value system, norms and the required behavior patterns of the society, organizations, or group which the person is entering."[27]

Specifically, socialization occurs in the following instances. A new college student reads many ads for "smart" attire aimed at young women entering college; she soon learns from her peers, however, that casual dress is considered more appropriate. A new homeowner plans to spend her limited funds on decorating her home, only to discover that the neighbors consider a well-kept lawn a higher priority.

Socialization may also be defined in terms of behavior appropriate to a member of society in general. In this context, it has been referred to as "the process by which individuals develop the attitudes, beliefs, and behavior necessary for them to be effective members of their society."[28]

While socialization is a lifelong process, the intensity of socialization in terms of the amount of learning acquired is stronger early in life than at any later age.[29] In fact, some consumer-behavior theorists have defined consumer socialization as the processes by which young people acquire skills, knowledge, and attitudes relevant to their functioning as consumers in the marketplace.[30]

There are indications that young people in different socioeconomic classes have different motives for consumption and that social class is related positively to consumer skills. This relationship may result from the fact that adolescents in families of higher socioeconomic status have more opportunities for consumption, and therefore may be socialized faster and better to the consumption role. The data do not indicate, however, whether better consumer learning occurs as a result of structural factors present in higher socioeconomic classes (for example, greater opportunities for consumption) or because of socialization practices that may be emphasized by families of these social groups.[31]

In view of these findings, it is suggested that marketing communication stressing the economic or functional aspects of a product (for example, cost or performance) would be more likely to be received favorably by adolescents in upper social classes than in lower social classes.

A clear understanding of the way children learn "appropriate" behavior is still to be uncovered. Recently the influence of television in the process of children's socialization has come under attack. Hearings currently under way by the Federal Trade Commission are addressing the issues of whether television advertising to children encourages the development of undesirable consumption habits and creates excessive demand by children for unnecessary purchases. Depending on the findings, some changes may be made in television advertising aimed at children.[32]

It is true that through the process of socialization, children learn the values and behaviors appropriate to their culture, to their social class, and to the various groups to which they belong or desire to belong. Socialization, however, occurs throughout the life cycle. As people get older, they learn new attitudes and behavior appropriate to the college student, the parent, the individual living alone, the professional, the retired worker, and so on.

In the process of socialization, the individual deals with social norms, social status, and social roles, as well as with reference groups. Specific research related to socialization and consumer behavior has been limited, but there are indications that such research will increase in the future.

SUMMARY

Numerous social groups may influence the consumer's marketplace activities. Groups may be primary or secondary, and the extent of their influence may vary widely. A knowledge of group influence requires an understanding of group dynamics. Group dynamics may be examined by noting the process of social influence and the effect of conformity and roles on the group members' marketplace decisions.

Reference groups are of particular significance in the consumer's behavior patterns, since he identifies with the standards and beliefs of these groups and then uses their standards to evaluate himself. Reference groups perform a number of functions, including such normative influences as pressures toward conformity and the provision of a means of social comparison. Research has indicated that reference-group influence enters the purchase decision but may vary by product and by consumer group.

DISCUSSION QUESTIONS

1. Designate a member of your primary group, a secondary group to which you belong, and a reference group that influences you.

2. Do you believe that the normative function or the comparison function of a reference group is more important? Why?

3. For what reasons do people conform? How may conformity affect purchase decisions?

4. What is meant by "anticipatory reference group"? "negative reference group"? Provide an example of the way in which an anticipatory and a negative reference group have influenced your behavior.

5. Describe how the role you play in one group conflicts with the role you play in another group.

6. On the basis of your own perceptions, do you believe that the role of women as portrayed in advertising has changed significantly? What suggestions would you offer in this regard?

7. Present or describe some ads that reflect changes in the ways in which women are presented.

8. How could marketers influence the socialization process so that children will learn "appropriate" behavior?

NOTES

1. Kurt Lewin, *Resolving Social Conflicts* (New York: Harper & Row, 1948), p. 54.

2. Lyman E. Ostlund, "Role Theory and Group Dynamics," in *Consumer Behavior: Theoretical Sources*, ed. Scott Ward and Thomas Robertson (Englewood Cliffs, N.J.: Prentice-Hall, 1973), p. 232.

3. George Katona, *The Mass Consumption Society* (New York: McGraw-Hill, 1964), p. 304.

4. George P. Moschis, "Social Comparison and Informal Group Influence," *Journal of Marketing Research* 13 (August 1976), pp. 237–244.

5. James E. Stafford and Benton Cocanougher, "Reference Group Theory," in *Selected Aspects of Consumer Behavior*, prepared for National Science Foundation, Directorate for Research Applications, Research Applied to National Needs, p. 372.

6. Francis S. Bourne, "Group Influences in Marketing and Public Relations," in *Some Applications of Behavioral Research*, ed. Rensis Likert and Samuel P. Hayes, Jr. (Paris: UNESCO, 1957).

7. Whan Park and V. Parker Lessig, "Students and Housewives: Differences in Susceptibility to Reference Group Influence," *Journal of Consumer Research* 4 (September 1977), pp. 102–110.

8. Herbert C. Kelman, "Three Processes of Social Influence," *Public Opinion Quarterly* 25 (1961), pp. 57–78.

9. Robert E. Burnkrant and Alain Cousineau, "Informational and Normative Social Influence in Buyer Behavior," *Journal of Consumer Research* 2 (December 1975), pp. 206–215.

10. Marie Jahoda, "Conformity and Independence: A Psychological Analysis," *Human Relations* 12 (1959), pp. 99–120.

11. Gerald Zaltman and Melanie Warrendorf, *Consumer Behavior: Basic Findings and Management Implications* (New York: John Wiley, 1979), p. 125.

12. M. Venkatesan, "Experimental Study of Consumer Behavior: Conformity and Independence," *Journal of Marketing Research* 3 (November 1966), pp. 384–387.

13. William Whyte, Jr., "The Web of Word of Mouth," *Fortune*, November 1954, p. 117.

14. James E. Stafford, "Effects of Group Influence on Consumer Brand Preferences," in *Perspectives in Consumer Behavior*, ed. Harold Kassarjian and Thomas S. Robertson, rev. ed. (Glenview, Ill.: Scott, Foresman, 1973), pp. 312–322.

15. Robert E. Witt and Grady D. Bruce, "Purchase Decisions and Group Influence," *Journal of Marketing Research* 7 (November 1970), pp. 533–535.

16. Whyte, "Web of Word of Mouth."

17. Thomas S. Robertson, "Group Characteristics and Aggregate Innovative Behavior: Preliminary Report," in *Models of Buyer Behavior*, ed. Jagdish N. Sheth (New York: Harper & Row, 1974), pp. 310–326.

18. Ostlund, "Role Theory and Group Dynamics," p. 231.

19. Alice E. Courtney and Sarah Wernick Lockeratz, "A Woman's Place: An Analysis of the Roles Portrayed by Women in Magazine Advertisements," *Journal of Marketing Research* 8 (February 1971), pp. 92–95.

20. Ahmend Belkaoui and Janice M. Belkaoui, "A Comparative Analysis of the Roles Portrayed by Women in Print Advertisements: 1958, 1970, 1972," *Journal of Marketing Research* 13 (May 1976), pp. 168–172.

21. Kenneth C. Schneider and Sharon Barich Schneider, "Trends in Sex Roles in Television Commercials," *Journal of Marketing* 43 (Summer 1979), pp. 79–84.

22. Lawrence H. Wortzel and John M. Frisbie, "Women's Role Portrayal Preferences in Advertisements: An Empirical Study," *Journal of Marketing* 38 (October 1974), pp. 41–46.

23. Michael B. Mazis and Marilyn Beuttemuller, "Attitudes toward Women's Liberation and Perception of Advertisements," in *Proceedings, 3rd Annual Conference of ACR, 1972,* ed. M. Venkatesan (Association for Consumer Research, 1972), pp. 428–435.

24. Beverlee B. Anderson, "Are We Missing the Ms?" in ibid., pp. 436–445.

25. Jacob M. Duker and Lewis R. Tucker, Jr., " 'Women's Libbers' versus Independent Women: A Study of Preferences for Women's Roles in Advertisements," *Journal of Marketing Research* 14 (November 1977), pp. 469–475.

26. William J. Lundstrom and Donald Sciglimpaglia, "Sex Role Portrayals in Advertising," *Journal of Marketing* 41 (July 1977), pp. 72–79.

27. Edgar H. Schein, "Organization, Socialization, and the Profession of Management," in *Organizational Psychology,* ed. David A. Kolb, Irwin M. Rubin, and James M. McIntyre (Englewood Cliffs, N.J.: Prentice-Hall, 1971), pp. 1–14 (at p. 3).

28. *Psychology Today: An Introduction,* 3d ed. (New York: Random House, 1975), p. 473.

29. O. G. Brim, "Adult Socialization," in *Socialization and Society,* ed. John A. Clausen (Boston: Little, Brown, 1969).

30. Scott Ward, "Consumer Socialization," *Journal of Consumer Research* 1 (September 1974), pp. 1–14.

31. George P. Moschis and Gilbert A. Churchill, Jr., "Consumer Socialization: A Theoretical and Empirical Analysis," *Journal of Marketing Research* 15 (November 1978), p. 606.

32. This subject is discussed in greater detail in Chapter 19.

CHAPTER 6

FAMILY

In 1955 Clairol, Inc., and its advertising agency took a hair-coloring product that was primarily associated with actresses, models, divorcees, and "fast women" and turned it into an acceptable cosmetic accessory for wives and mothers. Their subsequent advertising campaigns for this product reflect the changes in women's self-image and independence from traditional family roles:

1955	"Does she or doesn't she?"
1960	"What would your husband do if suddenly you looked ten years younger?"
1970	"How long has it been since your husband took you out to dinner?"
1979	"This I do for me."

Hallmark, the undisputed leader in the greeting-card industry, generally holds to what could be described as old, conservative ways. Nonetheless, it is apparently recognizing changes in American mores and family life-styles. Its Christmas line includes cards that can be used by unmarried couples living together, and it recently received a note from an unmarried mother of a biracial baby, thanking the company for offering a birth announcement that was general enough to fit her situation.[1]

The housewares industry grew from a total annual retail volume of under $2 billion to more than $25 billion in three decades. Whereas housewares used to be $2.99 to $4.99 items, food processors now sell for $250 and espresso coffeemakers for $150. This development reflects efforts of appliance makers to match their products to changing family life-styles. At one time, one member of the family, usually the mother, prepared three meals a day for all the others. Today the kitchen has become a place where anybody in the family may drop in to fix and eat something whenever the urge strikes.[2]

As we noted in Chapter 5, the family is a social group that has a major impact on consumer behavior. The above illustrations reflect the changing nature and role structure of the family as well as the strength of traditional relationships.

This chapter examines the family as a social influence and discusses such issues as:

> What are the various types of families and what roles do family members play in buying behavior?
> What are some of the demographic characteristics of the family and what changes are anticipated?
> How do family members influence consumer decision making?
> What is meant by "stage of the life cycle" and how do these stages affect consumer behavior?
> How is the changing role of women reflected in family structure and purchasing decisions?

THE FAMILY AS A SOCIAL GROUP

The family is one of a number of social groups that has a significant influence in consumer behavior. As we saw earlier, such groups are generally viewed as being either *primary* or *secondary*. The primary group is characterized by intimate, face-to-face association and cooperation. The family is one of the most important primary groups, if not the most important. It is the first group to which an individual belongs, and under normal circumstances it is the group to which one belongs for the longest period of time. Consequently, the ability of the family group to influence the personality and behavior of its members is paramount.

It is obviously appropriate to focus on the family as a critical decision-making and consumption unit.[3] Such items as food, shelter, and transportation are often jointly "consumed." Despite his strong preference for a sports car, a husband may buy a station wagon to accommodate the reality of having to transport his children. The purchase of a husband's ties, socks, and underwear is often made by the wife. A housewife bases her product and brand decisions to some extent on orders or requests from family members. The family offers feedback on products that are individually consumed, in such comments as "Gee, Mom, that dress makes you look fat," or "This cake is great."

Occasionally the family may emerge as a more useful market segment than its individual members. Gillette introduced Right Guard deodorant several years ago as a product for men. It was soon discovered, however, that all members of the family were using it, because the spray permitted sanitary use by several people. As a result, the advertising strategy was changed from male-oriented appeals in male-oriented media to such general appeals as "Hey! Who's got my Right Guard?" and "Don't leave your family defenseless!" in such general-appeal media as TV situation comedies.[4]

In the process of making decisions, the family is a major source of values for its individual members. One of the first sets of ideas and life-styles to which children are exposed is that of their own parents. The family performs a mediating function and interprets society's values. Attitudes toward certain products take shape within the context of the family, and the parents may exert a positive or negative influence on those products. The same effect may be found in the husband-and-wife relationship. The values of an individual family member may exert a significant influence in the purchase decisions of other members when one assumes the responsibility of interpreting society's values for them. For example, parents may protest their children's preferences in hair styles or clothing, while the children may indicate that the parents' preferences are out of date or "out of it."

Types of Families

There are conceptual differences regarding what constitutes the family. In the United States, we tend to think of husband, wife, and children as the basic family unit. In other parts of the world, the family may be conceived of as all blood relatives or kin, whether living or dead. One of the most important facets of the family's effect on consumer behavior is the fact that the family is an important source of interaction. Family interaction occurs between individuals who manifest these kinds of distinct characteristics:[5]

1. They are related by birth, marriage, or adoption.
2. They consider themselves as constituting a family group, and as being subject to family definitions of their group norms and roles, whatever they may be.
3. They engage in interaction sufficient to support these family definitions.

Just exactly who is included when one uses the term "family" varies from one group to another, and within one group various types of families can be identified. One categorization of family types includes:[6]

1. Nuclear (core) or conjugal family: husband and wife and children, if any.
2. Extended or consanguine family: husband and wife and their children, plus one or more other persons related to them by biological descent.
3. Family of orientation: family into which the individual is born.
4. Family of procreation: family established by marriage ceremony.

The family historically has many functions, including reproduction, socialization, social placement, and affection. The family also has been viewed as having the functional responsibility of status placement, emotional maintenance, and social and sexual control.

Most of the research into family influence on consumer behavior focuses on the nuclear family—husband, wife, and children. Despite changes, such families still predominate in the United States—approximately 77 percent of the population lives in a nuclear family.

DEMOGRAPHIC CHARACTERISTICS OF THE FAMILY

The marketer should be aware of the nature of the current family and the anticipated changes in family structure. Some of the demographic characteristics of the family in the mid-1970s can be seen in Table 6.1.[7] In 1978 there were approxi-

TABLE 6.1 CHARACTERISTICS OF ALL U.S. FAMILIES AND THOSE HEADED BY PERSONS AGED 25–44, 1975

Characteristics	All families	Family head aged 25–44		
		Total	25–34	35–44
Families				
Thousands	55,712	23,561	12,708	10,853
Distribution	100.0%	42.3	22.8	19.5
Average family size	3.42	3.97	3.57	4.45
Distribution all persons	100.0%	49.2	23.8	25.4
Type of family				
Husband-wife	84.3%	84.6%	85.6%	83.5%
Other	15.7	15.4	14.4	16.5
Number of children				
None	46.0%	16.3%	19.8%	12.1%
One	19.7	22.3	25.3	18.7
Two	18.0	30.8	32.7	28.6
Three	9.3	17.6	14.6	21.1
Four or more	6.9	13.1	7.6	19.5
Families with children	100.0%	65.6	33.9	31.7
Average number	2.09	2.28	2.03	2.55
Distribution of children	100.0%	71.8	33.0	38.8
Education[a]				
Elementary school or less	18.9%	9.6%	6.7%	13.5%
Some high school	15.4	12.5	10.9	14.7
High school graduate	34.3	37.1	37.3	36.8
Some college	15.7	17.2	19.7	13.8
College graduate	15.8	23.6	25.4	21.2
Occupation[b]				
White-collar workers	42.0%	46.8%	46.8%	46.9%
Professional/technical	15.2	19.9	21.0	18.5
Managers, administrators	14.1	15.1	13.0	17.8
Clerical workers	6.6	5.8	6.5	5.0
Sales workers	6.1	6.0	6.3	5.6

TABLE 6.1   (Cont.)

Characteristics	All families	Family head aged 25–44		
		Total	25–34	35–44
Blue-collar workers	44.6	43.2	43.6	42.8
Craft workers	20.1	21.4	20.8	22.2
Operatives	17.4	16.8	17.6	15.8
Laborers	7.1	5.0	5.2	4.8
Service workers	8.8	6.9	6.9	6.9
Farm workers	4.5	3.0	2.7	3.4
Residence[c]				
Metropolitan areas	66.6%	68.5%	68.9%	67.9%
Central cities	26.2	25.1	26.3	23.6
Suburbs	40.4	43.4	42.6	44.3
Nonmetropolitan areas	33.4	31.5	31.1	32.1
Central cities	100.0%	40.6	23.3	17.4
Suburbs	100.0%	45.6	24.4	21.2
Work status of wife[c]				
Wife working	43.2%	48.5%	49.0%	47.9%
Wife not working	56.8	51.5	51.0	52.1
Family income[d]				
Under $3,000	5.3%	4.1%	4.6%	3.5%
$3,000–5,000	7.8	5.5	6.2	4.7
5,000–7,000	8.9	6.6	6.9	6.3
7,000–10,000	13.8	12.6	14.1	10.9
10,000–15,000	24.4	27.4	30.1	24.2
15,000–25,000	28.3	33.9	31.7	36.5
25,000 and over	11.5	9.9	6.5	13.9
Distribution by income class				
Under $5,000	100.0%	30.9	18.7	12.1
$5,000–10,000	100.0%	35.8	21.1	14.8
10,000–15,000	100.0%	47.6	28.2	19.4
15,000–25,000	100.0%	50.6	25.5	25.1
25,000 and over	100.0%	36.6	12.9	23.6
Mean income	$14,502	$14,830	$13,552	$16,325
Median income	$12,836	$13,870	$13,000	$15,117
Distribution all income	100.0%	43.2	21.3	21.9
Mobility status[e]				
Moved between March 1970 and March 1975	41.7%	57.8%	71.4%	41.6%
Ownership				
Homes[f]	74.0%	7.03%	62.2%	79.4%
Cars[g]	81.5%	87.9%	87.3%	88.6%
Two or more	32.7%	37.1%	31.8%	43.2%

[a] Male population 18 years and over.
[b] Employed civilian males 16 years and over.
[c] Based on husband-wife families.
[d] Data refer to income earned in 1974.
[e] Based on mobility of married males, wife present.
[f] Data are based on husband-wife families and refer to October 1973.
[g] Data are based on households and refer to fall 1974.

Source: Fabian Linden, "Consumer Markets: The Post-War Generation Comes of Age," *Conference Board Record* 13, no. 9 (September 1976), pp. 3–4.

mately 60 million families. It is projected that there will be a significant growth in the number of families in the coming years, and an extraordinary growth in the number of young families. In 1985 there will be roughly 9 million more families than there were ten years earlier. Of that number, slightly more than 7.5 million will be in the 25–44 age group.

The spending power of this young family age group is expected to increase 80 percent over the next ten years. Thus, $1 of every $2 that will find its way to the nation's retail counters in 1985 will come from families in that age group.

Families with Heads Aged 25–34 Years

The 25–34 age group is currently the fastest growing age segment of the population. In the 1970s the size of this group expanded by more than 35 percent, over twice the rate of the total population. When these families are compared with their counterparts of the 1960s, many significant differences are found—in marital status, family composition, educational achievement, occupation, and working status of wives, among others.

Young adults are marrying much later than they did in the past. Some 43 percent of the married women in this age group are still childless, compared with 28 percent in 1965. Some 45 percent of the family heads aged 25–34 had at least some exposure to college in 1975, compared with 30 percent ten years earlier. Both in education and in occupation, the upcoming generation ranks significantly higher on the socioeconomic scale than any preceding one.

From the marketer's viewpoint, there are significant implications in the increasing tendency of women to work outside the home. The participation of wives in the labor force has been rising in all age groups, but the increase is especially pronounced in the 25–34 age group. Some 60 percent of all wives aged 25–34 were working for pay in 1978, compared to roughly 32 percent thirteen years earlier, and a larger proportion of mothers with young children were holding down jobs.

Families with Heads Aged 35–44 Years

The demographic characteristics of families aged 35–44 are not very different from those found in the comparable age group in the mid-1960s, but they are expected to change significantly in the future. This will be the fastest growing segment of the market in the mid-1980s. In 1975, about 19.5 percent, or 10.8 million, of the nation's families were in this age group—marginally fewer than ten years earlier. Much as in the mid-1960s, about 95 percent of all women in this age group were married in 1975 and about 88 percent of all families included at least one child. Only 41 percent of all homes had three or more children, however, down from about 44 percent, and the rate of this decline is expected to increase.

The educational accomplishments and occupational profile of the 35–44 group have undergone significant upgrading, and the income profile has improved considerably. Despite this relatively favorable financial picture, however, only 22 percent of total income flowed to this class in 1975 (compared with 26 percent ten years earlier) because the size of this group/has declined over the years. Nonetheless, because their numbers will grow quite rapidly, by 1985 this family group will probably account for 25 percent of total income.

Families with Heads Aged 45–64 Years

Some market researchers see the older family group as an important untapped market, since it represents combined household incomes totaling $400 billion a year. These people comprise approximately one-third of all U.S. households and represent more than half of all households in the country with annual incomes of more than $25,000. They include people of high occupational status and income and offer a potential market for many products that the younger segment uses as well as those that can be purchased by people who have a substantial amount of discretionary income to spend.

FAMILY ROLES IN BUYING BEHAVIOR

While demographic data on the family are useful to marketers, additional insights emerge from an understanding of the roles that family members assume in regard to buying behavior. These roles relate to the kinds of activities undertaken by the husband and wife, and to the parts played by family members in the actual purchase process.

Instrumental and Expressive Leaders

The family generally has an instrumental and an expressive leader. *Instrumental* refers to task-oriented activities, and *expressive* refers to those activities that involve the social-emotional area. Expressive values are those that have worth in themselves, such as love, personal dignity, religion, and art. Instrumental values are mainly economic, and relate to means rather than ends.[8]

In the traditional family the husband performs the instrumental role and the wife performs the expressive role. Each may maintain the ascribed role in the marketplace even when the major user of a product purchased will be the other person. For example, men's clothing, jewelry, and toiletries are frequently purchased by women. Styles, design, and fashion are considered within women's province. Items that have a utilitarian purpose are frequently the husbands' concern. When the family needs a new refrigerator or washing machine, for example, the wife will generally consult with her husband.

Family roles are also differentiated in regard to external and internal activities. Husbands generally are considered to be concerned with matters *external* to the family and wives with matters that are *internal.* With the changing nature of women's activities in our society, this distinction is less firm than it once was. Generally it still holds, however, and the man takes the lead in dealing with the major external institutions of the society.

When the internal-external roles are combined with the expressive-instrumental classifications, they suggest areas where the husband's and wife's roles overlap. For example, in matters that are internal-instrumental (home repairs) or external-expressive (entertainment outside of the home), in which husband and wife share an interest, they may make joint decisions.

Purchase-Process Influences

All family members can assume roles in the actual purchase process. These roles emerge in the course of determining the need for the product or service, securing and processing the information relevant to the purchase decision, making the purchase, and consuming the product or service. The roles in the purchase process may be defined as the influencer, the decider, the purchaser, and the user.

INFLUENCERS

Influencers may be defined as those who inform, persuade, or establish certain requirements to be met in the buying situation. There is considerable evidence that teen-age children exert an influence on the decision to buy an automobile. Traditionally, the wife is likely to be the influencer in the purchase of most household products, while the husband is the influencer in the decision to buy leisure items or do-it-yourself items, such as a power drill. In recent years, however, the traditional roles in the marital relationship have undergone a change. Male influence in purchase decisions that were once regarded as the almost exclusive interest of the female homemaker has increased. Table 6.2 shows that men believe they play a substantial role in selecting consumer household products. These data seem to indicate an expansion of the man's involvement in the household.

Ad campaigns reflect such male influences in purchases traditionally made by wives, such as food and household products. Now that she knows her husband prefers Stove-Top Stuffing, the wife declares, she will purchase it, and she will buy White Cloud toilet tissue, too, since her husband perceives it to be softer after comparing it with some other brands.

DECIDERS

Final authority in buying decisions often resides in a single member of the household. In some cases, the family member who takes on the role of decider is fairly obvious. The housewife decides on the purchase of cosmetics, the husband decides on the purchase of cigars, and the child decides on the purchase of candy or a comic book with his allowance.

TABLE 6.2   MEN'S PERCEPTION OF THEIR INFLUENCE IN FAMILY
SELECTION BY BRANDS, BY PRODUCT (PERCENT)

Products	Male users with "high" influence
Regular ground coffee	58.4%
Deodorant	57.8
Regular cola	55.6
Instant coffee	54.8
Other-flavor carbonated soft drink, regular	53.1
Toothpaste	53.0
Mouthwash	52.8
Thirst-quenching, quick-energy drinks	51.7
Other-flavor carbonated soft drink, low calorie	50.1
Frozen pudding	49.4
Salad dressing, prepared	49.2
Shampoo	48.7
Regular tea	48.3
Canned corn beef hash	47.1

Source: "The Male Expression of His Brand Influence," supplied by *Reader's Digest* (a syndicated study prepared by The Simmons Organization, 1972).

In other cases, the family member who takes on the role of decider may vary from household to household. In research to determine who makes the decision of when to buy an automobile, it was disclosed that the husband was the primary decider in 68 percent of the cases, the wife the primary decider in 3 percent, and there was an equal decision in 29 percent of the cases. The decision on the color of the automobile was influenced primarily by the husband in 25 percent of the cases, by the wife in 25 percent, and equally in 50 percent of the cases.[9]

Sometimes the dominating influence in the decision is not easily revealed. Research into this area has provided conflicting reports. The influence can be very subtle. A husband may report that he had a major influence in choosing the make of the car, although in reality his wife may have exerted a determining influence:[10]

Verbal, explicit: "We must buy a sports car." (Demand)
"Buy a sports car or I'll be unhappy." (Threat)
"I hope you will buy a sports car." (Request)
"A sports car would be best." (Advice)
Verbal, implicit: "Let's have a fun car this time." (Hint)
Nonverbal: She stands by the sports car beaming. (Enthusiasm)
She stands by the sedan sulking. (Despondency)

PURCHASERS

An individual member of the family is usually responsible for the actual purchase. In the family buying group, the wife and mother is most often the "purchasing agent." She has an established routine of shopping trips, and as a result of the repetitive nature of this task, she tends to develop shopping habits and favorite outlets.

The role of the wife in purchasing is evident in products that are used by the husband. C. B. Hathaway's research revealed that 68 percent of its men's dress shirts were purchased by women.[11] In a national campaign for its designer apparel, Hathaway geared the advertising of its Christian Dior men's dress shirts and neckwear largely to women. The copy declared, "Give him a Christian Dior shirt and tie for Christmas and stay home New Year's Eve." (See Exhibit 6.1.)

This situation seems to be changing, however, as traditional roles are being overturned and shopping conditions are altering to meet this change. Thus we find the shopping situation becoming more and more of a family outing, with husbands actively participating. Stores are open during evening hours, Saturdays, and even Sundays. With the emergence of shopping centers and enclosed malls, retailers have made efforts to provide the amenities necessary for family shopping.

Children have taken on an increased interest in the role of purchasing agent. Teen-agers have money at their disposal, much of it earned at odd jobs, and increased freedom in undertaking marketing activities. The shopping center performs a social role for teen-agers, permitting them to gather and exchange ideas, and at the same time offering them convenient outlets at which to purchase.

EXHIBIT 6.1

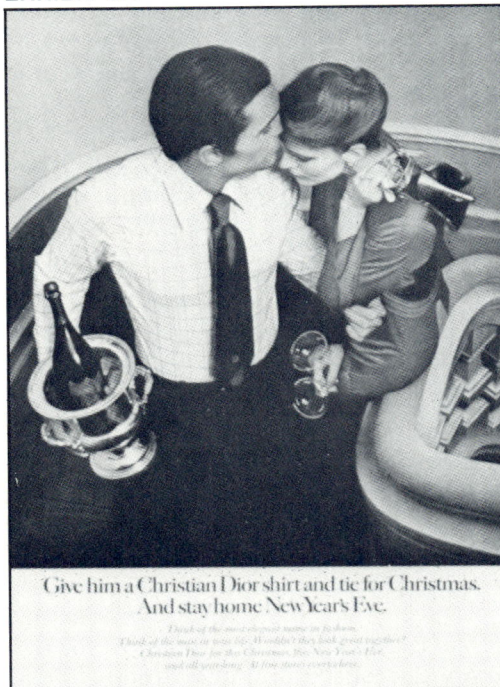

Give him a Christian Dior shirt and tie for Christmas.
And stay home New Year's Eve.

C. B. Hathaway Company's print campaign for the Dior men's dress shirt is aimed squarely at women.

USERS

The user, as the term implies, uses or consumes the product. In some cases, the same family member is the influencer, decider, purchaser, and user—for example, the teen-ager who purchases records. In other instances, the user may not be involved in any aspect of the buying decision. The parents buy their baby's crib, many wives buy underwear for their disinterested husbands, and all family members buy gifts. Traditional users may change, as we saw at the beginning of this chapter. Mothers and housewives color their hair, and all members of the family use kitchen utensils.

An interesting case in which the user is not involved in any aspect of the purchasing decision is that of the purchase of pet foods. Although a pet is not a biological member of the family, it is usually perceived to be an important part of the group. Many pet-food strategies are based on the concept that the user is not involved in the purchasing decision, particularly those tactics that include variations on the kinds of foods offered to dogs. It appears that dogs will gladly eat the same type of food day after day, as long as they like it; it is their owners who feel they need variety in their diet. It should be noted, however, that the pet is an important element in the repurchase decision, since if he will not eat the dog food, the owner will not purchase it again. In fact, many users are significant influencers in the repurchase decision, and mothers will ask their children if they like the cereal purchased for them, or ask their husbands if they like the underwear.

For the marketer, it is important to identify each of the family members involved in the purchase decision process. She should understand the role each one plays, the information they require, the outlets at which they may purchase the product, the media that may best reach them, and so on. Awareness of these roles permits her to develop a more efficient strategy than one that tries to reach the family as a group. Of equal importance to marketers is an awareness of the changing nature of these roles. As we saw at the beginning of this chapter, the purchase of housewares, traditionally the responsibility of the wife, may now generate interest among all members of the household.

FAMILY DECISION MAKING

The influence of the family on the consumer's decision process can be examined from various perspectives. Some researchers have studied this influence from the viewpoint of the extent to which joint decision making or role specialization occurs within the family. Others investigate the influence of various family members on specific product and brand decisions.

Role Specialization versus Joint Decision Making

One conceptual framework for family decision making provides four basic patterns representing role specialization or joint decision making.

Autonomic decision making: an equal number of separate decisions is made by each partner.
Husband dominance: the husband makes most of the decisions.
Wife dominance: the wife makes most of the decisions.
Syncratic decision making: most decisions are made jointly.

A study conducted in Belgium examined the extent to which husbands or wives exert greater influence in the purchase of 25 products.[12] The extent of role specialization in these 25 decisions is presented in Figure 6.1, in which each decision is positioned in relation to two axes. The first is a scale of the relative influence of husband and wife. The second axis is a scale of the extent of role specialization as measured by percentage of families reporting that a decision is jointly made.

There are four decision areas. "Husband dominant" decisions are those for which the mean relative influence is 1.5 or less on a scale of 3.0, while those with means of 2.5 or greater are "wife dominant." By definition, in both of these areas, the proportion of families that decide jointly is less than 50 percent. Decisions with mean relative influence between 1.5 and 2.5 fall into either a "syncratic" or an "autonomic" pattern. If more than 50 percent of the families make a decision jointly, it is classified as syncratic. If this percentage is less than 50 percent, the decision is classified as autonomic.

As Figure 6.1 shows, decisions concerning furnishings for rooms other than the living room, food, children's clothing, and kitchen products tend to be wife dominant. Insurance decisions are husband dominant. Decisions on appliances, cars, savings, and housing upkeep tend to be autonomic. Vacation, school, and housing decisions are likely to be syncratic.

This classification system suggests the need for various communication strategies. When decisions are dominated by the husband or the wife, messages may be designed in reference to the particular spouse. When decisions are syncratic, messages may be designed for the couple as a unit, showing, for example, the way in which the purchase of a particular brand or service can resolve certain decision conflicts within the family. For autonomic decisions, the communicator must realize he is communicating to two audiences. In the case of alcoholic beverages, for example, it may be justifiable to develop two campaigns, one stressing husband-oriented appeal and the other wife-oriented appeal, rather than one campaign that attempts to mix the two.

This research also indicated that marital roles vary throughout the phases of the decision process. The researchers examined the influence exerted by husbands and wives in three stages of the decision process: problem recognition, search for information, and final decision. The results revealed that in 16 of the 25 decisions, the same pattern of influence occurs in all phases of the decision process. Life insurance remains husband dominant; decisions regarding kitchenware, household cleaning products, and wives' and children's clothing remain wife dominant. The syncratic pattern characterizes decisions about housing, living-room furniture, children's toys, and schools and family vacations in all three phases. Decisions

FIGURE 6.1   MARITAL ROLES IN 25 DECISIONS

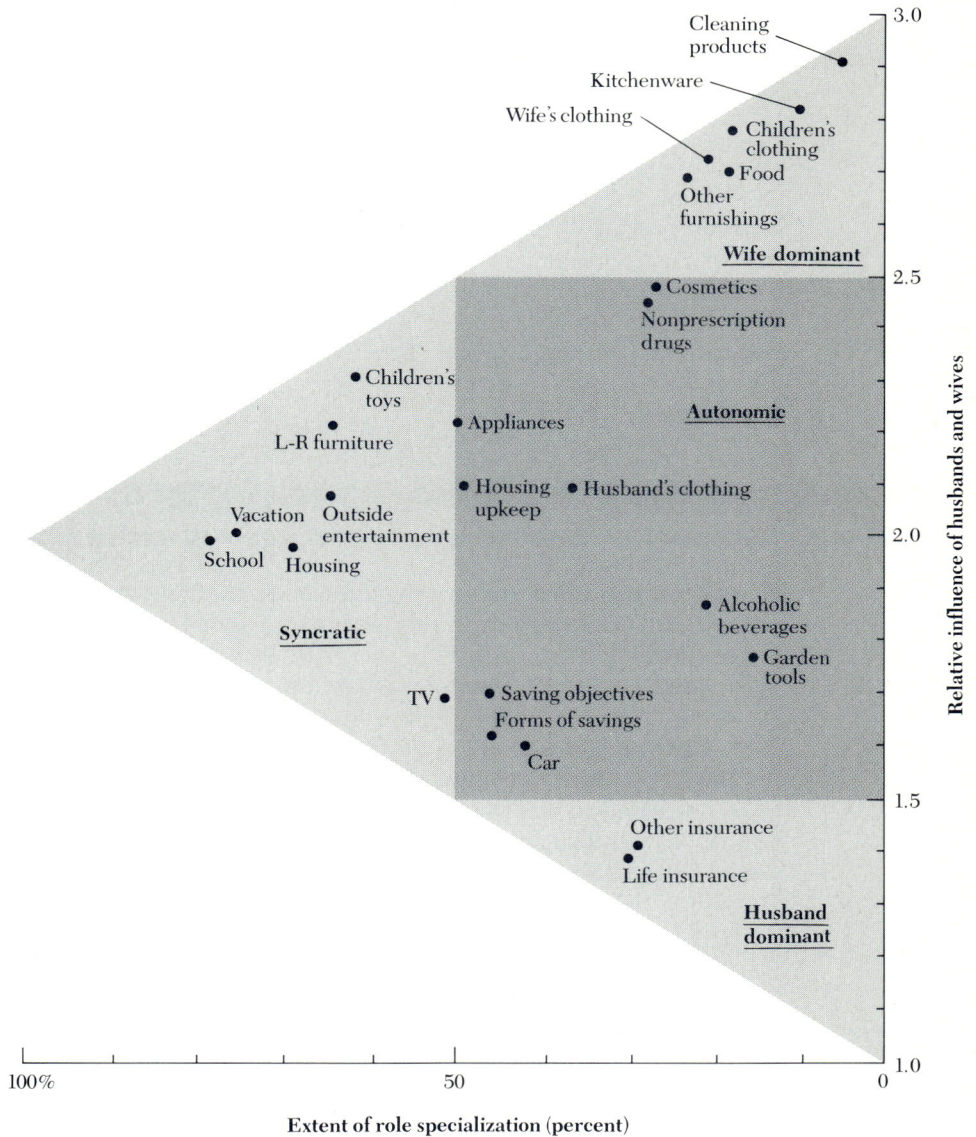

Source: Harry L. Davis and Benny P. Rigaux, "Perception of Marital Roles in Decision Processes," *Journal of Consumer Research* 1 (June 1974), p. 54.

concerning garden tools, alcoholic beverages, and nonprescription drugs remain in the autonomic pattern.

Five of the remaining nine decisions, which change patterns at least once over the three phases, move from autonomic in the first two phases to syncratic in the final decision. These decisions include those on housing upkeep, household appliances, husband's clothing, and savings. Of the four other decisions, the purchase of a car is most varied, moving from autonomic for problem recognition to husband dominant for search, and finally to syncratic for the final decision. This finding may suggest different campaigns relevant to the various decision stages. For the early stage of awareness of the need for a car, for example, messages may be directed toward either husband or wife. During the phase designed to create brand preference, messages may concentrate on the husband. To secure conviction concerning the purchase, messages may be delivered to the husband and wife as a unit.

FACTORS THAT INFLUENCE JOINT DECISION MAKING

In many family decisions, the husband and wife act jointly. A number of influences appear to determine the extent of joint decision making in the family.[13]

Life Cycle. Joint decision making appears to decline over the life cycle. The tendency is usually explained in terms of the increased efficiency or competence that people develop over time. Thus their decisions become acceptable to their partners, and the need for extensive interaction is eliminated.

Product Type. Joint decision making appears likely to occur in connection with purchases that represent significant outlays, whereas smaller purchases are likely to be delegated to one partner. When specialization does occur, certain products tend to be handled by men and others by women. This tendency has been discussed in the examination of the internal-external, instrumental-expressive roles.

Social Class. A "curvilinear hypothesis" postulates that joint decision making is less common at both extremes of the socioeconomic hierarchy than at the middle, with women playing the most important role in lower-class families and men dominating upper-class families.

Some empirical data have revealed that in family decisions in general, there is low joint involvement in the low income group, high in the middle income group, and again low in the high income group.[14] The explanation for this finding may be that one would expect less debate between husband and wife at the lower income levels because the available income must be allocated to routine and necessary purchases. At the upper income level, more autonomous decisions by the husband or wife may be expected because more discretionary income is available, so that the family has greater leeway in its choices. At the middle income level, it is possible that there is some discretionary income, but not in large amounts;

therefore, alternative purchases may require greater consideration and thus greater consultation between husband and wife.

It also appears that the amount of responsibility taken by the wife increases inversely with the status of the family. The least amount of responsibility is taken by the wife in a high-status group and the greatest in a low-status group. In support of this concept is evidence that lower-class families are more matriarchal. This situation, coupled with the fact that purchases in low income families are likely to be routine, suggests that the wife in such a family is more likely to make the decisions.

Ethnic Considerations. The question of who in the family makes most of the decisions may be influenced by ethnic backgrounds. In some ethnic groups, joint husband-wife activities are sanctioned; in others, the husband is the head of the house and chief decision maker. Research data suggest that among American couples, joint decision making is most pronounced among whites, husband dominance is most pronounced among those of Japanese descent, and wife dominance is most pronounced among blacks.[15]

Product and Brand Decisions

Responsibility for some product and brand decisions generally resides in a specific family member. Some of these decisions were earlier labeled "wife dominant" and "husband dominant." Such domains are not constant; variations are emerging, owing in part to the changing nature of the roles of men, women, and children in our society. As we noted earlier, decisions on the purchase of kitchen appliances, once considered the province of the wife, may now be relevant to all members of the family.

While the role of purchasing agent is frequently assigned to the mother, this role may vary from one product class to another. Furthermore, an important influence of product or brand selection is the authority of the adviser. In some circumstances, he may be the buyer and the user as well; in others, he merely acts as an adviser in product choice. For example, some men may express a preference for a certain kind of toothpaste. The wife may then be a purchasing agent for a product that her husband uses. Or the husband may express a preference for a particular fragrance among perfumes. The wife is then the purchasing agent and the user, but the husband has taken the role of adviser. Some research findings present useful insights into these variations.

THE WIFE AND PRODUCT DECISIONS

One study of family product choice gave some interesting insights into the influences exerted on the housewife as the purchasing agent.[16] It was found, as was to be expected, that other members of the family exert considerable influence on the housewife's brand decisions. The housewife tends to know the family brand preferences in some product classes better than others, however. Those in which she is likely to know her family's brand preferences involve products whose brand names are visible to the family when they are using them. Brands that are likely to be visible when the products are in use by adults are those of such products as beer, cigarettes, and deodorants. Children's products whose brands are clearly visible in use include candy bars, chewing gum, and cold cereals. Products whose brands are not visible in use include canned peas, canned spaghetti, and cake mixes.

The housewife, in her role as purchasing agent, is most receptive to the brand preferences of her family when buying products whose brands are highly visible. This characteristic may also be due to the element of risk the housewife may perceive in her use of products that may be highly visible to others. To reduce such risk, she may tend to select well-known brands of highly visible products. The additional authority provided by the family in the choice of highly visible products may also act as a risk reducer.

THE HUSBAND AND PRODUCT DECISIONS

We have less empirical evidence of the husband's actions as family decision maker in product choices than we have of the wife's. An obvious reason is that the wife is most frequently designated as the purchasing agent. Some recent findings, however, suggest the extent of husband decision making in family purchases.

A number of magazines commissioned a study to determine the extent of husbands' and wives' influence in decisions regarding the purchase of food.[17] The study found that wives' and husbands' indirect influence—that is, the extent to which one spouse buys a product and brand in order to please the other, without being told to do so—was roughly the same as their direct influence on both the products and brands purchased. Husbands proved to have the greatest influence in beer and wine purchases, but the wife has the greatest influence in all other food and beverage categories measured.

Husbands came closest in influence in hamburgers from fast-food restaurants, canned luncheon meat, liquid salad dressing, and regular instant coffee, but their wives still had the most influence in the buying decisions for all of those items.

Some general findings about husband involvement in consumer decisions emerge from a number of studies:[18]

1. Husband involvement varies widely by product category.

2. Husband involvement within any product category varies by specific decisions and decision stages. The automobile purchase illustrates how variable husband/wife involvement really is. According to some reports, wives were as involved as their husbands in gathering relevant information. Some 60 percent of couples interviewed in another study classified the decision about make of automobile as husband dominant, but only

25 percent considered the husband to be dominant in the choice of color.

3. Husband involvement in a consumer decision is likely to vary considerably among families.

CHILDREN AND PRODUCT DECISIONS

The importance of children to marketing strategies is apparent. The funds available to children are increasing. Children's behavior differs from that of adults. But children eventually become adults, and their adult behavior may be influenced by their behavior as children. Children exert extensive influence in family decision making.

Children, even the youngest, influence their parents to buy products. In a study of children aged 2 to 8 relating to products that were advertised on television, 9 out of 10 of the responding households indicated that children influenced their purchases.[19] Children can successfully use a variety of effective appeals to promote purchase. Most effective seems to be the direct request. In more than one-fifth of households a child can induce purchase by putting the product in the shopping cart. (See Table 6.3)

One researcher found that advertisers have done a much better job in some product categories than in others of making children want the brand as distinguished from the product.[20] Cereal advertising, for example, makes them want a specific brand of cereal. This is less true of soft drinks and peanut butter. One possible reason is the greater differentiation that exists among brands of cereal

TABLE 6.3   HOUSEHOLDS INFLUENCED BY CHILDREN'S APPEALS TO PURCHASE, BY AGE GROUP OF CHILDREN (PERCENT)

Form of appeal	Households with children 2–8 (N = 221)	Households with children 2–5 (N = 155)
Asks for product	79.6%	79.4%
Puts product in cart	21.3	20.6
Says good, nourishing, economical	39.8	34.8
Says product is new	22.2	15.5
Says other children use	8.1	6.5
Wants boxtop	26.2	18.1
Wants premium	49.8	43.9
Wants to try product	64.7	59.4
Does not affect purchase	9.0	6.5

Totals add to more than 100.0% since each respondent was to check all applicable appeals.

Source: Mark Munn, "The Effect on Parental Buying Habits of Children Exposed to Children's Television Programs," *Journal of Broadcasting* 2, (Summer 1958), pp. 253–258.

than among brands of peanut butter. An alternative explanation is that the advertiser who is successful in securing such a distinction does so by neglecting to provide the generic name of the product in his advertising, and instead making his brand a unique conceptual entity. While the peanut butter advertiser can hardly avoid mentioning peanut butter in conjunction with his brand name (for example, Skippy Peanut Butter), the cereal advertiser speaks only of Wheaties or Post Toasties.

PARENT/CHILD INTERACTION

Researchers have examined the child's role in influencing consumer decisions by studying the interaction between parent and child. One study focused on the impact of television advertising on mother-child interaction. Specifically, it examined children's attempts to influence their mothers' purchases of various products and the mothers' yielding to these attempts. The study was conducted through questionnaires sent to 132 mothers of 5- to 12-year-olds in the Boston area.[21]

The results indicated that across most product categories, the older the child, the more likely the mothers are to yield to influence attempts. This result may have been obtained because older children generally asked for less. It may also be due to the mothers' belief that older children have greater competence in making judgments about products. The kinds of products mothers are most likely to buy in response to their children's urgings are food products. These are also the kinds of products that children most often ask for. The study also revealed that mothers with positive attitudes toward advertising are more likely than mothers with negative attitudes to yield to influence attempts. (See Table 6.4.)

Cereals emerge as a product whose purchase patterns exhibit a high percentage of parental yielding to children's requests. A number of studies of parent/child interaction have focused on cereals. In one such study, the direct-observation method was used to examine the interaction between parents and children in supermarkets in an effort to determine the processes and effects of decision making on the selection of breakfast cereals.[22] In two-thirds of the episodes studied, the child initiated the interaction sequence by expressing a desire for cereal. (See Figure 6.2.)

According to the researcher, the child plays the dominant role in family cereal selection in the supermarket either by asking for a brand or by choosing one upon parental invitation. Children appear to rely on preestablished preferences based more often on premium incentives than on the product's nutritional features. Furthermore, the child's desire for the premium is met with a high rate of acceptance by the parent. Similar findings were reported in another study based on the interview method, which revealed that although there was much parental objection to the use of premiums in television advertising to children, the premium appeal is an effective persuasive tool for the child involved.[23]

From a sales viewpoint, these findings suggest that advertising and promotion efforts for child-oriented cereals should emphasize premium offers more than nu-

TABLE 6.4   FREQUENCY OF CHILDREN'S ATTEMPTS TO INFLUENCE PUR-
CHASES AND PERCENTAGE OF MOTHERS "USUALLY" YIELD-
ING, BY AGE OF CHILD

Products	Frequency of requests[a]				Percentage of yielding			
	5–7 years	8–10 years	11–12 years	Total[b]	5–7 years	8–10 years	11–12 years	Total[b]
Relevant Foods								
Breakfast cereal	1.26	1.59	1.97	1.59	88	91	83	87
Snack foods	1.71	2.00	1.71	1.80	52	62	77	63
Candy	1.60	2.09	2.17	1.93	40	28	57	42
Soft drinks	2.00	2.03	2.00	2.01	38	47	54	46
Jell-O	2.54	2.94	2.97	2.80	40	41	26	36
Overall mean	1.82	2.13	2.16	2.03				
Overall percentage					51.6	53.8	59.4	54.8
Less relevant foods								
Bread	3.12	2.91	3.43	3.16	14	28	17	19
Coffee	3.93	3.91	3.97	3.94	2	0	0	1
Pet food	3.29	3.59	3.24	3.36	7	3	11	7
Overall mean	3.45	3.47	3.49	3.49				
Overall percentage					7.6	10.3	9.3	9.0
Durables for child's use								
Game, toy	1.24	1.63	2.17	1.65	57	59	46	54
Clothing	2.76	2.47	2.29	2.52	21	34	57	37
Bicycle	2.48	2.59	2.77	2.61	7	9	9	8
Hot wheels	2.43	2.41	3.20	2.67	29	19	17	22
Record album	3.36	2.63	2.23	2.78	12	16	46	24
Camera	3.91	3.75	3.71	3.80	2	3	0	2
Overall mean	2.70	2.58	2.73	2.67				
Overall percentage					25.6	28.0	35.0	29.4
Notions, toiletries								
Toothpaste	2.29	2.31	2.60	2.39	36	44	40	39
Bath soap	3.10	2.97	3.46	3.17	9	9	9	9
Shampoo	3.48	3.31	3.03	3.28	17	6	23	16
Aspirin	3.64	3.78	3.97	3.79	5	6	0	4
Overall mean	3.13	3.09	3.26	3.16				
Overall percentage					16.8	16.3	18.0	17.0
Other products								
Automobile	3.55	3.66	3.51	3.57	2	0	0	12
Gasoline brand	3.64	3.63	3.83	3.70	2	0	3	2
Laundry soap	3.69	3.75	3.71	3.72	2	0	3	2
Household cleaner	3.71	3.84	3.74	3.76	2	3	0	2
Overall mean	3.65	3.72	3.70	3.69				
Overall percentage					2.0	.75	1.50	1.75

[a] On a scale from 1 (often) to 4 (never).
[b] 5–7 years, $n = 43$; 8–10 years, $n = 32$; 11–12 years, $n = 34$; $N = 109$.

Source: S. Ward and D. B. Wackman, "Children's Purchase Influence Attempts and Parental Yielding," in *Perspectives in Consumer Behavior*, ed. Harold Kassarjian and Thomas S. Robertson (Glenview, Ill.: Scott, Foresman, 1973), p. 370.

FIGURE 6.2   FLOW OF PARENT-CHILD INTERACTION IN SELECTION OF BREAKFAST CEREAL

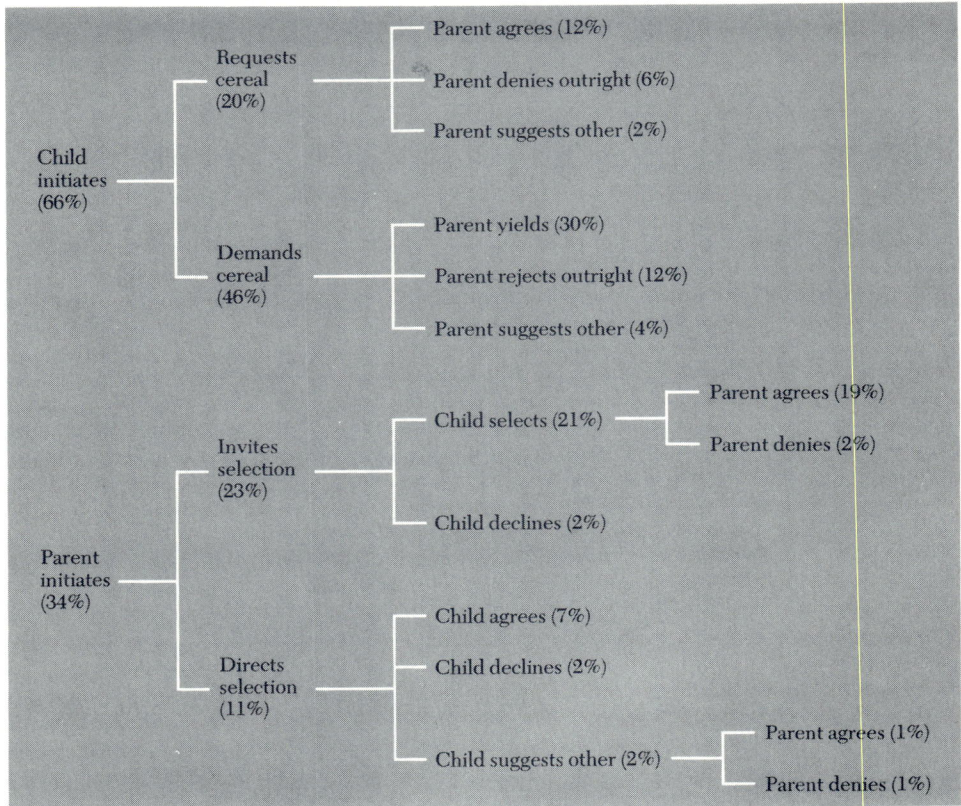

Source: Charles K. Atkin, "Observation of Parent-Child Interaction in Supermarket Decision-Making," *Journal of Marketing* 42 (October 1978), p. 43.

tritional content. With the widespread public interest in advertising to children, however, the social implications of these findings suggest that efforts should be made to increase the audience's attention to and interest in a product's nutritional benefits.

The Gatekeeper Effect. A study examined the mother's purchase behavior of the child's preferred cereal to determine if it was related to the child-centeredness of the mother.[24] Interestingly, it was found that child-centered mothers, instead of showing a greater tendency to purchase their children's favorite cereals, tend to purchase these cereals less frequently.

This finding appeared to emerge from the "gatekeeper effect." A child-centered mother may have a greater tendency to rely on her view of what is right and healthful in purchasing cereals. Since the child usually prefers presweetened cereals, the mother, in her concern for the child's well-being, tends to ignore the child's preference and to purchase what she thinks will do him the most good. The mother low in child-centeredness may be more likely to purchase the brands the child prefers to placate him.

A knowledge of the gatekeeper effect may be useful in devising a promotional strategy for a product in which a child is eventually involved. If the mother is not only a purchasing agent for the child but also an agent who puts her preferences above those of the child, advertisers might be more successful if they directed some of their advertising to the mother, even if she is not the user of the product. Messages stressing nutritional benefits may be an effective as well as appropriate strategy in such circumstances.

General versus Product-Specific Studies. An evaluation of the research relevant to the interaction between parent and child in purchase decisions indicates that such research is most useful when it is product- or service-specific.[25] General-category descriptions may imply general strategies that are unsuited for specific products or services. For example, in an examination of the process of arriving at a decision concerning a fast-food restaurant, the data indicated a high degree of interaction between adults and children at all stages of the process: initiation of the purchase idea, provision of information on alternatives, and the final decision.[26] In a decision regarding a family trip, however, adult-child interaction was less pronounced at each decision stage. This finding suggests that advertising showing all members of the family involved in a decision may be more effective for fast-food restaurants than for travel service companies.

LIFE-CYCLE INFLUENCES ON FAMILY DECISIONS

Although family structure is usually studied in terms of such demographic factors as age and income, research has suggested that the life cycle of the family may be a more sensitive indicator of purchase decisions in many kinds of consumer analysis. The life cycle is a composite of several variables, including age, marital status, and presence or absence of children. Intuition suggests that two people of the same age may be in different stages of the life cycle and thus may have widely varying purchasing patterns, which are influenced by their marital status and the number of children they have.

The stages of the life cycle most frequently named (see Table 6.5) are:

1. Bachelor stage: young, single people not living at home.
2. Newly married couples: young, no children.
3. Full nest 1: youngest child under 6.
4. Full nest 2: youngest child 6 or over.
5. Full nest 3: older couples with dependent children.

TABLE 6.5 FAMILY FINANCIAL CHARACTERISTICS AND PURCHASING PATTERNS, BY LIFE-CYCLE STAGE

Life-cycle stage	Financial characteristics	Purchasing patterns
Bachelor	Few financial burdens; fashion opinion leaders; recreation-oriented	Basic kitchen equipment; basic furniture; cars; equipment for the mating game; vacations
Newly married couples	Better off financially than they will be in the near future; highest purchase rate; highest average purchasers of durables	Cars; refrigerators; stoves; sensible and durable furniture; vacations
Full nest 1	Home purchasing at peak; liquid assets low; dissatisfied with financial position and amount of money saved; interested in new products; prefer advertised products	Washers; dryers; TVs; baby food; chest rubs and cough medicines; vitamins; dolls; wagons; sleds; skates
Full nest 2	Financial position better; some wives work; less influenced by advertising; buy larger-sized packages and multiple-unit "deals"	Many foods; cleaning materials; bicycles; music lessons; pianos
Full nest 3	Financial position even more improved; more wives work; some children get jobs; hard to influence with advertising; high average purchase of durables	New, more expensive furniture; automobile travel; nonnecessary appliances; boats; dental services; magazines
Empty nest 1	Home ownership at peak; most satisfied with financial position and money saved; interested in travel, recreation, self-education; make gifts and contributions; not interested in new products	Vacations; luxuries; home improvements
Empty nest 2	Drastic cut in income; keep home	Medical appliances; medical care; products that aid health, sleep, and digestion
Solitary survivor 1	Income still good, but likely to sell home	
Solitary survivor 2	Same medical and product needs as other solitary-survivor group; drastic cut in income; special need for attention, affection, security	

Source: Adapted from William D. Wells and George Gubar, "Life Cycle Concept in Marketing Research," *Journal of Marketing Research* 3 (November 1966), p. 362.

6. Empty nest 1: older couples with no children living with them, head in the labor force.
7. Empty nest 2: older married couples, no children living at home, head retired.
8. Solitary survivor 1: in labor force.
9. Solitary survivor 2: retired.

Some studies have, in fact, indicated that the life cycle discriminates better than age in the family's consumption patterns. For example, it was found that life-cycle analysis showed a sharp drop in the proportion of homeowners among older single people as compared with older couples.[27] It appeared that the relevant factor here was widowhood rather than age. In another comparison, the data relating to age gave the impression that young women tend to work indefinitely without interruption, while the life-cycle data reflected the fact that young wives without children are more likely to work than those who have children. Life-cycle data were also able to reveal more clearly than age data that new-car buying takes a dip in the "youngest child under 6" group, while television buying hits its peak in this group.

Other products for which the life cycle discriminated better than age included washing machines, dryers, refrigerators, home freezers, clothes, some foods (flour, cornflakes, sugar, macaroni, syrup, milk), bicycles, games, music lessons, auto operating expenses, boats, and magazines. For some products, however, age is a better discriminator than the life cycle: expenditures for medical care, luxuries, hi-fi components, and homeowner's insurance.

An early study of life-cycle influences disclosed that most washing machines are bought by young married couples with children under 6 years of age (a finding that could be anticipated).[28] These families also appear to be the best prospects for houses, used cars, and television sets. Purchases of furniture, refrigerators, and stoves are frequent among all married people under 45 years old, but less common in the older groups.

Families with young children are the most frequent purchasers of chest-cold remedies, cough syrups, and packaged detergents. Newly married women are prime prospects for cake mixes, precooked foods, new recipes, and new labor-saving devices.

A study of furniture buying conducted for the Kroehler Manufacturing Company showed that interest in furniture buying is highest during two separate life-cycle stages, and that the type of furniture bought varies from one stage to the other.[29] The first important stage is the early years of marriage, for it is at that point that the couple has to acquire furniture to fit its basic needs. At this stage, however, the young family tends to place somewhat greater emphasis on sensibility and practicality than on style and beauty.

For middle-class parents, the second stage occurs when their children have started to date and hold parties. At that stage, attractiveness and reflection of good taste become more important than sturdiness and low cost. For working-class parents, the second stage of furniture buying may be delayed until all of the children have left home. This group, however, tends to emphasize attractiveness rather than durability in both stages.

The Process of Adjustment and Family Life Cycle

While life-cycle research has indicated that it can be more useful as a basis for market segmentation than specific demographic characteristics, such as age, other variables may be superior segmentation correlates. A study of frequency of entertainment activity noted that older respondents in the later stages of the life cycle bowled most often. The frequency with which respondents attended movies, however, was found to be positively correlated with social class and negatively correlated with both age and life cycle.[30]

In considering family life-cycle influences, one must examine the effects of the process of adjustment within the family as a social group. As the family has the characteristics of a social group, such concepts as group dynamics apply to it. Like any other social group, the family must have some degree of consensus regarding its goals, objectives, and modes of operation if it is to exist and operate efficiently: ". . . the specifications of the marriage impose choices. The partners cannot . . . go to the party and to the concert together at the same time; they cannot rear the children as Catholic and as Protestant; they cannot spend the same money for slip-covers and for the power mower."[31]

In most cases, it is necessary for these things to be determined through negotiation, since group and individual goals rarely coincide completely.[32] The period of early marriage is one in which intensive negotiation takes place. Long-range plans are discussed regarding the mode of raising children, career goals, and such major purchases as houses, furniture, and automobiles. There is a great deal of both joint decision making and joint purchase activity, in which special preferences and skills are revealed. In many areas, husbands and wives may not be able to agree and may have to compromise.

It is believed that as the marriage progresses, these compromise decisions are replaced by consensus decisions. That is, the perceptions and preferences of husbands and wives involving items purchased by the family become more similar. This process is called "adjustment" and is the result of several forces. First, since the family is a reference group, it shapes the attitudes of its members. Second, since the husband and wife probably share membership in other reference groups, they tend to move toward views commonly held by these groups. Third, members of a family tend to use the same mass information sources, such as magazines and newspapers. Finally, a need may be common to all members of the family, such as a large car so that they may travel together.

The fact that the process of adjustment accelerates as the marriage progresses was examined in a study of automobile preferences. This study suggested that the preferences of husbands and wives in automobiles would be more similar in couples who had been married longer.[33] Rather than merely use length of marriage for this purpose, however, the researchers used the family life cycle to explain this process of adjustment. The stages of the family life cycle used for this study were:

1. Establishment: married less than 5 years with no children.
2. New parents: first child less than 6 years old.
3. School-age family: first child between 6 and 12.
4. Adolescent family: first child between 13 and 19.
5. Launching family: first child has left home.
6. Older family: all children have left home.
7. Childless family: married more than 5 years with no children.

The results of the study did indicate that the similarity between the husband's and wife's automobile preferences generally seems to increase as families enter the later stages of the family life cycle and as years of marriage lengthen. This finding seems to suggest that as the marriage progresses, the process of adjustment accelerates. The data did indicate, however, that agreement declines after 26 years of marriage, as well as in the last two stages of the family life cycle.

The analysis tends to suggest that the presence of children is one of the principal pressures toward the goal-congruent behavior that is designated "adjustment." Thus families who do not have children and those whose children no longer live at home are less likely to be goal-congruent.

Changes in Family Structure and Life-Cycle Stages

The character of the family has been changing in the past two or three decades, and these changes most certainly will have many repercussions in the marketplace.

In 1960, 77.2 percent of American households—groups of people who live in the same dwelling, regardless of relationships—consisted of families headed by men.[34] Only 7.8 percent were headed by women, and the remaining 15.0 percent of households were made up of unrelated or primary individuals. Life-styles had changed by the time of the 1970 census. The proportion of male-headed family households had decreased to 71.6 percent, while primary-individual households had increased to 19.7 percent. By 1975, almost 1 in 4 households contained primary individuals or unrelated persons. Today, young singles, both working and student, are free to move to their own apartments or share houses apart from the parental home. Senior citizens, many of whom are widows, have a greater desire to live on their own rather than with their children.

Along with the decrease in fertility of women and increases in separation and divorce have come other developments that have shrunk the typical cluster of persons who live together as a household. Very few married couples live with relatives, as many once did during some period of their lives. In the 1940s, only 1 in every 10 households was maintained by persons living apart from relatives, but now 1 in 5 households is of this type, and 1 in every 6 households consists of one person living entirely alone.[35] As evidence of the shrinking family size, from 1890 to 1910 the average household consisted of 5 persons; now it consists of approximately 2.97 persons.

The shrinking household size and the growing number of small households consisting of single-parent families, unmarried couples, and persons living entirely alone are evidence that large families are no longer regarded with favor by many persons and that new life-styles are being tried by persons who want to learn whether the new ways are more satisfying to them than more conventional patterns.

"MODERNIZING" THE FAMILY LIFE CYCLE

Future life-cycle analysis will have to incorporate the many changes taking place in the "family." For example, families who never have children, single parents, divorced persons, those who cohabit without getting married, the extended family resulting from the longer life of the older population—all create variations in the typical stages of the life cycle.

A modernized family life cycle has been proposed which bases its stages on the age of the household head, marital status, and, to a lesser extent, children's ages. The major features that distinguish it from the traditional life cycle are the recognition of divorce and childlessness as optional life-cycle stages.[36] Table 6.6 (pp. 120–121) presents this "modernized" version and compares population distributions between this life cycle and the concept of William Wells and George Gubar, described in Table 6.5.

MARKETING IMPLICATIONS OF CHANGES IN FAMILY STRUCTURE

Changes in living arrangements have significant implications for marketers. For single-parent families and nonmarried groups, purchases for the "family as a unit" are less important than individual needs. Leisure pursuits may require separate promotional strategies for the unmarried groups, as distinct from the "family outing" programs.

Unmarried Couples. An eightfold increase occurred during the 1960s in the number of household heads who were reported as living apart from relatives while sharing their living quarters with an unrelated partner of the opposite sex. Among older men sharing their living quarters with nonrelatives only, 1 in every 5 lived with a female partner. These older couples include a substantial proportion of widowed persons who are living in this manner in order to avoid losing survivor's benefits through remarriage.

This situation appears to project a change in the mores concerning marriage and the family structure. It should be noted, however, that unmarried people living together still represent only about 1 percent of the population.

Nonetheless, marketers should realize that this group represents a significant target market, and that they have specific needs that should be met. They need appropriate residential facilities and lease agreements that incorporate the relative independence of the residents, as well as banking services and loan facilities that also take this relationship into account. Some marketing strategies are indeed taking unmarried couples into account, and do not make reference to wife, husband, or spouse in their promotional efforts. There is also a tendency to eliminate wedding rings and couples surrounded by children in advertisements aimed at this market.

Singles. The proportion of young adults at every age who are single has increased markedly over the past two decades. While the changes this increase in single people has brought about have not been fully documented, it is a fact that single-person households make up the fastest growing category of newly formed households.[37] According to Lawrence Wortzel, this life-cycle stage is evolving from one in which the principal activities seemed to be searching for a mate and preparing for marriage to one in which the principal concerns are personal growth, the establishment of a personal identity and credentials, and the accumulation of a variety of personal experiences.[38]

Interviews conducted among young single college graduates indicated that a well-furnished, well-decorated apartment makes a strong statement about the owner's independence, her ability to support herself, and her career progress. These statements may be formalized not only in the purchase of furniture and decorative accessories, but in the transition of cooking from a necessary to a recreational activity.

Such changes have significant consumer-behavior implications. Traditionally, the purchases of many household durables tended to be concentrated in the period between the engagement and the first few months of marriage. When purchases of durables are independent of marriage plans, the accumulation period is bound to be longer, and a new set of variables will be required to identify prospective purchasers.

Marketers are obviously becoming aware of the proliferation of single-unit households. Many food offerings are produced in smaller portions. Soup cans are appearing in single servings—Lipton's "Cup-a-Soup" and Campbell's "Soup-for-One" are advertised extensively—as are single portions of chocolate pudding and other desserts. Furniture and other furnishings are also being designed for the single life-style. Support for the single life-style and reassurances for the parents are provided in such advertisements as Stouffer's frozen-food ad in which a young woman settling in her new apartment declares, "Don't worry, Mom, I'm eating good food." Hallmark, as we saw at the beginning of this chapter, provides greeting cards for the single population.

Future surveys will be required to determine the continued importance of the singles segment that represents changing life-styles in living arrangements. Four of every 5 divorced persons eventually remarry, and the single-parent family has been, in large part, a temporary arrangement serving as a transition for the parent from one marital partner to another. And most unmarrieds, of course,

TABLE 6.6   POPULATION DISTRIBUTIONS ACROSS THE STAGES OF TWO FAMILY LIFE CYCLES, 1970[a]

	Murphy and Staples	
Stage	Number of individuals or families (thousands)	Percent of total U.S. population[b]
1. Young single	16,626	8.2
2. Young married without children	2,958	2.9
3. Other young		
a. Young divorced without children	277	0.1
b. Young married with children	8,082	17.1
Infant[c]		
Young (4–12 years old)[c]		
Adolescent[c]		
c. Young divorced with children	1,144	1.9
Infant		
Young (4–12 years old)		
Adolescent		
4. Middle-aged		
a. Middle-aged married without children	4,815	4.7
b. Middle-aged divorced without children	593	0.3
c. Middle-aged married with children	15,574	33.0
Young		
Adolescent		
d. Middle-aged divorced with children	1,080	1.8
Young		
Adolescent		
e. Middle-aged married without dependent children	5,627	5.5
f. Middle-aged divorced without dependent children	284	0.1
5. Older		
a. Older married	5,318	5.2
b. Older married	3,510	2.0
Divorced		
Widowed		
All other[d]	34,952	17.2
	203,210[e]	

[a] Figures for this table were taken or derived from U.S. Bureau of the Census 1973, Tables 2 and 9.
[b] As there are single and divorced individuals in some of the stages, the numbers were calculated as a percentage of the entire population, not just the number of families. Also, the percentages of the total for families were determined by multiplying the number of families by 2.3 (average number of children per family in 1970) and adding the parents (or parent, in divorced instances) to the number. For example, the 17.1 percent in the young married with children was computed here as follows:

$$\frac{8{,}082 \ (2.3 \text{ children}) + 16{,}164 \ (\text{parents})}{203{,}210} = 17.1\%.$$

Stage	Number of individuals or families (thousands)	Percent of total U.S. popu- lation[b]
Wells and Gubar		
1. Bachelor	16,626	8.2
2. Newly married couples	2,958	2.9
3. Full nest 1	11,433	24.2
4. Full nest 2	6,547	13.2
5. Full nest 3	6,955	14.7
6. Empty nest 1	5,627	5.5
7. Empty nest 2	5,318	5.2
8. Solitary survivor in labor force	428	0.2
9. Solitary survivor retired	3,510	2.0
All other[d]	46,738	23.3
	203,210[e]	

[c] As many families have children at more than one of these age levels, it is not meaningful to compute the numbers for each of these ages independently.
[d] Includes all adults and children not accounted for by the family life-cycle stages.
[e] From U.S. Bureau of the Census 1970. The numbers do not add to this total because of the calculations explained in footnote b.

Source: Patrick E. Murphy and William A. Staples, "A Modernized Family Life Cycle," *Journal of Consumer Research* 6 (June 1979), p. 16.

eventually do marry. New surveys will provide evidence of the stability of these living arrangements.

The Changing Role of Women

The last decade has witnessed a substantial change in the role of women in U.S. society. The diminishing distinction between the roles that men and women perform in society has resulted in the merging of traditional sex roles. Women are increasingly performing tasks traditionally assigned to men, and vice versa. In addition, women are achieving greater autonomy, so that they are no longer dependent on men for economic and social support and recognition.

The changing role of women affects family life-style patterns in a number of ways that have relevance to marketers. For example:

> The distinction between men's and women's work in the home has blurred and a sense of shared household duties prevails. Appliances that formerly had an image of being a female appliance such as a vacuum cleaner tend to take on unisex image.
>
> The family dominated meal scene and the wife's role have changed. Prepared foods, particularly convenience foods, fast-food and family-style restaurants occupy a significant position in the family feeding function.
>
> The availability of household services beyond the usual morning and afternoon household hours, e.g., repair services during weekends, will become increasingly important.
>
> Women are becoming more cosmopolitan in their tastes and expectations as they become more involved with and exposed to the world external to their home.[39]

Major shifts in societal role structures should be reflected in the marketplace. Role changes of women could mean substantial changes in the buying behavior patterns associated with a wide variety of goods and services. Marketing managers have, in fact, responded to the changing woman's role through the introduction of new products designed to appeal to these emerging attitudes and partial repositioning of existing products. For example, new prepared foods appear on the market and the number of fast-food outlets is increasing substantially. The Clairol hair-coloring advertising campaigns noted at the beginning of this chapter reflect these changes. Similarly, an advertisement for Fantastik spray cleaner declares, "Don't call me a housewife—I'm not married to a house."

Nevertheless, the extent to which the changing roles have influenced the woman's performance in family purchasing patterns is not clearly delineated. As we have seen, previous research has indicated that the decision-making roles of the two sexes differ with respect to many products.[40] Decisions regarding some products, such as groceries, still tend to be the domain of the wife. Some variations are also related to age; for example, the participation of wives in life-insurance decisions increases among older couples.

It would appear that the changing nature of sex roles in society will produce changes in family purchasing roles. More specifically, it may be thought that the power of the husband in family purchasing decisions has generally declined. Such may not be the case, however. One study examined the extent to which wives make decisions in families with more contemporary role orientations, compared to those in families with traditional role orientations.[41] The study's sample consisted of 257 randomly selected married women who were divided into three groups: conservatives, moderates, and liberals. Conservatives held attitudes identified with the traditional female role. Liberals had contemporary attitudes toward the female role. Moderates represented an intermediate group whose role perceptions vacillated.

When the results of the total number of husband, wife, and joint decisions made by the three groups were computed, they did indicate that the husbands of liberated wives tended to make fewer purchase decisions than husbands of conservative and moderate women. These results should be interpreted cautiously, however. They turned out to be product-specific; that is, they applied to such items as major appliances, automobiles, and vacations. The purchasing-decision patterns were the same for all three groups for such items as groceries (wife dominated), life insurance (husband dominated), and furniture and housing (jointly decided items).

The findings also imply that the changes in purchase decision making one would expect to associate with the changes in the female role may be more pervasive among liberals in the younger age groups and in the upper income groups. Upper income liberals were characterized by significantly less husband decision making than upper income conservatives and moderates. Age categories revealed a similar pattern, with younger and middle-aged liberal housewives more involved in decision making than corresponding conservative and moderate wives.

The results of this study suggest that marketers should exercise caution in assuming that women who hold contemporary attitudes toward the female role are "liberated" or nontraditional in their purchase decisions.

From a marketing viewpoint, campaigns that attempt to segment the market on the basis of female role perceptions should take note of research that indicates that this criterion is relevant to the particular product or service, and that the target market actually represents the decision maker for the purchase or adoption of this item. Some marketers attempt to resolve potential problems by incorporating dual roles. For example, an advertising campaign for a fragrance called Enjoli adopted this approach in a parody of the song "I'm a Woman." The lyrics describe how a working woman can "bring home the bacon, fry it up in a pan, and never let him forget he's a man!" (See Exhibit 6.2.)

WORKING WIVES

Increasing numbers of women with husbands present have entered the work force, and in recent years small children are no longer a significant impediment to employment for many women.[42] The resulting changes in women's perceptions of their roles should cause variations in purchasing patterns between the working wife and the nonworking wife. Some studies, however, do not completely support

EXHIBIT 6.2

You can feed the kids and the gerbils.
Pass out the kisses.
And get to
work by
5 of 9!

You can bring home
the bacon.
Fry it up in a pan.
And never let him
forget he's a man!
Because you're a
woman!

ENJOLI

Compliments of Charles of the Ritz

the new 8 hour perfume
for the 24 hour woman.

A woman's dual role as perceived by some marketers

this conclusion. For example, a research project revealed that a wife's participation in the labor force was not an important determinant of the purchase of durable goods or services, or, in fact, of the amount that was spent on such purchases.

A study was conducted to determine whether a wife's employment outside the home increased her family's purchases of such major durable goods and services as dishwashers, dryers, television sets and furniture, hobby and recreation items, and vacations.[43] The results indicated that when account is taken of the fact that wives' earnings raise family income, families with wives in the labor force do not spend any more or less frequently or heavily on the durables studied than do families with only one wage earner. The study did not examine expenditures of work-related goods and services or nondurable goods and services.

Another study concluded that working wives do not differ significantly from nonworking wives in the use of convenience products and services.[44] In fact, the nonworking wives appear to be heavier users of take-out dinners and several other products, such as instant dusting sprays and baked goods. Furthermore, there is little to indicate that employed wives rely more on the use of domestic help or on mechanical labor-saving devices to aid in their cooking and housekeeping chores. On the contrary, the nonworking wives appear to be better equipped than their working counterparts, especially with washing machines and dryers, freezers, electric carving knives, and self-defrosting refrigerators. It may be that since non-working women spend more time in the home, they attach more importance to possession of these appliances than do women who have jobs to go to.

These findings suggest that families in which the wife is employed are unlikely to be prime targets for time-saving convenience products and services or pioneers in the use of such products. On the other hand, since the wives with jobs appear to seek ways of saving time on shopping, emphasis by retailers on speed of service and home delivery services could prove an attractive selling point to them.

Some evidence exists, however, of differences in behavioral patterns between working and nonworking wives. Such differences were revealed in a study conducted in Dallas, Texas, to compare the shopping behavior, attitudes, and use of leisure time of the two groups.[45] In shopping for food, the employed wife shopped less often than the homemaker and exhibited a greater preference for evening and weekend shopping. In selection of a food store the two most important factors for employed wives were convenience and quality of assortment. One of the more significant differences was that employed wives delegate major shopping activities to other persons. These findings led the researchers to conclude that with the increase in employment among married women, the demand for products and services will increase in proportion to the convenience they provide, with price considered of secondary importance.

The conflicting findings may be resolved as additional insights are applied to the study of jobholding wives and homemakers. Appropriate research requires further clarification of these two segments. For example, it is suggested that four categories of women be examined: (1) the employed woman who believes her work is a career; (2) the housewife who plans to seek work; (3) the working woman who views her work as just a job; and (4) the stay-at-home housewife.[46]

1. The career woman is the most affluent and best educated. She has a strong self-image and is efficient, broadminded, sociable, and creative.

2. The "plans to work" is also affluent and well educated, but she has children at home. She views herself as tense and awkward. She's stubborn, creative, sociable, and not egocentric.

3. The "just a job" woman works in a clerical or sales position. She has less education than women in the first two categories, and is less affluent than the career woman. Her income is on a par, however, with "plans to work." She thinks she's awkward, tense, affectionate, and not very intelligent or creative.

4. The "stay-at-home" woman is least affluent, is least educated, and has fewer children than the career woman. She sees herself as tense, refined, and low on ego and humor.

It may be helpful to understand the important determinants of women's decision to work outside the home, since their motives may have relevance to consumption behavior. Women seek employment for various reasons, and these reasons may incorporate both socioeconomic and social-psychological variables.[47] The items purchased by women who work for monetary reasons, for example, may differ from those purchased by women who work for nonmonetary reasons.

SUMMARY

Families may be classified into types designated as nuclear, extended, family of orientation, and family of procreation. Most studies related to the family and decision making involve the nuclear family—husband, wife, and children.

Families generally have an instrumental and an expressive leader. The husband usually performs the instrumental role in engaging in task-oriented activities, while the wife is expressive in activities that involve the social-emotional area. Family members may adopt varying roles in the purchase process. They may act as influencers, deciders, purchasers, or users. The family member who adopts any specific role in the purchase process may vary by product and by household.

Husbands, wives, and children influence the family's product choice. The patterns of decision making in the family may be described as husband dominant, wife dominant, autonomic (equal number of decisions made by each partner), and syncratic (most decisions made jointly).

Life-cycle stages may be more sensitive indicators of consumer behavior than such demographic characteristics as age and income. The life cycle is a composite of several variables, including age, marital status, and children. The life cycle has a number of stages, ranging from the bachelor to the solitary survivor. The life cycle appears to be an important discriminant in product choice, particularly with regard to such products as washing machines, home freezers, milk, bicycles, and magazines. Some research discloses that consensual decisions within the family increase in the later stages of the life cycle. Thus the process of adjustment tends to accelerate as the marriage progresses. Life-cycle analysis requires an acknowledgment of changing life-styles.

The nature of women's role has undergone a change, so that women are increasingly performing tasks traditionally assigned to men, and achieving greater autonomy. The extent to which these changes have influenced women's performance in the family purchasing pattern is not clearly delineated. Some research indicates that "liberal" women tend to make more purchase decisions than "moderates" and "conservatives," but these decisions are product-specific. With the steady increase in the number of working wives, these purchasing patterns may change significantly in the future.

DISCUSSION QUESTIONS

1. What major changes do you anticipate in family structure in the 1980s?

2. Discuss several purchase decisions in which you have acted as, respectively, the influencer, the decider, the purchaser, and the user.

3. What is meant by "role specialization" and "joint decision making" in reference to purchase decisions?

4. What are the factors that lead to joint decision making in your family?

5. Under what circumstances should marketers direct their communication strategies to children?

6. What is the "gatekeeper effect" and what is its significance to marketers?

7. Why may the life cycle be a more sensitive indicator of purchase decisions than demographic factors?

8. If you were asked to develop a family life-cycle chart, what stages would you incorporate? Why?

9. What kinds of changes should a marketer incorporate in his strategy to accommodate the changing roles of women in the family structure?

10. Select several ads that indicate some of these changes in women's roles.

NOTES

1. "Hallmark Now Stands for a Lot More than Cards," *Business Week*, May 29, 1978, pp. 57–58.

2. See B. G. Yovovich, "His Eyes Have Seen Housewares Soar," *Advertising Age*, July 2, 1979, p. S-8; Leo J. Shapiro and Dwight Bohmback, "Of Kitchen Tools and Lifestyles," ibid., 5–4.

3. Harry L. Davis, "Decision-Making within the Household," *Journal of Consumer Research* 2 (March 1976), p. 241.

4. Frederick E. Webster, Jr., *Marketing Communication* (New York: Ronald Press, 1971), p. 93.

5. Glen M. Vernon, *Human Interaction: An Introduction to Sociology* (New York: Ronald Press, 1965), p. 327.

6. Bernard Berelson and Gary Steiner, *Human Behavior: An Inventory of Scientific Findings* (New York: Harcourt Brace Jovanovich, 1964), p. 297.

7. Fabian Linden, "Consumer Markets: The Post-War Generation Comes of Age," *Conference Board Record* 13, no. 9 (September 1976), pp. 3–4.

8. J. H. Myers and W. H. Reynolds, *Consumer Behavior and Marketing Management* (Boston: Houghton Mifflin, 1967), p. 245.

9. Harry L. Davis, "Dimensions of Marital Roles in Consumer Decision-Making," *Journal of Marketing Research,* May 1970, pp. 168–177.

10. Philip Kotler, *Marketing Analysis, Planning, and Control,* 3d ed. (Englewood Cliffs, N.J.: Prentice-Hall, 1976), p. 82.

11. Robert Z. Chew, "Hathaway Paradox: Shirts for Men, Ads for Women," *Advertising Age,* October 31, 1977, p. 10.

12. Harry L. Davis and Benny P. Rigaux, "Perception of Marital Roles in Decision Processes," *Journal of Consumer Research* 1 (June 1974), pp. 51–62.

13. Donald H. Granbois, "The Role of Communication in the Family Decision-Making Process," in *Consumer Behavior: Selected Readings,* ed. James F. Engel (Homewood, Ill.: Richard D. Irwin, 1968), pp. 146–157.

14. Mirra Komarovsky, "Class Differences in Family Decision-Making," in *Perspectives in Consumer Behavior,* ed. Harold Kassarjian and Thomas S. Robertson, rev. ed. (Glenview, Ill.: Scott, Foresman, 1973), p. 327.

15. Thomas S. Robertson, *Consumer Behavior* (Glenview, Ill.: Scott, Foresman, 1970), p. 77.

16. John S. Coulson, "Buying Decisions within the Family and the Consumer-Brand Relationship," in *On Knowing the Consumer,* ed. Joseph W. Newman (Huntington, N.Y.: Robert E. Krieger, 1960), pp. 59–66.

17. "Purchase Influence: Measures of Husband/Wife Buying Influence on Buying Decisions," *Advertising Age,* September 29, 1975, pp. 28, 30.

18. Davis, "Decision-Making within the Household," p. 246.

19. Mark Munn, "The Effect on Parental Buying Habits of Children Exposed to Children's Television Programs," in *Consumer Behavior: Contemporary Research in Action,* ed. Robert J. Holloway, Robert Mittlestaedt, and M. Venkatesan (Boston: Houghton Mifflin, 1971), pp. 267–271.

20. William D. Wells, "Children as Consumers," in *On Knowing the Consumer,* ed. Newman, p. 143.

21. Scott Ward and Daniel B. Wackman, "Children's Purchase Influence Attempts and Parental Yielding," in *Perspectives in Consumer Behavior,* ed. Kassarjian and Robertson, pp. 368–374.

22. Charles K. Atkin, "Observation of Parent-Child Interaction in Supermarket Decision-Making," *Journal of Marketing* 42 (October 1978), pp. 41–45.

23. Pat L. Burr and Richard M. Burr, "Parental Responses to Child Marketing," *Journal of Advertising Research* 17 (December 1977), pp. 17–24.

24. Lewis A. Berey and Richard W. Pollay, "The Influencing Role of the Child in Family Decision-Making," *Journal of Marketing Research* 5 (February 1968), pp. 70–72.

25. Sunil Mehrotra and Sandra Torges, "Determinants of Children's Influence on Mothers' Buying Behavior," in *Advances in Consumer Research,* vol. 3, ed. Beverlee B. Anderson (Association for Consumer Research, 1976), pp. 56–60.

26. George J. Szybillo and Arlene Sosanie, "Family Decision Making: Husband, Wife, and Children," in *Advances in Consumer Research* 4, ed. William D. Perreault, Jr. (Atlanta: Association for Consumer Research, 1977), pp. 46–49.

27. William D. Wells and George Gubar, "Life-Cycle Concept in Marketing Research," *Journal of Marketing Research* 3 (November 1966), pp. 355, 360.

28. John B. Lansing and James N. Morgan, "Consumer Finances over the Life Cycle," in *The*

Life Cycle and Consumer Behavior, vol. 2 of *Consumer Behavior,* ed. Lincoln H. Clark (New York: New York University Press, 1955), pp. 36–45.

29. Ibid., p. 359.

30. Robert D. Hisrich and Michael P. Peters, "Selecting the Superior Segmentation Correlate," *Journal of Marketing* 38 (July 1974), pp. 60–63.

31. Jessie Bernard, "The Adjustment of Married Mates," in *Handbook of Marriage and the Family,* ed. Harold T. Christensen (Chicago: Rand McNally, 1964), p. 676.

32. Eli P. Cox, III, "Family Purchase Decision-Making and the Process of Adjustment," *Journal of Marketing Research* 12 (May 1975), p. 190.

33. Ibid., pp. 190–194.

34. Barbara E. Bryant, "Respondent Selection in a Time of Changing Household Composition," *Journal of Marketing Research* 12 (May 1975), p. 129.

35. Paul C. Glick, "Some Recent Changes in American Families," *Current Population Reports,* ser. P-23, no. 52, Bureau of the Census (Washington, D.C.: U.S. Government Printing Office, 1975).

36. Patrick E. Murphy and William A. Staples, "A Modernized Family Life Cycle," *Journal of Marketing Research* 16 (June 1979), pp. 12–22.

37. Frances E. Kobrin, "The Fall in Household Size and the Rise of the Primary Individual in the United States," *Demography* 13 (February 1976), pp. 127–138.

38. Lawrence H. Wortzel, "Young Adults: Single People and Single-Person Households," in *Advances in Consumer Research,* vol. 4, ed. Anderson, pp. 324–329.

39. William Lazer and John E. Smallwood, "The Changing Demographics of Women," *Journal of Marketing* 41 (July 1977), pp. 14–22.

40. Robert T. Green and Isabella C. M. Cunningham, "Feminine Role Perception and Family Purchasing Decision," *Journal of Marketing Research* 12 (August 1975), p. 326.

41. Ibid., pp. 325–331.

42. H. Hayhe, "Marital and Family Characteristics of the Labor Force, March 1974," *Special Labor Force Report 173* (Washington, D.C.: U.S. Department of Labor Statistics, 1975).

43. Myra H. Strober and Charles B. Weinberg, "Working Wives and Major Family Expenditures," *Journal of Consumer Research* 4 (December 1977), pp. 141–147.

44. Susan P. Douglas, "Working Wife vs. Non-Working-Wife Families: A Basis for Segmenting Grocery Markets?" in *Advances in Consumer Research,* vol. 3, ed. Beverlee B. Anderson (1976), pp. 191–198.

45. Suzanne H. McCall, "Meet the 'Workwife,' " *Journal of Marketing* 41 (July 1977), pp. 55–65.

46. Rena Bartos, "Insight on Selling the Working Woman," *Marketing Times,* May–June 1976, pp. 3–6.

47. Jeanne L. Hofstrom and Marilyn M. Dunsing, "Socioeconomic and Social Psychological Influences on Reasons Wives Work," *Journal of Consumer Research* 5 (December 1978), pp. 169–175.

PART THREE
INDIVIDUAL INFLUENCES

**PERCEPTION
LEARNING
MOTIVATION
PERSONALITY AND LIFE-STYLE
ATTITUDES
ATTITUDE CHANGE**

This section examines individual influences or the internal states that affect consumer behavior. It discusses perception, learning, motivation, and personality and their relationship to consumer behavior, as well as the effects of attitudes and attitude change.

CHAPTER 7

PERCEPTION

We are all aware that we have five major senses, which serve as links between ourselves and the physical world of things and events. The senses—sight, hearing, touch, taste, and smell—have been called the windows of the world. Stimulation of the sense organs results in sensations. Perception, the subject of this chapter, refers to the interpretation of sensations. The significance of such interpretations by consumers can be seen in the following marketing illustrations.

Sight: In 1978, R. J. Reynolds discontinued use of a large, spectacular outdoor advertising sign that had occupied a prominent spot in New York's Times Square for many years, depicting a man smoking Winston cigarettes. The decision to discontinue this advertisement was based in part on the negative reaction it generated in many people, who felt that the "smoke" (in reality vaporized water) emerging from the mouth of the illustrated model contributed to the pollution of the environment.

The structure was taken over by the A&P Company, which used the plumbing facilities already incorporated in the electrical display to show a cup of one of its brands of coffee emitting what now could be accurately perceived as steam.

Hearing: Starting in 1960, Ford began a probe into front-end problems of automobiles in Springfield, Illinois. The probe revealed that bumpy railroad tracks in the heart of Springfield were shaking up front ends and producing body rattles about equally among Ford and Chevrolet cars. This crucial difference emerged: Chevrolet owners more often blamed their dealers or their particular cars than Chevrolet as a make.[1] By contrast, Ford owners tended to place blame for the front-end problems on the maker. Since standard engineering tests indicated that both Ford and Chevrolet cars were about equally well built, these comparative perceptions did not reflect objective reality.

Further probing revealed that this perception of Ford derived from a persisting stereotype: Ford was still seen as the pioneer of mass production, and the resulting connotation of "tin lizzies" lingered on. Research indicated that the main signal to the driver that his car was "well built" rather than a product of "sloppy mass production" was the perceived sound of the car while it was being driven: "tight and quiet" indicated "well built"; "rattly and noisy" signaled "sloppy mass production."

As a result of these findings, tens of millions of dollars were invested in additional quality controls that achieved a measurable improvement in the noise level of Fords over competitive makes. Such efforts included ensuring that the doors of the car closed with an audible *thunk*. Beginning in 1963, a number of advertising campaigns were designed to communicate this difference to the public, incorporating a "quiet" theme.

Touch: Some product attributes that cannot be seen are determined through the sense of touch. Ripeness and freshness, for example, are often assumed to be "felt." A standard procedure in the selection of fruits and vegetables is to feel the food, to determine its level of ripeness. Bread manufacturers encourage consumers to feel their products to determine their "freshness." Interestingly, a more effective method of ensuring continued freshness would be to package bread in a thicker material. A thicker material, however, would camouflage the bread, so that its softness would not be so easily discernible.

Taste: A major food processor, hoping for a large share of the catsup market, set out to develop a tastier catsup. The company spent millions to perfect a process that captured the natural flavor of the tomato and preserved its delicate aromatic qualities. The new product was a failure.

The processor learned that the new process had eliminated the overcooked, scorched flavor that inadvertently seeps into catsup made by conventional processing methods. The company learned that it is precisely this flavor that most people identify as the taste of "real" catsup.

Smell: An early psychological study used women's silk hose to test the influence of scent on the perception of quality.[2] Women were asked to judge the quality of four pairs of identical hose packed in identical boxes which differed only in the following way: one pair was left with the normal, slightly rancid scent characteristic of the chemicals used to lubricate the fibers; another pair contained a faint narcissus scent; the third pair was given a faint fruity scent; and the fourth pair was given a faint sachet scent. The results of the test showed that the subtle influence of the various scents (which were consciously noticed by less than 3 percent of the subjects) dramatically affected the subjects' perceptions of quality.

In the late 1960s, Procter & Gamble introduced Lemon Joy, considered the first product of this type to incorporate smell as a significant attribute of a product whose primary function—in this case, cleaning dishes—was not necessarily improved by fragrance. The adaptation of this strategy to many other products suggests the recognition that consumers' perception of a product may be favorably enhanced by a fragrance that provides no functional benefit.

These illustrations should not be considered to delimit the concept of perception. While it is true that perceptions are primarily determined by the stimuli that impinge on the sense organs of the individual, it is equally true that factors other than the reactions of the sense organs modulate the resulting experience. Such factors may reflect the individual perceiver's history and present psychological status. Despite intensive efforts on the part of many scientists from a number of fields, the mysteries of the perceptual system remain hidden. The knowledge that is available concerning perception, however, provides some insights useful for marketing strategy.

In the process of perception the individual organizes and interprets sensory stimulation and thus develops an understanding of the world that surrounds him. These perceptual constructs operate in the marketplace, where the consumer faces sensory stimulation in a variety and complexity of forms. Numerous external forces—the many products and services available, the extensive and varied promotional efforts, the distinctive outlets for purchase—all serve to provide sensory stimuli that the consumer interprets in order to develop a meaningful and coherent picture of his purchasing world.

This chapter is designed to answer some questions about perception that are relevant to consumer behavior and marketing strategies:

> What determines whether a particular stimulus will pass all barriers so that a consumer will become aware of it?
>
> Is there such a thing as subliminal perception—that is, perception without awareness—and can the inducement of such perception be equated to brainwashing?
>
> Since so many stimuli in the environment face the individual simultaneously, what factors determine which ones will be selected?
>
> If a stimulus is perceived, what factors affect the manner in which it is interpreted?
>
> What kinds of research are relevant to perception and consumer behavior?

Subsequent chapters will examine the way in which perception influences the consumer decision process, particularly in reference to the use of some perceptual cues as evaluative criteria, and in the concept of perceived risk as a consumer choice strategy.

SENSATION AND PERCEPTION

In order to understand perception, it is necessary to understand some terms that will be used frequently in this discussion. Three such terms are closely interrelated: stimulus, sensation, and perception.

Physical energy that can excite a sense organ and thus produce an effect on the organism is called a *stimulus.* Light, sound, and heat are stimuli. A precise definition of this term requires a distinction between a stimulus and a stimulus object. A stimulus object is an object in the environment that is the source of the stimulus. Thus, for example, a red ball placed in front of a child's eyes is a stimulus object. The corresponding visual stimulus is the pattern of physical light energy that emanates from the ball and strikes the retina of the eye. For the purposes of this discussion, however, the single term *stimulus* may mean an object in the environment, a sensory event, or something experienced as a unit, such as a new product, a new package, or a 30-second TV commercial.

Sensation is the immediate and direct apprehension of a stimulus. When we sit before a TV set and a commercial appears, if we continue to watch, the light and sound reach our sense organs; these organs respond so that we have sensations of color, loudness, and so on.

Perception refers to an interpretation of the sensation. The following paradigm illustrates perception:[3]

$$\text{To perceive} = \begin{Bmatrix} \text{to see} \\ \text{to hear} \\ \text{to touch} \\ \text{to taste} \\ \text{to smell} \\ \text{to sense internally} \end{Bmatrix} \text{some} \begin{Bmatrix} \text{thing} \\ \text{event} \\ \text{relation} \end{Bmatrix}$$

Perception is the complex process by which people select, organize, and interpret these sensory stimulations in such a way as to produce a meaningful and coherent picture of the world.[4]

If an individual with no prior knowledge of a rattlesnake encounters one, his immediate apprehension of the rattlesnake will result in a number of sensations. He will *see* a long, thin, shiny, moving object; he will *hear* a sound that may be similar to that emitted by a baby's toy; he will *feel,* if the snake strikes, a slight tactile sensation in which his skin may be pricked.

Most people, however, have some prior knowledge of rattlesnakes, even when they have had no direct experience with them. Thus the sensory stimulation emanating from the rattlesnake will be interpreted in a more meaningful manner. The individual will perceive a slithery, slippery creature that incorporates evil; he will "hear" a death rattle, and he will "feel" a deadly venom coursing through his veins. His knowledge of the world, his prior experience, his understanding and background all have been incorporated in his perception or his interpretation of the stimuli before him.

SENSORY THRESHOLDS

To understand how perceptions provide interpretations of sensations, it is necessary first to examine briefly how sensory experiences are related to forms of energy. Sensation occurs when the sensory receptors (eyes, ears, nose, mouth, and skin) receive some sensory input from a form of physical energy—light, sound, and the like. People may not be able to sense all ranges of physical energy, however. Some lights are too dim to be seen, some sounds are too low to be heard, and some pressures too slight to be felt. Moreover, even when changes occur in these stimuli—lights are made brighter, sound is made louder, and so on—it is possible that the individual may not note these changes. The study of the relationship between the amount of a stimulus and the sensation it produces is called *psychophysics*. Such studies are designed to answer such questions as "How much of a stimulus is necessary for a person to notice it at all?" "How much of a change of stimulus is necessary for a person to notice a difference?"

Absolute Threshold

The minimum stimulus necessary to produce a specific sensation—a sound that can be heard or a light that can be seen—is called the *absolute threshold*. It is difficult to establish a universal standard for absolute thresholds, for they tend to vary with individuals and some extraneous "noise" in the environment usually prevents accurate measurement. There are devices, however, that make possible extremely brief and precisely timed exposure to a stimulus. The *tachistoscope*, for example, measures physical perception under varying conditions of speed, exposure, and illumination. (See Figure 7.1.) It may be used to determine how much light is needed to illuminate a billboard to make it visible in a nonlighted area, or the best design for a package to make it quickly identifiable in a TV commercial. While such a measured response may not be universally applicable, at least it can help to set the minimum standards of illumination and exposure time.

The absolute threshold does not remain constant. With disuse or rest, the threshold becomes lower (that is, the ability to detect stimuli increases). Under conditions of constant stimulation, however, sensitivity decreases. The latter experience is frequently referred to as "getting used to" something.

The fact that people get used to repeated stimulation has varying implica-

FIGURE 7.1   A SIMPLE TACHISTOSCOPE

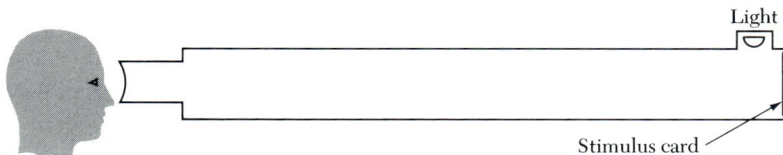

tions for marketers. It suggests, on the one hand, that if a consumer has gotten used to a certain stimulus, a variation in the stimulus is much more likely to be noticed. On the other hand, people tend to resist change, and such variations may have an adverse effect. This may have been the problem of the catsup manufacturer who reformulated his product.

Another interpretation of sensory adaptation suggests that if the consumer has gotten used to a constant repetition of a stimulus and become less sensitive to it, a "wear out" effect can occur, and the consumer tends not to notice it. It is on the basis of this presumed wear out that many advertisers change their advertising campaigns periodically. Although the White Knight was considered successful in creating awareness of Ajax scouring powder, the company discontinued its use of this symbol. The decision was apparently based on findings that suggested that although repeated presentations of the White Knight continued to attract attention, the viewer began to "turn off" the message that followed his appearance.

Unfortunately, it is not quite clear when repetitious campaigns tend to wear out. Schaeffer discontinued use of its highly successful jingle "Schaeffer is the one beer to have when you're having more than one" on the premise that consumers had gotten overly used to it. After numerous other campaigns, none of which had the same impact, Schaeffer restored its jingle. It is possible that these companies' decisions were appropriately based on the concept that disuse increases sensitivity to a stimulus. Nevertheless, it is frequently noted in advertising circles that campaigns wear out much earlier for the advertiser than for the consumer.

Differential Threshold

Distinguishing the absolute threshold may be less important to the marketer than determining when a change in stimulus produces a change in sensation. The point at which a change in stimulus will cause a change in sensation is known as the differential threshold. Efforts have been made to determine the change in stimulus that is necessary before the individual notices a difference. This smallest change is called the "just noticeable difference," frequently written as j.n.d.

A significant fact about the differential threshold, or more specifically the j.n.d., was discovered by a physiologist named Ernst Weber in the mid-nineteenth century. He found a relationship between the size of the stimulus and the size of the just noticeable difference. According to what became known as *Weber's Law*, the amount of a stimulus necessary to produce a just noticeable difference is always a constant proportion of the intensity of the original stimulus. That is, the stronger the intensity of the initial stimulus, the greater the changed stimulus must be for it to be noticed. For example, if you enter a brightly lit room (the initial stimulus) and light a candle (the change in stimulus), the change in visual brightness will scarcely be noticeable. Should you, however, enter a dark room and light a candle, the change in visual brightness will be clear and obvious.

Weber's Law is expressed mathematically as:

$$\frac{\Delta I}{I} = K$$

where I is the intensity of the initial stimulus

ΔI is the smallest increase in stimulus intensity that will be just noticeably different

K is a constant that varies according to the specific dimensions—visual brightness, loudness, taste, and so on.

The constant (K) varies with the sense that is being tested. A change of a little less than 2 percent in visual brightness, for example, can be detected, while taste must change by about 20 percent before the difference can be detected.

Whether a concept that has been established in the physics laboratory is applicable to consumer behavior in the marketplace is yet to be determined. Nevertheless, it suggests some strategies for product design and pricing that future research may validate.

In these days of product proliferation, a manufacturer may intensify the color, taste, and odor of his products, so that they stand out from his competitors'. Such changes not only are uncertain in their effects, but frequently require added expense. Research may suggest methods that will enable a manufacturer to limit the expense by determining the j.n.d. for his product attributes—the exact amount of additional odor or color intensity that is necessary to make consumers notice the difference. As in the case of the scented hose that we examined at the beginning of this chapter, a faint scent may be sufficient to be noticed.

Although such formulas are yet to be developed, marketers of deodorants, for example, have used light variations in tactile sensations to create minor but noticeable differences. One deodorant manufacturer advertises that his product goes on dryer than his competitor's, and that his competitor's product is "runnier" than his. Another declares how easy it is to "roll on" his product; another claims that his deodorant gives a "powdered" feeling; while still another declares, through advertising spokespeople laughing somewhat hysterically, that his deodorant "tickles." While the success of these strategies is yet to be proven (in fact, although the name Tickle has been retained, the appeal for this product was changed to "strength," in an apparent response to those who objected to the earlier campaign as "silly"), it is clear that Charmin's "squeezeable softness" caused problems for its competitors' generally similar products.

Weber's Law may also have applications to the consumer's perception of price. An application of the formula suggests that markdowns are best made on a percentage basis. For example, if an item costs $5, a 50-cent (10 percent) markdown may provide a sufficient change in the original stimulus to be noticed:

$$\frac{\Delta I}{I} \frac{\text{(50 cents)}}{\text{(\$5)}} = 10\%$$

If the item sells for $50, however, a 50-cent change will result in a markdown of only 1 percent, and therefore is not likely to be noticed. This concept of relative change is used by many retailers in making markdowns, which are more frequently quoted on a percentage rather than an absolute basis. Similarly, a banking institution that increases its interest rate for home mortgages from 12 to 14.0 percent may advertise it as "now 14%," but when the rate reverts to 12 percent, it may be designated as "a reduction of over 14%."

It has been suggested that Weber's Law may be responsible for the apparent effectiveness of pricing strategies involving rebates. Recently, manufacturers of automobiles and other durable products have offered potential rebates (say, of $500) on the purchase of a car (priced at $5,000). The rebate is said to be perceived differently by consumers from an offer of a $5,000 car for $4,500. A $500 reduction on a car that previously cost $5,000 is presumed to have less impact on consumers than an offer providing $500 back on an item that originally offered $0 back. Although the absolute change in both cases is the same, the percentage change is obviously higher in the rebate than in the price reduction. It should be noted, however, that a further justification of this tactic is that a rebate appears better for the image of the automobile than a price reduction. A price reduction may reflect a product of inferior quality, whereas a rebate indicates a temporary promotional tool to sell a quality product.

There is no general agreement, however, as to the applicability of Weber's Law to pricing. A "fair price" theory suggests that the absolute difference in price becomes more significant to consumers as the price of the product increases, even though the percentage difference is relatively insignificant. Thus consumers may be more acutely aware of an increase in the price of a color television set from $500 to $520 (a 4 percent increase) than of an increase in the price of a steam iron from $20 to $22 (a 10 percent increase).[5]

Another concept relating to the consumer's reaction to variations in price thresholds suggests that individuals have a range of acceptable prices for considered purchases—prices outside of the acceptable range, both high and low, are considered objectionable. An experiment related to prices of men's sports coats and women's shoes confirmed the hypothesis that the subjects would have a range of acceptable prices for a considered purchase.[6]

SUBLIMINAL PERCEPTION

The question of whether perception can occur without conscious awareness is controversial, in terms of both the extent to which it occurs and the ethical implications involved in its applications. "Subliminal perception" is the term used to designate perception of a stimulus that is beneath (*sub*) the threshold (*limen* in Latin) of awareness. The term does not imply that the stimulus is not received at all—that is, the stimulus is not below the absolute threshold of the receptors involved.

Subliminal communication, which is the most frequently studied subject in this area, has been defined as "the sending, reception and effects of physically weak visual or aural messages which people receive in a physiological sense, but of which they are not consciously aware."[7]

As early as 1938 the word "subliminal" was used in conjunction with perceptual experiments seeking to determine the distinct threshold or limen for each individual above which a visual impression is consciously perceived and immediately below which a visual impression is perceived without awareness.[8] Thresholds appear to vary among individuals; that is, your threshold may be higher or lower than mine. As long as these experiments were confined to the laboratories, they aroused little controversy.

Public interest was aroused when subliminal perception was applied to subliminal communication, or more specifically, was seen as subliminal persuasion. In a now-famous experiment in 1957 by James Vicary, the Subliminal Projection Company flashed the words "Drink Coca-Cola" and "Eat popcorn" in a New Jersey theater at a speed of 1/3,000 of a second, estimated to correspond to the lowest threshold of any member of the audience. In the six-week period during which these messages were projected, popcorn sales were said to increase by 57 percent and Coca-Cola sales by 18 percent.

Unlike the previous laboratory experiments, this study aroused controversy. In 1958 a committee was established in Great Britain to make an exhaustive study of the available information concerning subliminal communications in the United Kingdom, the United States, and elsewhere. The committee concluded: "Present evidence shows little if any effect from subliminal communication in the fields of selling and persuasion. The dangers of this method of communication—which have given rise to public comment—are therefore not justified by any evidence submitted." Nonetheless, the committee felt that the "free choice of the public to accept or reject is an integral part of all forms of professionally acceptable advertising, and does not appear to be available to recipients of subliminal communication," and its recommendation that it be banned by law was ultimately accepted in Great Britain.[9]

Similar concern was not exhibited in the United States until December 1973, when it was disclosed that a 60-second television commercial for Husker-Do, a children's game, contained a statement flashed intermittently and of such short duration that most viewers were not consciously aware of it. The message broadcast in this manner was "Get it"—"it" being the product advertised in the commercial. Obviously, the message was supraliminal for some parents, who complained to the Federal Communications Commission and the broadcasting station.

As no instance of such televised messages had come to the FCC's attention before that time, the commission had considered it unnecessary to adopt any covering rules and regulations. The National Association of Broadcasters' Television Code, however, did prohibit the use of "any technique whereby an attempt is made to convey information to the viewer by transmitting messages below the threshold of normal awareness."

As a result of this incident, the FCC issued a public notice stating that it believed the use of subliminal communication to be inconsistent with the obligations of a license and wished to make clear that broadcasts employing such techniques were contrary to the public interest.

In addition to the legal and ethical implications of subliminal techniques used to present persuasive messages, there are questions of effectiveness. Bernard Berelson and Gary Steiner, after reviewing much of the research on subliminal stimulation, concluded in the 1960s:

> There is no scientific evidence that subliminal stimulation can initiate subsequent action, to say nothing of commercially or politically significant action. And there is nothing to suggest that such action can be produced "against the subject's will" or more effectively than through normal, recognized messages.[10]

Another researcher, whose work indicated that people can be motivated through a subliminally presented stimulus, nevertheless declared that the new behavior pattern growing out of long-term exposure to subliminal advertising may not necessarily be associated with the specific content of the subliminal message.[11] Instead, it may be of a general nature, designed to reduce a specific drive. That is, subliminal advertising for Coca-Cola might arouse the viewer's thirst, but the viewer might very well quench his thirst with a bottle of Fresca. This evidence tends to alleviate the fear of those who believe such stimulation can act as a "hidden persuader" or a manipulative tool.

In recent years, psychologists have shown renewed interest in subliminal perception. Norman Dixon has maintained that the weight of evidence from experimental investigations firmly supports the view that registration of perceptual stimulation outside of conscious awareness does occur.[12] According to other psychologists, reluctance to accept the existence of subliminal perception may stem from the fact that effects attributable to subliminal perception are often weak and difficult to replicate.[13] They hypothesize that these differences relate to situational or individual factors, a hypothesis that is in keeping with the concept of selective perception, discussed in the next section.

The evidence seems clear that under certain conditions, material presented subliminally can have some effect on the viewer. The marketer, however, must consider the extent as well as the implications of this effect. Whether advertising messages are presented subliminally or supraliminally, they are faced with competition. If the effectiveness of an advertiser's supraliminal messages are curtailed by competitive efforts, why should she feel encouraged to spend a similar amount of funds on subliminal messages when, by definition, 50 percent of these messages will be below the threshold of perception? There is no indication that the remaining 50 percent of messages will be more influential than those that are received through traditional channels. That is, no evidence supports the view that you can brainwash the viewer more easily with a subliminal message than with a supraliminal one.

SELECTIVE PERCEPTION

As we noted in the previous section, some of the stimuli in the environment are of insufficient intensity to cause an effect—or more specifically to pass the sensory thresholds. Furthermore, even when those below the sensory threshold are eliminated, so many and such diverse stimuli exist in a person's environment that he or she can effectively perceive only a small portion of them.

What determines which of the many stimuli in the environment will be effectively perceived by the consumer? Consumers can employ numerous strategies, such as "chunking" or lumping information and storing it in short-term memory.[14] These strategies are discussed in Chapter 8. *Selective perception*, the tendency for the consumer to perceive some aspects of his or her environment selectively, is examined here.

The marketer who wishes to maximize the probability that consumers will perceive their products and communications should note some of the factors that influence selectivity. These factors may relate to the nature of the stimulus; they also may relate to the nature of the individual, but the internal states of the individuals themselves are amenable to influence.

The Nature of the Stimulus

The nature of the stimulus—that is, its physical, chemical, electromagnetic, and other observable factors—influences perception. Some of the more significant of these factors for consumer-behavior theorists relate to the effects of contrast, novelty, size, and color.

CONTRAST

Contrast is the phenomenon of perceiving a difference greater than that which is called for by the variations in the intensity of the stimuli. We all know that gray tones appear darker when placed next to white objects. Contrasts can be achieved by variations not only in color but in size (large items look larger when placed among small objects and vice versa), intensity (loud or normal sounds may appear louder in conjunction with soft sounds), and even mood (a humorous presentation may stand out among more somber offerings).

There have been complaints that television and radio commercials are designed to ensure that their sound is significantly louder than that of the program they accompany. In fact, the FCC has occasionally noted this tendency and suggested that the decibel level of commercials be moderated to meet required standards. Producers have responded to this criticism by claiming that the decibel ratings of commercials are not necessarily higher than those of the programs; the contrasting effects of many low-keyed programs, they say, make the commercials seem louder than in fact they are.

Care must occasionally be taken to keep contrasts from emerging unexpectedly to create undesirable impressions. In selecting programs for its advertisements, Kraft rejects those that are considered excessively violent. Kraft notes that it makes good sense not to select programs that contain scenes in which excessive blood is spilled, only to fade out and fade in to a Kraft cheese spread. Many viewers of "Holocaust," the television series that portrayed the plight of Jews under the Hitler regime, were extremely antagonized by the bright and generally cheery commercials that appeared just after scenes of horror. It has even been suggested that the clusters of ads seemed almost deliberately designed to offend; the viewer's mind was forced to make the transition from Auschwitz to Bottoms Up pantyhose.[15] In one grotesque juxtaposition, Lieutenant Dorf was seen sitting with Adolf Eichmann and other SS officers in their dining room at Auschwitz. Eichmann sniffed the air and disgustedly remarked that the stench of the chimneys kept him from enjoying his meal. The scene cut to a Lysol commercial, in which a woman character known as "Snoopy Sniffer" arrived at a housewife's kitchen and informed her she had house odors.

NOVELTY

People tend to notice the distinctive or surprising aspects of the environment. When a stimulus is obviously different from all the rest, it tends to stand out and be noticed more easily. Creators of advertisements are aware of this effect and strive to put it to use through the use of humor, animation, unusual graphics, and so on.

A series of ads that appeared in the *New York Times* began with an initial advertisement consisting almost entirely of white space, with just the tip of a spire emerging for a short distance from the bottom of the page. In subsequent ads, the Chrysler Building appeared slowly until the full ad, prepared for the rental agency for the building, appeared (see Exhibit 7.1). While the effectiveness of this

EXHIBIT 7.1

This series of ads uses a novel approach to attract attention.
Source: "Perspectives in Creativity," *Advertising Age*, June 4, 1979, p. S-14.

novel approach in securing tenants for the Chrysler Building has not been revealed, it was clearly successful in gaining attention, since it became the subject of numerous discussions on television talk shows and elsewhere.

Novelty may be used in various aspects of a marketing program. One particularly successful strategy was devised by Hanes Hosiery in the introduction of a new brand of hose. In developing a brand name, Hanes devised an unusually descriptive name, L'Eggs. A well-known designer created a novel egg-shaped package, which reinforced the name. An attractive and unusual award-winning display stand was also designed, one that permitted the product to be easily stocked and removed. A significant part of this total strategy was the novel outlet selected for distribution—the supermarket. Although stockings had been sold in supermarkets before, they were usually inferior and inexpensive hose and had been displayed on the familiar stands traditionally used for nongrocery merchandise. Hanes's ultimately successful strategy was designed to introduce a better grade of hose in the supermarket. A distinctive campaign was considered necessary to attract the attention of supermarket shoppers and to encourage them to try this new hose.

SIZE

While advertisers generally agree that large ads are more likely to be perceived than small ones, the relationship between increasing ad size and increasing perception has not been determined. One study concluded that when the size of an ad was increased, the tendency of people who used the advertised product to notice and read the ad also increased.[16] This effect, however, reached a peak and then declined as ad size increased further. The increase in size appeared to have no effect on people who did not use the product.

The finding of a tendency toward greater attention to advertisements by product users suggests that strategies involving variations in the size of ads directed toward users may differ from those involving ads designed to attract new users.

COLOR

Novelty and contrast, as well as variations in intensity, can be secured through the use of color. An early study indicated that on the average color TV commercials were at least 50 percent more effective than black-and-white commericals.[17] This advantage appears to have diminished now that most commercials appear in color. In fact, many of my students have reported that a commercial for L'Oréal hair coloring was especially noticed since part of it appeared in black and white. In newspapers, however, where most ads appear in black and white, color ads may command greater attention.

Color is considered useful in emphasizing some special part of an advertising message or product, and in fastening visual impressions in memory.[18] Most food products look better when depicted in color, and color is usually used in packages and labels. A study of advertising readership disclosed that the greater the number of colors in an advertisement, the greater its readership.[19] Interestingly, color seems to affect women more than it does men.

Color may also attract attention through the creation of symbolic representations and subjective impressions. In guiding its creative group in the manner in which color can be used, an advertising agency noted: "Through the ages, colors have been used as symbols of good, evil, wisdom, and sex: A scarlet letter is sin. A 'blue moon' is something to look for. People 'see red' in anger. They 'turn green' with envy. They have 'purple passions,' etc."

In suggesting how to use color, the agency noted that green creates the "objective impression" of quiet, refreshingness, and peace and the "subjective impression" of ghastliness, terror, disease, and guilt. The impression that is operative at any given time appears to depend to some extent on the nature of the situation in which the color is presented. It is apparent that the green streaks in Irish Spring soap do not create the same impression as the green Wicked Witch in *The Wizard of Oz*.

The Nature of the Individual

Consumers are more likely to perceive environmental stimuli that are related to their needs and motives, values and cultural backgrounds. If you are interested in purchasing a new car, you are more likely to note the various car advertisements, the new cars on the road, the cars displayed in dealers' windows, and so on.

The stronger the need, the stronger the tendency to perceive objects and events relevant to that need. The consumer who shops at the supermarket when she is hungry is probably surprised at how luscious and appetizing even the less frequently purchased foods appear. As a matter of fact, one suggestion for the economy-minded is to be sure not to go shopping when you are hungry.

Perception of stimuli is influenced by people's values and cultural backgrounds. For example, efforts of a soft-drink company to create awareness of the thirst-quenching properties of its product by use of such phrases as "glacier fresh" and "avalanche of taste" were unsuccessful in the Near East, where most people have never experienced wintry mountain temperatures.[20] While the novelty of humor or animation generally tends to increase perception, some cultures are too literal-minded to make such distinctions routinely. Even in his heyday, the friendly Esso tiger was regarded with suspicion by the literal Swiss, who could make no sense of a tiger in a gas tank. Pepsi Cola ads rely in part on the use of color and movement as attention-getters; a campaign based on the theme of "feeling free," however, fared badly in a country where a particular political party always won at the polls. Numerous examples of misperception due to cultural backgrounds were cited in Chapter 2.

Various tests of advertising readership have indicated that the average consumer is exposed to anywhere between 1,500 and 3,000 advertisements a day. According to one research study, however, the average American adult is aware of only 76 advertisements in the major media a day.[21] The extent of this selectivity is indicated by further findings. Even when consumers are aware of advertisements, 84 percent of ads did not make a sufficient impression to be categorized further. The remaining 16 percent were categorized by the respondents as annoying, enjoyable, informative, or offensive.

PERCEPTUAL DEFENSE

A concept relevant to an understanding of the manner in which the nature of the individual interacts with stimuli to influence perception is called *perceptual defense*. Perceptual defense is related to thresholds of awareness, discussed earlier. Thresholds of awareness may be raised as a defense against unacceptable or threatening stimuli. It should be noted that normal thresholds vary from consumer to consumer. Perceptual defense suggests that we set up a barrier against unacceptable stimuli—those that threaten us, create fear, or in some manner are inconsistent with our preconceptions.

Although pleasant or sympathetic scenes and messages are sought out, painful or threatening ones may be actively avoided. Studies have been conducted on reactions to taboo and neutral words. Subjects reacted more slowly to taboo words than to neutral ones—that is, they took a longer time to recognize them. This finding led to the conclusion that threatening or otherwise damaging materials may be less likely to reach consciousness than neutral material at the same level of exposure.

The raising of identification thresholds for taboo words is seen as a kind of blocking of recognition for classes of materials that are personally or culturally unacceptable to the perceiver. In tachistoscope tests for the SX 70 Polaroid, for example, the tendency of some respondents to report the same as SL 70 was interpreted by some researchers to be rejection of the implied SEX in the message.

There is no clear consensus on such findings. Some people indicate that the taboo words may in fact be seen as quickly and easily as the neutral words, but the viewer may not be willing to report them or vocalize them. Studies of pupil dilation, however, seem to support the concept of perceptual defense, for when a person looks at interesting or pleasant materials as compared to neutral ones, the pupil dilates measurably. Conversely, distasteful or disliked materials cause the pupils to contract.

Although the idea of perceptual defense is widely accepted, some theorists believe there is reason to reject this selective-avoidance hypothesis.[22] Nevertheless, marketers should use threatening messages with care, for it is possible that fear appeals, for example, interfere with the reception and comprehension of the message. This effect is examined at greater length in Chapter 15.

PERCEPTUAL INTERPRETATIONS

Although sensations provide the link between the individual's senses and the physical world of things and events, the raw sensory data are insufficient to give it meaning. An individual may have experiences with no sensory input, and some sensory inputs are not represented in conscious experience. The stimuli we receive or the patterns these stimuli form are often ambiguous. Sometimes they are physically weak and incomplete, that is, they may be briefly exposed, partly obscured, dimly illuminated, and so on. Much of perception is based on interpretations of these somewhat ambiguous stimuli.

Furthermore, different objects can produce the same stimuli (for example, a large advertisement far away and a small one nearby; or a jingle emanating from an eighty-piece orchestra in a studio and the same jingle coming from a twelve-inch hi-fi speaker). As a consequence, perception imposes the task of interpretation, of deciding what objects or events the sensory pattern actually does represent. Such interpretation is not usually a matter of conscious thinking through, but an instantaneous perceptual response.

Many of the bases for perceptual interpretation discussed here come from the principles of Gestalt psychology. Gestalt (from the German word for "form" or "pattern") psychologists have developed a concept involving a relationship between the whole and the part that suggests that perception of an object is determined by the pattern of its constituent parts. Thus the whole may remain the same even though its parts undergo changes, provided the pattern of the parts remains unchanged. The converse of this whole-part relationship is also true; that is, perception of the properties of a part depends on the nature of the whole in which the part is embedded.

The manner in which an object is perceived is influenced by the way in which the object and the environment are structured or organized. Perception, however, is a complex process that involves more than the physical properties of the entities involved. Both mental and emotional variables play roles in the perceptual process.

Structural and Object Variables

The principles of Gestalt psychology that may be useful in helping marketers to design a sound marketing program include the concepts of constancy, organization, and frame of reference.

CONSTANCY

People perceive objects as having certain constant properties, despite changes in the sensory information they receive from these objects from moment to moment. Thus familiar objects achieve a state of permanency in terms of size, shape, color, and so on, despite the changing nature of these stimulus patterns. Memory is a major element in perceptual constancy.

Size Constancy. The farther an object is from us, the smaller the size of the image it projects onto the eye. Because we know that it is far away, however, our perceptual process takes account of the distance and translates the object's projected size into its real size. Size constancy enables the viewer to interpret the distant 30-sheet poster and the close one-inch ad in a newspaper in a different manner, although the images they project on the eye may be the same.

Shape Constancy. The tendency to see a coin as round no matter what angle it is viewed from and to see a book as a rectangle even when it is placed on its edge is known as shape constancy. Shape constancy helps the consumer to interpret correctly a package that may be "misfaced" on a supermarket shelf or held at an angle in an advertisement.

Brightness and Color Constancy. Objects tend to maintain the same brightness and color to the viewer even though the amount or kind of illumination that surrounds them changes. Color constancy helps the viewer to see products and packages as always having the same color, despite variations in illumination from outlet to outlet.

ORGANIZATION

The defining characteristic of a perception is that it is a unified, organized experience. Imagine you were to walk into the average supermarket with its approximately 10,000 items available for sale, in various packages, colors, and sizes. You would face additional sensory inputs in the form of the many customers, sales personnel, point-of-purchase displays, and the like. If you had no mechanism for dealing with this vast variety of sensory inputs, you would probably quickly leave the store in utter confusion. But through perceptual organization you can place bits and pieces of information into meaningful patterns. The principles of organization first developed by Gestalt psychologists are illustrated by visual demonstrations, but they apply to the other senses as well.

Figure and Ground. One of the simplest and most primitive forms of perceptual organization is called *figure-and-ground* differentiation. When a scene with any detail is viewed, one part stands out distinctively from the rest. The perceptual properties of the figure differ from those of the ground. The figure tends to be better defined, better localized, more solid and integrated, whereas the ground appears to be less definite and less structured.

A number of factors determine what is viewed as the figure. In general, the more meaningful pattern will become the figure—a familiar face or a familiar voice in a crowd of people, or a familiar package on a crowded shelf.

Efforts to create familiarity with brand names and packages may help to increase the potential of certain products to stand out among their competitors on the supermarket shelf. Advertisers frequently create ads that are designed to ensure that the viewer focuses on the element of the ad they wish to accentuate. Special photographic techniques, drawings, and animation permit the advertiser to create a more solid, better defined figure, which may stand out from an amorphous background.

FIGURE 7.2   PERCEPTUAL AMBIGUITY

It is important to be aware of the potential for perceptual ambiguity, that is, the reversal of the figure and ground. Such reversals may be continuing, as we can see in the familiar figure that alternately appears as a white stemmed goblet against a black background and as two black faces in profile against a white background. (See Figure 7.2.)

The *oculometer*, originally developed for the U.S. space program to measure astronauts' eye fatigue,[23] may be useful in determining which element in an advertisement is viewed as the ground. The device tracks viewers' eye movements and focus points through an invisible infrared light beam that "locks into" their eyes. Some of the findings from oculometer research are helpful to commercial preparers, particularly in measuring their arousal impact in the rough stages.

Oculometer findings have indicated that people respond to people, that is, people in commercials command attention. The viewer tends to scan rapidly, however, then focus in on one element at a time. In fact, some viewers may never get to look beyond the model, even if the model is holding a product. When the oculometer was used in research on TV commercials, for example, it was found that even if the model holding a product speaks about the product, the viewer tends to focus on the mouth of the model rather than on the product.

Closure. Occasionally, when gaps exist within a stimulus, people will nevertheless tend to report it as complete. This tendency in perceptual organization is known as *closure.* Closure may occur when the resulting figure is familiar and meaningful. It has been hypothesized, although not verified, that when an individual perceives a stimulus that contains a gap and closes it, he may pay particular attention to this stimulus and remember it. On this basis, some trademarks have been designed with the principle of closure in mind. Figure 7.3 shows two trademarks that apparently make use of this concept.

FIGURE 7.3   THE CLOSURE EFFECT IN TWO TRADEMARKS

Seatrain, by Chermayeff & Geisman   Westchester County, by Mickey Smith

The tendency toward closure may be generated in advertisements through the presentation of incomplete messages or through requiring the viewer to make the clear connection between the copy and the illustration. Salem cigarettes had a successful advertising campaign that featured the jingle "You can take Salem out of the country, but you can't take the country out of Salem." After the jingle was repeated several times, it was concluded after the "but," leaving the listener to fill in the rest of the phrase.

A type of closure is accomplished by requiring a viewer of an advertisement to make the connection between the copy and the illustration, on the theory that this presentation may have more impact than one that clearly relates these elements. The illustration may feature a cool, babbling brook, a shady glen, and a sense of peacefulness, while the copy features taste attributes of a bottle of wine. Cigarette ads are illustrated by cowboys riding the range, while the copy speaks of low tar and nicotine.

Grouping.   Some of the principles of perceptual organization have been designated as *grouping*. Objects may be grouped by proximity or by similarity.

Objects that are in close proximity to one another have a greater tendency to be grouped than those farther apart. (See Figures 7.4 and 7.5.) Supermarket managers help to provide organization for purchase experiences by grouping products in a manner that has relevance for the buyer. The placement of the aisles, the separation of fruits and vegetables from the meat counters, in general the total store layout, is designed to ensure appropriate grouping.

The principle of proximity is frequently used in advertising to suggest a relationship between the product being advertised and other desirable products or situations. Cereals are grouped with fruits, automobiles with attractive men and women, and tennis rackets with successful tennis players.

A successful retailing innovation was the development of "boutiques" in department stores, where products that had previously been located in separate de-

FIGURE 7.4 COMPETITION BETWEEN GROUPING BY PROXIMITY AND GROUPING BY CLOSURE

‖ ‖ ‖ ‖ ‖ ‖ | | |[ ][ ][ ]|

The seven lines on the left tend to fall "naturally" into three pairs, and one, isolated by virtue of proximity relations. But the same lines (repeated on the right), with the addition of the short horizontal lines, tend to be grouped by closure with the more distant partners, overriding the influence of proximity.

partments were now grouped to attract a specific type of market segment and project a particular life-style.

Objects that are alike in physical attributes—intensity, color, size, shape, and so on—have a greater tendency to be grouped than those that are not alike. This concept is frequently applied in packaging and branding. For example, a firm may group its varieties of salad dressings by using bottles of the same shape for all of them, while another firm may use its family brand name to cover a wide variety of product lines.

FIGURE 7.5 GROUPING BY PROXIMITY AND BY SIMILARITY

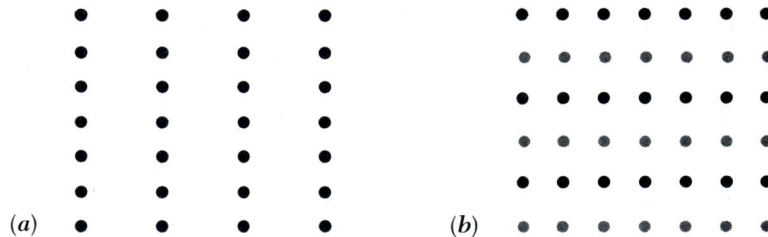

(a)   (b)

In *a*, the dots are perceived in vertical columns because their spatial proximity is greater in the vertical than in the horizontal direction. In *b*, where proximity is equal, the rows are perceived as horizontal because of grouping by similarity.

FRAME OF REFERENCE

Perceptual interpretation of ambiguous stimuli frequently involves some judgment on the part of the individual. The whole-part principle of the perceptual process suggests that such judgments may be made by establishing a frame of reference consisting of other relevant stimuli. An example of use of such a frame of reference appeared at the beginning of this chapter, in the illustration of the spectacular billboard. Here the emission of water vapor was interpreted as smoke when it accompanied cigarette smoking, but when it was presented in conjunction with a cup of hot coffee, it was more accurately perceived as steam.

To judge stimuli, individuals develop an *adaptation level*, particularly when they wish to judge magnitudes, as of size, weight, lightness, or loudness. To do so, people set a subjective standard based on a pooling of stimuli to form a scale for judgment. The neutral or medium point of such a scale is called the adaptation level. Sounds above this level may be perceived as loud, those below as soft, while weights are heavy above and light below.

The adaptation level varies as the frame of reference varies. Thus, when the medium point changes, some stimuli previously seen as large may be seen as small, and some stimuli previously perceived as small may be seen as large. In the frame-of-reference illusion appearing in Figure 7.6, two central circles are precisely the same size but are perceived to be unequal.

In designing new products, manufacturers take note of the adaptation level, particularly in the area of food products. Individuals develop an adaptation level in their sense of taste—oranges taste sweeter after lemons, sour after sugar. Moreover, as we noted earlier, after one is exposed to a stimulus for a period of time, sensitivity to it may be lost. In developing a sweet soft drink or salty pretzels, the

FIGURE 7.6 A FRAME-OF-REFERENCE ILLUSION

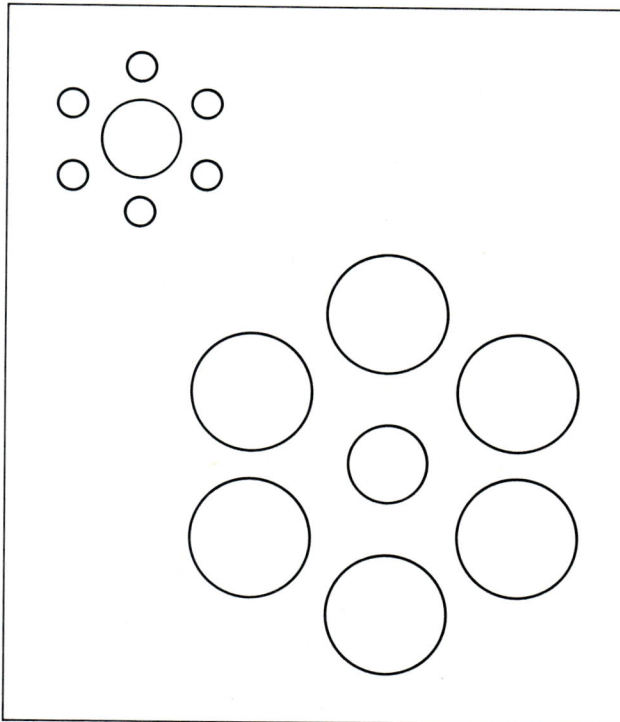

The two central circles are the same size but are seen as unequal because of the disparity in the size of the surrounding circles with which they are associated.

manufacturer may take into account the other foods that are likely to be used in conjunction with the product and use a disproportionately larger amount of sugar or salt so that consumers will perceive the attributes of sweetness or saltiness. In the catsup example at the beginning of this chapter, the manufacturer had to burn the tomatoes to achieve the acceptable catsup taste.

Levels of adaptation may also influence pricing decisions. As we saw earlier, a consumer establishes a range of acceptable prices for a considered purchase, and both higher and lower prices are considered objectionable.

Mental and Emotional Variables

MENTAL SET

"Mental set," "perceptual set," and "present expectation" are all terms that have been used to designate a similar concept—that a person tends to notice in the environment what he or she expects to find there. For the marketer, this concept may be a two-edged sword. On the one hand, a consumer may attach undesirable and perhaps unwarranted interpretations to a product or communication on the basis of his mental set; on the other hand, the marketer may benefit from desirable interpretations based on such expectations. The example of the tin-lizzy connotations of rattles in Fords, while rattling problems in Chevrolets were blamed on bumpy roads, illustrates the former condition.

"Perceptual set" refers to an individual's readiness to perceive a stimulus in a particular manner, even if the stimulus is presented differently. The Campbell Kids, a chubby boy and girl, were included as trade characters in Campbell's advertisements for a number of years. In time the company considered the effectiveness of these characters to be worn out and discontinued their use. Years later, when consumers were asked to recall Campbell's advertisements that they had seen recently, their descriptions included the Campbell Kids. Their readiness to perceive these advertisements in a particular way caused them to report "seeing" stimuli that were not present.

Perceptual set can be influenced by previous experience and by such personal factors as emotions and values. If someone is told what he will see in an ambiguous picture (that is, one that can be interpreted in several ways), he tends to see what he expected to see. An example of such an ambiguous stimulus is the famous "wife or mother-in-law" picture of E. G. Boring. (See Figure 7.7.) As we have noted, such ambiguity may occur in advertisements. To some extent, television commercials have an advantage over print advertisements in dispelling ambiguity, since the announcer's explanations can prepare the viewer.

THE HALO EFFECT

The so-called *halo effect* in perception refers to the fact that the favorableness (or unfavorableness) of our prime impression of another often leads us to attribute to

FIGURE 7.7   WIFE OR MOTHER-IN-LAW?

him all kinds of good (or bad) traits.[24] In a sense, the halo effect can be regarded as an instance of stereotyping, that is, creating a set of beliefs and expectations about people.

Although the halo effect is generally discussed in relation to the perception of people, the concept has been applied to the perception of products and brand names as well. The halo effect suggests that the perception of one characteristic is colored by the emotions we attach to a related characteristic. In general, the halo effect is concerned with the tendency to blur one characteristic or attribute of a product into another.

This concept may be useful for marketers in the development of their programs. For example, the tendency to blur brand names and taste has been examined in regard to beer. In a blind test (competing products were not identified) to determine whether or not beer drinkers could distinguish among various brands, the researchers concluded that participants did not appear to be able to do so. In this blind test, the labels had been completely soaked off and the crowns had been wire-brushed to remove all brand identification from the 12-ounce brown bottles used in the test.

When the same test was conducted with properly labeled bottles of beer, however, the overall ratings for all of the brands increased considerably. Moreover, when beer drinkers were categorized according to the brand most frequently drunk, they consistently rated "their" beer higher than comparison beers in the positive-identification taste test. This finding led the researchers to conclude that labels and their associations apparently did influence evaluation of beer.[25]

In other words, product distinctions or differences arose in the minds of the participants primarily through their receptiveness to the various firms' marketing efforts rather than through perceived differences in the physical products.

In a widely publicized advertising campaign in 1976, Pepsi Cola challenged the leadership of Coca-Cola. According to the Pepsi Cola Company, a blind taste test indicated that more Coke drinkers actually preferred Pepsi to their own brand. The campaign escalated into a competitive battle apparently based on taste preferences. Coca-Cola retaliated by stating that Pepsi was always labeled *M* and Coke was labeled *Q* in these tests, and that a distinct consumer bias for *M* over *Q* destroyed the validity of the test. Pepsi changed the letters used in the test, and Coca-Cola continued to object to the findings. Ultimately Coca-Cola introduced the campaign slogan "One taste is not enough," which made fun of all blind taste tests.[26] One advertisement, for example, showed a man drinking from a glass containing a golf ball, and declaring he likes the taste of golf balls. To some observers, it appeared that Coca-Cola's campaign was designed to cause consumers to distrust taste-testing, so that Coca-Cola would continue to prevail as a market leader. Coca-Cola's distributors, however, viewed the entire campaign with disfavor and considered it demeaning, and ultimately it was dropped.

While the research findings of these blind taste tests have been questioned, they suggest the potential of a halo effect for soft drinks and brand names and present some interesting questions that may be answered through further research.

The ability to measure the halo effect has promise as a marketing tool, to the extent that the individual's perceptions are contaminated by this effect. If the halo effect has led to a specific preference, it is unlikely that further communication contradicting this preconception is going to be accepted,[27] and strong persuasion techniques may be necessary. Empirical research in this area has been limited. Indications exist, however, that the strength of the halo effect has wide variability among types of products, and until more is known about which types of products generate the greatest halo effects, each product will have to be investigated on its own.[28]

PERCEPTION RESEARCH

Some research techniques involving perception and consumer behavior have already been discussed in this chapter. These techniques include the use of physiological devices designed to test awareness of an item, such as the tachistoscope, which measures visual perception under varying conditions, and the oculometer, which tracks the movements of the eye. A more obvious way to determine such awareness would be to ask consumers to recall the stimuli that they have perceived.

As we saw earlier, the perceptual process involves more than awareness. Knowing that the consumer is aware of a product, brand, or communication does not mean that the market knows how the individual perceives it.

Knowledge of a product's physical attributes and the way they affect a consumer's perception of the product should be valuable in the planning of product development and marketing strategy, particularly in regard to "positioning." One valuable approach is offered by multidimensional scaling.[29]

Multidimensional Scaling

In analyzing marketing data, many researchers have used metric scales. Metric scales are those that contain a natural origin or zero point from which all distances can be measured, or those in which the size of the distance between pairs of measurements has meaning. Evidence indicates, however, that people cannot ordinarily provide accurate and reliable information about equality relationships among competing brands or about brand characteristics.[30]

To secure such information, researchers have tended in recent years to use nonmetric multidimensional scaling. "Multidimensional" merely means "many dimensions"; that is, the relationships of brands are examined along a number of dimensions of significance: softness, strength, potency, and so on. "Nonmetric" means that the scaling technique simply describes the inequality of the relationships, that is, which one is larger or smaller. Thus one brand of facial tissue may be perceived as softer than another and one brand of paper toweling may be perceived as stronger than another, though no objective measurement has been done.

Perceptual Mapping

Data from the results of multidimensional scaling are frequently reported in chart form; and since such data develop not from accurate measurements but from the perceptions of individuals, the resultant findings are designated as perceptual mapping. A perceptual map consists of the consumer's perceived locations of several brands on a number of attribute dimensions.[31]

A perceptual map of brands of ethical pharmaceuticals developed in a study using multidimensional scaling appears in Figure 7.8. It should be noted that this is a relatively simple perceptual map involving only two product characteristics, while this technique may incorporate the analysis of many (multi) dimensions.

An analysis of the data collected in this study provided two salient dimensions for ethical drugs, identified as potency and side effects. Thus brands 2 and 4 were perceived to be highly potent, but also to induce undesirable side effects. Brands 1, 3, and 5 were perceived to be considerably weaker than the other two brands, yet brand 1 was still associated with undesirable side effects.

An "ideal brand" is frequently incorporated in such a map. By definition, the ideal brand is simply the most preferred one. It is assumed that the ideal brand of pharmaceuticals is one that has average potency and few side effects; thus in Figure 7.8, brand 6 is the ideal brand.

The introduction of an ideal brand has a number of advantages. It suggests how close each brand may come to the ideal and indicates that consumers would have greater preference for those brands closest to the ideal. In our illustration,

FIGURE 7.8   A PERCEPTUAL MAP OF BRANDS OF ETHI-
CAL DRUGS

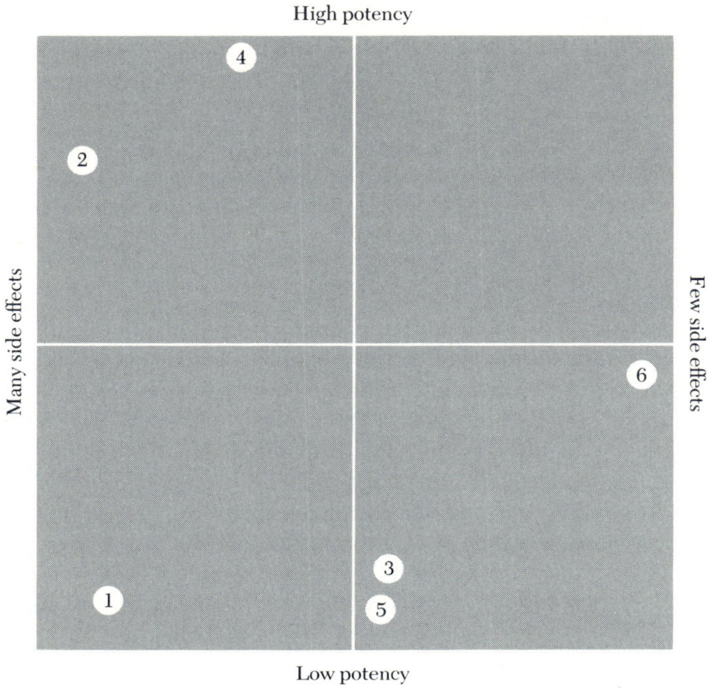

High potency

Many side effects

Few side effects

Low potency

Lester A. Neidell, "The Use of Non-Metric Multidimensional Scaling in Marketing Analysis," *Journal of Marketing* 33 (October 1969),
p. 41.

the position of brand 6 suggests that a good marketing strategy would incorporate
the introduction of a new brand containing average potency and few side effects,
since none of the competing brands appears to occupy this perceptual space.

Positioning

In connection with the development of nonmetric multidimensional scaling for
comparison of consumers' perceptions of product attributes, a product strategy
known as "positioning" has won wide acceptance. "Positioning" refers to the ability to find an "attractive space" within a range of competitive brands and to place
a product in that space. In the perceptual map in Figure 7.8, a valid competitive
position would occupy the attribute spaces of average potency and low side effects. In perceptual terms, positioning may be seen as analogous to providing the
consumer with an appropriate frame of reference for perception of the marketer's
product. Furthermore, for the consumer who engages in selective perception, it
clarifies the competitive group in which the product is designed to exist.

EXHIBIT 7.2

In this ad, Arm & Hammer Baking Soda is repositioned as a product that eliminates "kitty odors."
Source: "McMahan's '100 Best,' " *Advertising Age*, January 29, 1979, p. 58.

Many firms have used positioning in their product strategies, either in the introduction of a new product or in the repositioning of an old one. Proper positioning can focus on the specific attributes that may be uppermost in the consumer's mind. Kimberly Clark noted that among the best selling paper towels, two rated high in one basic dimension each—absorbency for one, strength for the other. Kimberly Clark positioned its new paper towel as high in both dimensions by naming it "Tough and Thirsty."

Anheuser-Busch found an appropriate space for its new "not-so-soft" drink by combining consumers' perceptions of the desirable attributes of beer and soft drinks. Chelsea pours like beer, contains natural ingredients, and is a blend of lemon and lime juices and apple and spice flavors.

When sales of a product are declining, or at best remaining stable, it may be desirable to use a repositioning strategy to develop a new product space in order to change consumers' perceptions of an old product. (See Exhibit 7.2.) Ginger ale, widely assumed by consumers to be a mixer and therefore primarily bought as such, was repositioned as a soft drink. Manufacturers of dog food, noting the change in consumers' perceptions of the desirable characteristics of dog food, redesigned their products' ingredients and designated them as "moist."

SUMMARY

Sensation occurs when stimuli reach the sense organs. Perception involves an interpretation of these stimuli.

In order to provide an understanding of the range of sensations that can be produced by various stimuli, psychologists have developed the field of psychophysics for the study of the relationships between sensation and perception. Among the concepts they have developed is that of thresholds of perception. The minimum stimulus necessary to produce a specific sensation is called the absolute threshold. The point at which a change in stimulus will cause a change in sensation is known as the differential threshold.

The extent to which an individual can receive stimuli below his level of awareness is difficult to measure. The concept of subliminal perception represents a controversial issue. Moreover, the use of subliminal communications is a questionable tactic, from the viewpoints of both potential effectiveness and ethical communications.

The manner in which the consumer interprets the items and events in the marketplace depends to a great extent on his perception of them. Perception is selective, so that the consumer perceives some items and events and ignores others. The factors that influence perceptual selectivity relate to the nature of the stimulus (for example, the effects of size, intensity, novelty, and color) and the nature of the individual (for example, his or her needs, motives, social values, and cultural background). Consumers may set up barriers against unacceptable items and events. The tendency to do so is called perceptual defense.

Because raw sensory data alone are insufficient to provide meaning and because the stimuli we receive are often ambiguous, we engage in perceptual interpretation. Thus objects that provide sensory information that changes from moment to moment are nevertheless perceived as having constant properties—that is, they are perceived to possess size constancy, shape constancy, and color constancy.

One of the basic principles of perception incorporates the fact that we organize stimuli in a meaningful fashion, through such techniques as figure-and-ground differentiation, closure, grouping, using a frame of reference, and developing a level of adaptation.

"Perceptual set" refers to our readiness to perceive a stimulus in a particular manner. Our perceptual set can be influenced by expectations, by previous experience, and by such personal factors as emotions and values.

Consumer research relevant to perception can take various forms, including the use of physiological testing devices and multidimensional scaling. Findings from multidimensional scaling techniques have good potential use in the development of new products and in the devising of positioning strategies.

DISCUSSION QUESTIONS

1. How does the fact that the absolute threshold does not remain constant affect decisions to repeat or vary advertising campaigns?

2. Discuss ways in which the concept of differential threshold may be incorporated in a strategy designed to add a "lemony" scent to a detergent.

3. How can the just noticeable difference be incorporated in a pricing strategy?

4. You are asked to evaluate an advertising campaign that includes heavy emphasis on subliminal communications. Discuss.

5. What factors should be incorporated in an ad to increase the probability that it will be perceived?

6. What is meant by perceptual defense? How is it important in communication strategy?

7. Describe and give examples of figure and ground and closure.

8. How can the halo effect be incorporated in a marketing strategy?

9. Give examples of products that have been positioned or repositioned. Explain.

NOTES

1. Albert Shepard, "How Comparative Segment Analysis Helps Identify and Validate New Communication Strategies," *Proceedings, Advertising Research Foundation*, 12th Annual Conference, New York, October 1966.

2. Donald A. Laird, "How Consumer Estimates Quality by Subconscious Sensory Impressions—With Special Reference to the Role of Smell," *Journal of Applied Psychology* 16 (June 1932), pp. 241–246.

3. Paul Thomas Young, *Motivation and Emotion: A Survey of the Determinants of Human and Animal Activity* (New York: John Wiley, 1961), pp. 289–299.

4. Bernard Berelson and Gary A. Steiner, *Human Behavior: An Inventory of Scientific Findings* (New York: Harcourt Brace Jovanovich, 1964), p. 88.

5. Joseph M. Kamen and Robert J. Toman, "Psychophysics of Price," *Journal of Marketing Research* 7 (February 1970), pp. 27–35.

6. Kent B. Monroe, "Measuring Price Thresholds by Psychophysics and Latitude of Acceptance," *Journal of Marketing Research* 8 (November 1971), pp. 460–464.

7. *Subliminal Communication*, a report prepared by the Institute of Practitioners in Advertising (London, July 1958), p. 7.

8. John Brooks, "The Little Ad That Isn't There," *Consumer Reports* 13 (January 1958), pp. 5–11.

9. *Subliminal Communication*, pp. 5–6.

10. Berelson and Steiner, *Human Behavior*, p. 95.

11. Del Hawkins, "The Effects of Subliminal Stimulation on Drive Level and Brand Preference," *Journal of Marketing Research* 7 (August 1970), p. 325.

12. Norman F. Dixon, *Subliminal Perception: The Nature of the Controversy* (Maidenhead, Berkshire: McGraw-Hill, 1971).

13. Harold A. Sackheim, Ira K. Packer, and Ruben G. Gur, "Hemispherity, Cognitive Set, and Susceptibility to Subliminal Perception," *Journal of Abnormal Psychology* 86 (1977), pp. 624–630.

14. William J. McGuire, "Some Internal Psychological Factors Influencing Consumer Choice," *Journal of Consumer Research* 2 (March 1976), pp. 302–319.

15. "Television and the Holocaust," *Time*, May 1, 1978, pp. 52–53.

16. Alvin J. Silk and Frank P. Geiger, "Advertisement Size and the Relationship between Product Usage and Advertising Exposure," *Journal of Marketing Research* 9 (February 1972), p. 25.

17. *Are Television Commercials Worth the Extra Cost?* (New York: Association of National Advertisers, 1966).

18. H. William Bockus, Jr., *Advertising Graphics* (New York: Macmillan, 1969), p. 63.

19. Daniele S. Diamond, "A Quantitative Approach to Magazine Advertisement Format Selection," *Journal of Marketing Research* 5 (November 1968), pp. 376–386.

20. J. Killough Anchor, "Improve Payoffs from Transnational Advertising," *Harvard Business Review*, July–August 1978, pp. 108–109.

21. Raymond A. Bauer and Stephen A. Greyser, *Advertising in America: The Consumer's View* (Cambridge: Graduate School of Business Administration, Harvard University, 1968), p. 176.

22. W. J. McGuire, "Selective Exposure: A Summing Up," in *Theories of Cognitive Consistency: A Sourcebook*, ed. Robert P. Abelson et al. (Chicago: Rand McNally, 1968), pp. 797–800.

23. James P. Forkan, "Oculometer Is Finding Out What Viewers See in Those TV Commercials," *Advertising Age*, April 11, 1977, p. 56.

24. David Krech, Richard S. Crutchfield, and Norman Livson, *Elements of Psychology*, 3d ed. (New York: Alfred A. Knopf, 1974), p. 785.

25. Ralph I. Allison and Kenneth P. Uhl, "Brand Identification and Perception," *Journal of Marketing Research* 1 (August 1964), pp. 80–85.

26. "One Sip Not a Taste Test, Coke Tells New Yorkers," *Advertising Age*, August 16, 1976.

27. Joel Huber and William James, "A Measure of Halo," in *Advances in Consumer Research*, vol. 5, ed. H. Keith Hunt (Ann Arbor: Association for Consumer Research, 1978), p. 472.

28. William L. James and Forrest S. Carter, "Halo Effects and Location Preferences," in ibid., p. 476.

29. K. James McCullough, Charlene S. Martinsen, and Reza Moinpour, "Application of Multidimensional Scaling to the Analysis of Sensory Evaluations of Stimuli with Known Attribute Structures," *Journal of Applied Psychology* 63 (1978), pp. 103–109.

30. Lester A. Neidell, "The Use of Non-Metric Multidimensional Scaling in Marketing Analysis," *Journal of Marketing* 33 (October 1969), p. 38.

31. Robert C. Blattberg and Subrata K. Sen, "Market Segmentation Using Models of Multidimensional Purchasing Behavior," *Journal of Marketing* 38 (October 1974), pp. 17–28.

CHAPTER 8

LEARNING

Burger King's research among consumers revealed that a major criticism of their hamburgers was their uniformity. Regardless of how the customers wanted them, the hamburgers were served in one way. Burger King changed this standardized format and created a new advertising campaign incorporating the jingle "Hold the pickle, hold the lettuce, special orders don't upset us . . . Have it your way." Now, if a consumer stops at a Burger King outlet, she can order a hamburger and get it to her own specifications (a reward). If she is satisfied with the reward, she may then repeat this experience. Moreover, her positive attitude toward Burger King may be reinforced when she later hears the jingle "Have it your way." If she is not satisfied, however, she will avoid eating hamburgers at Burger King. This may be considered an example of learning through instrumental conditioning.

The association of black leather jackets, delinquents, switchblades, and rowdy behavior with motorcycles is a stigma that manufacturers had to remove in order to mass-market the motorcycle. After Honda's introduction of the theme "You meet the nicest people on a Honda," its dealer organization more than doubled and its sales increased approximately 200 percent in one year.[1]

The sight of attractive, well-dressed women and men in business suits riding motorcycles added imagery to the advertising theme "You meet the nicest people.

. . ." Honda's advertising used such key words as "nice," "easygoing," "friend," "family," and "frugal." The information in the ad was organized through the use of key words and visual imagery; it was meaningful (particularly to a population increasingly concerned with economy and pollution) and relevant to an emerging life-style. This could be considered an example of cognitive learning.

How do consumers learn? Answers to this question offer many potential benefits not only to businessmen in the implementation of their marketing strategies, but to public policy makers in the development of societal policies and programs. In recent years, in fact, consumerists have shifted the focus of their efforts from consumer protection to the provision of information—so that consumers may learn.

Unfortunately, as with many other facets of consumer behavior, there is no clear knowledge of either the learning process or its influence on consumers' activities in the marketplace. The marketing illustrations at the beginning of this chapter can only present assumptions about consumer learning. Educators have been struggling with an understanding of learning for years, only to be faced with declining test scores and controversies as to the validity of their measurement devices. Despite these disappointments, numerous psychological theories have been developed about the learning process, many of which have relevance to consumer learning.

In Chapter 7 we saw how consumers pay attention to and interpret sensations aroused by stimuli in their environment. Although awareness and interpretations of such sensations may be prerequisites to the learning process, these factors alone do not ensure learning. This chapter attempts to answer some of the following questions:

> What are the major theories of learning and how do they explain consumer learning?
> What are the learning concepts of generalization and discrimination and how do they apply to marketing strategy?
> What can be done to reduce forgetting?
> How can retention and retrieval of information be facilitated?
> What are some of the methods used to measure learning?

LEARNING THEORIES

The theoretical constructs in consumer learning derive from the learning theories developed by psychologists. Although psychologists have been studying the learning process for many years, new theories continue to be developed, as do controversies and the refinement of older theoretical concepts. The theories of learning that have been applied most widely to consumer learning are classical conditioning, instrumental conditioning, and cognitive theories.

Classical Conditioning

Classical conditioning (sometimes called Pavlovian conditioning) involves a stimulus and the response to it. The noted Russian physiologist Ivan Pavlov discovered classical conditioning in 1904. Pavlov was originally studying how the stomach prepares itself, by secreting digestive juices, for food that is placed in the mouth. He found that the mouth also prepares itself, by secreting saliva, when food is merely seen or smelled. In Pavlov's terms, the food in the mouth is an *unconditioned stimulus*, which elicits the *unconditioned response* of salivation. The term "unconditioned" is used because the response usually does not depend on the organism's previous experience with the stimulus.

Pavlov discovered that if a previously neutral stimulus (one that did not cause this response, in this case the sound of a tuning fork) regularly occurs just before food is placed in a dog's mouth, this stimulus itself gradually comes to elicit salivation. The new stimulus (the tuning fork) that now elicits salivation is called the *conditioned stimulus*.[2]

The salivation that it evokes is called the *conditioned response.* Any one of a large variety of stimuli can serve as a conditioned stimulus for salivation: the sight of food, the sound of a bell, or a flash of light.

John Broadus Watson demonstrated the direct implications of classical conditioning for human behavior, particularly the conditioning of emotions.[3] In a classic experiment by Watson, an eleven-month-old child named Albert, who initially was quite comfortable, even playful, in the presence of a white rat, was conditioned to fear the rat (to cry, to escape from it) by a loud, intrinsically startling and frightening noise that was presented each time he reached for his playmate. Since Watson's time, researchers have classically conditioned a wide range of behaviors in people of all ages, using a variety of stimuli.

Early psychological approaches to advertising incorporated much of this "behaviorism"—the term used to denote Watson's theses. Under this concept, in which the conditioned response was seen as "habit,"[4] it was assumed that the child enters the world with little except the capacity to receive impressions and develop habits and attitudes implanted by his elders. Accordingly, the consumer entering the market was like a clean slate on which an advertiser could leave any impression he wished. When Watson entered the advertising field, this view spread, and advertisers began a campaign of endless and massive repetition. It was thought that the habit of buying was brought about by simple and constant repetition.

Although most psychologists now reject the empty-slate theory, there may be examples of classical conditioning of consumers. In addition to advertising, the stimuli in the conditioning process can be products, services, ideas, packages, prices, and so on. The response can be noticing, remembering, understanding, evaluating, and loyalty, among others. It has been suggested that repeated exposure to brand names, logos, labels, and package designs of certain products in the marketplace may result in such learning.[5]

Instrumental Conditioning

One of the major operational features of Pavlovian conditioning is the purely passive role played by the organism in the delivery of the conditioned or unconditioned stimulus. A second type of learning can be distinguished when the organism assumes some active role in the learning situation. Situations can be arranged so that the organism is not rewarded or cannot escape from punishment of some kind until it somehow makes the response the experimenter wants it to make. In such *instrumental conditioning,* as the name implies, the organism plays an instrumental role in producing rewards for itself or in escaping from or avoiding punishment.[6]

In a typical experimental procedure in instrumental conditioning, a hungry bird pecks at random while wandering about a Skinner box (named for B. F. Skinner, the behavioral psychologist who first described its use). Eventually the bird chances to peck at the illuminated window, and then the automatic mechanism delivers a food pellet; this response is rewarded.

A central statement of conditioning is known as the *law of effect.* Edward Thorndike, a psychologist who studied the behavior of animals in problem-solving situations, formulated this law, which states simply that "an action that leads to a desirable outcome is likely to be repeated in similar circumstances."[7] The desirable outcome is frequently designated as "reinforcing," or more simply as "reward."

Illustrations of instrumental conditioning are more readily found than those of classical conditioning in consumer learning and decision making (for example, having a hamburger "your way"). Much advertising today declares that consumers can get "fast relief" for stomach aches and headaches or can eliminate sink stains and "ring around the collar" by using the advertiser's product. The assumption is that if the consumers are pleased with the outcome (reinforced or rewarded), the use of Rolaids, Excedrin, Wisk, or Ajax (the response) is likely to be repeated in the future.

Cognitive Learning

Cognitive psychology is concerned with the way people cognize or gain knowledge about their world and use that knowledge to guide decisions and perform effective actions.[8]

It seems clear that a description of the behavior of an organism can, in principle, be given in terms of stimulus and response. Demonstrations are seen routinely in the case of the animal trainer and in custodial institutions for the mentally retarded. But this explanation does not account for the behavior of the organism outside of a highly restricted environment. Such behavioral differences led to the development of cognitive psychology. Cognitive researchers were led to assume that response to a stimulus varies because of differences in the organism's state of knowledge regarding its environment and in expectancies regarding consequences of possible actions.

It was assumed that since changes in behavior are observed in conditioning situations, it must be changes in behavior that are learned.[9] Then the attention of cognitive investigators of human learning began to shift from a modification of response tendencies to the acquisition of information. The shift was accelerated by the research of psycholinguists and the advent of computer-based information-processing systems.

Theoretically, cognitive learning might be defined as the study of all aspects of information processing by organisms. When its application to consumer behavior is examined, however, it is more useful to focus on the storage, retrieval, and use of information than on the neurophysiological mechanisms by which these functions are accomplished. The most common research view sees the consumer as an information-processing system whose operations are somewhat analogous to those of a computer, in the sense that information is put in (received), that it is processed in an internal center, and that something is put out (a decision is made, an attitude changes, a fact or impression is added to memory).[10]

Under this concept, the importance of the outcome rests not on its reinforcing value but on its informational value. An operating principle is the *law of information feedback*, which declares that "the outcome of an event serves as information about that event."[11] Moreover, there is an assumption of causality—that is, for learning to take place, a person must perceive an apparent causal relationship between the action and its outcome. It should be noted that the causal relationship need not be real, but may be inferred.

Cognitive learning theory indicates that behavior is a function of the state of the person and of the environment. Consumers, however, behave according to the way things appear to them, and not necessarily according to the way things really are. Thus perception plays an important role. Many internal factors influence learning, including the insight developed from past outcomes of a response, past experience, thinking, expectations, and so on. Thus advertising campaigns designed to secure learning under this concept must do much more than simply repeat names and identifications. They may present alternative life-styles, offer promise of peer approval, provide the means of social acceptance, or suggest advancement for the upwardly mobile (as Honda did).

The heart of cognitive learning is memory.[12] Studies of learning tend to emphasize the acquisition of knowledge. Studies of memory tend to emphasize the retention and use of that knowledge. Clearly, the two are so interrelated that the study of one must necessarily be the study of the other.[13]

THE MEMORY SYSTEMS

At least three aspects of memory can be identified: a sensory-information storage system, a short-term memory system, and a long-term memory system.[14] (See Figure 8.1.)

Sensory-Information Storage. The sensory-information storage system maintains a rather accurate and complete picture of the world as it is received by the sen-

FIGURE 8.1   THE MEMORY SYSTEMS

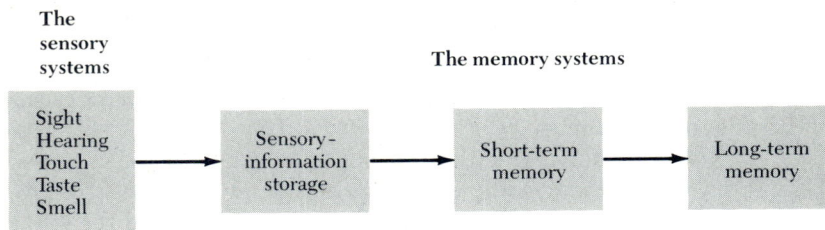

The
sensory
systems

The memory systems

Sight
Hearing
Touch
Taste
Smell → Sensory-information storage → Short-term memory → Long-term memory

Source: Adapted from Peter H. Lindsay and Donald A. Norman, *Human Information Processing: An Introduction to Psychology*, 2d ed. (New York: Academic Press, 1977), p. 304.

sory system. Its duration is short, perhaps 0.1 to 0.5 second. To illustrate this storage system, close your eyes, then open them for as short an interval of time as possible before you close them again. Note how the sharp, clear image that you picked up stays with you awhile and then slowly fades away. This system is of primary importance for the proper operation of perceptual processing. Perception is intimately related to the process of memory. Chapter 7 described some of the perceptual mechanisms that operate on sensory information, interpreting, classifying, and organizing arriving information.

Short-Term Memory. Information in the environment that is effectively perceived enters the short-term memory and is stored in meaningful units. The short-term memory has a severely limited capacity, which has been variously described as between five to seven and between four to six chunks of information. Although a chunk is a standard measure, the size of the chunk can vary. A single letter can be a chunk, or several words grouped in a meaningful manner can be a chunk. *C, A,* and *T* are three separate chunks, but *cat* is also a chunk; so is cat-o'-nine-tails.[15]

Information is stored in short-term memory for a brief time (perhaps no more than 18 seconds) unless it is "rehearsed." Rehearsal relates to a type of inner speech by which the memory trace is strengthened. Information in short-term memory may be forgotten or transferred to long-term memory.

The limited storage capacity of short-term memory is of significance to marketers. Its limitation tends to emphasize the need for the marketer's product or message to stand out from the myriad other stimuli in the consumer's environment (as discussed in Chapter 7), so that it can be stored in short-term memory. Furthermore, it suggests that information should be provided so that it can be processed as a meaningful chunk. It is possible that brand names provide an important chunking function, not only for short-term memory but perhaps in facilitating retrieval of information from long-term memory.[16]

Short-term memory is the active partition of memory. The individual has easier access to short-term memory than to long-term memory and can retrieve information from short-term memory faster than from long-term memory.

Long-Term Memory. Long-term memory is assumed to be the repository of the individual's more permanent knowledge and skills. The information structures in long-term memory include knowledge, beliefs, values, skills, and ability to interpret and understand. Thus much of the information relevant to culture and interpersonal relations is stored in it.

Whether or not information in short-term memory is transferred to long-term memory is dependent on numerous factors. Certain characteristics of such information are more likely to ensure its transfer to long-term memory for permanent storage. *Meaningfulness* is the most important characteristic, but material that is *familiar* or similar to what was previously retained is also likely to be stored. *Relevance* also influences whether material will be transferred to long-term memory.[17]

In the learning of new information, the problem is not getting the information into memory; it is making sure that it will be found later on when it is needed. Current theory favors the view that, theoretically, information that gets into long-term memory is never lost (or forgotten), though there may be no access to it and it may never be retrieved.[18] The manner in which information entering the long-term memory system is integrated with information already there affects its ability to be retrieved.

INFORMATION PROCESSING AND CONSUMER BEHAVIOR

The significance of information processing to consumer-behavior theory has been understudied in the past but is currently receiving attention.

According to some theorists, when a consumer makes a purchase, product information may come from two sources.[19] The external environment for the purchase situation contains package labels, point-of-purchase displays, posted prices, and the like. Much of the information relevant to the purchase decision, however, is retrieved from memory. Information concerning use, experience, family preferences, word-of-mouth communications, and advertising must all be mediated by memory. Further, if all brands are not available from a single vendor, then information about the missing ones must come solely from memory.

According to some theorists, product information retrieved from memory plays an essential role in almost all purchase decisions.[20] A processing history of product information has been outlined as follows:[21]

1. Encoding of product information from external sources.
2. Retention of product information in memory.
3. Retrieval and use of product information in the purchase-decision process.

Encoding

As we noted earlier, the external environment for the purchase situation contains many stimuli that can be used as inputs to the purchase situation. The nature of a stimulus input not only affects perception, as we saw in Chapter 7, but also determines how a person will encode and process information. Furthermore, it is not the stimulus itself (or its objective characteristics) that determines the consumer's judgmental process, but the cues that emanate from the stimulus.

For example, although the color red can be objectively defined in terms of physical qualities, the psychological perceptions of red vary greatly.[22] Even in prerevolutionary China, red played an important role in wedding ceremonies. Yet in our culture, a bride-to-be might react negatively to a suggestion that she be married in a red dress. In fact, a late-night movie, *Jezebel*, focuses on the outrage caused by a Southern belle who dared to appear at a ball in a red gown. Although a red dress might connote sin, red roses might be happily received as a sign of warmth and passion. In these two cases, different subsets of encoded information are used to decode the same objective stimulus, red. The information used by the subject may vary according to the perceived nature of the stimulus cue.

To encode product information, the consumer uses information cues to make judgments about the product. This is particularly true in relation to judgments about quality. Cues may be intrinsic to (or inherent in) the product, such as size, color, scent, or feel.[23] Others are extrinsic (external) to the product: price, store image, brand image, promotional message. It should be noted that it is not the objective characteristics of these cues that determine the way they are encoded, but the consumer's perceptions of these characteristics, as we saw in Chapter 7.

Retention of Information

Pieces of information stored in long-term memory seem to be interconnected in a meaningful manner so that it is possible to trace a path among related items. Such interconnections may be represented in long-term memory in the form of *semantic networks* or *list structures*.[24]

SEMANTIC NETWORKS

A *semantic network* is a representation of interconnections among meaningful (semantic) components of memory. The semantic network of an item is quite complex and includes interconnected knowledge about the class (the generic group) to which the item belongs, its properties, and examples.[25] A simple hypothetical semantic structure for peanut butter is shown in Figure 8.2.

According to John Howard, the semantic structure provides the meaning of a brand to consumers. Furthermore, a well-developed semantic structure will make it easier for consumers to construct a meaning for a radically new brand that they have never heard of before.[26]

LIST STRUCTURES

List structures suggest that product knowledge is stored in long-term memory by brand or attribute.[27] Storage by brand suggests that each person's knowledge of a

FIGURE   8.2   HYPOTHETICAL   SEMANTIC   NET-
            WORK   FOR   PEANUT   BUTTER

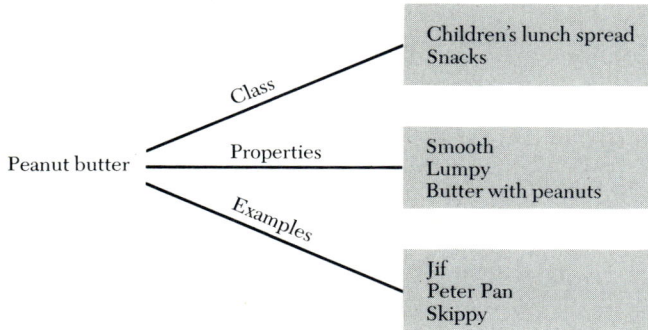

product class is organized according to brand. For peanut butter, for example, a verbal statement of brand-organized knowledge may be "Skippy tastes very good, it contains 17 grams of fat, and it costs $1.25 for an 18-ounce jar."[28] Attribute-organized knowledge could be organized around price: both Skippy and Jif cost $1.25, but Peter Pan costs $1.29. As to fat content, both Skippy and Peter Pan contain 17 grams of fat, but Jif contains 16 grams of fat. (See Tables 8.1 and 8.2.)

These storage structures may lead to different choice strategies. Storage by *brand* suggests an "elimination by aspects" strategy, in which each brand is scored separately on a personal value scale that incorporates, for example, taste, use of preservatives, and price.[29] In the "one dimension at a time" strategy, the consumer selects the *attribute* judged most important first (for example, taste) and eliminates the one or more brands that score relatively poorly on this dimension; then she considers the next most important (for example, price), eliminating those

TABLE 8.1   ORGANIZATION OF PRODUCT KNOWLEDGE
            BY BRAND

Brand	Attribute	Knowledge
Skippy	Taste	Very good
	Price	$1.25
	Size	18 oz.
	Fat content	17 grams
Jif	Taste	Good
	Price	$1.25
	Size	18 oz.
	Fat content	16 grams
Peter Pan	Taste	Very good
	Price	$1.29
	Size	18 oz.
	Fat content	17 grams

**TABLE 8.2   ORGANIZATION OF PRODUCT KNOWLEDGE
BY ATTRIBUTE**

Attribute	Brand	Knowledge
Taste	Skippy	Very good
	Jif	Fair
	Peter Pan	Very good
Price	Skippy	$1.25
	Jif	$1.25
	Peter Pan	$1.29
Size	Skippy	18 oz.
	Jif	18 oz.
	Peter Pan	18 oz.
Fat content	Skippy	17 grams
	Jif	16 grams
	Peter Pan	17 grams

that fail to meet this criterion, and so on until one brand remains. If "contains less fat" is an important dimension for the consumer, Jif will probably be selected.

Although such strategies may seem complex, given the vast number of brands and the many attributes inherent in each, consumers have apparently developed modes of dealing with these complexities. When a consumer needs to buy a product, say coffee, not all brands that he or she is aware of come to mind, or to use Howard's term, are "evoked." Instead, the consumer selects only two, three, or four brands that best meet the need. These brands constitute the "evoked set." The evoked set is defined as "the subset of brands that a consumer will consider buying out of the set of brands in the product class of which he or she is aware."[30] According to some research studies, four brands of coffee and three brands of toothpaste comprised the evoked set for these products.

It is not clear whether people prefer attribute-based or brand-based memory structures. On the basis of limited research in this area, it appears that consumer decision rules are flexible and depend on the structure of the available product information.[31] At least one study tentatively concluded that attribute structures are preferred.[32]

Retrieval

As in other areas of research on consumer information processing, a great deal more study is necessary before we have a clear understanding of information retrieval by consumers. The complexity of this subject is compounded by individual differences. As we noted earlier, cognitive psychologists assume that the response to a stimulus varies because of variations in the person's state of knowledge regarding his or her environment and in expectancies regarding the consequences of possible actions. It appears that the consumer will look ahead in an attempt to assess the potential usefulness of information.[33] Motivations may cause variations in information retrieval. Motivation, in this context, relates to the energy dimensions of consumer information processing—that is, what causes it to be stored and how it is sustained.[34] In addition to the effect of experience, expectations, and motivation, the consumer's predispositions, attitudes, and preferences for alternative brands may influence the manner in which information is processed or retrieved.

A general recommendation for marketers is that information be provided in a manner that makes it easy to process and retrieve. Specific recommendations, however, have not yet been developed.

One relevant study conducted in this area was related to the effects of unit-pricing requirements instituted by a number of states and localities in an effort to simplify the task of comparing prices for consumers.[35] A number of studies had indicated that unit pricing was relatively ineffective. Most unit prices were located on tags near the relevant brands. In an application of the concept of information storage by list structure, an experiment was conducted in a chain of supermarkets that had been using shelf tags (that is, listing by brands). This procedure was changed so that a single organized list of the various brands was displayed with their corresponding unit prices (that is, listing by attribute—in this case, price), as in Table 8.3. When the new method was used, consumers showed a significantly greater tendency to shift to cheaper brands. The reasons for this change have been variously interpreted. Howard suggests that consumers shifted because the data for comparison of brands were presented close together, permitting them to by-pass long-term memory—that is, consumers did not have to go through the "cognitive strain of storing information in the long-term memory."[36] Bettman suggests that this may be a case in which processing by attribute (a list of prices) is a more effective presentation of information than processing by brands. Bettman notes, however, that there is a need to determine which forms of processing are most effective; in fact, there may be occasions when processing by brand is more desirable.[37]

It is obvious that much additional research is needed to provide a clearer understanding of consumer information processing. Many studies in this area emerge from considerations of public policy and the development of appropriate programs to assist consumers in their "awareness and understanding of objective product information pertinent to the purchase and use of goods and services."[38] Research has also focused on the information processing characterizing special populations, such as children and the elderly.[39] Such research could be useful to marketers for whom these groups form a significant portion of the target market. Other studies are being currently conducted to determine the effect of information overload, as there are limits to the ability to assimilate and process information during any given unit of time. It is said that once this limit is passed, decision making may become confused, less accurate, and less effective.[40] These studies have implications for both public policy makers and marketers in suggesting that limits should be set for the amount of information presented to consumers.

TABLE 8.3 BRANDS OF SOAP PRODUCTS LISTED IN ORDER OF INCREASING PRICE PER QUART

Brand and size	Price	Price per quart
Par 48 oz.	54¢	36.0¢
Par 32 oz.	38¢	38.0¢
Sweetheart 32 oz.	55¢	55.0¢
Brocade 48 oz.	85¢	56.7¢
Sweetheart 22 oz.	39¢	56.7¢
Supurb 32 oz.	59¢	59.0¢
White Magic 32 oz.	59¢	59.0¢
Brocade 32 oz.	63¢	63.0¢
Brocade 22 oz.	45¢	65.5¢
Supurb 22 oz.	45¢	65.5¢
White Magic 32 oz.	45¢	65.5¢
Brocade 12 oz.	27¢	72.0¢
Supurb 12 oz.	29¢	77.3¢
Ivory 32 oz.	80¢	80.0¢
Dove 22 oz.	56¢	81.5¢
Ivory 22 oz.	56¢	81.5¢
Lux 22 oz.	56¢	81.5¢
Palmolive 32 oz.	85¢	85.0¢
Ivory 12 oz.	32¢	85.3¢
Palmolive 22 oz.	60¢	87.3¢
Palmolive 12 oz.	34¢	90.7¢

Source: J. Edward Russo, "The Value of Unit Price Information," *Journal of Marketing Research* 14 (May 1977), p. 194.

LEARNING CHARACTERISTICS

The previous discussion of learning theories is obviously incomplete. Furthermore, older theories of learning are continually being revised while new ones are developing. An understanding of consumer behavior also requires an analysis of the processes involved in learning attitudes and in learning to act and make decisions. Some of these forms of learning will be discussed in later chapters. The rest of this chapter is devoted to the characteristics of learning that have emerged from previously discussed theories relevant to consumer behavior.

Generalization

Generalization in classical conditioning is the process whereby a response that has been conditioned to a specific stimulus is repeated in the presence of a similar but not identical stimulus. In the experiment by Watson discussed earlier, little Albert's fear of the white rat was generalized to other furry objects, such as a fur neckpiece and a Santa Claus mask.[41]

In information-processing theory, such generalization is considered characteristic of the integrative nature of memory. Thus a response to common knowledge that is stored in memory can be generalized to a new concept or item to which the old knowledge is relevant.[42]

Generalization suggests that marketers may transfer previous satisfactory experience from one stimulus to another, similar stimulus. Business firms use generalization through family branding techniques, as in the cases of Kraft cheeses and General Electric appliances. It is assumed that the consumer's previous satisfactory experience with a Kraft cheese or a General Electric appliance will be generalized to other Kraft cheeses or GE appliances. Marketers may also attempt to generalize favorable responses to their products by relating them to their competitor's successes. An advertising campaign for a relatively inexpensive Ford automobile declared that many consumers could not distinguish between this car and a Cadillac.

The attribution of favorable characteristics to a product because of a previous satisfactory experience with other products is similar to the halo effect, discussed in Chapter 7. In this case, however, the effect is transferred from one product to another rather than from one characteristic of a product to another characteristic of the same product.

The success of strategies incorporating generalization depends on a number of factors. Most important is the nature of individual differences. Two different memories would follow exactly the same path of development only if they received identical inputs and if identical procedures were used in organizing them. It is extremely unlikely that any two people will develop precisely the same conceptual structure to represent the world they experience.[43] Furthermore, even the nature of the input varies, as the name Kraft or General Electric may be seen or noticed under quite dissimilar circumstances.

Generalization may work to a company's disadvantage if an unfavorable experience with its product is transferred to a new product introduced by the firm. Moreover, unsatisfactory experience may be generalized to a product that is in fact different from the one the consumer disliked but is perceived to be similar. For example, it appears that perceptions based on initially low-quality instant coffee and the public's belief that caffeine extraction detracts from the taste of coffee are generalized to new low-caffeine instant coffee. In a study of the perceptions of coffee, both low-caffeine ground and low-caffeine instant were seen as having poor taste, as indicated in Figure 8.3. Earlier studies indicate that consumers' perceptions of low-caffeine coffee as having poor taste are not entirely justified by the taste characteristics of contemporary low-caffeine products. Furthermore, extensive advertising campaigns aimed at correcting this bias have obviously been very slow to change these perceptions.[44] One company appears to have been successful in removing the undesirable generalized response and replacing it with a more favorable generalization by relating the product to the successful coffee brands. In an extensive advertising campaign, Sanka proudly proclaimed, "We're the third largest coffee in America."

FIGURE 8.3   PERCEPTUAL SPACE OF SEVEN TYPES OF COFFEE

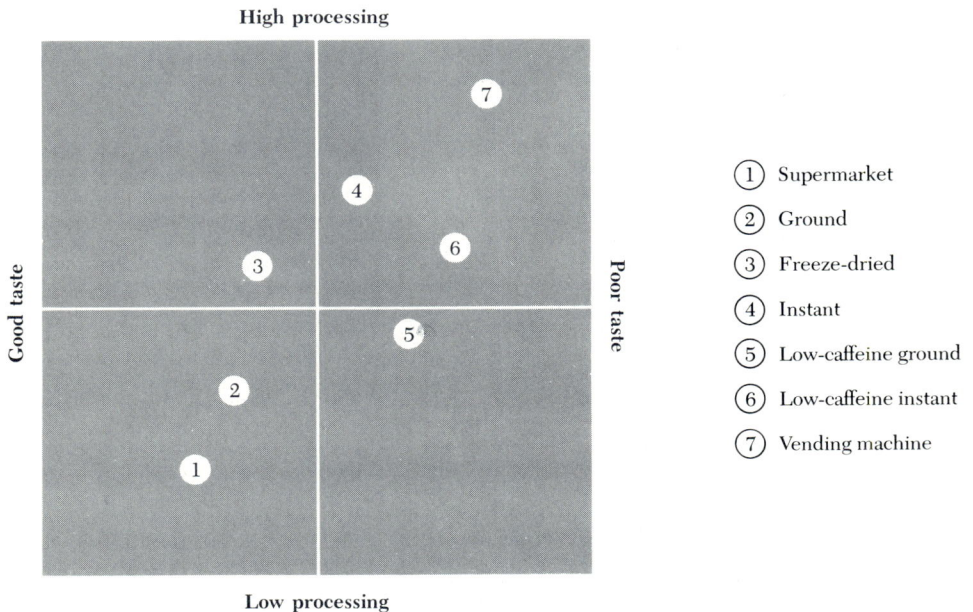

Source: Mary Lou Roberts and James R. Taylor, "Analyzing Proximity Judgments in an Experimental Design," *Journal of Marketing Research* 12 (Febraury 1975), p. 69.

Discrimination

Just as an individual learns to economize her behavior by generalizing stimuli, she also learns to respond in distinctive ways to specific stimuli. In an empirical sense, discrimination is the opposite of generalization. Discrimination is the process of responding in dissimilar ways to two similar but not identical stimuli.

It has been indicated that it is to the obvious advantage of a seller to have a pattern of cues for his offerings unlike that of his competitors, so that the expectation associated with his product will not be generalized to include the competitors' brands.

In marketing terms, the concept of discrimination is frequently employed in positioning (discussed in Chapter 7), whereby a clearly discriminative position is established for the specific product in the consumer's mind. This position can be established through product name, product or package design, price, or any of a variety of other marketing factors. Miller successfully discriminated its beer from others by making it "light"; the initial success of Procter & Gamble's potato chips was based on its uniform and unbroken chips; recently Jovan won an award for its outstanding package design, "Man and Woman"; Tiffany's continues to reign as the "expensive" jewelry outlet; and Chivas Regal is the "expensive" Scotch. (See Exhibit 8.1.) V-8 vegetable juice positioned itself as a drink for all occasions in an advertising campaign based on the slogan "Wow! I could have had a V-8."

Discrimination through positioning may also be achieved in the development of a new product. In a recent survey in which 100 of the 250 top industrial firms in *Fortune*'s 1977 list responded to the question "Why do new products succeed?" "unique appeal" ran a close second to the number-one response, "superior quality."[45] (See Table 8.4.) Firms are in the process of developing "unique appeals" in such products as vitamins for dogs that contain a contraceptive ingredient and men's socks that contain a deodorizing element.

It should be emphasized that a unique appeal does not guarantee success. In 1966 General Foods introduced Post cereals with freeze-dried fruits. Product tests had not fully revealed a problem: the fruit did not reconstitute fast enough and became soggy. General Foods lost close to $5 million.[46] Uniqueness is not enough; it must have relevance for consumers. The failure of the deodorant Mennen's with E is presumed to have been the result of consumers' lack of interest in the inclusion of a vitamin in their deodorant.

The psychological concepts of generalization and discrimination have been applied to buyers' reactions to price. Price generalization suggests that when buyers are not able to compare prices directly with those charged by competitors for similar items, they tend to evaluate prices on the basis of what they believe to be the overall price level of the store.[47] If a store's prices are believed to be higher than those of competing stores, consumers tend to believe that individual items offered by that store are relatively expensive if they have no specific information indicating otherwise.

Price discrimination may take place by direct comparison of price levels.

EXHIBIT 8.1

Chivas Regal discriminates itself as the "expensive" scotch.

TABLE 8.4 RESPONSES OF 100 TOP INDUSTRIAL FIRMS TO THE QUESTION *"WHY DO NEW PRODUCTS SUCCEED?"* BY RANK

Response	Rank	Mean of frequency
Superior quality	1	2.47
Unique appeal	2	2.63
Broad appeal	3	3.66
Good service	4	3.90
Many features, options, or uses	5	4.55
Superior advertising	6	4.95
Low price	6	4.95

Source: Elaine Sherman, "An Analysis of New Products: Success and Failure," master's thesis, Hofstra University, 1978.

One may compare the prices of competing brands sold by various retailers, or various prices charged over time for one brand in a given store. Direct comparison may not be necessary for discrimination to take place. The mere fact that a brand is advertised as price-reduced may lead to more favorable price evaluations by consumers.

In setting prices, then, stores would probably do well to consider not only the pricing of individual items, but also the need for a favorable overall price image. It also appears that uncertainty about comparative prices—resulting from lack of price information or difficulties in comparing prices—may well lead to both lack of discrimination and unfavorable price evaluations.[48] By providing information concerning a recent price decrease, then, a marketer may achieve a more favorable price evaluation than she would by just lowering the price without providing such information.

Marketers frequently use such terms as "new" and "improved" as discriminatory cues for their products. Care should be taken, however, in the use of these traditional claims. While additional research is needed, a study of such efforts indicated that promotional package copy proclaiming that the contents are "new" and "improved" has no significant effect on evaluations of certain household and personal-care products.[49] It may well be that the continuing influx of new products has deadened the impact of these frequently used words. Perhaps consumers have become satiated by "newness" and hence discount such claims. Another possible explanation is that in the past claims may have raised expectations that subsequently were not met. Should a marketer decide to designate his product as new and improved, he should be certain that these distinctive characteristics are obvious to consumers.

In addition to providing cues for discrimination, the seller must attempt to offer rewards for the consumer's response to his pattern of cues that are greater than the rewards provided by his competitors. Sometimes the perceptions of rewards may be interpreted through *sign expectancies,* that is, indications or signs that the consumer can use to anticipate a certain quality of performance from a product or service.

Consumers use many signs, some of which may be developed through their interpretation of sensations, as discussed in Chapter 7. For example, a cereal manufacturer uses sound to discriminate his cereal from his competitors'; his product, he declares, can be distinguished by its "snap, crackle, and pop." The indicated sounds may serve as a "sign expectancy" indicating that this cereal is fresher and crunchier than its competitors, and the long life of this campaign appears to attest to its effectiveness. A more recent campaign for Doritos corn chips humorously depicts their explosive crunchiness. Another apparently successful campaign suggests the thick consistency of one tomato juice by the "plopping" sounds that occur when it is poured and declares that these sounds are different from the "dripping" and "plipping" sounds of its competitors.

Some consumers have learned to use their own sign expectancies, such as the "slushing factor" by which they choose canned fruits and vegetables. When the information on the contents of the package fails to reveal the amount of liquid included in the total weight of various offerings, the consumer may discriminate by shaking the can to detect the extent of "slushiness" that can be heard. The slushier the can, the more liquid it is expected to contain.

Forgetting

To facilitate the understanding of learning, it is necessary to define two terms, *retention* and *forgetting.* "Retention" refers to the extent to which the material originally learned is still retained, and "forgetting" refers to the portion lost. It appears that most forgetting occurs soon after learning.[50] The extent and rate of forgetting, however, vary with the material that is learned.

In conditioning theories of learning, forgetting is similar to extinction. Thus the failure of a learning response to be connected with a reward will result in extinction of the response; it will be forgotten. Generally, the more frequently the unconditioned stimulus is paired with the conditioned stimulus, the more quickly learning occurs. Repetition, under this concept, may be seen as a means of both increasing retention and reducing forgetting.

REPETITION

If marketers could determine the amount of repetition that is necessary for the learning of the desired responses, such as awareness of a product, favorable reaction, and even purchase, such information would be beneficial both in increasing the effectiveness of their marketing efforts and in eliminating waste. That is, they might determine that a small number of exposures have little effect on learning and that a great many are unnecessary to achieve a desired learning objective.

The effects of repetition on consumer behavior have been most widely studied in the field of advertising. Many studies have been conducted to determine the amount of repetition of messages necessary to induce the desired response; unfortunately, results are not definitive. Research conducted in the 1960s indicated that awareness and learning peak when a person is exposed to verbal stimuli. The point beyond which they begin to decline is called the satiation point. These studies did not, however, provide a specific frequency at which satiation occurs.[51]

The shape of the repetition function may vary with the product advertised, the appeal used, the audience involved, the media setting, and what is being measured.

A study by Michael Ray and Alan Sawyer indicated that repetition may be more effective in creating awareness than in influencing purchase intention. The kind of goods being advertised may also influence the effectiveness of repetition: repetitive advertising created more awareness of convenience goods than of shopping goods.[52]

More recently it has been hypothesized that an individual requires a minimum of three exposures to a commercial to learn its message.[53] During the first exposure, the viewer probably notices the novel commercial situation and may notice the brand advertised. The second exposure may result in partial learning of the message and a personally evaluative "what of it" type of response. The third exposure acts both as a reminder and as the beginning of disengagement.

What happens in the range of exposures immediately above three is not clear. It is possible, for example, that between four and ten exposures, additional learning may not take place, but attitude reinforcement may. Evidence seems to indicate that more than ten exposures during a four-week period may actually have a negative effect. Learning may decline as an individual becomes satiated.

Research by Du Pont supported this theory and suggested that learning tends to peak somewhere between three and five exposures. Once the amount of information learned is maximized, additional exposures tend to result in negative consumer reaction.

Thus repetition alone does not ensure against forgetting. Forgetting may occur as a defense mechanism. It may also stem from dissociation. When a message has been received several times, the consumer may feel she has become familiar with it and may devote less and less attention to the message with each additional exposure. If the consumer adopts this strategy, she is dissociating the most overt cues of the message from other components and thus may eventually forget some of the latter—copy content, for instance—or overlook some important new attributes of a message (for example, a change in price).[54]

Consumers become satiated with stimuli; standardized and repetitive advertising messages tend to become boring. Some responses, regardless of the extent and degree of reinforcement, tend to become less satisfying over time. Thus forgetting may occur even with repetition.

To offset the consumer's tendency to forget through dissociation, advertisers frequently vary the presentation of their messages even though the messages remain the same. Cora asserts to a variety of visitors to her general store the good taste of Maxwell House Coffee, while the peripatetic Mrs. Olson proclaims the superiority of Folger's to various couples in various settings. And even Mr. Whipple has begun to notice that Charmin is also being squeezed in Hoffmeier's store. The effect of repetition on attitudes and attitude change will be discussed in Chapter 12.

FORGETTING IN SHORT-TERM MEMORY

In cognitive theory, forgetting is said to be due to lack of rehearsal in short-term memory. Rehearsal, the silent repetition of material, is one way to improve retention in short-term memory. Rehearsal can occur, however, only if the amount of material to be retained is very small. Forgetting in short-term memory may result from interference of other material or simply from the passage of time.[55]

Forgetting by Interference. Forgetting in short-term memory may occur because of the arrival of a new item. If, for example, you refer to a telephone book to find someone to repair your television set, you may see several telephone numbers but pay little attention to most of them. Once you have selected a repairman, you will mentally rehearse his number so that you may dial it. Once you have completed your call, the telephone rings and someone invites you to dinner next Friday. The arrival of this new information may "bump" the repairman's telephone number from your short-term memory.

As we saw earlier, short-term memory may retain between five and seven bits of information at one time. Marketers should take special note of consumers' limited ability to learn brand names, packages, advertising appeals, and the like because of the limited capacity of short-term memory. The tendency toward advertising clutter in television broadcasting (the grouping of a number of commercials so that they appear one after another during a station break) was seen as the major factor in the decline of television copy-testing (recall) scores during the 1960s.[56]

Furthermore, the increase in the number of commercials appearing in any one time period, caused by decreases in commercial length from 60 seconds to 30, 20, and even 10 seconds, is considered responsible for the rise in misidentification of brands advertised on television.[57] To limit the possibility of brand misidentification, many broadcasters offer "product protection" to their advertisers, which means they will not present competitors' products within 15 minutes of each other. This practice has been questioned by the Federal Trade Commission as anticompetitive.

Retention and Retrieval

As we saw earlier, material that enters long-term memory is more or less permanently stored. Forgetting in long-term memory, therefore, is seen as a failure to retrieve. Thus the problem for the marketer is to get new information into long-term memory so that it can be effectively integrated and retrieved when needed.

Although little is known of the way such activities occur, it appears that motives play a most important role in determining when the retrieval process starts and how it is sustained. In addition, the "rules" the consumer uses to guide information processing, her knowledge of the product class and available alternatives, and her predispositions all play their roles.[58] These factors will be discussed in later chapters. This section suggests some techniques that may aid in effective integration and retrieval of information. They are based on the earlier discussion of the factors that affect transfer of information to long-term memory (meaningfulness, similarity, and relevance) and those that relate to integration and retrieval (semantic networks and list structures).

MNEMONICS

For information to be meaningful, it must have an organized structure. *Mnemonics* is a method for remembering items that imposes a structure of organization on the material being memorized. In fact, the point of all mnemonic devices is organization. One mnemonic device is the *key-word* system, wherein certain key words are associated with the items to be remembered. The key words may be incorporated into vivid images in a story, and they frequently are alliterative. Du Pont's "Better things for better living," Clairol's "Does she or doesn't she?" and "Which twin has the Toni?" are all parts of successful, long-remembered advertising campaigns. More recently, Prell shampoo has made effective use of "I was flat til I went fluffy." Alliteration is not necessary for key-word association, however: "I'd rather fight than switch," "The disadvantages of Benson and Hedges," "Try it, you'll like it," and the single word "gusto" are also effective.

Another mnemonic device is the *method of loci*, in which people or objects to be remembered are imagined in specific spots in a familiar location. It requires that one walk, in one's imagination, through a familiar environment and put items to be remembered in conspicuous places. This method works because it takes advantage of the organization already present in a person's memory. Kool cigarettes have used a long-continuing campaign that provides a method of loci for the cigarette smoker, who views himself as relaxing in the woods near cool, idyllic waters. (See Exhibit 8.2.) Morton Salt continues to note, "When it rains it pours." By naming its new line of cosmetics Charlie, Revlon succeeded in creating an imaginative picture of a particular life-style for the user.

Many of the popular mnemonic devices rely on visual *imagery*. (See Exhibit 8.3.) It has been learned that people do learn verbal materials better when they are connected with some visual image. Manufacturers incorporate such imagery in their brand names, as in Thick and Zesty tomato sauce and Easy-Off oven cleaner, and in such advertising campaigns as "Good to the last drop."

Imagery may be a powerful aid in the recall of verbal material, not just be-

EXHIBIT 8.2

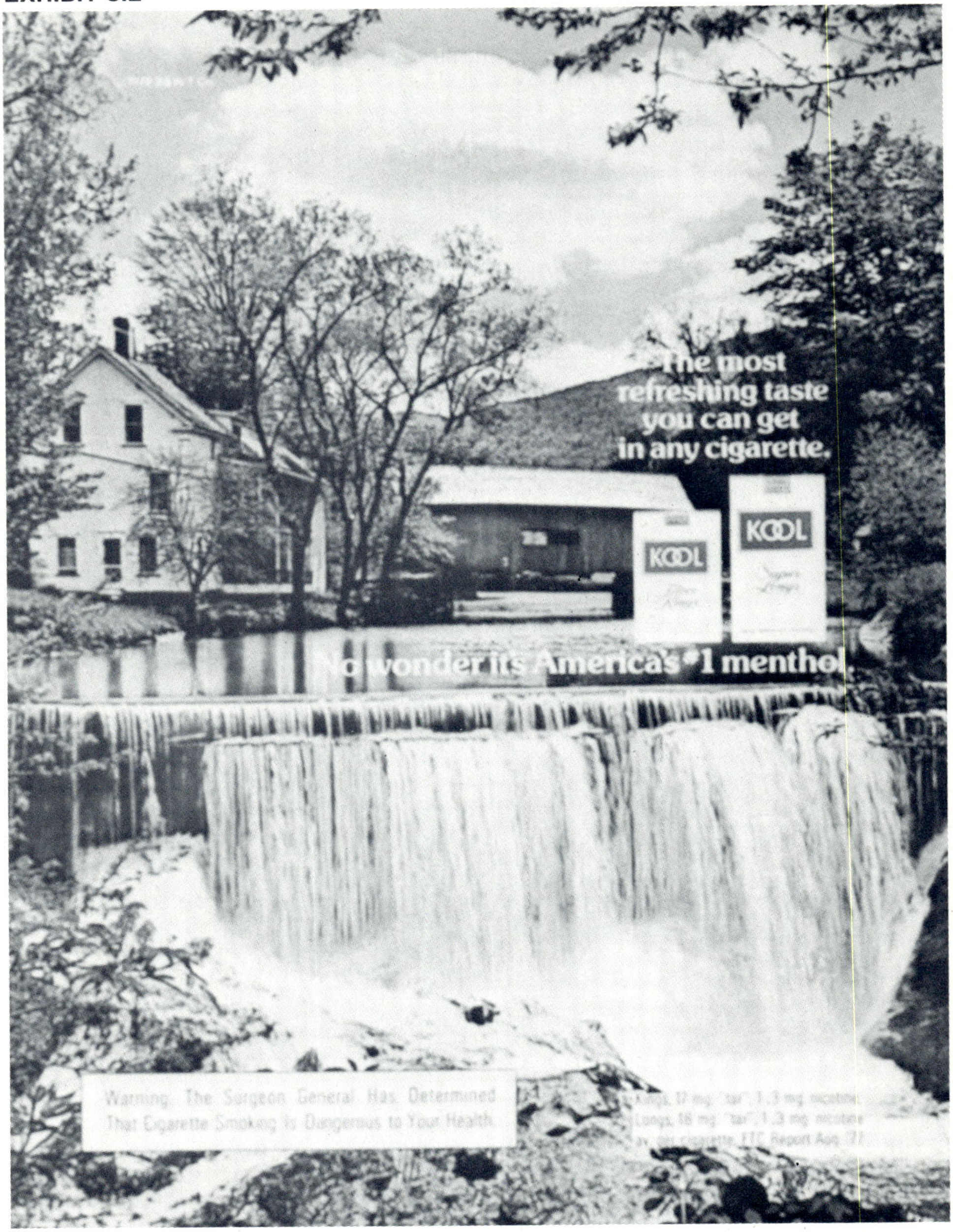

Cigarette ads make use of the method of loci.

EXHIBIT 8.3

GIVE YOUR BATHROOM A BUBBLE BATH.

When the Scrubbing Bubbles in Dow Bathroom Cleaner give your bathroom a bubble bath, they don't take time to relax.

They dig in fast to give dirt the brushoff.

They disinfect and deodorize too.

All that, without ever leaving any grit. What's more, they never scratch. They're kind to chrome, porcelain, even fiberglass.

So give your bathroom the shine of its life. With Dow Bathroom Cleaner.

The Scrubbing Bubbles work hard so you don't have to. And they can't wait to get on the job.

Advertisers use visual imagery.

cause images are inherently memorable, but also because imagery is processed in a nonlinguistic location in the memory. You are more likely to remember words plus images than words alone for the same reason that it is better to leave two reminder notes for yourself—one at home and one in your pocket—than to leave only one. The two notes make it twice as likely that you will remember the message. A particularly successful use of this mnemonic device was a picture of a finger pressing into a soft Q in the printed brand name "Q-tip."

One of the prime requisites for radio commercials is the creation of word imagery, since the time allocated for the message is short. To improve the learning situation, words rich in visual imagery are used so that recall of the message can emanate from a nonlinguistic as well as a linguistic location. This factor is not quite so important in television commercials, where the verbal message is supported by a visual counterpart.

POSITIONING

Meaningfulness, as well as discrimination, can be created through positioning, discussed in Chapter 7. Through positioning, a manufacturer may place his product within the appropriate product space, thus indicating where it should fit in the consumer's semantic network. A company may position its new car as "economical" or "similar to a foreign sports car" through its advertising and promotional efforts. Dannon built brand preference for its yogurt by adjusting its positioning to meet market needs. Dannon was first promoted as a diet food, next as a natural food, and then as a fresh and nutritious snack. A product whose sales have appeared to reach the saturation level may be repositioned in a new product space. Arm & Hammer's Baking Soda was repositioned as a deodorant for refrigerators, and witch hazel is being repositioned from an aid for minor cuts to a more meaningful product space as an astringent aid to complexions.

QUADRANT ANALYSIS

A technique incorporating concepts similar to multidimensional scaling may be helpful in determining relevance. "Relevance" refers to the degree to which information relates to a concept the buyer values highly.

Through the use of quadrant analysis, or more specifically importance–satisfaction analysis, efforts are made to determine how important each one of a series of attributes is to consumers, and how satisfied consumers are with the manner in which each attribute is incorporated in products or services currently available. This technique places attributes in one of four quadrants of a grid according to consumers' ratings. The grid is made up of two axes, representing the dimensions of satisfaction and importance. (See Figure 8.4.)

The best potential for competitive advantage appears to be in quadrant A. Attributes positioned here represent product or service characteristics that consumers consider important but do not find adequately represented in the market-

FIGURE 8.4   QUADRANT ANALYSIS GRID

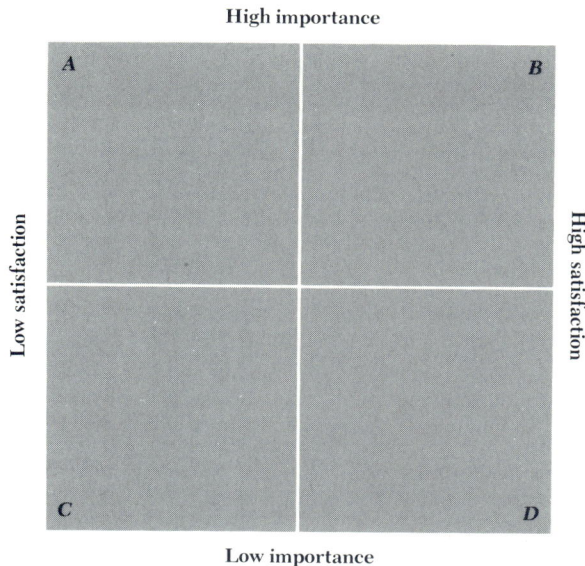

place. Quadrant *B* includes attributes that are highly important but are well satisfied by available products, and thus are not likely candidates for a competitive strategy. Attributes in quadrant *C* are of little importance and are offered unsatisfactorily. The potential for improving these attributes exists, but as they are of little importance to consumers, they have a lower priority for a competitive strategy than those in quadrant *A*. Quadrant *D* offers the least likely candidates for an effective marketing program, since it includes characteristics that are low in importance to consumers, yet are presented to them in a highly satisfactory manner.

This technique was applied to the selection of important attributes to be stressed by an automobile dealer's service department.[59] Since all of the attributes dealt with performance of the service department, the study was designated as importance–performance analysis.

A literature search and conversations with service and sales personnel and factory representatives identified fourteen attributes that were felt to be relevant to service department patronage. More than 600 respondents who had purchased new cars from the dealer within the last two years were then asked two questions about each attribute: "How important is this feature?" and "How well did the dealer perform?"

The mean ratings for each of these attributes in terms of importance and performance are shown in Table 8.5 and are plotted on the importance–performance grid in Figure 8.5.

**TABLE 8.5   IMPORTANCE AND PERFORMANCE RATINGS OF 14 SER-
VICE ATTRIBUTES**

Attribute number	Attribute description	Mean importance rating[a]	Mean performance rating[b]
1	Job done right the first time	3.83	2.63
2	Fast action on complaints	3.63	2.73
3	Prompt warranty work	3.60	3.15
4	Able to do any job needed	3.56	3.00
5	Service available when needed	3.41	3.05
6	Courteous and friendly service	3.41	3.29
7	Car ready when promised	3.38	3.03
8	Perform only necessary work	3.37	3.11
9	Low prices on service	3.29	2.00
10	Clean up after service work	3.27	3.02
11	Convenient to home	2.52	2.25
12	Convenient to work	2.43	2.49
13	Courtesy buses and rental cars	2.37	2.35
14	Send out maintenance notices	2.05	3.33

[a] Ratings obtained from a four-point scale of "extremely important," "important," "slightly important," and "not important."
[b] Ratings obtained from a four-point scale of "excellent," "good," "fair," and "poor." A "no basis for judgment" category was also provided.

Source: John A. Martilla and John C. James, "Importance–Performance Analysis," *Journal of Marketing* 41 (January 1977), p. 78.

The importance–performance grid is helpful in highlighting the relevance of the attributes in each of the four quadrants:

A. *Concentrate here:* Customers feel that low service prices (attribute 9) are very important, but indicate low satisfaction with the dealer's performance.

B. *Keep up the good work:* Customers consider courteous and friendly service (attribute 6) important and are pleased with the dealer's performance.

C. *Low priority:* Although the dealer is rated low in his provision of courtesy buses and rental cars (attribute 13), the customers do not perceive this feature to be very important.

**FIGURE: 8.5   IMPORTANCE-PERFORMANCE GRID FOR 14
SERVICE ATTRIBUTES**

Extremely important

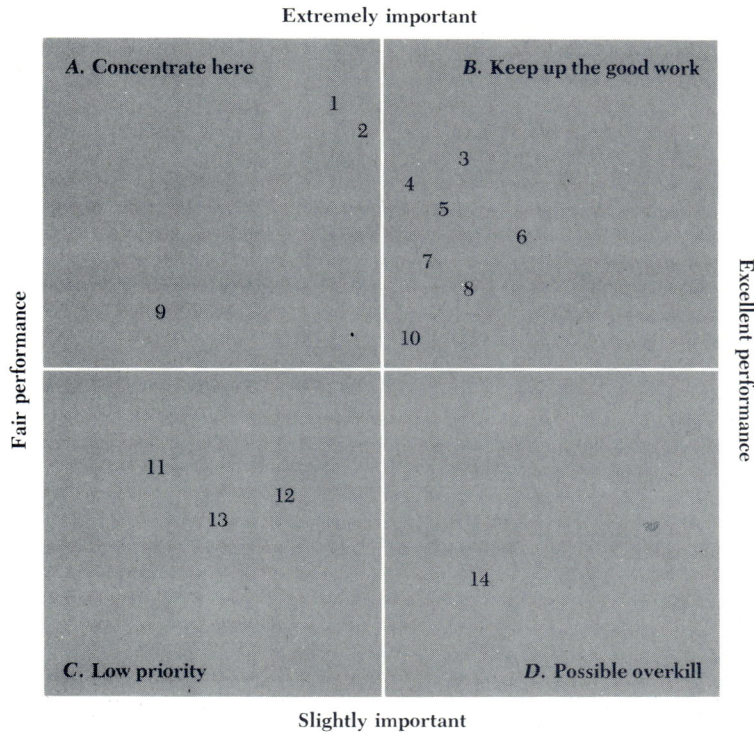

Source: John A. Martilla and John C. James, "Importance–Performance Analysis," *Journal of Marketing* 41 (January 1977), p. 78.

> *D. Possible overkill:* The dealer is judged to be doing a good job of sending
> out maintenance notices (attribute 14) but customers attach only slight
> importance to them.

A successful marketing strategy based on this analysis might be to concentrate on attribute 9. Consumers perceive low prices as very important and judge
the extent to which they are offered as only fair. A strategy for the dealer who
charges low prices might be to use informative advertising to indicate that his
rates are lower than those available at service stations. Such an approach might
accelerate learning, since the information is clearly relevant.

COMPARISON ADVERTISING

As we noted earlier, research into the development of appropriate list structures
for effective integration and retrieval of information is limited. Nevertheless, on

the assumption that some consumers may prefer the listing of attributes, comparison advertising offers a potentially useful device.

In comparison advertising (sometimes called comparative advertising), a manufacturer explicitly identifies one or more competitors of his advertised brand and claims superiority for his own on the basis of one or more attributes.

Such advertising contains a number of elements that may affect the integration and retrieval of information. Since comparisons are usually made with reference to top brands, such advertising provides consumers with a means of categorizing information about the manufacturer's brand and suggests its similarity to the top sellers. Comparative ads for automobiles, for example, declare that "the Ford Granada consistently rode as quietly as the Mercedes-Benz" and that "up front, a Volvo has as much legroom as a Cadillac de Ville. In back, as much as a Buick Electra." Bristol Myers claims that "in the early minutes Bufferin puts much more pain reliever into the bloodstream than Bayer or Anacin."

It should be noted, however, that there are legal and ethical considerations in the use of comparative advertising claims. Both competitors and the FTC have instituted complaints against questionable comparative claims. Furthermore, questions concerning consumers' reactions to comparative advertising and its effectiveness remain to be answered. A recent study relevant to consumers' perceptions of the usefulness of comparative advertising indicated that they tend to consider it more important in regard to shopping goods than convenience goods, since the former tend to involve attributes they find more difficult to judge. A laboratory experiment on the effectiveness of comparative advertising revealed that comparative advertising can enhance recall to some extent.[60] The results indicated, however, that consumers may perceive the claims in comparative ads to be of low credibility. Because of the complexity of comparative advertising, definitive answers to these and other issues require much more research.[61]

MEASURING LEARNING

It is frequently important to marketers to determine to what extent people have retained information about their products, services, advertising, and general communications. Two basic methods for testing memory are recall and recognition.

Recall

In a recall test a person is asked to retrieve the items that were learned with no helpful information other than the particular instructions in the experiment. For example, "Recall four brand names for coffee"; "Recall two commercials you saw on television last night."

In general, recall tests show the poorest performance among memory tests. A person may fail completely at the recall of an item even though there is some knowledge of that item within her memory system.

Recall is widely used as a measure of advertising effectiveness, as the recall of an advertisement is believed to be a necessary condition of change in attitude and behavior. Some advertisers hypothesize that if the purpose of advertising is to sell, it must communicate, and that the ads that communicate best are the ones that produce the greatest memory impression.[62]

Other researchers have assembled data that contradict these assumptions. On the basis of several studies, Haskins concluded that "learning and recall of factual information from mass communication occur. However, recall and retention measures seem, at best, irrelevant to the ultimate effects desired, the changing of attitude and behavior."[63] There appears to be general agreement, however, that recall and recognition measures may be used to establish the degree to which an advertisement attracted attention.[64] Yet it should be noted that variations may occur in such measurements as a result of the intervening variable (for example, the medium used) between the particular advertisement and the recall effect.

The efficiency of increasing the length of an advertising message to increase advertising recall scores has been examined. Studies have indicated that a 60-second commercial resulted in recall of more sales points than a 30-second one. Nonetheless, advertisers have tended to shorten commercials to 45, 30, 15, and 10 seconds. The current most popular length is 30 seconds. When the findings of the studies of the length of commercials and their recall scores are examined against a recall–cost criterion, the heavy use of 30-second commercials appears to be justified. Even though longer commercials may produce better recall scores than shorter ones, the marketing manager must consider the cost of each message unit. Recall of the 60-second commercial is rarely twice that of the 30-second one.[65] Thus, if the recall score of a 60-second spot is one-third greater than that of a 30-second spot, the marketer must determine how much he is willing to pay for the one-minute ad. The answer appears to depend most heavily on the advertising objectives, the complexity of the message, and the duration of the campaign.

Recognition

In a recognition test a person is presented with something and asked whether he has seen or heard it before. Recognition tests of memory are generally thought to be more sensitive measures of the amount a person has stored in memory than other methods, because more information is presented to the person, and the only task is to decide whether the presented information matches what is already in memory.

Recognition is also used in tests of the effectiveness of advertising. One of the most widely used methods for testing print media is the Starch Readership Service. This service attempts to appraise the readership of magazine advertisements, on the premise that whatever else the advertisement is designed to accomplish, its initial goal is to be read.

The studies are conducted through personal interviews of from 200 to 300 people per issue. The respondents qualify themselves as readers by telling something of the content of the magazine. The respondent is asked to go through the magazine page by page with the interviewer, giving the following information about each advertisement:

> "Noted": the reader remembers having previously seen the advertisement in the issue.
>
> "Associated": the reader also saw or read some part of the advertisement that clearly indicates the brand or company.
>
> "Read most": the reader read half or more of the written material.

These classifications are then combined to provide a "recognition index report," which presents the results for each advertisement for men and women separately.

Obviously, the most important benefit offered by this service is the information that the advertising is being read. The accuracy of these data depends on the extent of error that occurs during the interviewing and recording procedure. The noted scores, the most widely used Starch data, may be affected by factors other than the content of the advertisements—for example, the number of advertisements in the issue and their tendency to generate fatigue and boredom in respondents, the degree of reader interest generated by each issue's editorial content, the time spent reading each issue, and the exposure to the same and similar advertisements in other media.

Whether recall or recognition is the more desirable test of memory is subject to debate. Herbert Krugman has proposed a theory of "low involvement" with advertising that suggests that learning can occur as faint impressions from television commercials build up into an in-store-triggered purchase, with very little trace of the advertising effect before the purchase.[66] And this idea may extend to print advertisements. Thus, quick and faint perceptions of product advertising may do their job even when they are not remembered. Krugman suggests that as these types of quick exposure seem to result in the storing of a picture memory without words, recognition is a better test than recall, which requires that the picture be described in words.

This concept will no doubt become further developed as a result of research currently being conducted on the specialized functions of the right and left hemispheres of the brain.[67] It appears that while reading and speaking are functions of the left hemisphere of the brain, perception of images is a function of the right hemisphere. Thus the medium of print is seen as a left-brain function and television largely or relatively a right-brain function. Furthermore, high involvement appears to be a left-brain activity; low involvement, a right-brain activity, may result in learning through TV commercials without "recall." This theory may influence the kinds of tests that may best be used to determine learning, as well as the relationship between attitude change and purchase behavior, which will be discussed in Chapter 12.

Protocols

The obvious difficulty in studying the effects of learning on consumer behavior and problem solving is that much of what goes on is not directly observable. People go through their internal mental operations quietly, by themselves. One way of getting around this difficulty is to have people present their thought processes by asking them to describe aloud what they are doing as they attempt to make a purchase. The result is a word-by-word compilation of their verbalized thought processes, or *verbal protocol*.[68] Although interpretation of these protocols is difficult, they may provide useful information about the thought processes involved in information processing and behavior.

Protocols may be obtained by having the consumer think out loud while in the process of actually making choices. Such data potentially allow a great deal of information to be collected on the use of memory, whether consumers build rules for making such choices on the spot, and so on. In addition, the actual choice process may be observed. The use of protocols in analyzing consumer behavior has been limited but may increase in the future.

One recent study gathered protocols from consumers while they shopped for groceries.[69] The protocol data were then given to judges, who attempted to categorize the data by the nature of the information processing used. The results of this study suggested several biases and limitations in protocol research. According to the researcher, however, this exploratory study suggested ways in which the methodology may be improved. Consumers should be instructed in making protocols, for instance, and told not to provide rationales when they are buying what they always buy. Judges, for their part, can be told to ignore obvious retrospection—explanations of why the consumer bought the particular brand in the first place, because such reasoning is not relevant at that time. It is possible that protocol research may provide useful insights if the methodology is refined and improved. This may be particularly true when such protocols are gathered at the moment of shopping, since some consumer-behavior researchers feel that information gathered in more artificial situations, such as surveys and experiments, is likely to be biased.

SUMMARY

A variety of theories of learning have applications to consumer behavior. Conditioning theories assume that the stimuli that occur in the marketplace can in some manner be linked to consumer responses. Classical conditioning concerns involuntary behavior while instrumental conditioning concerns voluntary behavior. Reinforcement is an important factor in instrumental conditioning and is frequently equated to reward. Behavior that is reinforced tends to be repeated.

Cognitive learning theory assumes that responses to a stimulus vary with the consumer's knowledge of his environment and his expectations regarding possible outcomes.

The heart of cognitive learning is memory. Memory has three aspects: the sensory storage system, which interprets arriving sensory information and provides the means for the processing of perception (discussed in Chapter 7); the short-term memory system, which has a limited capacity and stores information for a relatively short period of time; and the long-term memory system, whose storage capacity and time limit are extensive but undetermined. Long-term memory is a repository of an individual's knowledge, beliefs, values, skills, and ability to interpret and understand.

Cognitive learning is equated to information processing. As applied to consumer behavior, it is concerned with the manner in which consumers store, retrieve, and use product information.

Product information to be stored is encoded by consumers on the basis of informational cues—size, color, brand image, and the like. It is stored in long-term memory in the form of integrated networks called semantic networks or list structures. Motivation, experience, expectations, and individual differences all influence the manner in which information is stored and retrieved from long-term memory. Meaningfulness, organization, relevance, and similarity seem to play important parts in the retention and retrieval of information.

Several concepts that have emerged from learning theory are relevant to consumer behavior and useful to marketers. Stimuli can be generalized—that is, the individual may respond the same way to similar but not identical stimuli. Discrimination also occurs: the individual responds in different ways to somewhat similar stimuli.

According to conditioning theories of learning, if a learning response is not reinforced (or rewarded), it will end in extinction (or be forgotten). Repetition may increase retention and reduce forgetting. Repetition alone, however, may not ensure against forgetting, since repetitive messages may become boring and less satisfying to consumers.

Cognitive psychologists assume that material that enters long-term memory is more or less permanently stored. Assuring that information is properly retained and can be retrieved when needed is of major importance. Various techniques may be used for facilitating the retention and retrieval of information—mnemonics, positioning, quadrant analysis, and comparative advertising, for example.

Two basic methods for testing memory are recall and recognition. Recall requires a person to retrieve an item that was learned with no other helpful information. In recognition, a person is presented with an item and asked whether he has seen it or heard of it before. Protocol is a technique useful in examining the effects of learning on consumer behavior and problem solving, since it requires consumers to describe aloud what they are doing as they attempt to solve a purchase problem.

DISCUSSION QUESTIONS

1. Describe marketing strategies that may involve each of the three learning theories discussed in this chapter.

2. From a marketing perspective, what are the significant differences between the long-term and short-term memory systems?

3. What are some of the intrinsic cues you would use to make judgments about a refrigerator? Extrinsic cues?

4. Provide a simple semantic network for toothpaste.

5. Develop a brand-organized and attribute-organized list structure for toothpaste.

6. How are generalization and discrimination interrelated in brand-name decisions?

7. Describe some techniques used by marketers to enhance learning and retention.

8. Which do you consider to be the superior measuring device for learning—recognition or recall? Why?

NOTES

1. Ronald D. Michman, "Behavioral Theories and Alternative Strategies of Product Differentiation and Market Segmentation," *Business Perspectives* 6 (Winter 1970), pp. 24–27.

2. James Deese and Stewart H. Hulse, *The Psychology of Learning*, 3d ed. (New York: McGraw-Hill, 1967), p. 10.

3. Ibid., p. 220.

4. Gregory A. Kimble, *Hilgard and Marquis' Conditioning and Learning*, 2d ed. (New York: Appleton-Century-Crofts, 1968), p. 24.

5. Michael L. Ray and Peter H. Webb, "Three Learning Traditions and Their Applications in Marketing," in *1974 Combined Proceedings of the American Marketing Association*, ed. Ronald C. Curhan, ser. 36 (Chicago, 1975), pp. 100–103.

6. Deese and Hulse, *Psychology of Learning*, pp. 10–11.

7. Peter H. Lindsay and Donald A. Norman, *Human Information Processing: An Introduction to Psychology* (New York: Academic Press, 1977), p. 500.

8. W. K. Estes, *Handbook of Learning* (New York: Halsted, 1975), vol. 1, p. 25.

9. Ibid., p. 253.

10. William L. Wilkie, "Consumer Information Processing: Issues for Public Policy Makers," in *Research for Consumer Policy: Proceedings Conducted by the Center for Policy Alternatives, Massachusetts Institute of Technology*, ed. William Michael Denney and Robert T. Lund, for National Science Foundation (prepared for Center of Policy Alternatives, Massachusetts Institute of Technology, Cambridge, Mass., 1978), p. 88.

11. Lindsay and Norman, *Human Information Processing*, p. 502.

12. Estes, *Handbook of Learning*, vol. 1, p. 12.

13. Lindsay and Norman, *Human Information Processing*, p. 499.

14. Ibid., p. 304.

15. John A. Howard, *Consumer Behavior: Application of Theory* (New York: McGraw-Hill, 1977), pp. 74–75.

16. Jacob Jacoby, George J. Szybillo, and Jacqueline Busato-Schach, "Information Acquisition Behavior in Brand Choice Situations," *Journal of Consumer Research* 3 (March 1977), pp. 209–216.

17. Howard, *Consumer Behavior*, p. 76.

18. Lindsay and Norman, *Human Information Processing*, p. 339.

19. Eric J. Johnson and J. Edward Russo, "The Organization of Product Information in Memory Identification by Recall Times," in *Advances in Consumer Research*, vol. 5, ed. H. Keith Hunt (Ann Arbor: Association for Consumer Research, 1978), pp. 79–86.

20. Jerry Olson, "Theories of Information Encoding and Storage: Implications for Marketing and Public Policy," paper presented at the Conference on the Effect of Information on Consumer and Market Behavior, Carnegie-Mellon University, 1977.

21. Johnson and Russo, "Organization of Product Information," p. 79.

22. Francesco M. Nicosia, *Advertising, Management and Society: A Business Point of View* (New York: McGraw-Hill, 1974), p. 252.

23. George J. Szybillo and Jacob Jacoby, "Intrinsic versus Extrinsic Cues as Determinants of Perceived Product Quality," *Journal of Applied Psychology* 59 (February 1974), pp. 74–77.

24. Lindsay and Norman, *Human Information Processing*, pp. 351, 385.

25. Ibid., p. 385.

26. Howard, *Consumer Behavior*, pp. 47, 148.

27. James R. Bettman and Jacob Jacoby, "Patterns of Processing in Consumer Information Acquisition," in *Advances in Consumer Research*, vol. 3, ed. Beverlee B. Anderson (Association for Consumer Research, 1976), p. 318.

28. Johnson and Russo, "Organization of Product Information," p. 80.

29. William J. McGuire, "Some Internal Psychological Factors Influencing Consumer Choice," *Journal of Consumer Research* 2 (March 1976), p. 311.

30. Howard, *Consumer Behavior*, p. 32.

31. James R. Bettman and Pradeep Kakkar, "The Effects of Information Presentation Format on Consumer Information Acquisition Strategies," *Journal of Consumer Research* 3 (March 1977), pp. 233–240.

32. Johnson and Russo, "Organization of Product Information."

33. Wilkie, "Consumer Information Processing," p. 104.

34. Ibid., p. 102.

35. J. Edward Russo, Gene Kreiser, and Sally Miyashita, "An Effective Display of Unit Price Information," *Journal of Marketing* 39 (April 1975), pp. 11–19.

36. Howard, *Consumer Behavior*, p. 81.

37. Bettman and Kakkar, "Effects of Information Presentation Format," p. 233.

38. "Public Policy and Product Information: Summary Findings," from *Consumer Research*, a report prepared for ANA National Science Foundation Research Application Directorate (RANN) (Washington, D.C.: Government Printing Office), p. 11. Consumer information processing will be discussed in greater detail in Chapter 14.

39. Bobby J. Calder, Thomas S. Robertson, and John R. Rossiter, "Children's Consumer Information Processing," *Communication Research* 2 (July 1975), pp. 307–316; Lynn W. Phillips and Brian Sternthal, "Age Differences in Information Processing: A Perspective on the Aged Consumer," *Journal of Marketing Research* 14 (November 1977), pp. 444–457.

40. Jacob Jacoby, "Information Load and Decision Quality: Some Contested Issues," *Journal of Marketing Research* 14 (November 1977), pp. 569–573.

41. Kimble, Hilgard, and Marquis, *Conditioning and Learning*, pp. 328, 424.

42. Lindsay and Norman, *Human Information Processing*, p. 404.

43. Ibid., p. 405.

44. Mary Lou Roberts and James R. Taylor, "Analyzing Proximity Judgments in the Experimental Design," *Journal of Marketing Research* 12 (February 1975), pp. 68–72.

45. Elaine Sherman, "An Analysis of New Products: Success and Failures," master's thesis, Hofstra University, 1978.

46. Theodore Angelus, "Why Do Most Products Fail?" *Advertising Age*, March 24, 1969, p. 85.

47. F. E. Brown, "Price Image versus Price Reality," *Journal of Marketing Research* 6 (May 1969), pp. 185–191.

48. Harry Nystrom, Hans Tamsons, and Robert Thams, "An Experiment in Price Generalization and Discrimination," *Journal of Marketing Research* 12 (May 1975), pp. 177–181.

49. Michael L. Dean, James F. Engel, and W. Wayne Talarzyk, "The Influence of Package Copy Claims on Consumer Products," *Journal of Marketing* 36 (April 1972), pp. 34–39.

50. Deese and Hulse, *Psychology of Learning*, p. 382.

51. Howard Kamin, "Advertising Reach and Frequency," *Journal of Advertising Research* 18 (February 1978), pp. 21–25.

52. Michael L. Ray and Alan G. Sawyer, "Repetition in Media Models: A Laboratory Technique," *Journal of Marketing Research* 8 (February 1971), pp. 20–29.

53. Herbert Krugman, "Why Three Exposures May Be Enough," *Journal of Advertising Research* 12 (December 1972), pp. 11–14.

54. Francesco M. Nicosia, *Consumer Decision Processes: Marketing and Advertising Implications* (Englewood Cliffs, N.J.: Prentice-Hall, 1966), p. 170.

55. Lindsay and Norman, *Human Information Processing*, p. 320.

56. Russell I. Haley, "Beyond Benefit Segmentation," *Journal of Advertising Research* 2 (August 1971), p. 5.

57. Harry McMahan, "Brand Misidentification Grows with Clutter of 30 Spots," *Advertising Age*, May 10, 1971, pp. 53–54.

58. Wilkie, "Consumer Information Processing," p. 107.

59. John A. Martilla and John C. James, "Importance–Performance Analysis," *Journal of Marketing* 41 (January 1977), pp. 77–79.

60. V. Kanti Prasad, "Communications-Effectiveness of Comparative Advertising: A Laboratory Analysis," *Journal of Marketing Research* 13 (May 1976), pp. 128–137.

61. Michael Etgar and Stephen A. Goodwin, "Comparative Advertising: Issues and Problems," in *Advances in Consumer Research*, vol. 5, ed. Hunt, pp. 63–71.

62. R. C. Lavidge and G. A. Steiner, "A Model for Predictive Measurements of Advertising Effectiveness," *Journal of Marketing* (October 1961), pp. 59–62.

63. J. B. Haskins, "Factual Recall as a Measure of Advertising Effectiveness," *Journal of Advertising Research* 4 (March 1964), pp. 2–8.

64. Michael Perry and Arnon Perry, "Ad Recall: Biased Measure of Media?" *Journal of Advertising Research* 16 (June 1976), pp. 21–26.

65. James E. Wiek, "Advertising Recall as Influenced by the Number, Length, and Position of Commercials," *1974 Combined Proceedings*, ser. 56 (Chicago: American Marketing Association, 1975), pp. 406–410.

66. Herbert E. Krugman, "Memory without Recall, Exposure without Perception," *Journal of Advertising Research* 17 (1977), pp. 7–11.

67. R. W. Sperry, "Lateral Specialization of Cerebral Function in the Surgically Separated Hemispheres," in *The Psychophysiology of Thinking*, ed. F. J. McGuigan and R. A. Schoonover (New York: Academic Press, 1973), pp. 209–229.

68. Lindsay and Norman, *Human Information Processing*, p. 544.

69. James R. Bettman and Michel A. Zins, "Constructive Processes in Consumer Choice," *Journal of Consumer Research* 4 (September 1977), pp. 75–85.

CHAPTER 9

MOTIVATION

Over two generations ago, in St. Louis, Missouri, a young man in an obscure chemical firm suggested a magazine advertisement to his employer. It was simple. A group of people are seen talking together at a party. Apart from the group is a young man, alone and unsmiling. Beneath the picture is the caption: "Even his best friend won't tell him."[1] The ad appeared and Lambert Pharmacal Company ultimately became a giant in the industry, as Listerine continued to be sold as a mouthwash, a gargle, a dandruff repellent, and even an antifungal cure for athlete's foot. The message in the ad can be viewed as triggering the need to avoid feelings of inferiority among others and as indicating that the use of Listerine is the best means of satisfying that need.

Advertisements designed to trigger security motives (for example, situations to be avoided) currently abound. Party givers are depicted frowning over spotty glasses, and housewives wonder "what kind of mother" their friends and neighbors will think them if they don't use a "whitener" in their children's clothes.

An early Cadillac ad that first appeared in the *Saturday Evening Post* in 1915 was headed "THE PENALTY OF LEADERSHIP" and began, "In every field of human endeavor, he that is first must perpetually live in the white light of publicity. Whether the leadership be vested in a man or in a manufactured product, emulation and envy are ever at work." "The Penalty of Leadership" appears regularly on every list of great advertisements compiled. The message stimulates the need to attain feelings of achievement and self-esteem and offers Cadillac as the means of satisfying those needs.

Self-esteem motives continue to be represented in advertisements for automobiles and many other products. Such ads now tend to enhance self-esteem for women as well as for men. In an ad for an Audi sportscar, a female engineer proclaims, "I pick the car and my husband picks the color."

The psychology of motivation is a field that deals with those factors that influence the arousal, direction, and persistence of behavior.[2] Most study in this area has focused on social and work situations; relatively little effort has been devoted to consumer behavior. This chapter is designed to examine some aspects of motivation that have specific relevance to consumer behavior and presents some research findings. For example:

> What is the significance of motives?
> How are motives classified and what is the relevance of these classification systems to consumer behavior?
> How can motives be aroused?
> What situations represent motivational conflicts?
> What kinds of research can be conducted to uncover motives?

Discussion of some of the specific motivational forces, such as fear, is presented in Chapter 15.

CONCEPTS AND DEFINITIONS

Motivation is a concept familiar to us from personal experience; it has been written about by poets, philosophers, psychiatrists, biologists, and psychologists, and is frequently discussed in television detective programs. It forms an exciting area of inquiry in many disciplines as well as in marketing. Like so many other concepts, however, it is not readily delimited.

We do not smell, see, or touch motivation; we infer it. We make the inference that a person is "motivated" on the basis of specific behaviors the person manifests or specific events we observe to be taking place.[3] If we see a person running, we may not be sure why he is doing so, but if we see a man with a gun chasing him, we may feel confident regarding his motivation—that is, the person is motivated by fear, or by the desire to reach safety.

Some psychologists see motivation and learning as closely related. As we saw in Chapter 8, psychologists distinguish between events that can be observed and events that can be inferred. The observable events have traditionally been categorized as stimulus and response events. Stimulus events are described as environmental inputs and response events as the behavioral output of the individual. Many psychologists expanded this *S-R* model of behavior to an *S-O-R* model. The

S-O-R model relates the stimulus (S) and the response (R) to processes going on within the organism (O)—often called "intervening variables."

Variations in the intensity of activity in a single individual from time to time, as well as from individual to individual, suggested to psychologists the desirability of developing a concept to deal with the energy characteristics of behavior.[4] "Motivation" is the term used for this concept, and is considered an intervening variable inferred to exist inside the O (that is, the processes going on within the organism).

"Drive" was a term used by scientists early in the twentieth century for this energizer of behavior, but the broader term "motivation" came to replace it. In modern usage, motivation is said to direct as well as to energize behavior. In the field of consumer behavior, "motivation" may be used to refer both to the conditions under which purchase behavior is activated and to the general direction of the behavior.

Efforts are made to distinguish among various aspects of this concept, such as motives, needs, and goals. Precise distinctions are difficult, since goals and needs are only special aspects of motivation and cannot be construed as independent. Some explanations, however, may be useful.

Motives

A *motive* is an inner state that energizes, activates, or moves and that directs channels of behavior toward goals. The field of psychology that deals with those factors—the influence on the arousal of behavior, the direction of behavior, and the persistence of behavior—is called *motivation*.[5]

Certain generalizations are made concerning motives. One motive may have diverse effects, while a single effect may result from several motives. Motives act in concert or in conflict, and they vary in intensity. They are related to goals and needs, but are also related to the individual's perception of goals and needs.

Needs

Needs are internal forces that prompt behavior toward solutions. Unlike motives, they do not necessarily affect behavior; that is, an individual may have a need and do nothing about it. Needs vary among individuals; people with the same need may seek to fulfill it in different ways.

Human needs are diverse and insatiable. They are usually treated under two broad categories: biological and personal-social (or psychogenic) needs. Biological needs are basic conditions that are necessary to the maintenance of life and the normal processes of health, growth, and reproduction. Psychogenic needs are less objectively described as personal security, self-confidence, group status, prestige, and so on. In a society that consumes at a high level, many goods and services are sought not necessarily to serve biological urges, but rather to fulfill the consumer's desire for psychogenic satisfactions.

Goals

A *goal* is the object, condition, or activity toward which the motive is directed; in short, that which will satisfy or reduce the striving. Goals are the product of the individual's personality, his life-style, his self-image, and his individual unique striving. They are also part of his culturally determined existence.

Goals vary according to a person's performance level, and at the same time they alter that performance level. The standards set for us or that we set for ourselves can alter our performance significantly. When we do well, we tend to raise our goals; when we do less well, we tend to lower them.[6]

A "goal object" is defined in a marketing context as any product or service that does or is expected to reduce or eliminate a need. According to Gerald Zaltman, "A product that satisfies a physiological need or a psychological need (such as prestige) thus becomes the reinforcement agent or as it is often called a *goal object.*"[7] In the illustrations presented at the beginning of this chapter, Listerine and Cadillac may be considered as goal objects.

CLASSIFICATION OF MOTIVES

There is no single way of classifying motives. Various writers have constructed lists of motives, ranging from very short and highly general lists to more specific ones containing as many as fifty or sixty motives. Some of these classification systems are discussed below.

Deficiency Motives: Survival and Security

Motives that emerge from the need for survival and security are directed toward securing something that is lacking. The concept of deficiency motivation assumes that the individual is impelled to act only when he lacks some important ingredient. In this view, some motives may be no more than the result of a physiological imbalance.

The physiological system functions as a whole in order to maintain the equilibrium of conditions necessary to keep the organism alive. This self-regulation process is called *homeostasis.* The body has automatic physiological mechanisms by which it maintains its temperature within narrow limits, by which the volume of blood is kept constant, and so on. Wide variations in the temperature of the external environment are regulated through the automatic body adjustments of sweating, shivering, panting, and other mechanisms. Disequilibrium is thus corrected by the automatic responses of homeostatic mechanisms.

The assumption that a need results from some kind of deficiency and will cease only when that deficiency is removed has been extended to broader conceptions of motivation. In this view, if a person is hungry, uncomfortable, or faced with danger, she will be aroused to act. When the response occurs (for example, the person eats), the physiological system returns to a state of proper balance. In brief, the homeostatic view holds that motivation occurs initially with the arousal of tension, and that it ceases when tension is reduced.

Deficiency motives pertain not only to bodily needs, but to avoidance of various circumstances and situations that may affect the survival and security of the individual. Such motives include avoiding disagreeable body states, avoiding dangerous objects and seeking objects necessary to future survival and security, avoiding interpersonal conflict and hostility, avoiding feelings of inferiority among others, and the like. (See Table 9.1.)

In this view, to arouse the consumer to act, the marketer should call attention to potential dangers to survival and security. More specifically, he can call attention to the problems inherent in house fires, particularly when there is no signaling system to alert the occupants to potential danger. He can suggest that a signaling system is necessary for future security and demonstrate that his smoke

TABLE 9.1   THE HUMAN MOTIVES

	Survival and security (deficiency motives)	Satisfaction and stimulation (abundancy motives)
Pertaining to the body	Avoiding hunger, thirst, oxygen lack, excess heat and cold, pain, overfull bladder and colon, fatigue, overtense muscles, illness, and other disagreeable body states.	Attaining pleasurable sensory experiences of tastes, smells, sounds, etc.; sexual pleasure, bodily comfort, exercise of muscles, rhythmical body movements, etc.
Pertaining to relations with environment	Avoiding dangerous objects and horrible, ugly, and disgusting objects; seeking objects necessary to future survival and security; maintaining a stable, clear, certain environment, etc.	Attaining enjoyable possessions; constructing and inventing objects; understanding the environment; solving problems; playing games; seeking environmental novelty and change, etc.
Pertaining to relations with other people	Avoiding interpersonal conflict and hostility; maintaining group membership, prestige, and status; being taken care of by others; conforming to group standards and values; gaining power and dominance over others, etc.	Attaining love and positive identifications with people and groups; enjoying other people's company; helping and understanding other people; being independent, etc.
Pertaining to the self	Avoiding feelings of inferiority and failure in comparing the self with others or with the ideal self; avoiding loss of identity; avoiding feelings of shame, guilt, fear, anxiety, etc.	Attaining feelings of self-respect and self-confidence; expressing oneself; feeling sense of achievement; feeling challenged; establishing moral and other values; discovering meaningful place for self in the universe.

Source: David Krech, Richard S. Crutchfield, and Norman Livson, *Elements of Psychology*, 3d ed. (New York: Alfred A. Knopf, 1974), p. 459.

detector is the best solution to that need. Whether or not the success of smoke detectors is the result of this strategy, it is clear that a rapid rise in sales followed campaigns that advertised these products as necessary to ensure "the safety of yourself and your family."

Although physiological needs may be a powerful source of motivation, they are not the only basis of motivation. Recognition of other deficiency motives are seen routinely in campaigns for mouthwashes, deodorants, and even chewing gum ("Brush your breath with Dentyne") that present situations that are to be avoided. Moreover, it is clear that people strive for objects and conditions not essential to their security and survival and occasionally detrimental or even fatal to them; the appeal of skydiving is certainly not that of safety.

Abundancy Motives: Satisfaction and Stimulation

Not all motives are necessarily related to deficiencies, that is, the lack of some important ingredient. *Abundancy motives* are so called since they involve satisfaction and stimulation, that is, a state of abundancy beyond the needs of immediate survival and security. (See Table 9.1.)

Hunger as an energizer of behavior was noted as early as 1863 in a publication that declared: "When a man is hungry he enjoys the smell of food; when sated he is indifferent to it and, if overfed, even has an aversion to it."[8] More recently, however, people have come to agree that a response to the smell of food may not be predictable even with knowledge of a person's state of hunger. For example, a sated gourmet may persist in his report of pleasure when he smells food despite the lack of need for it, whereas a sated nongourmet may report no pleasure at all.

People yearn to attain pleasurable sensory experiences—enjoyable possessions, love, feelings of achievement, and the satisfaction of expressing themselves. These human motives relate to satisfaction and stimulation and may increase rather than reduce tension.

While the sales of smoke detectors were climbing, another product was introduced so successfully that at Christmastime in 1977, retailers were selling empty boxes for $225 to be filled when production caught up with the demand for Cuisinart food processors. No vast advertising campaign launched this product; it appears that it had an innate appeal. It is evident that the food processor was more clearly related to a sense of achievement or self-expression than to survival and security.

Maslow's Hierarchy of Motives

An attempt to encompass deficiency and abundancy motives in a single scheme was made by Abraham Maslow in 1954.[9] In his treatment, all motives, whether they involve the increase or the reduction of tension, are combined in one interrelated scheme. Maslow arranges human needs in a ladder-like scheme, with the basic physiological needs at the bottom. As these needs are satisfied, others come into play. At the top is the need for *self-actualization*—the need to express one's potentialities in their most effective and complete form.

1. Physiological needs: the need for oxygen, food, water, warmth, shelter.
2. Safety needs: the need for security and stability.
3. Belongingness and love needs: the need for affection (as distinct from the biological sex drive).
4. Esteem needs: the need for prestige, self-respect, and success.
5. Need for self-actualization: the desire for self-fulfillment.

Maslow stressed the developmental nature of motivation: a lower need must be adequately satisfied before the next higher need can fully emerge. One must meet physiological requirements before devoting oneself to ensuring safety. A basic sense of security must be attained before love and belongingness motives are attended to. Love needs must be satisfied before one can strive for self-esteem. After all of these levels have been successively achieved, then the need for self-actualization can be felt.

It should be noted, however, that each lower need does not have to be completely satisfied before the next higher need emerges. The progression is more in the nature of a succession of waves, in which predominance among the various needs gradually shifts from one to another. (See Figure 9.1.)

The concept of prepotency (the relationship among motive strengths) may be useful in understanding consumer buying, because previously ignored desires frequently exert themselves only after a purchase has satisfied a predominant (and perhaps lower order) motive. For example, a home may be purchased in response to the needs for safety and for belongingness and love. In time, the homeowner

FIGURE 9.1   PROGRESSIVE CHANGES IN THE RELATIVE SALIENCE OF MASLOW'S FIVE CLASSES OF NEEDS

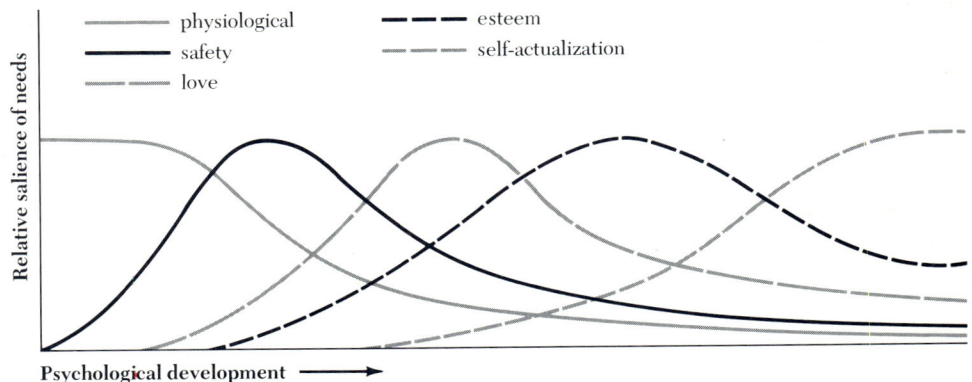

Source: David Krech, Richard S. Crutchfield, and Norman Livson, *Elements of Psychology*, 3d ed. (New York: Alfred A. Knopf, 1974), p. 462.

may add a two-car garage (esteem needs) and buy fine paintings to exhibit in the home (self-actualization). Moreover, a lower order motive can reassert itself, as in the purchase of a smoke detector.

According to Maslow, when a person self-actualizes instead of moving toward defense or safety, he moves toward growth. Maslow argues, as do other self-actualizing theorists, that human beings have the capacity for a meaningful potential-fulfilling existence, but they are prevented from achieving their potential because of the conditions of the environment. The circumstances of human existence conspire to prevent the satisfaction of all lower order needs, so that relatively few people ever become self-actualizers.[10] Nonetheless, many advertising appeals are directed to these higher order needs, as in ads for Revlon's Charlie and Benson & Hedges' "I like your style" ads.

Rational and Unconscious Motives

One view of motivation sees man as a *rational* animal. In this view, we behave as we do because we take account of our situation, calculate and weigh consequences, and finally act in accordance with rational analysis. Motives are therefore reasonable, and the reason for an action is synonymous with its motive.

According to the notion of unconscious motivation, people are often unaware of the real reasons for much of their behavior. The real reasons for deep-seated tendencies are manifested in complex ways. A person's actions are not always the outcome of a deliberate weighing of consequences. In this sense, the person's actions are irrational. This does not mean that people fail to make sense of their behavior. They experience needs and desires, goals and intentions, and tend to see most of their behavior as meaningfully related to them. But the motives they consciously experience are often elaborate, false fronts for the real unconscious motives, and their understanding of their motivation is merely a rationalization.

These two concepts of motivational theory are derived from Gestalt psychology and psychoanalysis. Gestalt psychology is concerned with conscious mind and rational decision; psychoanalysis introduced and popularized such concepts as the unconscious or subconscious mind. Gestalt psychology is concerned with goal-directed behavior and the rational use of environmental resources to attain conscious ends; psychoanalysis, at least in its earlier versions, held that behavior is primarily determined by instinctive drives and contends that we are unconsciously motivated to seek goals that we do not recognize or may be unwilling to acknowledge even to ourselves.

Obviously, these two views have very different implications as to the way consumers will react toward goods or toward the various appeals presented in advertising. If the Gestalt view is correct, the consumer might be expected to regard a product as primarily an instrument to be used toward a given end, and to judge it in terms of its *instrumental* efficiency. If the psychoanalytic view is correct, the consumer might be expected to be much more preoccupied with the *symbolic* aspects of goods, to use them as means of giving vent to suppressed desires, and to be more interested in symbols of mastery than in working tools.[11]

If goods are *instruments* for the attainment of specific ends, advertising might be expected to take on an educational character. Consumers, from this viewpoint, are seen in their social roles as members of households, as income earners, and as purchasing agents for the household. Advertising talks to them in terms they can use in talking to their family and friends. Its appeals are made through public channels and are directed to what may be called the public life of the individual, in contrast to what is peculiarly personal and private.

The consumer in this view considers many things bearing on the well-being and happiness of herself and her family. For example, an advertising campaign for Aim toothpaste generally presents a friend or neighbor declaring, "If you're such a concerned mother, how come you let Bobby use that toothpaste?" to which the mother responds, "Aim fights cavities."

The instrumental approach assumes that behavior patterns are convergent; that is, consumers with precisely the same problems will tend to adopt precisely the same solutions. The symbolic approach tends to be divergent. When a product is regarded as an instrument, each user wants to get results as good as his fellows get. When the product is regarded as a symbol, the individual may be more interested in characteristics that will help to set him apart from his fellows. An advertising campaign for Close Up toothpaste declares, in effect, "You'll be noticed by the opposite sex if you use Close Up."

The symbolic approach is justified as an attempt to achieve variety in advertising copy and presentation. In a given case, anything that can be said about the instrumental value of a product may have been said many times over. The advertiser may suspect that his potential audience has become bored and inattentive, so that these instrumental messages are no longer registering. He may then use the symbolic approach as a way of developing new copy slants. There is just so much, for example, that can be said about the benefits of men's cologne in eliminating offensive odors or creating "freshness." A more interesting copy approach can suggest that if a man uses this cologne, he will have to defend himself against a horde of ardent women. Overall, the symbolic view suggests an advertising strategy that continues to present repetitive messages, but makes them more palatable through various fresh approaches.

Social Motives

Historically, personality theorists have provided the major theoretical systems that incorporate motivation. Sigmund Freud, Alfred Adler, and Carl Jung provided broad theories of behavior that largely centered on motivational constructs. These early theorists were psychiatrists who attempted to provide explanations of and treatment for psychopathological disorders; their theories were extended to normal behavior as well. Adler, for example, theorized that the basis for an individual's motivation is provided by the goals and concepts she develops regarding her place in the social environment, which in turn shapes her personality and many crucial aspects of her behavior. The term "social" applied to these motives implies both an original goal and a further goal behind the motive.

One list of social motives was generated in the investigation of personality characteristics by Henry Murray.[12] Murray acknowledged that his total list of needs or motives does not occur in everyone. (See Table 9.2.) Two social motives designated by Murray (which can also be subsumed under Maslow's hierarchy)—affiliation and achievement—have been fairly well researched and appear to be incorporated in marketing strategies.

TABLE 9.2   HENRY MURRAY'S LIST OF SOCIAL MOTIVES

Social motive	Brief definition
Abasement	To submit passively to external force. To accept injury, blame, criticism, punishment. To surrender. To become resigned to fate. To admit inferiority, error, wrongdoing, or defeat. To confess and atone. To blame, belittle, or mutilate the self. To seek and enjoy pain, punishment, illness, and misfortune.
Achievement	To accomplish something difficult. To master, manipulate, or organize physical objects, human beings, or ideas. To do this as rapidly and as independently as possible. To overcome obstacles and attain a high standard. To excel oneself. To rival and surpass others. To increase self-regard by the successful exercise of talent.
Affiliation	To draw near and enjoyably co-operate or reciprocate with an allied other (an other who resembles the subject or who likes the subject). To please and win affection of a cathected object. To adhere and remain loyal to a friend.
Aggression	To overcome opposition forcefully. To fight. To revenge an injury. To attack, injure, or kill another. To oppose forcefully or punish another.
Autonomy	To get free, shake off restraint, break out of confinement. To resist coercion and restriction. To avoid or quit activities prescribed by domineering authorities. To be independent and free to act according to impulse. To be unattached, irresponsible. To defy convention.
Counteraction	To master or make up for a failure by restriving. To obliterate a humiliation by resumed action. To overcome weaknesses, to repress fear. To efface a dishonor by action. To search for obstacles and difficulties to overcome. To maintain self-respect and price on a high level.
Defendance	To defend the self against assault, criticism, and blame. To conceal or justify a misdeed, failure, or humiliation. To vindicate the ego.
Deference	To admire and support a superior. To praise, honor, or eulogize. To yield eagerly to the influence of an allied other. To emulate an exemplar. To conform to custom.
Dominance	To control one's human environment. To influence or direct the behavior of others by suggestion, seduction, persuasion, or command. To dissuade, restrain, or prohibit.
Exhibition	To make an impression. To be seen and heard. To excite, amaze, fascinate, entertain, shock, intrigue, amuse, or entice others.
Harmavoidance	To avoid pain, physical injury, illness, and death. To escape from a dangerous situation. To take precautionary measures.
Infavoidance	To avoid humiliation. To quit embarrassing situations or to avoid conditions which may lead to belittlement, the scorn, derision, or indifference of others. To refrain from action because of the fear of failure.

TABLE 9.2   **(Cont.)**

Social motive	Brief definition
Nurturance	To give sympathy and gratify the needs of a helpless object: an infant or any object that is weak, disabled, tired, inexperienced, infirm, defeated, humiliated, lonely, dejected, sick, mentally confused. To assist an object in danger. To feed, help, support, console, protect, comfort, nurse, heal.
Order	To put things in order. To achieve cleanliness, arrangement, organization, balance, neatness, tidiness, and precision.
Play	To act for "fun" without further purpose. To like to laugh and make jokes. To seek enjoyable relaxation from stress. To participate in games, sports, dancing, drinking parties, cards.
Rejection	To separate oneself from a negatively cathected object. To exclude, abandon, expel, or remain indifferent to an inferior object. To snub or jilt an object.
Sentience	To seek and enjoy sensuous impressions.
Sex	To form and further an erotic relationship. To have sexual intercourse.
Succorance	To have one's needs gratified by the sympathetic aid of an allied object. To be nursed, supported, sustained, surrounded, protected, loved, advised, guided, indulged, forgiven, consoled. To remain close to a devoted protector. To always have a supporter.
Understanding	To ask or answer general questions. To be interested in theory. To speculate, formulate, analyze, and generalize.

Source: Henry Murray, *An Exploration in Personality: A Clinical Experimental Study of Fifty Men of College Age* (London: Oxford University Press, 1938), pp. 80–83.

AFFILIATION

Affiliation has been defined as a concern with the establishment and maintenance of positive affectionate relations with other persons, with the desire to be liked and accepted.[13] Consumers who are motivated by affiliation are likely to seek social acceptance and to purchase goods that will meet the approval of others. They are not likely to want to shop alone, but instead seek the companionship of a friend or relative during shopping expeditions. They may rely on friendly salespeople for information and opinions.

Reference- and social-group influences such as those discussed in Chapter 5 should be useful in marketing strategies incorporating affiliation.[14] Examples of successful campaigns using this concept include "Like a good neighbor, State Farm is there." Similarly, Hallmark's strategy is to represent itself as a "social expression industry," not a greeting-card industry.[15] Its slogan, "For those who care enough to send the very best," adopted in 1944, is reported to be one of the best recalled in the United States.

ACHIEVEMENT

Achievement motivation may be associated with a wide variety of goals—money, goods, status, power, dominance, and so forth. Those who have a high achievement motivation find satisfaction in striving and achieving for their own sakes. The extrinsic rewards are not necessarily the only goals sought. The achievement-motivated individual generally is an information seeker. But unlike the affiliation-motivated individual, who is likely to use personal sources of information for purposes of decision making, such as friends, relatives, and salespeople, those motivated by achievement are likely to use nonpersonal and secondary sources of information. They seek the attainment of individual success, which is usually signalled by the acquisition and display of wealth. Such wealth quite frequently takes the form of goods and high levels of consumption activity.

M. D. Vernon points out that certain persons have a strong and persistent desire for achievement, especially of long-term goals. They are willing to sacrifice immediate rewards and take moderate risks to achieve more impressive rewards in the end.[16]

The idea of categorizing people according to their achievement motives has interesting implications for the development of a market segmentation strategy. People motivated strongly by achievement will respond to an appeal that plays on individuality or success symbols differently than those whose achievement motivation is low. Moreover, if the marketer has a product that requires skill or involves some risk, he might more usefully direct his efforts to those with high achievement motivation.

The marketer should be aware, however, that people do not have general achievement motivation. As a person matures, she seems to identify particular areas of interest in which she desires to achieve. For example, "You've come a long way, baby" has been singled out by a task force of women in advertising as a "misguided attempt to portray today's woman. Other than smoking in public and wearing fashionable clothes, what else does the Virginia Slims woman do?" The group approved the Audi ad described at the beginning of this chapter, portraying a woman engineer.[17]

It should also be noted that some people who seem to have high achievement motivation may suppress it. Their positive desire for achievement is outweighed by their fear that they may fail. A useful strategy for the marketer in such a case may be reassurance that success can be attained.

Consistency Motivation

Consistency motivation emerges from homeostasis theory, which reflects the desire to restore one's equilibrium or balance when imbalance occurs. Some earlier psychologists noted the need for balance in social and physiological areas as well. For example, a "strain toward consistency" was seen in the adoption of cultural norms and folkways.[18] The perceptual phenomena discussed in Chapter 7, such as constancy of shape, brightness, and size in the perceptions of environmental stimulation, are considered indicative of a desire to attain a steady psychological state. Moreover, the concept of consistency is basic to the cognitive models of behavior: individuals strive to maintain consistency among their values, beliefs, knowledge, images, and actions.

Consistency motivation has been applied to consumer behavior primarily through the theory of *cognitive dissonance*, developed by Leon Festinger in 1957. According to Festinger, the individual strives toward consistency within himself. The theory states that a person has certain cognitive elements that are "knowledges" about himself, his environment, his attitudes, his opinions, and his past behavior. If these cognitive elements follow logically from one another, they are said to be consonant. If they do not follow logically from one another, they are said to be dissonant. Dissonance, according to Festinger, is a negative motivational state that one wishes to reduce when it occurs. The basic behavioral prediction is that the greater the amount of dissonance, the more likely behavior will be undertaken to reduce the dissonance.[19]

In the mid-1960s and early 1970s, many studies examined empirically the arousal and reduction of cognitive dissonance in the context of consumer behavior. Although some of these studies examined the effects of dissonance arousal on tendency to repurchase and selective information seeking by consumers, by far the greatest amount of dissonance-related research in consumer behavior has been concerned with its effects on attitude change.[20] Some of these latter findings are discussed in Chapter 12.

Relatively few empirical studies have been specifically designed to examine the relationship between consistency motivation and actual behavior. One study of particular relevance to marketers examined the effects of initial selling price on subsequent sales.[21] The study was based on a concept of consistency motivation that postulates that the more effort a person exerts to attain a goal, the more dissonance is aroused if the goal turns out to be less valuable than expected. The individual reduces this dissonance by increasing her liking for the goal. The greater the effort, therefore, the more she should like the goal.

In applying the concept to a marketing situation, the researchers predicted that the higher a price a person initially pays for a product, the more he will come to like it. Thus, even if an "introductory" price will initially attract more customers, the greater liking for the same item when it carries a higher price will produce "brand loyalty" in the form of repeat purchases, and ultimately higher final sales.

The hypothesis was tested in a chain of discount houses for such products as mouthwashes and cookies introduced in matched stores under house brands. In some stores the item was introduced at discount prices, in others at a regular price for a short period of time. The prices were then made the same at all stores. The results were consistent with the prediction from dissonance theory: subsequent sales were higher when the initial price was high. The researchers noted, however, that there may be other explanations for these findings, such as the tendency of consumers to adapt to price levels.

Reviewers of cognitive dissonance literature have concluded that no single study has provided evidence that conclusively supports the application of dissonance-reduction theory to consumer behavior. They do declare, however, that evidence in favor of its applicability is somewhat more substantial than evidence against it.[22] Moreover, although the magnitude of dissonance appears to have little, if any, effect on consumer information-seeking behavior, it does seem to be related to a tendency toward repurchase and attitude change.

Some psychologists note that this is an area that needs further study. Suggested directions for future dissonance research include an investigation of a possible relationship between the cues that emanate from the external environment and the nature of inconsistency that together may account for the arousal and direction of behavior—or motivation.[23]

Additional Motives

Several recent studies into motivated behavior have described consumer behavior that does not fit the classical molds of biological and psychogenic needs. These studies have used such terms as "activity seeking," "curiosity drive," "novelty seeking," and "sensation seeking." As we noted earlier in connection with skydiving, such motives may occur despite the need for security and survival. While they have not received significant attention in the consumer-behavior literature, they appear to be used in a variety of marketing strategies.

Canadian Club recently resurrected its long-running "Hide-a-Case" campaign.[24] People were given the opportunity to participate in a kind of daredevil adventure with an exotic flair. The first hidden case of Canadian Club whiskey, found by a young couple on their honeymoon, was buried under Angel Falls, the highest waterfall in the world, located in South America. Cases were also buried on Mount Kilimanjaro, at Loch Ness, and in Death Valley. A campaign for a new liqueur named Ambrosia features such questions as "Are you an Ambrosiac?" "Would you fly to Europe for the weekend?" "Did you ever swim nude?" "Have you ever seen the same movie three times?" "Do you tell a client he's wrong when he's wrong?"[25]

Such campaigns have to be designed with care, however, to avoid unfavorable publicity. A new perfume introduced by Yves St. Laurent in 1978 was called Opium in an effort to convey an exotic image. Several consumers complained and a moral issue was raised, especially when some of the ads used the the word "addicted" in the copy.[26] To some observers, however, the resulting publicity may have been beneficial to the product's introduction. At this writing, it is too early to determine the ultimate effect of this campaign to reach the sensation seeker.

In conjunction with these notions, one author identifies a "variety drive": under certain conditions we all have a need for variety in our lives.[27] Steak may be an individual's favorite food, but if he were to receive steak every night, he would quickly tire of it and want something else. While this concept has not received significant attention in the consumer-behavior literature, it provides interesting suggestions for marketing strategy.

When the variety drive is operative, even though a consumer is completely satisfied with the brands he is buying, he occasionally buys another brand just for a new experience. This observation suggests that when a new product is introduced, the advertiser, rather than trying to switch dissatisfied customers to the new brand, should simply encourage them to try it as a change of pace. This strategy may be particularly useful when older brands are well entrenched. There are apparently numerous situations in which the consumer's desire for variety can be incorporated in marketing strategies, and studies are under way to examine this technique.[28]

MOTIVE AROUSAL

Motives are manifested through arousal. The diversity of motives and their variations among individuals, however, make it difficult for marketers to adopt strategies to arouse motives that are most satisfying to groups of consumers. Nonetheless, it appears to be possible to uncover groups with common strivings and goals, and although "motives are individually acquired . . . certain situations will produce pleasure or pain with such regularity either through biological or cultural arrangements that the probability of certain common motives developing in all people is high."[29]

According to some authorities, efforts to arouse motives are more useful in strategies involving generic choice (among product classes) and less useful in those involving specific choices (within product classes).[30] John Howard notes "that arousal determines whether the consumer will buy, brand concept influences what he or she buys—that is, which brand."[31] This observation suggests that motive arousal by the marketer should be accompanied by some attempt to create preferences for his brand.

Motives may be aroused in three general ways: physiological activation, cognitive arousal, and environmental stimulation.

Physiological Activation

Physiological arousal has been discussed earlier in connection with homeostasis. The physiological cues that may arouse a person's awareness of hunger or thirst are stomach contractions and dryness of mouth. Such motivation usually leads to a change in the level of activity channeled toward goals that have satisfied the aroused state in the past. Thus the individual who in the past found cola drinks to be less thirst-quenching than iced tea will attempt to secure the latter.

While marketers cannot cause physiological arousal, they may suggest the means of satisfying the state once it has been aroused. For example, the "Nestea Plunge" campaign featured hot, perspiring people falling backward into a swimming pool fully dressed. This campaign used various learning concepts to distinguish iced Nestea from other drinks in its class as the one most likely to satisfy thirst and the desire for coolness. The ads featured mnemonic devices (such as visual imagery and methods of loci, discussed in Chapter 8) for retention. At the same time, they presented the significant "thirst-quenching" properties of Nestea, which consumers could incorporate in either the semantic networks or the list structures used to organize information in long-term memory.

Cognitive Arousal

Our earlier discussion of consistency motivation indicates that motives may be aroused through cognitive inconsistency and the need to reduce the resulting dissonance. Motives may also be triggered, however, by information stored in memory. The "mentalistic" concepts of cognitive theory, such as feelings, perceptions, expectations, attitudes, and beliefs, may serve to arouse motives.

In this connection, Jerome Kagan defined a motive as a "cognitive representation of a future goal state that is desired."[32] This definition suggests that an individual may think about a person or object not present and imagine the consequences of engaging in some type of activity. Rather than being aroused by contractions of the stomach, a consumer's motive for food may be activated merely by the thought of a juicy steak smothered in onions. These thoughts may be viewed as a cognitive representation of the future consumption of food in order to feel better.

An activated motive for food is said to call up a belief-value matrix within the individual.[33] A belief-value matrix is a representation of that part of the individual's cognitive structure believed to be relevant to the satisfaction of the aroused needs. More specifically, if the aroused need is food, the matrix is said to contain images of those objects that the individual has learned through past experience are relevant to the satisfaction of the need for food. Thus a person may be activated to eat merely by thinking about a food object, even though no hunger drive was felt earlier. Many of us certainly have felt a desire for food just thinking about a juicy steak smothered in onions.

The concept of cognitive arousal offers implications for product formulation and design. It suggests the importance of creating a product that occupies a favorable position in the belief-value matrix used in the satisfaction of cognitively aroused needs. According to Jagdish N. Sheth, products satisfy five motives: functional, aesthetic-emotional, social, situational, and curiosity motives.[34]

1. *Functional motives* are related to the technical functions the product performs.
2. *Aesthetic-emotional motives* are related to the style, design, and comfort of a product. The product class is evaluated in terms of the fundamental values of the consumer in the emotional areas of fear, social concern, respect for quality of life, and so on.
3. *Social motives* are related to the impact that consumption makes on relevant others. Status, prestige, and esteem may be derived from the possession and use of products and their conspicuous features.
4. *Situational motives* are related to long-term desires to reach a certain goal.

5. *Curiosity motives* are supposed to promote trials of new or innovative products.

Environmental Stimulation

Cues coming from the environment can trigger motives. The smell of fresh-baked bread, the sight of a luscious ice cream cone, the sound of the twelve-o'clock lunch buzzer, the jingle of the Good Humor man's bell, all serve as cues to arouse expectation of pleasure and thus arouse the hunger motive. Suggestions to increase the sales of a bakery, for example, include the recommendation that the odor of fresh baking go beyond the store's front door.

The sight of the goal object itself may serve as a cue and activate a need for a product, or cause dissatisfaction with the present product. Seeing a neighbor use a motorized snow blower may cause an individual to experience a need for such a device.

Advertisements are used by marketers to trigger motives by providing information about the probability of reaching a goal or offering potential rewards for consumers. They frequently present problem situations to be avoided, such as disagreeable body states and feelings of inferiority, or offer suggestions for the attainment of love, self-esteem, and feelings of achievement. These conditions are usually interrelated with the use of the advertiser's product or service.

Although Listerine can no longer claim that it kills germs that cause colds, its advertisements state that the product helps one to avoid bad breath. Scope declares that it avoids "medicine breath," and Signal intimates its strength by noting that it eliminates garlic odor. The success of Wisk, according to one advertising authority, is due primarily to its claim that it eliminates "ring around the collar," which goes to the heart of a woman's need for belongingness and love and her desire for positive identification in her role as a concerned wife.[35]

Such themes as "I love New York," "A little like love" (Bolla wine), "When your kids take a fall and you can't give them more than love" (Johnson & Johnson Band Aids), and pictures of mothers with babies or babies alone in appealing situations are all used as potential activators of love and affection motives. If you drink Schlitz beer, you will have "gusto" (achievement motives), and if you drink Pepsi you will "have a Pepsi day" (happiness in a group, or affiliation motive).

MOTIVATION AND CONFLICT IN PURCHASING BEHAVIOR

Many forces operate simultaneously on the individual, and a person may be attracted to and repelled by many activities at the same time. At Christmastime the college student is frequently faced with the need to finish a term paper and the desire to go to Florida on vacation. Or he may have to choose between a down payment on a car and air fare to Europe.

Although frustration and conflict are commonly regarded as bad for the individual, they may also build tension, and so facilitate goal attainment. According to tension-reduction theorists, once a person is motivationally aroused, he typically engages in action that reduces or abolishes the aroused state. The specific patterns of directed action may vary widely, depending on the particular motives, the particular individual, and the particular situation. Despite this specificity, we can group such directed action into two general categories: approach and avoidance behavior.

Three short-term motivational conflicts are designated under this concept: approach-approach conflict, avoidance-avoidance conflict, and approach-avoidance conflict.[36]

In the *approach-approach* conflict, the individual must decide on only one of two favorable alternatives—like the student who can have either a car or a trip to Europe, but not both. This is likely to be the least painful of the conflict situations because the person can choose between two desirable things. But choosing one necessitates losing the other, so the need to choose can be a source of conflict.

Some products or services have features that may resolve such approach-approach conflicts. The various "buy [or fly] now, pay later" credit plans offer opportunities to have both car and vacation. Such products as Betamax provide the consumer with an opportunity to see a major football game and later view an interesting movie, although these desired opportunities occur simultaneously.

The *avoidance-avoidance* conflict occurs when a person is confronted with two negative things, one of which he or she must choose. For example, a housewife may be faced with the choice of being called lazy because of her dirty oven or getting down on her knees and cleaning it. Another individual noticing questionable symptoms may face the choice of going to a doctor or continuing to worry in silence. Some marketers see great potential for the design of new products in resolving this conflict by transforming one of the negative alternatives into a positive one. The self-cleaning oven and the self-testing kit for pregnancy are two products designed to resolve such conflicts.

The *approach-avoidance* conflict is probably the truest conflict. It occurs when a person is both attracted and repelled in the same direction. This situation may arise because the goal object itself has both positive and negative features— for example, ice cream and its high caloric content, or an attractive store and its high prices. Resolutions of these specific conflicts are offered by ice milk and by the provision of warrantees, return privileges, and private labels that identify the merchandise as expensive to others.

Examples of the negative aspects of products that may attract consumers are numerous. The marketer's response to them has led to the development of such special product forms as buffered aspirin and nonaspirin analgesics, peroxide-free hair coloring, hypoallergenic toiletries, biodegradable laundry detergents, decaffeinated coffee, and low-cholesterol foods.[37]

Another relevant strategy is seen in marketers' efforts to make product-related problems salient for the consumer, presumably as a means of strengthening a possible aversion and directing the consumer toward the marketer's brand.[38] Although a consumer may agree that a mouthwash or deodorant soap leaves a medicinal smell, however, it does not necessarily follow that the mouthwash or soap is therefore undesirable. Odor, as we noted in Chapter 7, results in varying perceptions, and to some people a medicinal smell may connote freshness and cleanliness, while to others it may be regarded as intrinsically unpleasant.

These analyses of short-term conflict situations are overly simplified; they fail to reflect all of the dynamics of the motivational processes. Moreover, most conflicts are likely to include more than two goals. Nevertheless, approach and avoidance patterns of conflict in motivation may be useful in suggesting the conditions under which purchase behavior is activated and do suggest the general direction of the behavior activated.

RESEARCHING CONSUMERS' MOTIVES

Research on consumers' motives is difficult and to some extent controversial. The problem is due in part to the nature of motives. Motives are not observable, but must be inferred from the actions of individuals. They cannot be seen, felt, touched, or smelled. Difficulties in the development of measurement indexes are further complicated by the fact that needs and goals vary among individuals and are constantly changing. Furthermore, the unfavorable connotation of the term "motivation research" has generated negative attitudes toward some of these efforts.

In an effort to understand this complex area, researchers have used a number of methods that fall under the broad headings of physiological research and motivation research. Physiological changes often accompany changes in motivation;[39] therefore, physiological recordings are used to determine the extent of arousal and attention. Such techniques, while not widely used, continue to be regarded as acceptable by most researchers.

Research that seeks to relate behavior to such underlying processes as desires, emotions, and intentions is usually designated as motivation research. Although it has fallen into some disrepute, a review of motivation research is useful, as some of its concepts are currently incorporated by researchers into qualitative or life-style research, while some of its methods, such as the depth interview, appear in a revised form in the widely used focus-group interviews. Additional research techniques have been designed to uncover product benefits and product problems in an effort to determine specific consumer needs that may act as motivating forces.

Physiological Research

Laboratory techniques are frequently used to measure emotion. There has been considerable controversy over the years regarding the distinction, if any, between motivation and emotion. Psychologists sometimes distinguish emotion from motivation on the basis of whether or not the variable leads to action. For example, one can be happy and not do anything about it. Activating characteristics, however, can be attributed to emotion as readily as to motivation. For example, one can say, "Because I am happy [emotion], I will buy you a present."[40] It therefore seems useful for the purposes of this discussion to use the terms interchangeably.

To learn the strength of the individual's emotions, we must be able to measure them. One way to measure emotions is to ask the individual. Another is to measure the individual's physiological reactions, such as arousal and attention. Since verbal measures confound attention, it is useful to measure attention through laboratory techniques.

PUPILOMETER

A popular nonverbal measure of physiological response to visual stimuli is the pupilometer. Developed as an academic research tool to monitor and measure the linkage of dilation and constriction of the pupil of the eye with ongoing mental activity, it was later adopted for commercial use. It has typically been applied to the evaluation of advertising materials, packages, and products.

It is assumed that pupil response to a given stimulus can range from extreme dilation (positive effect) to extreme constriction (negative effect), depending on whether the material shown is pleasant and interesting or unpleasant and distasteful to the viewer. Studies have indicated, however, that although dilation reflects the cognitive difficulty of generating mental images in response to words, it does not vary with pleasantness and unpleasantness.[41]

Empirical research seems to indicate that the pupil-dilation measure can be useful in determining the effectiveness of advertising.[42] The literature seems to leave some doubt, however, as to just what psychological processes, and thus advertising responses, are being monitored by pupilary responses. Some researchers believe that pupil dilation should be a measure of the arousal quality, and thus the emotional value, of the stimulus itself. Others believe pupil response can be expected to monitor the degree of mental activity accorded by the organism to the incoming stimulus—in other words, the pupilometer measures the awareness of the ad.

GALVANOMETER

The galvanometer, like the pupilometer, measures the amplitude of the response to a stimulus. The galvanometer, a device that looks something like a lie detector, has been used to measure changes in body responses as the viewer looks at advertisements. Such a device is used by Audience Studies, Inc. (ASI), a service that tests television commercials. Seats located in a special theater are equipped with dials that the members of the audience are instructed to turn clockwise to indicate interest and counterclockwise for lack of interest. The dials are linked to an electronic device that records the reaction of the entire audience second by second throughout a series of commercials.

To provide an unconscious measurement of interest, ASI also includes a type of galvanometer known as BSR (basal skin resistance), which picks up the sweat-gland responses from sensors applied to the second and fourth fingers of the viewer. The purpose of this measurement is to compare the conscious responses that are recorded when the viewer turns the dial with those that reflect physiological changes. Responses from the recorder disc and the BSR are recorded by computer and presented graphically on charts to indicate the consumer's interest in and involvement with the commercials.

According to one research firm, use of a psychogalvanometer to test people's responses to ads indicated the selling power of ads more effectively than did tests of what the consumer liked or remembered.[43] In postarousal test interviews, the firm found that verbal responses (for example, recall, belief, attitude) were frequently diametrically opposed to the subjects' reactions while they were attached to the instrument. The psychogalvanometer results correlated with sales test results, while the conscious verbalizations of recall, awareness, believability, and attitude did not.

The use of such physiological measures has generated questions concerning both what is being recorded (the noting of a stimulus or a positive reaction) and the reliability of the sample (how typical is a sample of respondents who agree to be wired?). Another sampling question concerns the possibility of a geographical bias due to the fact that the bulkiness of the equipment necessitates testing in a single location.

EYE CAMERA

The eye camera is used to track the movement of the eye as it peruses various stimuli. The route the eye travels is superimposed on a package or an advertisement, for example, to determine the path it takes and the areas that attract and hold the person's attention. Such tests are objective measurements of the areas of interest in the objects presented and may help in improving their design. The artificial conditions under which they are conducted, however, may influence the route the eye takes. And they are expensive, they do not indicate the viewer's thoughts, and they do not indicate success in capturing attention.

TACHISTOSCOPE

The tachistoscope is a device that measures physical perception under varying conditions of speed, exposure, and illumination. Its use in determining thresholds of perception has been described in Chapter 7. It is also used as a fast method of pretesting advertising in a laboratory setting. It has been found that high readership scores correlate with the speed of recognition of the elements under analysis. The tachistoscope, however, can provide little more than a measure of physical perception.

STRENGTHS AND LIMITATIONS OF LABORATORY PROCEDURES

Intense levels of emotional arousal do result in changes in body processes. To determine the extent of emotional arousal, psychological researchers tend to look directly at the indicators of emotion—heart rate, galvanic skin response, pupil dilation, and the like. Thus, to determine the level of the emotional component of motives, these physiological measurements may be used. Moreover, to the extent that such laboratory procedures do not rely on verbal reporting, they are objective and free of bias. When used in conjunction with verbal response, they can point out areas of discrepancy and suggest further evaluation.

The expense of a laboratory, its equipment, and trained personnel is high, especially since few respondents can be accommodated in any one time period. Also, although these methods eliminate response bias, they do create an artificial exposure condition that may bias objective reactions. Furthermore, it is difficult to interpret the results of tests that focus on arousal and attention, and the relationship between objective responses and intent to purchase is not clear.

Motivation Research

Motivation research is a phase of consumer-behavior research that attempts to answer the question "Why?" Why do people behave as they do in relation to a particular advertising, marketing, or communications problem? While much consumer-behavior research identifies the people who behaved in a given way, motivation research seeks to relate behavior to underlying processes, such as people's desires, emotions, and intentions.[44]

Motivation research as a technique had its heyday in the 1950s. Ernest Dichter, called the "father of motivation research," believed it was a mistake to conduct research into motives by merely asking people, "Why did you do what you did?" He felt the researcher could get more information by letting the individual talk in a "free-associative" way.

Dichter's first motivational-research study was for Procter & Gamble's Ivory Soap. Instead of asking people why they used the soap they did, Dichter interviewed 100 people on their bathing habits. He found out, among other things, that young women would bathe in a particularly careful way on Saturday night, before going on a date, and that the Saturday-night bath had a kind of ritualistic meaning. Since, according to Dichter, "bathing in its old ritualistic, anthropological sense, is getting rid of all your bad feelings, your sins, your immorality, and cleansing yourself, baptism, etc.,"[45] he devised the slogan "Be smart, get a fresh start with Ivory Soap."

Other motivational-research findings of the period include the following:

Miles Laboratories, Inc., found that its stingless antiseptic, Bactine, was too soothing. Motivation researchers discovered that the mother who administered a cure that lacked any sting whatsoever never got any part of the credit—no chance to comfort the child. As a result of the finding, part of the sting was put back.[46]

An advertisement that featured identical hairdos for mother and daughter, with the headline "A Double Header Hit with Dad," would arouse deep resentment on the part of mothers, according to research by an advertising agency. Women do not want to be in competition with their daughters for their husbands' attention and affection.[47]

An ad campaign showing a considerate hostess graciously offering cigars to her men guests was considered unsuccessful in a motivational analysis by an advertising agency. When the picture in the ad was used as a stimulus for a free-association discussion, it was revealed that there is a strong element of protest in cigar smoking by men. The pleasure derived from a cigar is heightened, according to this study, by the belief that it is objectionable to women. Therefore, when a woman invites a man to smoke a cigar, she robs him of his chance to show his independence.[48]

Marketers questioned the interpretations of these studies, particularly since many of them seemed to attribute sexual connotations to the purchase of prosaic products. Furthermore, as the results of motivation research were difficult to validate through replication, their validity and reliability were questioned. The concept of brainwashing and the appearance in the literature of references to "hidden persuaders" accelerated the decline in the acceptability of motivation research, as well as efforts by marketers to apply its findings.

Nonetheless, motivation research encouraged marketers to go beyond the analysis of income, occupation, education, and other demographic factors. Researchers entered into the arena of qualitative research, as distinguished from the quantitative research that had previously been emphasized. Motivation research as it was known in earlier literature has taken on new directions, and efforts to understand the "why" of consumer behavior have also resulted in the development of other types of research activities. (Some examples of these research efforts are found in Chapters 11 and 12.) Motivation research includes projective techniques, thematic apperception test, depth interviewing, and focus-group interviews.

PROJECTIVE TECHNIQUES

In a projective test the subject is presented with an ambiguous stimulus and asked to make sense of it. The theory is that in order to make sense of it, the subject will have to add to it—to fill out the picture—and in doing so he will project his own needs and motive structure in his responses.

Maison Haire's classic "shopping list" study is one of the most familiar and most often cited pieces of marketing research to make use of a projective technique.[49] That study, reported in 1950, supported three general conclusions. First, many products (such as instant coffee) have meaning and significance for consumers that go far beyond the physical attributes of the products themselves. Second, these hidden values are a major influence on the consumer's purchase decisions. Third, the identification and assessment of such motives require indirect approaches, such as projective techniques.[50]

Haire conducted personal interviews with a sample of 100 housewives in the Boston area. The following verbal instructions were given to each respondent:

> Read the shopping list below. Try to project yourself into the situation as far as possible until you can more or less characterize the woman who brought home the groceries. Then write a brief description of her personality and character. Wherever possible indicate what factors influenced your judgment.

Two shopping lists were used; the only difference between them was that one contained Maxwell House Coffee and the other Nescafé Instant Coffee. Each list was given to 50 respondents. The respondents were not aware of the existence of two shopping lists.

SHOPPING LIST 1	SHOPPING LIST 2
Pound and a half of hamburger	Pound and a half of hamburger
2 loaves of Wonder Bread	2 loaves of Wonder Bread
Bunch of carrots	Bunch of carrots
1 can of Rumford's Baking Powder	1 can of Rumford's Baking Powder
Nescafé Instant Coffee	1 lb. Maxwell House Coffee (drip grind)
2 cans Del Monte peaches	2 cans Del Monte peaches
5 lbs. potatoes	5 lbs. potatoes

Of the respondents who described the Nescafé shopper, 48 percent said she was lazy, 48 percent said she was a poor planner, and 12 percent declared she was a spendthrift. The Maxwell House shopper was described as lazy by only 4 percent and as a poor planner by 12 percent; none described her as a spendthrift.

These results led Haire to conclude that convenience foods, such as instant coffee, carry a certain opprobrium. If asked directly why they did not purchase instant coffee, however, people had been found to say, "I don't like the flavor," since this is a much more acceptable explanation than, "People will think I am lazy and not a good wife."

This study was replicated in 1968, and this time results indicated no significant differences between characteristics ascribed to the Maxwell House shopper and those ascribed to the Nescafé shopper. (See Table 9.3.) According to the authors of the replicated study, convenience foods had become more acceptable to the American housewife in the years since the Haire study. In 1968, the consumer who bought instant coffee was more typical than the consumer who bought drip-grind coffee.

Reviewers of the replicated study note, however, that the Maxwell House shopper had taken on more negative characteristics. The percentages of respondents who described the Maxwell House shopper as "lazy," "poor planner," and "spendthrift" had increased. This finding may reflect the "old-fashioned" nature of the shopping list itself.

THEMATIC APPERCEPTION TEST

In the Thematic Apperception Test (TAT), another projective technique, the consumer is shown a picture portraying an ambiguous situation and asked to indicate what the people in the picture are thinking and saying. The Rosenzweig Picture Frustration Test is a variation on the TAT technique that uses cartoons or comic-strip characters, and the situation presented in the picture usually contains some

TABLE 9.3   PERCENTAGE OF RESPONDENTS ASCRIBING CHARACTERISTICS TO SHOPPERS

Ascribed characteristics	Haire study			1968 study		
	Nescafé shopper ($n = 50$)	Maxwell House shopper ($n = 50$)	Chi square	Nescafé shopper ($n = 22$)	Maxwell House shopper ($n = 20$)	Chi square
Lazy	48%	4%	22.921[a]	18%	10%	0.010
Poor planner	48	12	13.762[a]	27	25	0.034
Thrifty	4	16	2.778[b]	36	55	0.813
Spendthrift	12	0	4.433[c]	23	5	1.436
Bad wife	16	0	6.658[d]	18	5	0.706
Good wife	4	16	2.778[b]	18	25	0.026
Overweight				18	10	0.010
Time-saver				32	10	1.808
Does not enjoy homemaking				18	10	0.010
Enjoys homemaking				27	40	0.298
No imagination				41	30	0.172
Single girl, busy				18	10	0.010
Brand of coffee mentioned				50	35	0.447

[a] Significant at 0.001 level.
[b] Significant at 0.10 level.
[c] Significant at 0.05 level.
[d] Significant at 0.01 level.

Source: Frederick E. Webster, Jr., and Frederick von Pechmann, "A Replication of the 'Shopping List' Study," *Journal of Marketing* 34 (April 1970), p. 62.

elements of frustration. Balloons over the individuals pictured in the cartoon are left blank, to be filled by the respondent. Figure 9.2 presents a situation that may be typical for a consumer faced with a purchasing decision requiring a choice among a potentially confusing array of relatively expensive appliances.

An airline conducting a cartoon test used a picture of a man and a woman disembarking from an airplane. Respondents were asked to fill in the balloons above their heads with statements the man and woman might be making to each other. Many responses could be anticipated: "This was a good [bad] flight," "The food was good [bad]," and the like. The most frequently reported statements, however, included some variation on "Now we have a long wait for the luggage." Airlines now attempt to accelerate the luggage-retrieval procedure by various methods, including carry-on luggage capabilities.

DEPTH INTERVIEWING

One of the most popular and yet sometimes harshly criticized techniques of motivation research is the depth interview. Drawn from the field of clinical psychol-

FIGURE 9.2   PICTURE-FRUSTRATION TEST

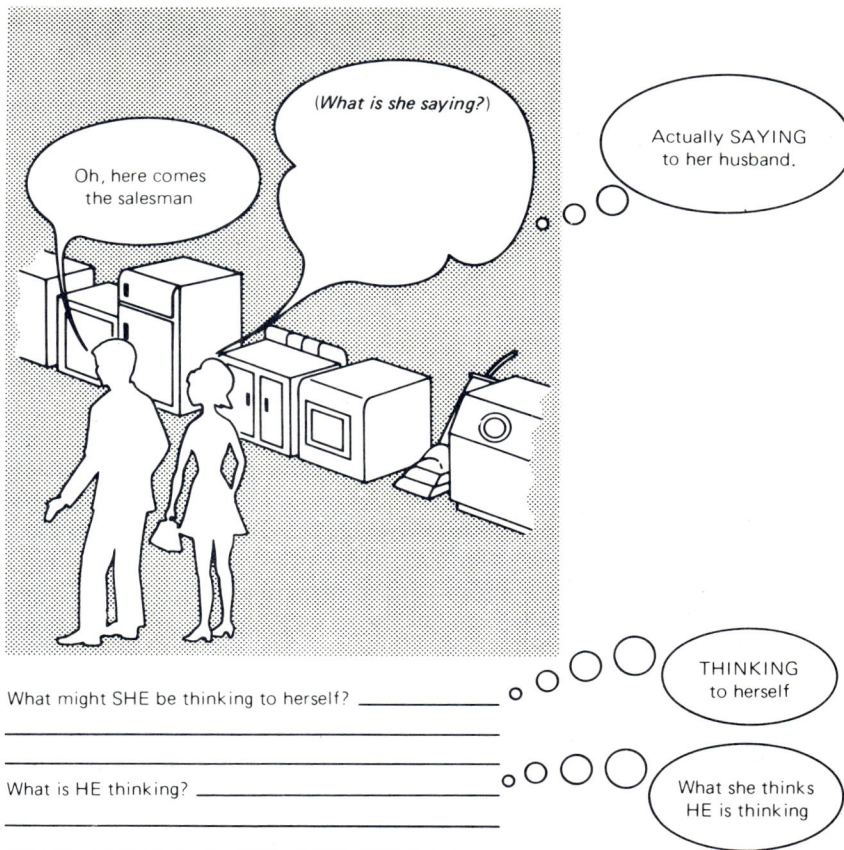

Source: "The Consumer Speaks About Appliances," copyright 1959 by Tribune Company.

ogy, this type of interview asks indirect questions that are interpreted along with the subtle reactions of the interviewee.

Usually these interviews were limited to from 50 to 200 individuals. The reason given for the small number of interviews is that basic motivations are common to a wide variety of people. This assumption itself has drawn strong criticism. After the responses to the interview are gathered, they were generally interpreted by analysts to determine common responses and other pertinent information. The lack of psychological training of many of the people engaged in this research and the human judgment that enters into the process of summarizing the findings have raised serious doubts as to the validity of these interpretations. Depth interviewing is infrequently used by marketers because of its high cost and questionable findings.

FOCUS-GROUP INTERVIEWS

A modification of the depth interview that is more widely used by researchers today is the focus-group interview. A small number of representative consumers, usually from six to twelve, are interviewed through informal group discussion headed by a trained discussion leader. In addition to providing the subjects for discussion, the group leader may also introduce various stimuli, such as products, packages, pictures, and advertisements. The discussion is recorded on tape and occasionally the group is observed through a two-way mirror so that additional significant reactions may be recorded.

There are some similarities between focus-group interviews and depth interviews. In fact, a recent focus-group study found, like earlier depth interviewers, that cigar smokers want to feel "big enough" to smoke a cigar. This finding led Muriel Cigars to portray a blatantly sexy, aggressive beauty, magically appearing at improbable times and settings (such as locker rooms). According to those who prepared the ad, this strategy satisfied the cigar smoker's need for fantasy and vicarious thrills.[51]

In fundamental contrast to depth interviewing, however, focus-group interviewing depends primarily on the interactions of ideas, attitudes, emotions, and beliefs among the group members. The focus-group interview allows people to discuss their true feelings, anxieties, and frustrations, as well as their conviction. In fact, one researcher indicates that the term "interview" is a misnomer, since it connotes questions and answers and therefore implies quantification.[52] The focus-group discussion method, on the other hand, is designed to provide information to direct further planning and research efforts.

For example, the Harris Meat Company, noting declining sales of its luncheon meats and frankfurters, wished to identify and isolate reasons for lack of sales growth. Focus-group interviews exposed a serious packaging problem and minor problems in shelf-space allocation and competitive pricing. Housewives in the group explained clearly why the packaging was a problem to them.[53] This information was used in a follow-up quantitative study to determine specific alternatives for improving the packaging strategy.

Focus-group interviews may be combined with TAT, according to a researcher, to design a more effective vehicle for in-depth probing of consumer needs.[54] Use of these two techniques in conjunction may eliminate potential problems, such as anxiety and defensiveness, which may lead respondents to be less than candid in their responses, or to distort past experiences.

Video TAT may be used to help marketers to understand consumers' motives for doing such things as coloring their hair. The process in question is videotaped in a logical, sequential manner. The tape then is shown to respondents in a focus group so they can get the "feel" of the complete process. The tape is repeated and stopped at various "end points," which represent the conclusion of specified activities within the process. In the hair-coloring example, the following end points may be used:

> Looking in a mirror at gray hair.
> Removing ingredients from the box.
> Mixing ingredients.
> Applying mixture to hair.
> Washing out mixture.
> Drying hair.
> Looking in the mirror at the finished job.

The respondents are then asked to react to the still frames presented. Other situations in which Video TAT may be applied as an analytical tool are baking a cake, washing or waxing a car, and a customer interacting with a salesperson.

While the results of focus-group interviews appear useful to management, there is concern about the subjectivity of the technique, and a feeling that different results might emerge with different moderators and respondents. A suggested alternative to the focus-group interview is phenomenological research, broadly defined as "research characterized by a period of intense social interaction between the researchers and the subjects, in the milieu of the latter."[55] It is assumed that interviews of consumers in their own kitchens, for example, may achieve results different from those attained by interviews conducted in the executive suite. Some researchers have attempted to duplicate this more natural environment by, for example, setting up typical kitchens in which consumers may be interviewed.

LIMITATIONS TO MOTIVATION RESEARCH

A number of questions have been raised as to the precise scope that should be assigned to motivation research. Many practitioners believe that motivation research is primarily a verbalizing device that helps to make respondents more articulate in expressing their reasons for buying a product or selecting one brand over another, rather than a procedure for discovering all-embracing hidden motivations.

The problems with applying these techniques to determination of consumers' motives are related to their initial development. They were created for use in the laboratory on a one-to-one basis, not for application to large groups. There is also a problem of interpretation: since results may not be expressed in a quantitative manner, interpretation becomes a personal matter. Moreover, many people who use these techniques have neither the psychological nor the sociological training necessary for accurate interpretation.

To improve the validity of interpretations, researchers have combined verbal responses with nonverbal or physiological responses. The attempt to reinforce objective with subjective measurement has given rise to such techniques as voice recording and latent response analysis. In *voice recording*, the respondent's verbal responses are recorded and mechanical devices are used to measure such vocal reactions as pitch. According to some researchers, such findings may aid in predicting, for example, which brand the respondent will choose, since both his verbalized response and the manner in which he speaks about the product are incorporated in the final judgment.

In *latent response analysis,* a record is made of the time it takes the respondent to make the response, on the assumption that responses made quickly are more likely to correlate with actual behavior than those that take a longer time. Neither of these tests, however, has met rigorous requirements of validity and reliability.

Detecting Product Benefits and Product Problems

Motivational concepts have been applied to marketing activities in efforts to determine product benefits and problems. The motivating forces that influence consumer behavior are seen as emanating from the salient benefits the product offers consumers or the important problems it solves. Such research may be useful in designing the appropriate "goal object" for satisfaction of consumers' needs. The earlier discussion of cognitive arousal suggested general motives that products may be designed to satisfy. This section discusses research techniques for more specific analysis.

DETERMINING BENEFITS

Multidimensional techniques can be used to determine the degree to which product benefits are desired by the consumer and the extent to which they are or are not being received. Such data may be useful in product development. One study, for example, indicated that a significant number of consumers perceived a deficiency in the desired benefit "removal of grease" in many household cleaning products.[56]

Multidimensional scaling was also used by a major soap company that wished to examine consumers' motives for adding a fabric softener to their wash. Specifically, why did many people use fabric softeners when almost an equal number did not? Multidimensional scaling was used to contrast user and nonuser perspectives on a number of relevant activities. Several activities were finally selected and used for detailed research. Only one was specifically related to the concept of "adding a fabric softener to the wash." Other activities ranged from "serving a special treat to the family" to "putting on perfume or cologne" to "cleaning out closets."[57]

Analysis of the data revealed that users perceived the use of a fabric softener as showing concern for family well-being and as giving the family a pleasant, pleasurable experience. Nonusers perceived the use of a fabric softener as a chore comparable to peeling potatoes or cleaning out a closet. That the product provides functional softness was assumed implicitly by both groups. This exploratory study of fabric softeners led to guidelines for product development and positioning, as well as advertising appeals (products could be developed with pleasant scents and advertised as offering pleasure to husbands, children, and so on).

It is difficult to provide a link between the emotional or psychological benefit derived from a product claim and the specific features of the product that will most credibly support that claim. To isolate product characteristics that provide psychological benefits, one advertising agency uses a "benefit chain."[58]

The Grey Benefit Chain begins with a description of the product and product attribute in question. Let us suppose that a manufacturer is interested in determining the emotional and psychological benefits of a hair spray that combines the holding ability of the normal hair spray with a cream conditioner that leaves the hair "just-washed soft." The latter factor is deemed to be a competitive advantage. Each member of a consumer group is asked to write two benefits that she associates with the "just-washed soft" attribute. Then on each of two successive layers of paper with carbon paper between them she writes two additional benefits derived from each of the previous benefits. This procedure produces a chain of fourteen product-related and emotional benefits. These items can be analyzed quantitatively to determine how often they are mentioned, how they are linked together in consumers' minds, the saliency or distance from the original attribute, and the precise language people use to communicate about these benefits.

The benefit chain derived in this manner might show that according to consumers' own perceptions and values, the product provides the following benefits:[59]

PRODUCT	FUNCTIONAL BENEFIT	PRACTICAL BENEFIT	EMOTIONAL BENEFIT
Hair spray that holds and leaves hair soft	Leaves hair easier to manage	I don't need to spend so much time on hair	Leaves me free to do other things I want to do

Analysis of such benefit-chain data might show that a marketing strategy directed toward enhancement of personal appearance would not be the best approach. A better positioning strategy would be to emphasize that the product leaves the hair easier to manage and therefore saves time and effort.

An analysis of product benefits may also provide a basis for market segmentation called *benefit segmentation*. Various analytical techniques may be used for this purpose, in addition to multidimensional scaling. Whatever the method used, researchers relate the ratings of each respondent to those of every other respondent and then seek clusters of individuals with similar rating patterns. If the items rated are potential consumer benefits, the clusters that emerge will indicate groups of people who attach similar degrees of importance to the various benefits.

A widely reported study of benefit segmentation examined the benefits to be derived by the consumer from the use of toothpaste. Four major benefits were identified: decay prevention, brightness of teeth, flavor and product appearance, and price.[60] These benefits were incorporated in a benefit segmentation strategy, in which each segment was identified by the benefits it was seeking. For example, the Worriers were seriously concerned with the possibility of cavities, the Sociables showed concern for the brightness of their teeth, the Sensory segment was concerned with the flavor and appearance of the product, and the Independent segment was price-oriented. The existence of various benefit segments suggests that copy, media choice, and even packaging decisions should vary in accordance with the segment that is chosen as a target. A review of the various techniques used by toothpaste manufacturers for their various brands indicates that benefit segmentation is part of their marketing strategies.

PROBLEM DETECTION

Some researchers declare it is more useful to probe consumers' problems in developing a successful marketing strategy than to concentrate on benefits. According to Tom Dillon, chairman of the board of BBD&O, International, one of the largest advertising agencies, "When you ask a consumer what he or she wants in a dog food, the reply will be, 'Something that is good for the dog.' If you ask what the problems with dog food are, you will learn that dog food smells bad when it is put into the refrigerator."[61]

Problem detection (similar to benefit analysis) can be used in the development of new products, advertising appeals, and market segmentation. In the latter situation, a group of individuals with common problems may be isolated and thus a submarket created. The S. C. Johnson Company considered the problem-solution approach desirable in introducing a shampoo. Rather than emphasize that Agree contains desirable ingredients, they declare in their advertising campaign that it "helps stop the greasies."

In the technique of problem detection, a list of problems is developed and then consumers are asked (1) whether the problem is important, (2) whether it occurs frequently, and (3) whether the solution to the problem has been preempted by some existing product or service.[62] A "problem score" is computed by combining importance, frequency, and preemptability in a single number. The larger the score, the greater the opportunity to solve the problem in the minds of consumers.

Examples of problems that may have been solved through the introduction of new products or variations on old ones are the "dry look" that replaced the wet look of Brylcreme and Wildroot Cream Oil; Cycle, which solved the problem of overweight dogs; and Pine-Sol, which added the natural scent of pine to the disliked odors of household cleansers.

The problem-solving technique may be useful in resolving some of the conflicts that arise in approach-avoidance situations, discussed earlier. Although problem detection is considered a useful technique by many researchers, others feel that the superior niche it provides for the manufacturer is only temporary, until another product comes along to solve another problem.

SUMMARY

"Motivation" refers to the reasons that people take certain actions. There are two primary dimensions to motivation: (1) it is a state of arousal, and (2) it gives direction to behavior. Motives may be classified in numerous ways. Those that are considered to emerge from the need for survival and security are designated "deficiency motives." They may result from a physiological imbalance: disequilibrium of the organism causes tension, which gives rise to motivation; when tension is reduced, motivation ceases. Deficiency motives also pertain to the avoidance of situations that may affect an individual's survival and security. Abundancy motives relate to satisfaction and stimulation and may increase rather than reduce tension. Maslow has provided a hierarchy of motives which attempts to encompass physiological, deficiency, and abundancy motives in a single scheme.

Motives may also be classified as rational and unconscious. Rational motives relate to the conscious mind and the rational use of environmental resources to attain conscious ends. Under this concept, the consumer is expected to regard a product as primarily an instrument to be used in the attainment of a given end, and to judge it in terms of its instrumental efficiency. Unconscious motives relate to the subconscious mind and to instinctive drives and goals that the individual does not recognize. The consumer impelled by unconscious motives might be expected to be concerned with the symbolic aspects of goods, and to value them as a means of satisfying suppressed desires.

Social motives provide the goals and concepts a person develops in regard to his place in the social environment. They may shape his personality and crucial aspects of his behavior. Various lists of social motives have been presented by researchers, and some of the relevant concepts, such as achievement and affiliation, have been incorporated in marketing strategies. Consistency motivation reflects the desire to restore one's equilibrium when imbalance occurs from a cognitive rather than a physiological perspective. The imbalance—or cognitive dissonance—is considered a negative motivational state that the individual wishes to reduce whenever it occurs.

Motives may be activated in several ways, through physiological arousal, cognitive arousal, and environmental stimulation. Conflict can build tension and therefore can motivate behavior. Conflicts can be designated as approach-approach conflict, in which the individual must choose between two or more favorable alternatives; avoidance-avoidance conflict, in which the individual is confronted with two negative choices and must choose one; and approach-avoidance conflict, which occurs when a person is simultaneously attracted and repelled by the same object.

Several physiological measurement devices may be used to measure emotions, among them the pupilometer, the galvanometer, and the eye camera. Although these devices may determine the level of the emotional component of motives, it is difficult to interpret the results of these tests, and the relationship between objective responses and intent to purchase is not clear.

Motivation research attempts to answer the "why" of consumer behavior. Techniques for this purpose include such projective methods as thematic apperception tests and focus-group interviews. Most of these techniques, however, were originally created for laboratory use on a one-to-one basis and require skilled interpretation.

Other research into consumers' motivation includes efforts to determine significant product benefits and product problems. These techniques are useful in devising promotional and target segmentation strategies relevant to consumers' needs.

DISCUSSION QUESTIONS

1. Present an ad that is based on deficiency motivation; abundancy motivation.

2. Can a campaign for such a product as a food processor have symbolic as well as instrumental aspects? Explain.

3. What kinds of motives do you believe would be most likely to activate you?

4. Describe some environmental stimulations likely to arouse motivation.

5. From your own experience, give examples of the motivational conflicts involved in approach and avoidance behavior.

6. Do you believe the use of psychological techniques in research on motives will increase or decline in the future? Why?

7. What research techniques might you use if you wished to gather "sensitive" information? Data on interactions? Explain.

8. In developing an advertising campaign, would you prefer the benefit-determination or problem-detection approach? Why?

NOTES

1. William Mason Morgenroth, "A Motivation Model of the Internalized Advertising Process," in *Making Advertising Relevant: Proceedings of the American Academy of Advertising, 1975*, ed. Leonard W. Lanfranco, p. 114.

2. Abraham K. Korman, *The Psychology of Motivation* (Englewood Cliffs, N.J.: Prentice-Hall, 1974), p. 2.

3. Eva Dreikurs Ferguson, *Motivation: An Experimental Approach* (New York: Holt, Rinehart & Winston, 1976), pp. 1–3.

4. Ibid., p. 14.

5. Bernard Berelson and Gary A. Steiner, *Human Behavior: An Inventory of Scientific Findings* (New York: Harcourt Brace Jovanovich, 1967), p. 240; Korman, *Psychology of Motivation*, p. 2.

6. Ferguson, *Motivation*, p. 256.

7. Gerald Zaltman, *Marketing: Contributions from the Behavioral Sciences* (New York: Harcourt Brace Jovanovich, 1965), p. 21.

8. I. M. Sechenov, *Reflexes of the Brain*, 1863, cited in Ferguson, *Motivation*, p. 194.

9. Abraham H. Maslow, *Motivation and Personality* (New York: Harper, 1954).

10. Abraham H. Maslow, "Self-actualization and Beyond," in *Challenges in Humanistic Psychology*, ed. James F. T. Bugental (New York: McGraw-Hill, 1967), pp. 279–286.

11. Wroe Alderson, "Advertising Strategy and Theories of Motivation," in *Motivation and Market Behavior*, ed. Robert Ferber and Hugh G. Wales (Homewood, Ill.: Richard D. Irwin, 1958), pp. 11–21.

12. Henry Murray, *An Exploration in Personality: A Clinical Experimental Study of Fifty Men of College Age* (London: Oxford University Press, 1938).

13. J. W. Atkinson and E. L. Walker, "The Affiliation Motive and Perceptual Sensitivity of Faces," *Journal of Abnormal and Social Psychology* 53 (1956), pp. 38–41.

14. Edward M. Tauber, "Why Do People Shop?" *Journal of Marketing* 36 (October 1972), p. 48.

15. "Nolan Says, 'Research Big Factor in Long Success of Hallmark Cards,' " *Marketing News*, August 13, 1976.

16. M. D. Vernon, *Human Motivation* (Cambridge: M.I.T. Press, 1969), pp. 121–122.

17. "Ad Women See Gains in How Ads Portray Women," *Advertising Age*, September 11, 1978, p. 54.

18. Korman, *Psychology of Motivation*, p. 153.

19. Leon Festinger, *A Theory of Cognitive Dissonance* (Stanford, Calif.: Stanford University Press, 1957).

20. William H. Cummings and M. Venkatesan, "Cognitive Dissonance and Consumer Behavior: A Review of the Evidence," *Journal of Marketing Research* 13 (August 1976), pp. 303–308.

21. Anthony N. Doob, J. Merrill Carlsmith, Jonathan L. Freedman, Thomas K. Landauer, and Soleng Tom, Jr., "Effect of Initial Selling Price on Subsequent Sales," *Journal of Personality and Social Psychology* 11 (April 1969), pp. 345–350.

22. Cummings and Venkatesan, "Cognitive Dissonance and Consumer Behavior," p. 305.

23. Korman, *Psychology of Motivation*, p. 179.

24. "Continuity Vital Factor in Marketing of Whiskey," *Marketing News*, May 19, 1978, p. 7.

25. Philip H. Dougherty, "Advertising," *New York Times*, August 4, 1978.

26. Pat Sloan, "Market for Opium Off on a High Note," *Advertising Age*, October 2, 1978, p. 100.

27. Edmund W. J. Faison, "The Neglected Variety Drive," *Journal of Consumer Research* 4 (December 1977), pp. 172–175.

28. Ibid., p. 174.

29. David C. McClelland, *Personality* (New York: William Sloane Associates, 1951), p. 474.

30. W. Fred va Raaij and Kassaye Wandwossen, "Motivation-Need Theories and Consumer Behavior," in *Advances in Consumer Research*, vol. 5, ed. H. Keith Hunt (Ann Arbor: Association for Consumer Research, 1978), p. 593.

31. John A. Howard, *Consumer Behavior: Application of Theory* (New York: McGraw-Hill, 1977), p. 25.

32. Jerome Kagan, "Motives and Development," *Journal of Personality and Social Psychology* 22 (1972), pp. 444–454.

33. Robert E. Burnkrant, "A Motivational Model of Information Processing Intensity," *Journal of Consumer Research* 3 (June 1976), p. 28.

34. Jagdish N. Sheth, "A Psychological Model of Travel Mode Selection," quoted in va Raaij and Wandwossen, "Motivation-Need Theories," p. 593.

35. "Big Ad Hits and Misses Hashed Out at Workshop," *Advertising Age*, August 28, 1978, p. 232.

36. Kurt Lewin, *A Dynamic Theory of Personality* (New York: McGraw-Hill, 1935), p. 575.

37. Geraldine Fennell, "Consumers' Perceptions of the Product-Use Saturation," *Journal of Marketing* 42 (April 1978), p. 42.

38. Ibid.

39. Ferguson, *Motivation*, p. 4.

40. Ibid., p. 98.

41. W. Pleavler and J. P. McLaughlin, "The Question of Stimulus Content and Pupil Size," *Psychonomic Science* 8 (1967), pp. 505–506.

42. Roger D. Blackwell, James S. Hensel, and Brian Sternthal, "Pupil Dilation: What Does It Measure?" *Journal of Advertising Research* 10 (1970), pp. 15–18.

43. "Psychogalvanometer Testing Most Productive," *Marketing News*, June 16, 1978, p. 11.

44. George Horsley Smith, *Motivation Research in Advertising and Marketing* (New York: McGraw-Hill, 1954), pp. 10–11.

45. Rena Bartos and Arthur S. Pearson, "The Founding Fathers of Advertising Research: Ernest Dichter: Motive Interpreter," *Journal of Advertising Research* 17 (June 1977), p. 4.

46. "The $ Billion Question: What Makes Her Buy?" *Printer's Ink*, October 18, 1957.

47. Smith, *Motivation Research*, p. 229.

48. Edward H. Weiss, "How Motivation Studies May Be Used by Creative People to Improve Advertising," reported in *Consumer Behavior and the Behavioral Sciences*, ed. Stuart Henderson Britt (New York: John Wiley, 1968), p. 104.

49. Maison Haire, "Projective Techniques in Marketing Research," *Journal of Marketing* 14 (April 1950), pp. 649–656.

50. Frederick E. Webster, Jr., and Frederick von Pechmann, "A Replication of the 'Shopping List' Study," *Journal of Marketing* 34 (April 1970), pp. 61–63.

51. *Advertising Age*, June 13, 1977, p. 23.

52. Roy Quiriconi, "Focusing on Focus Group Moderators . . . ," *Marketing News*, July 18, 1975, p. 6.

53. Keith J. Cox, James B. Higginbotham, and John Burton, "Applications of Focus Group Interviews in Marketing," *Journal of Marketing* 40 (January 1976), p. 79.

54. Donald Bernstein, "Video TAT Solves Two Problems, Makes Focus Groups More Effective," *Marketing News*, September 8, 1978, p. 11.

55. Bobby J. Calder, "Focus Groups and the Nature of Qualitative Marketing Research," *Journal of Marketing Research* 14 (August 1977), pp. 353–364.

56. James H. Myers, "Benefit Structure Analysis: A New Tool for Product Planning," *Journal of Marketing* 40 (October 1976), pp. 23–32.

57. *32 Capsule Cases from RAI's Project Files* (Bryn Mawr, Pa.: Robinson Associates, 1978), p. 9.

58. Shirley Young and Barbara Feigin, "Using the Benefit Chain for Improved Strategy Formulation," *Journal of Marketing* 39 (July 1975), pp. 72–74.

59. Ibid., p. 73.

60. Russell I. Haley, "Benefit Segmentation: A Decision-Oriented Research Tool," *Journal of Marketing* 32 (July 1968), pp. 30–35.

61. "Forget Wants, Needs, Listen to Consumers' Problems: Dillon," *Marketing News*, June 2, 1978, p. 6.

62. Harry E. Heller, "I Detect Some Problems with Problem Detection," *Advertising Age*, July 14, 1975, p. 76.

CHAPTER 10

PERSONALITY AND LIFE-STYLE

When the Ford Motor Company introduced the Pinto in 1971, its first television commercials presented it as a frisky, carefree little car. The Pinto was seen whisking down a country road, while superimposed on the television screen was a galloping pony.

When initial sales were disappointing, Ford decided to change the commercials. The new ones were based in part on a life-style study done by an advertising agency.[1] The study, which examined people identified as potential Pinto buyers, made it clear that they weren't looking for friskiness; what they wanted was a practical and dependable little car. Instead of comparing Pinto's performance with that of a pony, the new advertising campaign showed a Pinto on a split screen with the old Model A Ford, a car of legendary reliability and value. Pinto went on to become the largest selling subcompact in the United States.

Personality and life-style are two constructs that attempt to view the individual from the perspective of the interrelationship of a number of variables. Personality has been considered a valid subject for research by social scientists for many years. Its significance to consumer behavior emerges from the fact that personality is generally linked with tendencies toward consistent response to environmental stimuli.

Life-style analysis, as developed by marketers and consumer-behavior researchers, is of fairly recent origin. While life-styles emerge from various social influences, they are also derived from the individual's personal value system and personality. Their significance to marketers relates to the fact that life-styles are reflected in the patterns in which people live and spend their money.

This chapter examines some questions relevant to personality and life-style, such as:

> What are some of the major theories of personality?
> What relevance do these theories have to the prediction of the behavior of consumers?
> What are the limitations of personality research?
> What is meant by life-style?
> How has psychographic research been applied to life-style analysis?
> How are life-style profiles developed and what is their significance for marketing strategies?

PERSONALITY THEORIES AND RESEARCH

Early personality theories developed from a need to understand and treat persons who exhibited difficulty or discomfort in their functioning and life adjustment. Many modern personality theories are increasingly dependent on experimental or other nonclinical data, involving attempts to observe manifestations of normal personality in a systematic fashion.[2] As with many psychological terms, there is little consensus on the way "personality" is defined. Its meaning depends on the theorist whose constructs are adopted. According to one definition, personality consists of "the traits, modes of adjustment and ways of behaving that characterize the individual and his relation to others in his environment."[3]

An understanding of personality requires the study of the development and maintenance of many behaviors: social behavior, language behavior, intelligent behavior, problem-solving behavior, and so on.[4] Although personality theory is still in the course of development, it has received sufficient acceptance so that the means by which personality may affect the behavior of consumers is considered a legitimate area for examination.

Personality research has failed, however, to detect strong correlations between measures of personality and a person's actual behavior. This is particularly true of consumer-behavior research. The correlation between personality test scores and such consumer-behavior variables as product choice, media exposure, innovation, and segmentation are weak at best and thus of little value in prediction.

In his review of the literature linking personality to consumer behavior, Harold Kassarjian states, "A few studies indicate a strong relationship between personality and aspects of consumer behavior, a few indicate no relationship, and the great majority indicate that if correlations do exist they are so weak as to be questionable or perhaps meaningless."[5]

Some critics have questioned the value of efforts devoted to examining the manner in which personality influences consumer behavior. They note no more than 5 to 10 percent of a consumer's actions can be attributed to his personality. Others declare that any factor that explains even such a small proportion of a consumer's actions is useful and should be explored.

An examination of personality and its relationship to consumer behavior dates from Sigmund Freud and the motivation researchers of the post–World War II era. A number of psychological theories that have been applied to the concept of personality and its influence on consumer behavior are discussed below.

Psychoanalytic Theory

One of the most widely discussed theories of personality is the psychoanalytic theory developed by Sigmund Freud. Freud believed that every person is a dynamic system of energies. The personality is constructed of three main energy systems—the id, the ego, and the superego. According to Freud, much of the individual's behavior is related to the stresses within these systems.

The id includes all instincts and psychic energies that exist at birth and is the source of all driving energy. The id aims for immediate gratification of the individual's needs, and acts to avoid tension and to seek pleasure. Many of its impulses, however, are not acceptable to society. The ego therefore guides the urges of the id and mediates between the instinctual requirements of the individual and the conditions of the surrounding environment. The ego operates to postpone the release of tension until it can be effectively directed toward coping with the external environment.

The third structure, the superego, is considered the moral arm of personality. It represents the traditional values and ideas of the society in which the individual develops. The main functions of the superego are to inhibit the impulses of the id, to persuade the ego to substitute moral goals for instinctual ones, and to strive for perfection.

In Freud's interpretation, personality is determined by the ego's and the superego's interactions with the id. These interactions usually result in realistic compromises between basic strivings and socially acceptable behavior. An applicaton of this Freudian concept to consumer behavior suggests that potential conflicts between the id and the ego may be resolved by the manner in which products are presented in the marketplace. For example, the purchase of expensive gold jewelry is promoted as a "good investment," the luxurious car is offered as more "energy saving" than its competitors, and a costly gin is "forgivably expensive." (See Exhibit 10.1.)

An important contribution of Freud's is the idea that people are motivated by both conscious and unconscious forces. This concept is reflected in many product offerings that incorporate not only physical attributes but a variety of symbolic interpretations. Fantasy and wish fulfillment are represented in such advertisements as "The Man in the Hathaway Shirt" (with eyepatch) and Du Pont's Antron III, which makes you feel like "an heiress." (See Exhibit 10.2.)

EXHIBIT 10.1

An ad resolving conflict between the id and the ego

EXHIBIT 10.2

If you can't be an heiress, at least you can feel like one in slips and sleepwear of Antron® III.

You can't buy better lingerie nylon at any price than Antron® III nylon. So silky-soft and luxurious, it's used by the finest manufacturers of slips and sleepwear.

Almost too pretty to wear unseen. And what makes "Antron" III even more beautiful—it's anti-cling.

An heiress like you deserves the best. You've got it in "Antron" III. At nice stores near you.

As nationally advertised in: Glamour, Mademoiselle, McCall's, The New York Times Magazine, Redbook, and Vogue, throughout 1979.

Antron® III. DuPont's finest lingerie nylon.

MAN MADE FIBERS

DU PONT

This ad incorporates fantasy.

Freud also believed that in the first few years of life each individual passes through a number of stages that are decisive in the formation of the adult personality, and that sexual influences are evident in these processes. Sexual implications can frequently be seen in product development, packaging, and promotional campaigns. An advertisement for Jovan musk oil, for example, proclaims "the exciting scent that has stimulated passion since time began—It releases the animal instinct—Your sensual power is invincible."

Consumer research relevant to Freud's psychoanalytical theory of personality is evident in the early use of motivation research, discussed in Chapter 9. The depth interview, the most direct application of Freudian techniques to consumer behavior, is rarely used today. A modified form, the focus-group interview, is widely used. While the technique is not related specifically to personality research, focus-group discussions can offer insights into effective compromises between basic strivings and socially acceptable behavior.

Social Theories

Some of Freud's colleagues disapproved of his insistence on the biological basis of personality and stressed social considerations instead. Alfred Adler believed that the basic human drive is not the channeling of the id's libidinal urges but rather a striving for superiority. In striving to perfect the self and to feel less inferior to others, the individual selects his occupation, spouse, and even products accordingly. Erich Fromm stressed human loneliness in society and the search for love, brotherhood, and security.

These concepts are reflected in numerous marketing practices. Limited editions of artworks, books, and automobiles offer a feeling of superiority. Distinctiveness emerges through the purchase of Chivas Regal and V.O. Scotch and Blackglama mink. You express love by using the proper diaper for your baby, the right brightener for your children's clothes, and Pillsbury's "poppin'-fresh dough" for your entire family. "You're in good hands with Allstate," and to feel doubly secure, you can use Sure deodorant. Loneliness appears to be dispelled by drinking Coca-Cola, Pepsi, or Dr Pepper, all of which feature advertising campaigns showing groups of people enjoying themselves.

HORNEY'S CLASSIFICATION SYSTEM

One social theorist whose concepts have been specifically applied to consumer-behavior research is Karen Horney. Horney felt that childhood insecurities stemming from parent-child relationships create basic anxieties and that the personality is developed as the individual learns to cope with these anxieties.[6] Horney developed a classification system that places people in three groups according to the ways in which they respond to one another and cope with anxieties. According to this model, people can be classified as (1) those who move toward people (compliant), (2) those who move against people (aggressive), and (3) those who move away from people (detached). Each mode of response involves a different strategic method of coping with other people.

Compliant Orientation. Compliant people want to be part of activities. Such people tend to avoid conflict and subordinate themselves to the wishes of others. Among the most important attributes associated with compliance are goodness, sympathy, love, unselfishness, and humility. The compliant person dislikes egotism, aggression, assertiveness, and power seeking. Since many of his goals are tied to finding an accepted place in society, he will go out of his way to conform to what he believes are accepted forms of behavior.

Aggressive Orientation. Aggressive people want to excel, to achieve success, prestige, and admiration. Strength, power, and unemotional realism are seen as necessary qualities. The aggressive person seeks to manipulate others by achieving power over them. Yet he needs people to confirm his self-image, to bolster what may well be uncertainty about his competitive talents.

Detached Orientation. Detached people want to put emotional distance between themselves and others. Freedom from obligations, independence, and self-sufficiency are highly valued. Conformity is repellent; intelligence and reasoning are valued more than feelings.

Joel Cohen developed a CAD (compliant–aggressive–detached) instrument for the specific purpose of studying consumer behavior within a personality-related context. The instrument purports to measure a person's interpersonal orientation on the basis of Horney's tripartite model. It was used in a study designed to explore several possible relationships between CAD scores and consumer market behavior.[7] Results of the study indicated that people of different personality types tend to use different products and brands. Compliant types prefer well-known brand names and are heavy users of mouthwash and toilet soaps; aggressive types tend to use a razor rather than an electric shaver, are heavy users of cologne and after-shave lotion, and buy Old Spice deodorant and Van Heusen shirts. Detached types seem to be least aware of brands.

The CAD instrument is claimed to offer several appealing properties that should make it popular with marketing researchers. Its measurements are not sophisticated: respondents simply indicate their level of agreement with each of 35 statements. There is some evidence that CAD scores are related to several facets of consumer behavior. The instrument offers a relatively cheap, simple means of collecting primary data. Nonetheless, only a very few studies involving the use of the CAD have been reported. Further development and refinement are necessary to make the CAD a valid measuring instrument.[8]

Trait and Factor Theories

Some theorists see personality as a collection of "traits." Traits are underlying dispositions and can be inferred from the consistencies perceived in the individual's behavior. They may be general or specific to a particular situation. Refinement of statistical techniques has led to factor analysis, a technique to determine which of the underlying traits is most relevant in a situation. Factor theory assumes that if certain responses of a large number of people repeatedly occur together, then those responses reflect some underlying trait. For example, if, in a large sample, all individuals who bought sports cars also flew airplanes and responded on questionnaires that they enjoyed taking risks, a factor theorist would conclude that risk taking was an important trait underlying these behaviors.[9]

STANDARDIZED TESTS OF PERSONALITY TRAITS

There are over 17,000 available trait names, and they can be used in combination, increasing the potential number that can be identified.[10] Personality researchers, however, have developed a number of standardized tests that attempt to measure specified personality traits and factors. Some of these tests have been applied to studies of consumer behavior and are described below.

Gordon Personal Profile. The Gordon Personality Profile is designed to measure ascendency, responsibility, emotional stability, and sociability. An early study found correlations between one or more of these four variables and the use of headache remedies, vitamins, mouthwash, alcoholic drinks, automobiles, and chewing gum and the acceptance of new fashions.[11] In retrospect, however, the researcher has questioned his own methodology and findings.[12]

Thurstone Temperament Schedule. The Thurstone Temperament Schedule provides scores on seven traits: activeness, vigor, impulsiveness, dominance, stability, sociability, and reflectiveness. Each of these traits is believed to reflect a relatively separate and distinct aspect of human personality. An early effort to predict automobile choice on the basis of these traits found no differences between owners of compact and standard cars on the Thurstone variables. Personality characteristics did differ, however, between owners of convertibles and standard models.[13]

Edwards Personal Preference Schedule. The most widely used scale in consumer-behavior research is the Edwards Personal Preference Schedule (EPPS), which measures certain psychological needs. (See Table 10.1.)

An early consumer-behavior study that collected EPPS data from 9,000 persons throughout the United States presented some interesting findings.[14] The questions administered to the subjects consisted of pairs of equally desirable alternatives (determined by previous tests), each alternative representing a different need. The respondents' task was to choose one alternative in each of 225 pairs. For example, one pair representing the needs of dominance and exhibition is:

> I like to tell other people how to do their jobs.
> I like to be the center of attention in a group.

TABLE 10.1   EDWARDS PERSONAL PREFERENCE SCHEDULE

Need	Definition
Achievement	To do one's best, to accomplish something of great significance.
Deference	To find out what others think, to accept the leadership of others.
Exhibition	To say witty and clever things, to talk about personal achievements.
Autonomy	To be able to come and go as desired, to say what one thinks about things.
Affiliation	To be loyal to friends, to make as many friends as possible.
Intraception	To analyze one's motives and feelings, to analyze the behavior of others.
Dominance	To be a leader in the groups to which one belongs, to tell others how to do their jobs.
Abasement	To feel guilty when one does something wrong, to feel inferior to others in most respects.
Change	To do new and different things, to participate in new fads and fashions.
Aggression	To attack contrary points of view, to get revenge for insults.
Heterosexuality	To become sexually excited, to be in love with someone of the opposite sex.
Order	To have organized work, to have things arranged to run smoothly.
Succorance	To be helped by others, to have others sympathize about personal problems.
Nurturance	To help those in trouble, to forgive others, to show affection.
Endurance	To stay with a job until finished, to keep at a problem until solved.

Source: Reproduced from the Edwards Personal Preference Schedule. Copyright 1954, © 1959, by The Psychological Corporation, New York, N.Y. All rights reserved.

Each panel member was asked to choose the statement that "fits him better" in each of 225 pairs. Such choices indicate only the needs an individual expresses, not necessarily the way he really feels or behaves.

The results indicated highly significant differences between the average scores of men and those of women. Men scored higher on needs for achievement, autonomy, dominance, sex, and aggression. Women received higher scores on association, assistance, dependence, order, compliance, and self-depreciation. The younger people expressed high need for sex, change, and exhibition. The older groups expressed a greater need for order and compliance.

Efforts were made to determine whether the expressed needs related to the subjects' reported purchases. Findings indicated that the average male smoker scored significantly higher than the average man in his expressed needs for sex, aggression, achievement, and dominance, and significantly below average in compliance, order, self-depreciation, and association.

Personality traits differed not only between product purchasers and nonpurchasers, but also among buyers of different types of a product. For example, smokers of filter cigarettes scored higher than nonfilter smokers on dominance, change, and achievement, and lower on aggression, self-depreciation, and autonomy.

Another study examined the role of one trait only—achievement—and its relationship to consumer behavior. Subjects scoring high in need for achievement appeared to tend to favor products that might be thought of as virile and masculine—boating equipment, straight razors, skis, push lawn mowers.[15] Male subjects scoring low in need for achievement tended to favor products that might be thought of as meticulous or fastidious—automatic dishwashers, headache remedies, mouthwashes, electric toothbrushes, deodorants. This study did not indicate any clear-cut pattern in female purchase data. It appeared that products designated as "feminine" will not be purchased any sooner by women with low need for achievement than by women with high need for achievement.

The author of this study concluded that the need for achievement is probably more closely related to the male sex role than it is to the female sex role. The data appeared to reflect the belief that men are supposed to be aggressive and competitive and women are not. Men who are high in need for achievement strongly identify with their sex roles and project themselves via products that symbolize those roles. Women do not seem to follow this pattern.

NONSTANDARDIZED PERSONALITY TYPES

As we have noted, the data that have emerged from standardized personality tests have rarely provided empirical certainty as to the actual association of personality with specific behavior. Typically, only about 5 to 10 percent of the total variance in buyer behavior has been accounted for by personality construct measures. Suggestions to improve the efficiency of test instruments include the recommendation that personality "profiles" rather than personality traits should be the focus of such studies.[16] The benefit of the personality profile is that it reflects the interactions of various personality traits.

One such use of personality profiles occurred in an examination of banking behavior.[17] A set of profiles was developed contrasting people who have savings accounts but no checking accounts with those who have checking accounts but no savings accounts. As can be seen in Figure 10.1, the two groups have almost completely opposite personality profiles. This finding can be applied to the development of advertising copy: in talking to the savers who don't use checking, the bank should use a soft approach and the message should be delivered in a sort of "We know what's best" tone. The opposite approach should be used with the checkers who do not save: they would be uninterested in any soft-selling copy.

Another suggestion is the development of "modified" personality measures, which are usually shorter and easier to administer. An example of a modified personality instrument is this one by Kathryn Villani and Yoram Wind:[18]

Sociable

I am always glad to join a large gathering.
I consider myself a very sociable, outgoing person.
I find it easy to mingle among people at a social gathering.
When I am in a small group, I sit back and let others do most of the talking.

I have decidedly fewer friends than most people.
I am considered a very enthusiastic person.

Relaxed

I get tense as I think of all the things lying ahead of me.
Quite small setbacks occasionally irritate me too much.
I wish I knew how to relax.
I shrink from facing a crisis or a difficulty.

Internal Control

Sometimes I feel that I don't have enough control over the direction my life is taking.
Many times I feel that I have little influence over the things that happen to me.
What happens to me is my own doing.
Becoming a success is a matter of hard work; luck has nothing to do with it.
Getting a good job depends mainly on being in the right place at the right time.

In general, efforts to use trait and factor theory to predict consumer behavior have produced limited results. The statistical techniques used in factor analysis have been employed in more recent studies designed to relate personality characteristics to consumer behavior, but these psychographic studies, as they are called, have not led to a comprehensive theory either.[19] Psychographic research will be discussed later in this chapter.

FIGURE 10.1   PERSONALITY PROFILES OF SAVERS WHO DON'T CHECK AND CHECKERS WHO DON'T SAVE

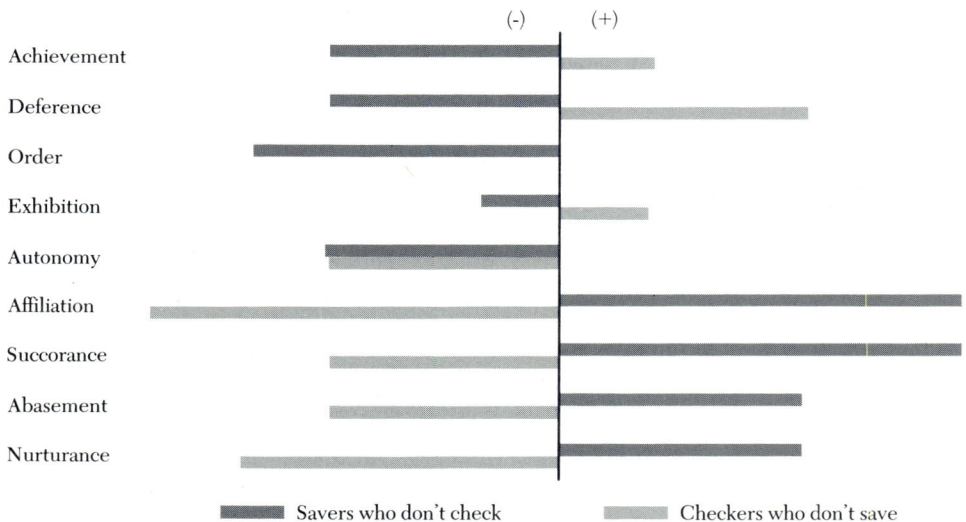

Source: Larry Percy, "A Look at Personality Profiles and the Personality-Attitude-Behavior Link in Predicting Consumer Behavior," *Advances in Consumer Research*, vol. 3, ed. Beverlee B. Anderson (Association for Consumer Research, 1976) p. 120.

Self Theory

Self theory provides some clarification of the dynamics of personality. Carl Rogers is credited with developing self theory in clinical practice. According to Rogers, although this construct emerged in client-centered therapy, there are clear indications that self-concept is an important variable in personality dynamics.[20]

Psychological research on self theory has examined it in the context of adjustment. Studies have indicated that the more congruence there is between what a person thinks she is and what she would like to be, the better adjusted she is.[21] Consumer-behavior research involving self theory has been based on the notion that people often strive to maintain and enhance their self-images in order to maintain a harmonious and internally consistent self. The consumer may see herself simultaneously as many things, however, depending on the perspective taken. According to self theory, more than one concept of self exists. There are, in fact, five such concepts: the real self, the ideal self, the self-image, the apparent self, and the reference-group image.[22]

The *real self* is the individual as an objective entity. The real self is never completely understood or observed, however. Most of us never acknowledge our own nature. We have many physical and mental quirks we will not acknowledge, and we deny many of our faults and foibles. We may have certain unconscious preferences, however, which derive from our real selves.

The *ideal self* is what the individual would like to be. The ideal self is never actually achieved; the individual always finds something new to strive for. We have aspirations that relate to what we wish to have and to be.

The *self-image* is the way we see ourselves. The self-image acts as a guide to much of consumer behavior. It is a combination of the real self and the ideal self. Consumers tend to buy products that either support or improve their self-images. The self-image may be the most important of all images in dealings with the consumer. Customers express their self-images in the stores they visit, the products they buy, and the way they react in the selling situation.

The *apparent self* is the self that outsiders see. In fact, outsiders may see a combination of the ideal self, the real self, and the self-image. What the outsider sees, however, may not be a true representation of the person.

The *reference-group image* is the self that the individual thinks others with whom he associates or identifies sees in him.

RESEARCH ON CONSUMERS' SELF-CONCEPTS

The notion that the consumer's concept of himself influences his behavior has been examined by researchers. Several studies have established a relationship between the individual's self-concept and his marketing behavior. Although such studies have been criticized for their theoretical and methodological shortcomings,[23] they offer some insights for marketers.

An early study examined the hypothesis that consumers of a specific brand of a product would perceive themselves as having characteristics that they attributed to other consumers of the same brand.[24] Further, consumers of a specific brand would have self-concepts significantly different from the self-concepts they attributed to consumers of a competing brand. This study examined owners of Pontiac GTOs and owners of Volkswagens.

The following descriptive words were selected for each of the products:

VOLSKWAGEN OWNERS	PONTIAC GTO OWNERS
Thrifty	Status-conscious
Sensible	Flashy
Creative	Fashionable
Individualistic	Adventurous
Practical	Interested in the opposite sex
Conservative	Sporty
Economical	Style-conscious
Quality-conscious	Pleasure-seeking

The results of the test were positive and supported the hypothesis. Consumers of the two makes of autos perceived themselves significantly differently and held definite stereotyped perceptions of the owners of each make. Further, they perceived themselves to be like others who owned the same make of car and quite different from owners of competing brands. The self-image of the GTO owners differed from their description of other GTO owners only on the adjective "flashy." Flashiness is apparently not a quality one wants to attribute to oneself.

After measuring the extent to which self-image is congruent with purchase, A. E. Birdwell concluded that self-image was significantly more congruent with make of car owned than with seven other brand categories studied. In addition, each car-ownership group had significantly different images of other car makes. Finally, Birdwell found that these findings were stronger for luxury cars than for economy cars. He reasoned that income is a factor in the consumer's ability to make purchases compatible with self-image.[25]

When I. J. Dolich studied self-image and the product images of most and least preferred brands within four product categories, he found greater congruity between self-image and most preferred brand over all four product categories.[26]

The relevance of self-concept to the consumer's choice of retail outlets has been researched. One study found that consumers select outlets that they perceive to be congruent with their self-image. In addition, consumers perceive stores they do not patronize to be significantly different in character from their perceptions of themselves. According to the researchers, "In order successfully to attract a desired market segment to one's store, the decor, merchandise and policies of the store need to be engineered so that they closely parallel the characteristics of the customer."[27]

MARKETING APPLICATIONS OF SELF-CONCEPT

There are clear indications of the applicability of self-concept to market segmentation, advertising, selling, and other marketing activities. The assumptions are that consumers will purchase products that preserve or enhance their self-image and avoid those that do not.

Cosmetics and toiletries companies develop products and promotional strategies for those who consider themselves to be "glamorous" or "independent" as well as for those who see themselves as "wholesome." An advertising campaign for Rive Gauche perfume presents an "independent woman" racing in a Ferrari to meet . . . not a man, but the sunrise. Ivory Soap features the "Ivory Girl" as one who conceives of herself as healthy, clean, and "average."

Retailers develop images designed to be congruent with the customers they wish to attract. Neiman Marcus, the exclusive Dallas retail store, promotes products in its Christmas catalog that are highly unlikely to be sold but which help to create an "exclusive" image. Items range from a matched pair of elephants to a matched pair of fur-lined automobiles. Other retailers deliberately promote the discount image for the consumer who perceives himself as "thrifty" by piling merchandise haphazardly on tables.

Future Personality Research Directions

Despite the paucity of significant findings, some researchers believe that personality remains a fertile field for consumer research. Personality research has been criticized for focusing on specific brand choice and brand loyalty rather than on the relationships between personality and the procedures that consumers adopt in approaching, modifying, simplifying, and reacting to their environment. A recent study supported the hypothesis that the personality traits of self-confidence and anxiety are related to the strategies consumers adopt in making choices.[28]

It is possible that more fruitful results may emerge from studies in which personality is examined in combination with other variables. "Self-monitoring" has been recommended as a moderating variable in research on personality and consumer behavior. A high self-monitoring individual is one who is sensitive to the expressions and self-presentation of others, and varies his behavior to accord with the people with whom he is interacting. It is hypothesized that while the behavior of high self-monitors will relate to social cues, the behavior of low self-monitoring individuals may be associated with personality traits.[29]

Situational factors can be incorporated in personality research. Situational factors (discussed in more detail in Chapter 16) are the various circumstances and conditions under which consumer decisions are made. Gift giving is considered to be a circumstance that may have particular relevance to studies of personality influence.[30] Other suggestions for future research directions include examination of personality in its relationship to consumer complaining behavior.[31]

LIFE-STYLE RESEARCH

When and where the term "life-style" was coined is not known. Life-style appears in the literature of poets and novelists as well as in that of economists and psychol-

EXHIBIT 10.3

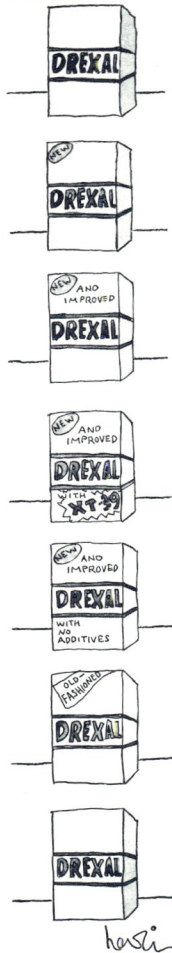

Changing life-style: back to basics
Drawing by Levin; © 1977 The New Yorker Magazine, Inc.

ogists.[32] While most people have some understanding of what is meant by "life-style," an analysis of this concept from a consumer-behavior perspective suffers from a lack of a universally accepted definition.

Some of the earliest uses of the term "life-style" in marketing-oriented studies of consumer behavior appeared in the mid-1960s. William Lazer described life-style as "the distinctive or characteristic mode of living of a whole society or a segment of a society." He emphasized environmental influences on the "mode of living," such as social class, life cycle, and the family.[33] Current life-style research examines internal considerations, such as personality and self-concept, also.

Life-style reflects the overall manner in which people live and spend their time and money. Its significance to marketing resides in the insights that life-style analysis reveals into the behavioral patterns of society as a whole, as well as its utility in distinguishing among market segments. Its relevance to segmentation strategy can be seen in the following description of two different life-styles:

If we think of a Chicago housewife who uses Crosse and Blackwell soups, subscribes to *Gourmet* magazine, flies live lobsters in from Maine to serve her guests, drives a Renault, and doesn't shave under her arms, we sense a value system that adds up to a life-style quite different from that of the woman who uses Campbell's, reads *Family Circle* for ideas on how to furnish a playroom, makes meat loaf twice a week, rides in her husband's Bel Air, and scrubs the kitchen floor three times a week.[34]

That life-styles and the value systems they reflect are not enduring is of significance to marketers.[35] The shopper who once eagerly snatched from the shelf the latest "new and improved" product "with additives" now scrutinizes labels in search of "natural" products that contain no preservatives.

Psychographics

Psychographics is a widely applied technique used in the measurement of life-style. Traditional demographic analysis, which examines age, income, residence, and the like, is useful in providing quantitative measures of consumers but does not present an adequate description of the consumer's life-style. Qualitative analysis, such as motivation research, examined consumers on relevant psychological dimensions, but these techniques required small samples and failed to offer quantifiable results. Psychographics combines the best features of both.

Psychographic research can be defined as quantitative research intended to measure the psychological—as distinguished from the demographic—dimensions of consumers.[36] The value of psychographic over demographic research may be seen in an effort to develop a profile on the heavy user of shotgun ammunition for communication purposes. (See Tables 10.2 and 10.3.) The demographic profile of the shotgun user revealed that the man who spends at least $11 a year on shotgun shells tends to be younger than the nonuser, lower in income and education, and more concentrated in blue-collar occupations. He is also more likely to be living in rural areas, especially in the South.

Psychographic data, however, can provide more pertinent information. From these data it is obvious that hunting is not an isolated phenomenon but rather is associated with other rugged outdoor endeavors. Buyers of shotgun shells not only like to hunt, they also like to fish and go camping. They are apt to be do-it-your-selfers, a finding that suggests that hunters are likely to be buyers of hardware and tools. The heavy user of shotgun ammunition is more attracted by violence than the nonbuyer, suggesting that detective, war, and violent Western TV programs ought to draw audiences with disproportionate numbers of shotgun users and that marketers ought to consider action and adventure magazines when placing advertising associated with hunting.

TABLE 10.2   DEMOGRAPHIC PROFILE OF THE HEAVY USER OF SHOTGUN AMMUNITION

Characteristics	Percent who spend $11 + per year on shotgun ammunition (141)	Percent who don't buy (395)
Age		
Under 25	9	5
25–34	33	15
35–44	27	22
45–54	18	22
55 +	13	36
Occupation		
Professional	6	15
Managerial	23	23
Clerical-sales	9	17
Craftsman	50	35
Income		
Under $6,000	26	19
$6,000–$10,000	39	36
$10,000–$15,000	24	27
$15,000 +	11	18
Population density		
Rural	34	12
2,500–50,000	11	11
50,000–500,000	16	15
500,000–2 million	21	27
2 million +	13	19
Geographic division		
New England–Mid-Atlantic	21	33
North and West Central	22	30
South Atlantic	23	12
East South Central	10	3
West South Central	10	5
Mountain	6	3
Pacific	9	15

Source: William D. Wells, "Psychographics: A Critical Review," *Journal of Marketing Research* 12 (May 1975), p. 197.

ACTIVITY, INTEREST, AND OPINION INVENTORIES

The first attempts to gather psychographic data on consumers employed standardized personality and interest inventories. Although these attempts generated considerable interest, they never quite succeeded in providing portraits of the consumer in action, partly because the traits that the inventories were designed to measure were only indirectly related to the consumption of goods and services.[37]

Ultimately, researchers assembled a large number of items similar to those found in standardized personality and interest inventories and then correlated re-

TABLE 10.3   PSYCHOGRAPHIC PROFILE OF THE HEAVY USER
OF SHOTGUN AMMUNITION

Base	Percent who spend $11 + per year on shotgun ammunition (141)	Percent who don't buy (395)
I like hunting	88	7
I like fishing	68	26
I like to go camping	57	21
I love the out-of-doors	90	65
A cabin by a quiet lake is a great place to spend the summer	49	34
I like to work outdoors	67	40
I am good at fixing mechanical things	47	27
I often do a lot of repair work on my own car	36	12
I like war stories	50	32
I would do better than average in a fist fight	38	16
I would like to be a professional football player	28	18
I would like to be a policeman	22	8
There is too much violence on television	35	45
There should be a gun in every home	56	10
I like danger	19	8
I would like to own my own airplane	35	13
I like to play poker	50	26
I smoke too much	39	24
I love to eat	49	34
I spend money on myself that I should spend on the family	44	26
If given a chance, most men would cheat on their wives	33	14
I read the newspaper every day	51	72

Source: William D. Wells, "Psychographics: A Critical Review," *Journal of Marketing Research* 12 (May 1975), p. 198.

sponses to these items with consumption of products and exposure to communication media. This procedure differed from those used in earlier research, since most of the items did not refer to generalized personality traits, but rather to budgeting, shopping, housekeeping, family relationships, leisure-time activities, and other matters likely to be directly related to the purchase of goods and services and so reflected consumers' life-styles.

The most widely used inventory for the measurement of life-styles incorporates the use of AIO (activities, interests, and opinions) rating statements. Such statements are designed to reveal psychographic characteristics. Although life-style analysis does not necessarily exclude demographic data, the emphasis on activities, interests, and opinions tends to make psychographics synonymous with AIO analysis. Joseph T. Plummer, a leader in this type of research, describes it as follows:

> AIO analysis is designed to answer questions about people in terms of their activities, interests and opinions. It measures their activities in terms of how they spend their time in work and leisure; their interests in terms of what they place importance on in their immediate surroundings; their opinions in terms of their stance on social issues, institutions and themselves; and finally basic facts such as their age, income, and where they live.[38]

Table 10.4 lists the elements included in each major dimension of life-style.

AIO measurements, designed to determine how people spend their time, their interests, and their opinions, incorporate a series of some 200 to 300 statements to which respondents indicate the extent of their agreement or disagreement. Such statements are frequently "dreamed up," but they are designed to have some relevance to the research issue. They may come from intuition, hunches, research, reading, or in-depth interviews. An example of some of the statements used to distinguish between the life-styles of the heavy user of eye makeup and the heavy user of shortening appear in Table 10.5.

GENERAL LIFE-STYLE PROFILES

A major benefit of life-style analysis is the development of life-style profiles, useful in describing potential targets for marketing strategies. Such profiles have emerged from a number of studies.

General life-style studies are presumed to describe the general population in psychographic terms. A major general life-style study was conducted by an advertising agency, Needham, Harper & Steers. More than 3,000 respondents were

TABLE 10.4 LIFE-STYLE DIMENSIONS

Activities	Interests	Opinions	Demographics
Work	Family	Themselves	Age
Hobbies	Home	Social issues	Education
Social events	Job	Politics	Income
Vacation	Community	Business	Occupation
Entertainment	Recreation	Economics	Family size
Club membership	Fashion	Education	Dwelling
Community	Food	Products	Geography
Shopping	Media	Future	City size
Sports	Achievements	Culture	Stage in life cycle

Source: Joseph T. Plummer, "The Concept and Application of Life Style Segmentation," *Journal of Marketing* 38 (January 1974), p. 34.

TABLE 10.5 LIFE-STYLES OF THE HEAVY USER OF EYE MAKEUP AND THE HEAVY USER OF SHORTENING

Dimensions measured	Heavy user of eye makeup	Heavy user of shortening
Demographic characteristics	Young, well-educated, lives in metropolitan areas	Middle-aged, medium to large family, lives outside metropolitan areas
Product use	Also a heavy user of liquid face makeup, lipstick, hair spray, perfume, cigarettes, gasoline	Also a heavy user of flour, sugar, canned lunch meat, cooked pudding, catsup
Media preferences	Fashion magazines, *Life, Look,* "Tonight Show," adventure programs	*Reader's Digest,* daytime TV serials, family situation TV comedies
Activities, interests, and opinions[a]	I often try the latest hairdo styles when they change I usually have one or more outfits that are of the very latest style An important part of my life and activities is dressing smartly I enjoy looking through fashion magazines I like to feel attractive to all men I want to look a little different from others Looking attractive is important in keeping your husband I like what I see when I look in the mirror I comb my hair and put on my lipstick first thing in the morning I take good care of my skin Sloppy people feel terrible I would like to take a trip around the world I would like to spend a year in London or Paris I like ballet I like parties where there is lots of music and talk I like things that are bright, gay, and exciting I do more things socially than do most of my friends I would like to have a maid to do the housework I like to serve unusual dinners I am interested in spices and seasonings If I had to choose, I would rather have a color televsion set than a new refrigerator I like bright, splashy colors I really do believe that blondes have more fun	I love to bake and frequently do I save recipes from newspapers and magazines The kitchen is my favorite room I love to eat I enjoy most forms of housework Usually I have regular days for washing, cleaning, etc., around the house I am uncomfortable when my house is not completely clean I often make my own or my children's clothes I like to sew and frequently do I try to arrange my home for my children's convenience Our family is a close-knit group There is a lot of love in our family I spend a lot of time with my children talking about their activities, friends, and problems Everyone should take walks, bicycle, garden, or otherwise exercise several times a week Clothes should be dried in the fresh air and out-of-doors It is very important for people to wash their hands before eating every meal You should have a medical checkup at least once a year I would rather spend a quiet evening at home than go out to a party I would rather go to a sporting event than a dance

[a] Subject agrees more than average with the statements indicated.

Source: S. Ward, T. S. Robertson, CONSUMER BEHAVIOR, THEORETICAL SOURCES, © 1973, p. 195. Reprinted by permission of Prentice-Hall, Inc., Englewood Cliffs, New Jersey.

asked to indicate, on a scale of 1 to 6, agreement or disagreement with each of 199 statements. The statements referred to personal preferences and habits, social and political views, activities, and various kinds of food products.

The results indicated that the U.S. consumer population could be broken down into ten life-style types, five female and five male, described as follows:

Thelma, the old fashioned traditionalist, is a devoted wife, doting mother, and conscientious housekeeper. Thelma has few interests outside her own family. She does not condone sexual permissiveness or political liberalism, nor can she sympathize with women's libbers.

Candice, the chic suburbanite, is an urbane woman, well-educated, probably married to a professional man. She is a prime mover in her community and is active in club affairs.

Mildred, the militant mother, married early, had children and now wishes the women's liberation movement had happened in time to help her. She likes soap operas and lottery tickets because they help her escape into a fantasy world.

Cathy, the contented mother, married early, had a big family and likes it that way. She thinks women's liberation opposes biblical teachings, is trusting and relaxed, and buys only the cereals her children demand.

Eleanor, the elegant socialite, says women's liberation is unnecessary if a woman has a man to take care of her. She spends little time preparing meals but spends a lot of time and money on cosmetics and high-fashion clothes, and thinks face creams are better if they cost more.

Herman, the retired homebody, has opinions that conflict with nearly everything in the modern world. He can neither change the world nor cope with it. His favorite meal is a hearty breakfast. He uses low-cholesterol products, and he is very concerned about high prices. He distrusts foreign-made products.

Dale, the devoted family man, married early, fathered a family, and is happy. A blue-collar worker with a high school education, he is more interested in knowing what a product can do for him than what star endorses it and worries about excessive sex and violence on TV.

Ben, the self-made businessman, believes you get what you pay for, values his time, eats bacon and eggs despite his doctor's disapproval because "there's no substitute," and thinks government should keep its nose out of private industry.

Fred, the frustrated factory worker, married young and is now unhappy and cynical. He likes to think that he is a bit of a swinger; he fantasizes and goes to the movies to escape from his everyday world.

Scott, the successful professional, is much smoother; his speech is more confident and his manner sure. He carries three major credit cards and uses them primarily to pay for business travel.[39]

According to those who conducted the study, such research can help the marketer to determine which segment or segments of those represented in the survey will want the product, and to select the right marketing strategy. Both Eleanor and Mildred, for example, buy nail polish, but they don't respond to the same marketing strategy. Fred and Dale may need insurance, but Dale will buy from the agent who sold insurance to his father, while Fred will go where he is made to feel like a person with some status.[40]

PRODUCT-SPECIFIC LIFE-STYLE PROFILES

Life-style profiles may also be developed for the users of specific products. When a life-style profile for potential users of a particular product is to be created, a target audience of interest must first be defined.[41] The target audience frequently consists of heavy users of a product or service, such as fast-food restaurants; readers of a particular magazine; members of a specific age group; or, in fact, any group of interest. Next, the target audience's responses to the activity, interest, and opinion questions are compared with the responses of the remainder of the population. Items that show significant differences are used to construct a profile of that audience.

In one study, a profile was developed of the male bank charge-card user. The profile showed that heavy users of commercial bank credit cards agreed more than nonusers with such items as:

"I would rather live in or near a big city than in or near a small town."
"I often have a cocktail before dinner."
"I enjoy going to concerts."
"I like to think I'm a bit of a swinger."
"I expect to be a top executive in ten years."
"I do more things socially than most of my friends."
"I am or have been president of a club or society."

The bank charge-card user disagrees with such items as:

"I stay home most evenings."
"There are day people and there are night people; I am a day person."
"My days seem to follow a definite routine, such as eating meals at a regular time."

In conjunction with the traditional demographics, a profile was developed of the male bank charge-card user. The portrait that emerged is one that seems "to typify the popular stereotypes of the successful man on the rise." The cardholder fits "the picture of the suburban businessman arriving home from the office and having a cocktail, settling down to a nice meal, and then going off to various activities. He is a busy young businessman on the rise who knows where he is going."[42]

Knowledge of such a portrait can be helpful in the development of a promotional campaign for the bank credit-card user. Such a campaign can emphasize how use of credit cards may help the busy man save time, reflect his success, and enhance his esteem in the eyes of others.

LIFE-STYLE SEGMENTATION

Life-style analysis can be useful in the development of profiles of various market segments. The apparel industry found that life-style analysis revealed significant characteristics of pertinent consumer segments. White Stag women's sportswear conducted a nationwide program of consumer research which defined five life-style segments, two of which proved to be White Stag's best customers.[43]

Segment *A* represented White Stag's traditional primary market: suburban, fortyish, upper-middle income, wearing misses' size 12–14, tending toward pantsuits and conservative, traditional clothing. Such women tended to shop in the "better" sections of large stores and represented a $41.4 billion market. Mrs. *A* was found to be more fashion-conscious and more interested in being well dressed than White Stag had anticipated. To meet her needs, White Stag updated the clothes designed for Mrs. *A* and met with excellent reaction at the retail level.

The other key segment, *B*, represented a new market. Mrs. *B*, in her mid-twenties, upper-middle income, wearing size 8–10, tended to shop in the "better" sections of department stores, specialty shops, and boutiques. She represented a $1.2 billion market. The surprise of the survey was that Mrs. *B* proved to be a younger primary-market target for White Stag. To exploit this marketing opportunity, the company designed younger, more spirited sportswear than their traditional lines. A film and a brochure explaining these five segments were used to convince retailers of the efficiency of these two segments, with some success.

Marketing Applications of Life-Style Analysis

Marketers have adapted to many of the more obvious changes in life-style in recent years. The "back to basics" life-style, for example, represents a desire for the genuine, the authentic, or the natural. This preference is reflected in product development of "no additive" cleansers and foods, and in such promotional campaigns as "Country Time—that good old-fashioned lemonade" or "Down Home Lemonade."

The shift in life-styles to casual living has led to the development of a fast-growing leisure-products industry. Blue Bell, a company that initially produced work clothes, switched to manufacturing jeans for casual wear. While sales of work clothes were $25 million in 1946, jeans sales for 1977 were projected at $800 million.[44]

Life-style analysis is used by marketers for product positioning and promotional decisions as well as market segmentation. As we saw at the beginning of this chapter, Ford changed its positioning strategy for Pinto after a life-style analysis of potential buyers.

Colonel Sanders' Kentucky Fried Chicken was originally advertised in a folksy, homey, small-town manner. Then it was found to be most heavily used by young housewives with an AIO profile that might be labeled "swinger." The advertising and packaging of the product were changed to reflect these findings.[45]

In the late 1960s Schlitz decided to freshen its previously successful campaign built around the line "When you're out of Schlitz, you're out of beer." One of the elements of a proposed new campaign was the word "gusto," which had been used in advertising in the early 1960s. Research was conducted to distinguish the life-style characteristics that significantly differentiated the heavy beer drinker from the nondrinker of beer.[46] (See Table 10.6.) The major life-style pat-

TABLE 10.6   PROFILE OF THE MALE BEER DRINKER

	Percent agreement		
	Non-users	Light users	Heavy users
He is self-indulgent, enjoys himself, and likes risks			
I like to play poker	18	37	41
I like to take chances	27	32	44
I would rather spend a quiet evening at home than go out to a party	67	53	44
If I had my way, I would own a convertible	7	11	15
I smoke too much	29	40	42
If I had to choose, I would rather have a color TV than a new refrigerator	25	33	38
He rejects responsibility and is a bit impulsive			
I like to work on community projects	24	18	14
I have helped collect money for the Red Cross or United Fund	41	32	24
I'm not very good at saving money	20	29	38
I find myself checking prices, even for small items	51	42	40
He likes sports and a physical orientation			
I would like to be a pro football player	10	15	21
I like bowling	32	36	42
I usually read the sports page	47	48	59
I would do better than average in a fist fight	17	26	32
I like war stories	33	37	45
He rejects old-fashioned institutions and moral guidelines			
I go to church regularly	57	37	31
Movies should be censored	67	46	43
I have old-fashioned tastes and habits	69	56	48
There is too much emphasis on sex today	71	59	53
. . . and has a very masculine view			
Beer is a real man's drink	9	16	44
Playboy is one of my favorite magazines	11	21	28
I am a girl watcher	33	47	54
Men should not do the dishes	18	26	38
Men are smarter than women	22	27	31

Source: Joseph T. Plummer, "Life Style and Advertising: Case Studies," *1971 Combined Proceedings of AMA Spring and Fall Conferences,* ed. Fred C. Allvine (Chicago: American Marketing Association, 1972), p. 294.

terns that emerged indicated that the heavy beer drinker was probably more hedonistic and pleasure seeking than the nondrinker. He seemed to have less regard for the responsibilities of family and job. More than the nondrinker, he tended to have a preference for a physical, male-oriented existence and an inclination to fantasize. He considered beer to be a real man's drink. These findings led to adoption of a new Schlitz beer campaign featuring the "Gusto Man." Similar life-style analysis led to advertising campaigns depicting users of Irish Spring soap as "independent" and "manly" and United Airline flights as "friendly."

Life-style analysis can reveal many additional marketing opportunities. As we saw in Chapter 6, the working/nonworking classification does not always provide an accurate reflection of women's attitudes toward food preparation and food shopping behavior. It appears that life-style factors, such as styles of food preparation, may contribute more to an explanation of general shopping patterns than do role orientations.[47]

Apparently the contemporary woman has multiple demands on her limited time, whether or not she is employed. Thus an effective marketing strategy may require the incorporation of life-style factors. Rather than appealing to jobholding women with "time-saving" features and directing "nutritional" appeals to home-makers, a food store might more successfully devote a specific section to quickly prepared foods for the "anticooking woman," who may or may not go out to work.

Limitations of Life-Style Research

Like many research techniques, life-style analysis raises methodological questions, and it may not be useful to all marketers. Some consider it most productive in determining the content and style of communications, developing new products, and positioning or developing new packaging. Life-style research may be more appropriate for products whose function is psychological gratification and relatively expensive,[48] and whose performance cannot be evaluated objectively. Such research is considered inappropriate for commodities (salt, for instance), which are purchased on the basis of price, or for products purchased by an expert or according to specifications.

Psychographic data may not always provide a basis for such strategic decisions as the selection of media. One recent study was designed to provide information concerning the personality and life-style characteristics of television audiences. The results indicate that audiences are relatively heterogeneous in terms of life-style characteristics. According to this study, such variables appeared to be of limited value in describing the composition of television audiences or predicting viewing behavior.[49]

More recently, Ronald Frank and Marshall Greenberg conducted a national survey of television audiences, and through cluster analysis they identified fourteen interest segments.[50] According to the researchers, these interest segments can be related to viewing behavior and thereby make significant contributions to decisions associated with television programming policy and strategy. Although they note this area requires further study, Frank and Greenberg suggest that interest segmentation may complement the demographic and socioeconomic measures traditionally used in audience classification.

Life-style patterns apparently provide a broad, three-dimensional view of customers so that one can think about them intelligently in terms of the most relevant product positioning, communication, and promotion. Further research is necessary before one can attest to the efficiency of life-style information in the analysis of consumer behavior.

SUMMARY

Personality can be thought of as those enduring traits that affect the manner in which the individual deals with his environment. A number of psychological theories have been applied to an understanding of personality's influence on consumer behavior. The psychoanalytic theory emphasizes the unconscious nature of personality, and suggests that three interacting forces—id, ego, and superego—combine to produce behavior. The social theory stresses social considerations, such as striving for superiority and the seeking of love and security, as the basic factors that influence consumer behavior. The trait and factor theory suggests that personality is composed of a set of traits and factors that can be measured on personality scales and have relevance to consumer behavior.

A number of personality scales have been developed to measure personality traits and factors, and these scales have been applied to research on consumer behavior. They include the Gordon Personal Profile, the Thurstone Temperament Schedule, and the Edwards Personal Preference Schedule. Recently efforts have been directed toward development of a modified personality-testing instrument—one that would have more relevance to studies in the field of consumer behavior.

There is evidence that the consumer's image of himself influences his behavior. Each individual, however, has five self-concepts: the real self, the ideal self, the self-image, the apparent self, and the reference-group image. The consumer may develop various patterns of behavior designed to protect these self-concepts.

Various research studies have been conducted to uncover a relationship between personality and consumer behavior. Results are subject to interpretation and raise questions as to the usefulness of the investigation of personality in predicting consumer behavior.

Life-style reflects the overall manner in which people live and spend their money. The development of psychographics has furthered efforts to consider life-style as a determinant of consumer behavior. Specifically, AIO inventories are used to gather life-style information for use in such marketing strategies as product positioning and promotion.

DISCUSSION QUESTIONS

1. How would you integrate Freud's personality theories with early motivation research efforts?

2. How would you incorporate the self-concept theory in marketing strategies?

3. What are some of the merging life-styles of the 1980s? What life-style trends do you anticipate will decline?

4. Why is life-style analysis considered more efficient than personality study in the field of consumer behavior?

5. What is meant by psychographics? AIO analysis?

6. Do you consider that Needham, Harper & Steers's general life-style studies provide valid information for marketers? What other segments might you include?

7. Assume you are preparing a marketing campaign for a company that sells through catalogs. How might life-style segmentation be used for such a campaign?

8. Select several ads that appear to incorporate various life-styles.

NOTES

1. Peter W. Bernstein, "Psychographics Is Still an Issue on Madison Avenue," *Fortune,* January 16, 1978, p. 80.

2. David Krech, Richard S. Crutchfield, and Norman Livson, *Elements of Psychology,* 3d ed. (New York: Alfred A. Knopf, 1974), pp. 708–709.

3. Clifford T. Morgan, *Introduction to Psychology* (New York: McGraw-Hill, 1961), p. 683.

4. Arthur W. Staats and C. K. Staats, *Complex Human Behavior: A Systematic Extension of Learning Principles* (New York: Holt, Rinehart & Winston, 1963), p. 285.

5. Harold H. Kassarjian, "Personality and Consumer Behavior: A Review," *Journal of Marketing Research* 8 (November 1971), pp. 409–418.

6. Karen B. Horney, *Our Inner Conflicts* (New York: W. W. Norton, 1945).

7. Joel B. Cohen, "An Interpersonal Orientation to the Study of Consumer Behavior," *Journal of Marketing Research* 4 (August 1967), pp. 270–278.

8. Jon P. Noerager, "An Assessment of CAD—A Personality Instrument Developed Specifically for Marketing Research," *Journal of Marketing Research* 16 (February 1979), pp. 53–59.

9. Gerald Zaltman and Melanie Wallendorf, *Consumer Behavior: Basic Findings and Management Implications* (New York: John Wiley, 1979), p. 391.

10. Gordon Allport, "Traits Revisited," *American Psychologist* 21 (1966), pp. 1–10.

11. William T. Tucker and John Painter, "Personality and Product Use," *Journal of Applied Psychology* 45 (October 1961), pp. 325–329.

12. Retrospective Comment to "Personality and Product Use," in *Classics in Consumer Behavior,* ed. Louis W. Boone (Oklahoma: Petroleum Publishing, 1977).

13. Ralph Westfall, "Psychological Factors in Predicting Product Choice," *Journal of Marketing* 26 (April 1962), pp. 34–40.

14. Arthur Koponen, "Personality Characteristics of Purchasers," *Journal of Advertising Research* 1 (September 1960), pp. 6–12.

15. E. Laird Landon, "A Sex-Role Explanation of Purchase Intention Differences of Consumers Who Are High and Low in Need for Achievement," *Association for Consumer Research,* Proceedings of 3d Annual Conference, ed. M. Venkatesan (Association for Consumer Research, 1972), pp. 1–8.

16. Larry Percy, "A Look at Personality Profiles and Personality-Attitude-Behavior Links in Predicting Consumer Behavior," in *Advances in Consumer Research,* vol. 3, ed. Beverlee B. Anderson (Association for Consumer Research, 1976), pp. 119–124.

17. Ibid., p. 120.

18. Kathryn E. A. Villani and Yoram Wind, "On the Usage of 'Modified' Personality Trait Measures in Consumer Research," *Journal of Consumer Research* 2 (December 1975), p. 225.

19. W. D. Wells and D. J. Tigert, "Activities, Interests, and Opinions," *Journal of Advertising Research* 11 (August 1971), pp. 27–35.

20. Carl R. Rogers, "A Theory of Therapy, Personality, and Interpersonal Relationships, as Developed in the Client-Centered Framework," in *Psychology: Theory of Science*, vol. 3, ed. Sigmund Koch (New York: McGraw-Hill, 1959).

21. Ralph H. Turner and Richard H. Vanderlippe, "Self-ideal Congruence as an Index of Adjustment," *Journal of Abnormal and Social Psychology* 57 (September 1958).

22. Carl R. Rogers, *Client-Centered Therapy* (Boston: Houghton Mifflin, 1951), p. 492.

23. George E. Belch and E. Laird Landon, Jr., "Discrimination Validity of a Product-Anchored Self-Concept Measure," *Journal of Marketing Research* 14 (May 1977), pp. 252–256.

24. Edward L. Grubb and Gregg Hupp, "Perception of Self, Generalized Stereotypes, and Brand Selection," *Journal of Marketing Research* 5 (February 1968), pp. 58–63.

25. A. E. Birdwell, "A Study of the Influence of Image Congruence on Consumer Choice," *Journal of Business* 41 (January 1968), pp. 76–88.

26. I. J. Dolich, "Congruence Relationships between Self-Images and Product Brands," *Journal of Marketing Research* 6 (February 1969), pp. 80–84.

27. Bruce L. Stern, Ronald F. Bush, and Joseph F. Hair, Jr., "The Self-Image/Store Image Matching Process," *Journal of Business* 50 (January 1977), pp. 63–69.

28. Raymond L. Horton, "Some Relationships between Personality and Consumer Decision Making," *Journal of Marketing Research* 16 (May 1979), pp. 233–246.

29. Richard C. Becherer and Lawrence M. Richard, "Self-Monitoring as a Moderating Variable in Consumer Behavior," *Journal of Consumer Research* 5 (December 1978), pp. 159–162.

30. Kenneth A. Coney and Robert R. Harmon, "Dogmatism and Innovation: A Situational Perspective," in *Advances in Consumer Research*, vol. 6, ed. William L. Wilkie (Ann Arbor: Association for Consumer Research, 1979), pp. 118–121.

31. Claes Fornell and Robert A. Westbrook, "An Exploratory Study of Assertiveness, Aggressiveness, and Consumer Complaining Behavior," in ibid., pp. 105–110.

32. William D. Wells and Stephen C. Cosmas, "Life Styles," in *Selected Aspects of Consumer Behavior*, prepared for National Science Foundation, Directorate for Research Application, Research Applied to Science, Washington, D.C., p. 299.

33. William Lazer, "Life Style Concepts and Marketing," in *Marketing and Its Environment: Some Issues and Perspectives*, ed. Richard A. Scott and Norton E. Marks (Belmont, Calif.: Wadsworth, 1968), p. 157, and "Life Style Concepts and Marketing," in *Toward Scientific Marketing: Proceedings of the American Marketing Association Winter Conference*, ed. S. A. Greyser (Boston, 1963), pp. 130–139.

34. Sidney J. Levey, "Social Class and Consumer Behavior," in *On Knowing the Consumer*, ed. Joseph W. Newman (New York: John Wiley, 1966), p. 156.

35. James M. Carman, "Values and Consumption Patterns: A Closed Loop," in *Advances in Consumer Research*, vol. 5, ed. H. Keith Hunt (1978), pp. 403–407.

36. William D. Wells, "Psychographics: A Critical Review," *Journal of Marketing Research* 12 (May 1975), pp. 196–213.

37. William D. Wells and Stephen C. Cosmas, "Life Styles," in *Selected Aspects of Consumer Behavior*, pp. 300–301.

38. Joseph T. Plummer, "Life Style Patterns," in *Journal of Broadcasting*, Winter 1971–72, p. 79.

39. Peter W. Bernstein, "Psychographics Is Still an Issue on Madison Avenue," *Fortune*, January 16, 1978, pp. 78–84, and "Film Findings Show Use of Lifestyle Research," *Marketing News*, June 17, 1977, p. 9.

40. "Film of Findings Shows Uses of Lifestyle Research," *Marketing News*, June 17, 1977, p. 9.

41. Stephen C. Cosmas, "The Advantages and Disadvantages of the Profile Approach to Analyzing Life Style Data," in *Advances in Consumer Research*, vol. 3, ed. Anderson, p. 501.

42. Joseph T. Plummer, "Life Style Patterns and Commercial Bank Credit Card Usage," *Journal of Marketing* 35 (April 1971), pp. 35–41.

43. Alan Weinman, "Discovering a $1.2 Billion Market: DeKupsa on Life Style Research," *Marketing Review,* November/December 1976, pp. 6–7.

44. *Marketing News,* February 25, 1977, p. 8.

45. William D. Wells and Douglas J. Tigert, "Activities, Interests, and Opinions," *Journal of Advertising Research* 11 (August 1971), pp. 27–35.

46. Joseph T. Plummer, "Life Style and Advertising: Case Studies," *1971 Combined Proceedings of AMA Spring and Fall Conferences,* ed. Fred. C. Allvine (Chicago: American Marketing Association, 1972), pp. 290–295.

47. Mary Lou Roberts and Lawrence H. Wortzel, "New Life-Style Determinants of Women's Food Shopping Behavior," *Journal of Marketing* 53 (Summer 1979), pp. 28–39.

48. "Lifestyle Research Inappropriate for Some Categories of Products," *Marketing News,* June 17, 1977, p. 9.

49. Kathryn E. A. Villani, "Personality, Life Style and Television Behavior," *Journal of Marketing Research* 12 (November 1975), pp. 432–439.

50. Ronald E. Frank and Marshall G. Greenberg, "Interest-based Segments of TV Audiences," *Journal of Advertising Research* 19 (October 1979), pp. 43–54.

CHAPTER 11

ATTITUDES

The American Can Company, faced with leveling sales and profits and "ban the can" litter campaigns, expanded its line of consumer products to include paper towels. To meet the competition in the field, American Can conducted market research that revealed that consumers' attitudes toward paper towels were influenced by the products' absorbency, strength, clothlike quality, and price, not necessarily in that order.[1] The company instituted a crash development program to introduce and position the new product appropriately.

In 1977 the R. J. Reynolds Tobacco Company introduced a new cigarette, Real. The new brand was calculated to enable Reynolds, which already made 1 of every 3 cigarettes sold in the United States, to gain an extra 1.0 to 1.5 percent share of the profitable $15 billion cigarette market within two years.[2] The new brand would compete with 170 other brands already on the market. In 1964 the surgeon general's report had provided evidence that linked the tar in cigarettes to increased risks of lung cancer, respiratory disease, and heart disease. New findings by the American Cancer Society in 1976 indicated that smokers of low-tar cigarettes have lower death rates from cancer and heart disease than smokers of "full-flavor" brands. Yankelovich, Skelly & White, Inc., a polling firm, conducted opinion surveys for Reynolds in 1971 and 1972 and found that consumers were shifting to "natural" products of all kinds. Thus it appeared that a good niche for the new cigarette was found—a low-tar, natural smoke.

The introductory advertising campaign for Real was the largest in the history of consumer packaged goods. An appropriation of $40 million was made for a six-month period. The money was allocated for 130 boxcar loads of display materials, more than 25 million free sample packages, the biggest billboard overlooking Times Square, the summer-long services of more than 2,000 salesmen to call on the nation's 360,000 retail stores that sell tobacco, and advertisements in various media. The Real advertising message was conveyed by tobacco leaves and rough-grained wood, focusing on one idea—a natural cigarette "with nothing artificial added." Although it was a low-tar cigarette, no mention of this fact was made in the ads. It was assumed that the "natural" characteristic would be sufficient to generate a favorable attitude toward Real.

However, "naturalness," an important characteristic of foods, seemed less significant for cigarettes. Acknowledging that taste may be a more important attribute than naturalness to smokers, Reynolds changed the campaign to emphasize Real as a "low tar" cigarette that "tastes" like it has "high tar." Real never captured more than one half of one percent of the market, and in 1980 R. J. Reynolds discontinued its Real brand.

Underlying these illustrations are a number of assumptions of attitude and attitude change and their relevance to consumer behavior. These assumptions will be clarified in this chapter, which examines such questions as:

What are attitudes?
How are they formed?
What functions do attitudes perform for individuals?
How are attitudes toward products and services developed?

DEFINING ATTITUDES

The psychological literature is replete with definitions of attitudes. One early definition, which appears to have survived with modifications, describes attitudes as "learned predispositions to respond to an object or class of objects in a consistently favorable or unfavorable way."[3] In a marketing context, the object may be a product, brand, service, company store, or even spokesperson.

Despite the relative simplicity of the definition, the concept of attitudes is complex and incorporates a number of theoretical constructs discussed in earlier chapters, such as learning, perception, and motivation. We are not born with attitudes; they are learned, and therefore are built partly from long-term memory. Perceptions both influence and are influenced by attitudes. Favorable or unfavorable attitudinal response may emerge from individual motives.

The "predispositions" of which the definition speaks are tendencies to perceive and to act in particular ways; an actual response may differ from a predisposition. Thus, if a bad experience with a "lemon" has resulted in a predisposition to distrust a certain make of car, other factors, such as low price or a new warranty, may overcome the unfavorable attitude in the final selection process. The word "consistently" indicates that attitudes do not develop from fleeting likes and dislikes; the favorable or unfavorable response must occur regularly. Since attitudes are not momentary whims, but relatively enduring, a means of judging and measuring consumers' attitudes might provide insights into the ways in which consumers are likely to behave in the future.[4]

THE LEARNING OF ATTITUDES

Attitudes are learned from many sources. The major sources generally considered to influence attitude formation are personal experience and social influence; attitudes also derive from emotional reactions.

Personal Experience

Attitudes may be learned through instrumental conditioning, as when a consumer's action is followed by or associated with a reward. The consumer's attitude toward a brand of detergent may be based on his favorable experience with such a product in a washing machine.

Cognitive learning also contributes to the development of attitudes. The beliefs, values, and knowledge stored in long-term memory provide a basis for evaluation of attitudes. If we believe, for example, that ecological concerns are valid, we may have a negative attitude toward "gas guzzlers" and a positive attitude toward small cars that get more miles per gallon.

Social Influence

It is commonly assumed that social influences are the single most important source of most attitudes. "The major influence on people is people."[5] Our shared beliefs, values, and expectations about the appropriate ways to behave in certain situations influence our attitudes. Parent-child interactions have enormous impact on a child's attitudes and values. The peer group is particularly influential among high school and college students in molding a wide variety of attitudes. Peer-group pressure is very influential in the formation of attitudes toward products and the appropriate fashion outlets to patronize.

Emotional Reactions

Some attitudes are formed as expressions of the individual's emotional reactions—either those momentarily aroused by some frustration or those more permanently related to the individual's personality. Conservative people tend to prefer cars that project a conservative image, while the adventurous are more favorably disposed to the car that presents a sporty image.

THE FUNCTIONS OF ATTITUDES

According to some researchers, the meaning and significance of attitudes are best understood at the functional level; that is, they strive to understand why people hold the attitudes they do and the purposes attitudes serve for them. According to Daniel Katz, attitudes serve four significant functions: utilitarian or instrumental, ego-defensive, value-expressive, and knowledge functions.[6]

The Utilitarian or Instrumental Function

Attitudes help the individual to adapt to the world of reality. If an item helped an individual to reach his goal, the attitude developed would be favorable; if the item interfered with attainment of the goal, the attitude would be negative. For example, if a person had pleasurable experiences with an automobile with which he completed a long, successful trip and a motel at which he stayed along the way, the car and the motel would be associated with the successful achievement of positive values and goals and would therefore become objects of favorable attitudes. Should the motel room have been uncomfortable and noisy and the automobile have broken down, the resulting attitudes would have been negative. Attitudes help the consumer to maximize his rewards in the marketplace and minimize his punishment, and he therefore makes his choices accordingly. This utilitarian function relates to approach-avoidance behavior, discussed earlier. It is also called "instrumental" to indicate that the individual's behavior is shaped by consequences—that is, consequences are instrumental in determining future behavior.

The Ego-Defensive Function

An attitude that serves an ego-defensive function is formed not on the basis of an item's ability to assist in attainment of a goal, but to protect oneself from internal anxieties or the dangers of the external environment. Attitudes may protect the individual from acknowledging her deficiencies and help her to defend her self-image. It is not necessary for a person to have deep feelings of inferiority for attitudes to serve an ego-defensive function. If forces in the environment are viewed as threatening, ego-defensive attitudes serve to reduce the anxieties they arouse. The idea that attitudes serve ego-defensive functions has its origin in Freudian theory.

Many marketing appeals are designed to bolster or defend the ego. The cigarette advertisement that states, "You've come a long way, baby!" and the cake-mix ad that assures a successful outcome are attempts at ego bolstering, while mouthwash and deodorant advertisements offer mechanisms for defense. There is little clear understanding of the ego-defensive function, and the marketer must be wary of behavior or communications that may trigger ego-defensive attitudes, since such messages may cause an unfavorable rather than a favorable predisposition toward the product.

The Value-Expressive Function

Attitudes give positive expression to the individual's values and to the type of person he conceives himself to be. When attitudes are expressed that reflect the person's cherished beliefs and self-image, they result in satisfactions. When attitudes serve as expressions of the individual as he would like to be, they serve a self-realizing function.

Attitudes rooted in the value-expressive function are those that attempt to project the social values and commitments of the individual. The surge in business school enrollments reflects increasingly favorable attitudes toward business and the commitment of many students to preparation for employment opportunities. Consumers express their values in the products they purchase, the stores they patronize, and the life-style they exhibit.

The Knowledge Function

Attitudes help to provide standards or frames of reference for an understanding of the world. People seek a degree of predictability, consistency, and stability in their perceptions of and interactions with the world. The notion that attitudes serve the knowledge function is related to the cognitive theory of learning and information processing. It assumes that the individual's information-processing ability will be inadequate, and that he will therefore be forced to rely on referents and stereotyping to simplify reality.[7] By forming cognitive categories, the individual is able to group cognitive elements in his task of defining and responding to (or developing attitudes toward) new stimuli. Through this mechanism, individuals give structure to a chaotic world.

Advertisements frequently provide new information to restructure the individual's perception of a given situation. For example, the presentation of microwave ovens permits people to develop favorable attitudes toward a new way of cooking and preparing food, while the "meal in a pouch" offers an alternative to eating out in restaurants.

In general, the concept of the knowledge function suggests that consumers are information seekers and that their need to know drives them to gain information that gives general meaning to their social world.

THE STRUCTURE OF ATTITUDES

Most researchers agree that attitudes pertain to that mental state of the individual which represents her positive or negative or neutral feelings toward an object, concept, or idea.[8] Attitudes have become an important area of study in the field of consumer behavior in part because of a widely held belief that they precede the individual's behavior toward an object (a product, brand, or firm) and hence may be used as predictors of behavior.

Efforts to understand this process have generated substantial research into the development of structural models that would both predict and explain attitudes. It is assumed that knowing the organization of attitudes and studying their parts and interrelationships will provide insight into the way attitudes are formed and changed. It should be clear, however, that such research frequently indicates that a distinction must be made between attitude toward an object and attitude toward the act of actually purchasing and using that object.

Attitudes and their structure cannot be observed; they are inferred. As bases for such inference, several models have been developed in consumer-behavior literature; two of the most widely discussed concepts are the three-component model and the multiattribute model.

The Three-Component Model

The single-component view treats attitude as a single dimension of affect for or against an object. In this view, it is the affective (feeling) component that is usually measured and treated as attitude. The failure of researchers to find consistent, strong relationships between the single-component view of attitude and behavior led to elaboration and clarification of the attitude construct and to further specification of its relationship to behavior.[9]

In another view of attitudes, three components are thought to be common to all attitudes, though their proportions vary: the cognitive component (or beliefs), the affective component (or feelings), and the action-tendency component.[10]

THE COGNITIVE COMPONENT

The cognitive component of an attitude includes the individual's beliefs about some object or class of objects. The beliefs in long-term memory summarize previous experience and make future interactions with the world more meaningful. The cognitive component influences the manner in which the attitude object is perceived. For example, previous knowledge may result in the beliefs that a deodorizing soap cleans and deodorizes and that "junk food" is unhealthy.

THE AFFECTIVE COMPONENT

The affective or emotional component involves likes and dislikes. Beliefs are interrelated with perception to provide this evaluative aspect of an attitude object, such as a product or its attributes.

While a belief that a soap cleans and deodorizes may cause some consumers to like the product, others may believe that deodorant soap dries the skin excessively and so may dislike it. Similarly, those committed to health concerns avoid junk food, while those who have developed the junk-food habit will like such products, despite a belief that they may be unhealthy.

THE ACTION-TENDENCY COMPONENT

The action-tendency component of attitudes is more commonly designated "behavioral intention," since it pertains to predispositions to behave or respond in a certain way. The transition from attitudes to actual buying behavior may occur through this action-tendency component.

THE CONSISTENCY OF ATTITUDE COMPONENTS

A significant aspect of the three-component model of attitudes lies in the presumed consistency of the components; that is, they support each other. Consistency is particularly important in attitude change, for it would seem that a change in one of the three components would tend to induce a change in the other two. Some studies do support the consistency of relationships among beliefs, emotions, and action tendency. Many marketing experiences, however, indicate differently. For example, it seems difficult to understand why, despite a "squeezably soft" ad campaign that has irritated and annoyed many consumers, Charmin continues to fare quite well in the toilet-tissue market. Consumers may have a negative reaction to the service in a restaurant but continue to patronize it.

Research results have indicated that whether beliefs and emotions are found to be translated into consistent behavior depends on a number of variables, including the attitude about other aspects of the situation, fear of punishment, and the extent to which the individual feels he is able to act on his attitudes and is personally involved with the issue.

Multiattribute Models

During the past several years, efforts to relate attitudes to behavior have resulted in the development of the multiattribute models of attitude. The basic proposition of these models is that consumers form attitudes toward products on the basis of product *attributes*, a hypothesis that has many implications for marketing strategies. Proponents of attitude-structure models have argued repeatedly for their diagnostic usefulness to decision makers in isolating those attributes that should be the targets of promotional appeals directed at the shaping of brand preferences.[11]

The term "attribute" does not appear to have a precise explanation in the marketing literature; however, attributes are frequently interrelated with definitions of "evaluative criteria"[12] or "choice criteria."[13] Thus attributes are considered to be specifications or criteria that consumers use in comparing product alternatives. In selecting an automobile, for example, a consumer may consider styling, convenience, economic value, miles per gallon of gas, or other specifications in evaluating a particular alternative. Attributes are not only specifications, however; they may be seen as beliefs about the consequences of using a product—prestige, protection of the environment against pollution, high trade-in value, and so on.[14]

In the marketing context, multiattribute models suggest that the consumer's choice of one brand or product over others on the basis of attitudes is not a case of simple likes and dislikes. The preferential attitude is rather a complex outcome of many separate judgments about the various attributes of a product. In general, these multiattribute models are good predictors of overall evaluation or attitude, but their ability to predict behavior is more varied.[15]

MEASURING ATTRIBUTES

The criteria used by consumers to make comparisons among alternative attributes are not always readily apparent. Further, the number of attributes that are to be included in a multiattribute model to ensure its predictive power is not specified. A relevant concept developed from learning theory is the "principle of information-processing parsimony." According to this principle, because of our limited cognitive capacity, we adopt heuristics (or rules of thumb) that permit us to process as few data as are necessary to enable us to make rational decisions.[16] Reliance on the three most important attributes would be such a strategy of information simplification.

In addition, it appears that frequently only a few attributes are sufficient in the model since in many cases few attributes are salient.[17] Though "salient" is frequently considered to be synonymous with "important," a "salient" attribute not only must be important to the consumer, but must also be seen as the basis on which various brands and institutions differ. According to Nelson Foote, manager of General Electric's consumer and public relations research program:

> In the electrical appliance business, we have been impressed over and over by the way in which certain characteristics of products come to be taken for granted by consumers, especially those concerned with basic functional performance, or with values like safety. If these values are missing in a product, the user is extremely offended. But if they are present, maker or seller gets no special credit or preference, because quite logically every other maker and seller is assumed to be offering equivalent values.[18]

Thus "browns more evenly" may be considered a more salient attribute of toasters than "safe to use," unless, of course, the consumer has accidentally received a shock or burn from a previously owned toaster.

Research into the structure of attitudes and attitude change has led to the development of techniques to determine salient or "determinant" attributes; that is, those that consumers are most likely to consider in choosing a product. The American Can Company, as we saw at the beginning of this chapter, relied on salient attributes in introducing its paper towels. Uncovering such attributes may be difficult, since some attributes take a long time to be accepted, while others gain fairly rapid acceptance and then wear out. Presweetened cereals for children were around for approximately fifteen years before they became popular. High-protein cereals, originally introduced for the geriatric market, became family cereals after several years. "Natural" cereals have had a faster acceptance rate, but observers expect them to top out with about 15 percent of the market. In fact, it is the wearout factor that causes new cereals to be continually introduced. As we saw in the case of Real cigarettes, naturalness apparently is not a salient attribute for cigarettes.

Attribute information may be secured through informal interviews with consumers. When a consumer is questioned as to the features of a product, frequently the first one elicited—and therefore designated as salient—may not be determinant, since it may come to mind as a result of heavily advertised slogans. Another problem with questioning consumers as to what it is they want is that they frequently do not know what they want until they know what they can have. When an appliance company interviewed housewives to determine what features they would like in ovens, typical responses were "Make ovens prettier"; "Move the dials back so that children can't reach them"; "Move the dials up front so I won't burn myself when I'm reaching for the oven"; not one woman had the nerve to say, "Make me an oven that cleans itself." Yet when the same housewives were interviewed a second time and exposed to the idea of a self-cleaning oven, they all declared, "That's just what I need!"[19]

In addition to informal interviews with consumers, several techniques may be used to provide a measure of the consumer's need for a product attribute and the relative importance they accord it. These methods include quadrant analysis, conjoint measurement, and magnitude estimation.

Quadrant Analysis. Marketers may use quadrant analysis, discussed in Chapter 8, in testing new products by including a scaled measurement of importance or necessity for each attribute, as well as attribute ratings. A four-part graph is then compiled, with each quadrant denoting a combined level of importance and satisfaction. Figure 8.5 in Chapter 8 not only revealed those attributes that consumers considered extremely important in automobile repair services, but indicated the consumer's satisfaction or dissatisfaction with their delivery by an automobile dealer's service department.

Conjoint Measurement. It is useful for marketers to be aware of the relative importance of product attributes. One method of determining their relative importance is conjoint measurement. This technique is useful in the early stages of product development. It attempts to determine the utility value of various attributes of a product so that eventually an "ideal" product can be built up from the utilities developed by the conjoint measurement model.[20]

FIGURE 11.1   UTILITIES FOR RIDING LAWN MOWERS

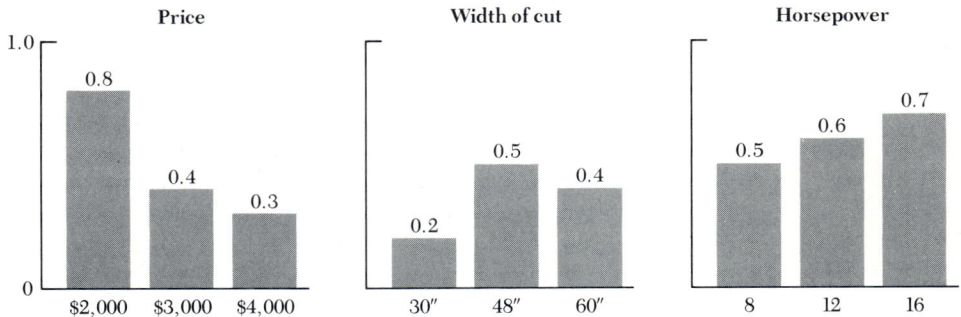

Source: Herbert Hupfer, "Conjoint Analysis Helps in Sorting Out Consumers' Weighting of Product Attributes," *Marketing News,* January 28, 1977, p. 10.

If an "ideal" riding lawn mower is to be developed, for example, the utilities of three major attributes can be determined through consumer research, and may emerge as shown in Figure 11.1. When the highest utility values for each of the attributes are added together, the "ideal" lawn mower would have these features:

ATTRIBUTE	LEVEL	UTILITY
Price	$2,000	0.8
Width of cut	48″	0.5
Horsepower	16	0.7
Total		2.0

If no lawn mower on the market currently has this set of characteristics, a manufacturer may consider developing one after learning the apparently high value accorded these attributes. If this choice is not feasible—as a result of engineering or cost problems, say—a lower sum of utilities might be considered. Two options are available to provide the next highest total utility, 1.9: one is to use the price of $2,000 (0.8 utility) with a 60-inch cut (0.4) and 16 horsepower (0.7); the other is a $2,000 price (0.8), a 48-inch cut (0.5), and 12 horsepower (0.6). As the 60-inch cut may offer lower maneuverability and be more costly, the second option seems preferable.[21]

The problem with conjoint measurement of attributes is that the process becomes unwieldy if the number of purchase criteria used by the consumer is large. Such analysis is also unnecessary if the product attributes are already known to be predominantly responsible for the respondent's purchasing behavior.

Magnitude Estimation.   When attributes are measured by magnitude estimation, each respondent is asked to use his own scale.[22] He is told that if he does not desire or need a given attribute, he should assign it a zero. He must, however, judge his need for each attribute in relation to the preceding ones. For example, let us assume that in rating attributes of mouthwashes he assigns taste a score of 20, and the next attribute to be considered is "kills germs." If he wants "kills germs" three times as much as taste, he assigns it a 60. If it is half as valuable to him, he assigns it a 10. Each respondent works with a personal scale, and data from each respondent are then translated into a common scale.

THE FISHBEIN MULTIATTRIBUTE MODEL

One of the most frequently cited multiattribute models was developed by Martin Fishbein. This model incorporates the belief and affective components of the tricomponent model, but it is based on attributes. Fishbein hypothesized that an attitude toward an object is a function of (1) beliefs about the object (or the probability that the object does or does not have a particular attribute) and (2) the evaluative aspects of those beliefs (the judgment that the attribute is good or bad).[23] The model takes the following form:

$$A_o = \sum_{i=1}^{n} (B_i a_i)$$

where A_o = attitude toward the object
B_i = the ith belief about the object
a_i = the evaluation of the ith belief
n = the total number of beliefs.

Fishbein developed another model to describe the attitude toward performing an act (rather than the attitude toward an object), which incorporates beliefs about the probability of *outcomes* resulting from the behavior, as follows:[24]

$$A_{\text{act}} = \sum_{i=1}^{n} (B_i a_i)$$

where A_{act} = attitude toward performing an act
B_i = the individual's belief about the likelihood that the behavior in question will result in outcome i
a_i = the person's evaluation of outcome i
n = the number of beliefs.

These are "expectancy value" models. It is hypothesized that object attributes are evaluated one at a time, and the ratings for all attributes are summed to arrive at a total evaluation of the object. The object with the highest sum "wins," or has the highest "expected value."

Variations of these models have been used in consumer-behavior research. A variation of Fishbein's model, which attempts to determine the consumer's attitude toward a brand, is similar to that of the A_o (attitude toward an object) but incorporates the "weight" or importance of each attribute.

The consumer's attitude toward a brand is hypothesized to be a function of the relative importance of each of the product attributes (W_i) and the consumer's beliefs about the brand on the basis of each attribute (B_{ib}), as follows:[25]

$$A_b = \sum_{i=1}^{n} (W_i B_{ib})$$

where A_b = attitude toward a particular brand
W_i = the weight or importance of attribute i
B_{ib} = the evaluative aspect or belief toward attribute i for brand b
n = the number of attributes.

The procedure for use of this model to determine attitudes toward mouthwashes, for example, may be as follows:

1. Determine the salient attributes (also considered choice criteria, or evaluative criteria) for mouthwashes. This information may be obtained by informal interviews with consumers. As a result of such interviews, the following salient attributes may be disclosed for mouthwashes:

Kills germs	Color
Taste/flavor	Effectiveness
Price	

2. Have respondents rank the importance of each attribute of a mouthwash (W_i). (See Table 11.1.)

The five attributes may then be ranked as follows:

1. Kills germs.
2. Effectiveness.
3. Taste/flavor.
4. Price.
5. Color.

TABLE 11.1   FREQUENCY OF ATTRIBUTE-IMPORTANCE RANKING (IN PERCENT)

Attribute	1st	2d	3d	4th	5th
Kills germs	49.3	31.9	11.9	5.9	1.0
Taste/flavor	15.1	22.6	43.0	18.5	0.7
Price	4.7	12.2	22.9	52.8	7.4
Color	0.2	0.3	1.1	9.3	89.1
Effectiveness	30.9	33.1	21.0	13.4	1.6

Source: "General Consumer Products," in *Cases in Promotional Strategy*, ed. James F. Engel, W. W. Talarzyk, and C. M. Larson (Homewood, Ill.: Richard D. Irwin, 1971), p. 91.

3. Respondents are next asked to rate the extent to which they believe each of various brands of mouthwash can satisfy each of these attributes (B_{ib}). To do so, respondents provide a scaled value from 1 (very satisfactory) to 6 (very unsatisfactory) for each attribute of each brand. Table 11.2 presents the average consumer ratings of several brands of mouthwash on the relevant attributes. (The lowest number therefore represents the highest ratings.)

The significance of this presentation emerges not so much from a summary score of A_b (or attitude toward a particular brand of mouthwash), which is not provided,[26] as from the detailed ratings. It is obvious that Listerine holds the highest ratings on the two most salient attributes, kills germs and effectiveness. It is equally obvious that Cepacol has consistently lowest ratings across all criteria. Such information is useful for management in determining how to improve ratings and ultimately attitudes. Unfortunately, as we noted earlier, although such models are considered good predictors of overall evaluations of attitudes, their ability to predict behavior is questioned.

Still, such information may be very useful in marketing strategies relevant to appropriate attitude development. It reveals a product's strengths and weaknesses and can be used to suggest specific changes in a particular brand and its marketing support.[27] The concept of "evoked set," discussed earlier, suggests that consumers consider only a number of the brands available in the marketplace, and that a desirable strategy is to move a manufacturer's brand into the frame of consideration. That is, efforts should be made to make it one of the brands that consumers consider.

Once the product is part of the evoked set, an effort may be made to increase the probability that the consumer will consider that brand superior to others in the group. In this strategy, the multiattribute model of attitude may be useful. Efforts should be made to determine the consumer's perception of the importance of an attribute and its delivery by the product. Some people see the role of advertising as creating perceptions of desirability or attribute importance and as announcing the product's delivery of a new idea or feature. For example, when Gillette introduced its Good News! razor, its advertising strategy was twofold. First, it was designed to notify consumers that a new disposable razor was available, and suggested the importance of disposability in shaving implements. Next, it indi-

TABLE 11.2   AVERAGE CONSUMER RATINGS OF MOUTHWASH BRANDS ON RELEVANT ATTRIBUTES

Brand	Kills germs	Taste/ flavor	Price	Color	Effective- ness
Micrin	2.22	2.46	2.60	1.85	2.21
Cepacol	2.40	2.92	2.70	2.29	2.36
Listerine	1.63	2.86	2.29	2.27	1.64
Lavoris	2.31	2.38	2.50	1.81	2.27
Colgate 100	2.35	2.52	2.68	1.87	2.32

Source: "General Consumer Products," in *Cases in Promotional Strategy*, ed. James F. Engel, W. W. Talarzyk, and C. M. Larson (Homewood, Ill.: Richard D. Irwin, 1971), p. 91.

cated that Good News! did indeed provide disposability, by its construction and cost.

Sometimes attributes gain in importance as a result of external factors, irrespective of marketing strategy. Recent research has indicated that foods with high fiber content may be beneficial to consumers. Thus products that are high in fiber have become more important to consumers without any change in the consumer's perception of the product's delivery of fiber. Similarly, the concern with aerosol cans caused an increase in the sale of products packaged with pump applicators. The interest in jogging has led many bra manufacturers to develop "sweat" and "support" bras for female joggers.

THE EXTENDED FISHBEIN MODEL

The early Fishbein multiattribute model was conceptualized to explain attitudes toward objects rather than the relationships between attitudes and behavior. An extended model, the Fishbein Behavioral Intention Model, was later designed to integrate attitudinal, normative, and motivational influences relevant to behavior.

The Fishbein Behavioral Intention Model is based on Don Dulaney's theory of propositional control, which states that a person's intention to perform (or his actual performance) is "based on (a) his attitude toward *performing* the *behavior* in a given *situation,* and (b) the *norms* governing that behavior in that situation and his *motivation* to comply with those norms."[28]

This model is consistent with the features-benefit argument advanced by many marketers, which contends that consumers purchase benefits, not product attributes. In fact, much promotional strategy is based on the presentation of benefits, and many advertising agencies proclaim, "We advertise product benefits, not product features." This concept suggests that consumers may purchase expected outcomes, not product attributes, and desirable attributes may be quite different from desirable outcomes. Fishbein provided the following example:

> . . . a woman might believe that "high-pile" carpeting is "warm," "comfortable," "luxurious," and "prestigious," and since she positively evaluates those attributes, she is likely to have a positive attitude toward "high-pile carpeting." However, what do you think the consequences of "buying high-pile carpeting" are for that woman if she has two dogs, a cat, and three children under nine?[29]

The Fishbein extended model is depicted in an equation:

$$B \sim (BI) = A_{\text{act}} W_1 + (SN) W_2$$

where

B = overt behavior

BI = behavioral intention to perform the specific overt behavior

A_{act} = attitude toward performing the behavioral act

SN = subjective norm

W_1 and W_2 = empirically determined standardized regression coefficients.

Generally speaking, the model states that a person's intention to perform any behavior is a function of (1) his attitude toward performing that behavior (A_{act})

and (2) his subjective norm concerning that behavior (*SN*). The individual's subjective norm reflects his perception about the feelings of those other individuals most important in the performance of the specific behavior (for example, his wife in the purchase of a car, his dentist in the purchase of toothpaste).

The model suggests that the weights of two of the variables may vary with the intentions they determine. That is, some intentions may be entirely under attitudinal control (A_{act}), other intentions may be entirely under normative control (*SN*), and still other intentions may be influenced by both attitudinal and normative consequences.[30]

Several studies have been conducted to test the extended Fishbein model in a marketing context, and the results suggest the usefulness of this model as a predictor of behavioral intentions toward toothpaste,[31] soft drinks, and beer.[32] The researchers noted, however, that brand attitudes for convenience products were of relatively greater importance than normative influences in the formation of intentions. This finding suggests that a simple attitudinal measure, rather than the extended model, may be sufficient to predict intentions for some convenience products. It appears that further research is needed to determine whether measurement of normative influence in attitude formation is likely to be a waste of time.[33]

SUMMARY

Attitudes are defined as "learned predispositions to respond to an object or a class of objects in a consistently favorable or unfavorable way." Attitudes are learned, and such learning derives from many sources, including experience, social influence, and emotional reactions. It is assumed that attitudes perform a number of functions for the individual, such as the utilitarian ego-defensive, value-expressive, and knowledge functions.

In order to understand how attitudes are formed and changed, researchers have developed several structural models both to predict and to explain attitudes. In one such model, attitudes are said to possess three components: the cognitive or belief component, the affective or emotional component, and the action-tendency or behavioral component.

Various multiattribute models have been developed by researchers. The basic proposition of these models is that consumers form attitudes toward products on the basis of product attributes. Martin Fishbein and others have developed multiattribute models that have been used in research in the field of consumer behavior. Many marketing efforts are directed toward determining the "salient" or "determinant" attributes that consumers refer to in making their purchase selections.

DISCUSSION QUESTIONS

1. Describe a situation in which you might learn an attitude through personal experience; through social influence.

2. Describe a personal experience to illustrate each of the functions of attitudes.

3. How would knowledge of the structure of attitudes aid a marketer?

4. What is the difference between the single-component model and the tricomponent model of attitude?

5. Provide an illustration of attitude inconsistency in terms of the components of the tricomponent model.

6. What is an attribute? Provide an illustration of an important attribute that may not be determinant.

7. How does the Fishbein attitude model differ from earlier attitude theories?

8. What implications does the Fishbein model have for marketing strategies?

NOTES

1. "Strategic Planning Shows Road to Profitable Innovations," *McClellan Marketing News,* August 11, 1978, p. 6.

2. This account is based on articles in the *New York Times,* May 15, 1977: "$40 Million for a Real Smoke," pp. 3, 4; "Real's Origin—A Public Opinion Survey," p. 5; and " 'The Product Is the Hero,' " p. 5.

3. Gordon W. Allport, "Attitudes," in *Handbook of Social Psychology,* ed. C. A. Murchinson (Worcester, Mass.: Clark University Press, 1935), pp. 798–844.

4. Milton Rokeach, *Beliefs, Attitudes, and Values: A Theory of Organization and Change* (San Francisco: Jossey-Bass, 1970), p. 112.

5. Daryl J. Bem, *Beliefs, Attitudes, and Human Affairs* (Belmont, Calif.: Brooks/Cole, 1972), p. 75.

6. Daniel Katz, "The Functional Approach to the Study of Attitudes," *Public Opinion Quarterly* 24 (Summer 1960), pp. 163–204.

7. W. J. McGuire, "The Nature of Attitudes and Attitude Change," in *The Individual in a Social Context,* vol. 3 of *Handbook of Social Psychology,* ed. Gardner Lindzey and Elliot Aronson, 5 vols., 2d ed. (Reading, Mass.: Addison-Wesley, 1968), pp. 136–314.

8. Secil Tuncalp and Jagdish N. Sheth, "Prediction of Attitudes: A Comparative Study of the Rosenberg, Fishbein, and Sheth Models," in *Advances in Consumer Research,* vol. 2, ed. Mary Jane Schlinger (Association for Consumer Research, 1975), pp. 389–404.

9. Richard P. Bagozzi and Robert E. Burnkrant, "Attitude Organization and the Attitude-Behavior Relationship," *Journal of Personality and Social Psychology* 37 (June 1979), pp. 913–929.

10. Virupashka Kothandapani, "Validation of Feeling, Belief, and Intention to Act and Three Components of Attitude and Their Contribution to Prediction of Contraceptive Behavior," *Journal of Personality and Social Psychology* 19 (1971), pp. 321–333.

11. Morris B. Holbrook, "Beyond Attitude Structure: Toward the Informational Determinants of Attitudes," *Journal of Marketing Research* 15 (November 1978), p. 554.

12. James F. Engel, Roger D. Blackwell, and David T. Kollat, *Consumer Behavior,* 3d ed. (New York: Holt, Rinehart & Winston, 1978), p. 388.

13. John A. Howard, *Consumer Behavior: Application of Theory* (New York: McGraw-Hill, 1977), p. 49.

14. Richard J. Lutz, "Changing Brand Attitudes through Modification of Cognitive Structure," *Journal of Consumer Research* 1 (March 1975), p. 49.

15. Fleming Hansen, "Psychological Theories of Consumer Choice," in *Selected Aspects of Consumer Behavior*, prepared for National Science Foundation Directorate for Research Application, RANN, pp. 33–69, at p. 50.

16. George H. Haines, "Process Models of Consumer Decision Making," in *Buyer/Consumer Information Processing*, ed. G. David Hughes and Michael L. Ray (Chapel Hill: University of North Carolina Press, 1974), p. 96.

17. William L. Wilkie and Rolf P. Weinreich, "Effects of the Number and Type of Attributes Included in an Attitude Model: More Is *Not* Better," in *Proceedings*, ed M. Venkatesan, 3d Annual Conference of the Association for Consumer Research, 1972, pp. 325–340.

18. Nelson N. Foote, *Household Decision-Making*, Consumer Behavior series, vol. 4 (New York: New York University Press, 1961), p. 11.

19. David M. Stander, "Testing New Product Ideas in an 'Archie Bunker' World," *Marketing News*, November 15, 1973, pp. 4–5.

20. Herbert Hupfer, "Conjoint Analysis in Sorting Out Consumers' Weighting of Product Attributes," *Marketing News,* January 28, 1978, p. 10.

21. Ibid.

22. "New Testing Methods Can Indicate Consumer Needs, Rank Those Needs," *Marketing News*, March 24, 1978, pp. 8–9.

23. Martin Fishbein, "An Investigation of the Relationships between Beliefs about an Object and the Attitude toward That Object," *Human Relations* 16 (1963), pp. 233–240.

24. Martin Fishbein, "Attitude, Attitude Change, and Behavior: A Theoretical Overview," in *Attitude Research Bridges the Atlantic*, ed. Philip Levine (Chicago: American Marketing Association, 1975), p. 12.

25. Frank M. Bass and W. Wayne Talorzyk, "An Attitude Model for the Study of Brand Preference," *Journal of Marketing Research* 9 (February 1972), p. 93.

26. A summary requires that the average rating of relevant attributes of each brand (B_{ib}) be multiplied by the attribute ranking (W_i) and the results summed.

27. William O. Bearden and Arch G. Woodside, "Testing Variations of Fishbein's Behavioral Intention Model within a Consumer Behavior Context," *Journal of Applied Psychology* 62 (June 1977), p. 352.

28. Martin Fishbein, "Attitude and the Prediction of Behavior," in *Readings in Attitude Theory and Measurement,* ed. Martin Fishbein (New York: John Wiley, 1967), p. 489.

29. Martin A. Fishbein, "Some Comments on the Use of 'Models' in Advertising Research," in *Proceedings: Seminar on Translating Advertising Theories into Research Reality* (Amsterdam: European Society of Marketing Research, 1971), pp. 297–313, cited in Michael J. Ryan, "The Fishbein Extended Model and Consumer Behavior," *Journal of Consumer Research* 2 (September 1975), p. 120.

30. Martin Fishbein, "Extending the Extended Model: Some Comments," in *Advances in Consumer Research*, vol. 3, ed. Beverlee B. Anderson (1976), pp. 491–497.

31. David T. Wilson, H. Lee Mathews, and James W. Harvey, "An Empirical Test of the Fishbein Behavioral Intention Model," *Journal of Consumer Research* 1 (March 1975), pp. 39–48.

32. Bearden and Woodside, "Testing Variations of Fishbein's Behavioral Intention Model," pp. 352–357.

33. Peter R. Dickson and Paul W. Miniard, "A Further Examination of Two Laboratory Tests of the Extended Fishbein Attitude Model," *Journal of Consumer Research* 4 (March 1978), pp. 261–266.

CHAPTER 12

ATTITUDE CHANGE

Allegheny Airlines, a regional carrier that covered the Northeast and North Central sections of the United States, in competition with Delta, United, TWA, and American, found that it was generally perceived to be a local carrier; thus, even when it had more convenient scheduling, it was frequently bypassed in favor of better known airlines. In research of airline users, it found that bigness inspired confidence in a carrier (that is, bigness was an important attribute in attitude ratings of airlines). As a result, Allegheny began a campaign designed to change the existing perceptions of the company from that of a small airline to that of a big airline—as in fact it was. Initially its advertising stressed bigness through attention-getting copy that compared Allegheny with better known carriers. Tracking studies revealed that within a relatively short time, there was a significant change in the percentage of people who perceived Allegheny to be a big airline.[1] Subsequently Allegheny changed its name to USAir.

In 1968 Procter & Gamble introduced a "newfangled" potato chip and immediately captured a significant share of the chip market. In fact, Pringles, a uniformly shaped chip in a canister package that provided long shelf life, was considered one of the most successful new products introduced during that period and attracted competition in the form of similar potato chips. In the 1970s, consumers became increasingly concerned about additives and artificial ingredients, and food products that were "natural" acquired greater value. Competitors of Pringles began to extol the virtues of their original potato chips, in, for example, an ad campaign that declared, "We're for real," while listing the artificial ingredients contained in the P & G canned chips. Pringles' sales began to decline; to many observers, the emphasis on the "natural" character of competitors' chips was responsible for an unfavorable attitude toward Pringles, which blunted its success. Procter & Gamble's strategy to recoup sales included a reformulation of the product and reintroduction of its chips as "all-natural."[2] In fact, Ernest Dichter, the motivational researcher, was consulted for package reformulation, and he declared that a major package change was necessary, since consumers perceived the original container as too "plastic" and therefore not "natural."

A knowledge of attitudes is important to the marketer since it may help him to predict consumer behavior. The predictive power of attitudes is not perfectly reliable—it is difficult to understand the complex processes that underly an attitude. Nonetheless, a knowledge of consumer attitudes may serve as a guide to marketing strategy. Almost as important as the knowledge of attitudes is an understanding of what causes them to change and how to bring about such changes. Much of a marketer's strategy is directed toward changing attitudes, as well as toward bolstering those that she considers desirable.

This chapter answers such questions as:

How may attitudes be changed?
What techniques are used in attitude research?
How may attitudes be used in market segmentation strategies?

THEORIES ON ATTITUDE CHANGE

Several theoretical approaches may be adopted in studying attitude change. Those most frequently used are *information processing, functional*, and *consistency* approaches.

Information Processing and Attitude Change

The information-processing approach to attitude change appears to be the most widely adopted in marketing.[3] Attitudes generally are represented in routine habits of thinking, feeling, and behaving. Outside influences, however, are likely to disturb an individual's attitudes toward many objects. When external events, such as the presentation of new information, do influence an individual, learning has occurred. The process by which learning occurs in this context is often *persuasion*. A great many promotional efforts are designed to change attitudes through persuasion.

The concept of an information-processing approach to attitude change, although speculative, shares a number of characteristics with the "hierarchy of effects" communications models. The theory behind these models suggests that a causal or predictive relationship exists between the changes in a person's knowledge about or attitude toward a product or service and changes in his purchase behavior in regard to that product or service. The "hierarchy of effects" theory hypothesizes that the consumer goes through a series of steps of increasing commitment to action.

A standard learning-hierarchy assumption has been in the literature for many years, beginning with the simple AIDA model developed in the 1920s. This model suggested that the steps in the advertising process are *a*ttention, *i*nterest, *d*esire, and ultimately *a*ction. The model has been revised in recent years. William McGuire has proposed a new series of steps: exposure, emotional response, encoding of information, acceptance of the claim, and overt behavior (buying).[4] The various factors that influence each of these steps will be described in greater detail in Chapter 14. The discussion here focuses on the presentation of information so that it may be properly encoded to increase the potential for attitude change.

As we saw in Chapter 8, decision makers encode information more easily if it is presented in terms of attributes rather than brands. Thus multiattribute models may be of particular significance in explaining and devising means of attitude change.

A discussion of attitude change through information processing incorporates the Fishbein A_{act} model, described in Chapter 11 as:

$$A_{\text{act}} = \sum_{i=1}^{n} (B_i a_i)$$

The B_i element estimates the likelihood that certain consequences will occur if the individual performs the act in question. Although many salient beliefs tend to center on consequences, not all beliefs an individual holds with respect to a particular brand will necessarily be beliefs about the consequences of using it. In the discussion below, therefore, the term "attribute" is substituted for "consequence" in discussion of the B_i component.

Three possible strategies for changing attitudes are suggested in using the above formula:[5]

1. Change an existing B_i (belief) element. An attempt is made to change the consumer's perception of a product or service on one or more attributes. This was the strategy used by USAir when, as Allegheny Airlines, it exerted efforts to change the perception of Allegheny from that of a small carrier to that of a big airline. Similarly, Pringles was redesigned to generate perceptions of "naturalness."

This strategy to change the structure of the belief about what a product can deliver has been discussed earlier in regard to positioning. For example, Arm & Hammer Baking Soda was perceived as delivering relief from upset stomachs and help in light house cleaning. When it was advertised as a refrigerator deodorant, it was then perceived to deliver a significant attribute that consumers had not considered earlier. A marketer may change the B_i component by declaring that a product does not deliver an inappropriate attribute. Clairesse, a hair-coloring product, was advertised as "the world's first no-ammonia shampoo-in haircolor."

2. Change the perception of an existing a_i (evaluative element). This strategy represents an attempt to persuade the consumer to reassess the value (the goodness or badness) of a particular attribute. "If Lestoil didn't smell so strong, it wouldn't work so good"; "Heinz's Ketchup is 'slow good' "; "We're only number two—so we try harder" (Avis); and Volkswagen's early campaign publicizing its unchanging style—all are examples of efforts to secure such reassessment.

3. Add a new $B_i a_i$ combination. A new attribute is introduced into the cognitive structure in an attempt to increase the overall attractiveness of the brand. Some examples of this strategy are the introduction of a birth-control element in dog food, the addition of a deodorizing feature to socks, the inclusion of a "light to show the way to escape" in smoke detectors, and the incorporation of protein in a dishwashing product for "softer hands."

Beliefs (B_i component of attitude) have often been assumed to be easier to influence than such components as attribute importance, salience, or desirability (a_i component), which are more directly linked to the consumer's value system.

Nevertheless, as we noted earlier, there may be occasions when external factors cause changes in the consumer's value system and the evaluative component of an attitude has been changed as a result of these external factors. Under such circumstances, marketers can emphasize that their products contain this currently more important attribute. As a result of research findings that roll-on deodorants are more effective than spray products, firms are now stressing their roll-on applicators.

Similarly, when the evaluative dimension associated with an attitude changes to a more negative position, firms may stress their products' lack of the undesirable attribute. Increased attention to the issue of excessive medication has led some pharmaceutical advertisers to declare: "Our competitors' products have other ingredients—which we chose not to include in ours." Pringles' competitors used this strategy with apparent success when they advertised, "We're for real."

Changing the Functional Components of Attitudes

The basic difference between a functional approach to attitude change and other approaches rests in an understanding of the motivational facets of the attitude itself.[6] Other approaches to attitude change place heavy emphasis on the person's belief structure. Functional theory is not solely concerned with a person's information about, perception of, or behavior toward some attitude object. In a functional approach, attitude change is seen as dependent on the motivational pattern supporting cognitive representations. The functional approach tries to assess why a particular attitude is held so that the proper appeal can be made.

Earlier we examined attitudes by discussing the functions they perform. Daniel Katz, who introduced the concept of attitude functions, also discussed ways in which attitudes can be modified. The concept of the instrumental function indicates that we hold attitudes toward a product because it can help us to attain a utilitarian goal or meet some need. Attitudes that fulfill the instrumental function may be changed if consumers can be shown that an older product no longer meets their needs. Procter & Gamble's introduction of disposable Pampers changed attitudes toward cloth diapers.

Ego-defensive attitudes may be difficult to change, since they appear to protect the individual from inner feelings of doubt. Rather than attempt to change these attitudes, it is sometimes easier to reinforce them by the presentation of ego-defensive benefits. This strategy can be effective for such products as cosmetics and personal hygiene aids.

As we noted earlier, attitudes express the individual's basic values, and while these values may change over time, there is little that the individual marketer can do to change them. He can, however, formulate his product and its promotion so that they are consistent with symbols of those values. "Natural" foods, food processors, and "Annie Hall" clothes represent such adaptations, as do "the Pepsi generation" and "Give me the Campbell life." When the motion picture *Saturday Night Fever* changed evaluations of appropriateness of white vested suits, dressy dresses with high-heeled shoes, and discos, numerous firms such as Ford, Dr Pepper, and Crazy Eddie (a New York discount store) used similar images in advertising their products and services.

The knowledge function of attitudes is becoming increasingly important in this complex world. This is the attitude function that organizes and classifies things so that they are easier to deal with. In the marketing context, this organizing function can be translated into positioning and repositioning, which places a product in a fairly precise category so that it is more meaningful to consumers. In positioning a new line of prepared foods, Nisson Foods noted that its "cup of noodles" is "more than a soup" and indicated its usefulness for children's lunches. With the decline in the sales of evaporated milk, Pet repositioned its product with the campaign theme "So rich you can use it as cream," and its advertisements featured creamy recipes for such dishes as chicken and potato soup.

Although relatively little research has been done in the area of functional components and attitude change, this approach suggests that without some comprehension of the functional structure of an existing attitude, a message designed to appeal to a nonsalient function may result in little attitude change, or it may result in change opposite that advocated in the message.[7] Suppose a tennis player was playing tennis to remain healthy and was told of the deleterious effects of playing. If the communication were to arouse ego defensiveness, the player might actually adopt a more positive attitude and persuade himself that playing is necessary to "be with his family" or "to relieve tensions."

Consistency Theory and Attitude Change

In Chapter 8 we discussed Leon Festinger's theory of cognitive dissonance. According to Festinger, the individual strives toward consistency within herself. A person has certain cognitive elements that are "knowledges" about herself, her environment, her attitudes, her opinions, and her past behavior. If these cognitive elements follow logically from one another, they are said to be consonant with each other. If they do not follow logically from one another, they are said to be dissonant. As dissonance is psychologically uncomfortable, a person will try to reduce it and achieve consonance.

Dissonance may be reduced in many ways, such as through search for and recall of consonant information, opinion change, behavioral change, and attitude change. An application of consistency theory to attitude change suggests that if consistency is disturbed by new information, it may be restored in two ways: (1) by discrediting the information and maintaining the attitude, and (2) by modifying the other attitude components so that a new attitude emerges.

Postdecision Dissonance

The concept of postdecision dissonance has particular relevance to attitude change. Since decision making entails the rejection of some alternatives, cognitive dissonance theory asserts that postdecision dissonance may be a consequence of decision making.[8] After deciding on one alternative, a person has to cope with the cognitive elements concerning the attractive attributes of the rejected alternatives. The possibility of postpurchase dissonance is greater under the following circumstances: (1) the purchase is important either financially or psychologically, (2) the rejected alternatives are very attractive, and (3) a large number of alternatives have been considered.

If a substantial outlay of funds is involved in the purchase decision or if the consumer's taste or intelligence will be judged on the basis of the purchase, strong dissonance may be present. Under these circumstances, an advertisement that emphasizes the desirable features of the chosen brand may reduce the dissonance so that in time the consumer will form a more favorable attitude toward the brand. For advertisers, the theory sheds new light on the role of advertising in increasing the probability of a product's repurchase. Automobile manufacturers, for example, tend to reassure the consumer as to the wisdom of the purchase and thus to reduce postpurchase dissonance. They may do so by emphasizing the car's desirable features, such as its high trade-in value or the long period during which the style will remain in fashion. Dissonance reduction may reinforce the purchase and increase the probability of future purchase of the same brand.

An experiment concerning automobile purchases seemed to support the concept of postdecision dissonance. The study found that the larger the number of alternative automobiles the consumer considered before his purchase, the more he tended afterward to read the advertisements of the make he bought.[9] This finding supports dissonance theory, and suggests that postdecision dissonance in this case was reduced through the seeking of consonant information.

There is some evidence that the reduction of postpurchase dissonance may operate more strongly in the case of shopping goods than of convenience goods.

The more frequently the product is purchased, as with convenience goods, the less important becomes the question of which brand is purchased at any one time, and the less the postpurchase dissonance. The consumer who has purchased a convenience good knows that she is not irrevocably tied to that particular choice, but can easily switch brands. Since her dissonance is not strong, advertising's role in reinforcing this purchase may be diminished. For the shopping good, however, dissonance reduction may be facilitated in several ways: advertising, warranties, hot lines for repair problems, easy return policies, and the like.

Another recommended strategy for avoiding postdecision dissonance is the follow-up call. The earlier discussion of learning focused on the role of reinforcement in the encouragement and maintenance of desired behavior. Conditioning theory suggests that behavior is more likely to be repeated if it is rewarded. It has been suggested that these concepts can be applied to consumers to generate after-purchase satisfaction and, it is hoped, repeat purchases. A "reward" may be provided through the follow-up call. A study conducted for a jewelry store indicated that this approach was successful.[10] Customers were separated into three groups following their purchases. One group was telephoned and thanked for their business; one group was called, thanked for their business, and told of a special promotion; and a third group, used as a control, was not called.

The customers' response was almost immediate. Many people from the first group came into the store to comment on the call. The most effective message seemed to be the simple "thanks." The second group apparently perceived the telephone call as a promotional effort. More important, the interest by customers was transformed into sales. There was a 27 percent increase in sales in the test month over the year before. These findings suggest that positive reinforcement of retail customers has a favorable effect on sales.

Changing Behavior before Attitude Change

Although the ultimate goal is to ensure change in behavior, some theorists hold that an attitude change is not necessary for behavior change; under certain circumstances, in fact, it may be desirable to secure a change in behavior in order to achieve the desired attitude change.

On the basis of consistency theory, generally it is assumed that the tricomponent model of attitude structure follows the change pattern: cognitive → affective → connative (behavioral). It has been suggested that this model is most relevant for a *high-involvement* situation, that is, one in which the audience is highly involved in either the medium or the message that is presented.

Herbert E. Krugman has proposed a *low-involvement* hierarchy,[11] which can be observed when products are not clearly differentiated and when the audience has a low level of involvement in both the medium and the message. The audience may receive some TV commercials, for example, with relaxed or inoperative perceptual defenses. In such situations, the primary effect of advertising is to increasing the level of awareness of the product. According to Krugman, under low-involvement conditions, advertising may create faint impressions that can build up into a triggered in-store purchase, with very little trace of advertising effect before that purchase. It is presumed that behavior change occurs as a result of subtle shifts in belief structures. Attitude (affect) will change to be consistent with behavior sometime afterward: cognitive **z** connative **z** affective.

One recent study supported these findings in regard to political advertising. Communications in both advertising and personal canvassing were found to have positive voter effect in a low-involvement political race, but not in a high-involvement race.[12]

The cognitive **z** connative **z** affective sequence may also have significance for areas other than advertising. Since attitudes are formed by personal experiences, the marketer's hope is to get the consumer to use her product or service. Such action is encouraged through samples, demonstrations, coupons, and the like. The makers of All detergent introduced their product into the consumer market through boxes of All placed in new washing machines sold by appliance manufacturers. More recently, in a campaign for Agree cream rinse and hair conditioner, the S. C. Johnson Company allocated $7 million for a sampling program to distribute small bottles of Agree to 31 million women.[13]

Magazine publishers offer cut-rate subscriptions and banks provide gifts in an effort to lure customers to try their products and services. Automobile companies have arrangements with car rental companies so that consumers who rent automobiles will experience their cars in use. Even when such trials are made by consumers, however, whether or not they ultimately change their attitudes is still in question.

ATTITUDE RESEARCH

In order to provide a greater understanding of the way attitudes influence consumer behavior, methods of measuring attitudes are increasingly being sought and developed. Most of the early research on attitudes can be categorized as essentially definitional and descriptive. A new phase emerged with the publication of Louis L. Thurstone's work, which attempted to measure attitudes quantitatively.[14] Considerable research has followed, and recent efforts have been directed toward the development of operational models of attitude structure by identifying factors that determine a person's attitude toward an object or concept and developing measurements for those factors. Many of the measurement devices are essentially scaling techniques.

Thurstone Scaling

Louis Thurstone believed that opinions are verbal expressions of attitudes. To get such opinions, a series of statements is made about an object, such as:

I think Chevrolet is the best auto on the road.
The Chevrolet is as good or as bad as other cars on the road.
Chevrolet is the worst car on the road.

These statements are printed on cards, and judges are asked to sort them in eleven piles, ranging from the most negative (score of 1) to the most positive (score of 11). Each statement is given a score based on the opinion of the majority of judges.

A shorter list of statements on which judges show strong agreement and which represent an evenly graduated scale, from most negative to most positive, comprises the attitude scale. This list of statements is presented to a group of subjects, who are asked to indicate (perhaps with a plus sign) all of the statements with which they agree and (with a minus sign) all of those with which they disagree. The final score is the average scale value of all of the statements that an individual has endorsed. The larger the score, the more positive the person's feelings toward the attitude object.

Summated Ratings

An approach developed by Rensis Likert in 1932 essentially constructs a verbal picture of a respondent's opinions on a given subject. The procedure is as follows:

1. A number of relevant statements about a subject are collected.
2. Respondents are asked to indicate degree of agreement or disagreement with each statement, using the choices:
   1. Strongly agree.
   2. Agree.
   3. Undecided, neither agree nor disagree.
   4. Disagree.
   5. Strongly disagree.
3. Each response is given a numerical weight (+2, +1, 0, −1, −2).
4. The numerical weights of all statements are summed to get each respondent's attitude score.

A variation of the Likert scale was used by the tea industry in an effort to improve the image of tea.[15] A series of statements about tea was developed, ranging from strongly positive to strongly negative. These statements were assigned numerical values from +3 to −3. One statement with a +3 (strongly positive) value was "I would specifically ask my (wife, hostess, waitress) for tea." A strongly negative (−3) statement was "I would refuse tea if offered to me."

The findings were cross-analyzed with tea-consumption habits, with the results shown in Table 12.1. From these data it appears that those with a positive attitude toward tea make up 20 percent of the population but consume 90 percent of the tea. The vast majority of people are either neutral or have a negative attitude toward tea. Such data are useful in developing both a market target and a promotional strategy.

TABLE 12.1   ATTITUDES TOWARD TEA AND TEA CONSUMPTION PER WEEK

Value	Percent of population	Tea consumption (cups)
+3	9%	10.0
+2	6	6.0
+1	5	2.0
0	35	1.0
−1	15	0.5
−2	20	0.2
−3	10	0.0
Total	100%	19.7

Semantic Differential

Another scaling technique widely used by marketers is the semantic differential. Originally the technique was developed by Charles Osgood, George Suci, and Percy Tannenbaum in their efforts to measure meanings; marketers typically use it to measure attitudes, frequently in the form of favorable or unfavorable images of a product or company.

The semantic differential uses a series of bipolar adjectives on a seven-point, equal-interval ordinal scale. The bipolar adjectives should be concerned with three basic factors: (1) evaluation (good–bad, beautiful–ugly); (2) potency (strong–weak, large–small); and (3) activity (active–passive, fast–slow). The seven points provide categories of agreement, for example: extremely good, good, somewhat good, neither good nor bad, somewhat bad, bad, extremely bad.

Findings relevant to attitudes toward three brands of beer developed by use of bipolar scales may be seen in Figure 12.1.

Constant Sum

The constant-sum scale is gaining popularity in marketing research as a means of evaluating alternatives. The scale requires the respondent to divide a constant sum, generally 10 or 100, among two or more stimuli. For example, respondents may be requested to divide 100 points among each of three brands according to preference for the brands. The results may be as follows:

Brand *A*	60
Brand *B*	30
Brand *C*	10

The constant-sum scale is useful since it measures the psychological distances between stimuli.[16] It also is less sensitive than the semantic differential to idiosyncratic interpretations of adjective cues. Constant sum requires a large number of

FIGURE 12.1   ATTITUDES TOWARD THREE BRANDS OF BEER
FOUND BY USE OF BIPOLAR SCALES

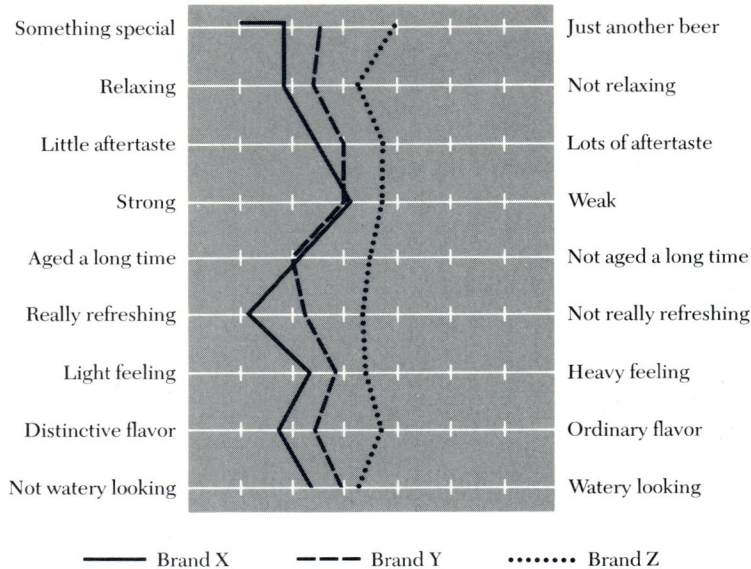

Something special	Just another beer
Relaxing	Not relaxing
Little aftertaste	Lots of aftertaste
Strong	Weak
Aged a long time	Not aged a long time
Really refreshing	Not really refreshing
Light feeling	Heavy feeling
Distinctive flavor	Ordinary flavor
Not watery looking	Watery looking

———— Brand X   – – – Brand Y   •••••••• Brand Z

Source: William A. Mindak, "Fitting the Semantic Differential to the
Marketing Problem," *Journal of Marketing* 25 (April 1961) p. 31.

comparisons, however, and may fatigue the respondent.

Constant-sum methods may be useful in tracking attitude change. Gallup &
Robinson, Inc., a research firm, makes use of constant sum, as well as other scaling
methods, in its In-View service, which evaluates the effectiveness of a commercial
designed to secure attitude change. For its In-View studies, Gallup & Robinson
has reserved air time on a UHF prime-time program, in which it schedules the
commercials to be tested.[17] On the day of the telecast, a selected sample of men
and women are invited to view the test program, with the understanding that they
may be interviewed the following day, but they are given no advance information
as to the nature of the interview. During the invitation call, respondents are questioned about six product categories, and their attitudes toward brands within each
category are scaled. The scaling method to be employed is selected from three
options:

Top-of-mind: The first three brands that come to mind.
Constant sum: Ten points, to be divided among three brands.
Purchase intent: First, second, and third choices.

The product categories asked about include three products that are advertised on the test program and three that are not.

On the following day, the same respondents are called back, and those who qualify by having watched the test program are questioned again, with the same scale used for measurement of brand attitudes. This procedure provides an opportunity to contrast the attitudes of viewers before and after their exposure to the test commercial.

Attitude Segmentation

With increased emphasis on market segmentation, attention has been focused on attitudes as segmentation variables. The key for use of attitudes as bases for segmentation lies in the link between attitudes and behavior. Only a few studies report direct evidence on the link between attitude and response to marketing stimuli. Nevertheless, identifying various attitudinal and use segments enables a firm to concentrate its efforts on those with positive attitudes, on the grounds that the cost of changing those with strong negative attitudes may be prohibitive.

In one study of the automobile market, four distinct attitude segments—which differed in their attitudes toward travel, safety, care of car, style, and power and speed—were identified. These segments provided guidelines for product and concept tests, advertising tests, media selection, and product-line extension.[18]

Attitude segmentation was applied in a project designed to elicit the importance of attitude in the purchase of paper napkins.[19] The product was to be marketed in a new type of package: when the wrapper was removed, an attractive box with no name on it remained. The questions raised in this research project were: How many people were concerned about the decor aspect of the package? How could they best be reached?

A long battery of statements was prepared concerning some forty aspects or benefits of the product, with consumers rating them on a six-point scale ranging from "extremely desirable" to "not at all desirable." The phrases used included: "It's a luxurious-feeling napkin," "It's extra-thick," "The box is pretty," "You don't have any advertising on the box," and the like.

An analysis of the responses indicated that in the total market, low price ranked fourth and attractive package ranked twelfth, or last. Segmentation analysis was conducted in an effort to find out how people clustered in terms of their desires on the entire battery of benefits. This analysis indicated that people fell into a number of groups. One was characterized by great interest in low price and utility. These people were more interested in a plain, functional napkin that would be practical for heavy users. Of minor interest to them, compared with the rest of the people in the study, were such attributes as "attractive package" and "elegant-looking napkin." For another segment, an attractive package was the main appeal, even though in the total market, attractive package was at the bottom. The analysis indicated that 47 percent of the people were in the first segment (price and function), and they represented 57 percent of the volume. The 16 percent who cared about attractiveness in both napkin and box accounted for 13 percent of the volume.

The results of this research indicated that a group did exist that was concerned about an attractive package, but it was relatively small. A very large segment was concerned about low price, economy, and basic utility. Thus the research helped to prevent the company from making the mistake of substituting an attractive package for the basic utility package. The company, moreover, was able to field a wide line of products, each designed to appeal to a different group of people, thus increasing its share of the market.

BENEFIT SEGMENTATION

A type of attitude segmentation that has received widespread attention is *benefit segmentation*. This approach, discussed earlier, stresses benefits rather than features. As we have noted, attributes in the attitude structure not only refer to specifications but may also be seen as beliefs about the consequences of using a brand—its benefits. An example of benefit segmentation in the toothpaste industry was described in Chapter 9.

General Foods' marketing strategy for its Cycle dog food is based on benefit segmentation. Its research disclosed varying attitudes among dog owners, some perceiving dogs as friends and others perceiving them as substitute babies. While the various "cycles" are presumably based on the stages in the life cycle of the dog, the strategy also incorporates such benefits as food for the overweight dog, which are intended to appeal to people who feel parental concern for their pets.

Benefit segmentation also enables a marketer to gain a foothold by finding a benefit not adequately provided by competitors. Pampers eliminates the need to wash diapers, Pringles provides long shelf life, and Aim makes children "brush longer." Gillette budgeted $18 million for an introductory advertising and promotion campaign for Dry Idea, a "revolutionary" roll-on antiperspirant that goes on dry.[20] The campaign features the slogan "Nothing will keep you drier."

Attitudinal factors can also be incorporated in varying strategies aimed at user and nonuser segments. On the basis of research on soft drinks and beer using the extended Fishbein model, different strategies have been suggested for different use segments.[21] For individuals who already consume soft drinks and beer (and therefore, according to the extended Fishbein model, are under more attitudinal control), advertising and promotional campaigns should include the use of product attributes as factors to influence the choice of a particular brand. For those who do not drink those beverages, it may be more useful to use reference groups in advertisements, as this appeal may be more relevant to "normative" influences.

The Halo Effect in Attitude Measurement

Despite the efforts to improve techniques of attitude measurement, such methods tend to be a source of concern. Some of this concern relates to the existence of halo effects. It is unclear to what extent halo effects are present in multiattribute measurement and how they can be accounted for and overcome.

Consumer ratings of a brand on a set of dimensions (attributes) are commonly used in consumer research. A consumer's rating of an attribute, however, may be determined by many other variables besides the cues directly related to the particular attribute. The tendency to be influenced by a general overall impression of a product when one is rating a particular attribute is designated as halo effect (discussed in Chapter 7).[22]

Substantial disagreement exists concerning just when and how much haloing occurs. It seems clear, however, that haloing is substantial in at least some circumstances: when the individual has little familiarity with the product, when an attribute is perceived ambiguously or subjectively, and when the product is perceived to be very popular or widely used.

Questions as to the extent of haloing came up in an FTC case against ITT Continental Baking Company, in which the FTC alleged that the company had falsely represented Wonder Bread to be nutritionally superior to competing brands of white bread. The charge was eventually dismissed on grounds unrelated to its merits. The FTC's investigation revealed some interesting facts, however. Both sides agreed that some percentage of the public believed (erroneously) that Wonder Bread stood out in nutrition. ITT claimed, however, that these beliefs were influenced by consumers' generally favorable overall attitudes toward Wonder Bread (based on familiarity, price, and intensive advertising); this positive overall feeling about the brand led to the belief that Wonder Bread was nutritionally superior. The FTC agreed that the halo effect had been operating, but named as its sources widespread use, generalized advertising claims, and claims about other specific attributes.[23]

There is significant controversy concerning the extent to which attitudes can be measured and used to predict behavior. Irving Crespi notes that the public appears to accept attitude surveys concerning political events, consumer products and services, and advertising and public information campaigns, yet critics declare that it is impossible to make reliable predictions of behavior from attitude measurements.

Crespi rejects the inference that the failure to demonstrate the existence of a clear relationship between attitudes and behavior is due to the lack of scientific worth of the concept. He suggests that this result stems from the manner in which attitude research has been conducted. He notes a tendency to rely on attitude scales of a high order of generality and abstraction and on theory that it is overly "particularized and concrete." According to Crespi, if measurements are highly particular and specific and the theory presents generalizable models, the goal of developing attitudinal measurements and theories that are predictive can be achieved.[24]

SUMMARY

A knowledge of the function and structure of attitudes helps marketers to assess the ways in which attitudes are formed and how they may be changed. Several theories have been proposed in regard to attitude change, including an information-processing concept and functional and consistency approaches. On the basis of these theories, marketers may develop strategies to encourage attitude change.

Attitude researchers have developed scaling techniques to measure attitudes, and variations of these techniques have been applied to consumer-behavior concepts. Attitude measurement has also been used in efforts to isolate market segments on the basis of attitudinal variations. While the reliability of predictions of behavior from attitude measurements causes some concern, future research may improve such capabilities.

DISCUSSION QUESTIONS

1. How might a manufacturer of microwave ovens use the Fishbein attitude model to change attitudes?

2. Provide illustrations of changes in the functional components of an attitude.

3. Describe from personal experience how a change in your behavior led to a change in your attitude.

4. Develop a semantic differential scale to depict the image of your school and compare it with others.

5. How may the halo effect distort attitude research?

6. Describe some environmental influences that have caused attitude change and affected purchase behavior.

NOTES

1. Nariman K. Dhalla, "Brand Positioning," paper presented at the Annual Convention of the Southwestern Marketing Association, March 24, 1977.

2. Larry Edwards, "WRG Picked to Work on Pringles' Turnaround," *Advertising Age*, July 10, 1978, pp. 2, 118.

3. William B. Locander and W. Austin Spivey, "A Functional Approach to Attitude Measurement," *Journal of Marketing Research* 15 (November 1978), p. 576.

4. Benjamin Lipstein and William J. McGuire, *Evaluating Advertising: A Bibliography of the Communication Process* (New York: American Research Foundation, 1978), p. xxviii.

5. Richard J. Lutz, "Changing Brand Attitudes through Modification of Cognitive Structure," *Journal of Consumer Research* 1 (March 1975), pp. 49–59.

6. Locander and Spivey, "Functional Approach to Attitude Measurement," pp. 576–587.

7. Ibid., p. 585.

8. Sadaomi Oshikawa, "Can Cognitive Dissonance Theory Explain Consumer Behavior?" *Journal of Marketing* 33 (October 1969), pp. 44–49.

9. Danuta Ehrlich, Isaiah Guttman, Peter Schonback, and Judson Mills, "Post-Decision Ex-

posure to Relevant Information," *Journal of Abnormal and Social Psychology* 54 (January 1957), pp. 98–102.

10. J. Ronald Carey, Steven H. Clicque, Barbara A. Leighton, and Frank Milton, "A Test of Positive Reinforcement of Customers," *Journal of Marketing* 40 (October 1976), pp. 98–100.

11. Herbert E. Krugman, "Memory without Recall, Exposure without Perception," *Journal of Advertising Research* 17 (August 1977), pp. 7–14.

12. William R. Swinyard and Kenneth A. Coney, "Promotional Effects on a High- versus Low-Involvement Electorate," *Journal of Consumer Research* 5 (June 1978), pp. 41–48.

13. "S. C. Johnson Tries Again on Personal Care," *Business Week*, February 14, 1977, p. 54.

14. Louis Thurstone, "Law of Comparative Judgment," *Psychological Review* 34 (1927), pp. 273–286.

15. Russell H. Colley, *Defining Advertising Goals for Measured Advertising Results* (New York: Association of National Advertisers, 1961), p. 76.

16. G. David Hughes, *Attitude Measurement for Marketing Strategies* (Glenview, Ill.: Scott, Foresman, 1971), p. 106.

17. *A Comprehensive Program for Evaluating Television Advertising* (Princeton, N.J.: Gallup & Robinson), pp. 20–21.

18. H. E. Heller, "Defining Target Markets by Their Attitude Profiles," in *Attitude Research on the Rocks*, ed. Lee Adler and Irving Crespi (Chicago: American Marketing Association, 1968).

19. Shirley Young, "Pitfalls Down the Primrose Path of Attitude Segmentation," in *Attitude Research Bridges the Atlantic*, ed. Philip Levine (Chicago: American Marketing Association, 1975), pp. 203–204.

20. "Dry Idea Gets Big Gillette Sendoff," *Advertising Age*, June 12, 1978, p. 1.

21. William O. Bearden and Arch G. Woodside, "Testing Variations of Fishbein's Behavioral Intention Model within a Consumer Behavior Context," *Journal of Applied Psychology* 62 (June 1977), p. 356.

22. Neil E. Beckwith, Harold H. Kassarjian, and Donald R. Lehmann, "Halo Effects in Marketing Research: Review and Prospects," in *Advances in Consumer Research*, vol. 5, ed. H. Keith Hunt (Ann Arbor: Association for Consumer Research, 1978), p. 463.

23. Ibid., p. 465.

24. Irving Crespi, "Attitude Measurement: Theory and Prediction," *Public Opinion Quarterly* 41 (1977), pp. 285–294.

PART FOUR
THE CONSUMER DECISION PROCESS

**PROBLEM RECOGNITION AND
INFORMATION SEARCH
INFORMATION PROCESSING
PERSUASIVE INFLUENCES
ALTERNATIVE EVALUATION
CHOICE AND OUTCOME
SPECIAL APPLICATIONS OF
CONSUMER DECISION THEORY**

In the next six chapters, the consumer decision process is discussed in detail. This discussion encompasses theoretical constructs relevant to the social, cultural, and individual influences on consumer behavior. The stages of problem recognition and information search are examined, as is the manner in which information is processed from marketer-dominated sources. Alternative evaluation, choice, outcome, and special applications of consumer decision theory are also described.

CHAPTER 13

PROBLEM RECOGNITION AND INFORMATION SEARCH

In order to gain a better understanding of consumer behavior, it is useful to focus on a particular manifestation of such behavior—in this case, the consumer purchase decision process. In this context, consumers may be viewed as going to the market to fulfill the dictates of their needs and wants. In engaging in this process, the consumer seeks solutions to his problems.

The consumer decision process, then, may be viewed as problem-solving behavior. Descriptions of problem-solving behavior abound in the literature. Generally, they consist of a sequence of activities designed to produce a solution to a perceived problem. John Dewey described these stages as follows:[1]

1. A difficulty is felt.
2. The difficulty is located and defined.
3. Possible solutions are suggested.
4. Consequences are considered.
5. A solution is considered.

The consumer decision process is a problem-solving process containing similar stages. The consumer recognizes or becomes aware of a problem related to the market; she seeks information to help her solve this problem; she evaluates alternative solutions to the problem by establishing various criteria for a choice; she makes a decision and engages in actions relevant to this decision; and she considers the consequences of those actions after making the purchase.

For the purpose of this presentation, the stages in the consumer's purchase decision process are considered to be:

1. Problem recognition.
2. Information search.
3. Alternative evaluation.
4. Choice.
5. Outcome.

As in all problem-solving behavior, these stages may not occur in the sequence presented. Moreover, except for the last stage, which by definition must occur after the item is bought, a time lapse may not necessarily exist between the stages. An impulse purchase, for example, may combine the first four stages in one. It should be noted, however, that some analysts do not believe that true impulse purchases actually exist. A felt need may have existed for the product at an earlier point in time and information sought and evaluated in the past, all of which are translated into what appears to be an impulse purchase at a later point in time.

This chapter discusses the first two stages of the consumer decision process: problem recognition and information search. It answers the questions:

How does problem recognition occur?
What factors determine the search for information?
What are the major sources of consumer information?

PROBLEM RECOGNITION

Problem recognition is a perceptual phenomenon. A problem is perceived when a goal is to be attained and uncertainty exists as to the best way to attain it. Problem recognition occurs when a person recognizes a difference of sufficient magnitude between what he perceives as the desired state of affairs and what he perceives as the actual state of affairs.[2] Most consumer problems can be related to some market factor—the choice of products, services, brands, stores, price, and so on.

Problem recognition is considered to be the first stage of the decision-making process, but it need not lead to subsequent stages. The difference between what is perceived as the desired state of affairs and what is perceived as the actual state of affairs may not be of sufficient magnitude to cause the individual to take further action. For a problem actually to exist, the consumer must have some desire that causes dissatisfaction. Even if the difference between the perceived desired state and the actual state is of sufficient magnitude, the consumer may lack the time, energy, or money to deal with it. In addition, an appropriate alternative must exist. Thus problem recognition may be necessary for the consumer purchase process to proceed, but its occurrence does not ensure that additional activity will ensue.

Influencers of Problem Recognition

Consumer problems may develop through many variables that influence either the actual state of affairs or the desired state. Some of the sources of consumer problems are assortment deficiencies, expanded means, expanded desires, new information, and changes in reference groups.

Assortment deficiencies arise when the individual's stock of goods is inadequate to satisfy his needs. He may have run out of shaving cream, razor blades, after-shave lotion. It should be noted, however, that should he decide to grow a beard, the depletion of such resources does not create a problem. It is only if he wishes to continue to be clean-shaven that such goods must be restocked.

A change in the individual's financial status can change her perception of her desired state. If the individual's income is rising or is expected to rise, the amounts of goods and services she desires are likely to increase.

Even without an expansion of means, the consumer may raise his level of aspirations. New motives may be triggered at various points in time. The individual may have become married or had a baby. Such changes lead to a desire for a home, furnishings, clothing, even new kinds of food.

A great deal of advertising effort is designed to impart new information to the consumer, to cause him to believe that his current product or service is not the best solution to his desires: "no preservatives" in our baby food, "crude fiber" in our bread, "44 channels." New information from friends and persuasive salespeople may put a currently used product in a new light, so that it no longer provides satisfaction.

Changes in reference groups can cause changes in consumer expectations. Moving to a new neighborhood, entering college, taking one's first job—all such experiences tend to influence the individual's perception of her desired state. The consumer may desire to emulate the clothing and life-style of her new reference groups and thus perceive a problem in securing the items that will permit her to do so.

Gathering Problem-Recognition Data

It would be useful for marketers to be aware of the specific factors that trigger problem recognition so that they could predict when problem recognition will take place. Since few empirical data are available, marketers examine consumers' intentions in the hope that such knowledge will enable them to predict when problem recognition will take place. Surveys of consumers' intentions provide a marketer with some estimate of the potential demand for his goods. Such surveys may contain simple intention questions—"Do you intend to buy a car within the next six months?"—or involve measures of subjective purchase probabilities—"How many chances out of ten are there that you will purchase a car within the next three months? six months? a year?" This type of question provides significantly better predictions of purchase rates than do intention questions.[3]

There are indications that certain family members may be better predictors of household behavior than others. For example, in one study of the roles of husbands and wives in problem recognition, wives initially recognized a problem related to refrigerators, vacuum cleaners, frozen orange juice, and rugs and carpets with much greater frequency than husbands. In fact, husbands initially recognized a problem more frequently than wives only in regard to automobiles. Such information may be useful in providing promotion targets for firms, by suggesting which family member should be reached.

It should be noted, however, that gathering data about intentions can be costly and time-consuming, and these data may not always be useful to the marketer in predicting problem recognition.[4] It is difficult to measure intentions data accurately, especially in regard to behavior twelve months in the future. Besides, intentions data may not be "actionable"—that is, the marketing manager may not be able to take action on such data to change overall demand.

Another technique for dealing with problem recognition is to identify widespread consumer problems. The focus-group interview, described in Chapter 5, is a common research method used for bringing consumers together to discuss problems within a product category. A variation of this technique involves a problem inventory analysis. Consumers are given a list of problems and asked for each item on that list what products come to mind as having that problem. An example of a problem inventory analysis used in a study conducted in the food industry appears in Table 13.1.[5]

The data provided in such an analysis should be used with caution. For example, while 16 percent of the sample believe that "it is difficult to get catsup to pour easily," it is likely that few would accept a thin, watery product. Nevertheless, a product inventory analysis may provide cues for further investigation of consumer problems.

Additional research may disclose more efficient techniques for evaluating problem recognition data and their relationship to subsequent stages of the consumer decision process. For example, purchase intention data may provide useful information for market segmentation. A study of purchase intentions in regard to various patterns of bed linen indicated the existence of market segments with distinctive expressed intentions to purchase.[6] Another study has recommended the use of purchase intention data as one input in the pretest market evaluation of new packaged goods.[7]

Other suggestions focus on the necessity of collecting, analyzing, and interpreting purchase intention and problem analysis data and the utility of developing a model that establishes intermediate links between stated purchase intentions and/or problems and actual purchase behavior.[8]

TABLE 13.1 RESULTS OF A PROBLEM INVENTORY STUDY ABOUT FOOD

Questions Asked and % of Respondents Answering

1. The package of _____ doesn't fit well on the shelf.
      cereal   49%
      flour   6%
2. My husband/children refuse to eat _____.
      liver   18%
      vegetables   5%
      spinach   4%
3. _____ doesn't quench my thirst.
      soft drinks   58%
      milk   9%
      coffee   6%
4. Packaged _____ doesn't dissolve fast enough.
      jello/gelatin   32%
      bouillon cubes   8%
      pudding   5%
5. Everyone always wants different _____.
      vegetables   23%
      cereal   11%
      meat   10%
      desserts   9%
6. _____ makes a mess in the oven.
      broiling steaks   19%
      pie   17%
      roast/pork/rib   8%
7. Packaged _____ tastes artificial.
      instant potatoes   12%
      macaroni and cheese   4%
8. It's difficult to get _____ to pour easily.
      catsup   16%
      syrup   13%
      gallon of milk 11%
9. Packaged _____ looks unappetizing.
      hamburger helper   6%
      lunch meat   3%
      liver   3%
10. I wish my husband/children could take _____ in a carried lunch.
      hot meal   11%
      soup   9%
      ice cream   4%

Source: Edward M. Tauber, "Discovering New Product Opportunities with Problem Inventory Analysis," *Journal of Marketing* 39 (January 1975), p. 70.

INFORMATION SEARCH

If a problem is recognized, it becomes necessary for the consumer to become aware of various alternatives for its solution. Lack of alternatives precludes action. To learn about these alternatives, the consumer may engage in information search; in effect, the decision-making process takes on a learning characteristic.

Several sources are available to consumers in search of information. *Internal search* provides information from the consumer's experiences, stored in long-term memory. *External search* involves a variety of sources. Information may come directly from marketers in the form of advertisements, packages, in-store displays, and so on. Much of the information that consumers receive, however, does not proceed directly from marketers. For example, the mass media present news stories and editorial statements that may contain information inputs. Public policy makers also provide information to consumers in, for example, their packaging and advertising requirements. Information may come from personal sources, such as friends, family, and acquaintances.

The extensive discussion of the information search stage in the consumer's decision-making process in this and the next two chapters reflects current theory that highlights the significance of information processing on consumer choice.[9] While the term "information search" appears to be restricted to actual search, a meaningful discussion of this learning situation requires an information-processing perspective, which incorporates exposure to and awareness of information and the manner in which it is encoded, stored, and ultimately retrieved. These latter aspects go beyond the search stage of the consumer's decision process and are of significance in alternative evaluation, choice, and even postpurchase behavior. In fact, information processing is relevant to all stages of the consumer's purchase decision process. Nevertheless, an effort is made to distinguish information processing in the search stage as concerning the sources of information and consumers' reaction to that information. The subsequent stages of the consumer's decision process are concerned with the integration of the new information with other information in such a way as to permit alternatives to be evaluated and choices made.

Factors Affecting the Extent of Search

Information search by consumers may be very limited or extensive. John Howard distinguishes among extensive problem solving, limited problem solving, and routinized response behavior.[10]

In extensive problem solving, the consumer may need a great amount of information in order to decide whether to buy a product. People wanted extensive information on instant coffee, for instance, when it was first introduced.[11]

Problem solving is limited when consumers already have criteria readily available in mind. Consumers probably needed little new information when other brands of instant coffee appeared on the market.

Routinized response behavior is characterized by little need for information and quick decisions. Now that consumers have become familiar with brands of instant coffee and have lost their reservations about convenience foods, the purchase of the same brand of instant coffee has become routinized or habitual for many consumers.

Thus the consumer may merely use prior experience to arrive at the best alternative, particularly if such experience was satisfactory. Conversely, the search may be quite extended and encompass many and varied information sources. A number of factors affect the extent of the consumer's search process. They are discussed below.

EXPERIENCE

As we have noted, satisfactory experiences in a similar situation will limit the extent of information search. A lack of experience will probably lead to at least some effort to secure information. Even if a consumer has had relevant experiences, not all experiences can be recalled, and even if they are, they may not be transferable to the present problem.

AVAILABILITY OF INFORMATION

Much information is readily available to the consumer, particularly in the mass media. In addition to advertising, feature stories in newspapers and magazines frequently give information about products and services. Store shopping services and consumer advisory services are also sometimes available to provide information.

KINDS OF INFORMATION AVAILABLE

Consumer information sources stress comparison between brands much more than that between products, even though the need for information is much greater in the latter case. There is, however, a level of subproduct information that is fairly common but not specifically related to brands.[12] An example is the "Take tea and see" advertising campaign that challenged coffee at the product level.

Products are generally more difficult to compare than brands, because the attributes are so rarely the same. (Should a quart of soda cost more or less than a pound of nuts?) Even at the brand level, the most carefully packaged information does not tell the consumer all he needs to know.

Information search is greatly reduced when well-known brands are available; apparently consumers lump these name brands into a "safe" or low-risk category on the basis of familiarity.

Advertising can provide information as well as familiarity with the product. Ads are more likely to be consulted when the product is costly, when it has not been purchased recently, and when the consumer has no favorite store in mind.

Price is one of the most common types of information sought by consumers, and to find out about it the consumer usually consults marketer-dominated sources of information, such as ads or price tags. Price is not the most important factor in brand decision, however, and it has been shown that price reduction bears no clear relationship to brand choice.

AMOUNT OF INFORMATION REQUIRED

The amount of information required in a purchase situation may vary with the individual and the situation. Some individuals require more or less information than others, depending on such characteristics as the extent of their current knowledge, their confidence in their ability to make decisions, their interest in the product, and its importance to them.

When researchers examined the type of information consumers acquired from package panels before making a purchase decision, they found that brand names and price were most frequently selected. Less information was sought when brand name was available, probably, according to the researchers, because brand name serves as an information chunk that can be easily encoded or retrieved for decision making. When brand-name information was available and used, consumers were more satisfied with their purchase decisions and tended to seek fewer kinds of information.[13]

In some cases, too much information may be offered. Researchers have found that automobile buyers at some point rush into the purchase from a sense of confusion and need to reduce frustration. A study concerning the provision of label information questioned the extent to which such information may aid in the making of choices. The researchers concluded that there are limits to the consumer's ability to accommodate substantial amounts of package information within a limited time span.[14]

It has been suggested that consumers do not use all of the information available to them and tend to obtain too little information instead of too much, seemingly because a psychic tension caused by extended search results in a psychological cost that is added to the monetary cost of additional information. Thus the total cost of the information is higher than the monetary cost.[15] Chapter 8 notes that the amount of information available is less important than the manner in which it is presented. Thus information should be material, relevant, and presented in a manner that is easily processable.

SATISFACTION DERIVED FROM SEARCH

To many consumers, shopping is a chore, and information seeking may also be a chore. To others, the process of gathering all the necessary information, sorting it out, and arriving at an informed choice provides enormous satisfaction. For such people, the search itself becomes a pleasurable activity. Making the appropriate choice may also be very important to this group, which therefore tends to engage in extended search.

PERCEIVED CONSEQUENCE OF SEARCH

If the consumer perceives the consequences of not searching as serious, then search activities will ensue. If the consequences of not searching are negligible, such activities will be reduced. Consequences are the expected outcomes for the consumer, the possibility of satisfaction or dissatisfaction, the inconvenience of selecting the wrong product, the financial outlay, and so on. If the consumer perceives that the wrong choice will provide great dissatisfaction, much inconvenience or an extensive financial outlay that is not justifiable, search may increase.

VALUE AND COST OF SEARCH

The extent to which a consumer shops for a particular product is governed by factors that are related both to the value of the search and to the cost of the effort involved. This hypothesis is derived from the rationale that the consumer is a profit-maximizing person who weighs the probable return from seeking a better price or superior quality against the out-of-pocket cost of shopping and the wear and tear on her psychic and physical well-being.[16]

This hypothesis was supported in part by a research project designed to test three basic generalizations:[17]

1. The consumer will shop more extensively when the cost of shopping is low.
2. The consumer will shop more extensively when she initially knows little about the product she is buying and the stores that sell it.
3. The consumer will shop more extensively when the value of the product is high.

The research project supported the hypothesis that consumers will respond to low shopping costs by making more interstore comparisons. The hypothesis that consumers will have a greater willingness to shop around for higher priced items was also supported. The hypothesis that consumers will shop when they are less informed about what they wish to buy was supported in part. For example, when consumers knew all of the features of the brand they wished to buy and had a favorite store, they shopped in two or more stores in only 6.8 percent of cases. When no brand was known, no store was preferred, and only some features were known, 41.8 percent of the products were shopped for in two or more stores. Although these concepts of rational consumer behavior have validity, they by no means explain all of the variation in shopping activity.

A behavioral definition of a shopping good (a good for which the consumer "shops"—that is, shops around—and therefore is gathering information) is a good for which the consumer's perception of the "probable gain from making a price and quality comparison among alternative sellers is high relative to the searching costs in terms of time, money and effort."[18]

The apparent economic basis for this definition is modified by the terms "perception" and "appraisal." There seems to be some question as to whether or not the consumer functions in a cost/benefit-analysis context or in monetary terms. In fact, a recent study indicated that the "economics of information" theory does not seem to be a useful framework for an explanation of gasoline-buying behavior.[19] An explanation emerges from Lester G. Telser: "One may well encounter empirical price distributions to persist such that the higher price is not more than twenty-five percent above the least price. . . . For such price distributions it may well be rational for shoppers regularly to patronize the same retailers and to do little search."[20]

CONSUMER CHARACTERISTICS

The findings from several studies unidimensionally investigating the role of economic and demographic characteristics in shopping behavior have indicated that age, income, education, family life-style, and other such variables are related to search behavior.

A study incorporating bivariate analysis to yield profiles of households associated with a variety of deliberation and search activities revealed that middle-aged female grocery shoppers are more prone to deliberate and to use shopping information than individuals in earlier stages of the life cycle. Income is correlated with external search activity (distance traveled, number and variety of trips). Education is consistently related to use of information.[21]

This study suggested that deliberation and search are not simple univariate phenomena. Certain households read food ads in many papers while preparing a shopping list. Others read only specific papers or just prepare a list. In the search activity, some households visited a variety of stores over a broad area. Others restricted shopping to a variety of stores in close proximity. The variety of personal characteristics that described the criterion variable appear to be related to pre-purchase deliberation and search behavior. One variation portrays a deliberate shopper, characterized by a mobile family, relatively high in income and education, and in one of the later stages of the family life cycle. Other combinations suggest that factors influencing the perceived cost of search (for example, children and the expense of a baby-sitter) are moderated by other demographic factors, such as education.

An analysis of consumer characteristics related to search behavior may be useful, particularly for purposes of market segmentation. It may be best, however, to view the total search process as a system of activities incorporating two or more variables (rather than to use single dimensions) in the development of profiles of households associated with a variety of deliberation and search activities.

In an effort to determine the characteristics of information seekers, studies have focused on the subscribers to *Consumer Reports*, a consumer information magazine. The *Consumer Reports* subscriber was found to be affluent, well educated, and likely to own a fairly wide range of durable goods, ranging from typewriters to cars. The subscriber also appears to be "communication active"—that is, he is articulate and is a reader of newspapers and magazines, but he does not watch much TV.[22]

INFORMATION IGNORED AND INFORMATION DISTORTED

Before information can have any tangible and direct impact on consumer choice behavior, it must be acquired, perceived, comprehended, and, in many cases, placed into memory and retrieved at some later point in time.

Information would seem to be an important component of most consumer decisions. Studies have indicated, however, that only about 1 shopper in 10 checks advertisements before shopping for shoes or personal accessories.[23] Even for such costly and heavily advertised purchases as appliances, auto accessories, and furniture, scarcely half of the sample reported checking ads before shopping.

A variety of reasons may account for this disinclination to seek out information.[24] Gathering and processing such information add to the total cost of the purchase. Furthermore, these activities postpone the purchase of items that may be needed, or at least desired, immediately. In addition, the total volume of information from a thorough search could be so confusing that the consumer might decide she would have been as well off without it.

As we noted earlier in the discussion of memory and information processing, individuals face limitations on their ability to deal effectively with large amounts of information within a limited time period. Psychological research has noted the phenomenon of "information overload."[25]

Recent research into the users of toll-free information services indicated some of the difficulties in getting such information used. The researcher concluded that if an information planner wants information to be sought and used, audience members must be shown that this information is relevant and meaningful to them.[26] This finding supports the earlier discussion on information processing and retrieval in Chapter 8. The researcher concluded that the information planner must "package" the information in an appealing manner and present it in a form that is understood by the target audience.

Distortion of information is a well-established principle in the field of voting and political information. Studies of presidential campaigns have indicated tendencies toward both selective exposure to campaign information and selective patterns of misperception of the candidates' stands on major issues. For example, despite Harry Truman's veto of the Taft-Hartley Bill and his many speeches against it, 4 of every 10 Democrats who favored the bill said they thought the president did also. (This error was made by only 10 percent of the Democrats who agreed with Truman in opposing the bill.)[27]

Although it is difficult to demonstrate empirically similar distortion of information in marketing studies, it no doubt exists. An apparent distortion occurred when Anheuser-Busch introduced Chelsea, its fruit-juice drink with a low alcoholic content, as we saw earlier. In its early market test, it was viewed by a nurses' association as encouraging children to imbibe alcoholic beverages by introducing them to the taste and supposed "acceptability" of alcohol. The company discontinued its initial promotion campaign and repositioned its product as the "natural alternative," suggesting its use for adults.

SOURCES OF INFORMATION

The major sources of consumer information are personal experience, nonmarketer sources, and marketer-dominated sources. Here we shall examine personal experience and nonmarketer-dominated sources of information. (Chapters 14 and 15 will examine marketer-dominated sources.)

Generally speaking, information from the mass media performs an *informing* function, whereas that from personal sources assumes a *legitimizing* or *evaluating* function.[28] This does not mean that mass media may not legitimize and personal sources may not inform. Still, consumers frequently use friends and relatives for information about quality but less frequently consult them about price. Generally, consumers will use mass media to learn about the availability and attributes of alternatives, and personal sources to evaluate them.

It appears that the various communication sources are not equally effective at the various stages of the purchase decision process. Marketer-controlled messages, which are the most likely source of initial information, decline markedly as a source of additional information, and further decline in ratings of the "most important" source. In contrast, personal communication is mentioned increasingly in the movement from "first" to "additional" to "most important" source of information. (See Table 13.2.)

Personal Experience

There are indications that the amount of information sought by many buyers is small, even though information is accessible, suggesting substantial selectivity of search. The findings do not necessarily mean, however, that the buyer is ill informed. He may have started with what he regarded as sufficient knowledge. It has been noted that use and purchase of a major durable product result in learning that influences later buying behavior.[29]

The consumer's excursion into the marketplace at any one time is generally preceded by a vast array of personal experiences. Frequently these experiences are sufficient for a decision. Past satisfactions with a brand lead to repeat purchases without search for additional information. These experiences can be designated as internal search, as distinct from information gathered from external sources. This type of internal search may provide all of the information necessary, and the consumer may forgo any additional search in arriving at a purchasing decision.

TABLE 13.2 USE OF INFORMATION CHANNELS IN THE PURCHASE DECISION PROCESS

Channels	Small appliances			Clothing			Food		
	First	Additional	Most important	First	Additional	Most important	First	Additional	Most important
Marketer-controlled									
Advertising	48	23	8	35	27	16	45	25	19
Salesmen	1	1	1	4	1	6	0	0	0
Sales promotion*	9	7	9	19	14	32	26	16	27
Nonmarketer-controlled									
Personal influence									
Friends, neighbors, relatives†	23	41	53	27	29	33	16	19	29
Immediate family	8	7	11	2	4	0	12	12	21
Professional advice	6	8	13	0	0	0	1	0	0
Editorial and news material‡	1	0	1	6	6	6	0	0	1
No mentions	4	13	4	7	19	7	0	28	3
Total (N = 99)	100%	100%	100%	100%	100%	100%	100%	100%	100%

Note: Three questions were asked:
"Could you tell me how this product came to your attention for the *very first time?*"
"How *else* did you hear about this product before you bought it?"
"Which *one* of these ways was your *most important* source of information in your decision to buy this product?"
* Includes sampling, displays, in-store shopping, packaging.
† Includes actual discussions as well as noticing the item or trying the item, for example, in the home of a friend.
‡ Includes *Consumer Reports.*
Source: Thomas S. Robertson, *Innovative Behavior and Communication* (New York: Holt, Rinehart & Winston, 1971), p. 156.

ATTRIBUTION THEORY

The significance of personal experience as an information source is taking on increasing importance with the development of *attribution theory*. While attribution theory is still in the developmental stage and involves a number of theoretical constructs (some of which are discussed in Chapter 18), one construct that should be noted at this point refers to the process whereby consumers infer meanings from outcomes. A simple explanation suggests that if the outcome of using a product is good, this experience may be used as a source of information for the consumer's future behavior, that is, he may purchase it again. Should the outcome be unsatisfactory, however, many inferences may be made by the consumer as to the causes. He may attribute the outcome to the product's inferiority or its inappropriateness for that particular situation; he may feel that the directions were not followed or believe that the item is a lemon, while the others of its kind are not.[30] Such inferences provide additional information based on personal experiences.

Self-perception theory is another aspect of the causal inference process. According to Daryl Bem, "Individuals come to 'know' their own attitudes, emotions, and other internal states by inferring them from observations of their own behavior and/or the situation in which this behavior occurred."[31] A simple illustration of a consumer's self-perception is "I drink coffee, therefore I must like coffee." Both object perception and self-perception may be important in the evaluation, choice, and postpurchase stages of the consumer decision process.

Nonmarketer Sources

Information may be available to consumers from a variety of sources other than the marketer: personal sources, mass media (through editorial or news content), and government sources.

PERSONAL SOURCES

Personal sources of information are people with whom the consumer has some contact. As we noted in Chapter 5, individuals establish reference groups throughout their lifetimes. The earliest of these groups is the family; then come school groups, peers, work groups, social contacts, and so on. All of these groups provide information for the consumer. Information exchanged via personal contacts is called *interpersonal communications*.

OPINION LEADERS

One of the most extensively researched phenomena relating to personal sources of influence is the role of opinion leaders. Elihu Katz and Paul Lazarsfeld described a *two-step flow of communication*—information flows from mass media to mass audience through the mediation of opinion leaders.[32] It has been pointed out that opinion leaders "act not only as channels of information but also as a source of social pressure toward a particular choice, and as social support to reinforce that choice once it has been made."[33]

Opinion leaders are a much-sought-after group through which marketers hope to influence others. In the two-step flow of information, the opinion leader, while not under the marketer's control, relays information from the marketer to the group members. The opinion leader is not merely a relayer of information; she also screens and evaluates the information before passing it on. The audience is not necessarily passive, however. Studies have shown that approximately 50 percent of product conversations are initiated not by the opinion leader, but by the consumer who is seeking information about the product.[34] Thus the consumer may be active in informal communication channels when her needs are not satisfied by the more formal channels.

A summary of the early literature on opinion leaders provides the following definition:

> Opinion leaders . . . exist in virtually all primary groups. . . . By and large, opinion leaders are like the rank and file of their associates but of slightly higher education or social status; they give much greater attention to the mass media on the topics of their opinion leadership; they are better informed, more partisan, and more active than their associates. Opinion leaders differ for different topics . . . but they have in common their channeling of the impersonal content of mass communications into the personal stream of influence.[35]

Characteristics of Opinion Leaders. Various research sources have disclosed that opinion leaders have certain distinguishing characteristics:[36]

1. They exert their influence primarily in one rather well-defined area of interest, such as marketing, fashion, or public affairs. Opinion leadership tends to overlap in product categories that have common interest dimensions, however.

    The question of how generalized opinion leadership is (discussed later) is still subject to considerable debate, especially with respect to some methodological issues involved in the measurement of opinion leadership. Current findings suggest, however, that if areas of consumer interest are strongly correlated, opinion leadership tends to overlap these areas.

2. Opinion leaders are usually found in approximately equal proportions in all strata of society. Although they are not equally effective at all social levels, opinion leaders are typically in the same social class as those they influence, or in a slightly higher class.

3. Opinion leaders personify certain values and show greater adherence to norms than those who are not opinion leaders.

4. They are perceived as competent and possess more knowledge than others about their areas of influence.

5. Opinion leaders are socially accessible, active in interpersonal relations, and more gregarious than other individuals. Findings in regard to institutional opinion leaders were similar to those regarding household opinion leaders.[37]

6. Opinion leaders are typically more exposed to mass media than other people.

Generally, opinion leaders do not seem to differ from nonleaders in the major demographic variables, with some exceptions (for example, influence in children's upbringing was more common among younger housewives and large households).[38]

Opinion Leader Overlap. Generalized opinion leadership represents influence in more than one narrowly defined area. Although researchers have disagreed as to the existence of generalized opinion leadership, there is some evidence of opinion leadership overlap.

A study of six product categories—packaged food products, women's fashions, household cleansers and detergents, cosmetics and personal grooming aids, and large and small appliances—found a large opinion leadership overlap across product categories. Some 46 percent of the sample qualified as opinion leaders in two or more product categories, 28 percent in three or more, and 13 percent in four or more categories.[39]

Several researchers have found evidence of opinion leader overlap. James Myers and Thomas Robertson found that influence in regard to household furnishings correlated highly with influence in regard to household appliances.[40] David Montgomery and Alvin Silk found overlap in opinion leadership across many but not all of the categories they studied.[41] It appears that opinion leadership overlap is greatest over product categories that involve similar interests. This research suggests there may be a quasi-general opinion leader in several consumer product contexts.

Methods of Identifying Opinion Leaders. Given the role of opinion leaders in providing information to others, marketers find it useful to be able to identify them. In a study to disclose relatively stable predictors of male fashion opinion leaders, two variables—fashion interest and fashion venturesomeness—consistently indicated that these characteristics were predictors of male fashion leadership.[42] By pinpointing such individuals and learning the media they use, the marketer can be in a position to use them as targets for their promotional efforts, as triers of their new and improved products, to generate word-of-mouth advertising, and so on.

A wide variety of measures has been used to identify opinion leadership. They may be grouped in three basic categories based on the means of identifying individuals who have influence in a given topic area.[43]

1. The *sociometric* method involves asking members of a sample from whom they get advice and from whom they seek advice or information in some

given topic area. The persons most often mentioned by the group are considered to be opinion leaders. This is the most expensive method.

2. The *key-informant* method requires the use of informed individuals in a social system to designate opinion leaders in a topic area. The number of respondents is usually smaller than in the sociometric method, but each response is assumed to carry more weight.

3. The *self-designating* method relies on the respondent to evaluate his own influence; for example, the individual may be asked, "Have you recently been asked your opinion about...?" This method usually contains the most bias. Some of the bias may be eliminated by later interviews with consumers who were supposedly influenced.

Data on self-reported opinion leadership may be usefully applied to two marketing areas: development of new products and copy testing.

A case history illustrates such application in the development of new products. The introductory campaign for a motor speedway in Los Angeles included a coupon with which to buy tickets for its opening event. As advance sales came in, records were kept of the first fifty purchasers, or "early adopters." These people were subsequently interviewed by telephone with a questionnaire that included a self-report measure of automotive opinion leadership. It was found that 60 percent of the early adopters were automotive opinion leaders. These findings provided clear directions for future advertising and public relations efforts on behalf of the speedway.[44]

It has been noted that opinion leaders legitimize the contents of a mass communication when they pass it on to their circle of friends and relatives. During a copy test, an advertiser might consider including a simple self-report question on opinion leadership in order to estimate the group's response to his message.

GOVERNMENT SOURCES

One consequence of the current interest in consumerism is a heavy emphasis on programs to provide consumers with full information on products and services. Two distinct arguments are made in support of such programs. One suggests that Congress has passed such laws as the Truth-in-Lending Law on the issue of the right to know rather than on any evidence that the consumer actually uses the information. A second argument for fuller provision of information flows from the free-enterprise economic model, in which maximal social welfare is assumed to result when consumers have the greatest opportunity to exercise free choice.[45]

A number of programs currently provide the consumer with information on products and services. Several *proactive* programs establish standards of information provision. Among them are truth-in-lending, fair packaging and labeling, unit pricing, and octane rating. Public agencies have increased their consumer education activities, and private concerns have offered expanded product-rating services and introduced consumer education programs.

Reactive programs, such as the advertising substantiation program and corrective advertising, are aimed at countering excesses of existing product claims.[46] In 1971 the FTC adopted a resolution designed to "assist consumers to make rational choices." The procedure outlined in the resolution required that advertisers submit on demand "tests, studies, or other data that purport to substantiate advertised claims regarding a product's safety, performance, efficacy, quality, or comparative price."[47] This rule was not intended to cast doubt on the continued propriety of "puffing" in advertising. Thus, if someone says a product "tastes great," no documentation is required; but if someone says a tire "stops three times as fast," the Commission may ask to see proof.

On the basis of this resolution, the FTC has issued a number of consent orders requiring various companies to discontinue claims that are not adequately substantiated. Whirlpool was ordered to stop referring to its "panic button" as unique (only the name, which was used to indicate fast cooling, was unique) and Fedders was told to stop stating that its "reserve cooling system" was a unique feature of its air conditioners. General Motors was told to stop declaring that "Vega handles better," and Firestone was ordered to stop advertising that its tires "stop 25% faster." In fact, the FTC ultimately charged Firestone with violating the consent order and required the company to spend $750,000 on "educational advertisements." Firestone disseminated a series of ads designed to inform the public that no tires are safe under all conditions of use and that proper tire safety depends on proper maintenance and operation of the car.

The FTC does not concern itself with all product claims and feels that some improper claims can be corrected by the market. In analyzing whether the market itself can correct false unsubstantiated representations, the FTC considers product claims to fall into three categories representing different "qualities" relevant to information processing.[48]

Search qualities concern product claims whose truth the consumer can and is likely to determine for himself before purchase (for example, a claim that a refrigerator door is "bright" yellow).

Experience qualities concern attribute claims that the consumer can assess only on the basis of actual experience with the product. If the product is safe and inexpensive, and the experience with the particular attribute is quickly realized, then the market may correct a deception when a product fails to perform as advertised (for example, a claim that one deodorant is "less runny" than another).

Credence qualities relate to claims that a consumer cannot evaluate for himself (for example, claims of efficacy of an over-the-counter drug or the lubricating effectiveness of a motor oil).

Because the market is least likely to correct deceptions having credence qualities, claims incorporating such qualities are more likely to be considered in enforcement procedures; but the decision to emphasize credence qualities is relevant only to the question of the ability of the market to correct the deception and does not eliminate the need to answer other questions relevant to substantiation.

Several state and federal agencies, including the Federal Trade Commission, the Department of Transportation, and the Food and Drug Administration, have begun programs to provide relevant product information to consumers. These programs require that marketers of certain products and services disclose particular information on their brand offerings, which in principle can be compared with baseline standards for those product categories.

Future thrusts in provision of consumer information are likely to be aimed at assisting brand-choice decisions.[49] The nature of information to be provided will reflect objective brand-performance characteristics. Greatest attention will probably be given to high-priced, infrequently purchased durable goods that are bought by most consumers and whose performance can potentially be described by relatively few dimensions susceptible to technical measurement against uniform standards. Possibilities include home appliances (refrigerators, freezers, air conditioners, vacuum cleaners, washers and dryers), carpeting, mattresses, and automobiles.

For such programs to be effective, channels must be provided for dissemination of the information. Such dissemination channels can be drawn in some combination from existing marketing contacts with the consumer. These forms of contact include the product or package, point-of-sale materials, retail salespersons, and print and broadcast advertising. Such existing channels could also be supplemented by public or private consumer education programs, consumer rating publications, and related voluntary programs by brand marketers (for example, comparison advertising, product booklets).

In addition to the problem concerning the proper format for such information and the channels for its dissemination, there is a question concerning the extent to which brand comparisons by consumers can or should be fostered, and when in the decision process these comparisons would be made. Some alternatives (for example, dimensional disclosure in broadcast offerings) would place heavy stress on consumer memory; others (for example, summary ratings at point of sale) could hinder comparisons with brands not available; still others (for example, dimensional disclosures on product or package) are likely to require complex processing within a constrained time period, thus impeding rational planning. It seems apparent, therefore, that combinations of channels and formats are required.

Types of Information to Be Provided. The type of information studied in the past in the context of consumer behavior has generally been "persuasive," that is, tending to be subjective, avowedly nonneutral, and often surpassing consumers' credulity. It has been recommended that in the future emphasis be placed on information processing. Information subsumed under this category relates to objective, neutral, credible brand ratings. It has been proposed that such information be viewed as including all product attributes capable of being objectively described or tested in terms of standards.[50]

Such information is multidimensional. Price of a given item is one dimension of objective consumer information that has typically been available. While price information may be necessary for informed choice, it is not sufficient; each consumer must somehow equate the "values" ("quality") of alternatives with their prices. The fundamental purpose of data for information processing is to assist in the consumer's evaluation of quality and its relationship to various prices. Provision of only a single dimension of information—a common approach in past programs—tends to assume that a single piece of information is sufficient for a quality determination. Further discussion of consumers' evaluation of quality will be presented in Chapter 16.

Problem Areas. As we noted earlier, a number of problem areas exist in the development of effective public policy programs to provide the consumer with adequate information. They include motivational factors, the capacity of consumers to assimilate and process information, existing consumer knowledge and predispositions, and individual differences.

Motivational factors relate to the willingness and ability of the consumer to process the information provided by a public policy program. Experience suggests that most consumers will not use such information.

In a study designed to test the recall of objective nutritional information presented in television commercials, respondents were able to recall and comprehend the overall message contained in the ad. Although the commercials appeared to convey accurate brand knowledge to respondents, brand preference/intention-to-buy seemed not to be affected by the information. Specifically, the researcher's findings suggest that consumers may have reasons other than superior "nutrition value" for preferring one brand or product over another.[51]

Research has consistently found that there are limits to human ability to assimilate and process information during a given time period. Quantities of information beyond these limits can create anxiety or psychological stress and can lead to confused and nonrational behavior.

Consumers have many varying cognitions and brand preferences before they are exposed to information. These attitudes are likely to have an effect on the new information that is provided. The nature and effect of such consumer predispositions require research in order to clarify the effect of new information provided for the consumer to process.

That consumers differ is perhaps the most tantalizing aspect of consumer behavior. Human variation raises real difficulties in arriving at meaningful generalizations and in developing public programs aimed at "the consumer." It has been suggested that research in consumer information processing will shed light on many of these questions.

SUMMARY

The consumer decision process is a problem-solving activity that encompasses five stages: problem recognition, information search, alternative evaluation, choice, and postpurchase behavior. In the first stage, problem recognition, a difference is seen between what is perceived as the desired state of affairs and what is perceived as the actual state of affairs. Problem recognition occurs in response to many variables that influence the actual state of affairs or the desired state: deficiencies in the individual's stock of goods, expanded means or expanded desires, new information, and changes in the consumer's reference groups.

In the second stage of the consumer decision process, the individual engages in a search for information to learn about the various alternatives available. The factors that influence the extent to which the consumer engages in information search are the amount of previous experience the individual has had, the availability of information without search, the availability of information when search is conducted, and the amount of information required. Other factors include the satisfaction derived from search, the perceived consequences of search, the value and cost of search, and particular characteristics of consumers that are related to search behavior. It should be acknowledged that available information can be ignored, and even if it is attended to, it may be distorted.

There are three major sources of information for the consumer: personal experience, nonmarketer sources, and marketer-dominated sources. Personal experiences may be designated as internal search, and when these experiences are satisfactory, they may lead to repeat purchases of a brand without search for additional information.

Reference-group sources of information include the family, school, peers, work groups, and so on. One important interpersonal source of information is the opinion leader. The opinion leader relays information from the marketer to group members. Opinion leaders appear to have certain distinguishing characteristics, but each area of interest is likely to have its own opinion leaders. Nonetheless, there seems to be some overlap in opinion leadership, especially in product categories that involve similar interests.

A number of methods may be used to identify opinion leaders: the sociometric method, the key-informant method, and the self-designating method. Identifying opinion leaders may be important to marketers, who can then determine useful targets for promotional efforts; these targets can in turn generate effective word-of-mouth advertising.

Current interest in consumerism places a heavy emphasis on programs to provide information for consumers. A number of programs already exist, including those aimed at countering excesses of existing product claims and those that establish standards for the information to be provided. There are recommendations that additional information be provided, and that programs be established to provide the means by which consumers may process this information more efficiently.

DISCUSSION QUESTIONS

1. Describe a recent personal situation that you can define as "problem recognition."

2. As a manufacturer of bicycles, you are using a purchase-intention survey to forecast sales. What would you consider to be the limitations of these data?

3. What factors would influence the extent of search in your decision to purchase a new car?

4. What sources of information would you examine for this decision?

5. What are the characteristics and functions of an opinion leader?

6. Have you recently been influenced by an opinion leader? Are you an opinion leader? Explain.

7. To what extent has government information helped you in recent purchase decisions?

8. Do you believe the government should be involved more or less in providing information for consumers? Why?

NOTES

1. John Dewey, *How We Think* (Boston: D. C. Heath, 1910), chap. 8.

2. James F. Engel, Roger D. Blackwell, and David T. Kollat, *Consumer Behavior,* 3d ed. (New York: Holt, Rinehart & Winston, 1978), p. 216.

3. Donald H. Granbois and John O. Summers, "On the Predictive Accuracy of Subjective Purchase Probabilities," in *Association for Consumer Research Proceedings, 3rd Annual Conference,* 1972, ed. M. Venkatesan, pp. 502–511.

4. C. Joseph Clawson, "Marketing Applications of Intentions Data," in *Association for Consumer Research,* 1973, pp. 522–525.

5. Edward M. Tauber, "Discovering New Product Opportunities with Problem Inventory Analysis," *Journal of Marketing* 39 (January 1975), p. 70.

6. Murphy A. Sewall, "Market Segmentation Based on Consumer Ratings of Proposed Product Designs," *Journal of Marketing Research* 15 (November 1978), pp. 557–564.

7. Alvin J. Silk and Glen L. Urban, "Pre-Test Marketing Evaluation of New Packaged Goods: A Model and Measurement Methodology," *Journal of Marketing Research* 15 (May 1978), pp. 171–191.

8. Donald G. Morrison, "Purchase Intentions and Purchase Behavior," *Journal of Marketing* 43 (Spring 1979), pp. 65–74.

9. See, for example, James R. Bettman, *An Information Processing Theory of Consumer Choice* (Reading, Mass.: Addison-Wesley, 1979), pp. 3–10.

10. John A. Howard, *Consumer Behavior: Application of Theory* (New York: McGraw-Hill, 1977), p. 9.

11. Chapter 8 describes consumers' initial resistance to instant coffee.

12. Steven H. Chaffee and Jack M. McLeod, "Consumer Decisions and Information Use," in *Consumer Behavior: Theoretical Sources,* ed. Scott Ward and Thomas S. Robertson (Englewood Cliffs, N.J.: Prentice-Hall, 1973), pp. 392–393.

13. Jacob Jacoby, George J. Szybillo, and Jacqueline Busato-Schach, "Information Acquisition Behavior in Brand Choice Situations," *Journal of Consumer Research* 3 (March 1977), pp. 209–216.

14. Jacob Jacoby, Donald E. Speller, and Carol A. Kohn, "Brand Choice Behavior as a Function of Information Load: Replication and Extension," *Journal of Consumer Research* 1 (June 1974), p. 41.

15. R. J. Markin, Jr., *Consumer Behavior: A Cognitive Orientation* (New York: Macmillan, 1974), p. 543.

16. Louis P. Bucklin, "Testing Propensities to Shop," *Journal of Marketing* 30 (January 1966), p. 22.

17. Ibid.

18. R. H. Holton, "The Distinction between Convenience Goods, Shopping Goods, and Specialty Goods," *Journal of Marketing* 1 (July 1958), p. 53.

19. Ariaeh Goldman and J. K. Johansson, "Determinants of Search for Lower Prices: An Empirical Assessment of the Economics of Information Theory," *Journal of Consumer Research* 5 (December 1978), pp. 176–185.

20. Lester G. Telser, "Searching for the Lowest Price," *American Economic Review* 63 (1973), pp. 40–49.

21. Stephen J. Miller and William G. Zikmund, "A Multivariate Analysis of Prepurchase Deliberation and External Search Behavior," in *Advances in Consumer Research*, vol. 2, ed. Mary Jane Schlinger (Association for Consumer Research, 1975), pp. 186–196.

22. William J. McEwen, "Bridging the Information Gap," *Journal of Consumer Research* 4 (March 1978), p. 248.

23. Louis P. Bucklin, "The Informative Role of Advertising," *Journal of Advertising Research* 5 (1965), pp. 11–15.

24. Chaffee and McLeod, "Consumer Decisions and Information Use," p. 387.

25. Jacoby, Speller, and Kohn, "Brand Choice Behavior," pp. 33–42.

26. McEwen, "Bridging the Information Gap," pp. 247–251.

27. Chaffee and McLeod, "Consumer Decisions and Information Use," p. 387.

28. Engel et al., *Consumer Behavior*, 3d ed. (1978), p. 250.

29. Joseph W. Newman and Richard Staelin, "Prepurchase Information Seeking for New Cars and Major Household Appliances," *Journal of Marketing Research* 9 (August 1972), p. 256.

30. Bettman, *Information Processing Theory*, p. 272.

31. Daryl J. Bem, "Self Perception Theory," in *Advances in Experimental and Social Psychology*, ed. Leonard Berkowitz (New York: Academic Press, 1972), p. 2.

32. Elihu Katz and Paul F. Lazarsfeld, *Personal Influence* (New York: Free Press of Glencoe, 1955).

33. Charles Y. Glock and Francesco M. Nicosia, "Sociology and the Study of Consumers," *Journal of Advertising Research* 3 (September 1963), p. 24.

34. Markin, *Consumer Behavior*, p. 378.

35. Katz and Lazarsfeld, *Personal Influence*, p. 550.

36. Ronald E. Frank, William F. Massy, and Yoram Wind, *Market Segmentation* (Englewood Cliffs, N.J.: Prentice-Hall, 1972), pp. 76–77 (for items 1 through 5).

37. Leon G. Schiffman and Vincent Gaccione, "Opinion Leaders in Institutional Markets," *Journal of Marketing* 38 (April 1974), p. 53.

38. James H. Myers and Thomas S. Robertson, "Dimensions of Opinion Leadership," *Journal of Marketing Research* 9 (February 1972), p. 45.

39. Lawrence G. Corey, "People Who Claim to Be Opinion Leaders: Identifying Their Characteristics by Self-Report," *Journal of Marketing* 35 (October 1971), p. 48.

40. Myers and Robertson, "Dimensions of Opinion Leadership," p. 45.

41. David B. Montgomery and Alvin J. Silk, "Patterns of Overlap in Opinion Leadership and Interest for Selected Categories of Purchasing Activity," in *Marketing Involvement in Society and the Economy*, ed. Philip R. McDonald (Chicago: American Marketing Association, 1969), pp. 377–386.

42. William R. Darden and Fred D. Reynolds, "Predicting Opinion Leadership for Men's Apparel Fashions," *Journal of Marketing Research* 9 (August 1972), p. 327.

43. Charles W. King and John O. Summers, "Overlap of Opinion Leadership across Product Categories," *Journal of Marketing Research* 7 (February 1970), p. 44.

44. Corey, "People Who Claim to Be Opinion Leaders," p. 53.

45. William L. Wilkie, *How Consumers Use Product Information: An Assessment of Research in Relation to Public Policy Needs,* report prepared for National Science Foundation (Washington, D.C.: U.S. Government Printing Office, 1975), p. 4.

46. Corrective advertising is discussed in Chapter 19.

47. "Documentation of Advertising Claims," Commerce Clearing House Trade Regulation Report no. C 7996 (June 1971).

48. Richard B. Herzog, "The Policy and Planning Protocol for Deceptive and Unsubstantiated Claims: A Management and Legal Perspective," address presented to the Institute of Advanced Advertising Studies, American Association of Advertising Agencies, New York Council, Tarrytown, New York, June 24 and 27, 1976, p. 9.

49. Wilkie, "How Consumers Use Product Information," p. 10.

50. Ibid., p. 51.

51. Debra L. Seammon, " 'Information Load' and Consumers," *Journal of Consumer Research* 4 (December 1977), pp. 148–155.

CHAPTER 14

INFORMATION PROCESSING

Many of the marketer's efforts to inform consumers emanate from his marketing communications in the form of advertising, personal selling, and sales promotion. "Sales promotion" is a broad term that encompasses various incentives to purchase—samples, coupons, contests, and the like—as well as communications that appear at the point of purchase, such as posters and displays. Sales-promotion techniques will be discussed in greater detail in Chapter 16. This chapter and the next focus on some of the effects of advertising and personal selling on the process of informing and persuading consumers. This chapter focuses on such questions as:

> What are the barriers to the processing of marketers' information?
> How do marketers communicate information?
> How are consumers persuaded?
> How does the information source influence persuasion?

BARRIERS TO COMMUNICATIONS

Despite marketers' best efforts, their communication strategies are not always effective. Over $40 billion was spent on advertising in 1978,[1] yet one still hears advertisers say, "I know I'm wasting half of the money I spend; the trouble is I don't know which half." This quip illustrates two typical communications problems: the difficulty of determining a message's effectiveness and the difficulty of pinpointing the reasons for success or failure.

One of the potential reasons for lack of success lies in the barriers to communications that emerge from the principles of selective perception, discussed in Chapter 7. In describing the consumer as a learner and the effects of perception, we noted that although stimuli abound in the individual's environment, she effectively perceives only a small portion of them. Such selective perception stems in part from the limited storage capacity of the individual's memory systems and from the need to organize the many and diverse stimuli in the environment into a coherent pattern. Although many messages may be disseminated to persuade consumers, the manner in which their information content is processed may be limited by selective exposure, selective attention, and selective distortion.

Selective Exposure

In rigid communication terms, exposure relates to the capability of receiving a message. Individuals may place themselves in situations where some messages can be received while others are avoided. The assumption is that if a stimulus is present, such as an advertisement in a magazine or a product on a supermarket shelf, and the consumer buys that magazine or goes to that shelf, the potential for exposure exists.

Advertising researchers have frequently found positive associations between measures of advertising exposure and those of favorable disposition toward the product, such as interest, prospect status, past use, and recent purchase. Such correlations have generally been interpreted as a manifestation of the process of selective exposure; that is, audiences tend to expose themselves selectively to those messages that best fit their existing predispositions or inclinations. Selective exposure, like selective perception, is related to the individual's needs, motives, social values, attitudes, and cultural background.

The concept of selective exposure is acknowledged in marketing in a variety of ways, including the growth of special-interest media and the development of market segmentation. Before the demise of the old weeklies *Look* and *Life*, both magazines had very large circulations. Their decline was in part a result of decreasing expenditures by advertisers, who considered the general nature of the magazines' audiences to present too unselective a target for their messages; too many of their subscribers did not share the beliefs, interests, and life-styles of potential purchasers of their products. Both radio and magazines are "fragmenting" audiences today, and *Life* and *Look* have been resurrected to reach more specialized interests.

While it is difficult to overcome this tendency toward selective exposure, marketing organizations may attempt to do so through "forced exposure." Thus, door-to-door sales of brushes and encyclopedias and party plans to sell Tupperware place the consumer in a position where the focus is on the product or service being offered, with few, if any, extraneous attractions.

Selective Attention

Just as the limitations on the ability to perceive all stimuli cause the individual to engage in selective exposure, these same factors lead to selective attention. Although various tests of advertising readership have indicated that the average consumer is exposed to 1,500 to 3,000 advertisements a day, one research study has found that the average American adult is aware of only 76 advertisements a day in the major media.[2] Even when consumers indicated awareness of advertisements, which they recorded through a counter technique, 84 percent of the ads they noticed did not make sufficient impact to be further categorized. Approximately 16 percent were categorized by the respondents as annoying, enjoyable, informative, or offensive.

Consumers tend to be more aware of stimuli that meet their needs and interests and are consistent with their beliefs. If a shopper is in the market for a stereo set, for example, the pages containing stereo advertisements will be noted. If a stereo is not a current or future purchase prospect, advertisements for such products will be ignored by the consumer.

In marketing segmentation strategy, an underlying concept is to devise techniques to reach consumers who either have a special interest or may be receptive to a particular approach. To meet the requirements of cholesterol-conscious consumers, for example, substitute egg products, such as Moor-Eggs and Egg Beaters, were developed. Morning Star Farms introduced a frozen breakfast from textured vegetable protein. One detergent is presented as a low pollutant for the "ecologically concerned" consumer; another cleans the clothes of the consumer beset by "problem stains," and a third is presented to the "conscientious mother" as one that will make her children's clothing white.

Selective Distortion

To some extent, we perceive what we want to perceive. Not only do we selectively expose ourselves to the media, messages, and appeals that support our predispositions, but those in conflict with our norms of behavior and our predispositions are converted, in the event of exposure, to positions more nearly compatible with our own.

People tend to misinterpret communications in accordance with their own predispositions. A classic study found that children overestimate the sizes of coins in comparison with discs of the same size, and poor children overestimate them more than rich children, presumably because of the greater value the coins have for the poor.[3]

In a recent study concerning the television program "All in the Family," featuring the highly prejudiced and narrow-minded Archie Bunker, selective distortion based on subjective traits was apparent. An audience survey showed that many people saw Archie Bunker as a hero. People who perceived him in this light tended to share Archie's prejudices; people who laughed at him as a ridiculous bigot did not.[4]

As we saw in Chapter 7, mental set may cause distortions in message interpretation. Several years ago an expensive television commercial (in fact, the most expensive at that time) presented Ann Miller dancing atop a can of soup, supported by a large chorus in an extravagant dance routine. The commercial had high word-of-mouth visibility—many people spoke about the "Campbell Soup ad." The distortion of this message, actually an ad for Heinz's Great American Soups, may have been the result of the consumer's tendency to lump all canned soups under the name Campbell. Heinz ultimately discontinued its Great American Soup line and instituted suit against Campbell. The suit, finally settled out of court, alleged that among other things, Campbell's "monopolistic practices" prevented Heinz from competing in the canned-soup market.

An unanticipated distortion occurred when several airlines introduced their "full-fare customer" plan, designed to cater to consumers who paid full fare for coach seats and traveled with others who had bought similar seats at a discount. The plan, which promised special treatment for full-fare passengers, drew criticism from many discount-fare passengers, who felt they were being downgraded. As a result of this reaction, the plan was abandoned by at least two airlines.

In a marketing context, the principle of selective distortion suggests that marketers should exercise care in developing messages in order to minimize misinterpretation. In reviewing consumer complaints about product performance, for example, some manufacturers have found that complaints have been related to a lack of clear understanding of the directions for product use. Consumers may also misinterpret the conditions of the warranty that is offered with the product. Such potential problems suggest that marketers provide clear explanatory material for product use and simple explanations of warranties. Such messages should be reinforced by duplicate presentations—that is, in hang tags and inserts or, in the case of television messages, through audio and visual presentations.

THE COMMUNICATION-PERSUASION MATRIX

From a marketer's viewpoint, communication of information is best considered in relationship to its effects on persuasion. Communication and persuasion are usually perceived as processes: the communication network is composed of a series of interrelated variables; the persuasion process is usually defined as a series of steps.

The variables in the communication process have been described as source, message, channel, receiver, and destination.[5] The persuasion process, as we noted earlier, includes the steps of exposure, emotional response, encoding, acceptance of the appeal, and overt behavior.

FIGURE 14.1 THE COMMUNICATION/PERSUASION MATRIX, INDICATING THE DIVISIONS ON THE INPUT (COMMUNICATION) SIDE AND ON THE OUTPUT (PERSUASION) SIDE

Output	Input	Source					Message				Channel	Receiver	Destination
Steps in being persuaded	Communication variables	Credibility	Likability	Power	Quantity	Demographics	Appeal	Style	Organization	Quantity			
Exposure	Simple exposure Attention to communication												
Emotional Response	Arousal Affect Attention to content												
Encoding	Perception Learning Remembering												
Acceptance													
Overt													
Behavior													
Consolidation													

Source: William J. McGuire, "The Communication/Persuasion Matrix," in *Evaluating Advertising: A Bibliography of the Communication Process*, ed. Benjamin Lipstein and William J. McGuire (New York: Advertising Research Foundation, 1978), p. xxvii.

To highlight the interrelationships of these two processes, William J. McGuire designed a communication/persuasion matrix (see Figure 14.1). This matrix emphasizes that each variable in the marketer's communication process may affect one or more steps in the process by which consumers are persuaded. For simplicity of presentation, the following discussion will focus on the communication variables, pinpointing their effects on the various steps in the persuasion process.

In 1975 a radio advertisement for Blue Nun wine won a CLIO award—an award for advertising excellence as determined by advertising professionals. (See Exhibit 14.1.) An analysis of this informational presentation in a communication context indicates the following:

1. Perceived source—makers of Blue Nun and/or Stiller and Meara as celebrity spokespeople.

2. Message strategy—humor involving entertaining characters who use frequent turns of meaning in their conversation. The basic appeal is that of a wine that is delicious, imported, correct with any dish.

3. Channel—radio, as often as possible. During the commercial flights, the aim is to accumulate 100 Gross Rating Points in the market per week.

4. Receiver—the primary target audience, selected on the basis of demographic characteristics, are men and women living in urban areas and who are between the ages of 18 and 34. A secondary group is between the ages of 35 and 52. Major psychographic considerations are heavy users who entertain or dine out frequently.

5. Destination—cognitive variables (a) Awareness—follow-up panel studies indicate that 98 percent of the respondents know Stiller and Meara and identify the pair as spokespersons for Blue Nun wines. (b) Attitude—the study indicates no negatives. The brand is perceived as a high quality table wine for use on any occasion.

6. Behavioral variables—sales of Blue Nun wine have climbed from a base of 68 thousand cases annually (140 thousand cases in 1970) to approximately 1.2 million in 1978). The increase is calculated as a gain of more than 2,000 percent.

Clearly, not every communication strategy is equally successful. Furthermore, there is no definitive validation that the success of Blue Nun in sales is based on the advertising communication. However, it appears the campaign has achieved some of its cognitive objectives relative to consumer targets in terms of significant awareness and favorable attitudes.

Bases of Source Influences

A communications source may be designated as the person or group of people whom the recipients perceive to be the source of the message—the perceived

EXHIBIT 14.1

Announcer:	Stiller and Meara
Stiller:	Good evening, Miss, will you be dining alone?
Meara: (in tears)	Yes.
Stiller:	What can I get you?
Meara:	Manicotti.
Stiller:	Oh, I'm sorry we're all out.
Meara:	No. I mean Carmine Manicotti. He just broke our engagement. He had his mother call and tell me.
Stiller:	Oh, the swine.
Meara:	No, she was very sweet about it.
Stiller:	No, I meant Carmine. Anyway, may I suggest the Surf and Turf tonight?
Meara:	Is that some new singles bar?
Stiller:	No, the Surf and Turf is our new delicious combination of lobster tail and filet mignon. Perhaps to raise your spirits, a very special wine.
Meara:	Can I get a wine that goes with seafood and meat?
Stiller:	Certainly, may I bring a little Blue Nun to your table?
Meara:	I'm sure she'd be very sympathetic, but I'd much rather be alone.
Stiller:	No, Miss, Blue Nun is a wine, a delicious white wine that's correct with any dish. It goes as well with meat as it does with fish. And, perhaps after dinner, cantaloupe.
Meara:	I don't see cantaloupe on the menu.
Stiller:	No, that's me. Stanley Cantaloupe. I get off at eleven. Maybe we could go out on the town.
Announcer:	Blue Nun, the delicious white wine that's correct with any dish. Another Sichel wine, imported by Schieffelin and Co., New York.

An example of effective information presentation

Source: *Campaign Report Newsletter*. New York: American Association of Advertising Agencies (January 1979), p. 6.

author of a written message, the announcer or the actor delivering a commercial, the sponsors to whom the viewers attribute the commercial, the politician who is giving a speech, and so on. Several characteristics of such sources appear to influence the persuasiveness of a message.

In studying the process of social influence, Herbert C. Kelman has hypothesized that three types of persuasive influences—compliance, identification, and internalization—are produced by three characteristics of communicators: *power*, *attractiveness*, and *credibility*.[6]

Source Power

According to the most generally accepted definition, social power is the ability of one person or group to cause another person or group to change in the direction intended by the influencer.[7] Power, however, is not an attribute or possession of an individual or group; it emerges from a relationship between persons. Source power derives from the source's being perceived by the audience members as having control over their means of satisfaction.[8] Furthermore, the source is considered to be able to observe whether or not the audience members are complying and to have the intention of rewarding and punishing them on the basis of their compliance.

Compliance to source power may be displayed when an individual declares he has changed his beliefs when in fact his attitude has not budged. A patient may tell his doctor he believes the doctor's statements concerning the need to lose weight but nevertheless continues to eat fattening foods.

Source Attractiveness

Generally, the more the audience likes the source, the greater the persuasive impact of the communication. This effect is based on the perceived attractiveness of the source, which is central to the identification process. *Identification* occurs when a person wants to define herself in terms of her relationship to some other person or group and consequently ascribes to herself characteristics or attitudes of that person or group. Identification differs from compliance in that the individual actually believes her adopted views.

When a baseball player endorses a particular brand of deodorant or hair tonic on television, he may not be especially knowledgeable about the merits of those products. Such testimonials can nevertheless be quite effective in persuading fans who identify with the star to use the product. A source that a viewer considers unattractive may produce a boomerang effect—he may respond by adopting attitudes opposite those the source advocates.

Attitudes adopted through identification are based on an emotional attachment, and if the emotional attachment to the group or the other person loses its importance, the attitudes are also likely to fade. A youngster may eat Wheaties because they are "the breakfast of champions" and Bruce Jenner eats them. Later in life, when his interest in becoming a sports star wanes, so does the attraction of Wheaties.

Source Credibility

The credibility of the communicator as perceived by the audience may have an effect on persuadability, the more prestigious communicator being the more persuasive. This difference is said to disappear over time, however, as a result of what is now called the "sleeper effect." In one experiment two groups of people were tested on the same persuasive material, the only variable being the degree of credibility of the communicator: one source was identified as a judge, and the other as a "suspicious character." There was less changing of opinion among the group that listened to the "suspicious character." When the groups were tested again after a time lapse of four weeks, a "sleeper effect" was noted, and the communication was found to have the same effect for both speakers. Thus the content of the message may be retained over time while the source of the communication is not.[9] When the sources were once again identified, however, the original differences were restored.

Using a source of great credibility can enhance the effectiveness of a communication advocating energy conservation, according to the results of one study.[10] In a field experiment, the source of the communication was found to influence the behavior of heavy users of electricity (likely to have air conditioners) in terms of requests for information on energy consumption and actual consumption of electricity.

The persuasiveness of a credible source can be explained in terms of cognitive response or information processing. Thus a message recipient's initial opinion is an important determinant of influence in response to a persuasive appeal. If the recipient's view is favorable, a moderately credible source may induce greater positive attitude and support argumentation. This result may be due to the message recipients' need to bolster a position they favor when the communicator is of questionable credibility. They may feel less inclined to engage in such cognitive work when a highly credible source presents the favored position.

When the recipient of a message is opposed to the view it expresses, a highly credible communicator may be more influential than one of questionable credibility. Individuals rehearse thoughts that are relevant to issues, as well as those presented to them. Messages are rejected when people opposed to the communicator's position rehearse or review counterarguments to statements made in the message. If a highly credible source inhibits counterarguing and a less credible source does not, the principle of cognitive response predicts the superior persuasive power of a highly credible communicator.

Other experiments have indicated that when a recipient was favorably predisposed to an issue and the communicator was identified before the message, a moderately credible source induced more agreement than a highly credible source.[11] These findings suggest that when a marketer must decide on a communicator, he is helped by a knowledge of the individual's initial opinion on the communication issue; if it is positive, moderately credible sources may be most desirable.

CELEBRITY SOURCES

Numerous companies have turned to the use of celebrities in both personal selling and advertising in order to enhance source effectiveness. Celebrities may influence the exposure stage of the persuasion process by providing a familiar face for an unfamiliar brand, by helping to break through advertising clutter, or by heightening awareness. A celebrity may have relevance to other stages of the persuasive process in adding credibility and lessening consumers' perceived risk in product choice.

Celebrity Choice

In the selection of a celebrity to deliver advertising messages, several criteria are used:

1. Familiarity of the individual to the target audience.
2. Attitudes toward the individual among the target audience, such as popularity, credibility, and sincerity.
3. Image of the individual among the target audience—desirable traits as well as potential negative ones.
4. Compatibility of the individual with the product or service.

Several research firms provide either syndicated or custom services that offer such analysis. Once the celebrity has been selected and used, other services are available to indicate the audience attitude toward the celebrity in the advertisements.

Credibility appears to be the most significant characteristic as a basis for celebrity choice. In the past, most product endorsers were connected with the entertainment or sports world. Their use was predicated, to some extent, on the premise that familiarity and likability would enhance the celebrity's credibility in the eyes of the viewing audience. One study of sports personalities, designed to identify the extent to which familiarity, talent, and likability were associated with the celebrity's credibility, disclosed that likability was most closely associated with the individual's credibility as a product endorser.[12] It is sometimes difficult, however, to separate likability and talent. The likable and talented Bill Cosby was selected on the basis of talent by editors of an advertising publication as the top star presenter of 1978, and General Foods, Ford, and other companies appear to be satisfied with his persuasive capabilities.[13]

A service called Tell-Back offers a group-response instantaneous poll that gives a quick evaluation of the appeal and impact of commercials and rates star presenters. Ten commercials were selected from "100 Best Commercials for 1977" with the Abraham Lincoln commercial for Lincoln Life as the norm or control.[14] (It seems Abraham Lincoln ranked number 1 in popularity in any test.) The method used was to compute a composite rating from a calculation that combined attitudinal changes with the respondents' conscious evaluations of each of the commercials. Paul Lynde for Manufacturers Hanover Bank rated highest, while Petula Clark and Robert Blake ("Baretta") rated lowest. (See Figure 14.2.) At this writing, Lynde and Blake no longer appear for their respective companies, and James Garner and Mariette Hartley have replaced Candice Bergen for Polaroid, with apparent success.

FIGURE 14.2   TELL-BACK COMPOSITE RATINGS (FIVE SESSIONS)

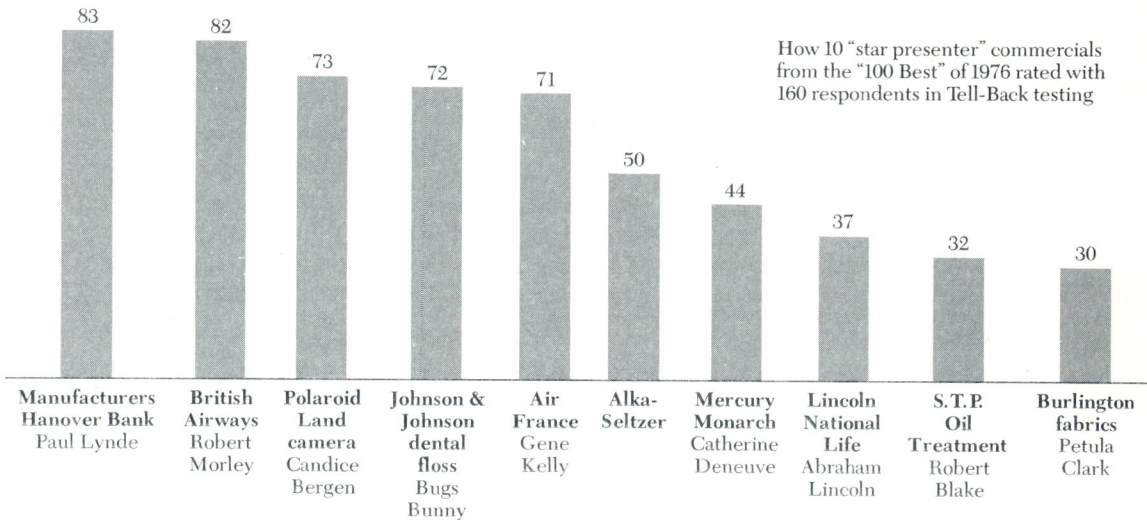

How 10 "star presenter" commercials from the "100 Best" of 1976 rated with 160 respondents in Tell-Back testing

Manufacturers Hanover Bank Paul Lynde	British Airways Robert Morley	Polaroid Land camera Candice Bergen	Johnson & Johnson dental floss Bugs Bunny	Air France Gene Kelly	Alka-Seltzer	Mercury Monarch Catherine Deneuve	Lincoln National Life Abraham Lincoln	S.T.P. Oil Treatment Robert Blake	Burlington fabrics Petula Clark
83	82	73	72	71	50	44	37	32	30

Source: Harry W. McMahan, "Rating the Stars in TV Commercials: Bugs Bunny vs. Catherine Deneuve," *Advertising Age*, August 22, 1977, p. 37.

Although in the past most celebrities used as endorsers were connected with the entertainment or sports world, recently there has been a tendency to use endorsers from other fields in order to generate greater credibility. Elliot Janeway, an economist, has been advertising that Mazda is a "great little car." Some companies expressed an interest in Walter Cronkite, in advance of his announced retirement from "CBS Evening News," as a celebrity who can provide extremely high credibility.

Functions of Celebrities in Communications

Celebrities may perform two major categories of functions for the advertisements in which they appear: they may be used as presenters or as spokespersons.

PRESENTERS

Presenters may be used for testimonials or endorsements. In *testimonials*, the celebrity attests to the excellence of the brand on the basis of his personal experience with it. Testimonials may be given by experts, such as Billie Jean King for a tennis racket, or by people who do not necessarily have such expertise, such as James Garner and Mariette Hartley for Polaroid's "One Step."

Endorsements may also come from nonexperts and need not indicate the celebrity's actual use of the product or service he endorses. Joe Namath endorsed a brand of pantyhose. According to the "Proposed Guidelines for Testimonials and

Endorsements" issued by the Federal Trade Commission, an expert endorsement is the same as an expert testimonial. Thus, when an expert endorses or provides a testimonial for a product (according to FTC guidelines), he must employ his expertise in evaluating the product in a way that is relevant to the ordinary consumer.

SPOKESPERSONS

When celebrities are used as spokespersons, the primary emphasis is generally on the company rather than on the product. The spokesperson is considered to be presenting the company's viewpoint rather than her own and therefore is not offering an endorsement or testimonial. The celebrity spokesperson may represent the company in its image advertising, as Robert Morley continues to do for British Airways. She may present an entire line of the company's products or serve a continuing role as a presenter for a variety of products over time, as Lauren Hutton does for Revlon products.

Actors and actresses are frequently used as company spokespersons, but they occasionally are presented in character roles rather than as themselves. Margaret Hamilton, as Cora, sells only Maxwell House Coffee in her country store, and Nancy Walker, as Rosie the waitress, wipes up spills with Bounty Paper Towels.

Risk in the Use of Celebrities

A number of risks are involved in the use of celebrities. A presenter or spokesperson may alienate certain market segments by activities unrelated to their roles as presenters. A celebrity may be perceived as lacking sincerity or as willing to say anything for money. Some unexpected event in the celebrity's personal life may alter the way in which he or she is perceived. A celebrity's endorsement may call forth complaints of unfair or deceptive practices. In 1978 Pat Boone entered into an agreement with the FTC to pay part of the penalties if a complaint of unfair and deceptive practices is upheld against Acne Staten, an acne-preparation product he endorsed.

In determining whether an endorsement is deceptive, the FTC considers endorsements and testimonials identically. Spokespersons and actors, however, who are perceived to speak on behalf of the company and to reflect the company's opinion rather than their own, are generally not considered to be endorsers. Nor are actors in "slice-of-life" commercials who provide a fictional dramatization of a real-life situation considered as providing testimonials or endorsements.

The use of experts in endorsements and testimonials may be considered deceptive if their expertise is misrepresented. According to the FTC guidelines, "An endorser who is represented as an expert must possess qualifications of an expert." For example, the FTC required a company to stop using racing car drivers to endorse toy cars, since these drivers were not experts on toys.[15]

Another guideline requires the celebrity endorser to use the product advertised when the advertisement so represents, and it permits the advertiser to use such an endorsement only so long as the advertiser has good reason to believe the endorser continues to use the product. In addition, endorsements must reflect the honest views of the endorser and may not contain distortions.

NONCELEBRITIES AS SPOKESPERSONS

In recent years there has been a movement toward the use of the nonprofessional as a spokesperson or presenter. One technique is to use the company president, such as Tom Carvel (ice cream), Frank Perdue (chickens), and the somewhat more polished Frank Borman (Eastern Airlines).

A variation of this technique is to use workers or relatives of the company executives. Luba Potemkin, who advertises her husband's Cadillacs in the New York metropolitan area, is considered to be effective in increasing the agency's sales. The success of such spokespeople may be an indication of the effectiveness of source likability—the fact that the targets see these people as similar to themselves in their lack of professionalism and their accessibility.

Advertisements frequently make use of "common man" techniques. The advertising campaign of the International Ladies' Garment Workers Union ("Look for the union label . . .") was particularly successful in creating recall with somewhat limited exposure. The spokespeople in this ad were working union members. The success of this ad may have been based on its unusual nature (its novelty characteristics).

CONSUMER ENDORSERS

Many advertisements now feature "workers" and "housewives" as endorsers in an effort to make the viewer feel familiar with, similar to, and ultimately trusting of the presenter. In the past this type of advertisement was generally treated as a presentation by a spokesperson and therefore was not subject to the same rules as an endorsement. The FTC, however, recently revised its "Guides Concerning the Use of Endorsements and Testimonials in Advertising"[16] and noted that an endorsement is an advertising message that consumers are likely to believe reflect the opinions, beliefs, or experience of a party other than the advertiser. Among the rules that the new guides incorporate are the following:

1. When an ad represents that "actual consumers" are making the endorsement, actual consumers should be used in both audio and video, or the ad must disclose that actors are appearing.
2. When an endorsement reflects the consumer's experience on a key attribute of the product or service, the advertiser must be able to show that the

average person can expect comparable performance. If the advertiser does not possess adequate substantiation for this representation, the ad must disclose that the endorsement has limited applicability.

3. Advertisers must disclose a connection between the advertiser and endorser that might materially affect the impact or credibility of the endorsement—when the audience cannot reasonably be expected to know the connection. Material connections that require disclosure include: compensation received prior to and in exchange for an endorsement; and the fact that the endorser knew or had reason to know that if the "right things" were said she would appear on TV. If the endorser is a celebrity or expert, promise of payment need not be disclosed. The following example is offered for clarification.

A restaurant patron who is neither a celebrity nor an expert is shown seated at a counter and asked his "spontaneous" opinion of a new food product served in the restaurant. If a sign had been posted on the door of the restaurant notifying customers that they would be interviewed by the advertiser as part of a TV promotion for a new soy protein "steak," this notification would be considered a material connection requiring disclosure in the ads. Alternatively, if there were no sign on the door of the restaurant and consumers who were interviewed had no reason to believe that their response would be used in advertisements—even if they are told after the interview that there was a "hidden camera" and that they would be paid for allowing the use of their opinions in advertising—these facts need not be disclosed.

Salespersons

Traditionally, a salesman's success has been viewed as a function of his job satisfaction, motivation, ability, and other attributes peculiar to his biographical or psychological profile.[17] In view of the fact that a salesperson, without varying his presentation, is not uniformly effective with prospects who have the same kinds of needs, questions have been raised about their use. One response is to view personal selling in the context of social interaction. It has been suggested, for example, that the "sale" is a social situation involving two persons. Their interaction, in turn, depends on the economic, social, physical, and personality characteristics of each of them. To understand the process it is necessary to look at both parties of the sale as a dyad, not individually.[18] The extent to which a salesperson can influence a customer is based on the concepts discussed earlier as source effects: power, credibility, attractiveness. In recent research concerning salespersons' influence, another conceptual approach focuses on the salesperson's expert power and referent power. Although these two conceptual approaches to source effects are not strictly congruent, for the purpose of this discussion expert power may be considered as encompassing *power* and *credibility*, while referent power incorporates *attractiveness*.

Expert power is based on the customer's perception that the salesperson has valuable knowledge, information, or skills in a relevant area. *Referent power* is based on the perceived attraction of the customer and salesperson to one another. The source of this power may arise from friendship, identification with a successful model, or feelings of shared identity.[19] Marketing studies suggest that perceived *similarities* in personal goals, interests, or values are sources that increase these feelings of shared identity.[20]

Both expert power and referent power are influential in gaining the customer's trust of the salesperson, although the salesperson's expertise appears to be more important than her referent power for this purpose.[21] This finding suggests that managers should design sales training programs to increase the salesperson's expertise and to encourage her to communicate information about this expertise to consumers.

Nonetheless, the effects of referent power cannot be ignored, particularly when the customer sees the salesperson as similar to himself. A study compared the selling efficacy of a paint salesperson perceived as similar but inexperienced against the same salesperson perceived as dissimilar but experienced. Results indicated that similarity was more important than experience in attempts to persuade customers to buy higher- as well as lower-priced paint than they originally intended.[22]

It also appears that a high-referent salesperson has a wider range of influence than a low-referent salesperson.[23] This finding suggests that if the salesperson sells a variety of products and services, it would be useful to develop her referent power. Thus, in a firm selling a wide variety of products, sales managers should screen and select prospective salespersons who can create a feeling of shared identity with customers. Another way to increase their referent power may be to use rewards, such as gratification of the customer's ego by entertaining and doing favors for her.

NONVERBAL COMMUNICATIONS

As we interact with others, we learn more about them. Eye contact, gestures, facial expressions, and voice are all important sources of interpersonal communication. For example, either too much eye contact (staring) or too little (avoiding all contact) has been found to create a negative impression. Persons with high-pitched voices have been perceived as good and small-framed; persons with loud voices were seen as bad and large.

While there has been a significant increase in the study of nonverbal communications in recent years, relatively little of this knowledge has been applied to marketing and consumer-behavior concepts. In an effort to encourage research in this area James Hulbert and Noel Capon devised a "paradigm of the individual in communication" that includes signs as part of the total set of stimuli bombarding the sense organs. (See Figure 14.3.) As a means of facilitating research into nonverbal communications, the authors provide a classification scheme for signs. (See Table 14.1).[24]

FIGURE 14.3   A PARADIGM OF THE INDIVIDUAL IN COMMUNICATION

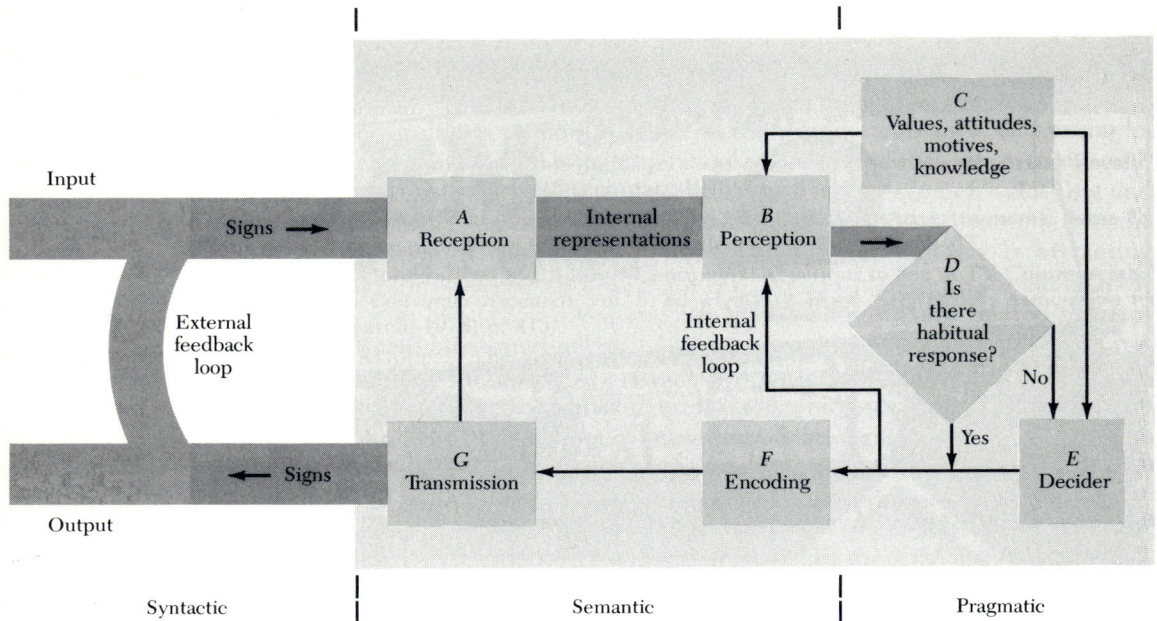

Source: James Hulbert and Noel Capon, "Interpersonal Communication in Marketing: An Overview," *Journal of Marketing Research* 9 (February 1972), p. 28.

TABLE 14.1   CLASSIFICATION SCHEME FOR INTERPERSONAL COMMUNICATION

Receiver role	Sender role			
	Static, uncontrollable	Static, controllable	Dynamic (low frequency)	Dynamic (high frequency
Visual	Physical features (race, sex, age, etc.)	Clothing (style, neatness)	Posture Axial orientation	Body movement Facial expression
		Physical features (hair style, facial hair)	Distance	Eyeline Gesture Head orientation
Auditory	Voice set	Accent	Temporal speech patterning Accent Voice qualities	Vocalizations Verbal
Tactile and olfactory		Personal odor	Touching behavior Thermal	

Source: James Hulbert and Noel Capon, "Interpersonal Communication in Marketing: An Overview," *Journal of Marketing Research* 9 (February 1972), p. 29.

TABLE 14.2   THE PSYCHOLOGICAL DIMENSIONS OF NONVERBAL COMMUNICATIONS

High status	Low status	Positive evaluation	Negative evaluation
Direct eye contact while speaking	Looking away before speaking	Head nods	Reclining position
Moderate eye contact when listening	Steady eye contact when listening	Uh-huh	Backward lean
Relaxed posture	Hesitations	Rhythmic following	Avoiding or shifting eye contact
Arm-position asymmetry	Halting speech with shifting eye contact	Close proximity	Avoidance of close proximity
Sideways lean	High speech error rate	Touching	Closed arrangement of arms
Hand relaxation	Inactive communication activity range	Eye contact	Torso orientation away from addressee
Neck relaxation	Depressed posture	Forward lean	Finger-tapping
Head nodding	Forward lean	Higher speech rate	n.d.
Gesticulation	Bowed head	Lengthier communication	n.d.
Increased facial activity	Dropping shoulders	Frequent verbal reinforcers	n.d.
Low speech error rate	Sunken chest	Gesticulation	n.d.
Halting speech with eye contact	Shifting body orientation	Smiling	n.d.
Active speech rate	n.d.	Less frequent self-references	n.d.
Strong speech volume	n.d.	Open arrangement of arms	n.d.
Chest expanded	n.d.	n.d.	n.d.
Backward lean	n.d.	n.d.	n.d.
Direct body orientation	n.d.	n.d.	n.d.

n.d. = no data.

Source: Thomas V. Bonoma and Leonard C. Felder, "Nonverbal Communication in Marketing: Toward a Communicational Analysis," *Journal of Marketing Research* 14 (May 1977), p. 176.

Information on nonverbal communications can be implemented in marketing in several ways. For example, the marketer may wish to improve his sales staff's behavior during interaction with customers to increase the efficiency of the communication source. In an effort to provide a mechanism by which relationships between verbal and nonverbal behavior might be extended to consumer-behavior research with marketing applications, Thomas Bonoma and Leonard Felder have offered a table describing the psychological dimensions of nonverbal behavior.[25] (See Table 14.2.)

The findings incorporated in Table 14.2 are based on the work of various researchers, such as that of Jay S. Efran, who found that high-status speakers receive much more eye contact than do low-status speakers in an interaction.[26]

Such a classification system may help marketers to answer such relevant questions as:

1. How does the person evaluate the person, product, or idea in question?
2. Is the evaluation strongly positive or negative?
3. Do the nonverbal cues to evaluation and status support, contradict, diminish, or intensify the verbal cues?

SUMMARY

When one explores consumers' search for information, it is apparent that a major information network emanates from the marketer. Several barriers confront marketers in their efforts to communicate. These barriers relate to the effects of selective perception, discussed earlier. Thus selective exposure, selective attention, and selective distortion may create some interference with the marketer's communication.

To gain a clearer understanding of the effects of marketer-dominated sources of information on consumers, it is necessary to examine such effects in the context of a communication/persuasion matrix. The communication process may be considered as a set of variables including source ⟶ message ⟶ channel ⟶ receiver ⟶ destination. The persuasion process is a series of steps through which consumers process information and which may culminate in action; specifically, exposure ⟶ emotional response ⟶ encoding ⟶ acceptance of the appeal ⟶ overt behavior. Each of the variables in the communication process may be examined in the context of one or more steps of the persuasion process.

Source effects may be considered in the context of power, attractiveness, and credibility, which may influence consumers through compliance, identification, and internalization. Celebrities serve important functions in securing appropriate source effects.

An analysis of the salesperson's effectiveness in communications may be based on concepts relevant to source effects. To understand the salesperson's influence, she should be viewed in the context of social interaction—that is, both parties of the sale must be considered as a dyad, not individually. Nonverbal communication, such as visual and auditory signs that emerge from the communicator, may be important in determining his persuasive influence.

DISCUSSION QUESTIONS

1. Provide a personal example of selective exposure, selective attention, or selective distortion.

2. Why is it desirable to examine the communication process in conjunction with the persuasion process?

3. Provide an illustration of an influential source and explain the reasons for its influence.

4. Do you believe you are personally influenced by a celebrity as a source? Why?

5. Explain the difference between an endorser and a spokesperson. What is the significance of this difference?

6. Would you prefer professionals or nonprofessionals as spokespeople? Why?

7. What kinds of nonverbal communications are useful to you in interpreting verbal statements?

8. Do you have any preference as to the characteristics of a salesperson? Explain.

9. Have you had any difficulty with a salesperson? How could the firm prevent such occurrences?

NOTES

1. "Ad Spending Outpaces Economy," *Advertising Age,* January 8, 1979, p. S-8.

2. Raymond A. Bauer and Stephen A. Greyser, *Advertising in America: The Consumer's View* (Cambridge: Graduate School of Business Administration, Harvard University, 1968), p. 176.

3. Jerome S. Bruner and Cecile G. Goodman, "Value and Need as Organizing Factors in Perception," *Journal of Abnormal and Social Psychology* 42 (1947), pp. 33–44.

4. Neil Bidmar and Milton Rokeach, "Archie Bunker's Bigotry: A Study in Selective Perception and Exposure," *Journal of Communication* 24 (Winter 1974), pp. 36–47.

5. William J. McGuire, "The Communication/Persuasion Matrix," in *Evaluating Advertising: A Bibliography of the Communication Process,* ed. Benjamin Lipstein and William J. McGuire (New York: Advertising Research Foundation, 1978), p. xxvii.

6. Herbert C. Kelman, "Three Processes of Social Influence," *Public Opinion Quarterly* 25 (1961), pp. 57–78.

7. R. A. Dahl, "The Concept of Power," *Behavioral Sciences* 2 (July 1957), p. 203.

8. McGuire, "Communication/Persuasion Matrix," p. xxix.

9. Carl I. Hovland and Walter Weiss, "The Influence of Source Credibility on Communication Effectiveness," *Public Opinion Quarterly* 15 (1951), pp. 635–650.

10. C. Samuel Craig and John M. McCann, "Assessing Communication Effects on Energy Conservation," *Journal of Consumer Research* 5 (September 1978), pp. 82–88.

11. Brian Sternthal, Ruby Dholakia, and Clark Leavitt, "The Persuasive Effect of Source Credibility: Tests of Cognitive Response," *Journal of Consumer Research* 4 (March 1978), pp. 252–260.

12. Alan R. Nelson, "Can the Glamour and Excitement of Sports Really Carry the Ball for Your Product?" *Marketing Review* 29 (February 1974), pp. 21–25.

13. John Revett, "Crosby Top Star Presenter of 1978," *Advertising Age,* July 17, 1978, p. 1.

14. Harry W. McMahan, "Rating the Stars in TV Commercials: Bugs Bunny vs. Catherine Deneuve," *Advertising Age,* August 22, 1977, p. 37.

15. Dorothy Cohen, "Surrogate Indicators and Deception in Advertising," *Journal of Marketing* 26 (July 1972), p. 13.

16. "FTC Endorsements and Testimonials in Advertising: Promulgation of Final Guides Concerning Use," 16 CFR Part 255, January 18, 1980.

17. Edward A. Riordan, Richard L. Oliver, and James H. Donnelly, Jr., "The Unsold Prospect: Dyadic and Attitudinal Determinants," *Journal of Marketing Research* 14 (November 1977), p. 530.

18. Franklin B. Evans, "Selling as a Dyadic Relationship—A New Approach," *American Behavioral Scientist* 6 (May 1963), p. 76.

19. G. R. Gemmill and D. L. Wilemon, "The Product Manager as an Influence Agent," *Journal of Marketing* 36 (January 1972), pp. 26–30.

20. Evans, "Selling as a Dyadic Relationship," pp. 76–79.

21. Paul Busch and David T. Wilson, "An Experimental Analysis of a Salesman's Expert and Referent Bases of Social Power in the Buyer-Seller Dyad," *Journal of Marketing Research* 13 (February 1976), pp. 3–11.

22. Timothy C. Brock, "Communicator-Recipient Similarity and Decision Change," *Journal of Personality and Social Psychology* 1 (June 1965), pp. 650–654.

23. Busch and Wilson, "Experimental Analysis," p. 10.

24. James Hulbert and Noel Capon, "Interpersonal Communication in Marketing: An Overview," *Journal of Marketing Research* 9 (February 1972), pp. 27–34.

25. Thomas V. Bonoma and Leonard C. Felder, "Nonverbal Communication in Marketing: Toward a Communicational Analysis," *Journal of Marketing Research* 14 (May 1977), pp. 169–180.

26. Jay S. Efran, "Looking for Approval," *Journal of Personality and Social Psychology* 10 (September 1968), pp. 21–25.

CHAPTER 15

PERSUASIVE INFLUENCES

As we saw in Chapter 14, the network of marketing communications consists of source ⟶ message ⟶ channel ⟶ target ⟶ destination. The hierarchy of steps in the process of persuading consumers was described as exposure ⟶ emotional response ⟶ encoding ⟶ acceptance of the appeal ⟶ overt behavior. Source effects were discussed in Chapter 14; here we will examine the remaining variables in the communication network and their effects on the process of persuasion.

A series of television commercials is credited with attracting an extra $38 million in tourist revenue to New York in 1978. The source—New York State—was not clearly designated. The basic message appeal was "Love," the major channel was television, the primary target was tourists (New Yorkers as well as out-of-towners), and the destination (variables targeted for change) were cognitive [attitude] and behavioral [action]).

The commercial, featuring four words, "I Love New York," was prepared by Wells, Rich and Greene Advertising Agency. The original campaign presented four commercials; three of them showed various areas around New York State. The fourth was a visual show tour of Broadway featuring actors and dancers from the cast of various Broadway shows, such as "Chorus Line" and "Dracula." The campaign was repeated for several years.[1]

This chapter examines these questions:

How does the manner in which the message is organized influence its effectiveness?

What effect does message repetition have on persuasion?

What kinds of creative strategies may be used to improve communication effectiveness?

How may the channel selected affect persuasion?

What kinds of research are used to test whether communications are remembered?

THE COMPONENTS OF MESSAGE ORGANIZATION

The message is the heart of the communication network. The kinds of information contained in the message and the manner in which it is presented have significant influence on its encoding and further processing.

Several of the factors relevant to the organization of the message have been discussed in Chapters 7 and 8. For example, novelty and contrast as a means of ensuring exposure and attention can be achieved through the use of animation, white space, unusual artwork, and so on. Exhibit 15.1 shows some ads that have made significant use of animation techniques.

Size, Color, Position

Size, color, and position have been the subjects of more research relevant to print messages than to telecast messages. Relatively little research, however, has been conducted on the effects of these factors and their specific effects on each of the steps of the persuasion hierarchy.

An early study examined the effect on readership of various components of advertisements. This study was based on data collected by Daniel Starch and Staff, who base their estimates of advertising readership on recognition of ads.

EXHIBIT 15.1

(a) PAPER-MATE

(b) ARM & HAMMER

Animation is used to capture attention
Source: "Animation," *Advertising Age*, January 26, 1976, p. 53.

Such recognition tends to validate the initial stages of exposure and awareness.

In evaluating the results of data for 1,070 of 1,197 advertisements, one-half page or larger, appearing in *Life* between February 7 and July 31, 1964, the researcher drew the following conclusions about the relationship of several independent variables and readership:[2]

1. The contribution of ad size to readership decreases in the following order: double page, single page, horizontal half page, vertical half page.

2. The greater the number of colors in an ad, the greater its readership.

3. Eliminating margins (bleed) increases readership very little.

4. An ad of one page or less will receive higher readership scores if it appears on a right-hand page than if it appears on a left-hand page.

5. An ad will generally receive higher readership scores if it has a photograph rather than another type of illustration, either of which is better than neither.

These results have not always been replicated, however, and it appears that the effects of size, color, and position depend on other factors involved in the presentation.

Order of Presentation

With the rise in the use of comparative advertising and the increasing "clutter" of television commercials, advertisers are concerned with the most effective order of presentation of information. In comparative advertising, the competitor's name usually appears as well as the sponsor's; in clutter, several advertising appeals are presented in quick succession.

Several concepts based on learning theory are significant for evaluation of the most effective order of messages. Through learning experiments, a serial position effect has been noted. If someone is given a list of words and then is asked to write down that list, items toward the beginning and the end of the series are more likely to be remembered than items in the middle of the list. The most frequently recalled items are those that were presented first; the last items will be recalled next; and the middle items are recalled last. Items recalled can be plotted on a graph, as in Figure 15.1.

When free recall is tested after one presentation of a list of items, the curve is roughly the reverse of the serial position curve—the greatest recall is for those items presented last. These concepts have also been designated as the law of recency and the law of primacy. The *law of recency* states that the items most recently reported are best remembered; the *law of primacy* states that the items first reported are best remembered.

Although these effects have been noted for unstructured material, they have been acknowledged in the preparation of more structured presentations. In copywriting, for example, frequently the most important selling points are inserted at the beginning and the end of the message. Research evidence concerning

FIGURE 15.1   SERIAL POSITION CURVE

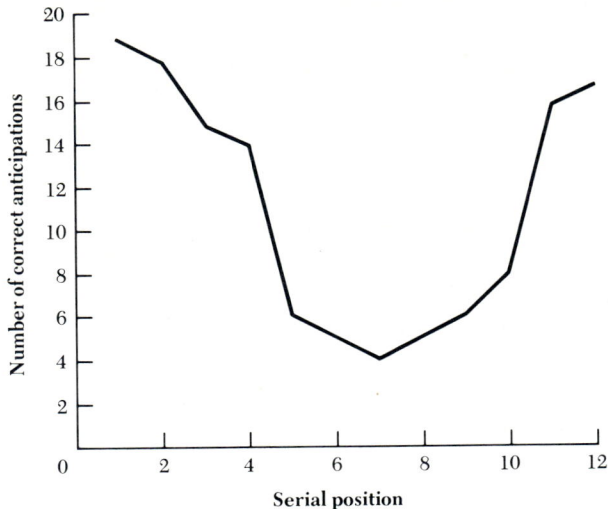

Source: James E. Deese and Stewart H. Hulse, *The Psychology of Learning*, 3d ed. (New York: McGraw-Hill, 1967), p. 283.

the best position in messages is conflicting. Nevertheless, many television copywriters agree that the sponsor's name should appear within the first few seconds of the commercial presentation.

Recent increase in commercial clutter has led advertisers to be concerned with the effects of a message when it appears in a string of other messages, that is, the effect on advertising recall of position in clutter.[3] When the effectiveness of advertising was examined in various clutter situations (ranging from "standard" to "very heavy" clutter), researchers found that first position in a string of commercials regularly produced the highest scores by all measures used; the last position usually attained the second highest scores; and the middle positions scored lowest, as in the serial position curve. (See Figure 15.1.)

On the basis of this research, advertisers obviously prefer the first or last position in a string of commercials. Unfortunately, unless they are sole sponsors of a program, advertisers have relatively little control over the positioning of their messages.

One-Sided Versus Two-Sided Messages

Research has focused on such factors as the extent to which the message presents only one side or both sides of an issue, as well as the order in which arguments are best presented. A one-sided message presents only the position advocated by the communicator; a two-sided message offers both the position advocated by the communicator and the opposing viewpoint. Recent research has indicated that the two-sided message may be an effective persuasive technique under some circumstances.

The one-sided argument may be more persuasive in influencing the attitudes of those unfamiliar with the issue and the less educated groups.[4] And if the audience doesn't know there are two sides and isn't likely to find out, a one-sided communication would obviously be more effective. The two-sided message may be more desirable when (1) the audience, regardless of its initial position, will be exposed to later counterpropaganda, and (2) the audience is opposed to the position advocated by the communicator.[5]

The two-sided message may be seen as more credible and may have an "inoculation" effect. In medicine, the individual can be given weakened dosages of the biological attack and, by overcoming this, develop an immunity to future attacks. So also is the case of persuasion: the individual can be presented with counterinformation that is subsequently weakened by refutation. The exposure to the counterinformation results in resistance to subsequent exposures to it.[6] (See Exhibit 15.2 on page 348.)

In deciding whether to present arguments first or last, an important consideration is the time that will elapse between the arguments and the attitude assessment. Although the primacy and recency effects are not sufficient to explain all of the findings in this area, it has been suggested that if the second communication is presented right after the first and attitudes are tested immediately after that, the two should be retained equally well, since neither primacy effects nor recency effects should occur. If a slight pause intervenes between the presentation of the two messages and the measurement of attitudes, the first argument should be slightly more influential, since the message of the first communication is usually learned better.[7]

MESSAGE REPETITION

While repetition of messages can increase the potential exposure to such messages, the effects of repetition on the subsequent steps of the persuasive process are less certain. Repeating messages at various times and in various places provides more consumers with the opportunity to see or hear them. In advertising terms, messages may be repeated to increase *reach*—the number of nonduplicated members of the audience—and *frequency*—the number of times each member of the audience is exposed to the advertisement. The quantitative aspects of advertising campaigns are frequently noted in terms of *gross rating points* estimated for a particular period, which combine reach and frequency.

As indicated in the previous chapter, the Stiller and Meara Blue Nun campaign was designed to achieve 100 GRP's per week. Gross rating points are determined by multiplying the reach by the average frequency. One gross rating point indicates that 1 percent of the audience (reach) had the opportunity to be exposed to the message one time (frequency). Three hundred gross rating points may be achieved in the following manner:

EXHIBIT 15.2

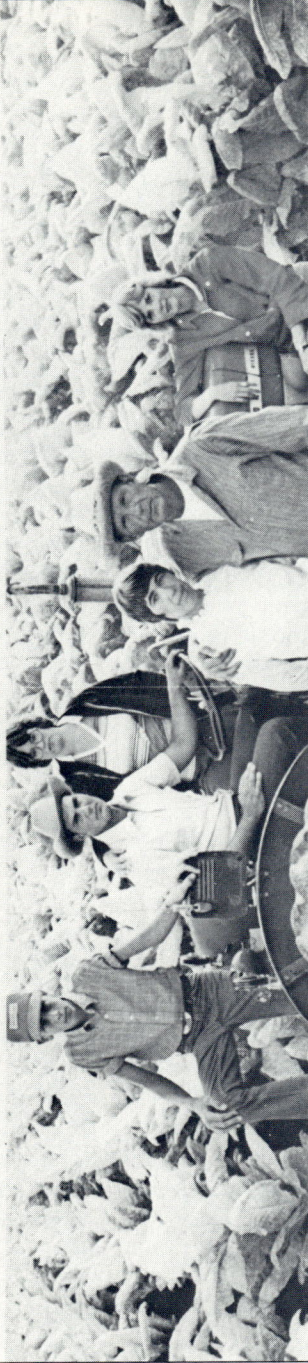

DOES THE GOVERNMENT SUPPORT THE TOBACCO FARMER?

NO, THE TOBACCO FARMER SUPPORTS THE GOVERNMENT.

Some people want to hear only one side of an argument. That's not you, obviously—or you wouldn't be reading this.

You've heard the side of the anti-smokers—that the government is, in some way, "supporting" or "subsidizing" the tobacco farmer.

Here is the other side of that argument. And if you're not a tobacco farmer, you'll probably be surprised, maybe even pleased, to hear it.

Because the truth is the other way around: It's the tobacco farmer who's supporting the government.

There *is* a government program called the tobacco price support program. It began in 1933, and for the past 45 years it has been the single most successful farm program the government has ever had. It costs next to nothing, and it pays enormous dividends to all taxpayers.

The heart of it is a simple businesslike arrangement. The government offers the tobacco farmer what *he* needs: a guaranteed price for his crop. If commercial buyers do not meet this price, the farmer receives a government loan and surrenders his crop. And the government gets, in return, what the *government* needs; the farmer's agreement not to plant any more than the government tells him he can.

The government's interest, and the taxpayer's, is in preventing economic chaos. Without the weapon of the loan agreement, the government would be powerless to limit the production of tobacco. The results would be as predictable as any disaster can be: overplanting of the crop by big farmers with extra land and by

newcomers, a fall in the price of tobacco, a drop in the income of small farmers to the point where many would be squeezed off the land and onto welfare rolls, sharp decreases in tax collections in the 22 states that grow tobacco, widespread disruptions in the banking and commercial systems and, if you want to follow the scenario out to its grim conclusion, very likely a regional recession.

The value of the program to the government, and to the taxpayer, is thus very great. And the cost is unbelievably low. Over the entire 45 years of its operation, the total cost of the government guarantee has been less than $1¼ million a year, or roughly what the government spends otherwise every 79 seconds. This is because the government has been able to sell, at a profit, almost all the tobacco it has taken as loan collateral.

From the farmer's viewpoint, the tobacco support program might as easily, and more justly, be called a *government* support program, since it does more to support the government than it does to support him.

One fact above all others tells you the true story. For all his labors in planting, growing and harvesting his crop, the farmer receives $2.3 billion. And from the products of his labor, the government (federal, state and local) collects $6 billion in taxes.

It's enough to make even an anti-smoker, at least a fair-minded one, agree that, on balance, it's the tobacco farmer who's supporting the government. And doing it superbly.

THE TOBACCO INSTITUTE
1776 K St. N.W., Washington, D.C. 20006

Warning: The Surgeon General Has Determined That Cigarette Smoking Is Dangerous to Your Health.

An inoculation ad

Source: "Tyler's Ten for November," *Advertising Age*, November 27, 1978, p. 58.

Gross rating points	=	Percent of reach	×	Average frequency
300	=	100%	×	3
300	=	50	×	6
300	=	1	×	300

or by any combination of numbers whose product is 300 (the maximum reach is of course 100 percent).

It should be noted that gross rating points project only the potential exposure, usually based on audience circulation of the particular medium. It does not ensure that the viewer will actually be exposed to the message.

Repetition and Attitude Change

A "mere exposure" hypothesis has been developed by some researchers who feel that mere exposure to an object is sufficient to enhance the attitude toward the object. One of the world's best known and seemingly best loved structures, the Eiffel Tower, has come to symbolize Paris and, to some extent, all of France. Although the Eiffel Tower has been referred to as the "subject of lyrical raptures," such impressions did not always exist. When the tower's completion was announced in 1889, the *Journal de Nature* noted that its construction took place despite a storm of protests from Frenchmen who considered it an unforgivable profanation of the arts. In the early 1900s the tower was almost demolished.

The cause of this shift in attitudes from condemnation and rejection to acceptance and affection is not clear. One fact *is* clear: because of its height in relation to other structures around it, the tower was inescapable; nearly everyone in Paris saw it day after day. One hypothesis relative to repeated exposure is that familiarity leads to liking. Perhaps attitudes toward the Eiffel Tower changed simply because it became a familiar part of the landscape.[8]

Robert Zajonc has formalized the "mere exposure" hypothesis, which suggests that repeated exposure to a stimulus is a sufficient condition for the enhancement of attitude toward the stimulus.[9] "Mere exposure" means that the stimulus is accessible to the organism's perception. This hypothesis does not preclude other bases for liking; it specifically allows that under some conditions liking can develop without repetition and that under some conditions liking accruing from increased exposure can be partially offset by other factors.

Support for Zajonc's hypothesis has come from a number of studies using a variety of objects, including musical compositions, works of art, and ideographs. Little has been done, however, to test the effects of repeated exposure on attitude change by use of such meaningful stimuli as public issues or advertised products.

A recent study tested the effects of repeated exposure to a political message, "Reduce foreign aid."[10] Thirty posters were placed on the walls in a university dormitory for four days. The results of these messages indicated that the repeated exposure to a persuasive message was sufficient to enhance the subjects' attitude toward the message. When 200 posters appeared for the next three days, however, overexposure appeared to dampen the positive attitudinal effect. This boomerang effect under excessive exposures seemed temporary; after a period of nonexposure, the evaluative ratings were significantly positive.

The results of this study indicate that exposure of a persuasive message (for example, on bumper stickers, billboards, media spots) should ideally be sufficient to familiarize the target population but not too great to cause a boomerang effect. If such a boomerang effect results, however, a period of nonexposure seems sufficient to correct the situation.

The "mere exposure" hypothesis has been deemed significant by those concerned about children's exposure to television advertising. Rita Wicks Poulos demonstrated that exposure of children to a cereal commercial in which an actor ate wild berries increased their willingness to consider all similar berries as edible.[11] The FTC issued a consent order requiring the company to cease this type of advertising on the basis of the fact that it was unfair to children viewers.

It has been suggested that TV messages that frequently feature heavily sugared food products influence children's preference for such products.[12]

Repetition and Learning

According to some learning theories, repetition is generally recognized as increasing learning. As we saw in Chapter 8, fewer than three exposures are usually regarded as insufficient for learning. The maximum number considered necessary to ensure learning varies on the basis of competitive advertising, creative strategy, product purchase cycles, and other marketing factors.

There are conflicting theories on the possibility that "excessive" repetition causes overexposure or "wearout." Some theorists argue that there is no such thing as overexposure, that the loss of appeal that appears to result from incessant repetitions reflects variables other than exposure itself.[13]

Evidence from field studies, however, suggests that beyond a certain level, repetition of advertisements will cause wearout. A laboratory experiment was designed to disclose the factors that account for the wearout phenomenon and its effects on brand-name recall. The findings indicated that wearout does occur and is attributable to the audience's inattentiveness to stimulus material and the loss of motivation for retrieval of brand names when repetitions are substantial.[14]

There are also indications that the likelihood of exposure effects is reduced when the stimuli are uninterrupted. That is, interrupting the presentation of stimuli may increase its effectiveness. Lengthening the interval between exposures may increase the likelihood of repetition effects, since the subsequent exposures are presented to the subject at a time when the effects of the initial exposure have decayed.[15]

Such findings suggest that it is useful for advertising practitioners to employ strategies that enhance attention when a high-frequency campaign is planned. One response to the problem of wearout is to mitigate the effects of excessive repetition by varying the execution of the theme: the advertiser may stress different benefits, use different spokespeople, or employ any other device that helps to maintain audience attention. Another technique (particularly important in view of the high cost of advertising) is to ensure that viewers get the desired frequency of exposures and interruption by incorporating "pooling" and "flighting" in media schedules: scheduling advertising noncontinuously in waves, such as several weeks on and several weeks off.

Repetition and Behavior

Repetition appears to have a smaller effect on behavior than on the other steps of the persuasive process. James Engel reports on a number of early studies that indicate that purchasing of some products increases with increases in the frequency of exposure to messages.[16] A more recent study, designed to examine alternate ways of promoting energy conservation, found that repetition had no effect on consumers' behavior.[17]

More research is necessary before accurate conclusions can be drawn as to the effects of repetition on behavior. One such study is in preparation by the Advertising Research Foundation (ARF) and is to be initiated in the late 1980s and is expected to run until 1982.[18] The ARF intends to test frequency by recording sales of six brands of advertised products for a period of 18 months. Advertising weight and frequency will be varied under controlled conditions to a panel of 3,000 homes. These homes will have cable television, which will permit variations of frequency, and family members will be provided with ID cards to present at checkout counters in supermarkets. The checkout counters will be equipped with scanning devices that will record purchases.

MESSAGE STRATEGY

In an effort to ensure the effectiveness of a message in moving consumers through various steps of the persuasion process, marketers employ numerous creative strategies. "Creative strategy" in this context refers not to what is said but how it is said.[19] Judging the sales effectiveness of advertising is difficult; one of the problems lies in isolating advertising as the variable responsible for the sale. And even when advertising is apparently responsible for sales, there are additional difficulties in isolating the specific aspect of the advertising campaign that is correlated most highly with sales.

Most frequently, advertising effectiveness is examined in terms of communication effectiveness—did the ad achieve the communication objective frequently specified as one or more steps in the persuasion process? There appears to be little consensus, however, concerning the message strategies that are most effective in ensuring proper exposure, emotional response, encoding, acceptance, and purchase.

TABLE 15.1 CREATIVE STRATEGIES

Strategy	Description
Information	Presentation of unadorned facts, without explanations or argument; just "news about" the product concerned.
Argument	Relating of facts (reason why) in some detail to the desired purchase; copy especially important; logical "playing on established desires" in presenting "excuses" to buy.
Motivation with psychological appeals	Explicit statement of how the product will benefit the consumer; use of emotion and appeals to self-interest in creating desires not previously readily apparent; interpretation of facts in an "especially for you" framework.
Repeated assertion	Hard-sell repetition of one basic piece of information—often a "generality" unsupported by factual proof.
Command	A "nonlogical" reminder (either hard-sell or soft-sell) to predispose audience favorably; may be reinforced by an authoritative figure.
Brand familiarization	Friendly, conversational feel; few or no "selling facts," but suggestion of "loyalty" to and "trustworthiness" of the advertiser; keeps brand name before the public.
Symbolic association	Subtle presentation of a single piece of information; links the product to a place, event, person, or symbol (any positive connotation), sales pitch usually not explicit, copy usually minimal, and product generally not "featured."
Imitation	Testimonial, by celebrity, "hidden camera" participant, or individual(s) unknown but with whom readers can readily identify (or whom they respect because of specified characteristics).
Obligation	Free offer of a gift or information, or a touching sentiment; some attempt to make the reader feel grateful.
Habit-starting	Offer of a sample or reduced price to initiate a "regular practice or routine"; product usually "featured."

Source: Julian L. Simon, *The Management of Advertising* (Englewood Cliffs, N.J.: Prentice-Hall, 1971), pp. 174–183.

One suggested list of creative strategies appears in Table 15.1. Researchers using Starch recognition scores to determine the relative effectiveness of these strategies concluded that the type of creative strategy used was not a good predictor of readership (exposure and awareness) of an ad. (See Table 15.2.) They concluded that the creative function remains resistant to attempts at quantification, but noted that other forms of analysis suggest its significance.[20]

Creative strategies are frequently judged by advertising professionals and

TABLE 15.2   READERSHIP SCORES OF ADS EMPLOYING EACH STRATEGY

Strategy	Number using	Noted Mean score	Range Min.	Range Max.	Associated Mean score	Range Min.	Range Max.	Read Most Mean score	Range Min.	Range Max.
Information	30	48	22	61	40	19	55	8	1	21
Argument	35	48	32	64	41	22	57	9	2	26
Motivation with psychological appeals	24	47	22	61	40	19	55	9	1	23
Repeated assertion	3	39	32	46	33	30	40	4	2	7
Command	2	50	47	52	43	42	44	6	4	7
Brand familiarization	10	49	38	61	42	28	55	8	1	17
Symbolic association	23	48	22	61	40	19	55	10	1	17
Imitation	2	34	22	46	30	19	40	4	2	6
Obligation	2	48	45	51	42	41	43	14	7	21
Habit-starting	5	46	38	58	38	28	41	7	3	10

Source: Alan D. Fletcher and Sherilyn K. Zeigler, "Creative Strategy and Magazine Ad Readership," *Journal of Advertising Research* 18 (February 1978), p. 30.

awards provided for those judged to be outstanding. Although some of these awards attempt to determine effectiveness (how well did the advertising achieve its objectives?), frequently they are based primarily on "creativity," such as the CLIO award for the "humorous" Blue Nun ad presented in the previous chapter. There appears to be a relationship between advertisements that advertising professionals consider the best and those that are considered outstanding by consumers. The Miller Lite campaign begun in 1975, which featured the slogan "All you want in beer—and less," was voted the "best made advertising outside their own place of business" by various executives of advertising agencies in 1978.[21] This campaign, which featured celebrities and humor, was also considered outstanding by consumers, who in December 1978 voted this ad the fourth "most outstanding TV commercial."[22] Number one in 1979 was Coca-Cola's "Mean Joe Green."

Creative strategies are frequently designated in terms of motivational appeals—humorous appeal, fear appeal, negative appeal, sex appeal, appeals to love and affection. The latter appeal was discussed in Chapter 9. This section reviews some of the findings relevant to the other motivational appeals.

Humor

During the past decade, marketers increasingly have employed humor as the motivational basis for their persuasive appeals. Evidence supporting the effectiveness of humor, however, is at best equivocal.[23] Humorous ads for Blue Nun, Benson & Hedges, and Miller Lite have been highly creative and commercially successful. Failures, however, have been at least as creative and as numerous: Betty Crocker rice, Quaker Oats, Rheingold beer.

Proponents of humor argue that it is a universal language that humanizes advertising, allowing the communicator to speak to members of the audience at their own level. The fundamental empirical question, however, is yet to be answered: Is humor an effective means of motivation? That is, is a humorous message more influential than a serious version of the same appeal?

Most advertisers agree that humor enhances audience attention, at least on the first few exposures to the persuasive communication. There is considerable debate, however, as to the degree of message comprehension afforded by humorous communications. Although humor improves attention, it may inhibit comprehension and thus reduce overall message reception and any attendant drive.

Advertisers who support the use of humorous commercials maintain that humor increases the probability of communication acceptance, and they suggest that humor may serve as a reward to the audience for listening. Even the proponents of humor, however, caution that a humorous appeal must be relevant, perceived as funny, and directed at the product rather than at the potential user if it is to facilitate communication acceptance and act as a motivating force. Still, humor finds considerable use as an appeal even in prescription-drug advertising. This finding is not inconsistent with the public image of the physician's ability to maintain a sense of humor in the face of adversity—an image promoted through such television shows as "M*A*S*H." It is clear, though, as seen in the choices by advertisers in professional journals, that some medical conditions are too serious to be laughed at.

A review of several professional medical journals in 1972 and 1973 revealed that what was perceived as appropriate targets for humor for a professional audience was not so different from what is considered fit for lay audiences: diarrhea, constipation, coughs and colds, obesity, and sex.[24] It is also notable that humor used to sell does not normally poke fun at physicians or drugs.

GUIDELINES TO THE USE OF HUMOR

There appears to be no prescribed formula for humor. Various sources have provided guides to its use, but no set of principles can ensure its success in communicating messages. Some suggestions for the development of humorous messages are these:[25]

1. Humor should have built-in, word-of-mouth possibilities (repeatability). Many people told their friends about the Benson & Hedges commercials detailing the "disadvantages" of the long cigarette. Perhaps the ads most widely disseminated by word of mouth are the earlier Alka-Seltzer messages—"I can't believe I ate the whole thing," the "spicy meatballs" commercials, and "Try it, you'll like it."

2. Humor should provide relief, especially emotional relief. Advertisements dealing with dandruff cures, reducing remedies, or relief from stomach disorders can all employ humor because it permits talking about an embarrassing problem without causing dismay.

3. Humor should be human. "Let Mikey try it," considered one of the most

successful ad campaigns, apparently was also effective in increasing the sales of Life cereal.

4. Humor should be tolerant. If it relieves us and gives us a feeling of having been forgiven and of having been able to look at the serious side of life in a removed fashion, it has been good. If it increases our anxieties and fears, it has been bad. A humorous ad with repeatability presented a funeral mourner driving a Volkswagen whose deceased relative had left him everything because the mourner's choice of automobile was consistent with the relative's penny-pinching nature.

5. Humor should involve exaggeration. Taking a simple fact and exaggerating it in such a way that the respondent must and can reduce it to its original meaning may be an effective form of communicating. The "man in the tank" Tidy Bowl ad and the "gorilla versus the American Tourister suitcase" are examples of such exaggeration.

6. Humor that belittles the brand or the subject matter is more effective than that which belittles the consumer. Some observers feel that despite the creative success of the Alka-Seltzer campaigns, the company's inability to maintain its market share may have been due to its tendency to belittle consumers in its ads.

Fear

Fear is frequently cited as a strong motivating force. The classical fear-drive model hypothesizes that increased amounts of induced fear tend to increase the potential for attitude change. As a result, many advertisers believe fear to be a potent advertising strategy.

The use of fear appeals in marketing has varied over the years. Life insurance ads of the 1920s featured a weeping child being led to an orphanage under the caption "Her daddy didn't have enough life insurance." While such appeals have undergone some modification in insurance ads, a 1970s' safe-driving ad by Mobil featured a middle-aged man and woman huddled together as they approached a door marked "Morgue" while the caption asked, "Are you coming home to visit your parents for Christmas or are they coming to you?"

In the early 1950s, Irving Janis and Seymour Feshbach reported the results of a study whose aim was to ascertain the amount of fear that best led to adoption of proper dental hygiene.[26] The experiment indicated that the least amount of fearfulness resulted in the greatest degree of adoption of the advocated oral hygiene technique. Other indications of a negative relationship between fear arousal and persuasion caused many marketers to discontinue fear appeals.

More recently, however, advertisers have come increasingly to agree that in some circumstances appeals to fear are effective. For example, the heavy and continuous reliance on fear appeals in the sale of such personal products as deodorants, fungicides for athlete's foot, and feminine hygiene aids suggest that fear may be employed with success in these situations. The reasons for fear's success in these cases are said to be threefold:[27]

1. The feared condition is avoided quickly and almost magically by application of the sponsor's product. This idea was applied in an ad for Dixie cups in which the mother declared that the child in her arms needed "seven stitches" after breaking a drinking glass.

2. There is no psychological investment in *not* using the product. In such cases, fear does not challenge a cherished habit (such as smoking).

3. What is feared is damage to the social image of the self rather than to the physical self, as in the Listerine "halitosis" ads.

Fear appeals may also be particularly effective with individuals whose arousal or anxiety about the product is low and with those who would not normally search for information about the product.[28] For example, insurance companies find that fear appeals work best with groups that typically do not see themselves as needing insurance; mouthwash advertisers find the fear appeal working with people who do not perceive themselves as having a breath problem.

A recent field experiment provided support for the use of a segmentation strategy in the investigation of fear appeals. A study designed to assess the effect of fear promotion on attitudinal and behavioral responses to a new group health insurance plan was conducted under the auspices of a health maintenance organization.[29] The results indicated that a response to fear is probably specific to the situation, topic, or person. For example, high-level fear appeals tended to produce the desired attitudinal results in two groups: the "older liberals" and the "older blue-collar blacks." The researchers concluded that segmentation of target consumers by demographic or psychographic characteristics appears to be a prerequisite in the use of fear appeals.[30]

Other research conclusions concerning the use of fear-arousal appeals indicated the following: (1) Increasing threat of physical consequences has generally been found to increase persuasion (though some studies report an adverse relationship between these variables); but (2) increasing the threat of physical consequences increases persuasion only when source credibility is high. When the credibility of the source is relatively low, any level of fear arousal is nonpersuasive.

Further research is required to determine when fear can be an effective message appeal. Such research may be forthcoming in efforts to understand information processing, as, for example, in the manner in which fear-inducing information is encoded and retrieved from long-term memory. Advertisers who wish to use the fear approach should consider the various findings with care.

Anxiety

Fear and anxiety are both considered to be learned motives but there is an important distinction between them. Fear occurs in response to a specific stimulus while anxiety is more diffused.[31] Anxiety depends on past experience and is anticipatory in nature. A person who anticipates failure in an enterprise or social disgrace becomes anxious. The anxiety is a product of experience and is aroused by events that are uncertain and unpredictable.

Two basic defense mechanisms may be used to ward off anxiety. We may seek relief through (1) increasing our mastery of or competence in the anxiety-provoking situation, and (2) securing reassurance or support from others.[32] In drug advertising, for example, both or either of these strategies may be used. The drug manufacturer may offer a simple, though somewhat clinical, explanation of the benefits of his drug to the customer. He may also provide the endorsements of doctors, dentists, and so on.

The degree of anxiety aroused by a particular message will affect the response pattern of the recipient. It is generally agreed that if a communication is to be effective, it must be strong enough to arouse the recipient to a "drive state" but not beyond that point. A moderately strong anxiety-arousing communication more effectively elicits an appropriate response than one that is stronger, in the sense of being more anxiety-arousing.

An experiment concerning anxiety used copy containing positive appeals and copy containing negative appeals. *Negative appeals* may be defined as those that warn about an annoying, repulsive, or uncomfortable situation that might be experienced as a result of not buying or using the advertised product or service. *Positive appeals* are those that describe the useful, beneficial, or desirable consequences of buying or using the advertised product or service. (See Exhibit 15.3.)

EXHIBIT 15.3

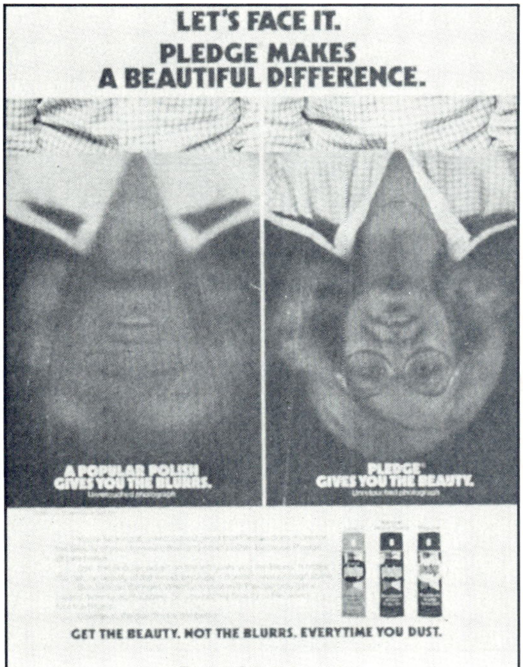

Both positive and negative appeals can elicit the desired response.
Source: "Tyler's Ten for December," *Advertising Age*, December 25, 1978, p. 16.

The results of the experiment indicated that both the positive and the negative copy brought about a small positive attitude shift. When the respondents were divided into low-anxiety and high-anxiety groups, however, the low-anxiety group exposed to the negative copy experienced a more favorable attitude shift than those who were shown the positive copy. The authors concluded that opportunities probably exist for the successful use of negative appeals in advertising, particularly with people of low anxiety.[33]

Sexual Appeals

While an increasing number and variety of products are being marketed with sexual overtones and the use of nudity in advertising is increasing, surprisingly little is known about the effects of either nudity or sexual overtones in marketing communications. The few empirical studies that have been conducted relied heavily on analysis of secondary data and were less than generalizable because the subjects employed (usually students) were not representative of the general population.

While explicit sex is rarely used in advertisements, implicit sex occurs in various forms; those that have been the subjects of research include sexual attractiveness, the use of the double entendre, and nudity.

SEXUAL ATTRACTIVENESS

The results of a study conducted to assess the impact on students of physically attractive models in advertisements suggested that the sex and physical attractiveness of an ad model influences people's evaluations of the aesthetic qualities of an advertisement. Attractive models therefore seem to be important determinants of the attention-getting value of the ad and the subject's liking of the ad. These two variables do not seem to affect a person's cognitions, however, and thus they may be relatively ineffective in getting the message accepted by the target audience. The results also suggested that in attempts to sell a nonromantic product to males, an unattractive female model may be more persuasive in creating eventual product purchase than an attractive one.

This study seems to contradict to some extent the theories of perception that suggest that the attractive model should have increased the credibility and thus the acceptance of the promotional message. This inconsistency may have occurred, according to the researchers, because the subjects were students and may be more skeptical of all advertising claims.[34]

NUDITY

In the current permissive climate, some companies have gone toward nudity; others, however, are trying to present a more "refined" image. White Rock's "Psyche" recently changed wardrobes for only the second time since she was presented at the 1893 World's Fair. Topless since that time, the newly attired Psyche now appears with her chest covered, but displays slightly more thigh than in the past.

Illustrations of nude or partly nude women in print advertising are not rare and are even found in "family" magazines. In terms of the persuasion process, little doubt exists concerning the attention-getting (exposure) value of a nude woman. More questions exist as to whether female nudity increases the encoding tendency (as measured by recall) or whether it leads to desired behavior.

An early study by Major Steadman concluded that nonsexual illustrations are more effective than sexual ones in achieving brand recall. Although the advertisements with illustrations depicting female nudity appear to possess attention-getting value, male viewers seem to attend solely to the illustration of the nude and ignore the brand name.[35]

A later study designed to test a number of hypotheses concerning the use of nudes in advertising supported Steadman's findings to some extent. Significantly more brand names were recalled for those advertisements containing a mountain or forest scene than for those with a nude model. In this study, however, brand recall did not significantly decrease as the degree of explicit nudity in the advertisements increased. Furthermore, unlike Steadman's finding, the number of brand names recalled was *little* influenced by the respondents' attitudes toward nudity in advertising. The difference in results was possibly due to the difference in methods of attitude scaling used in the two studies. According to these researchers, the study provided additional support for the proposition that when brand recall is the objective, a nude woman should not be used in advertisements directed toward men.[36]

Another study examined the role of a nude female model in an advertisement and its effect on consumer attitudes toward the advertisement, the product displayed, and the company that produced the product. Models presented to be perceived as demure, seductive, and nude were featured in advertisements for both a baby oil and a ratchet wrench set. Across products and respondents, the advertisement containing the nude model was consistently perceived as the least appealing, while the associated product and producing company were perceived as, respectively, possessing the lowest quality and being the least reputable.[37] While no effort was made to translate these perceptions into purchase behavior, and the results, like those in previous studies, cannot be generalized, the findings nevertheless merit further investigation. They suggest that marketers who employ nudity in their advertising may be making a mistake; rather than appearing as fashionably current, the use of nudity may ultimately produce deleterious effects.

DOUBLE ENTENDRE

Sexual overtones have been used for some time, particularly in the form of the *double entendre* (double meaning). An early example was the Clairol ad that asked, "Does she or doesn't she?" Although the ad was successful, at least in attracting attention and recall, whether this success was due to the sexual implication in the message has not been determined. In fact, a medium that at first rejected this ad accepted it when its secretaries declared they read the message as "Does she or doesn't she color her hair?"

Such double entendre ads continue to appear from time to time (see Exhibit 15.4), and occasionally are considered to be excessively and unacceptably sexist by some consumers. Particularly objectionable to women have been ads by airlines ("Fly me" and "We really move our tails for you").

As we noted earlier, however, reactions to double entendres in advertising vary. One study conducted in a focus-group format to determine how widely sexual innuendos are perceived used a Bic razor commercial in which a bride an-

EXHIBIT 15.4

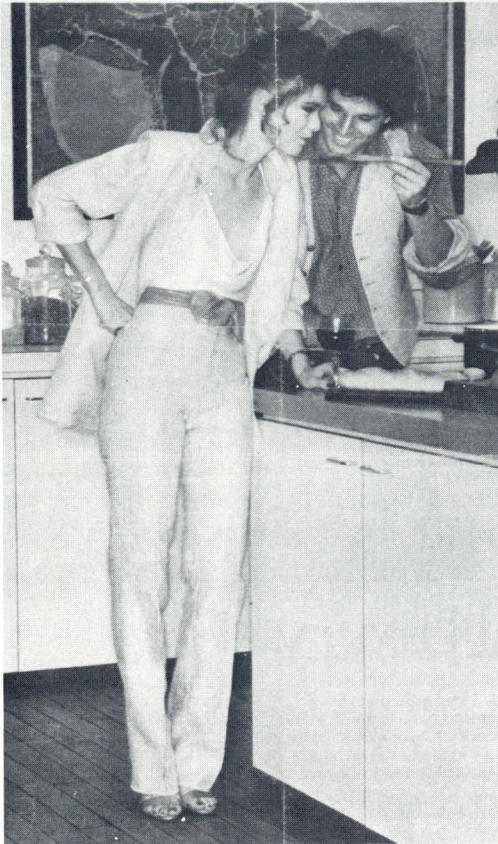

What to wear on Sunday
when you won't be home till Monday.

Happy Legs

Double entendre ad

nounced at her wedding that the groom was stroked that very morning and now would get stroked every morning. The group interviewed consisted only of women—those who had agreed with the statement "TV commercials place too much emphasis on sex." While the younger women in the group characterized sexual innuendo as crude locker-room humor, the older people saw nothing wrong in the commercial and thought it was kind of cute. How these perceptions affect purchasing behavior was not examined.[38]

THE CHANNEL

The effectiveness of a persuasive communication may depend on whether it is spoken or written, read in a newspaper or a magazine, or heard on radio or television. Marketers use a variety of channels to communicate information to consumers—the mass media, personal salespeople, and retail outlets. Personal salespeople may be sources as well as channels and were discussed in Chapter 14; retail outlets will be examined in Chapter 16. This section presents some recent findings relevant to the persuasive effects of mass media as channels for the marketer's communications.

Mass Media

The major significance of mass media as communication channels is obvious from the term—they are channels that reach "masses" of people with one message. Social scientists and public-opinion specialists have analyzed media in accordance with their relative advantages as instruments of pedagogy and persuasion. Their conclusions are rarely supported by objective data, but since they represent the careful thinking of acute observers, the advantages of each medium are reported.[39]

Print permits the audience to control the exposure. The reader sets his own pace, the continued availability of the printed matter allows for repeated exposure, and the treatment of the topic may be of any length. Publications designed for minority or special-interest groups are peculiarly effective persuasive agents, and print appears to possess greater prestige than other media.

Radio reaches an audience not so often reached by other mass media, and this audience tends to be less cultured and more suggestible than the audiences of other media. Radio approaches face-to-face contact in that it offers the spectator some degree of participation in the actual event being broadcast. Radio may be persuasive because it is usually the first medium to communicate given material to an audience.

Television is a medium of low involvement. High involvement in a medium leads to a dramatic conflict of ideas at the level of conscious opinion and attitude, which precedes changes in behavior. Low involvement, which occurs in commercial television viewing, leads to gradual shifts in perceptual structure, aided by repetition and followed at some time by attitude change.[40] Persuasion as such, then, may not occur through television advertising. Instead repetitive commercial messages change our ways of perceiving products and brands and our purchasing behavior without our thinking very much about it at the time of the television exposure or at any time before purchase, and without changing verbalized attitudes.

Research has been conducted to determine the effectiveness of various media in terms of specific steps in the persuasion process. In an effort to compare media on the basis of exposure and awareness, a study was sponsored by *Newsweek* magazine and conducted by Audits and Surveys.[41] The researcher found that the percentage of magazine readers who looked at the ads was larger than the percentage of viewers of a TV program who had an opportunity to see the ads. Specifically, readers of *Time, Newsweek,* and *U.S. News & World Report* looked at 85 percent of the news weeklies' ad pages. In contrast, only about 70 percent of a TV show's quarter-hour audience stayed in the room during commercial breaks, and somewhere between 23 percent and 30 percent remained mentally tuned to the ads. This finding of greater attention to print ads than to TV ads confirms earlier studies.

It is difficult to determine the relative strength of the medium in influencing attitude change. For example, comparisons between a one-minute commercial spot and a half-page advertisement are difficult to make. Effectiveness will vary with the audience sought, the objectives of the advertising, and so on. A media decision related to attitude change requires an overall evaluation of the objectives of a firm's marketing activities.

TABLE 15.3   CHANGE IN AUDIENCE ATTITUDES AFTER AN AVERAGE EXPOSURE TO TV COMMERCIALS AND MAGAZINE ADS (IN PERCENT)

Average effect for 13 brands	Magazines			Prime-time TV		
	Before	After	Percentage change	Before	After	Percentage change
Brand awareness	36%	48%	+33%	32%	53%	+66%
Belief in brand's claims	34	37	+ 9	33	39	+18
Positive brand evaluation	38	40	+ 5	33	40	+21
Desire to buy particular brand	35	40	+14	28	41	+46

Note: CBS-TV study conducted in 1960–61 by Audits & Surveys and Gilbert Research. In this study teenage "spies" who knew in advance which issues of *Life, Look, Saturday Evening Post,* and *Reader's Digest* and selected prime-time TV shows carried ads or commercials for products assigned to them queried other family members about the brands before and immediately after their exposure to the advertising. All told, 1,790 people were interviewed before and after TV exposures, while 1,589 magazine readers were observed and interviewed in the same manner.

Source: *The Media Book 78* (New York: The Media Book, Inc., 1978), p. 425.

Various types of media, however, claim to be more effective in securing attitude change than others, but their results appear to bear some relationship to the sponsorship of the studies and the conditions under which they have been conducted. A study sponsored by CBS-TV presented evidence that indicated, not surprisingly, the superior effectiveness of television over magazines in changing attitudes after an "average exposure." (See Table 15.3.) A magazine study conducted shortly afterward under the sponsorship of *Life* indicated that more readers of *Life* magazine than TV viewers remembered seeing an average ad or commercial the following day. (See Figure 15.2.)

FIGURE 15.2 PROPORTION OF "LAST NIGHT" TV VIEWERS AND "YESTERDAY" *LIFE* MAGAZINE READERS WHO REMEMBERED SEEING AN AVERAGE AD OR COMMERCIAL

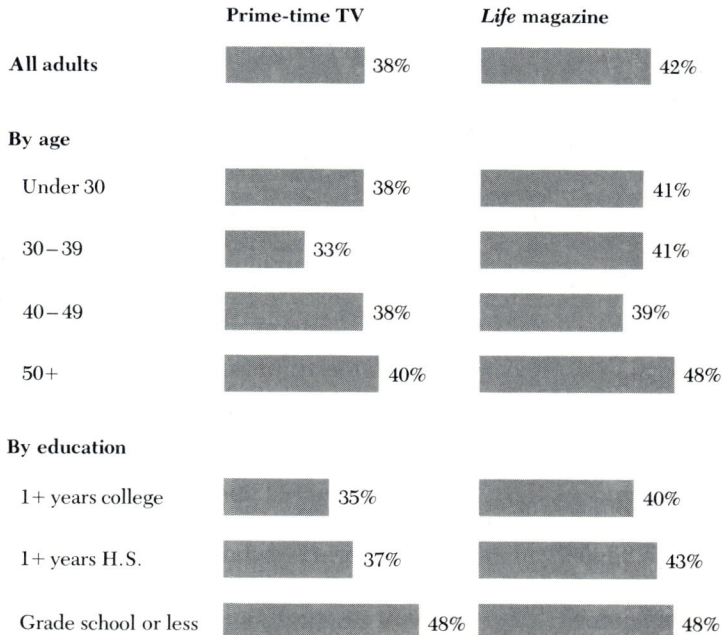

	Prime-time TV	*Life* magazine
All adults	38%	42%
By age		
Under 30	38%	41%
30–39	33%	41%
40–49	38%	39%
50+	40%	48%
By education		
1+ years college	35%	40%
1+ years H.S.	37%	43%
Grade school or less	48%	48%

Note: *Life* Magazine's "Ad Retention Study" conducted by W. R. Simmons & Associates in five major markets with 762 adult TV viewers and 1,173 *Life* magazine readers in 1964 and 1965. In this study, "last night" TV program viewers were shown commercials on a rear screen projector brought to their home by the interviewer. On average, 38% of those who claimed to have viewed a program that aired the average commercial remembered seeing it after this visual reminder. In the magazine phase, "yesterday" readers of a specific issue of *Life* magazine were shown a portfolio of ads that appeared in this issue (and some that didn't). An average of 42% of them remembered the average ad after seeing it again in the portfolio.
Source: *The Media Book 78* (New York: The Media Book Inc., 1978), p. 424.

TABLE 15.4 INCREASED COUPON REDEMPTION OF LOS ANGELES SUPER-MARKET SHOPPERS AFTER EXPOSURE TO MAGAZINE ADS AND TV COMMERCIALS FOR 12 BRANDS (IN PERCENT)

Brand	Magazine ad	TV commercial
Nabisco Saltines	+43%	+ 80%
Del Monte pineapple	+50	+102
Tang	+55	+ 91
Lysol Spray	+48	+ 87
Maxim freeze-dried coffee	+35	+ 67
Moisturelle cleanser	+32	+ 49
Ivory Liquid	+31	+ 55
Breck Shampoo	+50	+ 86
Cold Power	+34	+ 54
Jello 1-2-3	+78	+116
Campbell's Chunky Soup	+39	+ 78
Bounty	+48	+110

Note: Studies by Tele-Research Inc., sponsored by the three TV networks in 1970 and 1971. In these studies, samples of homemakers were interviewed before going into a supermarket about their brand preferences for the product classes involved. One group (the "control" group) was given a cents-off coupon packet and went into the store to do its shopping—*without* exposure to any commercials. Another group was exposed to either a radio or TV commercial and then was given a cents-off coupon packet which it used when shopping. Afterward, the coupon redemptions were compared for the control group (not exposed) and the ones exposed to radio or TV commercials. The basic assumption was that any difference between the control group and those exposed to a radio or TV message was caused by the impact of the ad.

The table reads as follows: women who saw a magazine ad for Nabisco Saltines redeemed 43% more coupons for Nabisco than a matched sample that didn't. The TV group, however, redeemed 80% more.

Source: *The Media Book 78* (New York: The Media Book, Inc., 1978), p. 426.

TABLE 15.5 INCREASED COUPON REDEMPTION OF LOS ANGELES SUPER-MARKET SHOPPERS AFTER EXPOSURE TO RADIO AND TV COMMERCIALS FOR 5 BRANDS (IN PERCENT)

Brand	Radio commercial	TV commercial
Sucaryl	+22%	+ 72%
Maxim	+79	+400
Excedrin	+35	+103
Laura Scudder potato chips	+26	+106
Action bleach	+16	+ 57

Note: Studies by Tele-Research Inc., sponsored by the three TV networks in 1968–1969. In these studies, samples of homemakers were interviewed before going into a supermarket about their branch preferences for the product classes involved. One group (the "control" group) was given a cents-off coupon packet and went into the store to do its shopping—*without* exposure to any commercials. Another group was exposed to either a radio or TV commercial and then was given a cents-off coupon packet which it used when shopping. Afterward, the coupon redemptions were compared for the control group (not exposed) and the ones exposed to radio or TV commercials. The basic assumption was that any difference between the control group and those exposed to a radio or TV message was caused by the impact of the commercial.

The table reads as follows: women who heard a radio commercial for Sucaryl redeemed 22% more coupons for Sucaryl than a matched sample that didn't hear the commercial. The TV group, however, redeemed 72% more.

Source: *The Media Book 78* (New York: The Media Book, Inc., 1978), p. 432.

More recent studies sponsored by the three networks indicated that supermarket shoppers in the Los Angeles area were apt to change their brand preferences as measured by increased coupon redemptions after exposures to a TV commercial than after exposure to a magazine ad or radio commercial. (See Tables 15.4 and 15.5.)

Current studies indicate no simple relationship between the type of medium and attitude change. One study using political candidates rather than products suggested that the type of medium will interact with the source to determine the influence a message will have on an audience. Specifically, television is the most effective medium for a trustworthy source, but the least effective medium for an untrustworthy communicator.[42]

Clearly, more research is required to enable us to understand the effects of media on communications. Suggestions by Emanuel Demby as to media research that should be undertaken include the following:[43]

1. Demographic profiles.
2. Purchasing behavior.
3. The propensity of a medium's audience to act on advertising and the kind of advertising it is likely to act on.
4. The influence of the medium's psychographic profile on the desire to go to specific places, buy specific goods, and so forth.
5. The contribution the medium might make to audience attitudes, behavior, and reaction to advertising.
6. The contribution the editorial or program environment might make to the effectiveness of the communication in the medium.
7. Of particular importance, the odds that a specific ad will be seen by the medium's audience.

THE RECEIVER

Much of this text is devoted to a discussion of the receiver of communications, in this case the consumer. Such factors as social, cultural, personality, life-style, and opinion-leader influences, discussed earlier, all have relevance to the persuasive aspects of communications. Perception, motivation, and learning are also important in this context. Specific note should be taken of market-segmentation techniques, which permit the isolation of target groups that incorporate demographic, psychographic, and use characteristics most relevant to efficient information processing. Chapter 18 will discuss another important aspect of communication, the diffusion process, which relates to the manner in which information is diffused (spread) among consumers.

Destination

More specific to this discussion of communications and persuasive information processing is the destination or target of the communication—that is, the variables having to do with the particular kind of change within the receiver that the communication is designed to produce. The *destination* of the persuasive communication may be defined in terms of specific targets, for example, cognitive variables and behavioral variables.

Behavioral target variables include actions, purchase, and intent, and are discussed in detail in Chapter 17. *Cognitive targets* are beliefs, attitudes, and liking, discussed in Chapter 11 and Chapter 12. The destination targets for the "I Love New York" campaign were both cognitive—to improve consumers' attitudes toward the state—and behavioral—to have more tourists select New York as the place to visit. Apparently the state believed both of these objectives had been achieved, as it purchased an additional $1.6 million of air time to feature these commercials in 1979.

COMMUNICATIONS RESEARCH

Many of the research techniques discussed in earlier chapters are relevant to communications research. When communications are prepared, efforts are made to determine salient attributes and benefits as well as significant motives—the former through perceptual mapping, quadrant analysis, and the like, and the latter through such motivational research techniques as focus-group interviews. The Gallup Robinson Impact Test for recall and the Starch Readership Test for recognition are used as posttests to determine the effectiveness of the memory of the communication.

Numerous pretest and posttest procedures are conducted to determine some of the persuasive effects of advertising communications. Testing can take place at various stages during the advertising campaign—in the creative process before the ads appear, during their appearance, or after they have appeared. Pretesting essentially measures awareness and comprehension. Although it attempts to offer insights as to what is acceptable and influential, it frequently consists of determining whether one advertisement is liked better than another. Pretesting in print media may consist of asking consumers to rank advertisements in terms of their relative merit (order-of-merit test), to compare advertisements in a series of pairs (paired-comparison test), or to discuss a series of advertisements presented in a binder (folio test). While these methods may offer insights into the advertisements' persuasive effect, they frequently result in the selection of the "best of the worst."

For advertisements prepared for broadcast media, in-home projectors and trailers may be used to determine awareness and comprehension or to offer diagnostic insights into problem areas. Attempts to overcome the artificiality of the situation in which tests are conducted have resulted in the development of live telecast tests through the use of closed-circuit television, cable TV, and UHF channels. Adtel, for example, has adapted cable TV for the testing of television advertising by using two cables instead of one to distribute pictures. This procedure permits homes to be wired to either of the dual cables, thus making it possible to hook up alternate subscribers to each cable. Adtel cuts in test commercials to one set of wired homes, while the other set of wired homes continues to get normal advertising exposure. Panels selected from the two sets of homes are provided with diaries in which they keep records of purchases. The diaries are compared in an effort to determine the impact of advertising communications on purchase measurements.

As we saw earlier, recall and recognition tests are used to determine posttest effects of advertising communications. A pre–post research technique designed to determine whether the advertisement *influences* a consumer to choose one brand over another in a forced viewing situation is called the theater test. Conditions for this test are not completely artificial, since the respondent does not know he is to rate the commercials, nor are they "natural," since the respondent is not viewing the commercial in an on-the-air context.

In the theater test, consumers are usually given a choice of brands when they enter the theater, having been informed that they have a chance to win a year's supply of the product. Several product categories with competing brands are listed, and the consumer is asked to choose the brand she would prefer if she should win. A series of commercials for several brands under test in various product categories is then shown to the viewers. After viewing the commercials, the respondents are asked to check off the brand they would now prefer. The effectiveness of the advertising is then computed by comparing the initial preferences (before the subjects saw the commercials) with the later ones (after they viewed the commercials for the brand in question).

An assumption in this test is that the only intervening factor between the pre and post brand choice is a commercial for one of the brands. A problem experienced with the pre–post method is that individuals seem to shift their preferences whether a commercial intervenes or not.

SUMMARY

Repetition of messages improves exposure, but there is conflicting evidence on the effects of repetition on the other steps of the persuasion process. Various message strategies are used to improve awareness, emotional responses, encoding, acceptance of appeal, and overt behavior. These strategies include use of humor, fear, anxiety, and sexual appeals.

In selecting a channel to disseminate the message, marketers most frequently use personal salespeople or mass media. Recent research has focused on the effects of the salesperson/customer dyad—that is, the interrelationships between the salesperson and particular types of customers—and nonverbal influences. Little research has examined the relative persuasive effects of various mass media.

Knowledge about the destination—that is, the variables having to do with the particular kind of change within the receiver that the communication is designed to produce—is based on research related to the manner in which beliefs and attitudes are organized and changed.

Earlier chapters have discussed specific research methods that may be applied to communication research. Other techniques have been developed by advertisers to pretest and posttest advertising messages.

DISCUSSION QUESTIONS

1. How are the laws of learning and the order of presentation in an advertising message interrelated?

2. Select some ads that present a two-sided message. What do you believe were the reasons for this type of presentation?

3. In which stages of the persuasion process is repetition of advertising messages more effective? Why?

4. Describe some humorous advertisements. What do you think are the benefits and/or deficiencies of the use of humor in these contexts?

5. How do you believe you would react to fear messages? Negative appeals?

6. A successful jeans manufacturer began its initial advertising campaign with a dancing scene. After sales skyrocketed, the campaign, particularly in print, incorporated some nudity. How do you react to this strategy?

7. For you personally, is one type of medium more persuasive than another? Why?

8. Most media research focuses on the number of people exposed to each medium. Should this criterion be changed? What kind of changes would you recommend?

NOTES

1. Hooper White, "Hooper White's Minireview: 'I Love New York,'" *Advertising Age*, December 25, 1978.
2. Daniel S. Diamond, "A Quantitative Approach to Magazine Advertisement Format Selection," *Journal of Marketing Research* 6 (November 1968), pp. 376–386.
3. Michael L. Ray and Pete H. Webbe, "Advertising Effectiveness in a Crowded Television Environment," Marketing Science Institute Working Paper (Cambridge, Mass.: Marketing Science Institute, September 1978).
4. Lauren Swanson, "Doceatur Emptor," *Journal of Advertising* 4 (Winter 1975), p. 25.
5. David Krech, Richard S. Crutchfield, and Norman Livson, *Elements of Psychology*, 3d ed. (New York: Alfred A. Knopf, 1974), p. 770.
6. Swanson, "Doceatur Emptor," p. 25.

7. Norman Miller and Donald T. Campbell, "Recency and Primacy in Persuasion as a Function of the Timing of Speeches and Measurements," *Journal of Abnormal and Social Psychology* 59 (1950), pp. 1–9.

8. Albert A. Harrison, "Mere Exposure," in *Advances in Experimental Social Psychology*, vol. 10, ed. Leonard Berkowitz (New York: Academic Press, 1977), pp. 39–83.

9. Robert B. Zajonc, "The Attitudinal Effects of Mere Exposure," *Journal of Personality and Social Psychology* 9, Monograph Supplement (June 1968), pp. 1–27.

10. Richard L. Miller, "Mere Exposure, Psychological Reactance, and Attitude Change," *Public Opinion Quarterly* 40 (Summer 1976), p. 229.

11. Rita Wicks Poulos, *Unintentional Negative Effects of Food Commercials on Children: A Case Study* (San Francisco: Media Action Research Center, 1975).

12. Marvin E. Goldberg, Gerald J. Gorn, and Wendy Gibson, "TV Messages for Snack Foods: Do They Influence Children's Preferences?" *Journal of Consumer Research* 5 (September 1978), pp. 73–81.

13. Harrison, "Mere Exposure," p. 41.

14. C. Samuel Craig, Brian Sternthal, and Clark Leavitt, "Advertising Wearout: An Experimental Analysis," *Journal of Marketing Research* 13 (November 1976), pp. 365–372.

15. Harrison, "Mere Exposure," p. 45.

16. James F. Engel, Roger D. Blackwell, and David T. Kollat, *Consumer Behavior,* 3d ed. (New York: Holt, Rinehart & Winston, 1978), pp. 433–445.

17. C. Samuel Craig and John M. McCann, "Assessing Communication Effects on Energy Conservation," *Journal of Consumer Research* 5 (September 1978), p. 87.

18. "Frequency, Part 2: ARF's New Project," *Marketing & Media Decisions* 15 (April 1980) pp. 108–114.

19. Chapter 16 will discuss what is said in the context of the evaluation of alternatives.

20. Alan D. Fletcher and Sherilyn K. Zeigler, "Creative Strategy and Magazine Ad Readership," *Journal of Advertising Research* 18 (February 1978), pp. 29–36.

21. Philip H. Dougherty, "Advertising," *New York Times,* January 5, 1979, p. D12.

22. Video Story Board Tests Inc., New York, 1978.

23. Brian Sternthal and C. Samuel Craig, "Humor in Advertising," *Journal of Marketing* 37 (October 1973), pp. 12–18.

24. F. M. Mburu, Mickey C. Smith, and Helen Wetherbee, "Humor in Prescription Drug Advertising," *Medical Marketing Media* (June 1976), p. 44.

25. Ernest Dichter, *Motivating Human Behavior* (New York: McGraw-Hill, 1971), pp. 35–50.

26. Irving L. Janis and Seymour Feshbach, "Effects of Fear-Arousing Communications," *Journal of Abnormal and Social Psychology* 48 (January 1953), pp. 78–92.

27. John R. Stuteville, "Psychic Defenses against High Fear Appeals: A Key Marketing Variable," *Journal of Marketing* 34 (April 1970), pp. 39–45.

28. Michael L. Ray and Wendell L. Wilkie, "Fear: The Potential of an Appeal Neglected by Marketing," *Journal of Marketing* 34 (January 1970), pp. 54–62.

29. John J. Burnett and Richard L. Oliver, "Fear Appeal Effects in the Field: A Segmentation Approach," *Journal of Marketing Research 16 (May 1979), pp. 181–190.*

30. Brian Sternthal and C. Samuel Craig, "Fear Appeals: Revisited and Revised," Journal of Consumer Research 1 (December 1974), pp. 30–31.

31. Eva Dreikurs Ferguson, *Motivation: An Experimental Approach* (New York: Holt, Rinehart & Winston, 1976), p. 298.

32. Paul Thomas Young, *Motivation and Emotion* (New York: John Wiley, 1961), pp. 566–567.

33. John J. Wheatley and Sadaomi Oshikawa, "The Relationship between Anxiety and Positive and Negative Advertising Appeals," *Journal of Marketing* 7 (February 1970), pp. 85–90.

34. Michael J. Baker and Gilbert A. Churchill, Jr., "The Impact of Physically Attractive Models in Advertising Evaluations," *Journal of Marketing Research* 14 (November 1977), pp. 538–555.

35. Major Steadman, "How Sexy Illustrations Affect Brand Recall," *Journal of Advertising Research* 9 (February 1969), pp. 15–18.

36. M. Wayne Alexander and Ben Judd, Jr., "Do Nudes in Ads Enhance Brand Recall?" *Journal of Advertising Research* 18 (February 1978), pp. 47–50.

37. Robert A. Peterson and Roger A. Kerin, "The Female Role in Advertisements: Some Experimental Evidence," *Journal of Marketing* 41 (October 1977), pp. 59–63.

38. Deborah E. Johnson and Kay Satov, "Consumers' Reactions to Sex in TV Commercials," in *Advances in Consumer Research,* vol. 5, ed. H. Keith Hunt (Ann Arbor: Association for Consumer Research, 1978) p. 413.

39. Joseph T. Klapper, "The Comparative Effects of the Various Media," in *Advertising Management: Selected Readings,* ed. Harper W. Boyd, Jr., and Joseph W. Newman (Homewood, Ill.: Richard D. Irwin, 1965), pp. 423–436.

40. Herbert E. Krugman, "The Impact of Television Advertising: Learning without Involvement," in *Dimensions of Communication,* ed. Lee Richardson (New York: Appleton-Century-Crofts, 1969), p. 356.

41. Bernice Kanner, "TV vs. Print Study Finds Reader More 'Attentive,' " *Advertising Age,* August 7, 1978, p. 2.

42. Virginia Andreoli and Stephen Worchel, "Effects of Media Communicator and Message Position on Attitude Change," *Public Opinion Quarterly,* Spring 1978, pp. 59–70.

43. " 'Propensity' May Be Key, Advertisers Need Help from Media Researchers," *Marketing News,* June 2, 1978, p. 3.

CHAPTER 16

ALTERNATIVE EVALUATION

Kimberly-Clark and Procter & Gamble both introduced a disposable diaper in 1978 to the "premium" marketing segment in an industry dominated by P & G's "Pampers." Kimberly-Clark's "Kleenex Huggies" and P & G's "Luvs" both presented a new attribute in diapers—elastic legs. The diapers were offered to the trade at similar prices, roughly 25 percent to 35 percent above "Pampers." Both companies offered consumers 25 cents off to try their products.

It appears that these two companies did not consider price as an important criterion for evaluation by the "premium" diaper market. However, the basic feature that distinguished this diaper from others on the market—the elastic leg—was presented in two different ways. Kimberly-Clark advertised its "Kleenex Huggies" as "the elastic leg diaper that helps stop leaking," while P & G's "Luvs" was presented as "the diaper designed for your baby's comfort."[1] These different appeals represent variations in the manner by which consumers evaluate alternatives, as perceived by the companies. Kimberly-Clark considered baby's comfort as an important consumer choice criterion, while P & G focused on solving the mother's problem. At this writing, the relative success of these campaigns cannot be judged.

In the fast-food industry, a motto expressing salient attributes is "quality, service, cleanliness, and value." While cleanliness and service may be determined by consumers fairly easily, quality and value are more difficult to ascertain. McDonald's, the leading firm in the industry, faced with extensive competition from Burger King and Wendy's, devised a new advertising campaign in early 1979. On the basis of the inflation/recession economic spiral, McDonald's decided to stress its image of "value."[2] Advertisements centered on the inexpensive nature of the product. They starred a young couple in their new house, eating at the McDonald's, a young teacher treating her class to lunch, and a young entrepreneur taking his dad out to eat.

Wendy's International, which grew from one store in 1968 to 1,407 in 1979, stressed "quality" as its product's important attribute. This attribute was reflected in its campaign theme "hot and juicy," which featured consumers wiping hamburger juice off their chins. Wendy's target market was primarily the young adult, unlike the competition that generally targets the family and children.[3] As is the case with the disposable diapers, so it is with the hamburger—which attribute to emphasize is open to debate.

Information processing continues beyond the search stage through the succeeding stages of evaluation of alternatives, choice, and outcome. The alternative-evaluation stage consists of the comparison of various alternatives for purchase and consumption against those criteria or product attributes felt by the consumer to be important in the decision. It is assumed that in making such judgments consumers use evaluative criteria, which are defined as "desired outcomes from choice or use of an alternative expressed in the form of specifications used to compare various alternatives."[4] John Howard defines "choice criteria" as mental counterparts of the attributes by which a consumer judges a brand. He distinguishes between attributes per se and the consumer's perception of those attributes, and notes that it is the perception that affects behavior, not the attribute itself.[5] While the distinction is a valid one, for practical purposes the term "evaluative criteria" will be used here.

Evaluative criteria can be either objective (specific physical features, such as low price or long service life or "elastic legs on diapers") or subjective (symbolic values or benefits, such as the perceived "naturalness" of Revlon's Charlie fragrance and the "sensuality" of its Jontue).[6] Subjective criteria may also involve beliefs about the consequences of using a product, such as enhancement of social acceptance, prestige, or the solution of a problem ("prevent diaper leaks").

In evaluating alternatives, the consumer may be seen both as an information processor and as a decision maker. A model is useful to indicate these dimensions. A representative decision matrix appears in Table 16.1. Its major dimensions are called *objects* and *evaluative criteria*, or attributes; objects are arrayed along the horizontal axis, evaluative criteria along the vertical. The entries in the cells are the *values* that are associated with each object, in terms of each specific attribute. An *object* is defined quite broadly as any element of the environment that exists psychologically for the person. In this model, an evaluative criterion is a dimension of judgment on which two or more objects can be compared. At least two objects and at least one evaluative criterion must be present for a decision to take place. The fast-food industry considers four attributes or evaluative criteria to be

TABLE 16.1   RELATIVE VALUES OF ALTERNATIVE OBJECTS (BRANDS OR PRODUCTS), BY CRITERION: SCHEMATIC MODEL OF A DECISION MATRIX

Evaluative criterion	Object A	Object B	. . .	Object Z
1	A_1	B_1	. . .	Z_1
2	A_2	B_2	. . .	Z_2
n	A_n	B_n	. . .	Z_n

Source: Adapted from Steven H. Chaffee and Jack M. McLeod, "Consumer Decisions and Information Use," in *Consumer Behavior: Theoretical Sources,* ed. Scott Ward and Thomas S. Robertson (Englewood Cliffs, N.J.: Prentice-Hall, 1973), p. 391.

of major importance in the consumer's purchase decision regarding fast foods: quality, service, convenience, and value.

Most decisions are somewhat complicated in that they involve many comparisons among more than two alternatives and a number of attributes. Furthermore, a decision matrix in which all of the information is available to the consumer is a theoretical goal that is rarely, if ever, found in real life.

To provide some understanding of the alternative evaluation stage, this chapter will answer some of the following questions:

What are the sources of evaluative criteria?
How do consumers make evaluations among product classes?
How do consumers make evaluations among brands of a product?
What kinds of evaluative criteria may be used?
How do "cues" offer a basis for evaluation?
How does the situation in which the decision takes place affect the evaluation process?
How does shopping behavior interrelate with the evaluation process?

SOURCES OF EVALUATIVE CRITERIA

Evaluative criteria can be shaped by values, motives, information, and experience.

Values

Perhaps the most basic criterion by which consumers choose a product or service is the value they perceive in it. As we saw in Chapter 2, a value is an especially important class of beliefs shared by the members of a society concerning what is desirable and what ought to be. Belief systems and the values they generate can influence an individual's social character, which in turn influences behavior. Some of these values find their expression in cultural norms, which dictate modes of conduct and appropriate and inappropriate behavior. Behavioral norms are in turn reflected in the evaluative criteria established by consumers to determine choice. As we saw in Chapter 2, relatively little research has been directed to ascertaining whether various value orientations lead to variations in preferences for products and brands. Values may be considered, however, in the selection and maintenance of ends or goals toward which human beings strive; at the same time, they regulate the methods and manner in which such striving takes place.[7] For example, if a young family man considers "taking care of loved ones" to be a value, he may settle for a station wagon, even though a two-seat sports car has more desirable attributes for him personally.

Motives

It is difficult to distinguish between values and motives in their effect as reference scales for evaluative criteria, and some authorities see values and motives as synonymous in the development of choice criteria.[8] A distinction between the two may be noted, however, in the definition of motives as an energizer of behavior. While both values and motives guide behavior, motives are more likely to initiate behavior. Motives help to establish goals and provide the energy and direction for their achievement.

As we noted earlier, motives are related to needs. Motives may shape the consumer's perception of those product attributes and benefits that will contribute most to need satisfaction. Development of a product with attributes that satisfy consumers' needs may be a complicated process for the marketer. To provide the consumer with a satisfactory pocket-size camera, Eastman Kodak had to develop 240 products in seven years. Even after the original Instamatic camera was introduced, market research revealed consumer needs that remained unfilled: needs for a camera that was easy to carry, easy to load, and could take clear, sharp pictures. To fulfill these needs, Kodak developed a new lens for a sharper image, a new film for clearer photos, and a new film cartridge.[9]

Motivating influences may also arise from an individual's self-concept. Evidence seems to indicate a connection between self-concept and buying behavior. Thus in evaluating alternatives, the individual may select products that she believes support her self-concept and reject those that do not. If she sees herself as "sporty" and "modern," she will purchase and wear clothing that reflects this image.

Information and Experience

Experience provides consumers with information that enables them to develop appropriate evaluative criteria. For example, while the initial choice of a cleanser may be based on such attributes as cleaning power and cost, after purchase and use an important criterion may become "does not scratch surfaces."

Information stored in long-term memory is an important source of evaluative criteria. Such information is based not only on use and experience, but on family preferences, word-of-mouth communications, and advertising. Some of the information gathered through the information-search stage becomes stored in long-term memory. Product information retrieved from memory plays an essential role in many purchase decisions.

As we saw in Chapter 8, information stored in long-term memory is interconnected. A semantic network provides the "meaning of a brand." Thus the significant specifications of peanut butter may be designated as smooth, lumpy, butter with peanuts, and so on. Further product knowledge may be stored in the form of list structures by attributes (taste, price, preservatives) or by brand (Jif, Skippy, Peter Pan). The brand name may be used as a chunk of information that combines various attributes as choice criteria.

Another important information source of evaluative criteria is the in-store environment and the "external memory" it provides.[10] Products and brands are available for inspection, and values for various attributes (price, nutritional values, and so on) can be obtained from the package, in-store displays, and inspection.

EVALUATING ALTERNATIVES AMONG PRODUCT CLASSES

Consumers may be faced with choices among product classes (Should I get peanut butter for lunch or fresh vegetables for a salad?), as well as among brands (Should I buy Jif or Skippy or Peter Pan?). Relatively little research has focused on choice among product classes, although current interest of public policy makers has tended to emphasize the need for such research in terms of nutrition, energy conservation, and so on.

Product-class choice appears to be difficult for several reasons. First, the attributes available may differ among product classes. As most marketer information deals with brand choice within a product class, consumers may see this as their normal task. In fact, there is little information available directly comparing product classes. Moreover, attributes may vary more across classes than within a single product class, making choice decisions among the former more complex. For example, nutritional value, cost, taste, and so on vary widely between peanut butter and vegetables, making it more difficult to eliminate any attribute as being the same among all alternatives. Howard notes that consumers often compare product classes in the extensive problem-solving stage of choice, during which criteria are not yet formed.[11] The lack of criteria complicates product-class choices.

From the marketer's viewpoint, providing information for choices among product classes represents a potentially useful strategy. One suggested approach is to focus on values as a means of classifying various kinds of products. Values can be terminal ("being") or instrumental ("doing"). (See Chapter 2, Table 2.1.) Terminal values appear to be more important than instrumental values in product-class choice.[12]

A study questioned homemakers who were considering the purchase of one or more of the following household appliances within the next three months:

Color television set.
Black-and-white television set.
Sewing machine.
Clothes dryer.
Dishwasher.
Vacuum cleaner.
Food freezer.
Refrigerator.

Terminal ("being") values were made operational as follows: "Being the kind of person who wishes":

"To have household possessions different from those of other people I know."
"To enjoy a high level of physical comfort at home."
"To have a beautiful home."

Instrumental ("doing") values included appearance, novelty, independence, and social consciousness. The researchers concluded that terminal values are related much more strongly than instrumental values to the product-class level of choice; instrumental values are related to brand choice.[13]

While further research is required in this area, the issue of choice among product classes has implications for some marketing decisions. When new products are being designed, for example, it would be useful to observe trends in changes in terminal values. Several syndicated services make periodic surveys of American values over a wide range of topics. Such surveys may be useful in indicating the sort of concept that can be easily incorporated in consumers' semantic networks. The terminal values of "a sense of accomplishment" and "self-respect" or "self-esteem" seem to be of importance to today's consumers. These values may account for the obvious success of such products as food processors and is reflected in the heavy emphasis on "this I do for me" in advertising campaigns.

In 1978 H. J. Heinz paid $121 million for Weight Watchers International, Inc., the largest weight-control chain in the world, and Foodways National, Inc., the U.S. licensee that produces Weight Watchers frozen entrées. Although other food giants declare that "it's very difficult to find low-calorie products that taste good and aren't too expensive," the Heinz acquisition is considered a "big step forward in an industry where new product development is time-consuming and costly." Clearly, Heinz's move indicates that the company sees a popular desire for weight-control food. According to one of its executives, the day may not be too distant when the symbol of beauty will be "a slender, athletic 'Heinz girl,' " who, of course, will owe her trim good looks to Weight Watchers classes and Heinz's foods.[14]

Terminal values may also be useful in the development of primary-demand advertising campaigns, such as those used by wool and cotton producers to limit the incursion of synthetics and by raisin producers to indicate that raisins are a good substitute for fresh fruit.

EVALUATING ALTERNATIVES AMONG BRANDS

In the marketplace, the consumer finds that the various product classes are represented by numerous brands. The consumer tends to devise a means of coping with the many brands of toothpaste, soap pads, frozen vegetables, and so on in making his purchase decision.

Evoked Set

One construct to explain a simplification method used by consumers in evaluating alternatives is the *evoked set*. A consumer is either aware or unaware of the existence of any product class. The set of brands in a given product class of which the consumer is aware can be called the awareness set. It is from among the brands in the awareness set that the consumer makes a purchase choice. But the consumer is likely to reduce his deliberative dilemma by narrowing the category further and making his purchase selection from a smaller group of brands, often referred to as an evoked set.

According to John A. Howard and Jagdish N. Sheth, "The brands that become alternatives to the buyer's choice decision are generally a small number, collectively called his 'evoked set.'" A brand "would be an element of the buyer's evoked set if he would consider it as an alternative if purchase decision were made now."[15]

Another concept has been used to provide a more complete explanation of the relative position of brands within the consumer's perception.[16] The *total set* concept can be seen in Figure 16.1. The total set (at any given time, *t*) is composed of all brands within a product category that exist in the market. The consumer may not be aware of all of the brands that exist, however; thus there is an *awareness set* and an *unawareness set*. The consumer may not consider buying some of these brands because she has insufficient information, she has tried and rejected them, she may already be satisfied with the brand she is currently using, she has received some negative feedback from word-of-mouth communication, and so on. These and other reasons lead to three subsets within the awareness set: *evoked set, inert set* (consisting of brands for which the consumer has insufficient information for evaluation), and *inept set* (consisting of those brands the consumer has rejected from purchase consideration).

In a research study, the minimum, maximum, and average number of brands in each set of several product categories were calculated. It was found that the minimum number of brands in any respondent's awareness set of toothpaste, for example, was 3; the maximum, 11; and the average, 6.5.[17] The sizes of other sets in the product categories of mouthwash, deodorant, and beer can be seen in Table 16.2.

FIGURE 16.1 THE "TOTAL SET" CONCEPT OF CONSUMER BEHAVIOR AND PRODUCT PERFORMANCE ($t'>t$)

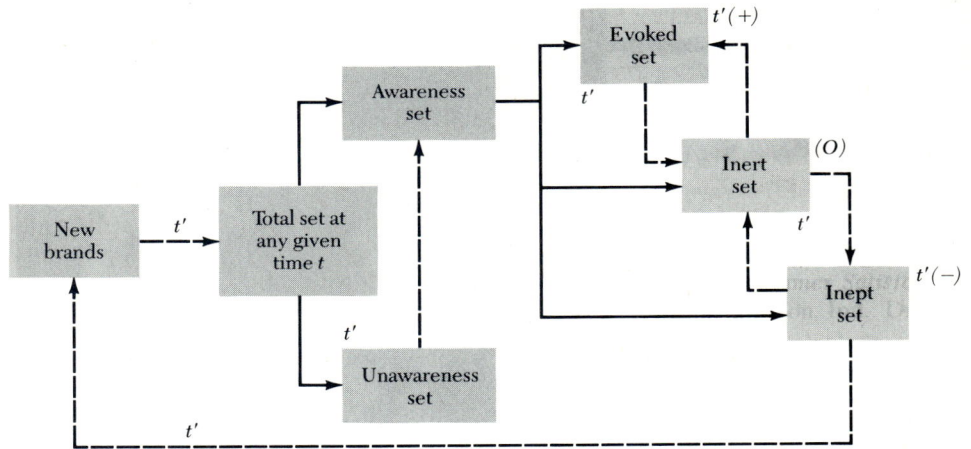

Source: Chem L. Narayana and Rom J. Markin, "Consumer Behavior and Product Performance: An Alternative Conceptualization," *Journal of Marketing* 39 (October 1975), p. 2

TABLE 16.2 NUMBER OF BRANDS IN FOUR PRODUCT SETS

Products and sets	Number of brands		
	Minimum	Maximum	Average
Toothpaste			
Awareness set	3	11	6.5
Evoked set	1	4	2.0
Inert set	0	8	2.0
Inept set	0	6	2.5
Mouthwash			
Awareness set	1	6	3.5
Evoked set	0	3	1.3
Inert set	0	5	1.2
Inept set	0	3	1.0
Deodorant			
Awareness set	1	11	6.0
Evoked set	0	4	1.6
Inert set	0	8	2.4
Inept set	0	8	2.0
Beer			
Awareness set	3	24	10.6
Evoked set	0	13	3.5
Inert set	0	15	4.7
Inept set	0	18	2.4

Source: Chem L. Narayana and Rom J. Markin, "Consumer Behavior and Product Performance: An Alternative Conceptualization," *Journal of Marketing* 39 (October 1975), p. 4.

With the exception of beer, none of the products had more than four brands in the evoked set of any respondent. A number of hypotheses were suggested from this study:

1. Consumers are aware of many more brands in any product category than they consider buying.

2. Consumers generally hold only a small number of brands in their evoked and inept sets.

3. A rather large number of brands about which the consumer is relatively neutral fall in the inert set, possibly because he lacks sufficient information about them. It is possible that if appropriate information were supplied, some brands in the inert set might move into the evoked set and thus enjoy consumer acceptance.

KINDS OF EVALUATIVE CRITERIA

Consumers can evaluate brands by many criteria, which vary from person to person, from product to product, and from situation to situation. Some criteria relate to the product's cost, such as price, installation cost, and maintenance cost. Others relate to its performance—durability, efficiency, materials used. Additional criteria encompass suitability—brand, image, appearance, style, color, size, and so on. Others include symbolic values or benefits, such as the perceived up-to-date characteristics of the product. Criteria for evaluation of alternatives may involve personal and interpersonal considerations, such as self-concept and social acceptance. Others relate to situational factors, such as the time and place of purchase and the reasons for purchase.

Typically, consumers use more than one criterion to evaluate alternatives; as we saw in Chapter 11, those selected are likely to be salient. While there are clearly many criteria, relatively few have been extensively investigated. Some of the evaluative criteria related to object (product) and situation variables that have been the subjects of research are discussed below.[18]

Price

A study on consumerism found that the number one problem that worries consumers is high prices.[19] It is clear that price is an important criterion for consumer choice. It is also clear, however, that price trade-offs occur; that is, many consumers are willing to trade off price for store cleanliness, quality of merchandise, convenience of shopping, and so on. Furthermore, although price may be seen as the amount of money exchanged for a product or service, it incorporates other factors, such as the amount and quality of the product, the time and place at which exchange will take place and payment will be made, the credit terms and discounts that apply to the transaction, guarantees, return privileges, and other factors.[20]

PRICE THRESHOLDS

As we saw in Chapter 7, consumers tend to establish price thresholds. The absolute threshold, which represents the minimum amount of a stimulus necessary to be noticed, is applied to pricing in the context of a hypothesis that suggests that consumers have a *range* of acceptable prices. Prices above this range may be perceived as too high, and those below it may be perceived as too low. One researcher reported the existence of a range for radios by asking the following:[21]

1. "Below what price would you suspect that a radio set was of poor quality?"
2. "Above what price would you judge a radio set to be too dear?"

Another study determined upper and lower price thresholds for nylon stockings, an underwear item, children's shoes, men's dress shirts, a gas lighter, and refrigerators.[22]

Little research has been reported on differential thresholds in pricing. Differential thresholds are based on Weber's Law, discussed earlier:

$$K = \frac{\Delta I}{I}$$

That is, the amount of stimulus change necessary for it to be noticed is a constant proportion of the initial stimulus. One of the difficulties involved in testing this thesis is that the K may not be constant for an individual over all price comparisons. According to Kent Monroe, "There is still no valid test of the applicability of Weber's Law to pricing."[23] Nevertheless, he suggests that in determining price differentials for products, marketers may consider the concept of just noticeable difference in reverse—that is, the prices of two products should not differ unless the products themselves are perceived by buyers to differ.[24]

DISCOUNT STRATEGIES

The widespread use of such practices as rebates seems to suggest that marketers assume the validity of Weber's Law. Rebates offer a greater change in stimulus than do discounts. Rebates, it should be noted, may offer protection against any improper evaluation of price-quality relationships on the part of the consumer, since the rebate may be seen as a temporary promotional effort, while a discount may seem to imply a reduction in product quality.

Other factors may affect the consumer's perception of a price-reduction strategy. To some consumers, a current reduction may be viewed as portending further cuts, so that they may defer their purchases. Moreover, in today's inflationary market, it appears that consumers may perceive a price increase as the first in a series, and therefore a price increase may accelerate their purchase decision.

ODD PRICE

The use of an odd price is based on an assumption that a price ending in an odd number will be associated in the consumer's mind with a lower price rather than with the next higher price. The demand curve for a product—the line on a graph indicating the number of units of the good that would be purchased at various prices—moves in a series of steps rather than in a smooth curve.[25] This finding suggests that sales will be greater at an odd price than at the next higher or lower even price. Therefore, we see more prices marked $1.95 or $4.98 than $2.00 or $5.00. Little published research, however, substantiates the supposed lure of the odd price.

Odd pricing is also used because it is assumed that prices ending with an odd number will increase price sensitivity. One early study concluded, however, that the dominance of pricing below the round figure in some markets may be largely an artifact.[26] That is, if sellers use odd pricing, then some consumers will consider the odd price as the real price and the round-figure price as incorrect and respond accordingly. No significant evidence, however, supports the psychological explanation of increased perceptual sensitivity. Before marketers adopt an odd pricing strategy, they should consider this lack of evidence of its efficiency and the potential losses from pricing each item a little less than a round number.

Package

While the package performs the functions of protection and containment and acts as a vehicle for information and promotion, it also provides the manufacturer with the final opportunity to persuade prospective buyers before brand selection. Through the introduction and promotion of the package, marketers may project a significant evaluative criterion for consumers' decision making.

Marketers devote a great deal of time to package development and often test packages to gauge consumer acceptance. Tests are also used to determine visibility and legibility of design elements by means of such devices as the tachistoscope, described in Chapter 7.

Manufacturers frequently make trade-offs in their packaging decisions on the basis of consumer preferences. Although dark bottles may provide greater protection for some contents, consumers' desire to see whether the contents are clear or contaminated may cause manufacturers to use the less protective light containers. Nevertheless, it is not always certain that consumers are willing to give up protection or that such trade-offs are desirable. Manufacturers frequently provide easy-open containers with pouring spouts and other convenience mechanisms even though these devices tend to minimize the package's protective elements. A research study to determine the extent to which consumers are willing to accept hard-to-open packages was conducted for potato chips. Consumers in two large supermarkets were offered potato chips in "easy-to-open" wax bags and in "hard-to-open" polyvinyl packages. Although the chips in the two packages showed no significant difference in earlier blind taste tests, a significant proportion of consumers perceived the chips in polyvinyl packages to be crisper and tastier than those in wax packages. Also, consumers appeared willing to sacrifice ease of opening for a fresher and crisper product. Taste, however, not packaging, was the most influential determinant in the purchase decision.[27]

While consumer package preference may be an important evaluative criterion, packaging decisions must incorporate ecological and manufacturers' requirements, as well as consumer requirements. Although consumers value convenience and adopted the spray can rapidly and extensively, ecological requirements now place restrictions on sprays that contain fluorocarbons. Consumer convenience also led to the popularity of nonreturnable containers, which are banned by a number of states. Some lightweight packaging, such as bottles made of plastic, are banned because they cannot be reused or destroyed.

Finding new packages designed to meet the requirements of all parties is sometimes difficult. The retort pouch, which was accepted by government agencies, had limited initial acceptance because of its relatively high cost, particularly in the packaging of such items as frozen foods.[28] The retort pouch was introduced as a means of encouraging comparisons among product classes (for example, dining at home with restaurant-type food as an alternative to dining out) and has been used to package food already processed and prepared.

The package may also serve as an information source for other evaluative criteria. Research has suggested that consumers select only limited amounts of information from available arrays of package information and tend to place substantial importance on prices and brand information.[29]

Cues

Frequently product attributes desired by consumers cannot be specified in terms of physical or even subjective characteristics—for example, quality and value. From an information-processing perspective, product brands in such cases consist of an array of cues (price, brand name, packaging, color). Rather than functioning as an evaluative criterion, each cue provides a basis for the development of various impressions of the product itself.[30] For example, the color red may be specified for the selection of a dress or an automobile, and therefore may be considered an evaluative criterion. It may also serve as a cue for an impression of products, such as the ripeness of an apple or the freshness of meat. Chapters 7 and 8 indicate that a consumer's response to a stimulus input is based on perceptual interpretations and encoding processes. Thus color, odor, package, and so on may be used as cues that permit the consumer to form judgments of products when such judgments are difficult to make merely on the basis of inspection or available information.

In 1973, when the feminist movement was in full swing, Revlon decided to emphasize the "natural look" with light lip gloss and subtle blushers, and introduced a "clean, fresh" blend of floral and herbal scents that Charles Revson, Revlon's president, named after himself: Charlie. Charlie was a great success, but when sales began to decline, Revlon concluded that although women want to "do their own thing," many still are romantic in the traditional manner. A new product that smelled more like gardenia—and that by common consent was a bit sexier than Charlie's jasmine—was introduced. The Jontue ads featured models wearing filmy white gowns amid swirling, silvery mists, and the copy proclaimed that thanks to Jontue, they were "sensual . . . yet with a touch of innocence." Jontue rocketed to second place in world fragrance sales, right behind Charlie.[31] Revlon's perfume strategy indicates the manner in which odor is used as a cue rather than as a specification to distinguish fragrances. In the same product area, Jovan won an award for package design with its distinctively sexual "Man" and "Woman" packages.

Cues may be either intrinsic or extrinsic.[32] Intrinsic cues are cues that, if changed, would produce a resultant change in the physical product itself (for example, flavor and aroma cues, size and color cues). Extrinsic cues are those external to the product, such as price and store image.

As noted in the illustration at the beginning of the chapter, marketers use varying strategies in selecting cues. Wendy's hamburger chain offers an intrinsic cue in its "hot and juicy" campaign as a means of judging quality, while McDonald's offers an extrinsic cue, low cost, as a means of judging value.

QUALITY CUES

While quality is important in the consumer's evaluation of brands, often it is difficult for consumers to discern quality differences. Under such circumstances, consumers may use cues to determine perceived product quality. The perceived quality of a product or brand is of considerable importance in consumer behavior.[33] In addition to being of interest in its own right, quality perception seems to be strongly related to actual purchasing behavior.[34]

When consumers cannot easily discern quality differences, they tend to use cues to evaluate product quality. A number of research studies have indicated that intrinsic cues, those that relate to physical product differences, have a greater effect on the perception of quality than do extrinsic cues.[35]

Marketers may use intrinsic cues as "surrogate" (substitute) indicators of product quality. Orange rinds are colored orange and apples red to indicate ripeness. Wonder Bread is produced and packaged so that its softness represents freshness. Odor is used to represent the cleaning power of cleansers either in strong ammonia scents or fresh pine scents.

Price/Quality Relationship. One area that has been the subject of a significant amount of research is the relationship between price and perception of quality. Originally, price/quality studies considered situations in which the only differential information available to respondents was price.[36] Harold Leavitt initiated these studies by asking respondents to choose between two differentially priced brands of four products (moth flakes, cooking sherry, razor blades, and floor wax) and then to indicate "degree of satisfaction" with their choice.[37] Subjects tended to be less satisfied when choosing lower priced brands and also tended to choose the higher priced brand when (1) price was the only differential information; (2) the products were perceived to be heterogeneous in quality; and (3) the price difference was large. When this experiment was replicated by Donald Tull and his associates with the use of table salt, aspirin, floor wax, and liquid shampoo, respondents tended to choose the higher priced brands of products perceived to be heterogeneous.[38]

A frequent criticism of the single-cue studies is that when price is the only information available, subjects naturally associate price and quality. To overcome this criticism, other price/quality studies have been performed that experimentally varied other cues in addition to price. Although single-cue studies unanimously observed a price/quality relationship, the multicue studies often found little direct relationship between price and perceived quality.

Nevertheless, at times marketers have found that low-priced products presented in a tawdry, unattractive way did not sell well. When this merchandise was reticketed to show a higher price, it sold more readily.

Brand Name/Quality Relationship. The findings of some multicue studies indicate that brand name is probably more important than price as a quality cue for relatively inexpensive grocery products and beverages. For clothing, there is an apparent increasing concern with price, although price may not always overcome the influence of brand name. In those studies in which brand names were part of the manipulations, the brand influence was seemingly stronger than the price influence.

One study of beer drinkers—a test in which the beers were labeled—clearly indicated that beer drinkers would assign superior ratings to the brands they regularly drank. It was assumed that if participants could identify their brands in the blind test, they would respond to them with superior ratings. In a blind test (all the labels and other identifying marks on the bottles were removed), *none* of the beer drinkers rated the taste of their brands over all of the others.[39]

It should be noted that the overall ratings for all of the brands increased considerably with brand identifications. Participants, in general, did not appear to be able to discern the taste differences among the various beer brands, but apparently labels and their associations did influence their evaluations. In other words, product distinctions or differences, in the minds of the participants, arose primarily through brand images rather than through perceived physical product differences. As we noted earlier, brand names appear to perform a chunking function, that is, they provide a means by which consumers can combine information about a product.

Brand Loyalty

The extent to which a brand name is significant as an evaluative criterion or cue relates to the concept of brand loyalty. Brand loyalty, which in general is the tendency of some consumers to purchase a particular brand consistently, is subject to varying interpretations. One definition of brand loyalty indicates that it is not simply repeat purchasing behavior but should be defined in terms of six necessary and collectively sufficient conditions. According to this definition, brand loyalty is a (1) biased (that is, nonrandom) (2) behavioral response (purchase) (3) expressed over time (4) by some decision-making unit (5) with respect to one or more alternative brands out of a set of such brands, and (6) is a function of psychological (decision-making, evaluative) processes.[40]

This definition suggests, among other things, that individuals can be and frequently are multibrand loyal, that is, loyal to two or more brands in a product category. It also indicates that brand loyalty is preferential behavior toward one or more alternatives out of a field containing competing alternatives. Brand loyalty serves an acceptance-rejection function. Not only does it "select in" certain brands, but it also "selects out" certain others.

As researchers tend to define brand loyalty in a number of ways, it is difficult to compare and synthesize their findings. Nevertheless, they have found conclusive evidence of the existence of brand loyalty.[41] One marketing strategy involving such findings suggests the use of brand loyalty as a basis for market segmentation. The marketer may create more brand-loyal consumers for the firm either by capturing users of competitors' products and nonusers or by increasing the use rate of brand-loyal consumers. The problem with this strategy is that in many cases it is difficult to distinguish between brand-loyal and other consumers.

Brand names may be more important for some products than for others. In a survey to determine which products were most often shopped for by brand, the J. Walter Thompson advertising agency determined that personal-care products rated highest.[42] The highest brand-loyalty rating went to toothpaste, with more than two-thirds of the respondents saying they looked for a particular brand. Other high-brand-loyalty personal products included deodorants, antiperspirants, mouthwashes, and toilet soaps.

In household products, there was significant brand loyalty for detergents, but only one-fourth of the respondents indicated that they looked for a particular brand of paper towels. More than half of those surveyed indicated they looked for brands in the purchase of TV sets and cameras. The lowest-ranking brand-loyalty score occurred for shoes.

The significance of brand names may undergo changes in the future. Of particular interest to marketers is the rather extensive inroads made by the so-called generic products—also known as "no-frills," "no-name," and brandless items—in the grocery marketing field. These products appear to have generated more sales than industry observers had expected. A review of companies offering generics made in the fourth quarter of 1978 revealed that some generic items were being offered in more than 8,000 supermarkets across the country, and the number appears to be growing.[43] The popularity of such products may be a reflection of growing consumer awareness of inflationary pressures (since the items are sold below national and store-brand prices). Some no-frills items that are being sold in supermarkets appear in Exhibit 16.1.

EXHIBIT 16.1

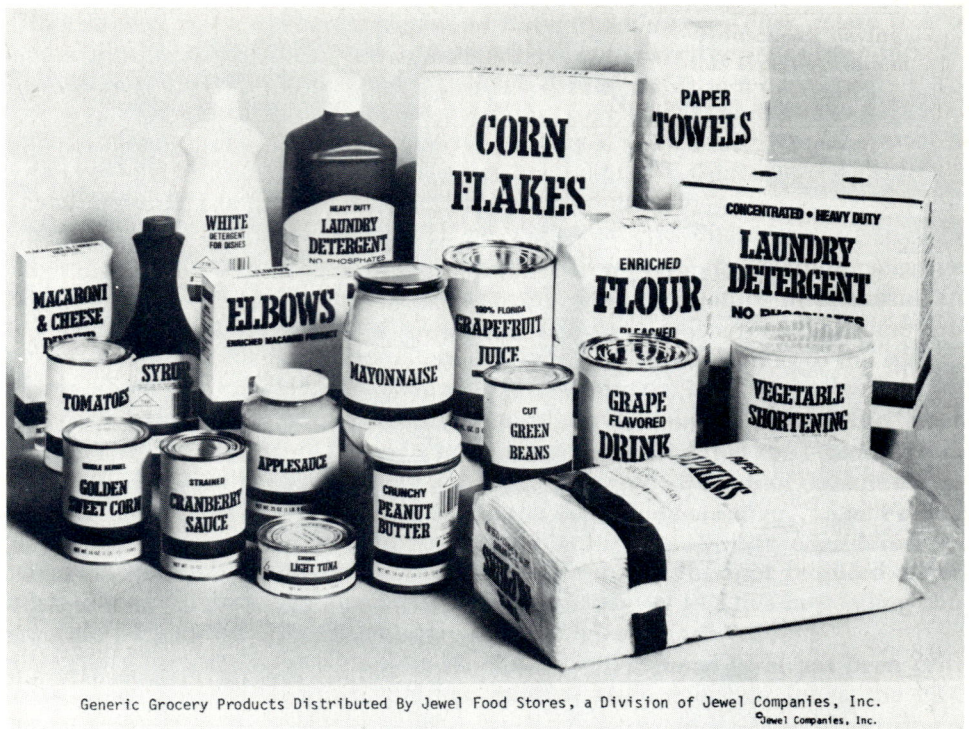

Generic Grocery Products Distributed By Jewel Food Stores, a Division of Jewel Companies, Inc.
                                                                    ᵒJewel Companies, Inc.

No frills personified
Source: "Products Step into the Limelight," *Advertising Age,* January 8, 1978, p. S6.

Advertising

The extent to which heavy advertising of a product may serve as a cue in the judging of quality and value is not clear. A study was conducted to examine the relationship between customer perceptions of brand quality and the extent to which the brand was perceived as being nationally advertised.[44] Three brands of peanut butter were displayed in identical and unmarked containers and female students were asked to taste one and rate it on their perceptions of product quality and the likelihood that the tested peanut butter was a nationally advertised brand. According to the researchers' findings, brands perceived by the respondents as being high in quality were also viewed as more likely to be nationally advertised than brands perceived as low in quality. Moreover, purchase intentions were positively correlated with perceptions of quality. The researchers concluded that advertising per se, by influencing perceptions of quality, may affect consumer purchase behavior.

SITUATIONAL VARIABLES

Psychologists have traditionally explained a person's behavior in general and consumer behavior in particular as a function of two classes of variables. One set of variables describes differences in persons. The other class of variables describes differences in environments—an environment being anything that is external to the person whose behavior is explained and that can be measured independently of that person, including both the objects purchased and the setting. Evidence has shown that behavioral variability remains when the person is the same but the environment changes.[45]

As differences in persons and in external factors relating to products purchased cannot explain all variations in buying behavior, attention has turned to the other environmental factors that may partially explain consumer choice. One environmental influence is designated as a situation. A simple definition suggests that a situation comprises a point in time and space. It is seen as a subunit within an environment; situations represent momentary encounters with those elements of the total environment that are available to an individual at a particular time.

A situation may then be defined as all of those factors particular to a time and place of observation which do not follow from a knowledge of personal and stimulus (object) attributes, and which have a demonstrable and systematic effect on current behavior.[46] The following five groups of situational characteristics are consistent with this definition:[47]

1. *Physical surroundings* are the most readily apparent features of a situation. They include geographical and institutional location, decor, sounds, aromas, lighting, weather, and visible configurations of merchandise or other materials surrounding the stimulus object.

2. *Social surroundings* include other persons present, their characteristics, their apparent roles, and the interpersonal reactions occurring. For example, in retail settings, the mere presence of children or a friend has been observed to alter purchase outcome.[48]

3. *Temporal perspective* is a dimension of situations that may be specified in units ranging from time of day to season of the year. Time may also be measured relative to some past or future event, such as time since last purchase.

Time, as an important variable relative to consumer behavior, is currently the focus of research interest. Relatively few empirical contributions, however, appear in the marketing literature concerning the importance of time in consumer behavior.

Philip Kotler notes that Americans are increasingly placing more value on time than on goods.[49] In discussing the determinants of choice process intensity—that is, the amount of information processing that is carried out by the individual—James Bettman notes that the intensity may be determined by the degree of conflict present.[50] Such conflicts were described in Chapter 9, in the discussion of approach-approach, approach-avoidance, and avoidance-avoidance tendencies. According to Bettman, time pressure can be one source of conflict; under time pressure the consumer may find simple choices if total conflict is too high.

Research by Peter Wright indicated that consumers under severe time pressure may use a simplifying strategy whereby they tend to place greater weight on negative product information than would consumers under less time pressure.[51] Others have indicated that "buyers under time pressure are less likely to adopt new brands";[52] there is some evidence, for example, that jobholding wives are less inclined to adopt new brands.[53] Findings that working wives generally spend less time grocery shopping, buy more convenience foods, and tend to be more brand loyal than nonworking wives appear to indicate that being brand loyal and purchasing national brands are the two most common strategies that consumers employ to reduce the time, risk, inconvenience, and effort spent in getting a product adjusted, repaired, or replaced.[54]

Other research indicates that the lack of available time prohibits adequate use of information.[55] This finding suggests that price information should be designed to reach the consumer during times of inactivity, rather than, for example, at the shopping site. Thus cable television, take-home price booklets, and even circulars distributed to the home provide price information that is more likely to be used.

4. *Task definition* includes an intent or requirement to select, shop for, or obtain information about a general or specific purchase. In addition, task may reflect different buyer and user roles anticipated by the individual. For example, researchers found that selection of a hair dryer as a gift depended on characteristics of the supposed recipient and that buyers of tableware used different types and sources of information depending on whether the purchase was intended for personal use or as a gift.[56]

5. *Antecedent states* are momentary moods (such as acute anxiety, pleasantness, hostility) or momentary conditions (such as cash on hand, fatigue, illness). One researcher was able to condition choice of specific cigarette brands to either stressful or boring situations and to consumption of a specific brand of beer.[57]

Most of the examination of situational effects in consumer choice behavior deals with differences across products. A recent study suggested that situational effects may vary across brands. According to the researcher, such situational variations of behavior may occur in a closely competitive product category—specifically, fast foods. Wendy's, for example, had a higher mean proportion of "evening meal for the family when rushed for time" than of any other situations.[58] From a strategic standpoint, if a product characteristic is more important in one situation than in others, it may be useful to promote it in that situation.

SHOPPING BEHAVIOR

Though shopping behavior does not precisely fall under the rubric of "consumer purchase decision process," it nevertheless is relevant to a discussion of alternative evaluation. The range of tasks performed by the consumer is very broad, with decisions being made not only at many levels (criteria, brand, and so on), but also in various task environments, from ordering out of a catalog to searching through a supermarket. Much of the information processed by consumers as they make their decisions comes from memory; the shopping site provides consumers with a form of "external" memory. The information on packages or other displays can serve as external memory for the consumer, available at the time the alternative is obtained; that is, the consumer can actually examine this information in the store, without needing to rely totally on her own memory.[59]

The significance of this external memory component is that the type of information presented may differ from that appearing elsewhere. Displays, counter cards, and other point-of-purchase materials provide information under conditions that differ from those in which decisions are made before the consumer enters the store. The consumer may have little prior experience, the decision may be difficult for some reason, or the consumer may feel low involvement in the decision.[60] External memory may be important even when the consumer has made the same sort of choice many times; if he feels low involvement in the choice, he may have stored little information in memory. Thus, alternatives may be evaluated during the shopping experience.

Shopping Motivations

To secure the products or services they need or desire, consumers engage in purchasing activity. For the marketer, the purchase activity is the outcome toward which all of her marketing efforts have been directed. The act of purchase occurs during a consumer's shopping experience, and therefore the marketer would like to encourage such shopping activity.

The simplest explanation of what causes people to shop is the need to purchase something. An analysis of various shopping expeditions, however, indicates that such activity may provide more than the utility of the merchandise purchased; the shopping process itself may, in fact, offer satisfaction. An understanding of the motives for shopping may be useful in encouraging such activity.

A number of motives have been hypothesized for the shopping experience. They can be either personal or social.[61]

PERSONAL MOTIVES

Role Playing. Many activities are learned behaviors, traditionally expected as part of a certain position or role in society—mother, housewife, husband, and so on. Thus grocery shopping is a customary activity of the housewife, and one in which she routinely engages.

Diversion. Shopping may represent a form of recreation and offer an opportunity for diversion from the routine of daily life. Shoppers frequently state they are "just browsing," and masses of people appear to stroll through shopping centers and engage in relatively little or no purchasing.

Self-Gratification. A person may go to a store to buy "something nice" for himself when he is depressed, or may merely alleviate depression by spending money on himself.

Learning about New Trends. An individual may learn about trends and movements and the symbols that support them when she visits a store. Many people are interested in keeping informed about the latest trends in fashion, styling, or products, and find they do so best through shopping activity.

Physical Activity. Shopping can provide people with a considerable amount of exercise. Some shoppers apparently welcome the chance to walk in shopping centers and malls that have been designed with internal throughways. The advent of enclosed malls has made it possible to walk comfortably from store to store in all kinds of weather.

Sensory Stimulation. Retail institutions may provide many sensory benefits for shoppers. Sounds that emanate from the shopping centers, smells that come from the various kinds of foods, and perfumes that pervade the air may be welcome influences on the shopping trip and may provide relief from boredom.

SOCIAL MOTIVES

Social Experiences Outside the Home. Shopping may offer the opportunity to make new acquaintances. Some shopping trips may result in direct encounters with friends or may just incorporate "people watching," thus minimizing loneliness.

Communication with Others with Similar Interests. Stores can offer hobby products and services—boating and fishing equipment, stamps and coins for collectors, needlework materials and instructions—and can offer a focal point where people with similar interests can interact.

Peer-Group Attraction. Sometimes people desire to be with their peer group or a reference group to which they aspire to belong. For instance, record stores are common hangouts for teenagers. Shopping in expensive stores offers satisfaction for strivers.

Status and Authority. Many shopping experiences provide an individual with an opportunity to command attention and respect. Many people can expect to be "waited on" and to appear in a superior rather than a subordinate position in few other contexts.

Pleasure of Bargaining. For many shoppers, bargaining is a degrading activity. Others, however, appear to enjoy the process, believing that bargaining can bring prices to more reasonable levels.

These hypothesized shopping motives may offer strategy suggestions to marketers. They may offer additional opportunities for market segmentation and store differentiation. Such product-related store benefits as quality lines, low prices, and credit can be easily duplicated by the competition. Thus the ability to gain a distinct differential advantage may depend on catering to shopping motives that are not product-related.

Shopping-Site Selection

The availability and popularity of many kinds of shopping sites attest to the variability of people's preference in the milieus in which shopping takes place. Some people prefer local stores, others nearby shopping centers, and still others choose sites that are quite distant from their homes. In addition, some people like to shop in their homes and purchase many items through catalogs or from door-to-door salespeople.

A search of the literature on buyer behavior reveals surprisingly little knowledge of the way people choose the stores in which they shop.[62] It appears that people establish evaluative criteria not only for the products they purchase but also for the stores where those products are sold. Some of these criteria are:

1. Ease of travel and access to the store.
2. Quality of merchandise.
3. Quantity and assortment of merchandise.
4. Price.
5. Demeanor of store personnel.
6. Store atmosphere (lighting, cleanliness, and so forth).
7. Feeling of comfort and ease while shopping.

In a study designed to examine the relationship between retail store patronage and some of these criteria, some of the results were predictable.[63] Ease of travel and access was the prime consideration in the choice of a store for a shopping trip for food and sundries; this criterion was less important in the choice of a store for clothing.

The importance of shopping-site attributes varies by store type. For example, one study found that except for dependable products, the top ten and the bottom five attributes were different for grocery stores and department stores. (See Table 16.3.)

For retailers and for manufacturers who display their merchandise in retail institutions, it may be useful to determine consumers' attitudes toward retail stores. Such information may be useful in determining how the site may be improved to encourage patronage and to enhance the purchase situation.

Scaling techniques, such as the Osgood semantic differential, discussed earlier, may be a useful device for detecting store attitudes. One method of increasing the effectiveness of this device is to develop tailor-made semantic differential in-

TABLE 16.3   TOP TEN AND BOTTOM FIVE ATTRIBUTES OF DEPARTMENT AND GROCERY STORES

	Attributes	
Rank	Department store	Grocery store
Top ten		
1	Dependable products	Dependable products
2	Fair on adjustments	Store is clean
3	High value for money	Easy to find items you want
4	High-quality products	Fast checkout
5	Easy to find items you want	High-quality products
6	Fast checkout	High value for the money
7	Helpful personnel	Fully stocked
8	Easy to return purchases	Helpful store personnel
9	Easy to exchange purchases	Easy to move through store
10	Store is clean	Adequate number of store personnel
Bottom five°		
1	Store is liked by friends	Easy to get home delivery
2	Many friends shop there	Lay-away available
3	Store is known by friends	Easy to get credit
4	Company operates many stores	Many friends shop there
5	Lay-away available	Store is liked by friends

° "1" indicates least important.

Source: Adapted from Robert A. Hansen and Terry Deutscher, "An Empirical Investigation of Attribute Importance in Retail Store Selection," *Journal of Retailing* 53 (Winter 1977–78), pp. 59–72.

struments. For example, a useful technique may be to use phrases rather than adjectives as descriptors of a store. Table 16.4 presents a list of such contrasting adjectives useful in analyzing a store's image, or consumers' attitude toward a store.

Display

Displays are considered important in many retail strategies and it is clear that a sizable percentage of total sales by a supermarket is secured through display. The effects of display on other retailing institutions, however, as well as the effect of display variations in supermarkets, are less certain. Despite the inadequacy of research evidence, many large manufacturers of grocery products intuitively feel that some shelf positions are better than others. Most studies that have been conducted relate to placement of grocery products.

Traditionally, the eye-level shelf is considered most effective in display of food products. It is obvious, however, that if the product displayed caters to chil-

TABLE 16.4 BIPOLAR NOMINALLY CONTRASTING ADJECTIVES AND PHRASES

crammed merchandise—well-spaced merchandise
bright store—dull store
ads frequently seen by you—ads infrequently seen by you
low-quality products—high-quality products
well-organized layout—unorganized layout
low prices—high prices
bad sales on products—good sales on products
unpleasant store to shop in—pleasant store to shop in
good store—bad store
inconvenient location—convenient location
low-pressure salesmen—high-pressure salesmen
big store—small store
bad buys on products—good buys on products
unattractive store—attractive store
unhelpful salesmen—helpful salesmen
good service—bad service
too few clerks—too many clerks
friendly personnel—unfriendly personnel
easy to return purchases—hard to return purchases
unlimited selection of products—limited selection of products
unreasonable prices for value—reasonable prices for value
messy—neat
spacious shopping—crowded shopping
attracts upper-class customers—attracts lower-class customers
dirty—clean
fast checkout—slow checkout
good displays—bad displays
hard to find items you want—easy to find items you want
bad specials—good specials

Source: John A. Dickson and Gerald Albaum, "Method for Developing Tailor-made Semantic Differentials for Specific Marketing Content Areas," *Journal of Marketing Research* 14 (February 1977), p. 89.

dren, lower shelves should be used. Moreover, the heaviest or bulkiest products may be sold more easily from low-level or waist-level shelves, since high shelves make it difficult for the customer to take them down. The highest shelves may also be inaccessible to many customers, and they may be reluctant to request help.

Nevertheless, the true effects of shelf placement are not clear. Most studies involving shelf positioning of grocery products have provided results that are confounded by the store itself, the size of the container, and the brand differences in sales. In one study contradictory results emerged: an analysis of some of the results for a specified product revealed that the lower shelves were more effective; other results suggested the middle and upper shelves were more effective.[64] The authors concluded that there was no interaction between the effect of shelf level and normal sales. Nevertheless, they indicated that the results may differ in the long run, since the study did not test the cumulative effects over time.

It appears that the impact of display on sales may depend on the product selected. One study attempted to isolate other factors that might increase this impact, such as the stage of the product's life cycle, the amount of advertising, the extent of the price cut that accompanied the display, and the competitive structure of the market for the product.[65] The findings may be useful to marketers who wish to adopt a display strategy.

When displayed with a price reduction, products that are in their growth stage (storage bags, semimoist dog foods, facial tissues) increase their sales *less* than products in the mature stage (bleach, mayonnaise, detergent, cooking oil).

The advertising-to-sales ratio of various products has no direct impact on the effectiveness of displaying these products with a price reduction. This finding suggests that the level of advertising in the product category has no impact on the effectiveness of display.

Variations in the amount of price reduction that accompanies the display do not appear to have any impact on its effectiveness. When the competitive structure is such that some products have similar positions and no one product has a clear market-share advantage, the average increase in sales resulting from a display with price reduction is higher than in competitive structures in which no such display is mounted.

These findings, which require additional research for verification, suggest that an appropriate product to select for display is one that is in the mature stage of its life cycle and has no competitors that enjoy strong market positions. They also suggest that a deep cut in price need not accompany such displays, since a threshold price cut may be as effective.

Impulse Purchases

Although many shopping trips are planned in the sense that the purchases are predetermined, many items are bought on impulse. "Impulse purchase" and "unplanned purchase" are often used synonymously. Unplanned purchases are not confined to any product or retail setting and in fact have included such products as jewelry, hardware items, furniture, drugs and toiletries, and grocery products.[66]

Although impulse purchasing is a widely recognized type of behavior, there is no clear consensus about the meaning of the phenomenon. The following definitions indicate the variety of explanations for this concept:[67]

1. An impulse purchase is an unplanned, spur-of-the-moment decision to purchase a product.

2. An impulse purchase is a logical and efficient way of making purchase decisions, since by waiting until one is in the store to finalize purchase intentions, one can often make a more comprehensive and realistic evaluation of the purchase alternatives.

3. There is no such thing as an impulse purchase. Rather, there are four types of unplanned purchases: (1) *pure impulse* is a novelty or escape purchase

that breaks a normal buying pattern; (2) *reminder impulse* occurs when a shopper sees an item or recalls an advertisement or other information and remembers that the stock at home is low or exhausted; (3) *suggestion impulse* occurs when a shopper sees a product for the first time and visualizes a need for it; and (4) *planned impulse* takes place when the shopper makes specific purchase decisions on the basis of price specials, coupon offers, and the like.

There are also differences of opinion about why impulse purchasing occurs. A widely accepted hypothesis is that in-store stimuli produce unplanned purchases because (1) shoppers make some purchase decisions at the store rather than relying solely on a shopping list and (2) in-store promotional techniques result in shoppers' recognizing new ways of satisfying needs.[68]

Several studies have indicated that in-store stimuli can trigger unplanned purchases. For example, it has been demonstrated that *store location* of such products as bread and dairy products is instrumental in precipitating unplanned purchases of surrounding products. Such promotional techniques as point-of-purchase *displays, signs,* and *shelf extenders* have in some instances proven effective in stimulating impulse purchases.

End-aisle displays, which do sometimes stimulate impulse purchases of the items placed at the end of the aisle, do not necessarily increase the total profit picture for the retail store. The purchasers may merely be stocking up on an item for future use. The displays, in fact, may discourage the customer from traversing the entire aisle, precluding additional purchases.

It would be useful if the concept of impulse purchasing became more precisely defined. If, for example, unplanned purchasing could be related to in-store purchase decisions, a manufacturer could use rates of unplanned purchasing of his brand as a measure of the effectiveness of both his advertising and his in-store promotional strategy.

Catalog Purchases

The rapid rise in catalog purchases presents an interesting phenomenon in retailing. More and more consumers are turning to catalogs for their purchasing activity. Some people say that catalog sales are increasing more rapidly than retail sales. Historically, the basic function of the mail-order catalog was convenient shopping—a highly desirable alternative to consumers faced with the need to travel long distances to stores, the frustrations of congested street traffic, the difficulties of finding parking spaces, and crowded stores.

Price, return privileges, and selections are believed to have provided the foundation for the acceptance of catalog retailing during its early years. More recent studies suggest that selection continues to be a primary appeal, particularly in smaller communities where the catalog is the "largest store in town." It is suggested that the current and future strength of the catalog lies in items that are unusual, new, and fashionable—those that provide the uniqueness or distinctiveness that appeals to the self-confident and venturesome frequent catalog buyer.[69]

One study explored three factors that affect catalog buying behavior: convenience, offering, and degree of risk. The researcher hypothesized that catalog buying is more likely to appeal to persons who can afford its convenience and to those who need it or think they need it because of the time it saves. The merchandise assortment was probably greater than can be found under one roof, if at all, in many localities, and it consists of more fashionable styles and unusual items, often at relatively low prices. As for the degree of risk, consumers must be willing to take some risk in catalog buying.

Catalog buyers reported lower opinions of local shopping conditions than their nonbuyer neighbors. This finding confirmed the impression that availability, quality, and assortment of merchandise and lower price were among the most frequent reasons for catalog ordering. The hypothesis that catalog buyers are more price-conscious than nonbuyers, however, was not supported by the data. As for risk taking, the data did, in fact, reveal that the catalog buyer tends to be younger, more venturesome, and more self-confident. As far as convenience was concerned, however, frequent catalog buyers seem to be motivated by a desire for convenient shopping in some situations but not in others. In general, the findings seem to indicate that catalog buying is to a great degree a result of the strength of catalog offerings.[70]

A useful marketing strategy might be one designed to reach the frequent catalog buyer. Special promotions and copy should be developed to be consistent with the life-style of the frequent-buyer segment. Announcement and display messages emphasizing the catalog merchant's assortment and unique items can subtly capitalize on poor attitudes toward local shopping conditions in smaller urban areas. Illustrations may be designed to depict user images congruent with the venturesomeness of the frequent buyers. Another strategy that might be useful is to employ greater use of smaller, supplemental catalogs that can be matched more closely with the life-styles of the key segment.

The key segment in the purchase of a particular product may be revealed through research of the heavy user. For example, a profile of the woman who buys over half of her cosmetics in the home was disclosed in a study. In comparison with the woman who buys over half of her cosmetics in a retail store, the heavy in-home buyer:[71]

1. Has less access to a car for daytime shopping.
2. Tends to be less well educated.
3. Is likely to have more children living at home.
4. Is more likely to have a family income under $15,000 annually.
5. Is a member of a household whose head will be a blue-collar worker, clerical employee, or salesman rather than a professional.

A useful strategy would be one that devised a catalog featuring cosmetics that provide for the needs of the consumer resembling this individual.

SUMMARY

Evaluative criteria by which consumers compare alternatives emanate from values, motives, information, and experience. Relatively little market information is available for consumer choice among product classes; much more is available for evaluation of alternatives among brands. In evaluating brand alternatives, the consumer considers an "evoked set"—that is, a relatively small group of the total brands available are included in the consumer's purchase selection process.

There are many kinds of evaluative criteria by which consumers may evaluate brands. Evaluative criteria may vary on the basis not only of person and object (product) variables but of situational variables. Product criteria may take the form of specifications (such as price and package requirements) or cues, which provide a basis for the development of various impressions (for example, quality and value) of the product itself. Changes in the environment can cause changes in behavior that are independent of the person and product. Such factors as physical and social surroundings, temporal perspective, task definition, and antecedent states incorporate situations that may have a demonstrable effect on consumer purchase behavior.

Shopping sites provide consumers with external memory and are therefore a source of information for the evaluation of alternatives. Consumers engage in shopping for personal and social motives. Various criteria may be used by consumers in selecting the stores they patronize. Displays may influence the alternative evaluation process, and impulse sales may be triggered by in-store stimuli.

DISCUSSION QUESTIONS

1. What kinds of evaluative criteria did you use when you made your last major purchase?

2. How many brands of coffee exist in your "evoked set"? How might a coffee manufacturer shift a brand from your "inert set" to your "evoked set"?

3. Why isn't price always a major evaluative criterion?

4. Describe a product in terms of its extrinsic and intrinsic cues.

5. How do you determine quality? Does advertising have any influence on this determination?

6. Do you agree that Americans are increasingly placing more value on time than on goods? Explain.

7. It has been suggested that the new computerized "at-home" techniques will virtually eliminate shopping in stores. Do you agree or disagree? Explain.

8. How do you select your shopping site? What suggestions would you make in regard to store layout that would increase your satisfaction in shopping at a store you patronize frequently?

9. How does the situation in which the purchase is made influence purchase behavior?

10. What is meant by the term "impulse-prone"? How would the marketer reach those who are impulse-prone?

NOTES

1. Larry Edwards, "Premium Diapers Gear for Eastern Clash," *Advertising Age*, September 25, 1978, p. 136.

2. Christy Marshall, "McDonald's '79 Plan: Beat Back the Competition," *Advertising Age*, February 19, 1979, p. 1.

3. "Wendy's Sales Growth Stays Hot and Juicy," *Advertising Age*, February 19, 1979, p. 89.

4. James F. Engel, Richard D. Blackwell, and David T. Kollat, *Consumer Behavior*, 3d ed. (New York: Holt, Rinehart & Winston, 1978), p. 365.

5. John A. Howard, *Consumer Behavior: Applications of Theory* (New York: McGraw-Hill, 1977), p. 28.

6. Engel et al., *Consumer Behavior*, p. 367.

7. Donald E. Vinson, Jerome E. Scott, and Lawrence M. Lamont, "The Role of Personal Values in Marketing and Consumer Behavior," *Journal of Marketing* 41 (April 1977), pp. 44–50.

8. Howard, *Consumer Behavior*, p. 139.

9. *Marketing News*, November 19, 1976, p. 6.

10. James R. Bettman, *An Information-Processing Theory of Consumer Choice* (Reading, Mass.: Addison-Wesley, 1979), p. 153.

11. Howard, *Consumer Behavior*, p. 87.

12. Ibid., p. 92.

13. Ibid., p. 100.

14. "Heinz Leaps into Low Calories," *Business Week*, March 5, 1979, pp. 57–58.

15. John A. Howard and Jagdish N. Sheth, *The Theory of Buyer Behavior* (New York: John Wiley, 1969), pp. 26, 212.

16. Chem L. Narayana and Rom J. Markin, "Consumer Behavior and Product Performance: An Alternative Conceptualization," *Journal of Marketing* 39 (October 1975), pp. 1–6.

17. Ibid., pp. 3–5.

18. Chapters 2–6 examine "person" variables. Chapter 11 describes some techniques to determine salient attributes.

19. "New Harris Consumer Study Causes Few Shocks in Adland," *Advertising Age*, May 30, 1977, p. 74.

20. D. V. Harper, *Price Policy and Procedure* (New York: Harcourt Brace & World, 1966), pp. 1–2.

21. Jean Stoetzel, "Psychological/Sociological Aspects of Price," in *Pricing Strategy*, ed. Bernard Taylor and Gordon Wills (Princeton, N.J.: Brandon System Press, 1970), pp. 70–74.

22. Daniel Adam, *Les réactions du consummateur devant le prix* (Paris: SEDES, 1958).

23. Kent B. Monroe, "Buyers' Subjective Perceptions of Price," *Journal of Marketing Research* 10 (February 1973), p. 76.

24. Kent B. Monroe and Albert J. Dalla Bitta, "Models for Pricing Decisions," *Journal of Marketing Research* 15 (August 1978), p. 419.

25. Matilda Frankel, "A Summary Report: What Do We Know about Consumer Behavior?" prepared for National Science Foundation Directorate for Research Applications, RANN, p. 18.

26. André Gabor and Clive Granger, "Price Sensitivity of the Consumer," *Journal of Advertising Research* 4 (December 1964), pp. 40–44.

27. Carl McDaniel and R. C. Baker, "Convenience Food Packaging and Perception of Product Quality," *Journal of Marketing* 41 (October 1977), pp. 57–58.

28. Larry Edwards, "Green Light for Retort Pouch; Marketers Go Slowly," *Advertising Age*, June 6, 1977, p. 36.

29. Jacob Jacoby, George J. Szybillo, and Jacqueline Busato-Schach, "Information Acquisition Behavior in Brand Choice Situations," *Journal of Consumer Research* 3 (March 1977), p. 214.

30. Jerry C. Olson and Jacob Jacoby, "Cue Utilization in the Quality Perception Process," *Association for Consumer Research, Proceedings of the 3rd Annual Conference* (1972), ed. M. Venkatesan, pp. 167–179.

31. "Cosmetics: Kiss and Sell," *Time*, December 11, 1978, pp. 86–96.

32. George J. Szybillo and Jacob Jacoby, "Intrinsic Cues versus Extrinsic Cues as Determinants of Perceived Product Quality," *Journal of Applied Psychology* 59 (February 1974), pp. 74–77.

33. Jacob Jacoby, Jerry C. Olson, and R. A. Haddock, "Price, Brand Name and Product Composition Characteristics as Determinants of Perceived Quality," *Journal of Applied Psychology* 55 (December 1971), pp. 570–579.

34. Jacob Jacoby, "A Model of Multi-brand Loyalty," *Journal of Advertising Research* 11 (June 1971), pp. 25–31.

35. Jerry C. Olson and Jacob Jacoby, "Cue Utilization and the Quality Perception Process," *Association for Consumer Research, Proceedings of the 3rd Annual Conference* (1972), ed. M. Venkatesan, pp. 167–179.

36. Monroe, "Buyers' Subjective Perceptions of Price," pp. 70–80.

37. Harold Leavitt, "A Note on Some Experimental Findings about the Meaning of Price," *Journal of Business* 27 (July 1954), pp. 205–210.

38. Donald Tull, R. A. Boring, and M. H. Gonsior, "A Note on the Relationship of Price and Imputed Quality," *Journal of Business* 37 (April 1964), pp. 186–191.

39. Ralph I. Allison and Kenneth P. Uhl, "Brand Identification and Perception," in *Perspectives in Consumer Behavior*, ed. Harold Kassarjian and Thomas S. Robertson, rev. ed. (Glenview, Ill.: Scott-Foresman, 1973), pp. 17–22.

40. Jacob Jacoby and David B. Kyner, "Brand Loyalty vs. Repeat Purchasing Behavior," *Journal of Marketing Research* 10 (February 1973), pp. 2–3.

41. Engel et al., *Consumer Behavior*, p. 474.

42. "Personal Care Area Has Most Brand Loyalty: JWT Study," *Advertising Age*, January 24, 1977, p. 12.

43. "Generic Groceries Keep Adding Market Share," *Marketing News*, February 23, 1979, p. 1.

44. Arch G. Woodside and James L. Taylor, "Consumer Purchase Intentions and Perceptions of Product Quality and National Advertising," *Journal of Advertising* 7 (Winter 1978), pp. 48–51.

45. James A. Russell and Albert Mehrabian, "Environmental Variables in Consumer Research," *Journal of Consumer Research* 3 (June 1976), p. 62.

46. Russell W. Belk, "An Exploratory Assessment of Situational Effects in Buyer Behavior," *Journal of Marketing Research* 11 (May 1974), pp. 156–163.

47. Russell W. Belk, "Situational Variables and Consumer Behavior," *Journal of Consumer Research* 2 (December 1975), p. 159.

48. William D. Wells and Leonard A. LoSciuto, "A Direct Observation of Purchasing Behavior," *Journal of Marketing Research* 3 (August 1966), pp. 277–288.

49. Philip Kotler, *Marketing Management: Analysis, Planning, and Control*, 2d ed. (Englewood Cliffs, N.J.: Prentice-Hall, 1972), p. 83.

50. Bettman, *Information Processing Theory*, p. 63.

51. Peter Wright, "The Harassed Decision Maker: Time Pressures, Distractions, and the Use of Evidence," *Journal of Applied Psychology* 59 (October 1974), pp. 555–556.

52. Howard and Sheth, *Theory of Buyer Behavior*, p. 325.

53. John G. Myers, "Determinants of Private Brand Attitude," *Journal of Marketing Research* 4 (February 1967), pp. 73–81.

54. Jacob Jacoby, George J. Szybillo, and Carl Kohn Berning, "Time and Consumer Behavior: An Interdisciplinary Overview," in *Selected Aspects of Consumer Behavior*, prepared for National Science Foundation, Directorate for Research Applications, RANN, p. 459.

55. Frederick W. Winter, "Laboratory Measurement of Response to Consumer Information," *Journal of Marketing Research* 12 (November 1975), p. 399.

56. Belk, "Situational Variables and Consumer Behavior," p. 161.

57. Ibid.

58. Kenneth E. Miller and James L. Ginter, "An Investigation of Situational Variation in Brand Choice Behavior and Attitude," *Journal of Marketing Research* 16 (February 1979), pp. 111–123.

59. Bettman, *Information Processing Theory*, p. 329.

60. Ibid., p. 330.

61. Edward M. Tauber, "Why Do People Shop?" *Journal of Marketing* 36 (October 1972), pp. 46–49.

62. Kent B. Monroe and Joseph B. Guiltinan, "A Path-Analytic Exploration of Retail Patronage Influences," *Journal of Consumer Research* 2 (June 1975), pp. 19–28.

63. Masao Nakanishi, "Attitudinal Influence on Retail Patronage Behavior," in *Advances in Consumer Research*, vol. 3, ed. Beverlee B. Anderson (Ann Arbor: Association for Consumer Research, 1976), pp. 24–29.

64. Ronald E. Frank and William F. Massy, "Shelf Position and Space Effects on Sales," *Journal of Marketing Research* 7 (February 1970), pp. 59–66.

65. Michel Chevalier, "Increase in Sales Due to In-Store Display," *Journal of Marketing Research* 12 (November 1975), pp. 426–431.

66. David T. Kollat and Ronald P. Willett, "Is Impulse Purchasing Really a Useful Concept for Marketing Decisions?" *Journal of Marketing* 33 (January 1969), p. 79.

67. Ibid., p. 80.

68. Ibid., p. 81.

69. Fred D. Reynolds, "An Analysis of Catalog Buying Behavior," *Journal of Marketing* 38 (July 1974), pp. 47–51.

70. Ibid.

71. William H. Peters and Neil M. Ford, "A Profile of Urban In-home Shoppers: The Other Half," *Journal of Marketing* 36 (January 1972), p. 64.

CHAPTER 17

CHOICE AND OUTCOME

In 1979, the Paper Mate division of the Gillette Company introduced a new pen in a $5 million advertising campaign, the most costly sales promotion effort in its history. While the new pen—Eraser Mate—was similar to other pens, its writing substance was "gunky," bluish, and thick, so that it required pressurized nitrogen gas to force it onto the paper.[1] Eraser Mate is neither priced inexpensively nor offered in a wide variety—it was initially introduced only in blue ink and with a medium point. According to Paper Mate, the pen will last as long as an ordinary ball point pen. The basic difference is that the Eraser Mate is erasable. Apparently, Paper Mate assumes consumer choice of pens will be based primarily on one salient attribute: erasability.

After choosing a product, dissatisfaction with the choice will lead some consumers to take strong steps, while others may not be so bothered. Complaints by consumers may not be severe as a result of dissatisfaction with an Eraser Mate; however, with more costly products, dissatisfaction may have widespread ramifications. This is apparent in a situation of a consumer dissatisfied with his IBM computer. (See Exhibit 17.1.)

Indeed, choices occur in all stages of the consumer purchase decision process. In the stage specifically designated as "choice," the consumer selects an alternative among those she has been evaluating.

EXHIBIT 17.1

A very dissatisfied consumer

At one time it was thought that the marketer-customer relationship ceased with the purchase act. This is no longer the case. In fact, the postpurchase phase is considered to be one of the most important in the consumer decision process, since outcomes influence future consumer decision making and activity.

This chapter examines such questions as:

What kinds of choice strategies do consumers use?
How are choices made on the basis of "perceived risk"?
What are some of the rules of thumb that consumers develop to simplify the choice situation?
What are the strategic implications of consumer choice strategies?
What are some of the outcomes of the purchasing act?
What are the sources of consumer satisfaction and dissatisfaction?
What are some of the findings relevant to consumer complaining behavior?
How can marketers handle consumer complaints?
What strategies can the marketer use to improve the postpurchase evaluation stage?

THE PROCESS OF CHOICE

A basic way to approach the study of choice is to view the consumer as a processor of information.[2] Thus the consumer interacts with his choice environment, seeks and takes information from various sources, processes this information as he evaluates alternatives, and makes a selection from among those alternatives.

As consumers have a limited capacity to process information, they do not typically engage in complex analysis or extensive processing. Rather they use simple heuristics, or rules of thumb: "Buy the same thing I bought last time," "Buy the brand that has the most peanuts," and so on. This section examines some of these choice strategies.

Choice Based on Perceived Risk

Consumers may combine various kinds of information to formulate some sort of judgment on alternatives. One method is to integrate information on the uncertainty and consequences of choice—to evaluate alternatives on the basis of perceived risk. A simple strategy may be stated as "Select the brand that minimizes expected loss."[3]

Risk is inherent in every purchase decision, because once the purchase is made, the buyer faces the consequences, good or bad. "Perceived risk" refers to the nature and amount of risk perceived by a consumer contemplating a particular purchase decision. To a consumer faced with a purchase decision, perceived risk is more important than actual risk.

Raymond A. Bauer, who formulated the concept of perceived risk, said, "Consumer behavior involves risk in the sense that any action of a consumer will produce consequences which he cannot anticipate with anything approximating certainty and some of which at least are likely to be unpleasant."[4] The perception of risk in the purchase decision is a function of the consequences and uncertainty involved. *Uncertainty* is the consumer's subjective feeling that the consequences of a purchase decision will be unfavorable, and *consequences* are the amount at stake that would be lost if the act were not successful.

Consequences may be categorized as functional and psychosocial. Functional risk is closely related to product performance and financial considerations; psychosocial risk involves the product's ability to enhance one's sense of well-being or one's self-concept.[5] Some products, such as clothing, are high in psychosocial risk, by their very nature. Others, such as drugs, are high in functional risk. Headache remedies were found to be higher in perceived functional risk than fabric softeners or dry spaghetti,[6] and a new telephone product was found to be low in perceived functional risk but fairly high in perceived psychosocial risk.[7]

THE CAUSES OF PERCEIVED RISK

Consumers may not calculate risk probabilities or expected outcomes on the same dimensions as the statistician. They deal with risk subjectively on the basis of loss of face among family and friends, inconvenience, annoyance of breakdowns, or time required to return an item and purchase another.[8]

Perceived risk may be caused by any one or a combination of the following factors:[9]

1. The consumer may not be certain what her buying goals are.
2. The consumer may be uncertain as to which purchase will best match or satisfy acceptance levels of buying goals.
3. The consumer may perceive possible adverse consequences if the purchase is made and the result is a failure to satisfy her buying goals.
4. The consumer has little past experience with the purchase decision.
5. The consumer's past experience was unsatisfactory.
6. All alternatives have both positive and negative consequences.
7. The purchase decision differs from that of an important reference group.
8. The consumer anticipates important changes in her economic or political environment.

REDUCING PERCEIVED RISK

There are basically two methods of reducing perceived risk. One is to reduce the uncertainty, and the other is to reduce the penalties involved in the consequences. The basic risk-reducing strategies involve additional information seeking, greater prepurchase deliberation, and brand loyalty.

The consumer has a choice of several risk-reduction methods:[10]

1. *Endorsements.* Buy the brand whose advertising has endorsements or testimonials from a person like you, from a celebrity, or from an expert on the product.
2. *Brand loyalty.* Buy the brand you have used before and have been satisfied with in the past.
3. *Major brand image.* Buy a well-known brand and rely on its reputation.
4. *Private testing:* Buy the brand that has been tested and approved by a private testing company.
5. *Store image:* Buy the brand that is carried by a store you think is dependable, and rely on the store's reputation.
6. *Free sample:* Use a free sample of the product on a trial basis before buying.
7. *Money-back guarantee:* Buy the brand that offers a money-back guarantee.
8. *Government testing:* Buy the brand that has been tested and approved by an official branch of the government.
9. *Shopping:* Shop around on your own and compare product features on several brands in several stores.
10. *Cheapest model:* Buy the least expensive model.

11. *Expensive model:* Buy the most expensive and elaborate model.

12. *Word of mouth:* Ask friends or family for advice.

A study conducted to test the effectiveness of these risk-relieving strategies suggests that buyers generally favor some and are relatively unimpressed by others. Three risk relievers (brand loyalty, major brand image, and government testing) evoked a response that was clearly favorable.[11] This finding suggests that it would be desirable for the marketer to develop a strong brand image and engage in activities that would increase loyalty to his brand. It may be useful, in some circumstances, to have the products tested and approved by an official branch of the government.

Another study indicated that the higher the socioeconomic risk involved in a purchase decision, the greater the importance of personal influence as compared to other sources of influence.[12] The findings suggest that promotional strategies in a high-risk purchase situation should try to reach consumers through personal channels (opinion leaders, word of mouth) rather than through general media. Greater emphasis should be placed on the social benefits of the purchase than on the economic ones. Some items that are considered to present high socioeconomic risk include color TV, automobile, sport coat, men's cologne, haircut, and men's hair spray.

Another study investigated why individuals appear reluctant to encourage and engage in generic drug practices. Many states have adopted legislation that encourages substitution of generic equivalents for more expensive brand names when feasible. Although generic drugs seem to offer substantial potential cost savings, general acceptance of generic drugs has been moderate. According to the researchers, future efforts designed to encourage the spread of generic prescribing and dispensing should consider stressing both the potential for consumer savings and the maintenance of quality care as a means of minimizing perceived risk and pinpointing benefits.[13]

Despite these findings, the level of interest in perceived risk as it affects consumer behavior has declined somewhat recently. It appears that the crucial problems of measurement and conceptualization must be addressed before research in this area can be considered fruitful.[14]

CHOICE RULES

As we saw earlier, consumers have limited capacity to process information. They do not generally have the resources or the abilities necessary to process the total amount of information available. Hence many comparisons among alternatives may be made by use of simple rules of thumb, or heuristics.[15] Heuristics (also described as choice strategies, decision rules, and judgment rules) are a way of simplifying the choice task and adapting to the limitations of one's information-processing capacity. Heuristic processes have been defined as problem-solving methods that tend to produce efficient solutions to difficult problems by restricting the search through the space of possible solutions.[16]

Many types of heuristics have been used by consumers in comparing alternatives in the selection process; moreover, different rules of thumb may be used by different individuals, or by the same individual in different situations. Some of these rules or choice strategies are discussed below.

Affect Referral

A relatively simple rule was proposed by Peter L. Wright.[17] It is designated *affect referral* and suggests that a consumer does not examine attributes or beliefs about alternatives, but simply elicits from memory a previously formed overall evaluation for each alternative. The most highly evaluated alternative is then chosen. Thus a "choose the best" criterion is used. This rule presumably is most applicable for choices that the consumer has had a great deal of previous experience in making. Affect referral may also be used for low-involvement product classes, as, for example, impulse purchases that may not justify much thought and consideration.

Compensatory Rules

In the compensatory model for choice, the weakness of one attribute of a product may be compensated for by the strengths of all others. This type of rule was described in the discussion on multiattribute models of attitudes (Chapter 11). Here the rule is applied in the choice process, so that the ultimate decision may be considered as "choose the best" among alternatives.

The expectancy-value model, described in Chapter 11, is a compensatory model. When it is applied to choice, it assumes that behavior is determined by two components—expectancy and value. The expectancy component (E_i) consists of beliefs that actions will lead to certain outcomes, and the value component consists of the value of these outcomes (V_i). The overall value of an action given by the $E_i V_i$ and the action chosen (or choice made) would be the one that maximizes this summation ($\Sigma E_i V_i$).

Some researchers do not consider attitude models to be adequate descriptions of a decision rule involving choice. The expectancy-value model, for example, fails to consider phenomena related to choice, such as the effect of information stored in memory.[18]

Noncompensatory Rules

In the noncompensatory model for choice, the weakness of one attribute of a product is not compensated for by the strengths of others. Noncompensatory models include conjunctive and disjunctive rules and lexicographic heuristics.

CONJUNCTIVE RULE

In conjunctive and disjunctive choice strategies, information is processed by *brand.* A consumer who wishes to purchase a typewriter may examine a number of makes of typewriters. Each typewriter make is examined on various dimensions (attributes or evaluative criteria). According to the conjunctive rule, a consumer is assumed to set up minimum cutoffs for each dimension. If an alternative does not pass all of the cutoffs, it is rejected. For example, a portable typewriter may meet or exceed all other requirements but be rejected because its carrying case is somewhat large.

The Tickle ad in Exhibit 17.2 offers information consistent with the conjunctive rule. According to the advertiser, the other brands pictured should be rejected because they do not keep you as dry as Tickle and do not offer a choice of "fresh, clean fragrances."

EXHIBIT 17.2

This ad supplies brand information for all attributes (conjunctive rule)

DISJUNCTIVE RULE

A consumer using a disjunctive strategy is assumed to develop standards of acceptability for several dominant attributes, usually above the cutoff levels in the conjunctive model, while other attributes are considered to be of little importance. A brand will be evaluated as acceptable only if it exceeds the minimum specified level on those key attributes. The key attributes in a portable typewriter may be size of case, 12-inch carriage, and cartridge ribbon. All other factors, such as size of type and number of characters, are unimportant. The ad for Sony in Exhibit 17.3 emphasizes the attributes of "small" and "lightweight" for a Sony cassette re-

EXHIBIT 17.3

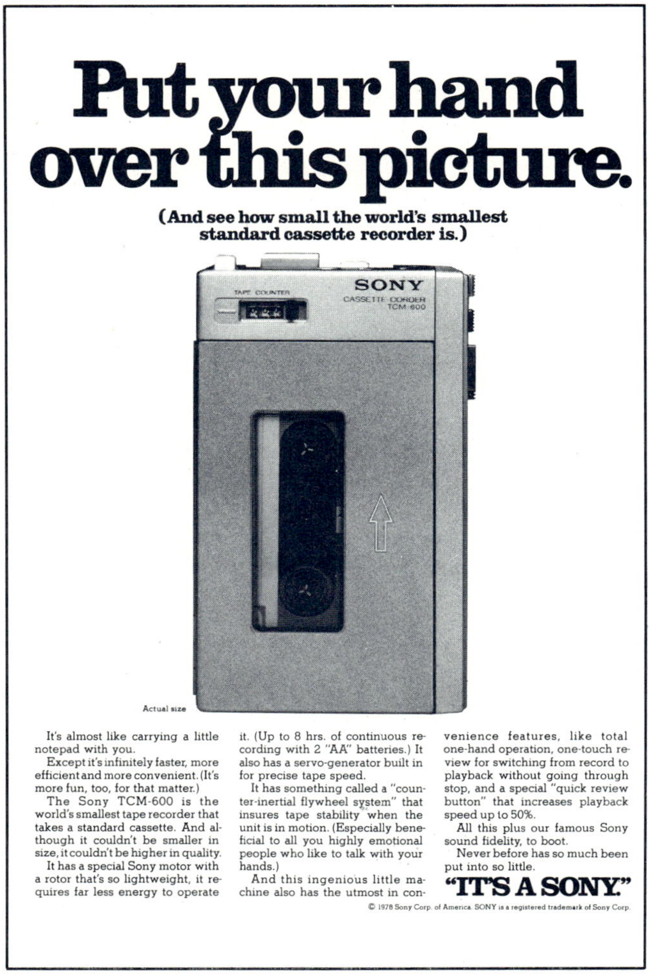
Put your hand over this picture.
(And see how small the world's smallest standard cassette recorder is.)
SONY
CASSETTE CORDER
TCM-600
TAPE COUNTER
Actual size
It's almost like carrying a little notepad with you.
Except it's infinitely faster, more efficient and more convenient. (It's more fun, too, for that matter.)
The Sony TCM-600 is the world's smallest tape recorder that takes a standard cassette. And although it couldn't be smaller in size, it couldn't be higher in quality.
It has a special Sony motor with a rotor that's so lightweight, it requires far less energy to operate it. (Up to 8 hrs. of continuous recording with 2 "AA" batteries.) It also has a servo-generator built in for precise tape speed.
It has something called a "counter-inertial flywheel system" that insures tape stability when the unit is in motion. (Especially beneficial to all you highly emotional people who like to talk with your hands.)
And this ingenious little machine also has the utmost in convenience features, like total one-hand operation, one-touch review for switching from record to playback without going through stop, and a special "quick review button" that increases playback speed up to 50%.
All this plus our famous Sony sound fidelity, to boot.
Never before has so much been put into so little.
"IT'S A SONY."
© 1978 Sony Corp. of America. SONY is a registered trademark of Sony Corp.

This ad supplies brand information for dominant attributes (disjunctive rule)

corder, as well as "uses less energy" and "offers the utmost in convenience." Price is not considered an important attribute.

LEXICOGRAPHIC HEURISTICS

A lexicographic strategy is an example of processing by *attributes*. Here the attribute or dimension that is most important is selected and the brands are examined on the basis of that dimension.

A consumer is assumed to be able to order attributes on the basis of importance. The brand that rates highest on the most important criterion receives the highest evaluation and is chosen, regardless of the values the alternatives have on the other attributes. If a cartridge ribbon is considered the most important attribute of a typewriter, and only one brand offers a cartridge ribbon, that brand will be chosen regardless of the value of its other attributes. If the most important attribute is judged equally good in two or more alternatives, the second most important attribute is considered. If two brands of a typewriter had a cartridge ribbon, the second most important attribute considered might be size of carriage. A general lexicographic rule may be "Buy the cheapest" when price is most important. The Hertz ad in Exhibit 17.4, which emphasizes "fast" reservations, presents information consistent with the lexicographic model. In the illustration of the Eraser Mate campaign in the beginning of the chapter, "erasability" was presented as the one most important attribute.

Strategic Implications of Choice Strategies

Other choice strategies are used by consumers, and additional research should provide more information on these strategies and further explanation of the rules described above. While it is useful for marketers to have an understanding of the rules of thumb that consumers use in making choice decisions, such information may be of particular relevance in devising marketing strategies. A marketer may attempt to direct the consumer toward a particular decision rule that favors his product. For example, a computer training school may develop a message that involves an "elimination by aspects" strategy, which is a combination of the disjunctive and lexicographic rules.[19] The ads present several key attributes by which this school may be compared with similar institutions, suggesting they should be examined in order of importance. The consumer is advised to eliminate computer schools that do not meet a criterion on one dimension (all those having no on-line facilities), then a second dimension (all that do not offer efficient placement services), then a third (all that lack approval for veterans' benefits). If the consumer adopts the judgment rule suggested, the message argues, then his choice of the advertiser's school is inevitable.

Marketers can also make assumptions concerning the choice heuristics that are most likely to be used and devise their presentations accordingly. The people who prepared the ads in Exhibits 17.2–17.4 obviously did.

EXHIBIT 17.4

Information offered on most important attribute strategy (exigraphic strategy)

To illustrate the concept of choice heuristics, let us assume that Mr. *X* has the following configuration of beliefs about a manufacturer's brand of toothpaste: (1) slightly below average in whitening power, (2) average in breath-freshening ability, (3) average in economy, and (4) slightly above average in decay prevention. If Mr. *X* were using a *compensatory* rule and the promotional tactics of the marketer succeeded in inducing a positive change in any one of his beliefs, then that change would have some positive effect on his overall judgment of the brand. If he were using a *conjunctive* rule—which establishes a minimum cutoff for each dimension—success of a promotional campaign in changing his beliefs about the brand's breath-freshening ability, economy, or decay prevention would be useless as long as he retained a below-cutoff belief about its whitening power.

If Mr. *X* uses a *disjunctive* rule, the brand may have to possess two attributes (say, breath-freshening ability and economy) which are far above average. Thus a

TABLE 17.1   CHOICE RULES

Rule	Strategy
Affect referral	Choose the most highly evaluated alternative elicited from memory
Compensatory rule	Choose the best by combining scores on all dimensions of each alternative
Conjunctive rule	Choose the brand that best meets or exceeds minimum requirements for each attribute
Disjunctive rule	Choose the brand that best meets or exceeds minimum requirements for dominant attributes
Lexicographic heuristics	Choose the attribute that is most important and select the brand on the basis of this attribute

campaign aimed at indicating that a brand of toothpaste is average in whitening power and slightly above average in breath-freshening ability would be ineffective.

With a *lexicographic* rule, Mr. *X* may rank the dimensions in such a way that whitening power is most important, economy second, decay prevention third, and breath-freshening ability last. Efforts on the last three dimensions would be wasted if the first were not improved. Furthermore, it might be useful just to differentiate the manufacturer's brand on whitening power positively and strongly and not worry about Mr. *X*'s other beliefs. In this choice, strategy has implications for highly salient attributes.[20] Table 17.1 provides a simple description of these choice rules.

OUTCOMES OF THE PURCHASE ART

This section examines several significant facets of the postpurchase stage. It discusses the possible outcomes of the purchase act, the effects of consumer satisfaction and dissatisfaction, and the consumer complaint process. Strategies to improve the postpurchase evaluation phase are offered.

In the Engel, Kollat, and Blackwell model of consumer decision making, two outcomes of the choice and purchase are immediately apparent:[21]

1. The triggering of new behavior in which there are three consequences: the need for the consumer to make financial outlays; product installation and use; and generated interest in related products and services.

2. Postpurchase evaluation, which can lead either to a continuation of search, particularly in cases of postdecision dissonance, or to a feedback loop into memory, whereby a comparison of the individual's expectations regarding the product and the purchasing situation can lead to either satisfaction or dissatisfaction.

Triggering New Behavior

As we have seen, a purchase can trigger new behavior in various forms. It may be necessary to make further financial outlays in this phase. The purchase of a new car, for example, may be accompanied by a need to secure financing and will surely require insurance. Financing may come through the individual's own source of funds, through banks or lending institutions, or from friends or relatives. Some car sellers offer their own financing. The widespread use of credit cards, particularly those that involve installment payments, indicate the consumer's acceptance of various types of funding.

The purchase act frequently triggers product installation and use. This is particularly true of expensive durable goods. Simple products may not require such new behavior; the purchase of a book merely requires that one open the cover and read. Some products have to be prepared for use, however. Children's bicycles have to be assembled, a new car may require a period of adjustment, a new washing machine has to be installed and directions read carefully before it is used. A formerly desired product may become undesirable as a result of misread or misunderstood instructions for use. This being the case, instruction manuals should be clearly and simply presented and checked for understandability.

The third type of behavior triggered by a purchase is the interest generated in related products and services. A new color television set may call for a cart to hold it, the installation of a new television antenna or cable, and a contract providing for repairs. Many people find that when a new sofa is purchased, other furniture may appear dingy and need to be replaced. Marketing strategists have long been aware of the benefit of offering complementary products in their lines: adding clothes dryers when they sell washing machines and stoves when they sell refrigerators.

The marketer must be aware that the purchase process does not stop when the consumer buys a product. Some firms provide financing for their customers or help them to secure such financing. Installation should be efficient and quick, and repairs should be executed as swiftly as possible. Again, information on product use should be clear and comprehensive. The marketer should be aware of related or complementary products that may be associated with the purchase and, if possible, offer these products or suggest how the consumer can secure them.

Postpurchase Evaluation

After an individual has made a purchase, she tends to evaluate its results. Such an evaluation may come from the use of the product or through new information the consumer has received about it. A new car may use an excessive amount of gasoline or have minor mechanical problems that lead to a negative evaluation. If it drives smoothly and causes no inconveniences, the evaluation will be positive. New information concerning a purchase may come from various sources, such as marketing literature, friends' and neighbors' comments, and peer-group statements. The information from these sources interacts with the experience derived from the use of the product and culminates in an evaluation of the purchase decision.

Postpurchase evaluation serves three purposes. First, it widens the scope of the consumer's experience and broadens his perceptions and understanding. Second, it serves as a means of measuring the success or failure of the consumer's marketing decisions. This measurement helps the consumer to determine how well he performs in selecting products and choosing outlets. Third, postpurchase evaluation provides the feedback necessary when the consumer is ready to make a new purchase decision. It enables him to adjust his future behavior in terms of products and stores selected and methods of making a purchase.[22] This phase will be examined further in Chapter 18.

CONSUMER SATISFACTION AND DISSATISFACTION

When the consumer compares the consequences of her purchase with her expectations regarding the product, she will be either satisfied or dissatisfied.

Consumer Satisfaction

Consumer satisfaction covers a wide number of factors, encompassing both objective product performance and psychosocial processes. The facets of consumer satisfaction can be subsumed under four major headings: product-related, process-related, psychosocial, and postpurchase satisfaction. Following is a partial list of some of the aspects of consumer satisfaction:[23]

1. Product-related satisfaction
   a. Cost
   b. Construction/durability
   c. Quality
   d. Performance
   e. Aesthetic qualities

2. Process-related satisfaction
   a. Convenience/accessibility/availability
   b. Information availability
   c. Sales assistance
   d. Decision analysis
   e. Alternative availability
   f. Personal treatment

3. Psychosocial satisfaction
   a. Contribution to psychosocial needs/wants
   b. Contribution to social needs/wants
   c. Image consistency
   d. Contribution to life-style

4. Postpurchase satisfaction
   a. Service convenience/accessibility/availability
   b. Environmental effects

These facets of consumer satisfaction can be either maintainers, which must exist if dissatisfaction is to be avoided, or satisfiers, which truly motivate and contribute to satisfaction. The relative importance of the facets may vary from individual to individual and from product to product.

A product that frequently rates high that provides consumer satisfaction is the television set. The product-related attributes that may provide this satisfaction are cost (which seems reasonable in relation to the amount of entertainment provided), performance, and durability. The process-related satisfiers include the many alternatives available and the convenience in purchasing. The television set provides psychosocial satisfaction in contributing to entertainment and enjoyment requirements, and offers postpurchase satisfaction in the numerous television repair services that are available.

An effective marketing strategy need not incorporate all of the facets listed, but some of them are necessary for almost all situations. The consumer expects performance in almost all circumstances. Research into desired benefits may disclose other facets of consumer satisfaction that are useful in a particular marketing strategy for a specific product or a designated target.

Consumer Dissatisfaction

The Random House dictionary states: "Dissatisfaction results from contemplating what falls short of one's wishes or expectations. . . ." Consumer dissatisfaction, then, might be measured by the degree of disparity between expectations and perceived product performance.[24]

Many of today's products perform better than their earlier models. Current refrigerators, for example, can hardly be compared with their earliest counterparts. Nevertheless, consumer dissatisfaction still continues.

Consumer dissatisfaction stems in part from consumers' rising expectations, which may be due to the increase in consumer affluence and sophistication. Expectations have been described as "subjective notions of things to come."[25] An expectancy is a type of hypothesis formulated by the consumer; the manner in which he perceives the product to perform after purchase will either confirm or invalidate this hypothesis.[26]

When one tries to predict how the disparity between expectations and actual product performance influences consumer satisfaction, four psychological theories must be considered: (1) assimilation, (2) contrast, (3) generalized negativity, and (4) assimilation contrast.[27] (See Figure 17.1.)

The assimilation theory declares that if there is a discrepancy between expectations and product performance, the consumer will minimize or assimilate the discrepancy by adjusting her perception of the product so that it is more consistent with her expectations. If this theory is true, the marketer should provide his

FIGURE 17.1   THEORIES OF DISCONFIRMATION OF EXPECTATIONS

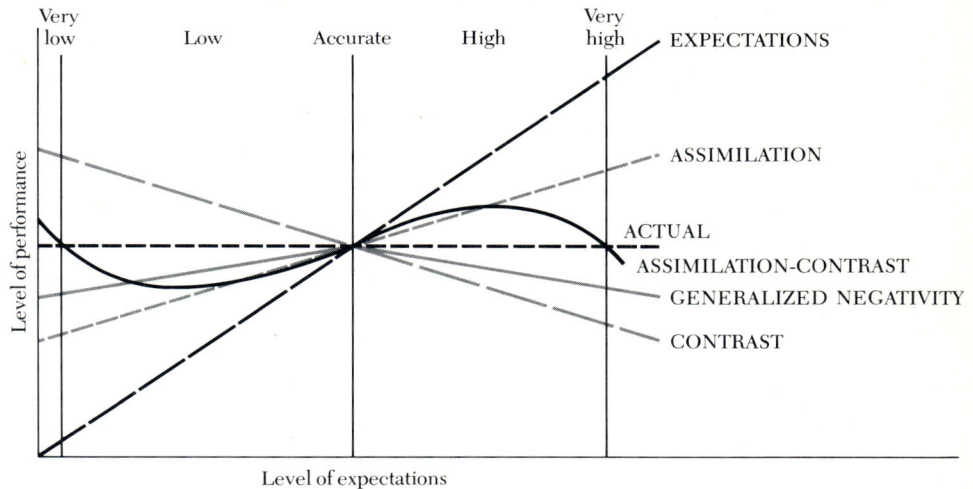

Source: Rolph E. Anderson, "Consumer Dissatisfaction: The Effect of Disconfirmed Expectancy on Perceived Product Performance," *Journal of Marketing Research* 10 (February 1973), p. 39.

product with a promotional mix that encourages expectations to be higher than product performance, so that the consumer will adjust her perception of the product until it receives a higher evaluation. This concept is illustrated by the dotted line in Figure 17.1.

The contrast theory assumes that the consumer will magnify the difference between the product performance and his expectations. If the objective performance of the product fails to meet his expectations, the consumer will evaluate the product less favorably than he would if he had had no expectations about it. This theory suggests that the marketer should understate his product's performance in advertising, a strategy that may lead to higher consumer satisfaction with the company's product. This concept is shown by the dashed line in Figure 17.1.

The generalized negativity theory indicates that any discrepancy between expectations and performance results in a generalized negative state, and thus the product will receive a less favorable rating than it would have received had it coincided with the consumer's expectations. This is thought to be true even if the product performance is superior to expectations: a generally negative attitude will cause it to be perceived as less satisfying than its performance would indicate. This theory suggests that the promotional activity of the marketer should create expectations that are as consistent as possible with product performance, because if the performance in any way differs from expectations (either better or worse), consumer satisfaction will be lowered. In Figure 17.1, the theory of generalized negativity is depicted by alternative dots and dashes.

The assimilation-contrast theory suggests that consumers have zones or latitudes of acceptance and rejection. If the disparity between the expectations and performance of a product is small, the consumer will assimilate it and perceive the product to be consistent with her expectations. If the disparity is wide, the product falls in the zone of rejection and the contrast theory is in effect. Thus the consumer will magnify the difference between the product performance and her expectations and evaluate the product less favorably than she would have done if she had had no expectations. The marketer who adopts the assimilation-contrast theory should use promotional messages that create high expectations for the product, but she should be sure that the level of disparity between the expectations and product performance is not wide enough to permit it to fall in the zone of rejection. Consumer perceptions of product performance in this theory take the form of the S-shaped curve in Figure 17.1.

No one theory is universally accepted as yet. Research has indicated that theories of expectation may vary across product classes. As indicated, however, the promotional strategy will vary with the theory of expectation that is adopted. High expectations of product performance should be created if the assimilation or assimilation-contrast theory is accepted. Low expectations of product performance are useful if the contrast theory is adopted, and expectations that are consistent with product performance if the generalized negativity theory is accepted.

CONSUMER COMPLAINTS

Few firms make public their volume of customer complaints. The following figures, however, were obtained from some United States firms: American Airlines heard from about 125,000 customers in one year. About 40,000 of these communications involved some complaint. Pillsbury keeps a staff of ten to answer the 2,500 complaints received per month. Corning Glass reports about 2,000 complaints per week.[28]

The number of complaints may not be an accurate barometer of dissatisfaction, however. Studies of Pan Am by a consumer action group suggest that on the average, for every person who complains, there are probably 35 others who are equally inconvenienced or dissatisfied but from whom the company does not hear.

A study found "brand switching" and talking to others the most important reactions of dissatisfied consumers.[29] Thus the volume of complaints may not reflect the full extent of customer dissatisfaction with the product or service.

> A malfunction or a frustrated expectation in a product costing $.89 or $1.49 is far more likely to result in a muttered expletive and a subsequent brand switch than in some kind of complaint. Recourse to litigation by an individual consumer for such a product failure . . . is almost beyond the realm of comprehension. Even a complaint to the manufacturer is unlikely when a low-priced item fails; the trade-off between consumer effort and the possibility of a satisfactory corporate response . . . is heavily weighted in favor of taking no action.[30]

Factors Leading to Consumer Complaints

It has been suggested that consumer complaint behavior be considered the function of four factors:[31]

1. The individual's propensity to complain when dissatisfied. The research data suggest that the propensity to complain is related to education, age, affluence, and a liberal-activist attitude.

2. Opportunities to become dissatisfied. The number-one product on complaint lists of consumer protection agencies is the automobile. This finding may be due to the fact that the automobile enjoys universal use, while at the same time it is a complex mechanism that most consumers do not understand. It is possible that many other products that are widely used are low in value so that consumers may neglect to complain about them.

3. Opportunities to obtain redress or complain. The ease with which consumers can obtain redress influences the quantity of complaints. In general, complaints are less likely to show up in consumer complaint data when the consumer deals with a local business.

4. Individual knowledge on the part of the consumer. The less knowledgeable consumer will be less able to judge product performance and to evaluate the goods and services he consumes. This consumer will tend to be less familiar with the procedures for registering complaints and securing redress.

To overcome some of the deficiencies in consumer complaint data resulting from the characteristics of consumer complaint behavior, it has been suggested that a formalized procedure be adopted. Rather than secure consumer complaint data on a voluntary basis, researchers should be encouraged to provide for a periodic collection of consumer data from a national probability sample of consumers interviewed in their homes.[32]

In 1974 the Technical Assistance Research Programs, Inc., under the sponsorship of the U.S. Office of Consumer Affairs, began a four-year study of the handling of consumer complaints. Initial findings of this study indicated that of the national sample of over 2,500 households, 32.4 percent reported consumer problems that occurred during the previous year. The most frequently designated problem was that the store did not have the product advertised for sale. (See Table 17.2.) According to the respondents, nearly 70 percent of their most serious problems were not satisfactorily resolved.[33]

Deficiency of Consumer Complaint Information

The problem with consumer complaint information is that the data on specific complaints reported by individuals and collected and summarized by various agencies are seriously flawed. One of the major problems is that the people who come forward with complaints are not a representative sample of the population.

TABLE 17.2   MOST PREVALENT TYPES OF CONSUMER PROBLEMS

Type of consumer problem	Households having this type of problem	
	Number	Percent
1. Store did not have product advertised for sale	203	24.9%
2. Unsatisfactory performance/quality of product (workmanship/ingredients)	182	22.4
3. Unsatisfactory repair	165	20.3
4. Unsatisfactory service (unrelated to repair)	127	15.6
5. Long wait for delivery	84	10.3
6. Failure to receive delivery	83	10.2
7. Overcharge or excessive price	78	9.6
8. Distasteful or offensive advertising	75	9.2
9. Product/service not as ordered/agreed on	72	8.8
10. Incorrect/deceptive or fraudulent billing	70	8.6
11. Deceptive advertising/packaging/pricing	66	8.1
12. Goods received in damaged condition	65	8.0
13. Manufacturer/dealer didn't live up to guarantee/warranty	58	7.1
14. Dealer/salesman misrepresented product/service	53	6.5
15. Failure to receive refund	43	5.3
16. Product unsafe	30	3.7
17. Item received different than one bought	27	3.3
18. Product harmful to environment	26	3.2
19. No return from repair or service	19	2.3
20. Instructions for use/care unclear/incomplete	19	2.3
21. Credit terms misrepresented	14	1.7
22. Unauthorized repair or service	13	1.6
23. Other	10	1.2

* $N = 814$ households that experienced consumer problem(s); 1,582 incidences or problems.

Source: Marc A. Grainer, Kathleen A. McEvoy, and Donald W. King, "Consumer Problems and Complaints: A National View," in *Advances in Consumer Research*, vol. 6, ed. William L. Wilkie (Ann Arbor: Association for Consumer Research, 1979), p. 496.

The former director of the Consumer Research Institute declared: "No one maintains that complaint letters which flow to governmental agencies or to private business firms come from a representative sample of the consuming public. In fact, the contrary is known to be true. Analyses of complaint letters show that they are heavily weighted by two groups: 1) people with time on their hands; and 2) highly educated, articulate people."[34]

There are indications that consumers who complain because they are dissatisfied differ from those who do not complain even though they are dissatisfied. One study was designed to distinguish between these groups. In a telephone study of 1,215 consumers, the respondents were asked, "Lately, have you gotten good and mad about the way you were treated as a consumer?"[35] A major proportion (64.5 percent) said they had not been upset about their treatment; 24.2 percent said they had been upset and had taken some action; and 11.3 percent reported they had been upset but had done nothing about it. There were differences among these three groups in demographic variables and political leanings. Those who were upset and complained were at one end of the spectrum (young, affluent, activist liberals), and those who were upset but did not complain were at the other end (older, poorer, politically alienated), while those who were not upset and obviously did not complain fell in between in most areas.

According to a study funded by the Administration on Aging, it appears that consumers over 65 are less likely to complain about unfair marketing practices or even to recognize some unfair practices as being wrong.[36] Older consumers are least likely to cite unfair practices that can lead to after-purchase problems, are most likely to be deterred by nonmonetary costs of complaining (embarrassment, fear of encountering angry reactions, fear of being a nuisance, "not worth the time," and so on), and, if they do complain, are least likely to go to an agency or consult a lawyer if they exhaust remedies within the store.

These studies suggest that the young and affluent are overrepresented among complainers, while they may not be typical of the population in their consumption patterns.

Handling Consumer Complaints

A tentative conclusion may be drawn from the data indicating that complaints are not a satisfactory barometer of consumer dissatisfaction. A continuing monitoring of consumer satisfaction or dissatisfaction by means other than complaints received might be necessary for the manufacturer. Thus cooperation with dealers in the postpurchase phase is very important, since customers tend to turn first to the dealer if they complain.

The importance of satisfied customers is clear. Satisfaction can lead to a more positive attitude toward the product or brand and a more pronounced intention to buy it again. It also can create loyalty to the brand and to the company, and can encourage interest in the other products the company carries. Furthermore, such satisfaction may result in word-of-mouth advertising, either spontaneously or in response to questions by friends who are in the market for a similar product.

Two kinds of marketer reactions to consumer complaints may lead to an improvement of the situation for the customer: (1) a *direct* reaction to a complaint of a single consumer, whereby the improvement of the situation is restricted to the complaining consumer only; and (2) an *indirect* reaction on the policy level, which results in an improvement of future performances offered to all customers.[37]

These two types of complaint reactions may be closely connected. If, for example, the treatment of any single complaint is connected with costs for the organization, when a certain number of complaints have been received it may be worthwhile for the organization to improve its services, so that complaints will be reduced.

In preparing his communications, therefore, the marketer may find it useful to direct his messages to the recent buyer rather than to all potential buyers. The recent buyer may be uncertain that he has made the right choice. He may need some support to indicate that the choice was appropriate, and advertising and publicity can offer such evidence.

REDUCING DISSONANCE

Chapter 12 discussed postpurchase dissonance and described strategies to reduce such dissonance and increase consonance. Three studies incorporating such strategies have employed a postpurchase reinforcement technique to increase the purchaser's satisfaction with the product. In two of the studies, the technique provided greater product satisfaction, while the third study obtained mixed results.

In a study carried out by Van Dyke, a supportive letter from the dealer increased consonance following the purchase of a new car. Purchasers who did not receive the supportive letter showed no such increase in consonance. According to a study by James H. Donnelly, Jr., and John M. Ivancevich, two supportive phone calls within two weeks following the purchase of a new car decreased the backout rate from about 6.0 percent to about 2.5 percent. Shelby D. Hunt, likewise, found that a supportive letter following the purchase of a refrigerator reduced posttransaction anxiety and increased disposition to repurchase. A supportive telephone call, however, had the opposite effect, although in content it was similar to the letter.[38]

Advertising, too, may be useful in reducing dissonance. When a consumer has purchased an expensive specialty good, she is likely to experience strong dissonance if her purchase is irrevocable and if it is important in a psychological sense. Thus, if the financial outlay for the purchase has been large or if it reflects the taste and intelligence of the purchaser, strong dissonance may be present. Under these circumstances, an advertisement that emphasizes the desirable features of the chosen brand can reduce dissonance and lead the consumer to form a more favorable attitude toward the brand.[39]

Dissonance, however, is reduced over time. Thus advertising may not operate effectively as a reinforcing agent long after the purchase. Nonetheless, it may be that the greater the postpurchase dissonance, the longer the period during which the seller's advertisement can act as a reinforcer. This reinforcing effect, however, does not necessarily ensure a repeat purchase because of the counteracting effects of competitive advertisements.

STRATEGIES FOR IMPROVING POSTPURCHASE EVALUATION

A number of strategies have been suggested to improve the marketer's chances of having his product favorably evaluated by consumers in the postpurchase phase. Suggested strategies include guidelines to improve the quality and service of the product, tactics designed to reduce the "dropout" rate, improved word-of-mouth communications, and adequate warranties.

Guidelines for the Producer

The postpurchase response pattern of the marketer may follow three normative patterns:[40]

1. *The "continuous quality" concept.* The basic idea behind the "continuous quality" concept is the manufacturer's conscious backing of her products from birth to death. Action patterns are built up in the prepurchase phase, during the purchase itself, and in the postpurchase phase. (See Figure 17.2.) By stressing the intertwining of company actions during all phases, this concept underlines the importance of the firm's continuous concern for quality.

2. *Guidelines for good after-sale service.* This area encompasses the warranty, use instructions, and repair and maintenance services. The requirements for warranties are spelled out in the warranty law (discussed in Chapter 19). Consumer education should be improved in relation to the use and maintenance instructions. In particular, manufacturers should urge the consumer to read and use the instructions. Consumer education material should be as simple and understandable as possible, and explicit demonstration of products and training of purchasers in their use should be provided. The core of any warranty program ultimately lies in the quality of the maintenance and repair services that are offered to customers.

    Dissatisfaction with repair service has been a powerful force in the consumer movement. There is some evidence, however, that during the depressed economy of 1974 and 1975, consumers' attitudes and experiences with respect to the servicing of durable goods improved.[41]

    A study was conducted to determine the relationship between product price and repair cost. The results indicated that respondents were

FIGURE 17.2   THE "CONTINUOUS QUALITY" CONCEPT

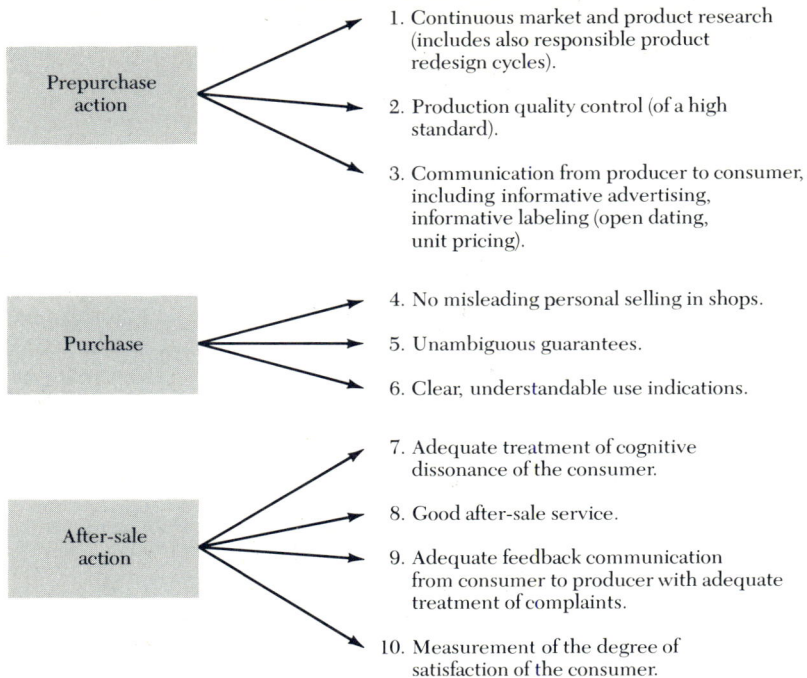

Prepurchase action

1. Continuous market and product research (includes also responsible product redesign cycles).

2. Production quality control (of a high standard).

3. Communication from producer to consumer, including informative advertising, informative labeling (open dating, unit pricing).

Purchase

4. No misleading personal selling in shops.

5. Unambiguous guarantees.

6. Clear, understandable use indications.

After-sale action

7. Adequate treatment of cognitive dissonance of the consumer.

8. Good after-sale service.

9. Adequate feedback communication from consumer to producer with adequate treatment of complaints.

10. Measurement of the degree of satisfaction of the consumer.

Source: Jacques de Rijcke, "Consumer Satisfaction and Dissatisfaction in the Post-Purchase Phase of Manufacturer Post-Sale Policies," in *Proceedings of the First Workshop on Consumer Action Research* (Berlin: International Institute of Management, 1975).

TABLE 17.3   MEAN PURCHASE PRICES OF TEN PRODUCTS AND MAXIMUM ACCEPTABLE REPAIR COSTS

Product	(A) Mean original price	(B) Maximum repair cost owners would be willing to pay	Ratio (B as percent of A)
Electric can opener	$ 16.93	$ 7.12	42%
Toaster	20.26	9.82	48
Pocket calculator	71.14	31.09	44
Typewriter	121.40	31.70	26
Vacuum cleaner	132.31	31.32	24
Stereo	282.74	54.87	19
Stove	302.81	69.54	23
Refrigerator	372.78	83.29	22
Television	392.90	79.94	20
Automobile	3,000.00	258.20	9

Source: Lee Adler and James D. Hlavacek, "The Relationship between Price and Repair Service for Consumer Durables," *Journal of Marketing* 40 (April 1976), p. 82.

willing to pay disproportionately higher amounts to have the lower-cost products repaired.[42] This finding may reflect the owner's expectations that there is some minimum cost of service regardless of the price of the original equipment, or perhaps it reflects faulty knowledge of actual service charges. Table 17.3 shows the mean purchase prices of ten products and the maximum amount owners would be willing to pay to have each product repaired. This research suggests quantitative guidelines that may assist marketers to determine acceptable repair charges. Misapprehensions concerning such costs may adversely affect the sale of a product, particularly a big-ticket item.

3. *Guidelines for adequate treatment of complaints.* A consumer-oriented complaint organization within a firm should have the capability to listen, to take action, to do a follow-up, and to initiate corrective action and ideas. To eliminate the mishandling of complaints, the company should take care to avoid delays in responding to complaints, not to attempt to shift the blame elsewhere, to avoid responding with a form letter, to take corrective action to forestall additional complaints, to avoid making promises it cannot keep, and, if a complaint proves unjustified, to explain the reasons for its rejection.

SUMMARY

In the choice stage of the consumer purchase decision process, the consumer makes a selection from among alternatives that have been evaluated. As consumers have a limited capacity for information processing, they use rules of thumb in making choices. Two consumer strategies are minimization of *perceived risk* and *affect referral* (the consumer elicits from memory a previously formed overall evaluation of each alternative and then chooses the one most highly evaluated).

Other rules of thumb include the *compensatory* model, in which the weakness of one attribute of a product is compensated for by the strength of all others and the consumer chooses the product with the highest "expected value." If the consumer uses the *conjunctive* rule, he sets a minimum cutoff for each dimension of a product alternative, and if the alternative does not pass all of the cutoffs, he rejects it. If he follows the *disjunctive* rule, he develops acceptable standards for several dominant attributes and considers other attributes to be of little importance. According to the *lexicographic* model, the attribute or dimension that is most important is selected, and alternatives are examined on the basis of this dimension.

The outcome of a choice decision is an important stage in the consumer decision process, since it influences future consumer decision making and activity. For example, the purchase act may trigger new consumer behavior in the form of financial outlays, installation needs, and interest in related products and services.

Outcomes may also result in postpurchase evaluation. Such evaluation may lead to consumer satisfaction or dissatisfaction. Despite the large number of reported complaints, the information available on complaints is not sufficient to provide firm guidelines for marketer strategies. It appears that the typical complainer may not be the typical consumer; in fact, older people are less likely to complain than others. One program to reduce complaints specifies continuous action by the firm before, during, and after the sale.

DISCUSSION QUESTIONS

1. Describe how a product choice might be influenced by perceived risk. Provide examples of functional and psychosocial risk.

2. What strategies do you tend to use to reduce perceived risk?

3. What problems might arise if consumers did not develop rules of thumb to use in making choices?

4. Select advertisements that might illustrate each of the choice rules discussed in the chapter.

5. Why has outcome become an important aspect of the consumer decision process?

6. For each of the psychological theories in the concept of "disconfirmation of expectations," explain whether consumer expectations should be raised or lowered before purchase.

7. What is your greatest personal complaint as a consumer? What do you tend to do about it? How should the firm be handling this situation?

8. Describe a situation in which the outcome of your purchase decision influenced your future purchase behavior.

NOTES

1. "News for Crossword Lovers," *Newsday,* March 15, 1979, Sec. II, p. 8.

2. James R. Bettman, *An Information-Processing Theory of Consumer Choice* (Reading, Mass.: Addison-Wesley, 1979), p. 1.

3. J. Paul Peter and Lawrence X. Tarpey, Sr., "A Comparative Analysis of Three Consumer Decision Strategies," *Journal of Consumer Research* 2 (June 1975), p. 29.

4. Raymond A. Bauer, "Consumer Behavior as Risk Taking," in *Dynamic Marketing for a Changing World, Proceedings of the 43d Conference of the American Marketing Association,* ed. Robert S. Hancock (Chicago: American Marketing Association, 1960), p. 390.

5. Donald F. Cox, "Risk Handling in Consumer Behavior: An Intensive Study of Two Cases," in *Risk Taking and Information Handling in Consumer Behavior,* ed. Ronald F. Cox (Cambridge: Division of Research, Graduate School of Business Administration, Harvard University, 1967), pp. 36–38.

6. Scott M. Cunningham, "The Major Dimensions of Perceived Risk," in *Risk Taking and Information Handling,* ed. Cox, pp. 507–523.

7. Thomas S. Robertson, *Consumer Behavior* (Glenview, Ill.: Scott, Foresman, 1970), p. 21.

8. James H. Myers and William H. Reynolds, *Consumer Behavior and Marketing Management* (Boston: Houghton Mifflin, 1967), p. 100.

9. Donald F. Cox, "Introduction," in *Risk Taking and Information Handling,* pp. 5–7.

10. Donald H. Granbois, "The Role of Communication in the Family Decision-Making Process," in *Consumer Behavior: Selected Readings,* ed. James F. Engel (Homewood, Ill.: Richard D. Irwin, 1968), pp. 153–154.

11. Ted Roselius, "Consumer Rankings of Risk Reduction Methods," *Journal of Marketing* 35 (January 1971), pp. 57–58.

12. Ibid., p. 59.

13. William O. Bearden and J. Barry Mason, "Consumer-Perceived Risk and Attitudes toward Generically Prescribed Drugs," *Journal of Applied Psychology* 63 (December 1978), pp. 741–746.

14. James R. Bettman, Harold H. Kassarjian, and Richard J. Lutz, "Consumer Behavior," in *Review of Marketing 1978,* ed. Gerald Zaltman and Thomas V. Bonoma (Chicago: American Marketing Association, 1978), p. 197.

15. Bettman, *Information-Processing Theory,* p. 174.

16. Myron L. Braunstein, *Depth Perception through Motion* (New York: Academic Press, 1976).

17. Peter L. Wright, "Consumer Choice Strategies: Simplifying vs. Optimizing," *Journal of Marketing Research* 11 (February 1975), pp. 60–67.

18. Bettman, *Information-Processing Theory,* p. 7.

19. Amos Tversky, "Elimination by Aspects: A Theory of Choice," *Psychological Review* 79 (July 1972), pp. 281–299.

20. Peter L. Wright, "Use of Judgment Models in Promotion Planning," *Journal of Marketing* 37 (October 1973), pp. 32–33.

21. James F. Engel, David T. Kollat, and Roger D. Blackwell, *Consumer Behavior,* 2d ed. (New York: Holt, Rinehart, and Winston, 1973), p. 529.

22. G. Glenn Walters, *Consumer Behavior: Theory and Practice* (Homewood, Ill.: Richard D. Irwin, 1974), pp. 559–560.

23. John A. Czepiel, Larry J. Rosenberg, and Adebayo Akerele, "Perspectives on Consumer Satisfaction," in *New Marketing for Social and Economic Process and Marketing's Contributions to the Firm and Society,* 1974 Combined Proceedings, ed. Ronald C. Curhan (Chicago: American Marketing Association, 1975), p. 120.

24. Rolph E. Anderson, "Consumer Dissatisfaction: The Effect of Disconfirmed Expectancy on Perceived Product Performance," *Journal of Marketing Research* 10 (February 1973), p. 38.

25. George Katona, "Business Expectations in the Framework of Psychological Economics (Toward a Theory of Expectations)," in *Expectations, Uncertainty, and Business Behavior,* ed. Mary Jean Bowman (New York: Social Science Research Council, 1958).

26. Rolph E. Anderson and Joseph F. Hair, "Consumerism, Consumer Expectations, and Perceived Product Performance," in *Proceedings, 3d Annual Conference, 1972,* ed. M. Venkatesan (Association for Consumer Research, 1972), p. 69.

27. Anderson, "Consumer Dissatisfaction," p. 38.

28. Jacques de Rijcke, "Consumer Satisfaction and Dissatisfaction in the Post-Purchase Phase and Manufacturer Post-Sale Policies," in *Proceedings of the First Workshop on Consumer Action Research, Berlin, 1974* (Berlin: International Institute of Management, 1975).

29. J. E. Swan and D. S. Longman, "Consumer Satisfaction with Automobile Repair Performance," in *Combined Proceedings of 1972 Spring and Fall Conference*, ed. Boris Becker and Helmut Becker (Chicago: American Marketing Association, 1973), pp. 249–255.

30. C. L. Kendall and F. A. Russ, "Warranty Policies and Practices of Consumer Packaged Goods Manufacturers," in *Proceedings of the 3d Annual Conference*, ed. M. Venkatesan, p. 350.

31. Ralph L. Day and E. Laird Landon, "Collecting Comprehensive Consumer Complaint Data by Survey Research," in *Advances in Consumer Research*, vol. 3, ed. Beverlee B. Anderson (Association for Consumer Research, 1976), pp. 263–264.

32. Ibid., p. 264.

33. Marc A. Grainer, Kathleen A. McEvoy, and Donald W. King, "Consumer Problems and Complaints: A National View," in *Advances in Consumer Research*, vol. 6, ed. William L. Wilkie (Ann Arbor: Association for Consumer Research, 1979), pp. 494–500.

34. Raymond C. Stokes, *Consumer Complaints and Consumer Dissatisfactions* (Phoenix: Food and Drug Law Institute, April 1974).

35. Rex H. Warland, Robert O. Hermann, and Jane Willits, "Dissatisfied Consumers: Who Gets Upset and Who Takes Action," *Journal of Consumer Affairs* 9 (1975), pp. 148–163.

36. "Marketing Briefs," *Marketing News*, July 14, 1978, p. 2.

37. Gerhard Ennemoser, "A Survey of Consumers and Their Complaints about the Services of the North Western Gas Board," in *Proceedings of the First Workshop on Consumer Action Research, Berlin, 1974* (Berlin: International Institute of Management, 1975).

38. The studies mentioned here are cited in William H. Cummings and M. Venkatesan, "Cognitive Dissonance and Consumer Behavior: A Review of the Evidence," in *Advances in Consumer Research*, vol. 2, ed. Mary Jane Schlinger (Association for Consumer Research, 1975), p. 26.

39. Sadaomi Oshikawa, "Can Cognitive Dissonance Theory Explain Consumer Behavior?" in *Buyer Behavior: Theoretical and Empirical Foundations*, ed. John A. Howard and Lyman E. Ostlund (New York: Alfred A. Knopf, 1973), p. 422.

40. de Rijcke, "Consumer Satisfaction and Dissatisfaction in the Post-Purchase Phase and the Manufacturer Post-Sale Policies."

41. Lee Adler and James D. Hlavacek, "The Relationship between Price and Repair Service for Consumer Durables," *Journal of Marketing* 40 (April 1976), p. 80.

42. Ibid., pp. 81–82.

CHAPTER 18

SPECIAL APPLICATIONS OF CONSUMER DECISION THEORY

Sometimes even a useful product may not be readily accepted by consumers as a necessity. The introduction of the shopping cart, currently an institution, was resisted by consumers. The developer introduced it to supermarkets in 1937 with an advertisement that asked, "Can you imagine winding your way through a spacious food market without having to carry a cumbersome shopping basket on your arm?"[1] At that time, the shopping basket was the traditional way of carrying supermarket merchandise. Despite the evident benefit of the shopping cart, consumers did not use it. To some people it looked too much like a baby carriage, and men considered it an offense to their strength. To encourage people to adopt the shopping cart, the inventor used the multistep hypothesis approach to acceptance of an innovation. Since he could not convince people of the advantage of the cart, he hired men and women of various ages to come into his supermarkets, pretending to be shoppers who were using the cart. By seeing this, other customers would come to accept the cart. This approach is consistent with the thesis that although mass media generate awareness, it is chiefly a favorable personal recommendation by a social contact that is thought to be instrumental in influencing an individual to adopt.[2] The inventor, by the way, became extremely rich on the royalties he subsequently received for every shopping cart that was sold.

Although the purchase is the final outcome of the consumer decision process, many activities occur between the introduction of an idea and its ultimate acceptance by the large majority of consumers. Two interrelated processes help to bring new ideas from their initial development to their final acceptance by consumers. These processes are called *adoption* and *diffusion*. The adoption process is a mental process through which an individual passes from the moment he first hears about a new idea or product to its final adoption. The diffusion process is the spread of new ideas from originating sources to ultimate users. In agriculture, for example, it is the process by which farm practices or ideas are communicated from sources of origin, usually scientists, to farmers.

Attribution theory is concerned with the way in which the consumer attributes effects to causes in an attempt to form a coherent view of the world.

This chapter examines such questions as:

What is the adoption process?
What is the relevance of the adoption process to marketers?
What is the diffusion process and what is the significance in the variations in adopters over time?
What is attribution theory?
How are the self-perception concepts, such as foot-in-the-door, door-in-the-face, and locus of control, relevant to marketing strategies?

THE ADOPTION PROCESS

The adoption process may be divided into stages. A division commonly used by sociologists is:[3]

1. *Awareness.* The individual knows of the new idea but lacks information about it.

2. *Interest.* The individual becomes interested in the idea and seeks more information about it.

3. *Evaluation.* The individual makes a mental application of the new idea to his present and anticipated future situation and decides either to try it or not.

4. *Trial.* The individual uses the new practice on a small scale to validate its workability.

5. *Adoption.* The individual uses the new practice on a full scale.

This model has been widely used in studies of the adoption process. Recent critics, however, cite at least three deficiencies in the model:[4]

1. It implies that the process always ends in adoption decisions, whereas in reality rejection may also be a likely outcome. Therefore, a term more general than "adoption process" is needed—one that allows for either adoption or rejection.

FIGURE 18.1   THE INNOVATION-DECISION PROCESS*

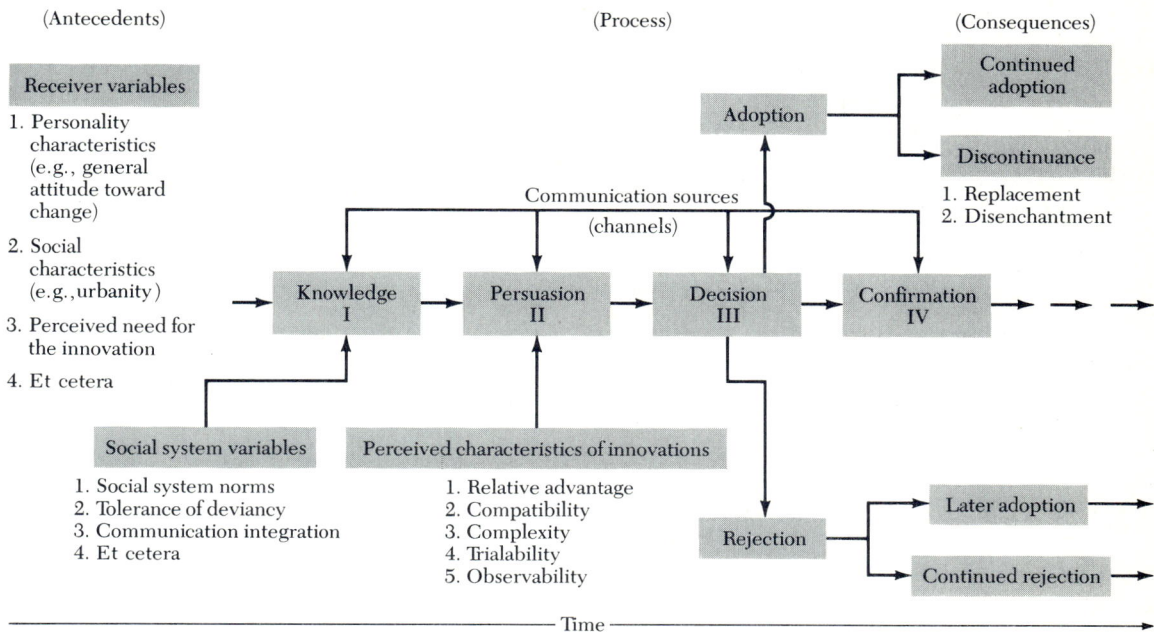

(Antecedents)   (Process)   (Consequences)

Receiver variables

1. Personality characteristics (e.g., general attitude toward change)

2. Social characteristics (e.g., urbanity)

3. Perceived need for the innovation

4. Et cetera

Communication sources
(channels)

Continued adoption

Adoption

Discontinuance

1. Replacement
2. Disenchantment

Knowledge
I

Persuasion
II

Decision
III

Confirmation
IV

Social system variables

1. Social system norms
2. Tolerance of deviancy
3. Communication integration
4. Et cetera

Perceived characteristics of innovations

1. Relative advantage
2. Compatibility
3. Complexity
4. Trialability
5. Observability

Rejection

Later adoption

Continued rejection

─────── Time ───────

* For the sake of simplicity we have not shown the consequences of innovation in this paradigm but only the consequences of the process.

Source: Reprinted with permission of Macmillan Publishing Co., Inc., from *Communication of Innovations*, by Everett M. Rogers and Floyd Shoemaker. Copyright © 1971 by Free Press, a Division of The Macmillan Company.

2. The five stages do not always occur in the specified order, and some may be skipped, especially the trial stage. Evaluation actually occurs throughout the process.

3. The process seldom ends with adoption, as further information may be sought to confirm or reinforce the decision, or the individual may later switch from adoption to rejection (a discontinuance).

Another model, called a "paradigm of the innovation-decision process," was developed by Everett Rogers and Floyd Shoemaker and consists of the following four stages (see Figure 18.1):[5]

1. *Knowledge.* The individual is aware of the innovation and has acquired some information about it.

2. *Persuasion.* The individual forms an attitude, pro or con, toward the innovation.

3. *Decision.* The individual performs activities that lead to an adopt-reject decision about the innovation.
4. *Confirmation.* The individual looks for reinforcement regarding his decision and may change his earlier decision if he is exposed to counterreinforcing messages.

The Rate of Adoption

New ideas or products may be adopted at varying rates of speed. The relative speed with which a new product is adopted depends partially on its characteristics. Some characteristics that affect the rate of adoption are:

1. *Relative advantage.* The degree to which an innovation is perceived to be better than an existing idea is termed "relative advantage"; "relative advantage" is a function of whether a person perceives the innovation as better than existing ideas; it is not a function of whether the innovation is, in fact, objectively better.

   Incorporated in the concept of relative advantage is the issue of cost and economic returns. New practices that are high in cost generally tend to be adopted more slowly than do less costly ones, and practices that produce quick returns on investments tend to be adopted more rapidly than those that produce deferred returns or returns spread over a long period of time.

2. *Complexity.* New ideas that are relatively simple to understand and use will generally be accepted more quickly than more complex ideas. Though the game of contract bridge became enormously popular, its diffusion rate was slower than that of the portable radio. Bridge requires knowledge of the play and complex bidding procedures; the portable radio requires only the twist of a knob.

3. *Communicability.* There is wide variation in the ease with which the operation of a product and the results obtained from it are seen or demonstrated. The more visible the product and its results, the more rapid its adoption. Everett M. Rogers cites "the case of preemergent weed killers that are sprayed on a field before the weeds emerge from the soil." The rate of adoption of this idea by Midwestern farmers was very slow in spite of its relative advantage, because there were no dead weeds that the farmers could show their neighbors.[6]

4. *Divisibility.* A practice that can be tried on a limited basis will generally be adopted more rapidly than one that cannot. For example, a computer requires extensive installation before it can be used, and this requirement tends to slow the rate at which it is adopted. A photocopying machine, however, can easily be installed on a small scale for a limited trial, and such an offer tends to accelerate the rate of adoption.

   If a product can offer the potential of trial use, the adoption process can be accelerated, as trial use is closely tied to the concept of perceived risk. A new vacuum cleaner tried in the home or a sample of grapefruit offered in the supermarket may be means of offering this trial use which may reduce the consumer's perceived risk and so encourage the adoption of the product. Products that are divisible in some manner—that is, a small part of the product or its performance can be separated from the total offering—offer the potential for trial use. For example, it is difficult to offer the consumer a small portion of an air flight in an effort to make him a user of airplanes. Trial use appears to be of greater importance to early adopters than to later ones because of the greater perceived risk inherent in the early decision.

5. *Compatibility.* A new idea or service that is consistent with existing ideas and beliefs will be accepted more rapidly than one that is not. Such innovations are thought to be less risky and more meaningful than those that are not compatible with a person's personal values and beliefs. For example, one research study showed that farmers who owned a power sprayer for the use of insecticides on crops adopted chemical weed sprays more quickly than those who did not own power sprayers. The slow adoption of acupuncture by American physicians may be due to the fact that the procedure does not fit into their accustomed methods of anesthetizing patients before an operation.

Once the shopping cart was presented in use, as noted in the beginning of the chapter, most of the criteria we have been discussing—relative advantage, lack of complexity, high visibility, divisibility, and compatibility—operated to ensure its widespread adoption.

Application of the Adoption Process Concept

The concept of the adoption process may be useful to the marketer devising a strategy to introduce an innovative product. Relevant characteristics of a product may be emphasized to accelerate the rate of adoption.

Perceived product characteristics appear to offer the greatest promise in the development of marketing programs for innovative products for two reasons: (1) a considerable body of research outside of the field of marketing testifies to their consistency, and (2) they embrace dimensions of the marketing program that are within the management's power to control.

Perceived product characteristics have been applied retrospectively to the marketing program used to launch the Mazda, an automobile with a rotary engine, in the Midwest.[7] The promotion campaign centered on the theme of the car's quiet operation and its smooth, rapid acceleration—qualities that indeed constituted its *relative advantage.* This theme appeared to be communicated successfully. Other aspects of the product that might have stimulated its rate of adoption seem to have been largely ignored, however. For example, little effort was made in the mass media to explain the basic principle by which the engine operated—a factor related to both *complexity* and *communicability.* While the

Mazda was sold with a warranty; no coherent effort was made to promote the idea of a test drive or possibly a short-term rental at special rates, although such offers would have provided the advantage of *divisibility*. Finally, no attempt was made to enhance the car's *compatibility* by pointing out that its size and low-pollution characteristics were in tune with the times. The rotary engine failed to attract buyers.

THE DIFFUSION PROCESS

The spread of new ideas or products from originating sources to ultimate users is referred to as the diffusion process. The diffusion of a new product is determined to a considerable extent by word of mouth.[8]

In studies of the diffusion process, adopters of a product are divided into categories that indicate the order in which they have adopted the product. In attempts to determine the distinct characteristics of each adopter category, early researchers discovered that if adopters were plotted on a graph over time, the curve resembled a normal bell-shaped curve. Researchers have found it useful to divide the adopters of any given innovation into five groups based on the relative time at which they adopt. (See Figure 18.2.) Many data have been compiled concerning the characteristics of each adopter group.

The Innovator

The "innovators of any one innovation are those members of society prepared to adopt the new product early in its diffusion and therefore without the personal or social support gained from discussions with prior users."[9]

A major goal of the new-product manager is to accelerate market acceptance of his product. Perhaps the most critical phase in the product life cycle is the introduction stage. Sufficient sales must be generated during this phase to develop

FIGURE 18.2   CLASSIFICATION OF ADOPTER GROUPS

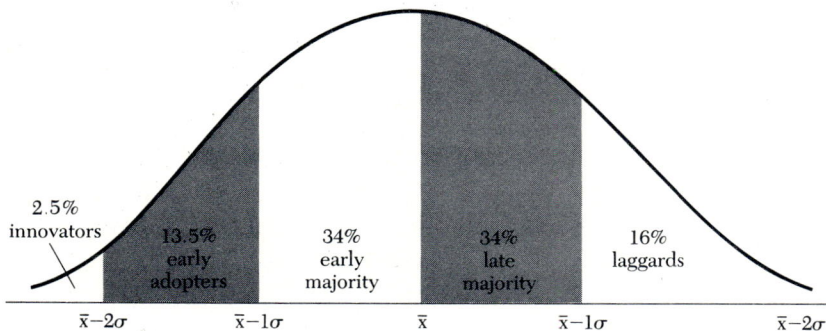

2.5% innovators

13.5% early adopters

34% early majority

34% late majority

16% laggards

$\bar{x}-2\sigma$ $\bar{x}-1\sigma$ $\bar{x}$ $\bar{x}-1\sigma$ $\bar{x}-2\sigma$

Source: Everett M. Rogers and Floyd Shoemaker, *Communication of Innovations* (New York: Free Press, 1971), p. 182.

and maintain retail distribution and to provide adequate promotional funds for the future. The marketer must attract a substantial group of early buyers in order to ensure survival of the new product. Early buyers directly affect the purchase decisions of other consumers. In their role as initiators of the diffusion process, they legitimize the new product. They also serve as an informal source of information through their visual display and word-of-mouth communication.

It is important for the marketer to appeal to those consumers who are most readily converted into buyers for his product—a group that may be considered the innovators. Marketers disagree on the proportion of potential adopters that constitutes the innovators. Estimates vary from 2.5 percent to 10 percent.

In an effort to reach these innovators, studies have been conducted to determine their psychological characteristics and media preferences. It should be noted that some of the findings on innovativeness are product-specific and therefore cannot be considered to be generally descriptive.

Five variables were studied in relation to their value as predictors of innovators:[10]

> *Venturesomeness:* the willingness to take risks in the purchase of new products.
> *Social integration:* the degree of participation with other members of the community.
> *Cosmopolitanism:* the degree to which an individual is oriented beyond his community to the world at large.
> *Social mobility:* the movement of individuals from one position to another in society—positions that by general consent have been given specific hierarchical values.
> *Privilege:* financial standing relative to other community members.

Innovators in the selection of the Touch-Tone telephone were found to be significantly higher on venturesomeness than noninnovators.[11] Since innovators perceive themselves as first buyers, the marketer may advertise to them as knowledgeable individuals who distinguish themselves by purchases of new products.

Innovators are more socially integrated within their neighborhoods than most people. They interact with more people and perceive themselves to be more popular. It is suggested that rather than ceasing to appeal to innovators once they have purchased a new product, marketers might encourage them to "tell their friends." Nonetheless, innovators are likely to be socially mobile. Marketers can make their products meaningful to the socially aspiring consumer innovator.

Innovators are more financially privileged than other community members. They have greater discretionary income than their neighbors and perceive themselves to be richer. Innovators are also found to be less concerned with cost than other people and should be appealed to accordingly.

It is also useful for the marketer to know the media habits of the consumers that comprise this innovative group. A study was conducted to disclose the media exposure of purchasers of such product categories as packaged food products, household cleansers and detergents, women's clothing, cosmetics and personal grooming aids, and both large and small appliances.[12] The data generated by the study supported the proposition that innovators are disproportionately more exposed to the mass media than noninnovators.

Innovators were also selective in their exposure to the mass media. The relationship between innovativeness and media exposure tended to be strongest when the media's editorial content was relevant to the product category. For example, innovativeness in packaged food products had a strong positive relationship with readership of women's magazines, and the same was true of women's clothing and women's fashion magazines. Romance magazines, whose editorial content appears to have little relevance to consumer products, were not effective in attracting concentrations of innovators for any of the six product categories. Readership of the local daily and Sunday newspapers, however, was positively related to innovation in small and large appliances.

Though relatively expensive, a standard practice in promoting mass-market paperbacks in recent years is the use of television commercials. Publishers of such books are aware, however, that the ultimate fate of the book does not rest with the advertising campaign. Rather it is designed to reach the innovators, those most alert members of the public for the book. If they can be persuaded to read it, they may recommend it to their friends.

It is interesting to note, however, that many publishers have their own indicators of potential success. In forecasting a book's fate, an editor of a large commercial house declared, "If Gloria doesn't like a manuscript, even if it's by a brand name author, we know we're in trouble." Gloria, it turns out, is a high school graduate with an average IQ whose title in the office is stenographer-clerk. As far as popular taste is concerned, she is a living sheet of litmus paper, reflecting average acceptance. Other publishers admit to having their own Glorias.[13]

The Early Adopter

Early adopters are the second group to adopt an innovation. The size of this group is defined statistically as 13.5 percent of all potential adopters. In contrast to innovators, who are cosmopolites, early adopters are localites.[14] The early adopter is well integrated with her small locality and is highly respected by her friends, who often seek her advice about new things. The respect such people are accorded by their peers makes them very important determinants of the success or failure of the innovation. Thus they are the people most frequently courted by the change agent. Opinion leaders are found to come primarily from the early-adopter group. Their characteristics were described earlier.

The Early Majority

The early majority comprise about 34 percent of all potential adopters of an innovation. Members of this group are deliberate and cautious in their adoption of an innovation. They have considerable contact with local adopters, change agents, and peers. Though the group displays some opinion leadership, it is well below that shown by early adopters. This group is slightly above average in education and social status, but below the early adopters.

The Late Majority

The late majority also make up 34 percent of potential adopters. A significant characteristic of the late majority is skepticism. These people require immense peer pressure before they finally adopt an innovation. Peers are the primary source of new ideas for the late majority; the late majority make little use of mass media. Demographically, they are below average in education, income, and social status.

Laggards

Laggards are the last group or segment of persons to adopt a product, service, or idea, although they do adopt eventually. Laggards probably comprise about 16 percent of the consumer market, and they are generally tradition-bound. They have the lowest income and social status of all adopter groups.

In a study designed to identify laggards, it was found that the variable that discriminated best between laggards and earlier adopters was family size.[15] The families of laggards tended to be smaller. The second most useful variable was stage in the life cycle: laggards tended to be in the categories of older and single; older (both over 45) and married with no children under 18; and older and married with children. Age was the third most important variable: the laggards, as suggested by the life-cycle variable, tended to be older. Laggards also reported lower income and indicated that the heads of their households were in lower status occupations.

Application of the Diffusion Process

In the past, most new-product marketers might launch their products by distributing them widely and informing anyone who might be a potential purchaser. For example, since women constitute the major market for cake mixes, a manufacturer of a new cake mix would try to reach and inform as many women as possible of his new product. This mass-market approach requires a heavy marketing expenditure and might involve a substantial number of wasted exposures to people who were not potential buyers.[16]

A later strategy was to aim communications at heavy users. A small percentage of the users of a product frequently account for a substantial share of all purchases. Thus the marketer attempted to identify the characteristics of the heavy user of a product class and then design a product to capture their specific interest. In the case of the new cake mix, the target would no longer be all women but rather women who were heavy users of cake mixes. An attempt would be made to identify their distribution over social classes, their family sizes, their educational levels, their media preferences, and so on. It might be found that the heaviest users of cake mixes were homemakers under 40 with families of three or more children and low income. The next heaviest group of users might be homemakers under 40 with families of three or more children and medium income. The company would build its marketing plan to reach the first or the first two target groups early and plan to extend the message to the lighter-using group later.

With the development of the adoption theory, it was noticed that there were differences in the speeds at which individuals would try new products. This finding gave rise to the concept of groups ranging from innovators to laggards. This theory indicated that it might be useful for the new-product marketer not to direct his communication equally to all heavy users of a class of products, but rather to try to reach those people who are most likely to adopt the product early. The early-adopter theory, whose premises were enunciated earlier, might be stated as follows:[17]

1. Persons within a well-defined target market will differ in the amount of time that passes between their exposure to a new product and their trial of the new product.

2. Early adopters are likely to share some traits that differentiate them from late adopters. That is, early adoption is associated with some common demographic, psychological, or situational factors. Early adopters are people who tend to be first in trying various new products in general or in particular product classes.

3. Efficient media exist for reaching early adopters.

4. Early adopters are likely to be high on opinion leadership, and therefore helpful in "advertising" the new product to other potential buyers.

More information may be necessary, however, before it can be assumed that early-adopter types are the best prospects to target. For example, it may be necessary to determine the magnitude and persistence of the early adopters. One way to secure this information is to add questions during the concept-testing stage of a new product.

When a new product is being developed, the appeal of its concept to a potential target user group is tested. Various potential users are asked to express, among other things, their understanding of the product concept, the degree of their interest in the concept, and the likelihood that they would buy the product. A number of other questions may be added to provide information as to the magnitude or persistence of the early-adopter effort:[18]

1. If you intend to buy the product, how soon after its appearance are you likely to buy it?
   a. ——immediately
   b. ——within a week

    c. ——within a month
    d. ——within a year

2. How do you see yourself with regard to buying new products?
    a. ——as one of the first persons to buy new products
    b. ——as an early adopter of new products after a few others have tried them
    c. ——as a late adopter of new products after a lot of people have bought them

3. If you liked the product, would you probably be:
    a. ——a heavy buyer (more than —— units per year)
    b. ——a medium buyer (between —— and —— units per year)
    c. ——a light buyer (fewer than —— units per year)

4. If you liked the product, would you probably:
    a. ——tell several other persons
    b. ——tell a few other persons
    c. ——not discuss

5. In what media or media vehicle do you think you would be likely to learn first about this product?

This type of questioning can provide useful information. The first two questions reveal those in the sample who are early-adopter types; the third question reveals those who are heavy-user types; the fourth question reveals the influential-adopter types; and the fifth question reveals the media expectations of potential buyers.

ADDITIONAL RESEARCH APPLICATIONS

While diffusion models have aided in the understanding of the consumer adoption process, new research directions are necessary to provide accurate representations of this phenomenon. A basic shortcoming of most of the previous research is that although it examines a type of communication process, the research in the field tends to lack a process orientation. Specifically, it has not analyzed adoption over time. Generally the research has been based on cross-sectional data gathered in one-shot surveys of respondents. Such research design cannot tell very much about the process of diffusion over time other than what can be reconstructed from recall data.

Another problem, according to Everett M. Rogers, is the tendency for most research to have an inherent pro-change bias, assuming that the innovations studied are good and should be adopted by everyone.[19] This may not be so, and many individuals for their own good should not adopt some innovations. The pro-innovation bias leads to a research of "what is" rather than "what could be" in regard to diffusion processes. Such research may be useful in suggesting methods of discouraging adoption of ecologically unsuitable products or those that consume unwarranted amounts of energy.

ATTRIBUTION THEORY

Attribution theory is relevant to many stages of the consumer decision-making process. The bulk of attribution theory research may be traced back to Fritz Heider's *Psychology of Interpersonal Relations,* published in 1958.[20] In that work Heider addressed the way people attribute causes to events or occurrences in the environment. Recent years have seen a significant growth of interest in applications of attribution theory to consumer behavior. Theorists have provided various definitions of attribution theory as well as various applications.

In the context of consumer behavior, attribution theory has generally been considered to relate to the manner in which the consumer attributes effects to causes so that he can maintain "a stable and meaningful picture of the world around him."[21] The consumer's attribution of effects to causes may involve various issues, such as the consumer's attributions of his own actions, his understanding of the reasons another person behaves in a certain way, or the reasons for a product's performance. Most of the studies in attribution theory have focused on self-perception and satisfaction/dissatisfaction. This section presents some of the current research into attribution theory that may be useful to marketing strategists.

Self-Perception Theory

According to the theory of self-perception (also called self-attribution), consumers tend to make use of their own past behavior as data in making inferences about their attitudes and beliefs. Simply, the theory focuses on the way individuals' beliefs cause events, the way they attribute causality, and what consumers learn from their own experiences. ("I eat hamburgers; therefore I must like hamburgers.") Several concepts have emerged from research in this area, including foot-in-the-door, door-in-the-face, and locus of control.

FOOT-IN-THE-DOOR

The foot-in-the-door notion has been developed in social psychology and under the pretext of nonprofit research. How to obtain compliance with minimal pressure is a concern in a wide variety of contexts—charitable giving, propaganda, buying a new product. In part foot-in-the-door is based on Daryl J. Bem's self-perception theory, which asserts that a person judges her own attitudes from observation of her own behavior.[22]

One of the first formal studies of this phenomenon was conducted by Jonathan L. Freedman and Scott C. Frazer, who found that California homeowners who first agreed to sign an auto-safety petition were significantly more likely to agree to the placement in their yards of large, unattractive signs promoting auto safety than were homeowners who were asked to accept the signs "cold."[23] Subsequent investigations have confirmed these findings.[24]

Carol A. Scott found that the foot-in-the-door technique is efficient in modifying behavior, provided the behavior is not too extensive.[25] (What constitutes extensive behavior may depend on a number of factors.) Also, the requests are more efficient when they are made in person, a finding that suggests that this technique requires more human than mass communication.

If a certain behavior is to be attributed to a certain stimulus, it must be perceived by the person as resulting from his true reactions to the stimulus, not to some controlling aspect of the environment. For example, if a person performs an act for a large reward, he attributes that behavior to the reward rather than to his own positive attitude toward the act ("I was paid to do this").[26] When attributions are made from such external contingencies, no belief inferences are made and no link between the behavior in one situation and behavior in another is expected. Attributions to oneself ("I did this because I wanted to") result in belief inferences and subsequent behavior may reflect initial behavior.

An interesting application of this thesis was used in a study to assess the advertising/selling interactions.[27] A standard belief in marketing is that "advertising paves the way for selling." When self-perception theory was applied to advertising, it was hypothesized that advertising may become more effective if it is preceded by a personal call. The hypothesis was based on the attribution-theory idea that a personal sales call can cause an attribution (can serve as a "foot in the door"). In other words, the sales call could form the basis for self-perception. Should the respondent mentally argue, "Why am I listening when nothing is forcing me to?" he may mentally respond, "It must be because I am the sort of person who participates in causes like this."

The study demonstrates a situation in which personal calls do appear to pave the way for advertising instead of the reverse common assumption. The authors indicate, however, that use of this finding in marketing practice may involve problems, since advertising does not, like personal selling, close a call. They suggest that advertising should follow missionary contacts, such as trade-show contacts, canvassers—all personal sales contacts that do not include a closing.

It is also suggested that other sales-promotional tools may provide a base from which a prospect can draw self-attributions, which lead the prospect to increased sensitivity to subsequent advertising. Among such tools are product samples (especially those involving some behavior commitment, rather than free and unsolicited samples), contests, cents-off coupons, and introductory offers. Using these promotional tools before advertising may have a more positive effect than using them after advertising.

DOOR-IN-THE-FACE

Another suggestion for inducing compliance with requests is called the door-in-the-face technique. Here an initial noncompliance with a large request may produce an increased rate of compliance with a second request.[28] A possible explanation is based on dissonance theory.[29] When a subject refuses to comply with an initial request for extensive help in a social cause, he probably feels some dissonance, which he can easily resolve by complying with the immediately following second request. Another possibility is a perceptual contrast effect. If the initial request is for an extreme response, the second request may be perceived as smaller than it would have been if it alone had been presented.

Suggestions for applying the door-in-the-face technique include situations in which donations are requested for the Heart Association, for example. Initial requests may be for a large sum or for a long-term donor program. Subsequent requests can be on the order of "Only a penny would help." It has been suggested that this technique may also be used in survey research: "Even answering five questions will help" or "Even completing one page will help."[30]

LOCUS OF CONTROL

"Locus of control" refers to the tendency to attribute causes to internal or external factors. Some people consistently tend to attribute the things that happen to them to causes that are within their own control, such as their own effort, preparation, or skill. Others tend to attribute their outcomes in life to factors beyond their control, such as luck, chance, or strong forces that they cannot counteract. The first group perceives an internal locus of control, while the second perceives an external locus.

In studying locus of control, Bernard Weiner developed a two-dimensional schema to represent the possible causes of an achievement behavior.[31] A success can be attributed to either something about the actor (internal) or something about the environment or situation (external). In addition, it can be attributed to something that does not vary over time (stable) or to something that does vary over time (unstable).

To believe that a good purchase was a result of one's ability to bargain is a stable internal attribution. The perception that a poor purchase was made because one was tired and in a hurry is an unstable, internal attribution. Blaming the manufacturer for producing a poor product is a stable, external attribution. Perceiving a product as a "lemon" or a "peach" (an unusual example of a poor or good product) is an unstable, external attribution.[32]

It appears that attributions to unstable causes may lead to expectancies that different outcomes might occur—"This particular car is a lemon, but another car of the same make may turn out to be all right." Or conversely, "This was a peach, but I can't be sure that another one would be as good."

Attributions to unstable causes may lead to information as to the sources of complaints and complaining behavior. People who believe that their choice represented a foolish action on their part will react differently from those who perceive the problem to be the fault of the manufacturer.

Satisfaction/Dissatisfaction

Recent research has focused on understanding the inferences consumers make about the causes of purchase outcomes—why a product performed the way it did. If marketers can learn to whom or why consumers attribute satisfaction or dissatisfaction with a product, they will have taken a first step toward determining appropriate actions.

If a consumer is dissatisfied with a product, the cause of (or blame for) this dissatisfaction may be attributed to the product, the manufacturer, the vendor, the advertising, a salesperson, a friend, himself, or external conditions. The marketing illustration at the beginning of Chapter 7—in which Ford owners' perceptions of the reasons for front end problems of their Fords in Springfield, Illinois, differed from Chevrolet owners' perceptions of reasons for similar problems with their Chevrolets—is an example of variations in attributions (that is, attributing different causes to similar effects). Although both Fords and Chevrolets were equally well-built, and the bumpiness of the ride in both cases was primarily due to the bumpy railroad tracks in the heart of the city, Chevrolet owners more often tended to blame their dealers or their particular car rather than Chevrolet as a brand, while Ford owners tended to place blame on Ford as a brand.

Ford's strategy to change these unfavorable attributions was to redesign the car and initiate an advertising campaign to change the perceptions of Ford as a noisy "tin lizzy."

A more recent study attempted to determine whether consumers attribute their satisfaction or dissatisfaction to specific reasons or persons.[33] First, students were asked to recall a product with which they were unhappy, and then they were asked the following questions: "What do you feel was responsible for that which caused your dissatisfaction?" and "Who, if anyone is to blame for your dissatisfaction?" They were asked the same questions concerning a product with which they were satisfied.

The responses indicated that most dissatisfaction stemmed from product performance that was worse than expected or that differed from advertising claims. This finding was consistent with the contrast theory, described in Chapter 17, which indicated that consumers will magnify the difference between product performance and their expectations.

Efforts were made in this study to determine locus of control (external vs. internal). A number of attributions were considered in regard to their psychological distance from consumers. "Self" and "known other," for example, were considered psychologically close to the consumer, while "system" was psychologically most distant. In other words, individuals feel that people they know are psychologically close to them, while retailers, manufacturers, and the marketing system are not close.

In Table 18.1, the locus of control is internal for self and external for all others. Of those respondents who attributed control over the situation to themselves, 14 expressed dissatisfaction with product performance and 11 expressed satisfaction. Most satisfactions and dissatisfactions were attributed to the manufacturer, who is only slightly less distant psychologically than the "system." While it is difficult to determine the reasons, it is apparent from the figures that the largest differences between attributions of satisfaction and dissatisfaction occur in the retailer category, and this category is perceived by the respondents as more responsible for dissatisfaction than for satisfaction.

TABLE 18.1   NUMBER OF RESPONDENTS ATTRIBUTING SATISFACTION AND DISSATISFACTION TO VARIOUS SOURCES, BY LOCUS OF CONTROL

Locus of control	Attributions	Dissatisfaction	Satisfaction
Internal	Self	14	11
External	Known other	5	6
	Retailer	16	7
	Manufacturer	27	24
	System	2	1

Source: Adapted from Valerie Valle and Melanie Wallendorf, "Consumers' Attributions of the Cause of Their Product Satisfaction and Dissatisfaction," in *Consumer Satisfaction, Dissatisfaction, and Complaining Behavior,* ed. Ralph L. Day (Bloomington, Ind.: Division of Business Research, Indiana University, 1977), p. 28.

SUMMARY

The adoption and diffusion processes and attribution theory are of particular relevance to the consumer purchase decision process.

While an actual purchase indicates acceptance, two interrelated processes help to bring new ideas from the source of their initial development to their final acceptance by consumers. These processes are called adoption and diffusion. The adoption process is a mental process through which an individual passes from the moment he first hears about a new product to its final adoption. This process is divided into five stages: awareness, interest, evaluation, trial, and adoption. More recently, the stages have been designated as knowledge, persuasion, decision, and confirmation.

Characteristics of a product that may affect the rate at which it is adopted include: the relative advantage the product offers, its complexity, its visibility, its divisibility, and its compatibility with existing ideas and beliefs.

During the diffusion process the new idea or product spreads from the originating sources to the ultimate users. The first people to adopt a product are called innovators; then, in turn, come the early adopters, the early majority, the late majority, and the laggards. Innovators tend to be venturesome and socially mobile. They are selective in their exposure to mass media.

Early adopters are localites in contrast with innovators, who are more cosmopolitan. Opinion leaders come primarily from the early-adopter group. The early majority are deliberate and cautious in their adoption of an innovation. The late majority require immense peer pressure before they finally adopt an innovation. Laggards, the last group of persons to buy a product, tend to be older than the other groups and have smaller families.

Attribution theory has recently been applied to an understanding of consumer behavior and relates to the manner in which consumers attribute effects to causes. Self-perception, as part of attribution theory, deals with the way in which consumers tend to use their own past behavior as data in making inferences about their attitudes and beliefs. The foot-in-the-door is a technique to modify consumer behavior. It implies that consumers who make an initially small contribution to some cause, for example, may be likely to make a larger contribution later because their judgments are made from observations of their own past behavior. This theory implies that the typical notion that advertising should precede selling might well be reversed. If such foot-in-the-door interactions exist, it is possible that advertising may be more effective when it follows (rather than precedes) the sales call, or more specifically when it follows the consumer's commitment to samples, contests, cents-off coupons, or the like.

The door-in-the-face theory suggests that noncompliance with a large request may produce an increased rate of compliance with a second request. This response may be due to the desire to reduce dissonance or the perceptual contrast effect: the small request is perceived as smaller as a result of the initial large request.

"Locus of control" refers to people's tendency to attribute causes to external or internal factors. This tendency may lead to variations in consumers' satisfactions or dissatisfactions with products. One study revealed that consumers perceived retailers as being more responsible for dissatisfaction than for satisfaction.

DISCUSSION QUESTIONS

1. The late 1970s saw the adoption of the use of carpet fresheners. Discuss this product in relationship to the characteristics that would accelerate the rate of adoption.

2. Are innovators and opinion leaders the same? Explain.

3. As a manufacturer of a new product,which adopter group would you emphasize in your first year's marketing strategy? Why?

4. What specific marketing techniques would you use to try to reach the innovator?

5. Have you been faced with foot-in-the-door or door-in-the-face strategies? Explain.

6. Explain how knowledge of the causes of dissatisfaction can aid marketers in their decision making.

NOTES

1. "The Man Who Put Your Groceries on Wheels," *New York Post*, April 28, 1977, p. 37.

2. David F. Midgley and Grahame R. Dowling, "Innovativeness: The Concept and Its Measurements," *Journal of Consumer Research* 4 (May 1978), p. 233.

3. Joe M. Bohlen, C. Milton Coughenour, Herbert F. Lionberger, Edward O. Moe, and

Everett M. Rogers, "Adopters of New Farm Ideas," in *Perspectives in Consumer Behavior,* rev. ed., ed. Harold Kassarjian and Thomas S. Robertson (Glenview, Ill.: Scott, Foresman, 1973), pp. 351–361.

4. Everett M. Rogers and F. Floyd Shoemaker, *Communication of Innovation,* 2d ed. (New York: Free Press, 1971), p. 7.

5. Ibid., p. 105.

6. Ibid., p. 156.

7. Laurence P. Feldman and Gary M. Armstrong, "Identifying Buyers of a Major Automotive Innovation," *Journal of Marketing* 39 (January 1975), p. 53.

8. Midgley and Dowling, "Innovativeness."

9. Ibid., p. 234.

10. Thomas S. Robertson, "Social Factors in Innovative Behavior," in *Perspectives in Consumer Behavior,* ed. Kassarjian and Robertson, pp. 363–364.

11. Ibid., pp. 367–370.

12. John O. Summers, "Media Exposure Patterns of Consumer Innovators," *Journal of Marketing* 36 (January 1972), p. 44.

13. Ray Walters, "Paperback Talk," *New York Times Book Review,* May 22, 1977, pp. 45–46.

14. M. Wayne DeLozier, *The Marketing Communications Process* (New York: McGraw-Hill, 1976), p. 154.

15. Kenneth Uhl, Roman Andrus, and Lance Pulsen, "How Are Laggards Different?: An Empirical Inquiry," *Journal of Marketing Research* 7 (February 1970), pp. 51–54.

16. Philip Kotler and Gerald Zaltman, "Targeting Prospects for a New Product," *Journal of Advertising Research* 16 (February 1976), p. 8.

17. Ibid., p. 9.

18. Ibid., p. 14.

19. Everett M. Rogers, "New Product Adoption and Diffusion," *Journal of Consumer Research* 2 (March 1976), pp. 290–301.

20. Fritz Heider, *The Psychology of Interpersonal Relations* (New York: John Wiley, 1958).

21. Robert B. Settle, "Attribution Theory and Consumer Behavior," in *Perspectives in Consumer Behavior,* rev. ed., ed. Harold Kassarjian and Thomas S. Robertson (Glenview, Ill.: Scott, Foresman, 1973), p. 64.

22. Daryl J. Bem, "Self-Perception Theory," in *Advances in Experimental Social Psychology,* vol. 6, ed. Leonard Berkowitz (New York: Academic Press, 1972), pp. 2–63.

23. Jonathan L. Freedman and Scott C. Frazer, "Compliance without Pressure: The Foot-in-the-Door Technique," *Journal of Personality and Social Psychology* (December 1966), pp. 195–202.

24. Peter H. Reinger and Jerome B. Kernan, "Compliance with an Interview Request: A Foot-in-the-Door, Self-Perception Interpretation," *Journal of Marketing Research* 14 (August 1977), pp. 365–369.

25. Carol A. Scott, "Modifying Socially Conscious Behavior: The Foot-in-the-Door Technique," *Journal of Consumer Research* 4 (December 1977), pp. 156–164.

26. Carol A. Scott, "Self-Perception Processes in Consumer Behavior: Interpreting One's Own Experiences," in *Advances in Consumer Research,* vol. 5, ed. Keith Hunt (Ann Arbor: Association for Consumer Research, 1978), p. 715.

27. William R. Swinyard and Michael L. Ray, "Advertising-Selling Interactions: An Attribution Theory Experiment," *Journal of Marketing Research* 14 (November 1977), pp. 509–516.

28. Robert B. Cialdini and Karen Ascani, "Test of Concession Procedure for Inducing Verbal, Behavioral, and Further Compliance with a Request to Donate Blood," *Journal of Applied Psychology* 61 (June 1976); pp. 295–300.

29. Peter H. Reingern, "On Inducing Compliance with Requests," *Journal of Consumer Research* 5 (September 1978), pp. 96–101.

30. Ibid., p. 101.

31. Bernard Weiner, Irene Frieze, A. Kukla, L. Reed, S. Rest, and R. M. Rosenbaum, *Perceiving the Causes of Success and Failure* (New York: General Learning Press, 1971).

32. Valerie Valle and Melanie Wallendorf, "Consumers' Attributions of the Cause of Their Product Satisfaction and Dissatisfaction," in *Consumer Satisfaction, Dissatisfaction, and Complaining Behavior,* ed. Ralph L. Day (Bloomington: Division of Business Research, Indiana University, 1977), pp. 26–30.

33. Ibid.

PART FIVE
THE CONSUMER ENVIRONMENT: REGULATORY AND SOCIETAL ASPECTS

CONSUMER BEHAVIOR AND PUBLIC POLICY CONSUMERISM

With the expansion of research activities in the area of consumer behavior, increasing concern has been shown for the strengthening of connections between consumer research and consumer policy formation. Research efforts have focused on the regulatory and societal aspects of the consumer's environment and its effect on consumer behavior and decision making. This section examines the interrelationships among consumer-behavior theory, public policy, and consumerism.

CHAPTER 19

CONSUMER BEHAVIOR AND PUBLIC POLICY

No discussion of consumer behavior can be complete without reference to the societal implications of consumer-behavior theory. A comprehensive discussion of this topic is beyond the scope of this book. This chapter and the next, however, examine some of the relevant areas, specifically those concerned with public policy and consumerism.

This chapter examines such questions as:

> How is the consumer defined for public policy purposes?
> What rights do public policy makers specify for consumers?
> How are these rights addressed from a behavioral perspective?

Public policy is a vague concept. It is variable and subject to change as the social, political, and economic climates change. As a result, public policy activities cannot be static. They must be adapted and molded to changing times and changing needs.

The basis for much public policy activity is the United States Constitution. Perhaps no part of the Constitution is so well known or held so sacred as the so-called Bill of Rights, the first ten amendments. We are all acquainted to some degree with the concepts of freedom of speech, press, religion, and assembly.

Usually we think of these matters as dealing with personal rights of individuals in a free society. Very important aspects of these freedoms, however, relate to economic opportunity and business activity.[1] In recent years, there has been increasing acknowledgment that the individual has special rights as a consumer.

PUBLIC POLICY AND CONSUMER RIGHTS

There is no precise definition of the consumer from a public policy perspective. Most efforts toward defining consumers occur when regulatory mechanisms are being devised for the consumers' protection. It is generally agreed that some consumers need more protection than others, but there is confusion as to the specific characteristics of those who require such protection.

Generally, the consumer-protection laws are designed to protect the "average purchaser." In 1942, however, a federal court declared that the Federal Trade Commission's control over deceptive practices covered all kinds of consumers, including "the ignorant, the unthinking and the credulous consumer."[2] The Federal Trade Commission, a major consumer-protection agency, has considered the "credulous" principle somewhat extreme and generally has not required advertisers to defend, for example, advertisements that are subject to a misleading connotation by those of the very lowest intelligence level.[3]

The FTC's tendency to ignore the lowest intelligence level has been criticized. According to former FTC Commissioner Mary Gardiner Jones, the FTC used an unacceptable model of a consumer in a case concerning the advertising of a fruit-juice drink. According to a majority opinion of the Commission, the advertising for the fruit-juice drink did not, as alleged in the complaint, convey the impression that it was being compared to citrus fruits, specifically orange juice. According to Commissioner Jones, however, the claims "high in Vitamin C" and "the sensible drink" were "nonclaims or incomplete claims" and have meaning only when consumers fill them in with their own perceptions.[4] The model used by the FTC in this case, according to Commissioner Jones, portrayed a consumer as "discriminating, sophisticated, and highly knowledgeable, as well as skeptical and unbelieving." The Commission ignored the standard model—"the ignorant, the unthinking and the credulous consumer."

Despite its reluctance to include those at the lowest level of intelligence in deciding whether or not a consumer is to be protected from deceptive practices, the FTC has decided that certain groups of consumers, such as the poor, the aged, and children, require special standards. The FTC, then, includes behavioral criteria of the various market segments in determining the need for protection.

A classification of consumer rights first made in an address by John F. Kennedy is fairly well accepted, but not necessarily considered all-inclusive. These rights included the right to information, the right to choose, the right to safety, and the right to be heard. Richard Nixon focused on the right to consumer education in his message to Congress in 1971. It should be noted that the right to protection is inherent in all of these rights.

THE RIGHT TO BE INFORMED

Although the consumer's right to information has been accepted for many years, concern with the behavioral aspects of the delivery and receipt of such information is of fairly recent origin. Such concerns are an outgrowth of the acknowledgment of behavioral influences in the processing of information—selective perception, source-related influences, symbolic interpretations, the arousal of dissonance, and so on. Public policy efforts to provide consumers with information necessary to make informed choices emerge through the elimination of some earlier restrictions on advertising, the requirement of disclosure of product information, and the elimination and correction of deceptive or misleading information.

Limiting Advertising Restrictions

In a 1976 decision that emphasized the consumer's interest in the "free flow of commercial information," the Supreme Court declared that commercial speech had the protection of the First Amendment.[5] Such information is necessary, according to the Court, in order to permit the consumer to make intelligent and informed decisions. In the following year, the Court extended First Amendment freedom to lawyers' advertising, paving the way for the elimination of many restrictions on professional advertising.[6] While these actions have led to some increase in the availability of information on professional services to consumers, the behavioral implications of this informational input are yet to be determined. At this time, there appears to be little agreement as to the kinds of information that should be made available or the way they should be presented to ensure receptivity and effectiveness.[7]

Disclosure Requirements

Recent years have seen an increase in legislative and regulatory requirements for additional disclosure of product information. The effects of these requirements on consumer behavior are difficult to determine; they have been in existence for too short a period of time.

The kinds of information that are legally required to be disclosed relate to comparative prices, comparative performance, ingredients, perishability, warning notices and clarifications, and warranties. (See Table 19.1.) An analysis of the effects of these disclosure requirements revealed information that may be useful in determining what their role should be in the future.[8] The effectiveness of disclosure information has been judged by various researchers on the basis of a number of criteria: awareness of information, comprehension of information, confidence in

TABLE 19.1   SOME RECENT AND PROSPECTIVE INFORMATION DISCLOSURE REQUIREMENTS

Type of disclosure	Implemented in past five years[a]	Probable in the future[b]
Comparative prices	Truth in lending Unit pricing Automobile list prices	Prescription prices Truth in life insurance Costs of operation of appliances and automobiles Truth in consumer leasing
Comparative performance and efficiency	Nutrition labeling of food products Lumen and life data for light bulbs Stereo amplifier power output Octane labeling Automobile performance (vehicle stopping distance, acceleration and passing ability, and tire creserve load)	Automobile gas mileage Appliance energy consumption and comparative efficiency Appliance performance Tire mileage, stopping ability, and high-speed resistance to heat Carpet and upholstery wear characteristics Quality grade labels for food products Sun screen efficacy of suntan preparations Standards of drug efficacy Detergent efficacy Vocational school drop-out rate
Ingredients (including additives)	Cosmetics Food Liquor Phosphate content of detergents	Labeling of fat content in food Presence of pesticides Pigment content of paint Labeling to explain purpose of food ingredients and additives
Life/perishability	Open dating of foods	Appliance durability and life Expiration dates for drug potency Automobile damage susceptibility and repair costs
Warnings/clarifications	Cigarette health hazards Lack of efficacy of vitamins Flammability (children's sleepwear)	Flammability of cellular plastic insulation

TABLE 19.1   (Cont.)

Type of disclosure	Implemented in past five years[a]	Probable in the future[b]
Form and usage of product/terms of contract and warranties	Size standards (i.e., TV screens and refrigerators) Truth in warranties and service contracts Tire construction and load rating	Standards specifying amount of product to use (i.e., detergents) Care labeling for clothing Terms of land sales contracts Truth in imports (country of origin) Truth in savings (interest payments) Disclosure of manufacturer, packer, and distributor of food products Net and drained weights of canned and frozen food

[a] Many of the disclosure requirements in this column will be the subject of future legislation designed to extend coverage (especially from state to federal jurisdictions) or clarify implementation problems. Some are primarily in existence as voluntary industry standards motivated by the threat of government involvement.
[b] As of the second quarter of 1975, none of these requirements had been implemented federally although serious proposals were being considered in virtually all cases.

Source: George S. Day, "Assessing the Effects of Information Disclosure Requirements," *Journal of Marketing* 40 (April 1976), p. 43.

judgments, use of information, and satisfaction and impact on behavior. Table 19.2 details the findings.

Between 60 percent and 70 percent of a sample of respondents were aware of the concept of unit pricing, 50 percent understood the meaning, and 30 percent to 50 percent used unit pricing in a buying situation. Only 26 percent had seen a nutrition label, 16 percent understood it, and 9 percent used such labels at least once.

EFFECTS OF DISCLOSURE REQUIREMENTS

An analysis of the effects of disclosure requirements revealed the following findings:[9]

The availability of information may increase buyer confidence. Consumers see themselves as benefiting, for example, from nutritional labeling because of the way it affects others—through advertising and through the accountability of food manufacturers for the nutritional quality of their food products. In stores where open dating was used, there was increased confidence in the freshness of all food. There are questions, however, about whether such increased confidence leads to

TABLE 19.2 EVIDENCE OF EFFECTS OF SELECTED INFORMATION DISCLOSURE REQUIREMENTS (UNLESS NOTED, PROPORTIONS REFER TO ENTIRE SAMPLE)

Effect	Disclosure requirement				
	Nutrition labeling[a]	Unit pricing[b]	Truth in lending[c]	Buying guide tags[d] (small appliances)	Open dating[e]
Awareness of information	26% saw label	60% to 70% awareness of concept	57% of all credit buyers noticed some credit information	50% noticed tag	65% noticed
Comprehension of information	16% understood label	50% understood meaning of concept	34% correctly reported interest rate on a recent purchase	—	36% knew that the pull date was used
Confidence in judgments	N/A	—	54% felt better knowing rates and charges	—	N/A
Satisfaction	—	—	—	—	Higher degree of satisfaction with freshness
Claimed use of information (one or more times)	9% used labels at least once	30% to 50% used in a buying decision	10% of all credit buyers used in last durables purchase	28% found tag helpful	39% used open dating on one or more products during last trip
Impact on behavior					
(a) Self-report	—	5% to 38% of claimed users said some element of a shopping trip was influenced	—	—	50% reduction in report of spoiled food
(b) Other evidence	—	—	Negligible relationship of knowledge and shopping behavior, choice of credit source, or decision to use cash or credit	No evidence of effect on pattern of sales for specific models	—

[a] R. J. Lenahan, J. A. Thomas, D. A. Taylor, D. L. Call, and D. I. Padberg, "Consumer Reaction to Nutritional Labels on Food Products," *Journal of Consumer Affairs* 7 (Spring 1973).
[b] Summary conclusions from a recent review of unit pricing studies: Ivan Ross, "Applications of Consumer Information to Public Policy Decisions," in *Marketing Analysis for Societal Problems*, ed. Jagdish Sheth and Peter Wright (Urbana: University of Illinois, 1974).
[c] George S. Day and William K. Brandt, *A Study of Consumer Credit Decisions: Implications for Present and Prospective Legislation* (Washington, D.C.: National Commission on Consumer Finance, 1973).
[d] Federated Department Stores, Inc., *Buying Guide Tag Pilot Program*, February 1970.
[e] R. C. Stokes, R. Haddock, W. J. Hoofnagle, and E. P. Taylor, *Food Dating: Shoppers' Reactions and the Impact on Retail Foodstores*, Report no. 984 (U.S. Department of Agriculture, Economic Research Service, January 1973).

Source: George S. Day, "Assessing the Effects of Information Disclosure Requirements," *Journal of Marketing* 40 (April 1976), p. 46.

increased satisfaction. Nevertheless, a laboratory study revealed that as the amount of information was increased, although the subjects made "poorer" purchase decisions, they felt more satisfied and certain regarding their selections.[10] Thus increased confidence may lead to increases in satisfaction.

Researchers who sought to discover whether the information that was disclosed was easy to use and relevant to the choice process have had conflicting findings. Truth-in-lending information, for example, is usually presented after the effective agreement—the oral agreement—is concluded; that is, after this information would be of use. There are problems with unit pricing in that coverage within stores is not uniform, labels are not uniformly understandable and legible, and in-store explanatory material is frequently lacking. Some people are confused as to how to interpret terms that are used in open dating—pull date, expiration date, pack date, display date. Moreover, some consumers assume that a label is a stamp of quality when no such meaning is intended.

Information disclosure requirements have the least effect on consumers who have the greatest need for consumer protection. Low-income consumers lack the education and knowledge necessary to choose the best buy, even if it is available. They often lack the freedom to go outside of their local community to engage in comparative shopping, and they lack the motivation to make improvements in their situation. As far as truth-in-lending information is concerned, low-income consumers are primarily influenced by the availability of credit and the size of the monthly payments rather than by the total cost of such credit. Whether the lack of use of disclosure information results from economic constraints or educational differences, these requirements mainly benefit the middle class.

Indirect effects of disclosure requirements on the retailer and the producer tend to benefit the consumer. It was found, for example, that buying-guide tags for small appliances provide more complete point-of-sale information and help to overcome the inadequacies of sales help. Price disclosure requirements may also lead manufacturers to increase quality or lower prices.

Some indirect effects, however, may be negative. Many retailers, for example, simply note that credit is available in order to by-pass the requirements of truth-in-lending legislation, which insist that when more information is made available, the retailer must also disclose annual percentage rates and credit charges. Furthermore, labels such as those attached to new cars with suggested retail prices have weakened the bargaining position of the buyer and encouraged retail price maintenance.

BEHAVIORAL DEFICIENCIES OF DISCLOSURE REQUIREMENTS

A review of the effects of information disclosure requirements suggests that these programs may require some modification. An analysis of the Truth-in-Lending Act revealed that improved knowledge of credit rates and charges that could reasonably be attributed to TIL have relatively little effect on credit search and use behavior. This finding, however, was not considered to constitute evidence of failure of TIL. It is possible that the small minority who understand and use the information to make a credit decision are sufficient to police the market. Moreover, it is not enough simply to provide consumers with more information. This may be the first step in a major educational task of getting consumers to understand the information and persuading them to use it.[11]

A study of grade labeling of beef disclosed that these standards do not truly reflect consumer preferences. Nor do such grades as Choice and Good indicate real differences in nutritional value, palatability, or tenderness of beef. Suggestions for improving this situation included a recommendation that the beef-grading system be modified.[12] Other researchers suggest that it would be useful to examine the extent to which consumers are deceived or misled by USDA-approved labels on products.[13]

Eliminating Deceptive Information

The responsibility for eliminating deception in business communications to consumers has been given to numerous federal regulatory agencies: the Food and Drug Administration, the Federal Trade Commission, the Securities and Exchange Commission, and others. The FTC, the agency most actively involved in this area, is empowered to eliminate "unfair or deceptive acts or practices." In the past, most of its activities relevant to consumer information have been concerned with eliminating deception in advertising; in recent years it has directed its attention to "unfair information" as well.

In determining deception, the FTC examines whether or not the communication has the "capacity or tendency to deceive." According to this standard, actual deception need not be proved; the potential for deception is enough to cause the message to be restricted.

The FTC has not clearly defined deception, but several criteria have emerged from its activities. Thus an ad may be deceptive if it presents a false claim, if the claim is true but presents a false impression, and if it provides insufficient information.[14]

An example of a *false claim* occurred in an advertisement by a company that insured credit-card holders against being held responsible for purchases made after their cards were lost or stolen. According to the ad, owners of lost or stolen cards might "find themselves liable for as much as $175,000." Since the Truth-in-Lending Act specifically limits the liability for lost or stolen credit cards to a maximum of $50, a consumer would have to lose 3,500 credit cards to incur such liability.[15]

A demonstration by a glass producer created a *false impression*. The commercial ad was designed to indicate the superiority of plate glass over plain glass, a claim that may be true. To demonstrate this superiority to the consumer, however, a scene was photographed through two automobile windows, one purported to contain plain glass and the other supposedly made of plate glass. For the plain-glass presentation, vaseline was streaked over the window, and the resulting view indicated obvious distortions. For the plate-glass presentation, the scene was photographed with the window rolled down.[16]

An advertisement for a bread product contained *insufficient information.* Recent medical evidence indicates that some foods containing fiber may be particularly beneficial to health. A bread product was widely touted for its fiber content. According to the FTC, the ads represented that the fiber in Fresh Horizons bread was the same kind as that in whole-wheat bread, when in fact the Fresh Horizons fiber was derived from wood.[17]

Criteria for unfairness are even more difficult to delineate. Some unfair practices include making claims without a reasonable basis or adequate substantiation, claims that offer promises unlikely to be fulfilled, and claims that may cause harm to special audiences, such as the elderly, children, and the handicapped. Many activities relevant to special target markets involve consumerist as well as public policy issues, and are discussed in the next chapter.

A BEHAVIORAL DEFINITION OF DECEPTION

One of the problems in establishing a standard approach to the issue of potentially deceptive communications is the difficulty of developing a precise definition. David M. Gardner suggests a behaviorally oriented definition of deception in advertising: "If an advertisement (or advertising campaign) leaves the consumer with an impression(s) and/or belief(s) different from what would normally be expected if the consumer had reasonable knowledge, and that impression(s) and/or belief(s) is factually untrue or potentially misleading, then deception is said to exist."[18]

The benefit of such a definition, according to Gardner, is that it permits a research approach to determining deception. For example, it assumes that some types of deception involve consumer attitudes. Attitude theory, discussed in Chapter 11, may be used to identify deception in advertising. According to attitude theory, the deceptively advertised claim may have its strongest impact on the cognitive element, that is, beliefs about the claim. Several researchers have advocated a belief criterion for deception. Potential problems with this approach emerge from the concepts discussed earlier—the halo effect, consumers' expectations, and the difficulties in determining consumers' perceptions. Moreover, any belief-oriented approach to deceptive advertising is likely to show that a given ad has created false beliefs for some consumers. Policy-oriented research in this area may require an answer to the question "When is a measured deception *serious enough* to warrant action?"[19] Some of these issues were discussed in Chapter 12.

REMEDIES FOR DECEPTION

In the past, most of the regulatory agencies responded to deception in promotional communication by seeking to eliminate the offending message. New insights into various aspects of consumer behavior have led to the development of other remedies.

Correcting Advertising Information. In recent years, eliminating the message has been deemed insufficient, since in many cases the message has been promulgated over a period of years, and it may be assumed that it has left a memory trace that has not dissipated.

To overcome the continuing effects of inaccurate information in past advertising, a remedy known as *corrective advertising* has been devised. Corrective advertising is designed to (1) dispel the residual effects of prior deceptive advertising, (2) restore competition to the stage that prevailed before the unfair practice, and (3) deprive firms from falsely obtained gains to which deceptive advertising may have contributed.

The first case in which such a remedy was suggested concerned an advertisement by Campbell Soups. Campbell was alleged to have placed marbles at the bottom of the soup bowl in advertisements designed to indicate the large amounts of meat and vegetables in its soup. The marbles forced the solid ingredients to the surface, creating, according to the FTC, the false impression that there was more stock than actually existed. A group of law students, designating themselves as SOUP (Stamp Out Unfair Practices), recommended that the Commission require Campbell to use corrective advertisements in order to dispel the memory trace resulting from its past advertising. The FTC accepted a consent agreement in which Campbell promised not to engage in such advertising in the future, but did not require correction. In several subsequent cases, settled by consent decree, the FTC did order such correction.

In the first litigated order (the firm appealed to the courts) to contain a corrective advertisement requirement, the Commission ordered Warner-Lambert to spend a specified amount on advertisements that included the following statement: "Contrary to prior advertising, Listerine will not prevent colds or sore throats or lessen their severity." According to the FTC, since 1921 Listerine's advertisements had contributed substantially to the belief that Listerine was effective in the treatment and prevention of colds and sore throats. Thus the FTC required that the amount to be spent by Warner-Lambert to dispel the belief that Listerine was effective for such purposes was to be equal to its average annual Listerine advertising budget for the ten-year period from April 1962 to March 1972. Some estimates indicated that the amount would approximate $20 million. Warner-Lambert appealed the decision, and an appeals court upheld the order but eliminated the "confessional" preamble "contrary to prior advertising." The Supreme Court's refusal to review the case supported the FTC's power to order such corrective advertising.[20]

Warner-Lambert's initial campaign to fulfill the corrective requirement incorporated the disclaimer "Listerine will not help prevent colds or sore throats or lessen their severity" in an ad comparing the product to its rival Scope. Ads depicted an "onion breath" sniff test during which it was noted, "While Listerine will not help prevent colds or sore throats or lessen their severity, breath tests prove Listerine fights onion breath better than Scope."

The FTC has retained a market research company to conduct a survey designed to assess the impact of corrective advertising for Listerine.[21] Questionnaires were to be sent to 14,000 households to inquire into consumers' beliefs and patterns of use of several brands of mouthwash. The results of this study were not available at this writing.

The effectiveness of corrective advertising in ensuring that consumers receive accurate information is an appropriate subject for behavioral research. One study that examined the effects of corrective advertising found that its impact on the audience varied, depending on whether the source of the messages was the affected company or the FTC. This finding was in keeping with the behavioral theory that the more prestigious the source, the more likely the message is to be believed. The results of this study indicated that when corrective messages were broadcast on the air, the FTC-source message increased brand recall.[22] When the corrective advertising appeared in print, intention to buy decreased when the corrective message was identified as originating with the FTC, but did not decrease when the company was named as the source. A recommended approach for future research is to examine the effects of corrective advertising measures in changing beliefs over time.[23]

Affirmative Disclosure. Affirmative disclosure is also designed to eliminate the potential for deception in promotional communications by providing information on negative attributes. Affirmative disclosure specifically requires a company to disclose in its advertising or labeling the deficiencies or limitations of its product or service so that the consumer may be aware of the negative as well as the positive attributes. The warning notice on cigarette packages and in cigarette advertising is an example of such disclosures.

A company offering a medical treatment to remove wrinkles and blemishes has been the subject of a complaint by the FTC for misrepresenting that the treatment was free from danger of infection and painful effects. According to a proposed consent order, the firm is to devote 15 percent of its advertising to disclosures of the inherent dangers of the treatment, or, as an alternative, to give this specific warning statement in all promotional materials and broadcast advertising:

> WARNING: This is a medical procedure—basically a chemical burn which peels skin away. It is extremely painful, takes a long time to heal, and exposes a person to risks of poisoning, infection, permanent scarring and other medical complications. If performed on the neck, the process may make it look worse....

Similarly, the Commission required the makers of Fresh Horizons bread to place the following statement in their ads: "The source of the fiber is wood" or "Contains fiber derived from pulp of trees."

The assumption is that the consumer will use such negative information in making purchase decisions, or at least in the development of attitudes toward products and services.

THE RIGHT TO CHOOSE FREELY

The extent to which the right to choose freely exists also depends on the nature of the market, the maintenance of open markets, the curtailment of monopolistic and antitrust activities, and the general state of the economy. Specific efforts are made by various federal agencies to eliminate deceptive practices that inhibit appropriate choice and to provide adequate buying criteria that can create the climate for right choice. Some of these efforts are described below.

Elimination of Bait-and-Switch Tactics

One of the longest continuing deceptive practices against consumers is the bait-and-switch tactic. Since its organization, the FTC has attempted to eliminate such practices but has had less than complete success. Sears, the "largest merchandising organization in the United States," was accused of conducting such activities in 1976.[24]

When companies bait and switch, they advertise a product at a very low price—the "bait." When the customer enters the store with the intention of buying the advertised product, she discovers it is "nailed down"—that is, the store has no interest in selling it. The customer, in fact, is discouraged from making the purchase and is urged instead to buy a "better" model at a higher price—the "switch."

It should be noted that there is nothing illegal in "trading up," a practice that is frequently engaged in by retail institutions. Trading up is the practice of encouraging the customer to purchase higher priced or better quality merchandise than that which he originally requested. Bait-and-switch, however, is illegal, for the retailer never intended to sell the advertised merchandise at all, merely using it as bait to lure prospective customers into the store so that they then could be sold higher priced merchandise. Although it may be difficult to make a distinction between these practices, the FTC has made such distinctions. It notes, for example, that in bait-and-switch the salespeople make no effort to sell the advertised merchandise and actually disparage it. Moreover, in some cases the advertising expenditures for such bait merchandise have exceeded the sales volume of those items. A number of firms have received orders to desist from bait-and-switch practices, thus providing consumers with free choice.

Consumer Warranties

Consumer groups and legislators have tried to secure reforms in product warranties for many years. One of the basic causes of warranty problems is that consumers and warrantors have quite different perceptions of the role that a warranty plays in the purchase situation.[25] For the consumer, the warranty may act as a positive influence. Given the choice of two similar products, only one of which is warranted, the consumer may prefer the warranted one, even at added cost. The warranty is taken as an assurance of product quality and value, even though this may not be the case.

The firm that offers the warranty considers it a promotional device in a market characterized by similar competing products rather than as an instrument offering real consumer benefit. Furthermore, while the consumer may regard warranty provisions as a grant of rights of redress that might not otherwise exist, the warrantor (before the passage of the warranty law) viewed the warranty as a legal instrument that limited his obligations to the purchaser.

Some of the provisions of the Magnuson-Moss Warranty–Federal Trade Commission Improvement Act, passed in 1975, were designed to overcome the problems consumers found with warranties. Before the passage of the act, warranty information was sometimes not available until after the purchase was made, since it was provided inside the closed appliance, for example. Now such information must be made available to the prospective consumer before the product is sold to him.

Information received by consumers about warranties had been misleading or obscure. The warranty is now required to contain such information as the identity and location of the warrantor, exceptions to warranty coverage, and the procedure to be followed by the consumer to obtain satisfaction under a warranty. Manufacturers of products costing more than $10 that are warranted (not every product need have a warranty) must designate their written warranties as either "full" or "limited."

If a seller designates her warranty as "full," she is required to repair an unsatisfactory product within a reasonable period of time. After the warrantor has made "a reasonable number" of unsuccessful attempts to repair it, the consumer may elect either replacement or refund without charge. The FTC has the power to establish different standards by product class as to what constitutes "a reasonable number" of repair efforts. A "limited" warranty does not provide the comprehensive stipulations offered by a "full" warranty.

To strengthen consumer recourse, the Magnuson-Moss act encourages warrantors to establish informal dispute-settlement procedures that meet FTC standards. It also provides for federal class-action suits when several consumers have been similarly damaged by a failure of the warrantor to perform, subject to certain conditions.

A true evaluation of how well this act works depends on the manner in which consumers behave in relation to warranties in the marketplace. For example, efforts should be made to determine the role the warranty takes in the sales transaction and the ways in which this role varies by product and the circumstances surrounding the sale. Some questions that should be answered are: What proportion of consumers wish to see the terms of the warranty before buying? Would it be more beneficial to have it printed on the carton as part of the sales display? Will consumers understand the significance of a "full" warranty as opposed to one that is "limited"? How will the answers to these questions differ by product class and circumstances of sale? Do the costs to consumers of these warranty-reform measures provide comparable benefits?[26]

Comparison Advertising

To improve consumers' ability to choose the FTC has recently encouraged the use of comparison advertising. Comparison advertising, as described in Chapter 8, occurs when advertisers mention competitors by name and directly compare specific attributes of their products with those of competitors. (See Exhibit 19.1.) According to the FTC, such advertisers improve the competitive environment and offer consumers specific information with which to compare brands.

EXHIBIT 19.1

A comparison ad

Whether comparison advertising is an efficient means of improving consumers' ability to choose is not clear. According to one study that tested commercials in packaged-goods industries, such as health and beauty aids and household and beverage products, such advertising may not provide benefits to consumers or advertisers.[27] According to this study, the comparative commercial appeared to create greater negative attitudes toward advertising. It also tended to generate greater sponsor misidentification, with the named competitor benefiting. It tended to create more skepticism toward commercial claims and more miscommunication. In most cases, comparative commercials were seen as no more persuasive than noncomparative versions. When only one comparative commercial was seen among a group of noncomparative commercials, however, it was found to be significantly more persuasive.[28]

Many companies currently use comparative advertising. Nonetheless, additional research is necessary to determine both its effectiveness in persuasion and its efficiency as a public policy measure. One study has indicated the need to find out whether comparisons that are "incomplete" are inherently ambiguous and susceptible to multiple meanings and therefore of dubious value to consumers. Incomplete comparisons are those in which the comparison attribute or object is not specifically designated, such as "Brand X tastes better" or "Brand X has more sudsing power." More than what? They don't say.

With the growing emphasis on comparison advertising, such advertisements are occasionally considered deceptive. According to the FTC, manufacturers of television sets have advertised the superiority of their sets over competitors' sets without having adequate substantiation for such claims. Some advertisements continue to provide survey evidence indicating the superiority of the manufacturer's product when in fact the manufacturer may have subsequent evidence that contradicted the survey data. The FTC is attempting to stop such practices.[29]

In a comparison advertising case concerning a sugar company, the FTC ordered the sugar refiner not to claim that there are differences between brands of granulated sugar or that its sugar is superior to others unless that difference or superiority is discernible to or beneficial to the class of consumers to whom the representation is directed.[30] The company had claimed that its sugar was superior to other kinds when, in fact, for purposes for which consumers generally purchase sugar, there are no differences between brands of granulated sugar.

The FTC does encourage comparison advertising, however, considering it to be a significant part of competition and a means of providing consumers with competitive information. It has, for example, expressed concern for codes adopted by broadcasting stations and other media which may place excessive restrictions on comparison advertising.

Eliminating Consumer Confusion

The FTC is concerned with promotional efforts that cause consumers to be confused as to what is being offered. In some cases, the FTC has issued orders designed to eliminate such confusion and to improve the consumer's ability to choose.

A finance company's offer of an "instant tax refund" led some consumers to believe that the main qualification for an instant loan was entitlement to a government refund. Actually, the loan, like all such loans, was based on the creditworthiness of the customer. The FTC had required that the company discontinue the use of the phrase "instant tax refund," since it confused consumers. A court of appeals revised the FTC's order that would have banned the use of this phrase and required that if it is used in advertising, it is to be qualified with explanatory material.[31]

According to the FTC, sales representatives of companies selling encyclopedias have used deceptive acts to gain entry into consumers' homes. Salespeople were trained to disguise the main purpose of the visit in a way that deceived the consumer as to the real reason the representative sought admittance to the home—to make a sale. They were trained to deliver verbatim a three-paragraph spiel that the encyclopedia company characterized as having the distinct advantage of allowing the representative to approach the prospect's door, not in the role of a seller, but rather in the role of a company representative who is delivering a free booklet and making an advertising-effectiveness survey.

An FTC order required the company's representatives, at the time admission is sought to the home to solicit a sale, to give the consumer a card that discloses (1) the name of the corporation, (2) the name of the sales representative, (3) the term "Encyclopedia Sales Representative," and (4) the statement "The purpose of this representative's call is to solicit the sale of encyclopedias."[32]

Suggesting Alternative Criteria

In the face of rapidly rising prices and declining energy resources, suggestions have been made to encourage the use of the concept of *life-cycle purchasing*.[33] Under this concept, the consumer evaluating alternatives would consider not only the initial cost of the product but three additional factors: operating cost, servicing cost, and disposal cost. As an aid to consumers in making such evaluations, regulatory programs are designed to provide performance labels for appliances and to encourage consumers to read them. As part of this program, tags are developed to be attached to appliances, providing such significant information as performance capability and energy efficiency.

THE RIGHT TO SAFETY

Programs to protect the health and safety of consumers may be approached in any of several ways. Historically, safety standards have been established in the manufacture of products. Such standards are continually being refined. In recent years failure to meet the standards has resulted in the recall of significant numbers of products. Other efforts have focused on the consumer in an attempt to generate increasing concern for safety.

Product Recalls

Product recall requirements have a significant impact on firms. Numerous legislative acts, as well as a variety of regulatory agencies, have provided for the recall of hazardous products. Figure 19.1, which lists a number of legislative mandates and products recalled, does not include state laws providing for recall.

As with many other consumer programs, the effectiveness of product recall requires further evaluation. While the safety implications are clearly desirable, some analysts suggest that these rules require a rigorous cost/benefit analysis before their overall usefulness can be ascertained.[34] From the point of view of consumers, the effectiveness of the program depends on their ability to receive the recall information, an issue that suggests the utility of consumer-behavior theories in the development of appropriate communication networks.

Consumer Safety Programs

If the health and safety of consumers are to be protected, they must be persuaded to change their behavior in some way. For example, campaigns have been designed to provide immunizations for children entering school, to provide for and encourage the use of seat belts, and to encourage people to have their blood pressure tested. Such campaigns require consumers to act, and unfortunately are rarely, if ever, 100 percent effective.[35]

Another method of protecting consumers is the passive approach. Laws have been passed to require milk to be pasteurized and drinking water purified before they reach consumers. Many other passive approaches, however, have been neglected. One widely recommended passive restraint is the air bag that inflates automatically in a severe crash. At this writing, it is not yet required equipment in any car. Break-away light poles that yield on impact are available and in use in some places, but are not required; nor are restraints on the speed capability of automobiles that are currently not supposed to be driven faster than 55 miles per hour.

An evaluation of mass-media campaigns to improve the consumer's health revealed that the actual effects of advertising on deeply rooted behavior may be small.[36] Such campaigns appear to be more effective in achieving intermediate goals, such as creating awareness of the topic and of its importance. If behavioral change is the goal, it may be necessary to combine mass-media campaigns with interpersonal and group reeducation programs. When behavior is particularly intractible, as in the use of seat belts, persuasive strategies may not achieve public health goals, and other solutions, such as legal sanctions or money incentives, may have to be sought.

FIGURE 19.1 LEGISLATIVE MANDATES FOR RECALL OF PRODUCTS AND PRODUCTS RECALLED

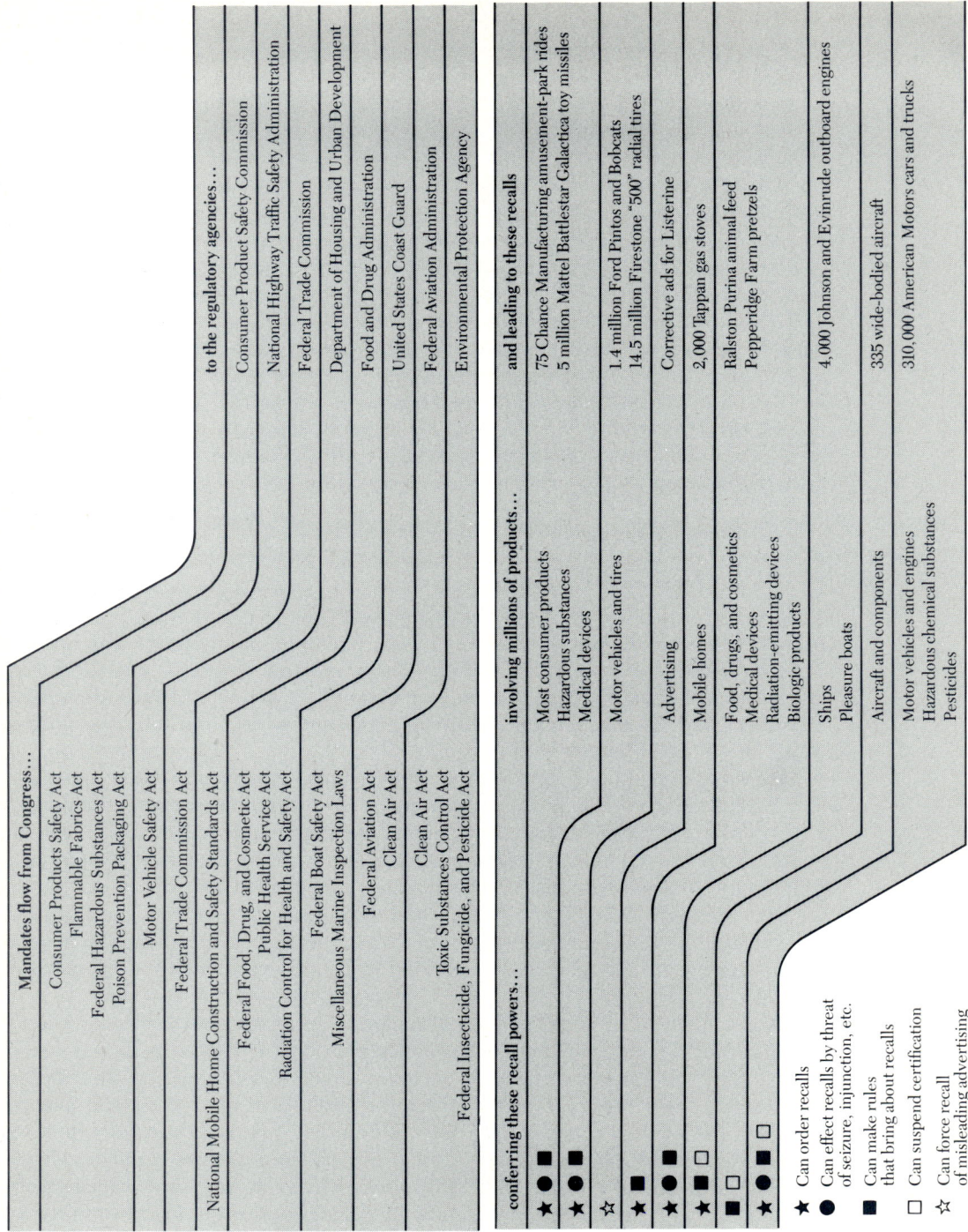

Mandates flow from Congress…

- Consumer Products Safety Act
- Flammable Fabrics Act
- Federal Hazardous Substances Act
- Poison Prevention Packaging Act
- Motor Vehicle Safety Act
- Federal Trade Commission Act
- National Mobile Home Construction and Safety Standards Act
- Federal Food, Drug, and Cosmetic Act
- Public Health Service Act
- Radiation Control for Health and Safety Act
- Federal Boat Safety Act
- Miscellaneous Marine Inspection Laws
- Federal Aviation Act
- Clean Air Act
- Clean Air Act
- Toxic Substances Control Act
- Federal Insecticide, Fungicide, and Pesticide Act

to the regulatory agencies…

- Consumer Product Safety Commission
- National Highway Traffic Safety Administration
- Federal Trade Commission
- Department of Housing and Urban Development
- Food and Drug Administration
- United States Coast Guard
- Federal Aviation Administration
- Environmental Protection Agency

involving millions of products…

- Most consumer products
- Hazardous substances
- Medical devices
- Motor vehicles and tires
- Advertising
- Mobile homes
- Food, drugs, and cosmetics
- Medical devices
- Radiation-emitting devices
- Biologic products
- Ships
- Pleasure boats
- Aircraft and components
- Motor vehicles and engines
- Hazardous chemical substances
- Pesticides

and leading to these recalls

- 75 Chance Manufacturing amusement-park rides
- 5 million Mattel Battlestar Galactica toy missiles
- 1.4 million Ford Pintos and Bobcats
- 14.5 million Firestone "500" radial tires
- Corrective ads for Listerine
- 2,000 Tappan gas stoves
- Ralston Purina animal feed
- Pepperidge Farm pretzels
- 4,000 Johnson and Evinrude outboard engines
- 335 wide-bodied aircraft
- 310,000 American Motors cars and trucks

conferring these recall powers…

- ★ Can order recalls
- ● Can effect recalls by threat of seizure, injunction, etc.
- ■ Can make rules that bring about recalls
- □ Can suspend certification
- ☆ Can force recall of misleading advertising

Source: *Fortune*, April 9, 1979, pp. 54–55.

Safety Message Strategy

Some suggestions have been offered in regard to the design of messages intended to promote the safe use of products. Three factors to be considered are the source of the message, its content and structure, and its timing.[37]

Earlier discussions of the use of fear appeals are relevant to the content and structure of such messages. In view of the conflicting evidence regarding fear appeals, care should be taken in their use. In other words, the use of fear appeals to promote the safe use of products may not always yield desirable results. Other persuasive methods should be tried, such as the appeal that makes the dangerous activity appear offensive to group or social norms rather than dangerous.[38] A seat-belt safety message, for example, can suggest that one shows one's care or love for one's passengers by making sure that they fasten their seat belts and that failure to do so implies lack of love or concern.

To ensure that messages of product safety are timed properly and achieve the greatest impact, the mood of the audience and its interest in the subject matter should be studied and a determination made of the proper sequencing of the messages. The seasonal pattern in the use of bicycles and sleds, for example, suggests the appropriate date of initiation and sequencing of messages promoting their safe use.

THE RIGHT TO BE HEARD

The right of consumers to be heard has received increased attention in recent years. Such attention is expressed in the passage and implementation of laws designed to regulate abuses and in actions by consumers and consumer groups. Consumer concerns about the right to be heard are manifested in boycott activities and class-action suits. Regulatory efforts in this area are exemplified by credit regulations and the use of informational input from consumers to formulate rules and determine the existence of deception in the marketplace.

Consumer Boycotts

Although boycotts are not widely used, their potential as an expression of dissatisfaction is always there. Consumers have boycotted meat, sugar, and coffee in protest against high prices. The most highly publicized and apparently effective boycott occurred in the meat industry in April 1973. Those who engaged in the boycott were found to be younger, more liberal, and better educated than nonboycotters and were more likely to attribute rising meat prices to external forces.[39] This finding is consistent with the belief inherent in their actions: that direct action by consumers could bring prices down by exerting pressure on cattlemen, middlemen, and the government structure.

A potential area for the boycott mechanism that is receiving some attention involves violence on television. A survey conducted by the J. Walter Thompson advertising agency revealed that of the 47 percent of the sample of people who thought television was getting worse, 32 percent posited excessive violence as a reason.[40] When asked directly about the amount of violence on television, 42 percent of the sample said it was "extremely" widespread or "very" widespread, and another 42 percent said it was "somewhat" widespread. The survey also disclosed that the correlation between viewing patterns and attitudes toward violence is very high. People who say they hate it stay away from it; people who like it or are not offended by it watch it.

Of particular interest was the issue of whether or not consumers would actually boycott the product advertised on a program they considered excessively violent. A very small percentage (less than 2 percent) indicated that they would, and another 5 percent said they had considered not buying a product advertised on a violent show. These potential boycotters, however, were in the age group 35–49, well educated, in the upper-income brackets, and were considered opinion leaders. Thus this group, if mobilized, might have a strong influence on elected officials and civic organizations. Of further significance to firms that advertise on violent programs was that one-fourth of all respondents indicated that they would approve of government intervention to reduce TV violence, primarily because it would be more effective than current controls.

Class-Action Suits

A strong opportunity for consumers to be heard exists in the class-action suit, a lawsuit in which a representative of a large number of people who have similar claims against the same defendant sues on behalf of himself and others similarly situated. In many cases of consumer deception, the loss to the individual is so small that the costs of the suit would exceed any damages that could be collected. When this loss is multiplied by the thousands of consumers who may have been deceived, however, such a suit is reasonable and desirable. Moreover, many individual consumers may fail to bring suit because they are ignorant of their rights.

The courts have set a number of stringent requirements for the class-action suit that have minimized the opportunities for such actions. Under recent legislation, however, both the Department of Justice and the Federal Trade Commission can institute suits on behalf of consumers to secure restitution resulting from deceptive practices and antitrust activities, and recent court rulings appear to acknowledge the rights of consumers themselves to institute class-action suits under the Federal Trade Commission Act and the Clayton Act. A district court declared that consumers could seek recovery from sellers of a freezer-food plan for sales practices that allegedly violated the FTC Act and an FTC consent order against the seller's franchiser.[41] The court declared that in view of the government's inability to act in more than a small fraction of cases of deceit, a private right of action is necessary. A change has also taken place in the consumer's right to sue under antitrust statutes. Recently the Supreme Court ruled that a consumer has the right to sue for treble damages in a case concerning price fixing of hearing aids.[42]

Consumer Credit Regulation

The dramatic increase in consumer credit over the past thirty years has caused certain problems relevant to the consumer's right to be heard. As a result, a number of legislative efforts have been designed to regulate various perceived credit abuses: the Consumer Credit Protection (Truth-in-Lending) Act (1968), the Fair Credit Reporting Act (1970), the Fair Billing Credit Act (1975), the Equal Credit Opportunity Act (1975), the Consumer Leasing Act (1976), and the Fair Debt Collection Practices Act (1977). The FTC also has prepared rules against abusive credit practices.

One problem emerged from a legal doctrine—the holder-in-due-course doctrine—that served to deprive customers of needed protection in credit sales. Under this policy, the consumer's obligation to pay for the goods or services he purchased was not conditioned upon the seller's corresponding duty to keep his promises.[43] Typically, the story went like this: A consumer, relying on the seller's representations of a product's characteristics, service warranty, and so on, made a purchase on credit. The consumer then found the product unsatisfactory; it failed to measure up to the seller's claims, or the seller refused to provide the promised maintenance. The consumer then sought relief from his debt obligation only to find that no relief was possible. His debt obligation, he was told, was not to the seller, but to a third party, whose claim to payment was legally unrelated to any promises made about the product. Before the sale, in fact, the seller had arranged to have the debt instrument held by someone other than himself; usually he sold it at a discount. The consumer was left without ready recourse. He had to pay the full amount of his obligation. He had a product that yielded less than its promised value. And he had been robbed of the only realistic leverage he possessed—his power to withhold payment.

A story in the *Phoenix Planner* reported the following incident:

> A consumer bought a car, paid 25 percent down and signed a note for the balance. The dealer sold the note to a bank. After a few days, the purchaser of the car realized he had a lemon, returned it, told the dealer to keep the money he had already received, and left thinking that was the end of the matter. But it wasn't, because the bank still held the note and demanded payment. The customer refused to pay, since he had taken the car back. The only thing he had worth money was a mobile home in which he lived with his wife and children. The bank got a court order and sent two deputy sheriffs out to claim it. The man resisted, with a gun. In the shootout, all three were killed.[44]

In order to avoid the occasions that can lead to such tragedies, in November 1975 the FTC issued a trade regulation rule concerning the "preservation of consumers' claims and defenses." According to this rule, consumer lenders must notify third-party holders of the instruments that they (the third parties) are subject to any consumer claims or defenses on the transaction. In fact, consumer credit contracts must contain the following provision in large type:

NOTICE

ANY HOLDER OF THIS CONSUMER CREDIT CONTRACT IS SUBJECT TO ALL CLAIMS AND DE-
FENSES WHICH THE DEBTOR COULD ASSERT AGAINST THE SELLER OF GOODS OR SERVICES
OBTAINED PURSUANT HERETO OR WITH THE PROCEEDS HEREFOR. RECOVERY HEREUNDER
BY THE DEBTOR SHALL NOT EXCEED AMOUNTS PAID BY THE DEBTOR HEREUNDER.

The effect of this requirement is to eliminate the procedure that made the consumer's duty to pay independent of the seller's duty to fulfill his obligations. It eliminates the consumer's obligation to make full payment to a creditor despite breach of warranty, misrepresentation, and even fraud on the part of a seller who has turned the debt over to a third party. It provides the consumer with the right to be heard and the leverage to make sure he will be listened to.

The extent to which credit legislation has protected consumers or influenced their behavior remains to be determined. Such findings may require intensive analysis of the behavior of specific segments, such as disadvantaged consumers. Public policy experts have suggested that such an analysis requires further investigation and inputs from regulators, consumers, industry, scholars, and other independent observers.[45]

Gathering Consumer Data

Regulatory agencies have begun to use consumers as sources of information to be used in designing their programs. The Magnuson-Moss Warranty Act authorized the FTC to provide compensation of up to $1 million for participation by the public in the agency's rule-making proceedings. Such funds have been made available, for example, to those who wish to be heard at the proceedings to determine whether or not limitations would be placed on television advertising directed to children.

Consumer surveys are used to gather information relevant to regulatory decisions. The FTC, for example, uses consumer surveys in determining whether or not advertising is deceptive. Such evidence was used in the Wonder Bread case discussed in Chapter 12. While the number of cases in which the FTC has used consumer evidence is relatively small, there are indications that use of such data will increase in the future, in part because of the FTC's desire to control more subtle forms of deception, such as those involving consumers' perceptions.[46]

CONSUMER EDUCATION

To President John F. Kennedy's Consumer Bill of Rights, President Gerald R. Ford added a fifth concept. The original four rights were those to information, choice, safety, and to be heard. In 1975 Ford stated, "The time has now come to recognize a fifth right—one without which consumers cannot gain the full benefit of the other four. This is the right to consumer education.''[47]

Before the fifth right was acknowledged, President Nixon directed the Office of Consumer Affairs to establish guidelines for consumer education programs in all grades from kindergarten through high school. The Office of Consumer Affairs prepared such guidelines and sent copies to every school district in the United States.[48] By 1975, only five states had made consumer education a required high school course, although several other states have listed it as an "educational priority."[49] In view of research that suggests that consumers do not make appropriate use of the information that is made available to them, additional education efforts ought to provide significant benefits.

A recent study, however, found little evidence that formal consumer education contributes much to the adolescent's learning of consumer skills; future research should examine the reasons for students' failure to learn consumer skills at school.[50] Such research may be directed, for example, to uncovering the relationships between knowledge and behavior.[51]

A consumer may not avail herself of the consumer protection laws because she does not feel that the issue is important enough, does not wish to spend the necessary time, or feels she will not win without a high-priced lawyer. Consumers are not alone in being insufficiently aware of all of the legal remedies available to them: some lawyers are not well versed in them, either. When a questionnaire containing questions relevant to consumer protection laws was submitted to consumers and attorneys in Texas, only 31 percent of the respondents answered correctly questions related to the legality of door-to-door selling practices. No more than 40 percent of questions dealing with false or deceptive advertising and deceptive retail practices were answered correctly. Although there were differences between lawyer and consumer samples in knowledge of the consumer protection laws, the magnitude of the differences was not large. In the area of false or deceptive advertising, for example, only 33.5 percent of the consumers' responses and 46.5 percent of the lawyers' responses were correct.[52]

A recent report concluded that although the FTC has broad authority to help consumers who have been the victims of unfair or deceptive practices, it has had limited success.[53] Part of this failure is attributed to the fact that the FTC's policies and procedures are not effectively communicated to consumers. In January 1975, for example, the Commission settled its case against a vocational school that offered such courses as keypunching, computer programming, and secretarial training. Commission staff estimated that students paid about $12 million in tuition for courses that were virtually worthless for future employment. The negotiated settlement required the school to refund up to $1.25 million to certain students. The school had difficulty locating students eligible for the refund and ended up paying back only about $675,000.

Current programs to educate the consumer appear to be inadequate to solve these problems. Several studies have indicated that educating families on poison prevention has little effect on the incidence of child poisoning. Research has indicated, however, that it is possible to reduce children's attraction to these products

EXHIBIT 19.2

Toy Safety Curriculum

Little
Leon
the
Lizard

U.S. Consumer Product Safety Commission

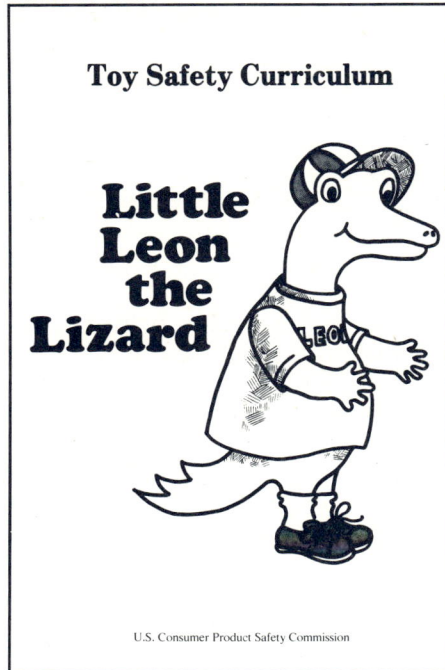

Consumer education begins in kindergarten
Source: U.S. Consumer Product Safety Commission

through package and label design.[54] A related technique has been adopted by the Consumer Product Safety Commission in the educational materials prepared by its Consumer Education and Awareness Division and distributed to public schools. Little Leon the Lizard, a bright-green baby reptile who wears a red baseball cap (see Exhibit 19.2), is one of a cast of characters in these materials, part of an educational program designed to reduce the number of product-related injuries and deaths among children under age 16, now estimated at 10 million annually.[55]

SUMMARY

Public policy considerations with respect to consumers find their expression in a number of consumer rights: the right to be informed, to choose freely, to safety, to be heard, and to consumer education.

In acknowledgment of the consumer's right to the free flow of information, the Supreme Court has ruled that commercial speech is protected by the First Amendment. Both the Food and Drug Administration and the Federal Trade Commission have designed programs to disclose nutritional information in the advertising and labeling of foods. The FTC also requires corrective advertising and affirmative disclosure by companies that have engaged in deceptive advertising practices.

An analysis of the effectiveness of the various information disclosure requirements adopted by regulatory agencies has indicated that they may increase buyer confidence and may indirectly result in beneficial consumer effects by leading manufacturers to increase quality and lower prices. The findings are conflicting, however, concerning the ease with which such information may be used and its relevance to the choice process.

To ensure the consumer's right to choose freely, efforts have been made to eliminate bait-and-switch tactics, and an extensive warranty program has been adopted. The use of comparison advertising has been encouraged to stimulate competition, and efforts have been made to eliminate confusion in the marketplace.

Programs designed to promote the health and safety of consumers involve product recalls and efforts to change consumer behavior. A more passive approach attempts to incorporate safety features in products before consumers purchase them. An understanding of the manner in which consumers react to various message sources and the use of fear appeals in advertising are useful in devising a message strategy to promote consumer safety.

The right of consumers to be heard finds its expression in legislation and in such consumer actions as boycotts and class-action suits. A number of legislative acts have been passed to give consumers an opportunity to be heard in areas where there are apparently widespread consumer problems, such as credit abuses. Data are gathered from consumers to be used in designing regulatory mechanisms and in determining the occurrence of deception.

Programs have been designed to educate consumers, but they have met with little success. Consumers continue to be largely unaware of the legal remedies available to them. Widespread programs to educate consumers as to legal remedies are not yet available, but some attempts should be made by both companies and regulatory agencies to educate consumers in the proper choice and use of products.

DISCUSSION QUESTIONS

1. How would you define a consumer for public policy purposes? Should intelligence be a significant characteristic in the setting of advertising standards?

2. How does the increase in professional advertising affect consumers, in your opinion?

3. To what extent do you use disclosure information? What kind of additional information do you believe should be disclosed?

4. Using Gardner's behavioral definition of deception, describe an advertisement that tends to deceive.

5. Have you ever seen any corrective ads? How did you react to them?

6. To what extent do you personally agree with the findings regarding the effects of comparative advertising? Explain.

7. Do you agree on the necessity of a cost/benefit analysis to evaluate the usefulness of product recalls? Explain.

8. How can behavioral insights be incorporated in a consumer education program? A safety program?

NOTES

1. Robert N. Corley and Robert L. Black, *The Legal Environment of Business* (New York: McGraw-Hill, 1973), p. 51.

2. *Aronberg* v. *FTC*, 132 F. 2d 165 (1942).

3. M. D. Bernachhi, "Substantive False Advertising Standards: Discretion and Misinformation by the FTC," *Journal of Advertising* 5 (Spring 1976), pp. 24–28.

4. "Legal Developments in Marketing," *Journal of Marketing* 38 (April 1974), p. 82.

5. *Virginia State Board of Pharmacy* v. *Virginia Citizens Consumer Council, Inc.*, U.S. 96 S. Ct. 1817 (1976).

6. *Bates* v. *State Bar of Arizona*, 45 U.S.L.W. 4895 (1977).

7. "Legal Developments in Marketing," *Journal of Marketing* 40 (July 1976), p. 96.

8. George S. Day, "Assessing the Effects of Information Disclosure Requirements," *Journal of Marketing* 40 (April 1976), pp. 42–52.

9. Ibid., pp. 45–51.

10. Jacob Jacoby, Donald E. Speller, and Carol A. Kohn, "Brand Choice Behavior as a Function of Information Load," *Journal of Marketing Research* 11 (February 1974), pp. 63–69.

11. George S. Day and William K. Brandt, "Consumer Research and the Evaluation of Information Disclosure Requirements: The Case of Truth in Lending," *Journal of Consumer Research* 1 (June 1974), pp. 21–32.

12. John A. Miller, David G. Topel, and Robert E. Rust, "USDA Beef Grading: A Failure in Consumer Information?" *Journal of Marketing* 40 (January 1976), pp. 25–31.

13. Philip G. Kuehl and Robert F. Dyer, "An Experimental Examination of Deception in Labeling: Consumer Research and Public Policy-making," in *Advances in Consumer Research*, vol. 5, ed. H. Keith Hunt (Ann Arbor: Association for Consumer Research, 1978), pp. 206–211.

14. Dorothy Cohen, "The Concept of Unfairness as It Relates to Advertising Legislation," *Journal of Marketing* 38 (July 1974), pp. 8–13.

15. *In re Credit Card Service Corp. et al.*, 3 Trade Reg. Rep. no. 20,215 (January 1973).

16. *In re Libby-Owens-Ford Glass Co. and General Motors Co.*, 3 Trade Reg. Rep. no. 16,509 (July 1962).

17. *In re ITT Continental Baking Co., Inc.*, 3 Trade Reg. Rep. no. 21,546 (March 1979).

18. David M. Gardner, "Deception in Advertising: A Conceptual Approach," *Journal of Marketing* 39 (January 1975), pp. 40–46.

19. Jerry C. Olson and Philip A. Dover, "Cognitive Effects of Deceptive Advertising," *Journal of Marketing Research* 15 (February 1978), p. 37 (italics in original).

20. "Legal Developments in Marketing," *Journal of Marketing* 40 (October 1976), p. 118.

21. Dorothy Cohen, "Anacin Ruling Indicates Research Role at FTC," *Marketing News,* December 15, 1978, p. 3.

22. Robert F. Dyer and Philip G. Kuehl, "The 'Corrective Advertising' Remedy of the FTC: An Experimental Evaluation," *Journal of Marketing* 38 (January 1974), pp. 48–54.

23. Robert F. Dyer and Philip G. Kuehl, "A Longitudinal Study of Corrective Advertising," *Journal of Marketing Research* 15 (February 1978), pp. 39–48.

24. "Legal Developments in Marketing," *Journal of Marketing* 41 (April 1977), p. 106.

25. Laurence P. Feldman, "New Legislation and the Prospects for Real Warranty Reform," *Journal of Marketing* 40 (July 1976), p. 41.

26. Ibid., p. 47.

27. Philip Levine, "Commercials That Name Competing Brands," *Journal of Advertising Research* 16 (December 1976), pp. 7–14.

28. Terence A. Shimp, "Comparison Advertising in National Television Commercials: A Content Analysis with Specific Emphasis Devoted to the Issue of Incomplete Comparative Assertions," in *Marketing in Turbulent Times, 1975 Combined Proceedings of the American Marketing Association Conferences,* ed. Edward M. Masse (Chicago: American Marketing Association, 1975), pp. 504–508.

29. "Legal Developments in Marketing," *Journal of Marketing* 41 (July 1977), pp. 119–120.

30. "Legal Developments in Marketing," *Journal of Marketing* 41 (April 1977), p. 106.

31. *Beneficial Corp. and Beneficial Management Corp.* v. *FTC,* 5 Trade Reg. Rep. no. 61,066 (September 1976).

32. *Encyclopaedia Britannica, Inc., and Britannica Library Home Services* v. *FTC,* 5 Trade Reg. Rep. no. 62,793 (August 1979).

33. Stanley E. Cohen, "Product Label Plan Forging Ahead Despite Protests from Appliance Area," *Advertising Age,* June 6, 1977, p. 18.

34. Walter Guzzardi, Jr., "The Mindless Pursuit of Safety," *Fortune,* April 9, 1979, pp. 54–64.

35. Leon S. Robertson, "Consumer Response to Seat Belt Use Campaigns and Inducements: Implications for Public Health Strategies," in *Advances in Consumer Research,* vol. 3, ed. Beverlee B. Anderson (Ann Arbor: Association for Consumer Research, 1976), pp. 287–289.

36. Mary Jane Schlinger, "The Role of Mass Communications in Promoting Public Health," ibid., pp. 302–305.

37. Joseph C. Miller and A. Parasuraman, "Advising Consumers on Safer Product Use: The Information Role of the New Consumer Product Safety Commission," *1974 Combined Proceedings of the American Marketing Association Conferences* (Chicago: American Marketing Association, 1975), pp. 372–376.

38. John R. Stuteville, "Psychic Defenses against High Fear Appeals: A Key Marketing Variable," *Journal of Marketing* 34 (April 1970), pp. 39–45.

39. Michael B. Mazis and John H. Faricy, "Consumer Response to the Meat Boycott," *1974 Combined Proceedings of the American Marketing Association Conference,* p. 333.

40. "TV Violence: In the Eyes of the Beholders," a survey by J. Walter Thompson Company (1977).

41. *Eugene and Jacqueline Guernsey et al.* v. *Rich Flan of the Midwest et al.,* 5 Trade Reg. Rep. no. 60,740 (March 1976).

42. *Kathleen R. Reiter* v. *Sonotone Corp. et al.,* U.S. Supreme Court no. 78-690 (June 1979).

43. *FTC Staff Guidelines on Trade Regulation Rule Concerning Preservation of Consumers' Claims and Defenses* (Washington, D.C.: Bureau of Consumer Protection, May 4, 1976).

44. Booton Herndon, *Satisfaction Guaranteed* (New York: McGraw-Hill, 1972), pp. 225–226.

45. See, for example, Alan R. Andreasen and Gregory D. Upah, "Regulation and the Disad-

vantaged: The Case of the Creditors' Remedies Rule," *Journal of Marketing* 43 (Spring 1979), pp. 75–83, and John R. Nevin and Gilbert A. Churchill, Jr., "The Equal Credit Opportunity Act: An Evaluation," *Journal of Marketing* 43 (Spring 1979), pp. 95–104.

46. Michael T. Brandt and Ivan L. Preston, "The Federal Trade Commission's Use of Evidence to Determine Deception," *Journal of Marketing* 41 (January 1977), pp. 54–62.

47. *Guide to Consumer Services* (Washington, D.C.: Office of Consumer Affairs, 1976), p. 2.

48. Department of Health, Education, and Welfare, *Suggested Guidelines for Consumer Education: K–12* (Washington, D.C., 1970), p. v.

49. Paul N. Bloom and Mark S. Silver, "Consumer Education: Marketers Take Heed," *Harvard Business Review*, January 1976, p. 33.

50. George P. Moschis, "Formal Consumer Education: An Empirical Assessment," in *Advances in Consumer Research*, vol. 6, ed. William L. Wilkie (Ann Arbor: Association for Consumer Research, 1979), pp. 456–459.

51. Richard Staelin, "The Effects of Consumer Education on Consumer Product Safety Behavior," *Journal of Consumer Research* 5 (June 1978), pp. 30–40.

52. William H. Cunningham and Isabella C. M. Cunningham, "Consumer Protection: More Information or More Regulation?" *Journal of Marketing* 40 (April 1976), pp. 63–68.

53. *Comptroller General's Report to the Congress: Victims of Unfair Business Practices Get Limited Help from the Federal Trade Commission* (Washington, D.C.: Comptroller General of the United States, October 1978), p. 9.

54. Kenneth C. Schneider, "Prevention of Accidental Poisoning through Package and Label Design," *Journal of Consumer Research* 4 (September 1977), pp. 67, 73.

55. U.S. Consumer Product Safety Commission, "CPSC Memo" (Washington, D.C.: September 1978).

CHAPTER 20

CONSUMERISM

To be effective, a public policy program must be adaptable to changing emphases and issues. Consumer issues shift and change. Public policy and consumerism are, in fact, closely related; but while effective public policy must accommodate all groups in society, including business, consumerism focuses on the rights and powers of consumers.

This chapter discusses the consumer movement and examines such significant questions as:

What is consumerism?
How can the consumerist be identified and reached?
How do firms respond to consumer issues?
What are the consumer's responsibilities?
How can consumer-behavior research be brought to bear on consumer issues and public policy decisions?

Consumerism has a long history in the United States. Since the early 1900s there have been at least three strong, distinct consumer movements. It is only with the current consumer movement, however, that efforts have been made to apply behavioral insights to consumer issues.

The first consumer movement was fueled by such factors as rising prices,

477

Upton Sinclair's writings, and scandals concerning ethical drugs.[1] It culminated in the passage of the Pure Food and Drug Act (1906), the Meat Inspection Act (1906), and the creation of the Federal Trade Commission (1914). The second consumer movement, in the mid-1930s, was also a result of an upturn in consumer prices, this time in the midst of a depression, and the sulfanilamide scandal. Dr. Samuel Massengell, a prominent druggist of Bristol, Tennessee, discovered a method of packaging sulfanilamide in a liquid form. He bottled nearly 500 gallons of the mixture and proceeded to sell it as a patent medicine called Elixir Sulfanilamide. He had not tested the mixture for toxicity, nor had he bothered to test its effects even on animals. The use of the patent medicine ultimately caused 73 deaths in 7 states. Under the existing law the Food and Drug Administration was unable to hold Massengell responsible, nor could the government have legally seized the drug had it not been for a technicality—an elixir by law had to contain alcohol and by sheer chance this one did not. The Food and Drug Administration seized the remaining stock, enough to kill 3,720 people, and ultimately Massengell was fined $200 for having misbranded a drug product.[2] The resulting publicity brought about the strengthening of the Pure Food and Drug Act and the Wheeler-Lea Amendment to the FTC Act, which gave the Commission the power to regulate against unfair or deceptive acts or practices.

The current consumer movement resulted from a complex combination of circumstances, including increasingly strained relations between standard business practices and long-run consumer interests. It is this movement that has gone beyond concern for fair prices and market practices to emphasize consumer rights. In the drive to secure such rights, attention has been focused on the application of behavioral insights to consumers' activities in the marketplace and on the behavioral implications of consumerist proposals.

DEFINING CONSUMERISM AND THE CONSUMERIST

Like those that preceded it, the current consumer movement does not emerge from a clear consensus of needs and objectives. For example, there is as yet no generally accepted definition of consumerism. Philip Kotler, focusing on consumer rights, defines consumerism as "a social movement seeking to augment the rights and powers of buyers in relation to sellers."[3] Another definition that has received some acceptance examines the remedies that should be made available to consumers and defines consumerism as "the organized efforts of consumers seeking redress, restitution, and remedy for dissatisfactions they have accumulated in the acquisition of their standard of living."[4] This definition does not encompass consumer concerns that occur despite lack of effort toward redress. Both of these definitions, however, relate in some manner to consumer rights, which are addressed in many aspects of public policy. While it is sometimes difficult to draw precise lines between public policy and consumer concerns, a major distinction emanates from the fact that public policy makers must consider the rights of sellers as well as those of consumers.

Just as there are difficulties in arriving at an acceptable definition of consumerism, similar problems are encountered in describing the consumerist. A recent work defines a consumerist as "a consumer active in pioneering and supporting consumer issues in order to upgrade and protect the well-being of consumers."[5]

Research efforts to isolate and identify the consumerist can be useful in devising strategies to reach them. Consumerists make up an important market segment, since they constitute at least 15 percent of the population and are likely to be particularly influential with other consumers.[6] Identification of the consumerist may also be useful for public policy purposes.

Demographic Variables

Many approaches have been suggested for understanding the consumerist segment. Demographic studies have revealed that the consumerist is considerably better educated than the average person, more likely to be employed in management or a professional position, of middle to upper-middle income, and a member of a smaller family.[7] Such information may be usefully applied, for example, to the design of communication programs directed toward consumerists. Messages are more likely to reach consumerists if they appear in travel and news magazines such as *Time* and *National Geographic*, and on documentary and public affairs programs on television.

Sociopsychological Variables

While some studies indicate that sociopsychological variables are not relevant to an understanding of the consumerist, others suggest that they are very relevant indeed. Research has examined "socially conscious consumers," described as those whose actions lead to improvement in the quality of life.[8] Such consumers were found to be less alienated than others, to feel less isolated, to be more involved in the community, and to be more inner-directed.[9]

Other studies indicate that personality may be an important indicator of the socially conscious consumer. It is suggested that insights relevant to such consumers may be offered by Abraham Maslow's theory, discussed in Chapter 9, of a hierarchy of needs, ranging from basic physiological needs to the need for self-actualization. A study indicated that individuals who are higher on the dimension of self-actualization will appear more often among socially conscious consumers than will those whose self-actualization level is lower.[10] Such campaigns as the one used by *U.S. News and World Report*, "We spare our readers unimportant news, we spare our advertisers unimportant readers," may be useful in capturing the attention of the self-actualizing consumer.

Public Policy Implications

A precise definition of the consumerist is of particular importance to public policy makers. Many consumerists lobby for consumer regulations. Such groups, however, may not be totally representative of the broad consumer interest. A study of consumerists who had written to governmental or regulatory agencies revealed the following demographic profile: they are likely to be white, married, female, 45 years of age or more, with some college education, residing in the northeastern or north central states, and with a family income well above the median.[11] This led to the conclusion that the consumer representative who testifies before regulatory bodies may not be truly representative of the American public.

TARGETED CONSUMERISM

In recent years consumer protectionists have focused on certain segments of the society in efforts to ensure their rights and to protect groups that need more help than those more favorably situated—the low-income consumer, children, the aged, the sick, and so on. The special consumer activities involving two such segments—the low-income consumer and the young—are discussed below.

Low-Income Consumers

Consumerism has become identified with problems associated with the social fabric, particularly those of the low-income consumer. These consumers suffer the most from fraud, excessive prices, exorbitant credit charges, and poor quality in merchandise and service.[12] Solutions aimed at improving the amount and quality of product information appear to have little relevance to low-income buyers, who lack most of the characteristics of the prototype middle-income consumer. For example:[13]

> Low-income consumers are often unaware of the benefits of comparative shopping.
> They lack the education and knowledge necessary to choose the best buy even if it is available and have fewer opportunities to learn through experience.
> They often lack the freedom to go outside of their local shopping communities to engage in comparative shopping.
> They lack an appreciation of their rights and liabilities in postsale legal conflicts.

Questions have been raised as to the extent of the protection afforded by consumer protection laws, particularly to low-income consumers. One study examined the attitudinal and cognitive readiness of consumers to accept such consumer legislation. The researcher hypothesized that the effectiveness of a statute often depends on consumers' ability to understand the law well enough to recognize illegal activities (cognitive readiness) and their confidence in the efficacy of the legal system (attitudinal readiness).[14]

The study examined the attitudes of consumers toward cooling-off laws —statutes that permit the consumer a cooling-off period during which he can cancel without penalty a purchase he has made from a direct-to-home salesperson. The evidence suggests that consumers in low-income areas are less attitudinally and cognitively ready to take advantage of cooling-off laws than are middle- and high-income consumers. The low-income respondents indicated the most favorable attitudes toward direct salespeople and the products they sell, the least favorable attitudes toward consumer protection laws in general and the cooling-off law in particular, and less knowledge of the provisions of the cooling-off laws. The results suggest that those consumers who are perhaps most in need of the protection this law can provide are those who are least likely to use it.

Another researcher found that the availability of unit pricing did not result in a significant reduction of cost of a selected set of grocery products to low-income consumers.[15] The researcher concluded that these results may be due to the low saliency of price as a purchase criterion in the grocery store. Since the addition of unit pricing information represents a rather small modification of the environment, it seemed unlikely that consumers would immediately incorporate it in their behavior patterns. To accomplish such changes of behavior, it may be necessary to determine the proper conditions for increasing the saliency of such pricing information.

The implications of these studies are being examined and no doubt will be used in the development of programs that offer increased protection for the low-income consumer. Some recent activities have indicated one direction such a program may take: ensuring better understanding of the information. One such effort has been designed to ensure that foreign-language-speaking customers understand information that is relevant to their purchasing decisions. For example, retailers who advertise in Spanish-language media and often make sales presentations in that language have been ordered to provide Spanish-speaking customers with a Spanish translation of retail installment contracts and related documents.[16]

In designing a trade regulation rule to eliminate deceptive practices by vocational schools, the FTC made its first use of the "Flesch Test" and applied it to consumer notices. The test, devised by Rudolf Flesch, is a readability test, and uses a scale designed to measure the ease with which material can be understood. Under this test, the notices contained in the rule were rated "very easy." The trade regulation rule would require vocational schools to disclose various kinds of information for those taking the courses, such as the dropout rates and placement and salary statistics.

Children

Much of current consumer concern related to children deals with advertising and its influences. Complaints have charged that advertising influences children to eat junk food and food excessively laced with sugar, to exert excessive pressure on parents to buy the merchandise advertised, and to engage in actions deleterious to themselves. Efforts have been directed toward curtailing, modifying, and reorienting the focus of such advertising.

A public-interest group concerned with children, Action for Children's Television (ACT), petitioned the FCC for removal of advertising from children's programming. The FCC denied the petition, but some controls have been established for advertising geared to children. The National Association of Broadcasters has adopted a code that limits the number of minutes of commercials on programs primarily directed to children. It also requires that commercial material be clearly separated from program content and prohibits the delivery of sales messages by program hosts. These requirements respond to findings that young children appear to be unable to distinguish clearly between program content and advertising and that program hosts appear to have strong persuasive influence on young children.

These efforts are somewhat limited because the question of whether children need special protection from the effects of advertising has not been definitely answered. One study did indicate that first-graders appear to be "quite persuasible"; roughly two-thirds of them indicated that they trusted all commercials and liked all commercials, and roughly half claimed they wanted the products they saw advertised.[17] This study also revealed, however, that these percentages declined dramatically among third- and fifth-graders. Thus the argument can be advanced that exposure to advertising is a necessary prerequisite for the development of cognitive defenses against advertising's persuasive effects. These findings led the researchers to suggest that the issue of advertising effects must be approached from multitheoretical and interdisciplinary research perspectives.

GOVERNMENTAL ACTIVITIES

Some governmental regulatory efforts have been directed toward protecting "special" consumer groups. The Federal Trade Commission has indicated particular concern with advertisements that may cause children to engage in conduct deleterious to themselves. A relatively new criterion established by the FTC for unfair advertising is the tendency to cause "unreasonable risk or harm." The Commission is particularly concerned with such influences as they involve children.

In one instance, the FTC issued a complaint against a manufacturer of a rice product for an advertisement that encouraged a four-year-old to "help" cook rice and therefore behave in a manner that led to unreasonable risk or harm.[18] The child in the ad is assigned the task of watching a pot of rice that has been removed from a stove and placed on a counter. The child places her face close to the pot and examines it. The company agreed to a consent order that prohibited it from presenting advertisements that showed children closely examining foods being cooked.

In another advertisement, naturalist Euell Gibbons was depicting eating certain wild plants and stating that they were edible and delicious.[19] The FTC ordered the cereal company that sponsored the advertisement to stop representing that wild plants are suitable for human consumption, since children might be tempted to try them and thus injure themselves.

FTC hearings were held to determine whether restrictions should be placed on television advertising to children. The proposals included a ban on all televised product advertising to audiences composed of a significant proportion of children less than 8 years old.[20] In addition, television advertising of sugared food products directed to audiences including children aged 8 to 12 would be banned. Televised advertisements for sugared food products not banned but seen by many older children would be balanced by advertiser-funded nutritional or health disclosures. However, criticisms by industry and advertising groups of such far-reaching proposals by the FTC ultimately led to the passage of the FTC Improvements Act of 1980 (Public Law No. 96–252), which limits the agency's activities. The act provides for a congressional veto of FTC rules and eliminates the agency's power to develop trade regulation rules relating to unfair (as opposed to deceptive) advertising. The FTC may still propose trade regulations rules on children's advertising on the basis of deception and may proceed against unfair advertising on a case-by-case basis.

CONSUMER RECOMMENDATIONS

Consumerists have suggested that an appropriate response to children's advertising is to turn this communication effort into a positive force. Suggestions have been made that television advertising become a vehicle for social messages to children. One area pinpointed for such an approach is the formation of food habits. Children learn through their culture what is considered fit to eat; however, it appears as though the forces that mold the eating attitudes and behavior of children and youth have, in recent years, been extended to television.

It is estimated that children under 13 who are moderate TV viewers see an average of 220 minutes of commercials per week and over 5,000 commercials per year for edible products alone. The foods most heavily advertised are snacks (including candy), cereals, and beverages. During the first six months of 1974, on weekend daytime programming, vegetables, cheeses, soups, and virtually all meats, fish, and poultry received a total of one commercial altogether.[21] There is obviously a vast opportunity to present good nutritional advertisements on children's programs and to improve the social and nutritional development of the children.

Commercials have special features that are likely to lead to later action by children. Inserted into popular programs designed to entertain are brief messages, appealing jingles, enchanting music and sound effects, repetition, and the delivery of a single concept with a pitch to purchase the product being advertised. These characteristics are designed to hold the child's attention, to provide information, and to motivate her to some specific action or response. It is possible that these basic educational principles as used in television commercials can be used also to communicate information on nutrition.

CORPORATE RESPONSES

Marketers and consumerists need not see each other as antagonists. A sense of social responsibility and an understanding of public policy should lead the prudent marketing manager to take note of consumers' concerns in his actions.

One suggested approach is a "strategy of accommodation."[22] Internally this strategy provides educational programs that instruct managers in new marketing and management regulatory policies and attempt to convince them of the need for compliance with the law. Externally, it focuses on the trade-off between traditional and new public expectations that somehow must be reconciled. A strategy of accommodation goes beyond internal dissemination of information and extends to self-policing activities in such areas as advertising, consumer rights, and product safety. A major emphasis should be on innovative approaches to corporate management and marketing policies that lead to more informed open relations with the public and government.

Many companies have adopted such policies in providing consumers with information, responding to complaints, and presenting the firm's side of relevant issues.

Corporate Information

An aggressive consumer-oriented program can have a favorable impact on the image of a company and even on its profits. In a study conducted for Giant Food Stores, which initiated such a program, consumers cited consumer information programs as a major criterion for supermarket selection. Giant Food Stores increased its sales, market share, and profits during the relevant period.[23]

Marketers can aid consumer educators by providing consumers with advice. Shell Oil Company had a campaign in 1977 that helped motorists to determine how to react in certain hazardous driving situations and taught them what to look for when they were confronted with automobile problems. General Foods has also presented consumer education messages in advertisements. One series of ads explained in clear language what processed foods are and how they may be prepared. General Motors acknowledges the right to be informed by providing information on the meaning of "sticker prices." (See Exhibit 20.1.)

Responding to Complaints

Some companies react directly to a widespread consumer complaint. One major source of consumer dissatisfaction concerns automobile repair services. General Motors, in evident awareness of this fact, uses symbolic representations to express

EXHIBIT 20.1

CUSTOMER INFORMATION FROM GENERAL MOTORS

WHAT "STICKER PRICES" REALLY MEAN

HOW TO GET THE BEST BUY ON THE CAR THAT'S BEST FOR YOU.

Every GM dealer is an independent businessman. No one can tell him what to charge. Not the government, and not the manufacturer.

But the government can and does require that manufacturers post a suggested retail price, or "sticker price," on every new car we build. It's a good idea, because it makes it easier for you to compare one car against another.

Remember, the "sticker price" is only the suggested price. The actual selling price may be different. That's because the law of supply and demand affects the prices of cars, just as it affects most other prices. And market conditions change all the time.

For example: a very popular model may sell at the suggested price, but frequently cars will sell for less, because the automobile business is highly competitive.

The difference between the "sticker price" and the wholesale price—that's what the dealer pays us—is called the markup, or dealer's discount. This changes from time to time, but as a general rule the markup on small cars is lower than on full-size cars.

The dealer's markup helps to pay his rent, taxes, salaries, utility bills—all that it costs to run a business. And he also has to make a profit, or he can't stay in business. Last year, GM dealers reported about two cents profit on each dollar of sales. As you can see, competition doesn't leave the average dealer a very big margin of profit.

You can affect the price you pay. It depends on the marketplace, for one thing. You may get a bigger break if you choose a slower-selling model or a car the dealer already has in stock. The latest sales figures published in many newspapers will give you some idea of how cars are selling, although the demand for a particular model may be greater or less in your area.

How much optional equipment you order on your car also makes a big difference in its price. Go over the list carefully, and equip the car just the way you want it. Then it will have most value for you, and you'll enjoy it more. You shouldn't buy what you won't use, although much of the equipment you add to your new car will make it worth more when you decide it's time to trade it in.

Most buyers trade in a used car when they buy a new one. And the value of used cars varies according to demand as well as to their condition. Performance and appearance count, so it's a good idea to maintain your car and keep it clean. The more you can get for your old car, the less will be your out-of-pocket cost to replace it with a new one.

But whichever car you choose, the price should never be your only consideration. The dealer's reputation and his service capability are also important.

Our interest is in helping both you and the dealer to get a fair deal. We want you to be satisfied with your car. That's good for you, good for the dealer, and good for us.

This advertisement is part of our continuing effort to give customers useful information about their cars and trucks and the company that builds them.

General Motors
People building transportation to serve people

A corporation provides information helpful to consumers

its concern with satisfactory repairs. An extensive promotional campaign emphasized that GM's "Mr Goodwrench" could solve the consumer's automobile repair problems. Companies may also respond by the creation of mechanisms to handle complaints, as described in Chapter 17.

Some marketers have turned to the use of hot lines for consumer complaints. In a study to determine which problems were considered most important by consumers, more than 3,000 calls received by a consumer hot line in 1971 were analyzed.[24] Six categories were most prevalent: prepurchase, purchase/transaction/delivery, product performance, guarantee/warranty/contract performance, service/repair, and deposits/credit/collections.

TABLE 20.1 CONSUMER PROBLEMS REPORTED TO CONSUMER HOT LINE, BY CATEGORY

Type of problem	% of hot-line sample (N = 150)	
Prepurchase		
Deceptive advertising	6	
Offensive advertising	8	
		14
Purchase/transaction/delivery		
Failure to deliver	15	
Wrong product delivered	2	
Product damaged	3	
Unsolicited advertising	2	
Excessive charge	5	
		27
Product performance		
Defective product	17	
		17
Guarantee/warranty/contract		
Deceptive or inadequate warranty	2	
Failure to honor guarantee/warranty	3	
Failure to honor contract	5	
Cancellation of contract	1	
		11
Service/repair		
Faulty repairs	9	
Merchandise exchange	3	
Refund/return	13	
Charge for services not rendered	1	
		26
Deposits/credit/collections		
Refused credit	2	
Interest-rate problems	1	
Security deposit problems	1	
		4
Other	1	
		1
		100

Source: Steven L. Diamond, Scott Ward, and Ronald Faber, "Consumer Problems and Consumerism: Analysis of Calls to a Consumer Hot Line," *Journal of Marketing* 40 (January 1976), p. 59.

TABLE 20.2   SOCIAL CLASS OF HOT-LINE CALLERS, BY CATEGORY OF PROBLEMS REPORTED (PERCENT)

Problem category	Social class			
	Low (N = 39)	Middle (N = 66)	High (N = 45)	Total (N = 150)
Prepurchase	13%	11%	20%	14%
Purchase/transaction/ delivery	10	31	31	27
Product performance	13	18	18	17
Guarantee/warranty/ contract	15	11	9	11
Service/repair	39	25	18	26
Deposits/credit/ collections	8	1	4	4
Other	2	3	0	1
	100%	100%	100%	100%

Source: Steven L. Diamond, Scott Ward, and Ronald Faber, "Consumer Problems and Consumerism: Analysis of Calls to a Consumer Hot Line," *Journal of Marketing* 40 (January 1976), p. 60.

Tables 20.1 and 20.2 indicate that although purchase/transaction/delivery and service/repair problems were most prevalent, the problems reported by consumers tended to vary by social class. Upper-class respondents were most likely to complain about advertising; purchase and delivery problems were most frequently reported by middle- and upper-class callers; and lower-class consumers reported considerably more problems in the service and repair area. (See Table 20.2.)

Even when follow-up calls indicated that the problems that initially occasioned the calls to the hot line had been solved, respondents held significantly more negative attitudes toward business than those held in the broader population. Some of these problems were not under the direct control of the large national manufacturer, but the findings suggest that such organizations should pay greater attention to the selection of retail outlets in order to gain better control over such major problem areas as delivery and retail service.

Advocacy Advertising

As a response to controversial social concerns, some corporations have engaged in "issue" or "advocacy" advertising. While attempts have been made to distinguish among these forms of advertising,[25] essentially they are designed to present the corporation's point of view on a significant issue. Monsanto, for example, has used an extensive advertising campaign in an effort to change the public's perception of all chemicals as "bad." (See Exhibit 20.2.)

Marketers should be aware, however, that the consumer is exposed to many

EXHIBIT 20.2

Corporations engage in advocacy advertising in efforts to change the public's perception of their products or operations.

other corporate images through alternative communications. Advocacy advertising can play a healthy role only if a company is making other efforts to bring its performance into line with public expectations. For example, Beechnut Foods indicated for some time its concern with excessive additives in baby foods. The company validated this concern by ceasing to add sugar to its baby foods and dropping desserts from its line. According to the company, the reformulation will remove 8.2 pounds of sugar from a baby's first-year diet.

CONSUMER RESPONSIBILITIES

A commitment to consumers' rights requires an equivalent commitment on the part of consumers to their own responsibilities. There are indications that consumers may not be aware of, completely acknowledge, or clearly understand their responsibilities in the marketplace. An evaluation of a number of consumer protective efforts has provided evidence that consumers do not take advantage of the informational or remedial opportunities offered to them. Conversely, some consumers take too much advantage of the potential protection available to them and in fact engage in fraudulent practices.

A partial list of responsibilities consumers should undertake includes:

1. The responsibility to expose themselves to consumer educational opportunities.
2. The responsibility to gather information from various sources, such as labeling information, required disclosures, and warranty data.
3. The responsibility to use such information in their purchase decisions.
4. The responsibility to articulate legitimate dissatisfaction.

Public policy officials, consumerists, and others have attempted to generate increased interest in consumer responsibilities in a variety of areas. Consumerist concerns have become identified with widespread interest in the quality of the physical environment. The problems of air, water, and noise pollution have become increasingly obvious, and recently energy problems have attained extremely high saliency. Federal agencies, in an effort to change attitudes in the direction of energy conservation, have engaged in an advertising campaign that exhorts consumers, "Don't be fuelish." In the late 1970s, the apparent ineffectiveness of persuasive messages in changing attitudes toward conservation of gasoline led to such governmental actions as odd–even-day gas rationing. Efforts to change awareness and attitudes are continuing, however, and the Department of Energy is considering a major test of paid advertising to tell the public how to save energy.[26]

The results of these actions will be seen in the future. It is clear that the energy shortage is one of the most significant problems facing the economy. Consumer-behavior theory may provide a vital link to programs that offer effective solutions.

Consumer Self-Protection

The consumer cannot rely on public policy measures and consumerist activities to provide total protection. In many areas the consumer clearly has to provide her own protection.

While product safety is a prime societal concern, the legal community recognizes the need for consumers to protect themselves. Product liability rules hold the firm responsible for injury to a consumer resulting from lawful use of a product for the purpose for which it was intended, but this liability does not extend to other uses of the product. To some extent, the limitations on liability are based on the concept of "foreseeability"—the results that could reasonably be anticipated by a manufacturer or supplier.[27] Liability of the manufacturer or supplier may be limited if the product user engages in misuse, abnormal use, or unintended use of the product.

A consumer may disregard a strong warning concerning a danger connected with the use of a product. If a cigarette smoker ignores the warning label on cigarette packages and suffers lung damage, the manufacturer cannot be held liable. Small children may use toxic substances in an unintended way—they may swallow them. If the manufacturer took reasonable measures to warn of harmful consequences, she cannot be held liable. If a consumer is injured when he picks up a lawn mower by hand and attempts to trim a hedge with it, it is doubtful that the manufacturer could be held liable.

Consumers may also be held responsible for protecting themselves against false advertising claims. As we saw earlier, the FTC holds that it is not in the public interest to challenge advertising claims whose truth or falsity the average consumer can judge by making one rather inexpensive purchase of the advertised product.

An FTC commissioner declared that consumer trial and error may be the quickest way to eliminate dishonest advertising claims when a product is relatively inexpensive and frequently purchased or when its attributes can be easily verified before purchase.[28] When consumers lack the expertise or resources to evaluate claims, however, deception through misrepresentation or silence may pay, even if the product is cheap. In other cases, the product may be so costly that a consumer's wrong choice based on deception may be extremely harmful. In such situations, the market is not always susceptible to self-correction, and a formal regulatory mechanism may be required.

RESEARCH DIRECTIONS FOR PUBLIC POLICY AND CONSUMER ISSUES

The consumer-behavior literature provides a fertile field for suggestions concerning research into public policy and consumer issues. Information-processing theory, the diffusion and adoption processes, attitude theory, and analysis of the consumer decision process may all provide insight into effective measures for consumer protection. Some suggested approaches are discussed below.

Segmenting Consumer Targets

As we have seen, public policy makers and consumerists segment consumers in accordance with the need for protection. Segmentation may also be applied in designing informational or other programs for consumers. For example, there are indications that ecologically concerned consumers differ in several ways from those who do not share environmental concerns. The following profile of the ecologically concerned consumer emerged from one study:[29]

> She tended to score high in perceived consumer effectiveness against pollution; that is, she believed consumers could be effective in reducing pollution.
> She was high in her openness and tolerance for new ideas.
> She was high in her need to understand the workings of things and to satisfy intellectual curiosity.
> She was moderately high in her need to obtain personal safety and avoid harm.

A behavioral approach suggests an education program directed at both those who are ecologically concerned and those who are not. For the concerned consumer, the educational program can incorporate a maximum arousal of the need for understanding, a mild arousal of the need to avoid harm, and a heavy emphasis on the effectiveness of consumers. These needs may be aroused by a presentation of factual evidence of a product's effectiveness in acting against pollution, indicating the reasons for its effectiveness, stressing how one could show social concern through purchase of the product, and stressing the impact consumers can have on pollution levels. Such an approach was supported by another study of ecologically responsible consumers that indicated that they preferred logical, factual appeals to those intended to arouse status motives or other essentially emotional appeals.[30]

For the consumer who does not base his actions on ecological concern, an education program should be designed to increase his confidence in his ability to contribute to pollution abatement.

Another study indicated that a psychographic profile was useful in constructing a welfare assistance program. The study, conducted in Canada, revealed that individuals who scored high on "independence from government" would tend to react favorably to a change in the welfare assistance program that resulted in tax savings, whereas those who scored higher on "altruism" would tend to prefer welfare reform that provided more generous benefits and did not require a recipient to move to a place where jobs were available.[31]

Decision Models

The multiattribute model is useful in understanding consumers' decisions that pertain to public policy. Such a model has been suggested, for example, in the development of programs to persuade people to switch from private automobile transportation to mass transit. A multiattribute model can be used to identify utilities and conjoint analysis can then be applied to determine trade-offs among attributes of both mass transit and private transportation.[32] Such information can assist the planner of public transportation to determine changes in the transit system most likely to increase ridership. A study that used this approach indicated that the policies most likely to improve the overall use of public transportation would be those directed toward improved total travel time, increased availability of service, protection against dangerous people, and comfort.

Research may also be directed toward the isolation of the factors that are most salient in socially relevant purchase decisions. This recommendation emerged from a study to determine the extent to which consumers are environmentally consistent in their purchase behavior; that is, if they select low-polluting product A, will they also select low-polluting product B?[33] The study focused on the purchases of gasoline, detergents, paper towels, and bathroom tissues. The sample of people tested were environmentally inconsistent in their purchases. This finding led the researcher to suggest that other factors may be more important in the purchase decision than the environmental aspects of the products studied. It may therefore be necessary to increase the saliency of ecological factors in consumer purchase considerations. Another approach may be to identify factors that are closely related to environmental characteristics of the product and emphasize these connected attributes in the purchase situation.

SUMMARY

There is no clear consensus on a definition of consumerism or, for that matter, the consumerist. Consumerism is generally defined in terms of the rights and powers of consumers or organized efforts by consumers to seek redress. The consumerist may be viewed as one who is active in pioneering and supporting consumer issues. Demographic and sociopsychological variables have been used to characterize the consumerist. Such data are useful in attempts to isolate and reach the consumerist.

The concept of segmentation has been applied to consumerism. Thus, certain segments of the society are considered in need of more protection than others. Studies have been conducted to determine the effectiveness of protective efforts as they relate to low-income consumers, with the aim of designing programs that will more efficiently protect the interests of this group. Children are also considered to require special protection, particularly in the area of advertising. Some controls have been placed over advertising to children, and suggestions have been made that advertisements may be useful in efforts to direct social messages to children.

A sense of social responsibility as well as prudent management should encourage firms to adopt practices responsive to the concerns of consumers and public policy. Such practices include the provision of corporate information, adequate response to consumer complaints, and advocacy advertising.

Consumers also have a responsibility to gather and use the information made available to them and to protect themselves by using products in a safe manner.

Consumer-behavior theory is in its infancy; much more research is required before its concepts will have widespread acceptance. Such research may support or reject current concepts, provide new directions for study, and suggest new applications of constructs. It will also generate many questions and criticisms, but we have reason to hope that it will offer aid to buyers, sellers, and public policy makers, and generate among these groups the desire and means to exercise social responsibility.

DISCUSSION QUESTIONS

1. Are you a consumerist? Explain.

2. Do you believe the FTC should eliminate television advertising to very young children? Explain.

3. What behavioral insights can be introduced into consumer programs by corporations?

4. To what extent do you believe consumers themselves are responsible for problems in buyer-seller relationships?

5. Provide three advocacy ads and discuss their objectives.

6. Do you believe a company should use its funds for advocacy advertising? Explain.

NOTES

1. Philip Kotler, "What Consumerism Means for Marketers," *Harvard Business Review,* May–June 1972, pp. 48–57.

2. Otis Pease, *The Responsibility of American Advertising: Private Control and Public Influence, 1920–1940* (New Haven: Yale University Press, 1958), p. 124.

3. Ibid., p. 50.

4. Richard H. Buskirk and James T. Rothe, "Consumerism—An Interpretation," *Journal of Marketing* 34 (October 1970), pp. 61–65.

5. Jacques C. Bourgeois and James G. Barnes, "Viability and Profile of the Consumerist Segment," *Journal of Consumer Research* 6 (March 1979), pp. 217–228.

6. Ibid., p. 227.

7. " 'It's Up to Marketer to Communicate,' " *Marketing News,* May 4, 1979, p. 10.

8. George Brooker, "The Self-Actualizing Socially Conscious Consumer," *Journal of Consumer Research* (September 1976), pp. 107–112.

9. Leonard Berkowitz and Kenneth G. Lutterman, "The Traditional Socially Responsible Personality," *Public Opinion Quarterly* 32 (1968), p. 169.

10. Brooker, "Self–Actualizing Socially Conscious Consumer," p. 227.

11. " 'It's Up to Marketer to Communicate.' "

12. George S. Day and David A. Aaker, "A Guide to Consumerism," *Journal of Marketing* 34 (July 1970), pp. 12–19.

13. Ibid., p. 16.

14. Dennis H. Tootelian, "Attitudinal and Cognitive Readiness: Key Dimensions for Consumer Legislation," *Journal of Marketing* 39 (July 1975), pp. 61–64.

15. William E. Kilbourne, "A Factorial Experiment on the Impact of Unit Pricing on Low-Income Consumers," *Journal of Marketing Research* 11 (November 1974), pp. 453–455.

16. *In re Busch's Jewelry Co., Inc.,* 3 Trade Reg. Rep. no. 21.057 (December 1975).

17. Thomas S. Robertson and John R. Rossiter, "Children and Commercial Persuasion: An Attribution Theory Analysis," *Journal of Consumer Research* 1 (June 1974), p. 20.

18. "Legal Developments in Marketing," *Journal of Marketing* 41 (July 1977), p. 119.

19. "Legal Developments in Marketing," *Journal of Marketing* 41 (April 1977), p. 106.

20. *In re proposed Trade Regulation Rules for Children's Advertising,* Trade Reg. Rep. no. 331 (May 1978).

21. Norge W. Jerome, "Children's Television Advertising: A Vehicle for Pro-Social Nutritional Messages," in *Marketing in Turbulent Times and Marketing: The Challenges and Opportunities, 1975 Combined Proceedings of the American Marketing Association Conferences,* ed. Edward M. Mazze (Chicago: American Marketing Association, 1975), pp. 511–513.

22. Douglas N. Ross, "Corporate Response to Social Challenges," in *New Marketing for Social and Economic Progress, and Marketing's Contributions to the Firm and to Society: 1974 Combined Proceedings of the American Marketing Association Conferences,* ed. Ronald C. Cuhan (Chicago: American Marketing Association), 1975, p. 228.

23. Marion C. Burke and Leonard L. Berry, "Do Social Actions of Corporations Influence Store Image and Profits?" *Journal of Retailing* (Winter 1974–1975), pp. 62–72.

24. Steven L. Diamond, Scott Ward, and Ronald Faber, "Consumer Problems and Consumerism: Analysis of Calls to a Consumer Hot Line," *Journal of Marketing* 40 (January 1976), pp. 58–62.

25. S. Prakash Sethi, "Institutional/Image Advertising and Idea/Issue Advertising as Marketing Tools: Some Public Policy Issues," *Journal of Marketing* 43 (January 1979), pp. 68–78.

26. Richard L. Gordon, "U.S. Mulls Paid Test on Energy," *Advertising Age,* June 25, 1979, p. 1.

27. William L. Trombetta and Timothy L. Wilson, "Foreseeability of Misuse and Abnormal Use of Products by the Consumer," *Journal of Marketing* 39 (July 1975), p. 49.

28. *Trade Regulation Reports,* February 1, 1977, p. 11.

29. Thomas C. Kinnera, James R. Taylor, and Sadrudin A. Ahmed, "Ecologically Concerned Consumers: Who Are They?" *Journal of Marketing* 38 (April 1974), pp. 20–24.

30. W. Thomas Anderson, Jr., Karl Henlon, and Eli P. Cox III, "Socially vs. Ecologically Responsible Consumers," in *New Marketing,* ed. Cuhan, pp. 304–312.

31. Sadrudin A. Ahmed and Douglas N. Jackson, "Psychographics for Social Policy Decisions: Welfare Assistance," *Journal of Consumer Research* 5 (March 1979), pp. 229–239.

32. Linda L. Golden, John F. Betak, and Mary I. Alpert, "Attracting Potential Switchers to Mass Transit: Mode Choice as a Multi-Attribute Decision Model," in *Advances in Consumer Research,* vol. 6, ed. William L. Wilkie (Ann Arbor: Association for Consumer Research, 1979), pp. 519–525.

33. David D. J. Fritzche, "The Environmental Consistency of Consumer Purchases," in *New Marketing,* ed. Cuhan, pp. 312–315.

INDEX

ABOUT THE AUTHOR

Dorothy Cohen is Walter H. "Bud" Miller Distinguished Professor of Business at Hofstra University. She is the author of *Advertising*, co-author of *Modern Marketing Management*, has published numerous articles and columns in professional journals, and has chapters appearing in a dozen books. Her writings on advertising regulation have influenced public policy decisions here and abroad.

Dr. Cohen served as national Vice President for the American Marketing Association from 1974–1976. She is now on the editorial review board of the *Journal of Marketing* and the *Journal of Advertising*. She received the Dean's Award and the Ademco Research Award from Hofstra University in 1978 and the Faculty Distinguished Service Award in 1979.

ABOUT THE AUTHOR

Dorothy Cohen is Walter H. "Bud" Miller Distinguished Professor of Business at Hofstra University. She is the author of *Advertising,* co-author of *Modern Marketing Management,* has published numerous articles and columns in professional journals, and has chapters appearing in a dozen books. Her writings on advertising regulation have influenced public policy decisions here and abroad.

Dr. Cohen served as national Vice President for the American Marketing Association from 1974–1976. She is now on the editorial review board of the *Journal of Marketing* and the *Journal of Advertising.* She received the Dean's Award and the Ademco Research Award from Hofstra University in 1978 and the Faculty Distinguished Service Award in 1979.